Personal Financial Planning

Personal Financial Planning

G. Victor Hallman, Ph.D., J.D.

Member of the Pennsylvania Bar
and Lecturer, Wharton School,
University of Pennsylvania

Jerry S. Rosenbloom, Ph.D.

Chair and Professor, Department of Insurance
and Risk Management, Wharton School,
University of Pennsylvania
and Academic Director of the Certified
Employee Benefit Specialist Program

Fifth Edition

McGraw-Hill, Inc.

New York   St. Louis   San Francisco   Auckland   Bogotá
Caracas   Lisbon   London   Madrid   Mexico   Milan
Montreal   New Delhi   Paris   San Juan   São Paulo
Singapore   Sydney   Tokyo   Toronto

Library of Congress Catalog Number: 92-402-74

4 5 6 7 8 9 0   DOC/DOC   9 8 7 6 5

ISBN 0-07-025680-2

*The sponsoring editor for this book was Caroline Carney, the editing supervisor was
Caroline Levine, and the production supervisor was Pamela A. Pelton. This book
was set in Baskerville by North Market Street Graphics.*

Printed and bound by R. R. Donnelley & Sons Company.

To Susan and Victor
and to Lynn,
Debra, Heather, and Amy

Contents

Part 2. Using Insurance Effectively

3. Basic Insurance Principles   **45**

4. Life Insurance and Social Security   **63**

5. Health Insurance   **118**

6. Property and Liability Insurance   **154**

Part 3. Accumulating Capital and Income Tax Planning

7. Basic Investment Principles   181

8. Common Stock and Other Equity Investments   217

10. Investing in Fixed-Income Securities   278

11. Income Tax Planning   299

Part 4. Planning for Retirement

12. Pension, Profit-Sharing, and Savings Plans   347

Part 5. Estate and Tax Planning

14. Estate Planning Principles   411

15. **Planning for Death Taxes**   **432**

16. **Will Substitutes in the Estate Plan**   **459**

17. **Planning for Business Interests**   **482**

Preface to the Fifth Edition

In the preface to the first edition of this book, written in 1975, we noted that consumerism has been a rising tide and that personal financial planning really is consumerism applied to an individual's or a family's personal financial affairs. We also noted that since the end of World War II, our economy has developed an almost unheard-of level of affluence that has made financial planning important for larger and larger numbers of people. We further observed that the increasing role of women in the work force, particularly at the executive and professional levels, and the rapid growth of multi-income-earner families in the United States are placing more and more persons in a position in which they need to apply sophisticated financial planning techniques to their personal and family affairs. At the same time, however, the economic uncertainties of potential recurring inflation, possible deflation (severe recession or depression), and a relatively high level of unemployment have made prudent personal financial planning all the more important for almost everyone.

It is surprising how well those statements apply today as they did then. The impact of all these forces simply has become stronger in recent years. In particular, as of the time of the preparation of the fifth edition, there is increasing concern in many quarters about the prospect for longer-term recession or depression in our economy. Thus, it is clear that an environment has been created in which personal financial planning is indeed an idea whose time has come and which is being widely applied. Further, it is increasingly being recognized that the personal financial planning concept applies to a very large number of middle-income persons and families and not just to the well-to-do. Many financial institutions have recognized this and are gearing their products and services toward the financial planning needs of the general public. In addition, there is an increasing number of professional financial planners who are applying the personal financial planning concept to the economic needs of the public.

In this edition of the book, as in the previous editions, we consider personal financial planning as the process of determining an individual's or a family's total financial objectives, considering alternative plans or methods for meeting those objectives, selecting the plans and methods that are best suited for the person's circumstances, implementing those plans, and then periodically reviewing the plans and making necessary adjustments. In this process, a person's or family's overall financial affairs—investments, savings programs, insurance and annuities, retirement plans, other employee benefits, income tax planning, estate planning, and so forth—should be considered as a coordinated whole, rather than on a piecemeal basis. This means that individual financial instruments, such as stocks, bonds, life insurance, annuities, mutual funds, real estate, trusts, and various kinds of employee benefits and compensation arrangements should be considered in terms of a person's overall financial objectives and plans rather than in isolation. It also means that the professional financial planners who are rendering financial planning services to the public should be knowledgeable in a variety of financial disciplines. It is an objective of this book to help achieve these results.

The development of appropriate, unbiased, and cost- and service-efficient methods for meeting the public's need for personal financial planning remains a problem. One possible approach to meeting this need would be to include a personal financial planning or counseling service for all or most employees and their families as a part of the employee benefits program of employers. Employers already provide or make available pension plans, profit-sharing plans, savings plans (often including several investment options), life insurance, disability insurance, medical expense coverage (often with several options), dental insurance, stock purchase plans, stock options, executive perquisites, and perhaps long-term care (LTC) insurance, as well as a variety of other employee benefits. Would not a broadly based personal financial planning service be a logical supplement and capstone for all these benefits? As another advantage, such a planning service could improve the employees' understanding and use of the employer's employee benefit plans. This would aid employers in the all-important, and sometimes neglected, task of communicating effectively to employees about the extent and value of the employee benefits the employer is providing to them. Thus, such an employee benefit would serve the objectives of both employees and their employers. The development in employee benefit planning of flexible benefits (or so-called "cafeteria compensation"), under which employees have wide latitude to choose the nature and composition of their employee benefits within a number of options offered by the employer, would seem to make such a personal financial planning or counseling benefit all the more valuable.

Since the publication of the fourth edition of this book, the Revenue Act of 1987, the Technical and Miscellaneous Revenue Act of 1988 (TAMRA), the Revenue Reconciliation Act of 1989, the Revenue Reconciliation Act of 1990, and recent changes in the taxation of distributions from qualified retirement plans have been enacted. These statutes, and particularly the landmark Tax Reform Act of 1986, have made very significant changes in income taxation, employee benefits and their taxation, and federal estate taxation. This fifth edition has been completely updated to include the changes made by the laws mentioned above. In addition, a number of areas have been added or expanded in this edition. These include: a discussion of evaluating the financial strength of insurance companies; the description of the types and taxation of life insurance products, including term products, variable products, and second-to-die policies; increased coverage of nonqualified annuities; a discussion of long-term care (LTC) insurance; increased coverage of mutual funds; increased attention to the asset allocation concept in investment planning; increased coverage of planning for retirement plan distributions; increased attention to employee stock plans and stock arrangements; and coverage of planning for property management in the face of physical or mental incapacity, including powers of attorney and revocable trusts; among others. Thus, the fifth edition has not only been updated, but it also has been expanded in these and other areas.

G. Victor Hallman
Jerry S. Rosenbloom

Personal Financial Planning

PART 1

Coordinated Financial Planning

1
Personal Financial Planning— The Process

Most people are in great need of personal financial planning. They have certain basic financial goals they want to attain, but such objectives usually are not precisely defined. To help meet their goals, a bewildering array of investments, insurance coverages, savings plans, tax-saving devices, retirement plans, and the like is constantly being offered to the public, but these financial instruments and plans often are presented in a piecemeal fashion. Furthermore, consumers are faced with a dilemma because the very affluence of our society, coupled with improving educational levels, helps create a situation in which more and more people can benefit from the more sophisticated financial planning techniques.

What Is Personal Financial Planning?

Personal financial planning is the development and implementation of total, coordinated plans for the achievement of one's overall financial objectives. The essential elements of this concept are the development of *coordinated* plans for a person's *overall* financial affairs based on his or her *total financial objectives*. The idea is to focus on the individual's

objectives as the starting point in financial planning, rather than emphasize the use of one or more financial instruments to solve only *some*
financial problems.

Most people, in fact, use a variety of financial instruments before they
can achieve all their objectives. Thus, such basic financial tools as common
stocks, bonds, mutual funds, insurance, fixed and variable annuities,
money market accounts, certificates of deposit, savings accounts, individual
retirement accounts, personal trusts, and real estate are essential elements
of many, if not most, soundly conceived financial plans.

Also involved in the planning process is the development of *personal
financial policies* to help guide a person's financial operations. Examples of
such policies in investments would be deciding what percentage of an
investment portfolio is to go into bonds (or other so-called fixed-dollar
securities) and what percentage into common stocks (or other equity-type
investments), or deciding to invest primarily in growth-type common stocks
to be held for the long pull, or deciding to invest the "equity" portion primarily in real estate. In the insurance area, the consumer might decide to
buy property and liability insurance and health insurance with the largest
deductibles he or she can afford in order to save on premiums and thereby
avoid the disadvantage of "trading dollars with the insurance company."
The consumer might also decide to buy the highest limits of liability available for liability insurance coverages (or "excess" or umbrella liability coverage) to protect against potentially catastrophic losses—the ones that can
destroy a person or family financially. When it comes to buying life insurance, the consumer may want to purchase mainly cash-value life insurance,
or he or she may decide to buy mostly term life insurance—which is pure
protection—and place the savings dollars elsewhere. There are many other
such financial policy decisions that people need to consider in their financial planning.

Unfortunately, many people do not follow any consistent policies in making these decisions, but rather make them as each day-to-day problem
comes up or as a result of some sales presentation. The more completely
consumers and their advisors can formulate the financial policies that make
sense for themselves and their families, the more rational their financial
decisions will be and the less likely they will be to be unduly influenced by
others. One of the most important functions of financial planners is to help
their clients develop sound financial policies within which they can make
well-conceived specific financial decisions.

In financial planning, people consciously or unconsciously make some
assumptions about the current economic climate and what the economy
holds for the future. A commonly held view, for example, has been that the
U.S. economy generally will experience real long-term growth, accompa-

nied by at least some price inflation, for the indefinite future. Such an assumption has clear implications for personal financial policies and planning. On the other hand, others may fear that economic conditions will deteriorate into a prolonged recession or even depression, and they plan their financial policies accordingly.

Focus on Objectives

Each person's financial objectives differ in terms of his or her individual circumstances, goals, attitudes, and needs. However, the total objectives of most people can be classified as follows:

1. Protection against the personal risks of
   a. Premature death
   b. Disability losses
   c. Medical care expenses
   d. Custodial care expenses (or long-term care expenses)
   e. Property and liability losses
   f. Unemployment
2. Capital accumulation for
   a. Emergency fund purposes
   b. Family purposes
   c. General investment portfolio
3. Provision for retirement income
4. Reduction of the tax burden
   a. During lifetime
   b. At death
5. Planning for one's heirs (estate planning)
6. Investment and property management (including planning for property management in the event of disability or incapacity)

This overall view of personal financial planning encompasses the work of several specialized fields. Tax planning, for example, involves planning for the reduction, shifting, and postponement of the tax bite and cuts across several specialties. Estate planning is concerned primarily with planning for the disposition of one's property to heirs (during one's lifetime as well as at death) in such a way as to accomplish one's objectives with minimum overall shrinkage in the estate. Life underwriting traditionally has involved all the uses of life insurance, health insurance, and annuities to meet a person's financial objectives. Now, however, life insurance agents also have at their disposal various equity products, such as mutual funds, variable annuities, and variable life insurance, to help meet investment needs. Similarly, the personal insurance survey deals primarily with a person's exposures to property and liability losses. Investment planning is concerned largely with the accumulation of capital and the management of a person's investment portfolio.

Lawyers, accountants, bankers and trust officers, investment advisors, insurance agents and brokers, financial planners, and others may all assist the public in meeting these financial objectives. In fact, a person may need to deal with several practitioners to receive all the expert advice needed. This makes coordination of effort among these experts important. What is needed might be termed a "systems approach" toward meeting a person's financial goals by integrating the basic principles of each specialty into a cohesive whole approached from the consumer's point of view. This kind of systems approach increasingly is being developed and is known as the field of *personal financial planning*. Further, a growing number of financial planners and others are now approaching the analysis of their clients' affairs in this logical manner.

Need for Personal Financial Planning

Who Should Plan?

Most people find themselves in need of financial planning to some degree. Some of the more sophisticated techniques tend to be used by those with higher incomes and larger property or business interests, but partly this is so because many persons of more modest circumstances lack information about financial planning. If they knew of the techniques, they would use them more. In fact, less affluent people actually may need such planning more than those with greater wealth, because each dollar of income or capital means relatively more to them.

Interestingly, our economic growth, the tax structure, and changes that have taken place in our social framework have increased tremendously the need for, and the complexity of, financial planning. One product of our "affluent society" is the large number of people who have enough income, assets, and possibilities of gifts and inheritances within their families to find themselves, as never before, with a real need for investment, tax, insurance, and estate planning services. For example, many people today, as a result of their hard work, education, and consequent success, have incomes that place them in federal and often state and local income tax brackets that make income tax planning advantageous. Similarly, a number of people, when both the husband's and the wife's estates are considered, potentially have estates that are large enough to be subject to a federal estate tax as well as state death taxes. For these and other reasons, they are logical candidates for financial planning, including estate planning.

As an illustration, let us take the case of a successful executive, George Able, and his wife, Mary. George is age 46 and Mary is 42. They have three children, ages 22, 18, and 14. George's 18-year-old is in college. In addition, George contributes to the support of his widowed mother, who is age 67. George currently earns $75,000 per year in base salary, and he and Mary receive about $20,000 more each year in taxable investment income. Mary presently does not work outside the home, but she had a successful career as an accountant before they were married and plans to return to this field after their 14-year-old enters college. George is employed by a large corporation whose stock has shown considerable growth in per-share earnings, price, and dividends paid over the last 20 years that George has been with the firm. George's asset picture may be briefly summarized as follows. He owns in his own name about $320,000 worth of his employer's stock, which he acquired under the company's employee stock purchase plan and in the open market. He also owns in his own name about $40,000 worth of other listed common stocks; $10,000 worth of mutual fund shares (a balanced common stock fund); $40,000 in a money market fund; and $30,000 worth of tangible personal property, including a valuable stamp collection. George and Mary jointly own their main home, worth about $180,000 on today's market and with a $20,000 mortgage note still due; their summer home, valued at about $100,000 and with a $30,000 mortgage note still due; and savings and checking accounts of $30,000. In addition to the above mortgages, George has a $40,000 bank loan outstanding, which he took out to help finance the purchase of some of the stock that he owns in his employer's company, and he has about $10,000 of other personal debts outstanding. Through his employer, George has group life insurance equal to three times his base salary (or $225,000), which is payable to Mary as primary beneficiary; a deferred profit-sharing plan with about $300,000 currently credited to George's account; and an employee savings (thrift) plan with about $100,000 currently credited to George's account. The benefits of the profit-sharing and savings plans are payable to George's estate at his death. Finally, George owns individually purchased life insurance policies on his life having total death benefits of about $200,000. This insurance is payable in a lump sum to Mary as primary beneficiary. George has a will which leaves everything outright to Mary if she survives him; otherwise, everything is left outright to his children in equal shares.

Mary owns some personal jewelry, furs, and other personal effects in her own name. However, her parents, in their wills, have left their farm, currently estimated to be worth $600,000, to Mary and her two brothers in equal shares. Mary has no will at present. Neither George nor Mary has made any gifts that would be taxable for federal gift tax purposes.

From these facts, George and Mary have gross income for federal income tax purposes of $95,000 per year ($75,000 from George's salary and about $20,000 from taxable investment income). Assume they have itemized deductions of $22,200 (deductible interest, deductible taxes, and charitable contributions), and four personal or dependency exemptions of $2300 each.[1] Assuming no other deductions and no credits, their taxable income would be $63,600, and at federal income tax rates for 1992, their federal income tax would be $13,154 if they filed a joint return. This puts them in the 28 percent federal income tax bracket. When this is added to the top rates George and Mary pay in state and local income taxes, the result is that about one-third of each additional dollar of taxable income is taken in income taxes.[2]

Thus, it can be seen that, on either a *marginal basis* or an *average basis,* income taxes represent a significant reduction in the Ables's spendable income. They also reduce the after-tax yield, and hence the ability to accumulate capital for retirement or other purposes, from their taxable investments. If, for example, George and Mary receive a current yield from the dividend on one of their common stocks of 5 percent, this current yield, taken alone, is worth about 3.6 percent $[0.05 - (0.28 \times 0.05)]$ after federal income taxes in the 28 percent bracket, and the Ables can retain only about two-thirds of the taxable dividends received from the stock (in the 28 percent bracket) for spending or reinvestment.[3] Thus, as part of the overall financial planning process, the Ables should consider income tax planning techniques that can eliminate, reduce, shift, or defer their current income tax burden. (See Chap. 11 for specific planning ideas toward these ends.)

To continue the illustration, let us turn now to death taxes and estate planning. From the facts given above, if George were to die today, survived by Mary, his federal estate tax picture would look like this:[4]

---

[1] This is the personal and dependency exemption for 1992. This amount may be adjusted annually for inflation.

[2] Note that this statement refers to their marginal taxable income (and marginal tax rates), not their total taxable income. Thus, in 1992 the $13,154 in federal income taxes constitutes about 21 percent of their $63,600 in taxable income and about 14 percent of their $95,000 in gross income.

[3] This, in itself, does not mean that such taxable investments as common stock are poor investments for the Ables. In fact, as far as current yield is concerned, such taxable investments have become relatively more attractive to the Ables since the lower individual income tax rates of the Tax Reform Act of 1986 than they were before that change in the tax law. It means only that such investment decisions depend on many factors, as explained in Chap. 7, and that income tax planning is an important part of investment planning, as well as of other personal financial planning.

[4] The computation of the federal estate tax in this illustration assumes a knowledge of tax principles that are explained later in the book (see Chaps. 14 and 15). The illustration is presented at this point only to show the need for planning.

Gross estate for federal estate tax purposes		$1,420,000
Less:		
George's debts	$75,000	
Estimated funeral and estate administration expenses	45,000	– 120,000
Adjusted gross estate		$1,300,000
Less: Federal estate tax marital deduction (includes full amount of all property in gross estate that "passes" to the surviving spouse so as to qualify for the marital deduction and, for the sake of simplicity, ignores the effect of state death taxes payable on the amount of property qualifying for the marital deduction).		–$1,300,000
Taxable estate (and tentative tax base in this case)		—0—
Federal estate tax payable		—0—

In this illustration, there is no federal estate tax payable at George's death. This is due to the deduction provided by the unlimited federal estate (and gift) tax marital deduction. However, George Able and his wife should not be lulled into a false sense of security by this, because in this case a heavy federal estate tax burden may fall on Mary's estate when she subsequently dies.

Also, using the inheritance tax law of one state for illustrative purposes, the state inheritance (death) tax at George's death would be about $47,000 on the basis of his present estate arrangements. Therefore, as matters now stand, the estimated reduction in the value of George's estate assets that would go to his family in the event of his death, referred to as estate "shrinkage," would be approximately as follows:[5]

Debts (including the full amount of mortgage notes on homes)	$100,000
Estimated funeral and estate administration expenses	45,000
Estimated federal estate tax payable	—0—
Estimated state death tax payable	47,000
Total estate "shrinkage"	$192,000

It is important to plan for both husband and wife.[6] This is true for many reasons, particularly today. First, the wife usually will be the key person in managing the family in the event of the husband's death or disability. Second,

---

[5] For purposes of simplicity, income taxes have been ignored in this example.

[6] It is desirable to plan for the whole family, and this may be possible. However, as a practical matter, it may be difficult in some cases to have coordinated planning beyond the immediate family of husband, wife, and children. For example, in some cases, grown, self-supporting children may find it difficult emotionally to coordinate their planning with that of their aged parents from whom they might expect an inheritance. But when this can be done, everyone benefits. Openness in estate planning usually pays handsome dividends for the whole family.

several important tax-saving devices, such as the federal estate tax marital deduction, split gifts for gift tax purposes, and joint income tax returns, depend on marital status. Moreover, today many wives are employed and receive good incomes, have an opportunity to acquire property and investments themselves, and are entitled to various employee benefits in their own right. Some women also have an active interest in a closely held business. Finally, a wife often will acquire substantial property upon her husband's death and may be the beneficiary of an inheritance from other sources.

In our hypothetical case of the Ables, for example, Mary can expect to receive a net amount of about $1,383,000 from all sources in the event of George's death. She also expects an inheritance of about $200,000 from her parents. This would give her an estate of about $1,583,000, with all the resulting property management and investment problems. Also, at Mary's subsequent death, her estate's tax burden and "estate shrinkage" will be significant, as shown below.[7]

Gross estate for federal estate tax purposes		$1,583,000
Less:		
Mary's debts (estimated)	$ 10,000	
Estimated funeral and estate administration expenses	70,000	– 80,000
Taxable estate (and tentative tax base in this case)		$1,503,000
Federal estate tax on tentative tax base		$557,150
Less available credits:		
Unified transfer tax credit	$192,800	
Credit for state death taxes payable	64,592	– 257,392
Federal estate tax payable		$ 299,758 (or about $300,000)

The credit for state death taxes paid, used in this illustration, is explained in Chap. 15. Any other possible credits have been ignored in this illustration for the sake of simplicity.

We can now see that the estimated "estate shrinkage" at Mary's subsequent death will be considerably greater than when George died. Again assuming a particular state's death tax law for illustrative purposes, this estimated "estate shrinkage" at Mary's death would be:

---

[7] This assumes that Mary does not remarry and thus does not have the marital deduction available to her estate. It also assumes that the mortgage notes (and other debts) were paid off following George's death and that estate property values remain the same. In fact, in most cases estate property values can be expected to change (increase or decrease, depending on economic conditions) between the first death and the subsequent death of the surviving spouse. This will affect the death tax burden of the survivor's estate.

Debts	$ 10,000
Estimated funeral and estate administration expenses	70,000
Estimated federal estate tax payable	300,000
Estimated state death tax payable	90,000
Total estate "shrinkage"	$470,000

Thus, assuming only the current values in the Ables's estates, and making some realistic estimates concerning funeral and estate administration expenses and state death taxes payable, when their estates are taken together, they will have potential "estate shrinkage" of $662,000 ($192,000 at his death and $470,000 at hers). This obviously represents a very significant reduction in the value of their property that ultimately will pass to their children. Proper planning of *both* their estates could substantially lessen this sizable drain on their family's assets as well as accomplish other objectives. (See Chaps. 15 and 16 for specific planning ideas in these areas.)

Clearly, George and his family could benefit from estate planning services, and it is quite likely that his estate and Mary's estate will even increase in value in the years to come. In addition, George and Mary undoubtedly have investment, insurance, and retirement planning needs that we have not yet considered. The point we are making by this analysis at the beginning of this book is that planning services which some may believe are only for the wealthy really have broad applicability in our society today.

Why Planning May Be Neglected

People fail to plan for a host of reasons. They often feel they do not have sufficient assets or income to need planning, or that their affairs are already in good order. Both these assumptions are frequently wrong. There also is the natural human tendency for busy people to procrastinate with respect to planning. Some people actually may fear planning, since part of it involves consideration of unpleasant events such as death, disability, unemployment, property losses, and possible incapacity. Finally, people may be deterred by what they consider the high cost of planning services. Actually, the real cost of planning may be lower than people believe, and, in any event, the true cost of not planning in terms of higher taxes, lost opportunities, and other personal losses may be the highest of all.

Knowledgeable consumers can secure some valuable planning services without additional cost. For example, stockbrokers, trust officers, insurance agents and brokers, and others stand ready to give valuable advice in the areas of their specialties without extra cost to consumers beyond that already built into the overall cost of their products or services. The consumers must pay this cost in any event, whether they use the planning services or not. Of course, consumers must evaluate carefully the advice they receive in light of the advisor's experience, knowledge of the field, and objectivity. The trick is for knowledgeable and discerning consumers to have the benefit of the knowledge and experience of these advisors and yet reserve for themselves the final decision as to what advice to accept and act upon and what advice to ignore.

Remember, too, that the fees charged for some planning services may be deductible for federal income tax purposes. The tax law permits the deduction of expenses, in excess of a certain limit, incurred for the management, conservation, or maintenance of property held for the production of income, except to the extent such expenses are incurred in earning tax-exempt interest or income. Thus, investment counsel and advisory fees, trustees' fees, custodian fees, legal fees for advice concerning the arrangement and conservation of income-producing property, and similar expenses incurred in connection with investments may be deductible on the income tax return of the person receiving or entitled to receive the income from the investments.[8] An income tax deduction also may be taken for expenses incurred in connection with the determination, collection, or refund of any tax (including gift and estate taxes). Such investment expenses, tax preparation expenses, and other miscellaneous itemized deductions, as well as most employee business expenses, are considered together as a single category of itemized deductions and are deductible only to the extent that combined they exceed 2 percent of the taxpayer's adjusted gross income.

Costs of Failure to Plan

While there may be understandable human reasons why people neglect to plan, the costs of failing to do so can be high indeed. A family may be unprotected or inadequately protected in the event of personal catastrophes such as death, disability, serious illness, an automobile accident, prolonged unemployment, incapacity to manage one's property, confinement in a custodial care facility or arrangement, or similar risks of life. There may not be enough money set aside for education and retirement, necessitating painful compromises when such predictable needs actually arise. On the other hand, some of these risks may be covered more than adequately, resulting in a waste of family resources.

---

[8] Except to the extent that such expenses relate to rents and royalties, they are deductible only from adjusted gross income to arrive at taxable income. Expenses incurred to earn rents and royalties are deductible from gross income to arrive at adjusted gross income.

Failure to plan can result in higher-than-necessary income, estate, and perhaps gift taxation. It can also cause larger estate settlement costs in general. The case of the Ables illustrates these dangers.

When there is a closely held business interest in the family, failure to plan for the future disposition of this interest can result in severe problems in the event of the death, disability, or retirement of one of the owners. This can cause severe business losses as well as bitter disputes within the family as to who will control the business. In the same vein, failure to engage in proper estate planning not only can result in higher-than-necessary death taxation and estate settlement costs but, perhaps more important, also can cause disputes and harsh discord within the family, resulting in unhappiness for the very persons the estate owner wishes to benefit. In an unplanned estate, for example, the bereaved and perhaps inexperienced surviving spouse may find himself or herself faced with a multitude of unexpected and complex problems in managing property and investing money at the very time the survivor is least capable emotionally of doing so. At the same time, in the wings all too frequently wait those who are anxious to "advise" the survivor but not always for the survivor's and the survivor's children's *benefit*. In many cases, these human problems of an unplanned estate can be more costly than higher taxes and estate settlement costs.

Last but not least, a very important cost of failure to plan is that a person's own individual objectives in life may not be realized. The person may not be able to achieve the degree of financial independence he or she wants. It is sad indeed when a person is tied to an employer or a job because he or she "can't afford to move." Yet this can happen even in our "affluent" society because so much of our personal financial security can be tied to a particular employer. It stands to reason that a properly planned personal investment and insurance program, within the control of the individual, can go a long way toward providing the individual and his or her family with a desirable degree of personal independence. Such a planned program will also enable the person and his or her family to achieve their financial objectives in life on an organized basis. Nothing is more common than the person who intends to "get my financial house in order" but never does. Planning is the first step toward achieving this.

Steps in the Planning Process

The financial planning process basically involves the translation of personal objectives into specific plans and finally into financial arrangements to implement those plans. To this end, the following are logical steps in the process. These steps are covered in greater detail throughout the book. The following is a brief overview of the whole process.

Gathering Information and Preparing Personal Financial Statements

A person's affairs cannot be planned well without certain basic information. Also, most experts with whom people deal customarily need some basic facts before they can really help the individual or family. Therefore, the first step in the planning process is getting together useful information about the person's financial situation to help develop intelligent plans.

The kinds of information needed vary with the situation, but they usually include information about the person's or family's *investments;* the *life, health, long-term care, and property and liability insurance policies* carried; the *retirement and other employee benefits available;* their *tax situation—* income, estate, and gift taxes; *wills, trusts, and other estate planning documents; powers of attorney* and related instruments; and similar financial documents and information. A number of people probably have many of these documents and much of this information in their possession now, and normally they can get more information about them from other sources, such as their stockbroker, insurance agent, employer, lawyer, accountant, trust officer or banker, financial planner, and the like. Of course, not everyone will have all these advisors, but most people at least some of them to go to for further information if needed.

In summarizing a person's present financial position, it may be helpful to prepare some simplified personal financial statements, much like those that business concerns use. These can include a *personal balance sheet,* a *personal income* (or *cash flow*) *statement,* and other financial statements that would be helpful. A sample family balance sheet (Table 1.1) and a sample family income statement (Table 1.2) are given at the end of this chapter. Of course, these can be modified as the individuals or their advisors wish for their own needs and purposes. They are meant only as examples, and other statements could be illustrated as well. Many people are surprised how much they are "worth" when everything is considered. As an illustration of how these statements can be used, the sample balance sheet and income statement are filled out for the Ables, whom we met earlier in this chapter.

In addition, many financial concerns and practitioners, such as banks, insurance companies, stockbrokers, and financial planners, have or use forms and reports that consumers or their advisors may find useful, particularly in the areas of their specialties.

This information-gathering step does not have to be overly extensive or burdensome. It is surprising how much can be done with relatively little additional information if a person knows what to look for. Of course, normally, the more information that is available, the better the planning process will be. Again, outside sources can be helpful in this regard if they are used and evaluated properly.

Identifying Objectives

The next step is the identification and setting of objectives, as outlined previously in this chapter. This is such an important step that the next chapter is devoted to it.

Analyzing Present Position and Considering Alternatives

The third step in the process is an analysis of the person's present position in relation to his or her objectives and then consideration of alternative ways of remedying any deficiencies found. There almost always are problems to solve in meeting at least some objectives. And sometimes a person actually will be overprepared in one area but seriously lacking in others. Thus, balancing the plan is important.

Therefore, at this stage, and under the guidance of appropriate advisors, consumers should consider the various alternatives available to meet their objectives, given their financial position, personal situation, and investment constraints. Depending on the circumstances and complexity of the situation, these alternatives may be relatively few and not difficult to accomplish, or they may be numerous and quite complex.

Developing and Implementing the Plan

Given the facts of the case, the person's objectives, an analysis of his or her present financial position, and consideration of alternatives, recommendations can be made for a financial plan to meet the indicated objectives. Naturally, reasonable people may differ on the specific recommendations that should be made for any such plan. It also goes almost without saying that consumers can reject those parts of a plan with which they cannot agree or feel they cannot afford.

Periodic Review and Revision

No plan, once developed and implemented, should be considered "engraved in bronze." Circumstances change, and so should financial plans. There are births, marriages, divorces, deaths, job changes, different economic conditions, and a host of other factors too numerous to mention that may make revisions in financial plans desirable or even necessary. Therefore, the final step in the process is adopting a procedure for periodic review and needed revision of the personal financial plan.

Use of Financial Planning Statements

Personal Financial Planning Checklists and Review Forms

To aid the reader in applying this process to his or her own situation, a *personal financial planning checklist* and *personal financial planning review forms* have been prepared for use with this book and will be found at the end. *It must be emphasized, however, that such materials can never be regarded as a substitute for sound professional advice in the areas where such advice is necessary.* Naturally, the authors do not intend them as such a substitute. In fact, the checklist and review forms may simply help the readers formulate the right questions to ask their advisors.

Other Financial Statements

As indicated above, the financial statements and review forms shown here and at the end of the book are not meant to be exhaustive. Other statements often are used in the personal financial planning process. Two of these are the *personal budget* and a personal *cash flow statement*. A budget is an advance plan for anticipated expenditures and income. It is very helpful in keeping a person's or family's expenditures under control and within their income. A cash flow statement shows the sources and timing of a person's or family's cash receipts and of their cash outlays.

Table 1.1. Family Balance Sheet (as of Present Date)

Assets		
Liquid assets		
Cash and checking account(s)	$ 5,000	
Savings account(s)	25,000	
Money market funds	40,000	
Life insurance cash values	15,000	
U.S. savings bonds	—0—	
Brokerage accounts	—0—	
Other	—0—	
Total liquid assets		$ 85,000
Marketable investments		
Common stocks	360,000	
Mutual funds	10,000	
Corporate bonds	—0—	
Municipal bonds	—0—	
Certificates of deposit	—0—	

Table 1.1. (*Continued*) Family Balance Sheet (as of Present Date)

Other	—0—	
Total marketable investments		370,000
"Nonmarketable" investments		
Business interests	—0—	
Investment real estate	—0—	
Pension accounts	—0—	
Profit-sharing accounts	300,000	
Savings (thrift) plan accounts	100,000	
IRA and other retirement plan accounts	—0—	
Tax-sheltered investments	—0—	
Other	—0—	
Total "nonmarketable" investments		400,000
Personal real estate		
Residence	180,000	
Vacation home	100,000	
Total personal real estate		280,000
Other personal assets		
Auto(s)	6,000	
Boat(s)	3,000	
Furs and jewelry	10,000	
Collections, hobbies, etc.	4,000	
Furniture and household accessories	15,000	
Other personal property	2,000	
Total other personal assets		40,000
Total assets		$1,175,000
Liabilities and net worth		
Current liabilities		
Charge accounts, credit card charges, and other bills payable	$ 10,000	
Installment credit and other short-term loans	—0—	
Unusual tax liabilities	—0—	
Total current liabilities		$ 10,000
Long-term liabilities		
Mortgage notes on personal real estate	50,000	
Mortgage notes on investment real estate	—0—	
Bank loans	40,000	
Margin loans	—0—	
Life insurance policy loans	—0—	
Other	—0—	
Total long-term liabilities		90,000
Total liabilities		$ 100,000
Family net worth		$1,075,000
Total liabilities and family net worth		$1,175,000

Table 1-2. Family Income Statement (for the Most Recent Year)

Income

Salary(ies) and fees			
The individual		$75,000	
His or her spouse		—0—	
Others		—0—	
Total salaries			$75,000
Investment income			
Interest (taxable)		6,000	
Interest (nontaxable)		—0—	
Dividends		14,000	
Real estate		—0—	
Realized capital gains		—0—	
Other investment income		—0—	
Total investment income			20,000
Bonuses, profit-sharing payments, etc.		—0—	
Other income		—0—	
Total income			$95,000

Expenses and fixed obligations

Ordinary living expenses			$24,000
Interest expenses			
Consumer loans	$—0—		
Bank loans	5,400		
Mortgage notes	4,400		
Insurance policy loans	—0—		
Other interest	—0—		
Total interest expenses		9,800	
Debt amortization (mortgage notes, consumer debt, etc.)		2,000	
Insurance premiums			
Life insurance	1,900		
Health insurance	500		
Long-term care insurance	—0—		
Property and liability insurance	2,400		
Total insurance premiums		4,800	
Charitable contributions		3,800	
Tuition and educational expenses		10,000	
Payments for support of aged parents or other dependents		6,000	
Taxes			
Federal income tax	13,154		
State (and city) income tax(es)	4,600		
Social security tax(es)	4,528		
Local property taxes	4,000		
Other taxes	—0—		
Total taxes		26,282	
Total expenses and fixed obligations			$86,682
Balance available for discretionary investment			$ 8,318

2
Setting Financial Planning Objectives

Since personal financial planning is concerned primarily with helping people meet their objectives, the nature of those objectives and the ways they can be met are of critical importance in the planning process. A problem defined and broken down into its component parts frequently is half solved. In this chapter we shall analyze the financial objectives common to most people and outline briefly the sources available to help meet these objectives.

Importance of Setting Objectives

As a general principle, it is desirable to formulate and then state one's objectives as *explicitly* as possible. This can have several advantages. *First,* it forces people to think through exactly what their financial objectives are. *Second,* by doing this they are less likely to overlook some objectives while concentrating unduly on others. *Third,* when objectives are carefully defined, one may see solutions that had been overlooked before. One is also less likely to be sidetracked by persuasive sales presentations into actions that run counter to personal long-range planning. *Finally,* the explicit determination of financial objectives establishes a rational basis for taking appropriate action to realize those objectives.

Once established, a person's financial objectives do not remain static. What may be entirely appropriate for a young married person with young children may prove quite inappropriate for an executive with college-age children or for a husband and wife approaching retirement.

19

How to Organize Objectives

While the emphasis on particular objectives will change during a family's life cycle, the following classification system of personal financial objectives provides a systematic way for identifying specific objectives and needs. It is used throughout the book as a framework for total financial planning.

Protection against Personal Risks

This category recognizes the desire of most people to protect themselves and their families against the risks they face in everyday life. These risks can arise from the possibility of premature death, disability, large medical expenses, loss of their property from various perils, liability they may have to others, unemployment, and custodial care needs.

Premature Death.   A major objective of most people is to protect their dependents from the financial consequences of their deaths. Some people also are concerned with the impact of their deaths on their business affairs or their estate's liquidity and conservation picture. At this point, let us note briefly the various financial losses that may result from a person's death.

Loss of the Deceased's Future Earning Power That Would Have Been Available for the Benefit of His or Her Surviving Dependents.   Most families live on the earned income of the husband or husband and wife combined. The death of an income earner results in the loss of that person's future earnings from the date of death until he or she would have retired or otherwise left the labor force. For most families, this represents a potentially catastrophic loss and usually is the most important financial loss arising out of a person's premature death. The so-called needs approach to valuing this potential loss of future earnings for insurance purposes is illustrated in Chap. 4.

Costs and Other Obligations Arising at Death.   Certain obligations are either created or tend to come due at a person's death. Perhaps the most important of these are funeral and burial expenses, cost of settlement and administration of the deceased's estate, and any federal estate and state death taxes that may be due. The deceased's estate also owes the federal income tax on the individual's income during the year of his or her death.

In addition to the costs created by death itself, there often are obligations that tend to come due at death. Most people have balances on charge accounts, credit cards, and other personal debts that their estate must pay in the event of their death. In addition, many people have larger debts outstanding that they may want to be paid at their death. Perhaps the most typical is the balance due on any mortgages on their homes. While there may be valid reasons why a family would decide not to pay off such a mortgage note after a breadwinner's death, many persons planning their affairs like to think that their families at least would be able to pay off all their debts and thus would not "inherit a mortgage."

Increased Expenses for the Family.   The death of certain family members, especially a wife and mother who works within the home, results in increased expenses for the family to replace the economic functions performed by that person as a homemaker. This potential loss frequently is overlooked, and yet it can be considerable. Another increasingly significant factor is that in a great many families today, the wife is an important income earner, and her premature death results in the loss of her present and future earning power in the outside job market.

Loss of Tax Advantages.   In some cases, the death of a family member can result in substantially increased taxation for the survivors. This results largely from the loss of income, estate, and gift tax advantages accorded to married persons under our tax laws. Generally, the tax benefit most discussed in this regard is the potential loss of the federal estate tax marital deduction on a spouse's death (see Chap. 15).

Loss of Business Values Because of an Owner's or Key Person's Death. When the owner or one of the owners of a business that can be called "closely held" (i.e., a sole proprietor, a partner in many partnerships, or a stockholder in many smaller corporations with only a few stockholders who actively run the business) dies, the business may die financially with the deceased or suffer considerable loss in value. These potential losses in business values are related directly to the owners' personal financial planning because such closely held business interests frequently constitute the major part of the owners' estates. Planning for such business interests is covered in Chap. 17.

Many businesses also have certain key employees, whether owners or not, whose premature death can cause considerable financial loss to the business until they can be replaced.

Sources of Protection against Premature Death.   Various kinds of death benefits may be available to a deceased person's family. While each is described in greater detail in later chapters, they are shown here in outline form to give an overview of the planning devices that may be available to meet this important risk.

1. Life insurance
   a. Individual life insurance purchased by the insured, his or her family, a trust, or others
   b. Group life insurance
      (1) Through the insured's employer or business
      (2) Through an association group plan provided through a professional association, fraternal association, or similar group
   c. Credit life insurance payable to a creditor of the insured person to pay off a debt

2. Social security survivors' benefits
3. Other government benefits
4. Death or survivors' benefits under private pension plans
5. Death benefits under deferred profit-sharing plans
6. Death benefits under savings (thrift) plans
7. Death benefits under tax-sheltered annuity (TSA) plans, plans for the self-employed (HR-10 plans), individual retirement account or annuity (IRA) plans, nonqualified deferred compensation plans, personal annuity contracts, and the like
8. Informal employer death benefits or salary-continuation plans
9. Proceeds from the sale of business interests under insured buy-sell agreements or otherwise
10. All other assets and income available to the family after a person's death

Disability Losses.   Another major objective of most people should be to protect themselves and their dependents from the loss of earned income arising out of their disability, either total and temporary or total and permanent. Loss of earned income due to the disability of the income earner can be referred to as the *disability income exposure*. Such a disability exposure, particularly total and permanent disability, is a serious risk faced by almost everyone. Yet, surprisingly, it is often neglected in financial planning.

Actually, the probability that someone will suffer a reasonably long-term disability (90 days or more) prior to age 65 is considerably greater than the probability of death at those ages. For example, the data below show that the probability of such a long-term disability at age 32 is about 6½ times the probability of death at that age. This is something for young income earners to think about.

Attained age	Probability of disability of 90 days or more per 1000 lives	Probability of death per 1000 lives	Probability of disability as a multiple of probability of death
22	6.64	0.89	7.46
32	7.78	1.18	6.59
42	12.57	2.95	4.26
52	22.39	8.21	2.73
62	44.27	21.12	2.10

Financial losses from disability generally parallel those resulting from death. An important difference from the consumer's viewpoint, however, is that there is a wide range of possible durations of total disability—from only a week or so to the ultimate personal catastrophe of total and permanent disability. Thus, a person must recognize in personal financial planning that he or she could become disabled for a variety of durations—from a few days to the rest of his or her life. Virtually all experts agree, however, that consumers should give greatest planning attention to protecting themselves against long-term and total and permanent disability rather than being unduly concerned with disabilities that last only a few weeks. For example, depending on individual circumstances and resources, it often is much more economical for a person or family to rely on their emergency investment fund for shorter-term disabilities than to buy disability income insurance to cover such disabilities.

The total and permanent disability of a family breadwinner actually is a greater catastrophe than his or her premature death because the disabled person remains a consumer, whose consumption needs may even increase because of the disability, and because other family members must devote at least some of their time to caring for the disabled one, and, of course, his or her spouse is not free to remarry as long as the disabled spouse is alive. In fact, total and permanent disability has been graphically, and rather heartlessly, characterized as "wheelchair death."

One final point about the disability risk is in order. The physical or mental incapacity of someone who owns property or investments may give rise to particular property and investment management problems because the incapacitated person might be in such a state as to be unable to manage his or her affairs effectively. Advance planning is desirable to provide a means for handling this unhappy contingency. This aspect of disability losses can be referred to as the *incapacity exposure*.

Sources of Protection against Disability Income Losses. As was done in the case of premature death, the various sources of protection against disability income losses are outlined below. They will be described in greater detail later.

1. Health insurance
   a. Individual disability income insurance purchased by the insured, his or her family, or others
   b. Group disability income insurance
      (1) Through the insured's employer or business
      (2) Through an association group plan
   c. Credit disability income insurance payable to a creditor of the insured person to pay off a debt
2. Disability benefits under life insurance policies
   a. Waiver-of-premium benefits included with, or added to, most individual life insurance policies
   b. Disability benefits under group life insurance
   c. Disability income riders sometimes available with individual life insurance policies

3. Social security disability benefits
4. Workers' compensation disability benefits
5. Other government benefits
6. Disability benefits under private pension, profit-sharing, and nonqualified deferred-compensation plans
7. Noninsured employer salary-continuation (sick-pay) plans
8. All other income, investment or otherwise, available to the family

This outline, and that for premature death, show that there often are more sources of protection available than many people may think. The problem is to recognize these sources and use them efficiently to meet an individual's or family's needs.

Sources of Meeting Property Management Problems in the Event of Physical or Mental Incapacity.   This is really another aspect of the disability or incapacity problem but is different in nature from dealing with the loss of earned income during disability and often becomes more important as a planning consideration as people reach more advanced ages. However, in reality such incapacity can strike people of any age, through accident or otherwise. Therefore, consideration of sources or ways for meeting this problem is important for almost everyone with property or investments to handle. The following is an outline of some ways to help meet this problem. They will be described in greater detail later.

1. Powers of attorney
    a. Existing durable powers of attorney
    b. "Springing" durable powers of attorney
    c. Health care powers of attorney
2. Revocable living trusts
    a. Funded revocable living trusts
    b. Revocable living trusts in conjunction with durable powers of attorney

This is a newly emerging area of planning and the law. Professional advice should be sought in planning for this risk. Sources of aid in planning for this risk, outlined above, are described in greater detail in Chap. 16.

Medical Care Expenses.   There is little need to convince most people of the need to protect themselves and their family against medical care costs. Mounting medical care costs have become a national problem, and they are no less for individuals and families.

For purposes of personal financial planning, it may be helpful to divide family medical care costs into three categories, as follows.

"Normal" or Budgetable Expenses.   These are the medical expenses the family more or less expects to pay out of its regular monthly budget, such as

routine visits to physicians, routine outpatient laboratory tests and X-rays, expenses of minor illnesses, and small drug purchases. Just what expenses are "normal" or budgetable depends a great deal on the needs, other resources, and desires of the individual or family. As a general principle, the larger the amount of annual expenses a family can afford to assume, the lower will be its overall costs. This is true because buying insurance against relatively small potential losses results in what is called "trading dollars with the insurance company," which usually is an uneconomical practice for the insured. (See Chap. 3 for a more complete explanation.) Also, to the extent an emergency fund is established to meet unexpected expenses and losses (of all kinds), the investment earnings on this fund will be available to the consumer. On the other hand, one of the features of the rapidly growing health maintenance organizations (HMOs) is the coverage of most kinds of medical expenses, including routine expenses, on a comprehensive basis. Thus, if the individual or family has HMO coverage, this category of medical expenses generally will be covered automatically.

"Larger than Normal" Expenses. These are medical expenses that exceed those that are expected or budgetable. If they occur, they probably cannot be met out of the family's regular income. To meet such expenses, most people need insurance or other coverage. The cutoff point between "normal" and "larger than normal" expenses depends on the individual's or family's circumstances.

Catastrophic Medical Expenses. These are expenses so large as to cause severe financial strain on an individual or family. They are important to plan for because they are potentially so damaging. Again, the dividing line between "larger than normal" losses and "catastrophic" losses depends on individual circumstances. One family, for example, may feel that uncovered medical expenses of over $1000 in a year would be a severe financial strain. Another family, however, with a larger income and an emergency fund, may feel that uncovered medical expenses of several thousand dollars could be tolerated, provided the annual savings in medical expense coverage costs were significant enough for the family to assume this much risk. The significance of the dividing line lies in the fact that insurance or other coverage generally is necessary to protect the family against truly catastrophic medical expenses, while the family may elect to assume at least some of the larger-than-normal expenses.

In many cases, however, this decision is, in effect, taken away from the individual because his or her employer provides medical expense benefits which the employee must either accept or reject. On the other hand, employees increasingly may choose among several medical expense plans or options offered by their employers. Also, when both husband and wife are employed outside the home, one of them often can elect to waive or limit coverage under his or her employer's medical expense plan and thus save or reduce the employee's contribution to the plan. In general, employees today are given more cost-saving options in this area than was formerly the case.

The traditional approach for protecting against catastrophic medical expenses is coverage under so-called major medical expense insurance. But even major medical expense insurance may prove inadequate under certain circumstances to meet some of the really large medical bills that are possible. There really is no way to know in advance just how large catastrophic medical expenses might be. Because they could be *very* large, individuals and families should plan for that possibility to the greatest extent they can.

Sources of Protection against Medical Care Expenses. The following are the major sources to which consumers may look for coverage of medical care costs.

1. Health insurance
    a. Employer-provided medical expense coverage [including insured plans, Blue Cross–Blue Shield plans, and health maintenance organization (HMO) plans]
    b. Individual medical expense coverages
2. Social security medical benefits (Medicare)
3. Medical payments coverage under liability insurance policies and "no-fault" automobile coverages
4. Workers' compensation medical benefits
5. Other government benefits
6. Other employer medical reimbursement benefits
7. Other assets available to the family

Custodial Care Expenses (or Long-Term Care Expenses). These generally are expenses incurred to maintain persons when they are unable to perform at least several of the normal activities of daily living, such as eating, bathing, dressing, toileting, taking medication, and general mobility. Thus, these expenses are associated with long-term custodial care for persons who are no longer able to care for themselves, rather than for the treatment and potentially the cure of acute medical conditions as covered in the preceding section. Sometimes, however, the dividing line between custodial care and medical care for acute conditions is not easy to determine. Nevertheless, group and individual medical expense plans and Medicare do not cover custodial care. Only Medicaid (the federal-state medical assistance or welfare program in which eligibility is based on financial need) covers some kinds of custodial care, such as nursing home care.

The type of private insurance that is designed to cover the custodial care exposure is *long-term care (LTC) insurance.* Therefore, if coverage for this risk is desired, as it generally should be, there should be planning well in advance of the need for the purchase of some kind of long-term care coverage.

The custodial care need can take a variety of forms, such as skilled nursing home care, intermediate institutional care, adult day care, and home health care. The financial exposure for an individual or family (including the children of the person needing care) can be very substantial and even ruinous for some families. For example, for uncovered care in a nursing home that charges $120 per day, the annual cost would be $43,800, not counting any other medical or other expenses of the person needing care. This kind of financial exposure is the reason why there is such intense interest today in long-term care coverage.

Sources of Protection against Custodial Care Expenses.   Long-term care coverages are a relatively new form of protection and are still in their developmental stage. Several forms of coverage are now available, and there almost certainly will be new developments and changes in this field as experience is gained in it over the years. As of this writing, the income tax status of LTC insurance is unclear.

Nevertheless, at this point in the development of this field, certain sources of protection for the custodial care risk can be identified as follows.

1. Long-term care (LTC) insurance
   a. Individual LTC insurance purchased by the covered person, his or her family, or others
   b. Group LTC insurance
      (1) Through the insured's employer or business
      (2) Through an association group plan
   c. LTC insurance as riders to life insurance policies
2. Accelerated death benefit provisions in life insurance contracts
3. Medicaid [This includes planning so that a person *may* be or become eligible for custodial care (and other medical) benefits under Medicaid. This sometimes is referred to as "Medicaid estate planning."]
4. Other income and assets available to the family

Property and Liability Losses.   All families are exposed to the risk of property and/or liability losses. For planning purposes, it is helpful to consider property exposures and liability exposures separately because somewhat different approaches may be used for each.

Property Losses.   Ownership of property brings with it the risk of loss to the property itself, or *direct losses,* and the risk of indirect losses arising out of loss or damage to the property, called *indirect or consequential losses.* Direct and consequential losses to property can result from a wide variety of perils, some of which, such as fire, theft, windstorm, and automobile collision, are common, while others, such as earthquake and flood, are rather rare except in certain geographic areas.

Some of the kinds of property owned by individuals and families that may be exposed to direct loss include:

Residence

Second home

Investment real estate

Furniture, clothing, and other personal property

Automobiles

Boats (and aircraft)

Furs, jewelry, silverware, and fine art works

Securities, credit cards, cash, and the like

Professional equipment

Assets held as an executor, trustee, or guardian, and assets in which the person has a beneficial interest

Some of the consequential losses that may arise out of a direct loss to such property are as follows:

Loss of use of the damaged property (including additional living expenses while a residence is being rebuilt, rental of a substitute automobile while a car is being repaired, etc.)

Loss of rental income from damaged property

Depreciation losses (or the difference between the cost to replace damaged property with new property and the depreciated value, called "actual cash value," of the damaged property)

Cost of debris removal

Many property losses are comparatively small in size, but some are of major importance. As with disability income losses and medical care expenses, what constitutes a "small" loss depends on the resources and attitudes of those involved. Also, like disability income and medical expense exposures, a financial planning decision needs to be made as to how much of a property loss exposure should be assumed and how much insured. Another decision is what property to insure against what perils.

Liability Losses.   By virtue of almost everything a person may do, he or she is exposed to possible liability claims made by others. Such liability claims can arise out of the person's own negligent acts; the negligent acts of others for whom the person may be held legally responsible; liability he or she may have assumed under contract (such as a lease); and liability imposed by statute (such as workers' compensation laws).

Some of the exposures that may result in a liability claim are:

Ownership of property (e.g., residence premises, vacation home)

Rental of property (e.g., vacation home)

Ownership, rental, or use of automobiles

Ownership, rental, or use of boats, aircraft, snowmobiles, etc.

Hiring of employees (e.g., domestic and casual)

Other personal activities

Professional and business activities (including officerships and director-ships)

Any contractual or contingent liability

Most people realize the financial consequences that could occur as a result of liability claims against them. However, they may not recognize all the liability exposures they have and may not protect themselves against the possibility of *very* large claims. Like medical expenses, there really is no way to know in advance just how large a liability loss one may suffer. Judgments and settlements for $1 million and more are not unusual today. Therefore, prudent financial planning calls for assuming that the worst can happen and providing for it.

Sources of Protection against Property and Liability Losses. For most persons, the main source of protection against property and liability losses is insurance. This insurance generally is available under individually marketed property and liability policies. In some cases, it may be possible for some individuals to protect themselves by not assuming liability under contract or by transferring a liability risk to others by contract. But this really is not feasible for most people.

Capital Accumulation

Many people and families do not spend all their disposable income, and thus they have an investable surplus; many also have various semiautomatic plans, such as qualified savings and profit-sharing plans, that help them build capital; and some receive gifts or inheritances that must be invested. Thus, in one way or another, an important and desirable financial objective for many is to accumulate and invest capital.

There are a number of reasons why people want to accumulate capital. Some of the more important are for an *emergency fund,* for the *education of their children,* for *retirement purposes,* and for a *general investment fund* to provide them with capital and additional income for their financial security. In other words, people want to accumulate capital to promote their own personal financial freedom. People also save with certain consumption goals in mind, such as the purchase of a new car or taking an extended trip or vacation.

The relative importance of these reasons naturally varies with individual circumstances and attitudes. A woman in her fifties may be interested primarily in preparing for retirement, while a younger family man or woman may be more concerned with educating his or her children or the capital growth of a general investment fund.

Emergency Fund. An emergency fund may be needed to meet unexpected expenses that are not planned for in the family budget; to pay for the "smaller" disability losses, medical expenses, and property losses that purposely are not covered by insurance; and to provide a financial cushion against such personal problems as prolonged unemployment.

This need for an *emergency unemployment fund* has received greater attention in recent years as many capable persons have lost their jobs because of economic uncertainties. A reasonable emergency fund can help prevent the problem of temporary unemployment from becoming a crisis by giving the affected family time to adjust without having to change their living standards drastically, alter suddenly their childrens' education plans, or disturb their other investments.

The size of the needed emergency fund varies greatly and depends on such factors as family income, number of income earners, stability of employment, assets, debts, insurance deductibles and uncovered health and property insurance exposures, and the family's general attitudes toward risk and security. The size of the emergency fund often is expressed as so many months of family income—such as 3 to 6 months. In times of economic uncertainty, this goal may even be increased somewhat.

By its very nature, the emergency fund should be invested conservatively. There should be almost complete security of principal, marketability, and liquidity. Within these investment constraints, the fund should be invested so as to secure a reasonable yield, given the primary investment objective of safety of principal. Logical investment outlets for the emergency fund include:

Bank savings accounts (regular accounts)

Savings and loan association accounts (regular accounts)

Money market mutual funds

U.S. savings bonds

Short-term U.S. Treasury securities

Short-term, high-grade municipal securities

Life insurance cash values

It may be desirable to *diversify* the emergency fund among several of these investment outlets so that all the emergency fund "eggs" are not in one "basket." The careful person also may want to have some ready cash available for emergencies, even if it is non-interest-earning.

Education Needs.   The cost of higher education has increased dramatically, particularly at private colleges and universities. For example, it may cost $20,000 or more per year in tuition, fees, and room and board alone for a student to attend some private colleges. This can result in a tremendous financial drain for a family with college-age children, and yet it is a predictable drain that can be prepared for by setting up an education fund.

The size of the fund obviously depends on the number of children, their ages, their educational plans, any scholarships and student loans that may be available to them, and the size of the family income. It also depends on the attitudes of the family toward education. Some people feel they should provide their children with all the education they can profit from and want. Others feel that children should help earn at least a part of their educational expenses themselves. There is also the idea in some cases that older children should help send their younger brothers and sisters through school after their parents have helped them. What types of schools the children plan to attend also has a considerable bearing on the costs involved.

An investment fund for educational needs often is a relatively long-term objective, and it is set up with the hope that the fund will not be needed in the meantime. Therefore, wider investment latitude seems justified than in the case of the emergency fund to secure a more attractive investment yield. All that is really necessary is for the principal to be there by the time each child is ready for school. However, as with most investment accounts, a diversified approach seems in order.

Retirement Needs.   This is a very important objective for many people in accumulating capital. They want to make sure they can live independently and decently during their retired years. Because of the importance and unique characteristics of retirement planning, it is dealt with as a separate objective later in this chapter.

General Investment Fund.   People often accumulate capital for general investment purposes. They may want a better standard of living in the future, a second income in addition to the earnings from their employment or profession, greater financial security or a sense of personal financial freedom, the ability to retire early or to "take it easier" in their work in the future, or a capital fund to pass on to their children or grandchildren; or they may simply enjoy the investment process. In any event, people normally invest money for the purpose of *maximizing their after-tax returns,* consistent with their objectives and the investment constraints under which they must operate.

The size of a person's investment fund depends on how much capital there originally was to invest, how much the person can save each year, any other sources of capital, and how successful the person or his or her advisors are at the investment process. There are, of course, wide variations in how much different people have to invest. However, it seems clear that there are many individuals and families in the United States today with capital to invest in one form or another. This certainly is one reason for the rapid growth of investment companies (including mutual funds) in recent years.

There are a number of ways people can accumulate capital and many possible investment policies they might follow. However, in terms of the objective of capital accumulation, an individual basically has the following factors to consider: (1) an estimate of how much capital will be needed at various times in the future (perhaps including an estimate for future inflation or deflation); (2) the amount of funds currently available (and possibly available in the future) for investment; (3) an estimate of how much will be saved each year in the future; (4) the amount of time left to meet the person's objectives; (5) the general investment constraints under which the person must operate in terms of security of principal, stability of income, stability of principal, tax status, and the like; (6) the net average annual rates of total investment return that are expected on various kinds of investments in the future; and (7) the adoption of an investment program that will give the best chance of achieving as many of the person's financial objectives as possible, within the limitations of his or her investment constraints.

Tables 2.1 and 2.2 give some growth rates for capital at assumed rates of return over various time periods. Table 2.1 shows how much an investment fund of $1000 will grow to at certain assumed rates of return for the number of years indicated. This is known as the future value of a sum.

Table 2.1. Values of a $1000 Investment Fund Invested for Specified Numbers of Years at Various Rates of Return (Future Value of a Sum)

Percent annual net rate of return (compounded)	Number of years the $1000 is invested							
	5	8	10	12	15	20	25	30
3	$1,159	$1,267	$1,344	$1,426	$1,558	$ 1,806	$ 2,094	$ 2,427
4	1,217	1,369	1,480	1,601	1,801	2,191	2,666	3,243
5	1,276	1,478	1,629	1,796	2,079	2,653	3,386	4,322
6	1,338	1,594	1,791	2,012	2,397	3,207	4,292	5,744
8	1,469	1,851	2,159	2,518	3,172	4,661	6,848	10,064
10	1,611	2,144	2,594	3,138	4,177	6,727	10,835	17,449
15	2,011	3,059	4,046	5,350	8,137	16,367	32,919	66,212

The dramatic effect of compound rates of return over a number of years can be seen from Table 2.1. Suppose a person is age 35 and has $10,000 to invest. If the *net* rate of return (after investment expenses and income taxes) is only 4 percent, the person can accumulate $14,800 by age 45, $21,910 by age 55, and $32,430 at age 65. But if this *net* rate of return can be increased to 6 percent, the person can accumulate $17,910 by age 45, $32,070 by age 55, and $57,440 at age 65. And with an increase of this *net* return to 10 percent, the comparable figures would be $25,940 by 45, $67,727 by 55, and $174,490 by 65.

Approached in a somewhat different manner, if, say, a woman age 35 with a $10,000 investment fund feels she needs approximately $20,000 in 12 years for her children's education, she can see from Table 2.1 that she will have to earn a net rate of return of about 6 percent on the money to accomplish her goal ($10,000 at 6 percent per year for 12 years = $20,120).

It may also be desirable to know to how much a certain amount saved each year will accumulate in a specified period, known as the future value of an annuity. This can be determined from Table 2.2, which shows to how much $100 per year will grow at certain assumed rates of return for the number of years indicated. Now assume that a person is age 35 and can save $1200 per year (about $100 per month). If the person receives a *net* rate of return of 8 percent on the money, he or she can accumulate $17,388 by age 45 ($1449 × 12), $54,912 by age 55, and $135,936 by the time the person reaches age 65. This kind of analysis is often used to show the growth of a periodic savings program for retirement.

It often is helpful to combine the results of Tables 2.1 and 2.2. People frequently have an investment fund and also are saving so much each year. Suppose, for example, that a person is age 35 and has $10,000 to invest now and expects to save about $1200 per year that can be invested in the

Table 2.2. Values of a Periodic Investment of $100 per Year at the End of Specified Numbers of Years at Various Rates of Return (Future Value of an Annuity)

Percent annual net rate of return (compounded)	Number of years at $100 per year							
	5	8	10	12	15	20	25	30
3	$531	$ 889	$1,146	$1,419	$1,860	$ 2,687	$ 3,646	$ 4,758
4	542	921	1,201	1,503	2,002	2,978	4,165	5,608
5	553	955	1,258	1,592	2,158	3,307	4,773	6,644
6	564	990	1,318	1,687	2,328	3,679	5,486	7,906
8	587	1,064	1,449	1,898	2,715	4,576	7,311	11,328
10	611	1,144	1,594	2,138	3,177	5,728	9,835	16,449
15	674	1,373	2,030	2,900	4,758	10,244	21,279	43,474

future. If the person can invest these amounts at a *net* annual rate of return of 8 percent, he or she will accumulate $38,978 by age 45 ($21,590 from Table 2.1 and $17,388 from Table 2.2), $101,522 by age 55, and $236,576 by age 65. It can be seen from the tables that substantially higher accumulations could be achieved by securing a net rate of return even 1 or 2 percentage points higher than the 8 percent assumed above. It also is clear that consistent saving and investment can produce startlingly favorable results.

Investment Instruments for Capital Accumulation.   A wide variety of possible investment instruments (or media) can be used as investment outlets. These are discussed in detail in Part 3, "Accumulating Capital," but they are outlined briefly below. The instruments are classified as *fixed-dollar* and *variable-dollar* (or *equity*) investments. Fixed-dollar investments mean those whose principal and/or income are contractually set in advance in terms of a specified or determinable number of dollars. Variable-dollar (or equity) investments are those where neither the principal nor the income is contractually set in advance in terms of dollars. In other words, both the value and the income of variable-dollar investments can change in dollar amount, either up or down, with changes in economic conditions.

1. Fixed-dollar investments
    a. Bonds
    b. Savings accounts and certificates
    c. Certificates of deposit, Treasury bills and notes, and other short-term debt investments
    d. Money market funds
    e. Preferred stock
    f. Annuity fixed-dollar (nonvariable) cash values
    g. Life insurance fixed-dollar (nonvariable) cash values
    h. Mutual funds consisting of investments in fixed-dollar-type investment media (e.g., bond funds)
    i. Variable annuities and variable life insurance with cash values invested in fixed-dollar-type investment accounts (e.g., bond or money market separate accounts)
    j. Qualified retirement plan account balances invested in fixed-dollar-type investment accounts [e.g., guaranteed investment contracts (GICs) or bond or money market separate accounts]
2. Variable-dollar investments
    a. Common stock
    b. Investment real estate
    c. Mutual funds consisting of investments in variable-dollar-type investment media (e.g., common stock and balanced funds)

d. Variable annuities and variable life insurance with cash values invested in variable-dollar-type investment accounts (e.g., common stock accounts)

e. Qualified retirement plan account balances invested in variable-dollar-type investment accounts (e.g., diversified common stock accounts or common stock of the employer)

f. Tax-sheltered investments

g. Ownership of business interests

h. Commodities

i. Fine art, precious metals, collectibles, and other tangible assets

Provision for Retirement Income

We noted previously that a basic personal objective is to provide a retirement income for an individual and also for his or her spouse. This objective has become increasingly important in recent times because of changes in our socioeconomic institutions and because most people now can anticipate living to enjoy their retirement years. As can be seen from the figures below, the life expectancy at all these ages exceeds the typical retirement age in the United States of 65. Also, at all these ages the probability of survival to age 65 considerably exceeds the probability of death before age 65.

Age	Life expectancy in years	Probability of death before age 65	Probability of survival to age 65 (1 − probability of death)
25	46	0.29	0.71
30	41	0.28	0.72
35	37	0.27	0.73
40	32	0.26	0.74
45	28	0.25	0.75
50	24	0.22	0.78
55	20	0.18	0.82
60	16	0.12	0.88
65	13	—	—

There are many ways a person can plan for retirement—some involve government programs while others rely primarily on private means, and some involve tax-favored retirement plans while others do not. The following is a brief outline of these sources.

1. Social security retirement benefits
2. Other government benefits
3. Private pension plans
   a. Employer-provided pension plans
   b. Retirement plans for the self-employed (HR-10 plans)

4. Savings (thrift) plans [including plans with a Section 401(k) cash or deferred option]
5. Deferred profit-sharing plans
6. Individual retirement accounts or annuities (IRA plans)
7. Tax-sheltered annuity (TSA) plans
8. Nonqualified deferred-compensation plans
9. Individually purchased annuities
10. Life insurance cash values
11. Investments, other assets owned by the individual, and other employee benefits

Many of these instruments for providing retirement income offer substantial tax advantages to the individual if the plan meets the requirements of the tax laws. The nature of these plans, the tax benefits afforded, and the requirements that must be met to secure them will be discussed in detail in Part 4, "Planning for Retirement."

Because many persons today have a variety of retirement benefits available to them, coordination of these benefits has become increasingly important. It does not make sense to either underprovide or overprovide for retirement income. Also, because the tax laws in this area have become so complex, planning for *how* and *when* to take benefits from certain tax-favored retirement plans is important for many people.

Reducing the Tax Burden

In many ways, we have a tax-oriented economy in the United States. Most people have the legitimate objective of reducing their tax burden as much as legally possible, consistent with their nontax objectives. Also, the tax implications of most transactions at least must be considered, and the tax aspects of some transactions are vital to their success. Thus, tax planning has an important role in personal financial planning.

People may be subject to many different taxes. These include sales taxes, real estate taxes, social security taxes, federal income taxes, possibly the federal alternative minimum tax on individuals, state and/or local income taxes, federal estate tax, state inheritance and/or estate taxes, federal (and sometimes state) gift taxes, and possibly the federal tax on generation-skipping transfers. The relative importance of these taxes varies considerably among families, depending on their circumstances and income levels. When engaging in tax planning, however, most people are concerned primarily with income taxes, death taxes, and perhaps gift taxes.

A wide variety of specific tax-saving plans are being used or proposed today. In general, however, they fall under one or more of the following *basic tax-saving techniques:* (1) tax elimination or reduction, (2) shifting the tax burden to others who are in lower brackets, (3) allowing wealth to accumulate without current taxation and postponing taxation, and (4) taking returns as capital gains. These techniques, along with many specific tax-saving ideas, are covered in detail in Parts 3, 4, and 5 of this book.

Planning for One's Heirs

Planning for one's heirs is commonly referred to as "estate planning." An *estate plan* has been defined as "an arrangement for the devolution of one's wealth." For a great many people, such an arrangement can be relatively simple and inexpensive to set up. But for larger estates or estates with special problems, estate plans can become quite complex. Estate planning is a technical and specialized field where such diverse areas of knowledge as wills, trusts, tax law, insurance, investments, and accounting are important. Thus, it frequently is desirable to bring together several professionals or specialists into an estate planning team to develop a well-rounded plan.

Unfortunately, the impression has developed over the years that estate planning is only for the wealthy. However, many persons who would not regard themselves as wealthy actually do have potential estates large enough to justify the use of estate planning techniques.

The specific objectives of estate planning; the various methods of estate transfer, both lifetime (inter vivos) and at death; and the use of common estate planning techniques are treated in greater detail in Part 5.

Investment and Property Management

Need for Management in General.   The need and desire to obtain outside investment or property management in dealing with one's general affairs vary greatly among individuals and families. Some people have a keen interest in investments and property management and hence seek little, if any, help in managing their affairs. Others who may be knowledgeable enough to handle their own investment and property management nevertheless prefer to devote their full time and energies to their business or profession and leave the management of their personal financial affairs to professionals in that field. Then, of course, there are those who by temperament or training are not equipped to manage their own investments and property.

However, the increasing complexity of dealing with investments, tax problems, insurance, and the like generally has increased the need for investment and property management. Also, these complexities tend to increase as personal incomes and wealth increase in our society.

Sources of Aid for Investment and Property Management in General.
There are many such sources now available. They vary considerably in the nature and scope of the aid they offer.

Use of Financial Intermediaries. Broadly speaking, a *financial interme-diary* is a financial institution that invests other people's money and pays them a rate of return on that money. Such institutions serve as conduits for savings into appropriate investments. In effect, they take over the invest-ment and money management tasks with respect to those savings. They may also offer subsidiary financial advice, but normally only within their partic-ular areas of interest. The important financial intermediaries as far as most individuals are concerned include:

Commercial banks [offering certificates of deposit (CDs), bank money market accounts, and various types of savings accounts][1]

Investment companies (mutual funds and closed-end investment com-panies)

Life insurance companies

Savings and loan associations

Mutual savings banks

Trusts. One of the basic reasons for establishing trusts is to provide experienced and knowledgeable investment and property management services for the beneficiary(ies) of the trust. The various uses of personal trusts, including the use of revocable living trusts to provide investment and property management services for the person creating the trust (called the *grantor* of the trust), are covered in greater detail in Chaps. 14, 15, and par-ticularly 16.

Investment Advisory Services. There are many separate investment advisory firms that offer their clients professional investment advice on a fee basis. These firms range from small advisory firms of one or a few per-sons to large firms handling hundreds or even thousands of clients and hav-ing sizable staffs of specialists in various phases of investments. Many commercial banks and investment banking firms also offer investment advi-sory services on a fee basis.

The investment advisory services that may be rendered include (1) anal-ysis of the client's investment needs and objectives, (2) recommendation of an investment program and specific investment policies to achieve the client's objectives, (3) recommendation of specific security issues to imple-ment the policies, and (4) continuous supervision and review of the client's investment portfolio. Banks and some investment advisory firms also pro-vide custody services for their clients, which include safekeeping of securi-ties, handling buy-and-sell orders with brokers, collection of dividends, dealing with rights under securities, and record keeping, as a part of their

---

[1] Commercial banks also provide trust and investment advisory services that are covered later in this section of the chapter.

advisory services. Banks also provide custody services separately if that is all the customer wants.

In terms of investment decision-making authority, investment advisors may operate in one of three ways: (1) on a strictly *discretionary* basis, under which the advisor actually makes investment decisions and buys and sells securities for the client without prior consultation on the transactions with the client; (2) under an arrangement whereby the advisor basically makes the investment decisions but does consult with the client to inform him or her of the reasons for the decisions before taking action; and (3) an arrangement under which the advisor and clients consult extensively before investment decisions are made, but clients reserve the actual decision making for themselves. There are advantages and disadvantages for the advisor and client in each of these methods of operation. In the final analysis, however, the worth of any investment advisor basically lies in how good his or her advice turns out to be over the long pull in terms of the client's objectives.

Annual fees charged by investment advisors vary, depending on such factors as the size of the client's portfolio, the extent of the services rendered, whether it is a discretionary or nondiscretionary account, and the kinds of securities (or property) in the portfolio. For example, an annual fee might start at ¾ of 1 percent of principal with a minimum annual fee of, say, $1000, or more. Unfortunately, use of investment advisors by smaller investors frequently is made impractical by the relatively large minimum annual fees charged. For an investor with a $75,000 portfolio, for example, a $1500 minimum annual fee would constitute an annual charge of 2 percent of principal. For this reason, many investment advisors discourage accounts of less than a certain amount. Some advisors, however, encourage smaller accounts, but with proportionally higher fees.

Investors, small and large, also can obtain valuable investment advice from account executives and others with stock brokerage firms. Many brokerage houses have active and well-staffed research departments that provide their customers with considerable investment information and often helpful recommendations. It must be pointed out, however, that the relationship between stockbrokers and their customers is not the same as that of investment advisors and their clients. Brokers typically are paid commissions based on the transactions in their customers' accounts, while advisors are paid on an annual-fee basis, as described above. However, professional-minded brokers recognize that long-term success ultimately depends on the investment success of their customers and act accordingly.

Other Advisors. There obviously are other important sources from which individuals can secure aid in managing their affairs. Many were mentioned in Chap. 1. Attorneys provide necessary legal and other advice. The old adage, "The person who acts as his or her own lawyer has a fool for a client," still holds true. In the area of estate planning, for example, costly mistakes can be made in the absence of professional advice. Accountants are depended on by many persons for advice concerning their financial affairs, particularly in the tax area. Mutual fund representatives and persons offering various tax-sheltered investments provide important advice on investments and how they can be used in financial planning. Life insurance agents and brokers can offer valuable advice concerning life insurance and annuities, health insurance, and pensions, as well as the other financial products and services their companies may offer. Similarly, property and liability insurance agents and brokers are becoming increasingly important for the advice they can provide on personal risk management, property and liability insurance coverages, and the other financial products and services their companies may offer.

The total-financial-services concept also has fostered the development of a new kind of financial services or financial planning organization. These organizations typically provide coordinated planning for their clients in such areas as investments, insurance, pensions and other employee benefits, and tax and estate planning. Their goal is to deal with the client's total picture. Independent financial planners as well as some banks, insurance companies, stockbrokers, and others, offer this kind of service.

Planning for Investment and Property Management in the Event of Disability or Incapacity. This is an entirely different issue than planning for investment and property management in general as just discussed. This point concerning investment and property management has to do with arranging for the management of one's affairs in the unhappy event that the person should become either temporarily or permanently incapacitated and thus be unable to manage his or her own affairs. This point really has nothing to do with the person's interests, present capabilities, or temperament. Tragically, virtually anyone could suffer either temporary or permanent incapacity or disability that could render him or her incapable of handling his or her affairs, and so almost everyone with property should be concerned with planning for investment and property management under these circumstances. As a practical matter, people tend to become more concerned with this need as they grow older and the risk of incapacity becomes greater. But incapacity can strike at any age, and so most people with property should give attention to planning for this need.

The planning techniques (or sources of aid for investment and property management in the event of disability or incapacity) are different from those just outlined for investment and property management in general. They essentially involve arranging in advance for a *trusted* person or persons and/or a trust institution (e.g., a corporate trustee) to take over the management of one's affairs in the event of physical or mental incapacity for the benefit of the incapacitated person. The arrangement should also provide for the returning of the property management to the person in the event any physical or mental incapacity should end before the person's death. These planning techniques have already been outlined in this chapter in the section dealing with "Sources for Meeting Property Management Problems in the Event of Physical or Mental Incapacity" on p. 24. They basically involve using *powers of attorney* or *revocable living trusts* or both. Use of these planning techniques involves legal and practical issues that should be explored with one's professional advisers. These techniques are described in greater detail in Chap. 16.

Adjusting Objectives
for Inflation and Deflation
(Recession or Depression)

Inflation has been a persistent worldwide economic problem for many years. Also, as the experience of the depression of the 1930s shows, deflation (recession or even depression) cannot be ruled out as an economic phenomenon which must be considered in personal financial planning. However, how to plan for inflation and deflation is difficult indeed. Obviously, since we cannot foretell the future, we cannot be sure which will occur, and when, and in what magnitude.

However, it is possible to adjust objectives as to future financial needs for assumed rates of inflation (or deflation) on the basis of a person's perceptions and beliefs as to what will happen in the future. Let us say, for example, that Mr. Jones, age 50, estimates that he and his wife will need a retirement income (after income taxes) of about $3000 per month by the time he reaches age 65, or in 15 years. If it is assumed that the price level in the economy (as measured, for example, by the Consumer Price Index or CPI) will remain stable over this 15-year period, then Mr. Jones and his wife need only plan to have retirement income of $3000 per month at his age 65. If, however, this assumption is not deemed to be realistic in view of past inflationary trends, and if an inflation rate of, let us say, 4 percent is assumed for the next 15 years (this may even be a conservative assumption over the long run), then their retirement income objective, to be realistic, should be adjusted for the expected inflation. Assuming a 4 percent compounded annual diminution in the value of the dollar, $1 today will be worth only 55.53 cents in 15 years. This is also the present value of $1 due at the end of 15 years at 4 percent compounded interest. (This present value is 0.5553; similar present values for different interest rates and/or time periods can be secured from present value tables published in financial texts or reference books.)

Therefore, to convert a retirement income objective of $3000 per month in current dollars to a corresponding dollar amount of equal purchasing power starting 15 years hence, assuming a 4 percent per year inflation rate for the 15-year period, we should divide the $3000 per month by the present value of $1 due at the end of 15 years at 4 percent compound interest (or 0.5553). The result is a retirement income objective expressed in terms of the assumed price levels (purchasing power) that will exist when Mr. Jones reaches age 65 (assuming 4 percent inflation) of $5402 ($3000 ÷ 0.5553). When thus adjusted for assumed inflation, the Joneses' retirement income objective might require somewhat different planning than otherwise would have been the case.

Planning for a severe recession or even a depression is a more difficult matter. While there has been more or less persistent inflation since the end of World War II, there has not been a depression in the United States since the 1930s. However, some still think current economic conditions can deteriorate into a *depression*. On that, of course, only time will tell.

During a severe recession or a depression, the general price level tends to fall and the values of certain kinds of assets, such as most common stocks, real estate, business interests, and other kinds of equity-type assets, generally collapse. Various kinds of incomes, such as from wages, businesses, rents, dividends from many common stocks, and the like, generally also fall, and sometimes severely. Thus, the fundamental problem during deflation is not maintaining the purchasing power of a given income stream (which purchasing power actually will increase due to the generally falling prices in the economy), but rather is to maintain, as much as possible, the person's or family's income stream and the values of their assets and investments. The modifications of objectives for deflation, then, generally involve attempting to secure conservative, guaranteed sources of income and to hold kinds of property interests that will maintain, or perhaps even increase, their values during severe recession or depression.

Unfortunately, the secure, guaranteed kinds of assets (and sources of income) that likely will maintain their values during deflationary times (which for that reason might be termed "deflation hedges") are often not the ones that will grow in value (or provide increased income) during inflationary times (which are often referred to as "inflation hedges"). The effect of this dilemma is that there really is a conflict of objectives in such important planning areas as determining an asset allocation (composition of investments) strategy for one's personal investment portfolio and for benefit accounts (such as qualified savings plans or IRAs) over which a person may have at least some control. While this conflict may be resolved by some by assuming that only one of these economic conditions will occur, and then by setting objectives and planning on that basis, perhaps the better approach for many people is to set objectives as if either economic scenario could occur and then to use the principle of *diversification* to try to protect themselves to some degree either way.

PART 2
Using Insurance Effectively

3

Basic Insurance Principles

Insurance provides an important means of meeting the financial objectives of most people. To understand how insurance may be useful in meeting a person's financial objectives, it will be helpful to look first at the broader field of risk management.

Risk Management

The term *risk management* normally means the use of all alternative methods of dealing with risk. Business firms are becoming increasingly aware of the benefits that can be derived from a well-developed risk management program. Although most people are perhaps less able to implement these techniques in a "personal risk management" situation, the knowledge of this concept can assist them in developing the proper philosophy toward handling the personal risks they face.

Approach to Risk Management

Risk management, in its simplest form, consists of knowledge of the existence of various forms of risk and their magnitude and the management of the various methods of dealing with those risks. The ultimate goal is the recognition and control of risk. The first steps in the risk management process are *risk analysis* and *risk evaluation*.

Risk Analysis. The logical start of any risk management program is the recognition of one's risk exposures. This may not be as easy as it seems at first glance. For example, if a person hires a domestic worker in his or her home, what liability for workers' compensation exposures may exist? Also, some losses can be avoided if knowledge of the cause of loss is known in advance.

Risk Evaluation. Once a risk is discovered, it should be evaluated to determine its cause and the probable degree of control that may be had over it.

Basic Risk Management Techniques

Avoidance of Risk. *Risk avoidance* is simply the act of eliminating risk by avoiding the causes of risk. As an example, if one does not choose to drive a car, there is little risk from the auto liability peril. Of course, such drastic measures are not necessarily recommended in dealing with risks of this nature. In some cases, however, risk avoidance may be quite logical. One of the factors a family may consider in deciding whether to put a swimming pool in the backyard, for example, is whether they want to be responsible for any accidents.

Risk Reduction (Loss Control). For our purposes, *risk reduction* is almost synonymous with loss control. First, it consists of all activities intended to prevent the occurrence of a loss (loss prevention). In addition, it includes those steps taken to minimize a loss should one occur (loss reduction). An example of the former would be the removal of combustible materials (such as paints, thinners, and gasoline) from a garage or basement and storing them in an outside shed to minimize the risk of fire to the dwelling. An example of the second would be placing fire extinguishers in certain areas of the house to control a fire should one occur.

Retention (Assumption) of Risk. *Risk retention* is the conscious act of keeping or assuming a risk rather than transferring it. In some cases, such as the risk of loss from war or insurrection, retention is the only practical method of handling the risk, since insurance usually cannot be purchased for such risks. In other cases, risk retention may be the most economical alternative. For example, this usually is the case with respect to the use of deductibles, which are discussed later in this chapter. In still other cases, whether retention is the proper or most economical alternative is debatable, such as in the case of the earthquake exposure or flood exposure in certain areas.

Transfer of Risk. *Risk transfer* (including insurance) consists of any measure by which the risk of one party actually is transferred to another. A noninsurance transfer of risk can perhaps best be explained by an example. Suppose Mrs. Smith volunteers her services to supervise a Girl Scout troop on a hike. However, the Scouts' parents all sign waiver agreements agreeing not to hold Mrs. Smith liable for any injuries. In this way, Mrs. Smith's liability risk has been at least partly transferred.

Insurance is the most important type of transfer device and usually is defined as the transferring of risk to a third party (the insurance company) in return for the payment of an amount of money (the premium). For the remainder of this chapter, we shall concentrate on this most popular technique for individuals to use in their personal risk management—*insurance.*

The Insurance Principle

Not all risks are insurable. In fact, most of the risks we are exposed to in daily life are insignificant and do not involve serious financial consequences. However, there are many potentially serious events, such as fire, automobile accidents, robbery, death, and disability, that can cause substantial losses when they occur. These are the risks that insurance is all about.

In essence, insurance is a means of eliminating or reducing the financial burden of such risks by dividing the losses they produce among many individuals. For example, assume that there are 1000 individuals age 35, each of whom needs $10,000 of life insurance protection. Further assume that the chance of a male age 35 dying during the next year is 0.002, or 2 out of 1000. To protect the entire group, since a person cannot apply the laws of probability to himself or herself (that is, no individual knows who will be one of the two to die during the year), each of the 1000 individuals could agree to contribute $20 to a common fund. This fund then would be used to reimburse the families of any individuals who die during the next year. The probability is that two persons will die, and so we would expect the fund to pay out $20,000 in the next year.

Therefore, for a "premium" of $20, each individual in the group will lose no more than $20, while the risk, as far as a major financial loss is concerned, will have been reduced. Of course, under the arrangement just described, each of the 998 individuals who did not die during the year could have saved money by not joining the plan. However, no one knew beforehand which particular individuals would die during the year; therefore, each of them was subject to a serious financial risk before the "insurance" plan was adopted. This risk was reduced when each contributed $20 to the fund. The assurance that his or her family's loss would be limited to $20, rather than as much as $10,000, was the return obtained by each of the 998 for the small sum ($20) paid.

Before leaving this illustration, we must note that the overhead expenses of running such an insurance plan would add to the cost of the plan. Thus, the amount that each of the 1000 persons would have to pay must be "loaded" to cover these overhead expenses. These are the costs of running an insurance business.

Insurance Purchase Decisions

Most people must make decisions concerning which risks should be insured and which risks should be handled in other ways. To help do this, a convenient kind of measure that quickly shows the types of risks that can wipe out an individual or family financially is contained in the following simple formula:

$$\text{Relative value of a risk} = \frac{\text{total amount at stake}}{\text{total wealth}}$$

The greater the result of this formula, the less able an individual is to assume any given risk and the more he or she needs to insure the risk.

To illustrate, suppose an individual has a home worth $150,000 and a total net worth of $225,000. Applying the above formula, we have

$$\text{Relative value of the loss of the home} = \frac{\$150,000}{\$225,000} = \frac{2}{3}$$

Obviously, the risk of the home being totally destroyed—say, by fire—is too great for the individual to bear alone, because two-thirds of his or her net worth could be lost. Thus, this person would be wise to purchase fire insurance.

Now, let us assume that the same individual is wondering whether to carry a $500 deductible on the collision insurance covering his or her car. If a covered loss does occur, the insured will have to pay the first $500 as the deductible. According to our formula, we would put the $500 over the individual's total wealth and come up with a value of 0.002, or about ⅕ of 1 percent. Thus, use of the deductible seems sound. Any such loss can be handled easily by the individual. Moreover, the administrative expenses of settling such a claim would be high relative to the actual loss itself.

These two examples illustrate that the first principle of insurance buying is to place primary emphasis on those risks that potentially could wipe out or substantially deplete the person's or family's net worth. This sometimes is called the "large-loss principle." Insurance against such losses is considered *essential*. Note that the *severity* of a potential loss, not its *frequency*, should be the determining factor.

Some losses cannot be handled out of current income but nevertheless are not large enough to bankrupt the family. However, they may impair the family's accumulated savings or saddle it with unwanted debt. Insurance against these losses is considered *desirable*, provided the family's insurance budget is large enough to provide more than the essential coverages.

The final category is *available* insurance coverages. Included in this class is insurance against small losses that can be paid out of current income or an emergency fund without seriously impairing the family's financial position.

Few families will be able to afford the luxury of insurance simply because it is available to offset some possible financial loss. For most families, premium dollars are needed for insurance necessities or other purposes.

Use of Deductibles and Other Cost-Sharing Devices

Whenever feasible, the use of deductibles should be considered in insurance planning. A deductible requires the insured to pay the first portion, such as the first $100, of a covered loss before the insurance comes into play. Use of deductibles can result in several benefits for the insured. For example, it makes the insurance *less expensive,* since deductibles eliminate small losses and hence the disproportionately high administrative expenses of settling such small claims. Thus, with a deductible, higher benefits may be purchased, or insurance costs may be reduced. For example, by taking a $500 instead of a $200 deductible on automobile collision insurance, an insured might save enough premium to increase his or her liability limit from $50,000 per accident to $300,000 or more for about the same premium. Thus, by forgoing an additional $300 recovery on a small collision loss, the insured is able to guard against the possibility of a much larger liability loss that possibly could destroy him or her financially.

Deductibles can take various forms. The use of deductibles in particular lines of insurance is discussed in later chapters. Other cost-sharing devices, such as coinsurance or copayment in medical expense insurance, also are discussed in succeeding chapters.

Types of Insurers

A starting point in intelligently selecting an insurer is for the consumer to have a basic understanding of the different types of insurers that offer their wares to the public. The several thousand private insuring organizations in the United States may be broadly categorized as to whether they seek a profit for those who own the organization or whether they are nonprofit in operation. Stock insurance companies constitute the major segment of the profit-seeking insurers, while mutual insurance companies are the most important nonprofit insurers.

Profit is an elusive concept, particularly for insurers. It should not be inferred, therefore, that "nonprofit" necessarily means lower operating costs. Any broad classification of insurers sets up an almost endless chain of qualifications that may be halted by a fundamental statement: *The purchaser of insurance generally can draw no meaningful conclusions about a particular insurer solely on the basis of its legal form of organization.* Later, we shall consider the significant factors to be considered in the choice of an insurer, *but early warning should be sounded against the all-too-common error of generalization, e.g., about the safety of an insurer, the price of its coverage, or the service it provides, based solely on the insurer's legal structure.*

Profit-Seeking Insurers

As just noted, stock insurance companies are the main type of profit-seeking insurer. They are owned by stockholders who provided the original capital for the company as required by law or who acquired the stock from other shareholders. Stock companies seek to pay dividends to their stockholders after the payment of claims and expenses and normally the provision for additions to surplus.

It has been traditional for stock insurance companies to sell coverage at a fixed price. Thus, until recent decades, most stock insurance companies issued nonparticipating policies; that is, they paid no dividends to policyholders in the event of underwriting (or investment) profits. There is a current tendency, however, for many stock insurers to offer "par" (participating) policies, particularly in the life insurance field. However, contracts with a fixed cost still constitute a large portion of the business of most stock insurers.

Lloyd's of London, one of the best-known insurance organizations in the world, also is considered a profit-seeking insurance operation. The operations of the underwriters at Lloyd's, however, do not directly affect most individual insurance consumers.

Nonprofit Insurers

There are various kinds of nonprofit insurers and comparable organizations from whom coverage may be purchased. There really is no uniform pattern among them.

Mutual Insurance Companies.   These companies have no capital stock and, therefore, no stockholders. Technically they are owned by their policyholders. This is the primary difference between mutual insurance companies and stock insurance companies. However, both are organized as corporations. In theory, the policyholders of a mutual company exercise control through their right to elect the corporation's board of directors.

Technically, mutual insurers may be assessable or nonassessable. Many of the early, smaller mutual insurers required no payment of premiums at the inception of the protection period. Rather, insureds had to pay their share of each claim as it arose, which was the insured's assessment. Thus, these insurers were termed assessment mutuals. This approach is not significant today however, because most mutual insurers have modified or eliminated the assessment concept, and the bulk of insurance currently written by mutual insurance companies is "nonassessable." This means that the premium the insured pays to the mutual insurer is the most the insured will have to pay for his or her insurance coverage. The insured cannot be assessed further. As a matter of fact, the charters of major mutual insurers generally prohibit assessment. The nonassessable arrangement is made possible by the fact that before mutual insurers can issue nonassessable policies in a particular state, they generally must meet the same financial requirements stipulated for stock insurers. A policy issued by a mutual insurer must indicate on its face whether it is nonassessable. While there may be arguments on the other side, in general, consumers should buy only nonassessable insurance, or possibly insurance where the right of assessment is strictly limited.

But even in nonassessable mutuals, the final cost of insurance coverage often is unknown, although insureds never have to pay more than the advance premium. This is because policyholders may receive policy dividends, thus reducing the cost of the coverage. Policy dividends are entirely different from dividends on common stocks. Policy dividends, at least to an important extent, amount to a return of unneeded premium and thus are a cost reduction for the policyholder. Therefore, they are not subject to federal income taxation. Dividends on stocks, on the other hand, are a type of investment income and normally are taxable income.

Not all mutual insurance is "participating," that is, entitled to the possible payment of dividends. Some mutual health insurance and property and liability insurance policies, for instance, are nonparticipating. Sometimes mutual property and liability insurers will write insurance at lower initial premiums than otherwise would have been the case, instead of paying dividends at the end of the policy period. Mutual life insurance is almost always participating.

A few insurers write "perpetual" property insurance in limited geographic areas. The perpetual approach requires the payment of a relatively large advance premium, which is invested by the insurance company; the investment earnings on the advance premium are expected to be more than sufficient to pay claims and expenses. In addition, perpetual companies frequently pay generous dividends to their policyholders along with providing insurance protection. Thus, perpetual insurance combines property insurance with investment returns. Normally, the insured may cancel the perpetual contract at any time and get back 90 to 100 percent of the deposit premium, depending on how long the policy has been in force.

Hospital and Medical Expense Associations.   Much early hospital, surgical, and medical expense protection was issued by nonprofit associations.

A substantial portion still is written by these organizations, which include Blue Cross-Blue Shield plans.

Most of these associations have been established at the instigation of hospitals, physicians, dentists, or civic groups. Covered persons, called "subscribers," are not the owners of the associations, nor do they generally have a vote in the selection of the board of directors. Technical control of a plan often rests with a "corporation," a body composed of various occupational and civic representatives.

Hospital service associations, of which Blue Cross plans are the most significant, were the first types of nonprofit health care associations to be organized on a wide scale. The hospital associations have sought in most instances to obtain hospital services on a cost basis for subscribers through contractual arrangements with hospitals and possibly other institutions that provide health care services.

Blue Shield plans and other medical service associations (e.g., organizations providing surgical and certain medical benefits) were developed after the hospital service associations. The two types of organizations ordinarily operate under similar rules and often cooperate in performing various functions.

The establishment and use of health maintenance organizations (HMOs) is an important development in this field. HMOs generally offer comprehensive benefits, little or no cost sharing (i.e., have few or no deductibles or coinsurance), and emphasize prevention. They generally operate either as group practice plans or as individual practice associations (IPAs). The participating physicians in a group practice plan are employed by or under contract with the HMO, while the participating physicians in an IPA-type plan operate in private practices under a contractual arrangement with the HMO to provide the plan's benefits to covered persons. Employers normally offer one or more HMOs to their employees as part of their employee benefit plan. Persons also may participate in HMOs on an individual basis. However, employees or others electing HMO coverage have restrictions placed on their choice of health care providers, which restrictions may or may not be significant to them.

Reciprocal Insurance Exchanges. Reciprocal exchanges (also called "interinsurance exchanges") are a type of nonprofit insurer resembling mutual insurance companies in many ways despite organizational, operational, and local differences between the two. In a reciprocal, those insured assume a proportionate share of every risk being pooled (except their own). Thus, each insured is individually liable for a portion of the risk presented by every other insured in the organization. Reciprocals may operate on an assessable or nonassessable basis. The bulk of the business written by reciprocals is automobile and fire insurance.

Considerations in Choosing
an Insurer

Selection of an insurer or insurers is one of the practical problems faced in buying insurance. In many cases, this problem may be resolved either by the selection (or acceptance) of an agent or broker, who then determines the insurer to be used, or by the use of direct insurance-buying facilities (e.g., through the mail or at a counter or booth in a place of business patronized by the individual). Unfortunately, some insureds may not even be able to identify the insuring organization with which they are placed. However, more insureds appear to be taking an interest in the actual choice of the insurers through whom they will obtain protection. This interest may be fostered by such factors as rising premiums in some lines of insurance, extensive advertising by insurers and others, consumers' guides issued by some state insurance departments, intense competition among all insurers, the general mood of "consumerism" in the country, or the concern in recent years over the financial soundness of some insurers.

We noted above that *no generalization should be made concerning a particular insurer solely on the basis of its legal form of organization.* Instead, insurers should be evaluated on the basis of such aspects of the insured-insurer relationship as the *financial soundness of the insurer,* the extent and quality of the *service it will render the insured,* the *types of coverage and policies the insurer offers,* and the *price* it charges for a particular coverage.

Financial Soundness

General Considerations.　The financial soundness of an insurer is of obvious interest to potential insureds. This has become particularly true as of this writing due to the well-publicized insolvencies of a few sizable insurance companies and the financial difficulties of some others.

Unfortunately, it is difficult for the average person to assess the financial status of an insurer. This problem arises in part from the specialized accounting methods used by insurers and their practices in setting up reserves. Also, the financial soundness and stability of an insuring organization are affected to a considerable degree by a number of factors, such as the types and quality of insurance it writes, its reinsurance arrangements, the nature and quality of its assets, the quality of its management, and many others. As a consequence, the asset–liability position of an insurer is not the only indication of its financial soundness.

Nevertheless, one measure of financial soundness that is used is the insurer's policyholders' surplus ratio. This ratio is shown by the formula

$$\text{Policyholders' surplus ratio} = \frac{\text{insurer net worth (i.e., assets - liabilities)}}{\text{insurer liabilities}}$$

While this ratio certainly is not the complete answer, it is used in the insurance industry. It can also be easily calculated from an insurance company's balance sheet. Note that the policyholders' surplus ratio compares net worth with liabilities, which is logical. Beware of insurance company claims of financial strength based on assets alone. Companies, in effect, may say, "Look how strong we are; we have over X million in assets." However, numbers of dollars of assets alone mean little in judging an insurer's financial strength.

Buyers of insurance also may receive some assurance about the strength and stability of insurers through the regulatory procedures of the various states. While the financial requirements that insurers must meet vary considerably among the states, there nevertheless may be some indication that an insurer is stable and financially sound if it is authorized to issue coverage in states that do have effective insurance regulation. People often cite New York State as an example in this regard. Some sources of information dealing with an insurer's financial strength are discussed later in this chapter.

Financial Ratings of Insurers.   Perhaps the most widely used, and most readily available to consumers, measure of the financial soundness or the claims-paying ability of insurance companies is the *financial ratings* given to many insurance companies, particularly the larger ones, by several *independent insurance rating services*. While there are several such services rating insurance companies (including both life and health insurers and property and liability insurers), probably the most widely followed are *A. M. Best, Moody's,* and *Standard & Poor's.* Two other frequently mentioned services are *Duff & Phelps* and *Weiss Research.* Each of these services differs at least to some degree from the others, and their rating grades and standards are not uniform. This has created a somewhat confusing situation in which a given insurer may have several ratings from different rating services, creating what some commentators have jokingly referred to as "alphabet soup."

Nevertheless, as a practical matter, the rating services' gradings for insurers are probably the main, or perhaps the only, measures that most consumers will have as to the financial soundness or claims-paying ability of particular insurance companies. Therefore, these financial strength ratings have become quite important, particularly in times of economic uncertainty. Before purchasing insurance from an insurer, consumers should check into whether the insurance company has been rated by one or more of the independent rating services, and if so, what its financial strength ratings are by each of the services that rated the insurer. Consumers also should inquire into whether the insurance company's rating or ratings have recently been downgraded (lowered) by any of the rating services, and if so, why. Some insurers are not rated by any of the rating services, and others are rated by one or more but not all of the services.

While the ratings of the different services do not exactly correspond to each other, and their standards may differ to some degree, it will be helpful at least to list here the hierarchy of the insurance company financial strength ratings as of 1992 for the three most widely followed rating services. These hierarchies of ratings, listed from highest to lowest, are as follows (the ratings of these services are not necessarily consistent with each other just because they are placed parallel in this listing):

Moody's	Standard & Poor's	A. M. Best
Aaa	AAA	A++
Aa1	AA+	A+
Aa2	AA	A
Aa3	AA–	A–
A1	A+	
A2	A	B++
A3	A–	B+
Baa1	BBB+	
Baa2	BBB	B
Baa3	BBB–	B–
Ba1	BB+	
Ba2	BB	C++
Ba3	BB–	C+
B1	B+	
B2	B	C
B3	B–	C–
Caa	CCC	D
Ca	CC	E
C	D	F

As noted above, consumers (both individuals and businesses) are now paying considerable attention to these independent rating services' financial strength ratings for insurance companies in making their insurance purchase decisions—as indeed they should.

State Insurance Guaranty Funds.   Some protection also is provided to consumers by state guaranty funds, which may reimburse insureds and claimants for certain of the losses they may suffer due to the insolvency of insurance companies in the state. All states now have such guaranty funds that separately cover life insurance companies and property and liability insurance companies. Except for New York State (which has a preinsolvency guaranty fund), the states have what are called postinsolvency (or postassessment) guaranty funds, under which the insurance companies of a certain type doing business in the state are assessed up to an annual limit to pay for losses to policyholders or claimants *after* the insolvency of an insurance company.

While these state guaranty funds offer valuable protection to policyholders and claimants in the event of insurer insolvencies, there are limits to the amount of protection they provide to individual claimants against the funds, and the funds may not be available to cover all losses or in all circumstances. Further, these state guaranty funds are of relatively recent origin, and so no one knows how they will perform in the face of sustained economic difficulties. Therefore, it does not seem prudent for buyers of insurance to place primary reliance on the state guaranty funds to protect them against the insolvency or financial weakness of insurance companies from which they may buy insurance. Instead, buyers of insurance should do their best to make sure that their *first consideration* is to purchase their insurance or annuities *only* from financially sound insurance companies in the first place, and then also try, to the extent they can, to move their insurance or annuities from any insurance company that becomes financially weak or in danger to a financially sound insurer.

General Observations on Insurer Financial Soundness for the Consumer.   Unfortunately, there are no hard-and-fast rules that can be provided to guide consumers only to financially secure insurers. All that really can be offered are some general observations that may prove helpful to buyers of insurance. No one can know what will happen in the future. Also, there can be honest differences of opinion regarding these solvency issues and regarding the economy in general. Further, no general observations can deal with all the particular situations that may arise. However, given all these caveats, the following are some general observations that may help consumers buy their insurance from financially sound insurers.

- It is very helpful for the insurer to be rated by *at least two* of the independent insurance rating services, and that their ratings be consistent with each other, stable, and on the high side of the hierarchy of ratings shown above. What the minimum acceptable ratings might be is very difficult to say, but an example might be that an insurer should be at least within the top four grades of at least two rating services, unless there is an adequate explanation of why it is not.

- It is also helpful for the insurer to do business in and be subject to the regulation of one or more states with capable, effective insurance regulation, such as New York State.

- Consumers should watch the general financial press for any unfavorable (or positive) news items about the insurer. Sometimes an insurer's financial condition can deteriorate relatively quickly (or the deterioration can come to light quickly), even though the insurer may have received relatively high grades from one or more rating services in the recent past.

- If the insurer's products or rates (such as the interest rates being paid on its annuity contracts or universal life insurance contracts) seem to be too good to be true, they probably are too good to be true for a sound insurer. Thus, if an insurer's product terms, prices, or rates of return are *way out of line* with those of comparable products generally available from other insurance companies in the industry, watch out!

- From the viewpoint of financial strength, there may be some advantages in dealing with insurers with proven track records of financial soundness and stability over a reasonably long period of time. However, it must be stated that this comment has not held true in a few recent cases of well-established, formerly highly regarded insurers that have unexpectedly (at least to their policyholders) run into financial problems.

- If an insurer does weaken financially, the insured or policyowner should evaluate whether to secure other coverage and then cancel the coverage with the weakened insurer in the case of property and liability insurance, or whether to exchange a life insurance policy or an annuity contract in the weaker insurer for a comparable contract in a stronger insurer (which would be a tax-free exchange under Section 1035 of the Internal Revenue Code, provided the tax law requirements for such exchanges are met). There may, however, be charges or disadvantages to such exchanges or cancellations that should be evaluated under the circumstances.

As noted above, generalizations in the area are difficult to make and are certainly not perfect. As of this writing, however, the issue of the solvency of insurance companies is of intense interest to the insurance-buying public, and this public needs at least some general guidelines for dealing with this issue. Before closing the discussion on the financial strength of insurers, however, it should emphatically be pointed out that historically the insurance industry has had an enviable record for financial strength and soundness. Further, the vast majority of insurers are sound and secure.

Service

There are many facets to the service an insurer might be expected to offer its customers. *Claims service*—the expeditiousness and fairness with which claims are settled—naturally is a major consideration. An insurer should be expected to provide equitable claims settlement that is neither too low nor

too high. An idea of the general reputation of a particular insurer relative
to claims settlement sometimes can be gained by asking several acquain-
tances about their experience with the insurer. Some people will always
think they have been cheated, whether in connection with insurance claims
or in any other business dealings; but by obtaining and evaluating the com-
ments of a number of individuals one may be able to get an impression of
an insurer's claims practices. Then, too, the reputation of the insurance
agent or broker in itself may testify to the type of claims service to expect.
In fact, in some instances agents have authority to settle certain claims for
an insurer. Even without claim settlement authority, an agent often is in a
position to present very effectively an insured's position concerning a claim
to the insurer. Thus, an agent or broker of good repute can be expected to
render considerable assistance to the insured if a claim arises.

A number of services in addition to claims treatment may be important
to insureds. For example, *life and health insurance programming and other
estate analysis services* in life insurance and *risk analysis and insurance sur-
veys* for property and liability insurance may be of importance. As noted in
Chap. 1, such services can be of considerable aid to the consumer in the
personal financial planning process.

Types of Coverage

The types of contracts a particular insurer offers in a given area of insurance are a consideration. Some insurers have a broader portfolio of policies to offer the public than others. Also, some insurers may offer
more attractive policies (in terms of coverage or price or both) in some
areas, while other insurers may have better contracts in other areas of
insurance. Therefore, it is not unusual or illogical for consumers to buy
insurance from several insurers to meet their insurance needs. There
may be reasons, however, for keeping some kinds of insurance with the
same insurer, such as liability insurance, for example, for claims-handling
reasons.

Price

It is self-evident that the price charged for a given amount of insurance is of
great significance to insurance buyers. It also goes almost without saying
that price considerations should never be placed above financial safety,
since protection in an unstable organization is a questionable buy at any
price. Also, if a particular policy is available at a lower cost because the
insurer provides less service of a particular type, such as claims service or
evaluating customers' risk situations, customers should evaluate how
important the service is to them.

To some extent, the price of a given policy may depend on the type of sales organization used by the insurer. Here again, the question of which services are important to the customer is a significant consideration.

It should be noted again in connection with price considerations that the legal form of organization of an insurer gives no direct clue as to the competitiveness of its premiums. For example, it would be incorrect to assume that the coverage of a stock insurance company, which may pay dividends to its stockholders, is necessarily more expensive than mutual insurance. Many stock insurance companies offer participating policies, and the total amount of dividends paid to stockholders in large stock companies generally is but a small fraction of their overall operating expenses. On the other hand, it is equally improper to think that the cost of mutual insurance is erratic. The dividends of most mutuals, for instance, have had a tendency to be stable over a period of years, and the final cost of mutual (participating) protection could have been predicted reasonably closely in the past.

In general, the selection of an insurer presents some of the same kinds of problems as the selection of a doctor or a lawyer or the choice of an important item such as a home. In relatively few decisions of this nature is the choice clear-cut; rather, one must weigh relative factors on the basis of information that is not always readily available or easily interpreted.

The existence of several thousand insurers in the United States virtually precludes an insurer-by-insurer comparison. Most individual insureds are limited to a selection from among insurers with sales representatives— agents, brokers, employees, or other sales methods—within their locale. Furthermore, many lines of insurance often are not purchased unless some type of sales effort is made toward prospective insureds. The range of choice then is reduced to those insurers who make themselves available to an individual. However, the more knowledgeable the consumer, the more likely it is that he or she will evaluate such aspects as financial strength, service, and price in an intelligent manner.

Sources of Information

Several sources of information are available to an insured or prospective insured who wants to know more about an insurer's financial strength, service, and cost. Published sources provide the most detailed information. The sources noted here are illustrative only and are not meant to be exhaustive. The annual reports that insurers must submit to state insurance departments provide extensive information on the financial affairs of the insurer and may be consulted by the public. Sometimes an insurance commissioner will issue a report which condenses much of this information, and many insurers will send interested parties copies of their reports to stockholders or policyholders.

Reporting services, however, are the most frequently consulted sources. In life insurance, illustrative reporting services include: *Best's Life Reports* and *The Spectator Insurance Year Book,* which present the background histories of most insurers, the lines of insurance they write, the states in which they operate, and detailed financial data; *Flitcraft* and *Life Rates & Data,* which indicate the principal policy provisions, premium rates and dividend rates (for participating policies), and the settlement option values used by most life insurers; *The Handy Guide,* which reproduces one insurance contract issued by each of the leading insurers and, in addition, presents important premium information; *Settlement Options,* which also contains tables of settlement option values but in addition describes in detail the practices of most insurers with respect to settlement options; *Who Writes What in Life and Health Insurance,* which lists the contracts and underwriting practices of the leading life and health insurers; and *Time Saver,* which analyzes the policies and rates of most health insurers.

In property and liability insurance, *Best's Insurance Reports, Fire and Casualty* occupies a position similar to *Best's Life Reports* in life insurance. For each insurer, this service describes the history, management, and general underwriting policy of the insurer and presents detailed financial data. *Who Writes What?* is similar for property and liability insurance to *Who Writes What in Life and Health Insurance. Best's Aggregates and Averages* reports important financial data for leading insurers and the industry. *The Fire, Casualty, and Surety Bulletins* provide up-to-date information on property and liability insurance coverages. A few state insurance departments have distributed tables of rates charged by different insurers.

Other sources of information are agents and insurers, who can supply specimen contracts and premium information; other consumers, especially those facing the same problems; and the consumer's own personal experiences.

The various insurance rating services providing ratings of the financial soundness or claims paying ability of life and health and property and liability insurance companies have already been noted in the discussion of financial ratings of insurers on pp. 54–55 of this chapter. Information on these ratings may be obtained by consumers from libraries, the insurance companies or their agents or brokers, state insurance departments, from reference sources sold by the rating services, and sometimes directly from the rating services.

Considerations in Choosing an Agent or Broker

General Considerations

How does an individual go about finding a good insurance agent or broker? What readily visible earmarks are there that will enable the insurance buyer to select an agent or broker wisely from the start? The answer is practically none—that is, practically none that are readily visible. There are several, however, that the individual buyer should try to evaluate. The consumer can ask pertinent questions, such as: What is the experience of agents or brokers in terms of years and extent of practice? Are they noted specialists in any certain line? Do they do business mostly with individual households, with business firms, or on a general across-the-board basis? How do they sell insurance? Do they engage in survey selling? Do they present a unified program of coverage based on a careful analysis of exposures? Do they represent a sound company or companies? The answers to all these questions offer some measure of the quality of agents or brokers.

In selecting an insurer, a consumer must pay attention to financial strength, service, and cost. In selecting an agent or broker, the consumer must realize that service and cost are the primary factors to be considered. The ability of agents or brokers to service their insureds depends on their knowledge of the insurance business, their understanding of special problems, and their ability (in terms of time, interest, analytical skill, markets, and facilities) to help the consumer design and implement, with minimum delay and cost, a proper program of protection. The agent's or broker's task does not terminate, however, with the design and implementation of the original program. Insurance needs change constantly, and the program must be kept up to date. In addition, when losses occur, agents or brokers can render valuable assistance. They also provide or request additional services, such as appraisals, when desirable or necessary.

Information about Advisors

Obtaining information about agents, brokers, and other sales representatives is much more difficult than investigating insurers. The service to be provided is the principal issue, and published sources cannot provide this type of information. Personal or business associates may be able to provide some useful evaluations of agents and brokers as well as insurers, but the most satisfactory source of information probably is personal contact with the agent or broker.

One positive indication of a financial planner's or an insurance representative's knowledge and basic professional commitment to his or her career is whether he or she has earned the Certified Financial Planner (CFP) designation, the Chartered Property Casualty Underwriter (CPCU) designation, the Chartered Life Underwriter (CLU) designation, and other corresponding professional degrees or designations. Depending on the particular program, to obtain these designations, a practitioner must have passed a series of examinations covering such diverse fields as insurance and risk management, law, economics, social legislation, finance, investments, accounting, taxation, estate planning, employee benefits, and management. Although it is true that many competent practitioners do not have these designations, and that designations do not always indicate competence, the consumer should be aware of the existence and meaning of CFP, CLU, and CPCU.

4

Life Insurance and Social Security

Once it is determined that some form of life insurance is needed to protect against the economic risk of premature death, many questions still remain. They include, among many similar questions: Should one buy term life insurance and invest the difference? Should one purchase traditional whole life insurance or certain newer forms such as universal life insurance? Is participating or nonparticipating life insurance the better buy? Should one buy what might be termed guaranteed principal (or nonvariable) life insurance or variable life insurance? What provisions are included in a policy? Should one purchase extra coverages such as double indemnity, guaranteed insurability, or other supplementary benefits? How does social security affect life insurance planning? This chapter responds to such questions concerning the decisions involved in life insurance planning.

Sources of Life Insurance Protection

But before responding to such questions, we shall consider the various sources (and forms) of life insurance available to consumers. As far as the consumer is concerned, they can conveniently be broken down into (1) individually purchased, (2) employer-sponsored, and (3) government-sponsored life insurance coverages.

Individually Purchased Life Insurance

Individually purchased life insurance is characterized by the sale of life insurance on an individual basis. That is, the individual typically applies for and, if found insurable, is issued an individual contract of life insurance. The various forms of individually purchased life insurance include ordinary life insurance, industrial life insurance, credit life insurance, fraternal life insurance, and savings bank life insurance.

Ordinary Life Insurance. This category of life insurance typically is sold through an agent or broker to the individual. An applicant for ordinary life insurance may obtain any amount he or she wishes, as long as the insurer is willing to write it and the applicant can afford the coverage. Premiums for ordinary life insurance policies usually are paid directly to the insurer on an annual, semiannual, quarterly, or monthly basis. There are three basic types of traditional ordinary life[1] insurance: term, whole life, and endowment. These are discussed later in this chapter. Universal life and variable life also can be considered types of ordinary life insurance in this sense and also are discussed later in this chapter.

Industrial Life Insurance. This form of life insurance normally is issued in small amounts, with premiums payable on a weekly or monthly basis, and with premiums generally collected at the home of the insured by an agent of the insurance company. In recent years, industrial life insurance in force has decreased. It generally is a high-cost form of life insurance. It also may be referred to as home service life insurance.

Credit Life Insurance. Credit life insurance may be written on either an individual or a group basis, but most of it is written as group insurance. This coverage is issued through a lender or lending agency to cover the payment of a loan, installment purchase, or other obligation in the event of the debtor's death. Credit life insurance protects both the debtor and the creditor against loss as a result of the debtor's death during the term of the loan. The debtor normally pays for this coverage.

Fraternal Life Insurance. This life insurance is available through membership in a lodge or fraternal order, religious group, or the like. In the past, the number of fraternal insurers was large and they operated on an almost pure assessment basis, with uniform assessments regardless of age

---

[1] There often is confusion concerning the term "ordinary" as it pertains to types of life insurance. The word "ordinary" can have two very different meanings. "Ordinary life" can be used to mean that type of insurance on which a minimum amount of insurance, such as $1000, is written on an annual premium basis. It is thus used to distinguish this type of insurance from group insurance and industrial insurance. This is how the term is used here. But "ordinary" also is commonly used to indicate the kind of policy where protection is furnished for the whole of life. In this regard, "ordinary" is used interchangeably with "whole life" and "straight life."

each time a death occurred. Today, however, fraternal insurers generally operate on a legal-reserve basis, as other life insurers do.

Savings Bank Life Insurance. The distinctive feature of savings bank life insurance, sold by mutual savings banks, is that it is transacted on an over-the-counter basis, or by mail, without the use of agents. Currently, only three states permit savings bank life insurance: Massachusetts, New York, and Connecticut. Savings bank life insurance is available only to residents of, or workers in, these states, but, of course, such coverage remains in force if the policyholder should leave the state. The amount of savings bank life insurance obtainable by any one applicant is limited by law.

Association Group Life Insurance. A person may become eligible to buy group or wholesale (see below) life insurance by being a member of one or more associations of individuals, such as professional, fraternal, alumni, and community service groups. The life insurance usually is sold to members of the group through the mail, with limited individual selection and with the insured person paying the entire cost. Only certain plans and amounts of coverage are normally available. Once insured, the covered person normally can continue term life insurance coverage until a certain age, such as 70 or 75, unless he or she terminates membership in the association or unless the association group policy itself is terminated.

Life insurance plans of this type are usually sold to association members on the basis of low cost. When deciding whether to buy coverage under an association group plan, however, it is important to compare its cost with that of other life insurance plans on the same basis. One association group plan written for the members of a college fraternity, for example, would provide $40,000 of group term life insurance (with waiver of premium) for members age 35 through 44 at a semiannual premium of about $100. This amounts to an annual premium of $5 per $1000 ($100 × 2 ÷ 40) for term insurance in that age bracket. With this information, the cost of this plan now can be compared with the cost of other term policies (or other life insurance plans).

Employer-Sponsored Life Insurance

The employer-employee relationship can result in providing employees with substantial life insurance protection. The vast bulk of this life insurance is provided as an employee benefit. However, the employment mechanism also sometimes provides a convenient means of purchasing life insurance on an employee-pay-all basis. The various employer-sponsored life insurance programs include group life insurance, wholesale life insurance, salary savings life insurance, and group universal life plans (GULP).

Group Life Insurance.   Group life insurance generally is available as an employee benefit through an individual's place of employment, with part or all of the cost generally being paid by the employer. Group life is generally issued without individual evidence of insurability, while individual life insurance generally requires some evidence of insurability. The amount of group life insurance on individual employees normally is determined by some type of benefit formula. Because of its importance to most people, group life insurance is discussed in greater detail later in this chapter.

Wholesale Life Insurance.   This is a hybrid between individual and group life insurance, utilizing some of the principles of each. Wholesale life insurance normally is used for groups too small to qualify for group life insurance and also for association group cases. Under wholesale life insurance, an individual policy is issued to each person in the group and there is some individual underwriting.

Salary Savings Life Insurance.   This plan was developed mainly as a marketing tool for selling regular forms of individual life insurance to employees under a convenient arrangement for paying their premiums through their employer. Its distinguishing characteristics are the collection of premiums on a monthly basis from the employer, who deducts the necessary amounts from the wages or salaries of the insured employees; the necessity of individual evidence of insurability; and the issuance of individual life insurance policies to the insured persons. There normally are little or no cost savings for the insured employees.

Group Universal Life Insurance.   This is a recent development and is a group employee-pay-all version of individual universal life (UL) insurance.[2] A group universal life plan (GULP) is made available to the employees of an employer on a voluntary basis, with the employees being able to decide, within limits, how much life insurance they wish to purchase and how much premium they wish to contribute to the savings element (cash value) of the plan. Employee premium contributions are deducted by the employer from their pay. The employee's contributions go to pay for the mortality cost ("pure" term cost) of the life insurance on his or her life, for any administrative expense charge for the plan, and normally for an addition to the cash value of the insurance that stands to the employee's credit under the plan. Interest is credited to these cash values by the insurance company at a rate set periodically by the insurer, but with a minimum guaranteed interest rate for the plan below which the rate set by the insurance company may not go. Participating employees may withdraw their cash val-

---

[2] Individual UL insurance is described in greater detail on pp. 76–78 of this chapter.

ues from the plan, take policy loans against them, and upon termination of employment continue the coverage by making their premium payments directly to the insurance company (this is referred to as the coverage's being "portable").

There is no direct tax advantage to participating employees in a GULP as compared with simply purchasing their own individual UL policies from an insurance company. This is because participating employees pay the full cost of a GULP from their after-tax pay (on a salary withholding basis). The employer does not contribute to the GULP.

However, there may be certain advantages to participating employees in purchasing their coverage through a GULP. Employees normally can secure certain amounts of life insurance on their lives through a GULP on a guaranteed issue basis (i.e., with no individual underwriting). In addition, periodic open enrollment times may be available during which employees may later decide to enroll in the plan (again with no individual underwriting). Thus, otherwise uninsurable employees or employees who might be rated for individually underwritten life insurance may be able to obtain some universal life insurance at standard rates under these plans. Further, some of the rating factors (e.g., the mortality charges, expense charges, or interest credited) may be somewhat more favorable under a GULP than for individual UL policies because a GULP is written on a group basis. However, this is not assured and depends largely on the insurance companies involved. It also may be somewhat more convenient to purchase UL insurance through a GULP.

Federal Government Life Insurance Programs

U.S. Government Life Insurance (USGLI) and National Service Life Insurance (NSLI) were government life insurance programs enacted during World War I and World War II, respectively. The issuance of new insurance under these plans has since been terminated and replaced with Servicemen's Group Life Insurance (SGLI), which started in 1965. All servicemen and servicewomen on active duty are eligible for up to $100,000 of group term life insurance at group rates. Upon separation from active duty, veterans can continue this group term life insurance, now referred to as Veterans' Group Life Insurance (VGLI), for up to 5 years at the group rates for their attained age. After this 5-year period, veterans have the right to convert all or part of this insurance into regular life insurance written by a participating life insurance company without individual evidence of insurability.

Although it is normally not thought of as life insurance, social security provides survivorship benefits which, in essence, represent significant death benefits. These survivorship benefits are described in this chapter.

Types of Individual Life Insurance Contracts

As indicated earlier, there have been three traditional basic types of individual life insurance contracts: term, whole life, and endowment. In addition, there have been various kinds of contracts, sometimes with imaginative names, which are, when analyzed, often found to be one of, or some combination of, these basic forms.

In recent years, however, a number of newer types of individual life insurance contracts have been developed. These contracts have tended to emphasize the investment aspects of life insurance and are quite different in concept from the traditional forms of cash value (or "permanent") life insurance contracts.

Considerations in Purchasing Individual Life Insurance

Assuming that a person (or persons) needs individual life insurance, one of the fundamental issues that must be decided is what type or types of individual life insurance contracts to purchase and from which insurance company or companies to purchase the coverage. However, in making this fundamental choice the consumer really has to make decisions on several subissues. The first of these subissues is whether the person wants to rely largely or entirely on term life insurance for his or her insurance needs. If so, then presumably the person will look to non-life-insurance investment media for his or her investment or savings needs and will not purchase much, if any, individual life insurance that accumulates a cash value as part of the contract (so-called permanent or cash-value life insurance). The question then becomes what kind of term insurance to buy.

On the other hand, if the person is interested in a cash value (in effect a savings or investment element) as part of the life insurance contract, then he or she must decide whether to buy cash value life insurance in which the cash value is guaranteed as to the principal amount and a minimum rate of return by the insurance company (what might be termed "guaranteed-dollar" or "fixed-dollar" policies) and for which the investment decisions and presumably the investment risks fall on the insurance company; or in which the investment of the cash value (asset allocation of the cash value) is decided upon by the policyowner from among the separate accounts (investment funds) made available under the policy (variable life insurance) and thus where the investment decisions and the investment risks inherent in the separate accounts fall on the individual policyowner. Thus, this subissue within cash-value life insurance is whether the buyer wants *guaranteed-dollar life insurance* or *variable life insurance*.

Another subissue is whether either of these approaches to cash-value life insurance should be on a *fixed-premium basis,* where the periodic premium essentially is set in advance based on the insured's age, sex, and whether the insured is a smoker or a nonsmoker; or on a *flexible-premium basis,* where the policyowner decides, within limits, what, if any, premium will be paid in any given year. While there are several kinds of flexible-premium life insurance, the most widely discussed and used is universal life insurance.

Thus, from the viewpoint of selecting the type of individual life insurance contract or contracts to buy, the consumer is faced with the following system of choices.

  I. Term Insurance
 II. Cash-Value or "Permanent" Life Insurance
    A. "Guaranteed-Dollar" Policies
      1. Traditional (Fixed-Premium) Cash-Value Life Insurance
      2. Flexible-Premium Policies [Universal Life (UL) Insurance]
    B. Variable Policies
      1. Variable Life Insurance (VL)
      2. Universal Variable Life Insurance (UVL)

Although there are numerous policy variations within each of the types in the above system, this classification shows the basic conceptual choices the consumer may make in buying individual life insurance contracts. This is the system of analysis used next to describe these types of contracts in greater detail.

The previous general outline of types of life insurance policies assumes only that one life is insured. In other words, there is a life insurance contract whose death proceeds will be paid upon the death of one person—the insured. Another approach to individual life insurance is to insure two lives under the same policy (i.e., have two insureds) with the death proceeds normally payable at the death of the second insured to die. These policies often are called joint last survivor or second-to-die policies and are also described in this chapter.

Term Insurance

Perhaps no other type of life insurance has generated so much confusion, and sometimes controversy, as term insurance.

Nature and Uses of Term Insurance. Term life insurance provides financial protection for a specified period. If death should occur during the specified period, the face amount of the policy is paid, with nothing being paid in the event the insured survives the period. Term insurance thus is comparable to most forms of property and liability insurance. Term policies generally have no cash or loan values. Since term insurance provides "pure" protection without also building up a cash value or investment fund in the life insurance contract, as of a given age at purchase, it has a low premium per $1000 of life insurance, as compared with whole life and endowment policies.

The very nature of term insurance suggests how it may be used in meeting a person's needs for life insurance protection. Term insurance often is used when the need for protection is temporary, or when the need is permanent but the insured cannot currently afford the premiums for some type of cash-value life insurance, or when the insured decides to use the strategy of using term insurance only for "pure" insurance protection and of investing his or her savings or investment dollars elsewhere (the "buy term and invest the difference" philosophy).

When term insurance is used where the need is permanent but the insured temporarily cannot afford the premium for a more permanent type of life insurance that the insured ultimately wants, as more funds become available, the policyowner may convert some or all of a term policy (assuming that it is convertible) to more permanent forms of insurance. Or the policyowner may undertake some other combination of term insurance and investment if that is his or her planned strategy.

Kinds of Term Life Insurance.   While term insurance is rather simple in concept, there are a number of different contracts on the market that the consumer might consider just for "pure" life insurance protection. Also, the prices charged for term insurance can vary considerably among life insurance companies, and so some "shopping" by the consumer, or by an agent or broker representing the consumer, may produce premium savings in this area. However, this said, it is important that the same kind of term contract be compared and that only financially sound (as described in Chap. 3) life insurers be considered.

In terms of amount of insurance, the two main kinds of term insurance are level term and decreasing term. *Level term insurance* provides a specified level amount of insurance for the indicated time period. This time period may be for 1 year [called yearly renewable term (YRT) or annually renewable term (ART)]; 5 years; 10 years; 20 years; to a certain age, such as 65; or for other time periods. The premium charged per $1000 of insurance increases for each successive time period as the insured's attained age increases. Thus, for a YRT policy of, say, $200,000 issued on a male age 35, at the end of the first year the premium rate per $1000 would be that for a male age 36 (the insured's then-attained age), and so on for each year the YRT policy is renewed. As a result, the cost of a level amount of term insurance will continually increase as the insured grows older. It will be quite low when the insured is younger (say, under age 40), but it will increase dramatically as the insured gets older.

Decreasing term insurance, on the other hand, provides a declining amount of insurance over the period of the contract. A good example is mortgage protection insurance designed to cover the insured for an amount that will pay off a home mortgage which decreases over time. Sometimes it also may be used to meet the currently sizable protection needs for a family where it is perceived that the need for life insurance may decrease over time as the children become self-supporting.

Many term policies are *renewable* for successive periods of time at the policyowner's option without having to show any evidence of insurability at renewal. The age to which such policies may be renewed often is limited. Term policies also generally are *convertible*. This means the policyowner has the right during the conversion period to change the term policy into a whole life or other "permanent" level-premium policy of a like (or lesser) amount of insurance without having to show any evidence of insurability at the time of conversion. Again, the age up to which a term policy may be converted usually is limited and often is lower than the maximum age for renewability. As an example, one large insurance company writes a YRT policy that is renewable to age 100, convertible to age 65, and will be issued by the insurer up to age 65. The renewable and convertible features of term policies can be particularly valuable for insureds who later become uninsurable or insurable only on a substandard basis.

In terms of the premiums charged, term policies may have guaranteed rate structures or may be indeterminate-premium policies. When there is a *guaranteed rate structure,* the term premium rates for each age are set when the policy is issued and cannot be increased in the future. Naturally, as the insured grows older, the premium rate applied will increase; however, the whole rate schedule by age is guaranteed once the policy is issued. *Indeterminate-premium policies,* on the other hand, have an initial rate structure which can be increased or decreased by the insurance company according to the expected actuarial experience of the insurer but cannot be increased beyond a maximum level of rates. Thus, if an insurer's term experience deteriorates, the insurer can raise rates up to the maximum under this approach. Often the initial term rates for indeterminate-premium policies will be lower than those for guaranteed-premium policies, but of course they lack the rate guarantees.

Some term policies are participating (i.e., they pay policy dividends), while others are not. Also, some term policies are referred to as reentry term or revertible term and provide initially low term rates, but these rates continue to be low only if the insured periodically reestablishes his or her insurability with the insurance company. Otherwise, the term rates normally increase considerably.

Cash-Value or "Permanent" Life Insurance

As noted previously, the broad classification of cash-value or permanent individual life insurance contracts embraces all those that are designed to develop a cash value inside the life insurance contract. For this reason, policies in this category necessarily involve some combination of "pure" life insurance protection and a savings or investment feature (the cash value). Traditionally, this cash value developed because of the level-premium approach to paying for this kind of life insurance, in contrast to the increasing premiums with attained age for term insurance. Periodic growth in the cash values of life insurance contracts is often referred to as the "inside buildup" of the cash value of permanent life insurance policies.

Also, as noted earlier, from the viewpoint of insurance purchase decisions by consumers, cash-value policies can further be divided into those in which, once amounts are allocated to the policy's cash value, the insurance company guarantees those dollar amounts plus a minimum investment return on them ("guaranteed-dollar" policies), and those in which the policy's cash value depends on the investment performance of one or more separate accounts into which the policyowner has directed that the cash value be invested. The choice is thus essentially a question of who makes the investment decisions (asset allocation) and who takes the resultant investment risks—the insurance company (in the case of "guaranteed-dollar" policies) or the policyowner (in the case of variable policies). Of course, the guarantees of an insurer will prove illusory if the insurance buyer does not select an insurance company that itself is financially strong.

"Guaranteed-Dollar" Cash-Value Policies

There are a variety of policies in the "guaranteed-dollar" category, but they can be divided into those with a fixed premium and those with flexible premiums.

Traditional (Fixed-Premium) Forms of Cash-Value Life Insurance. Until recent years, these were almost the only forms of cash value life insurance. Now, however, they share the market with newer, more interest-sensitive kinds of products.

These traditional forms have a *fixed premium* that is determined primarily by the insured's age at issue, sex, and whether the insured is a smoker or a nonsmoker.[3] Premiums per $1000 of life insurance may also be lower for policies with larger face amounts of life insurance. This may be done with constant policy fees per policy, lower premiums per $1000 at certain break points or face amounts (so-called bands), or effectively with minimum-size

---

[3] The premium for any life insurance policy also may be affected by the insured's health and other individual underwriting factors. Thus, so-called substandard policies that do not meet the insurer's underwriting requirements for standard policies normally are "rated" in that they have a higher premium per $1000 of insurance than do comparable policies issued at standard.

policies. For a given policy, one or more of these methods may be used. This may make it cheaper per $1000 of life insurance for the policyowner to buy larger-sized policies from one insurer, but it may be at the sacrifice of the policyowner's diversifying his or her life insurance purchases among several life insurance companies.

These traditional forms can be *participating* (pay policy dividends based on the actuarial experience of the insurer) or *nonparticipating* (pay no policy dividends). If they are participating, it is the gross premium (before dividends) that is fixed, and the final cost and financial results of the policy often will be substantially affected by the policy dividends (which are *not* guaranteed) that are declared on the policy in the future by the insurance company. These future and uncertain policy dividends on participating life insurance are a major reason it is so difficult to compare policies and life insurance companies.

The gross premiums for these policies are set when the policy is issued, and their guaranteed cash values increase according to a schedule contained in the policy. Thus, the cost elements (the mortality cost for death claims, the charges for expenses, and the interest rate credited by the insurer on policy values) of these policies are not shown to the policyowner separately, and hence these policies may be referred to as "bundled" contracts.[4]

Also, from the consumer's point of view, these policies in effect are "front-end loaded" for expenses. This is because for the first several years a policy is in force, normally there either is no cash value or the cash value is significantly less than the premiums paid for the policy. While there is no separately stated expense charge for these traditional cash-value policies, the effect of this cash-value growth pattern is at least to partially reflect the expenses of the insurance company in writing the policy. Therefore, the policyowner normally will lose money if such a life insurance policy is surrendered after it has been in force for only a few years.

There are various kinds of these traditional, fixed-premium, "bundled" life insurance contracts. By far the most common is whole life insurance. In addition, there are a variety of special contracts that in most cases are some combination of whole life insurance and term insurance.

Whole Life Insurance. This widely used policy furnishes protection for the whole of life regardless of how many years premiums are paid. Premiums may be paid throughout the insured's lifetime or over a limited period, such as 10, 20, or 30 years, or to a specified age. Premiums also may be paid in one lump sum at the inception of the policy, in which case the policy is referred to as a single-premium whole life policy (SPWL). Because of the special tax characteristics of SPWL contracts, they are covered briefly

---

[4] This is in contrast to policies that are "unbundled," such as universal life (UL), as discussed on pp. 76–78 of this chapter.

later in this chapter. When the insured is to pay premiums throughout his or her lifetime, the policy is commonly referred to as "ordinary life" or "straight life." When the insured is to pay premiums over a specified period, such as for 20 years or to age 65, it is referred to as "limited-payment life insurance."

In addition to permanent protection, other major distinguishing features of whole life insurance as compared with term insurance are the level premium for the premium-paying period and the combining in the insurance contract of savings (cash value) with insurance. The savings feature arises from the fact that in the early years of a whole life contract, the annual level premium is more than enough to pay the current cost of insurance protection. The excess of premiums in the early years, coupled with the effect of compound interest, makes up for the deficiency of premiums in the later years when the level premium is no longer sufficient to pay for the actual cost of insurance. The funds accumulated from the extra premiums in the early years are held by the insurer for the policyowner. This is the savings or investment element of a whole life policy.

Whole life policies can be participating (par) or nonparticipating (nonpar). In addition, some companies sell nonpar contracts as indeterminate-premium whole life policies, where the premiums may increase or decrease based on expected future experience of the insurer subject to certain guaranteed maximum premiums.

Endowment Insurance. The endowment life insurance policy offers insurance protection against death for a specified period of time, such as 10, 20, or 30 years, to age 65, and so forth; then, if the insured lives to the end of the specified period (term of the endowment), the contract pays the face amount either in a lump sum or in installments. Thus, the primary emphasis is on the savings feature, and if the primary need is for death protection, a great deal more such protection can be provided through either term or whole life insurance. There has been a clear tendency over the years for the sale of endowment insurance to diminish in importance.

Special Life Insurance Contracts. There are many fixed-premium life insurance policies with a variety of names sold by insurance companies. As mentioned before, such contracts really boil down to combinations or adaptations of the major types just discussed. We shall discuss only the more important types of these life insurance contracts here.

"Modified" Life Insurance Policies. Under this type of policy, the premiums are smaller for the first few years than for the remainder of the contract duration. It is typically a whole life contract in which the premiums are redistributed so that they are lower during the first three or five years than they are thereafter. Modified life may be useful for a young family person who wants to buy whole life insurance but who currently cannot afford to buy enough insurance on a regular whole life basis to meet his or her family's insurance needs.

Graded-Premium Whole Life. These contracts are somewhat similar in concept to modified life except that the initially lower premiums increase annually for a longer period of time (such as from 5 to 40 years, depending on the policy) until they level off. During this annually increasing premium period, there are no or low cash values developed under these policies. Thus, some of these contracts really are more akin to yearly renewable term (YRT) than whole life during this period. Again the fact remains: The consumer gets only what he or she pays for.

Family Income-Type Riders or Policies. This coverage is most commonly provided through a family income rider attached to another basic life insurance policy. Under the traditional family income contract, if the insured dies during a specified family income period, the proceeds of the whole life insurance are held at interest until the end of the family income period, at which time they are paid to the beneficiary. In the meantime, family income payments (which frequently are $10, $15, or even $20 per month for each $1000 of face amount) are paid to the beneficiary until the end of the family income period. Interest on the deferred proceeds and decreasing term insurance provide these family income payments. Assume, for example, that a person at age 33 purchased a 20-year, $50,000, $10-per-month family income policy and then died at age 38. In this case, the beneficiary would receive $500 a month for 15 years (i.e., to the end of the remaining duration of the family income period), and then receive the $50,000 face amount at the end of the 15 years.

Family Maintenance-Type Riders or Policies. This type of contract is similar to the family income policy or rider. The traditional family maintenance policy or rider consists of a basic life insurance policy, usually a form of whole life, plus level term insurance (instead of decreasing term, as used in family income contracts). The level term insurance provides income for a stated number of years after the insured's death, provided this occurs within the family maintenance period. If, for example, a person died at age 38 and had a $50,000, 20-year, $10-per-month family maintenance policy that the person had purchased at age 33, the contract would pay an income of $500 per month to the beneficiary for 20 years, and then the $50,000 face amount would be paid at the end of the 20-year family maintenance period.

Family Policy. This policy includes coverage on all family members in one contract. Most family policies provide whole life insurance on the breadwinner, designated as the insured, with the premium based on his or her age, while term insurance is provided on the spouse and children. All living children are covered, even if adopted or born after the policy is issued, until a stated age, such as 21. The children's term insurance usually is convertible to any permanent plan of insurance without evidence of insurability.

Interest-Sensitive Whole Life.   This is a newer, nontraditional whole life policy that can have several variations and can be called by other names. It basically is a cross between the traditional whole life policy just described and universal life (UL) insurance to be discussed next. The policy normally has an *initial premium* which can be *redetermined* (recalculated by the insurance company) periodically based on new actuarial assumptions and the level of the policy's current accumulation account. The insurance company does provide some guarantees as to minimum interest rates and maximum mortality charges in setting any new actuarial assumptions. In this sense, the policy is similar to indeterminate premium whole life.

The policy's current *accumulation account* (cash value) is determined by using the *current experience of the insurance company,* hence the term "interest-sensitive." From the periodic premium as currently set by the insurance company, an expense charge (if any is separately identified by the insurance company) is deducted and the net amount is added to the previous year's accumulation account. Then, interest is credited to this account at the current rate being assumed by the insurer (normally with a minimum rate guaranteed) and a mortality charge (normally with a maximum charge guaranteed) calculated on the "pure" life insurance protection (the policy face less the accumulation account) is deducted. The balance is the policy's accumulation account at the end of the year. A surrender charge may be deducted from this account if the policyowner surrenders the contract.

The result is a policy with periodic premiums that may be redetermined after an initial period by the insurer and whose accumulation account (cash value) is immediately impacted by the current interest and mortality rates being used by the insurer. However, once determined, this accumulation account is guaranteed by the insurer.

Universal Life (UL).   The keynotes of universal life (UL) insurance are flexibility for the policyowner and identifiable cost elements. Thus, it involves a flexible-premium concept that separates the "pure" insurance protection (term element) of a permanent life insurance policy from the investment element in the policy. The policy cash value is set up as a cash-value fund (or accumulation fund) to which is credited investment income on the fund, and from which is taken the cost of term insurance (as a mortality charge) at the insured's attained age on the net amount of death protection. There also may be certain expense charges deducted. This separation of the cash value from the death benefit has been referred to as "unbundling" the traditional life insurance product.

Premium payments for UL are at the discretion of the policyowner (i.e., are flexible), except that there must be a minimum initial premium to start the coverage and then there must be at least enough cash value in the policy each month to cover the mortality and any expense charges so that the policy will not lapse. Insurers also set maximum premium payments. Within these parameters, the policyowner can increase or decrease premium payments, discontinue them, or resume them at will.

There are two general types of death benefit systems under UL: option A and option B. Under option A, there is a level death benefit, and so if the cash value increases, the net amount of death protection (also referred to as the net amount at risk) declines. Under option B, the death benefit is equal to a specified amount selected by the policyowner when the policy is purchased plus the policy's current cash value. Thus, under this option the death benefit will increase if the cash value increases. Which of these options the policyowner should purchase depends on how much insurance protection is desired relative to the investment element in the policy. Option B provides more death protection relative to cash value than option A. Insurers also frequently permit policyowners to purchase a cost-of-living (COL) rider on UL policies so that the face amount of their life insurance will increase automatically with, say, the Consumer Price Index, without the insured's needing to show any new evidence of insurability. Such COL riders may be used with some other kinds of policies as well. Finally, insurers often allow policyowners to increase or decrease their policies' death benefits as they desire, except that if the death benefit is increased, individual evidence of insurability normally must be shown by the insured. There may be other limitations on such increases and decreases as well.

The cash-value accumulation under UL is credited with an interest rate (usually monthly). There is a guaranteed minimum interest rate specified in the policy, and then the insurer may actually pay a higher current rate. The rate actually paid will depend on the terms of the policy and current economic conditions. Thus, UL policies also have been termed "interest-sensitive products." The interest rate or rates actually paid by an insurer on its UL policies may be determined in one of three ways. One is a *portfolio rate*, which is one rate set by the insurer based on the investment performance of the insurer's whole investment portfolio. The second is a *new money approach*, where the insurer sets more than one interest rate for UL cash values depending on when the policy premiums were paid and what interest rate conditions were then. Third, some UL policies credit interest rates that are *indexed* to some outside measure, such as a percentage of an average of long-term corporate bond rates.

UL policies often are sold based on certain assumptions (projections) of the interest rates that will be paid on the policy cash values far into the future. The same kind of thing also is done for other kinds of life insurance policies as well. The consumer should beware of these long-term projections because no one can know what interest rates (or the other cost elements of life insurance, for that matter) will be 10, 20, or even 30 years from now. Instead, the consumer should note the interest rate currently being paid on any policy being considered (and perhaps also consider it in relation to what other insurers are paying and in relation to other long-term rates in the economy, such as those on investment-grade corporate bonds and investment-grade municipal bonds), what the past history of the insurer has been with regard to the interest rates paid, and the minimum guaranteed rate in the policy. Naturally, the financial strength and general reputation of the insurer are of paramount importance. High current interest rates on any kind of insurance or annuity product sold by a weak insurer are no bargain at all.

A *mortality charge* (in effect, a term insurance charge) is deducted each month (or other policy period) from the cash value based on the insured's attained age and the policy's current net amount at risk. UL policies typically have a schedule of guaranteed maximum mortality charges and then the insurer often charges less than the guaranteed maximum. However, the insurer can increase (up to the maximum) or decrease the mortality charges and so, in effect, they are indeterminate. Insurers can differ greatly in the mortality charges they make on their UL policies.

Insurers may also levy expense charges (policy loadings) against premiums or cash values. Some UL policies have so-called *front-end loads,* where an expense charge is made for the first policy year and then often lower charges are made in subsequent years. Other policies have so-called *back-end loads,* which are charges levied on the surrender or exchange of the policy. Such back-end loads or surrender charges normally diminish year by year as the policy remains in force, reaching zero at a certain point (say, after 10 to 20 years). Some policies have both front-end and back-end loads. Policies with no identifiable front-end loads sometimes are referred to as "no-load" life insurance.

Since UL policies are unbundled, they normally allow the policyowner to make cash withdrawals (partial surrenders) from the cash value while the policy is still in force. Any such withdrawals will reduce the policy's death benefit dollar for dollar. UL policies also have policy loan provisions like other permanent life insurance policies. Thus, the policyowner of a UL policy can get cash out of his or her policy while the policy is still in force by making withdrawals of a part of the cash value or by taking a policy loan.

The UL policies of different insurance companies can vary considerably. They can vary as to the current interest rate being credited to the cash value, the guaranteed interest rate, the method used to credit interest, mortality charges, and the nature and amount of any expense charges. All these factors will affect the current cost or return on a UL policy.

Variable Life Policies

General Features. As opposed to the "guaranteed" or "fixed" principal approach just discussed, variable life policies allow the policyowner, within limits, to allocate his or her premium payments to or among one or more separate investment accounts maintained by the insurance company and also to shift, with certain restrictions, the policy cash values among the separate accounts. The amount of the policy cash values and perhaps the death benefit depend on the values (investment performance) of the separate accounts to which the policyowner has allocated the funds under the policy. Hence, the investment decisions and the corresponding investment risks, within the separate accounts offered by the insurance company for its variable life products, fall on the policyowner rather than the insurer. On the other hand, the policyowner can fit the cash-value allocation under these policies to meet his or her own investment needs and overall investment strategy.

The kinds of separate accounts offered under variable life policies vary among insurance companies. Some common examples of such accounts might include: a conservative common stock account, an aggressive common stock account, an investment-grade bond account, a high-yield ("junk") bond account, a money market account, a balanced (stock and bond) account, and perhaps one or more zero-coupon bond accounts. Policyowners also may be given the option of having their funds invested in the general investment portfolio of the insurance company (a fixed principal account). Thus, these policies generally give policyowners reasonably wide latitude in the investment strategies they may want to follow. These separate accounts are much like a small group (or "family") of mutual funds and, in fact, in some cases the same investment management firms that manage mutual funds also provide investment management services for a fee to insurance companies for at least some of the insurers' separate accounts. [However, for tax reasons the separate accounts under variable life insurance (and variable annuities, which are considered in Chap. 13) cannot be the same as mutual funds offered to the public.] Since long-term investment results are critical to the decision to purchase variable insurance products, who is the investment manager for at least some of the accounts (such as common stock and high-yield bond accounts) may be a very significant factor for the consumer to consider. Investment management is an important advantage cited for variable life insurance (and variable annuities), just as it is for investment companies (including mutual funds).

One important reason for the development of variable life insurance was to allow policyowners to invest their premiums and policy cash values in whole or in part in common stock funds or diversified funds that would be more competitive with other kinds of investment media (such as mutual funds) and that would maintain or hopefully even enhance the purchasing power of policy values (cash values and possibly life insurance death protection) in the face of seemingly unending price inflation. How well these goals may be met will depend on the actual investment performance over a relatively long period of time (say, 10, 15, or even 20 years) of the particular variable life separate accounts. As in the case of investment companies (including mutual funds), the investment performance of separate accounts can vary considerably among life insurance companies. Also like investment companies' performance, an analysis by the consumer of insurance company separate account investment performance should be over a considerable period of time—such as 5, 10, 15, or even 20 years, if available—rather than for only one or a few good years.

Policyowners may follow other investment strategies in these tax-protected separate accounts as well. For example, some policies have one or more otherwise taxable zero-coupon bond accounts that enable policyowners to lock in current bond interest rates until some future time or need, such as the education of children or planned retirement. There is no current tax on these otherwise taxable zero-coupon bond accounts, as there would be if they were held by an investor directly, because they are held inside the cash value of a life insurance policy (or an annuity contract). Of course, when a life insurance policy (or annuity contract) is surrendered or when taxable distributions are otherwise made from them, then the investment growth (inside buildup) portion of the surrender value or taxable distribution will be taxable to the policyowner as ordinary income upon receipt. Thus, the income tax is only deferred on the investment growth (or inside buildup) of life insurance or annuity cash values.[5]

Still another strategy is to place at least some of the cash value in higher-yielding investments [such as otherwise taxable diversified bond accounts—investment-grade bonds, high-yield (junk) bonds, or possibly both] to shield the yield from current income taxation. As with other investment media, many people feel that a *diversified investment strategy* is to be preferred in allocating variable life insurance (or variable annuity) cash values among the available separate accounts. Alternatively, perhaps the variable life insurance (or variable annuity) cash values can be one part of an otherwise diversified overall investment portfolio. Of course, any investment strategy, including diversification, can be done only by using the separate investment accounts or funds that are available within the variable life insurance (or variable annuity) contracts. Therefore, this is another significant issue for the consumer to consider in buying such contracts.

Another investment advantage of variable insurance products (either variable life insurance or variable annuities) lies in the ability of the policy-

---

[5] In this regard, however, it should be noted that *life insurance death proceeds* paid by reason of the insured's death are entirely income tax-free to the policy beneficiary, and, in effect, such life insurance death proceeds include any policy cash value. Thus, in economic effect, at the death of the insured any *tax-deferred* inside buildup in a life insurance policy (either a "guaranteed-principal" contract or a variable contract) will be essentially converted into *tax-free* life insurance death proceeds. However, this is not true for annuities. For annuity contracts, the death benefit is equal only to the policy cash value (or premiums paid, if greater), and any difference between this death benefit and the net premiums paid for the annuity is ordinary income when received by the death beneficiary of the annuity policy.

owner to move the policy cash value among the separate accounts inside the policy without any current income tax liability due to the changed allocation. In effect, this allows the policyowner to make changes in his or her asset allocation strategy within the policy without adverse tax consequences. It thus avoids the capital gains tax lock-in problem discussed on pp. 337–339 of Chap. 11. For example, assume that Norman Wong purchased a universal variable life (UVL) insurance policy several years ago and has paid a total of $10,000 in premiums for the policy, which has a $200,000 face amount. He has elected to have the premiums and the policy's cash value placed in the policy's common stock separate account, which over the years has shown good investment growth and is now worth $25,000. However, Norman has become concerned that he has too much of his overall investment portfolio in common stocks [considering his directly owned investments, his investment options under his employer's 401(k) savings plan, his IRA plan, as well as the UVL policy]. Therefore, he has decided to change the UVL policy's $25,000 cash value from the policy's common stock account to its investment-grade bond account. This change (exchanging one separate account for another) is not deemed a sale or exchange of a capital asset for capital gains tax purposes. Further, if Norman should become dissatisfied with the investment management of the insurance company (or the investment firm hired by the insurance company) writing his UVL policy, he could exchange income-tax-free, under the provisions of Section 1035 of the tax code, his policy for another life insurance policy with a different insurer. Of course, any surrender charge (back-end load) applicable to his UVL policy would apply to such a tax-free exchange. Thus, it can be seen that the policyowner can have considerable investment flexibility in changing the asset allocation under a variable life (or variable annuity) policy.[6] If, however, Norman were to completely surrender his policy for cash, then the difference between its net surrender value (currently $25,000 in this example) and his investment in the contract or income tax basis in the contract (normally the net premiums paid, or $10,000 in this example) would be taxable to the policy-

---

[6] By way of comparison, if instead these investment funds had not been in separate accounts under a variable life policy (or variable annuity), but rather had been mutual funds in a "family" of mutual funds (as explained in Chap. 9), then the exchanging of one mutual fund (say, a common stock fund) for another mutual fund (say, an investment-grade bond fund), as in this illustration, would result in an exchange of a capital asset for capital gains tax purposes and hence either a currently taxable gain or a loss. In this illustration, there would be a currently recognized $15,000 capital gain [$25,000 value (amount realized) − $10,000 adjusted basis = $15,000 capital gain]. There would, of course, have been the same gain if Norman had held the stocks and then the bonds directly rather than through a family of mutual funds. On the other hand, if there had been a capital loss on this transaction, it would have been better tax-wise to have held the assets in a mutual fund or directly, because then Norman could have taken the loss currently against any capital gains he might have had that year and then against ordinary income to the extent of $3000 per year.

owner in the year of receipt. However, if instead Norman were to take a policy loan from the insurance company secured by his policy cash value (as described on pp. 89–90), then in the case of a life insurance policy (but not in the case of an annuity), it would be viewed for income tax purposes as a loan and not as a taxable distribution and thus would not attract any federal income tax liability.[7]

It must be noted, on the other hand, that there are *expense loadings and mortality costs* involved with variable life products. Depending on the situation, these loadings can be significant. As just noted, some variable life policies have initial sales charges (front-end loads), but many do not and instead may have *back-end loads* upon surrender—referred to as surrender charges or contingent deferred sales charges. There are annual (or periodic) *investment management fees* levied against the net assets of the particular separate accounts. The amount of these fees often varies depending on the nature of the separate account. There also are annual (or periodic) *mortality and expense risk charges* levied against the assets of each plan account to cover the possibility that mortality or administrative expenses incurred by the insurer for all policyholders may be greater than the insurer had anticipated. [Note that this risk charge is in addition to the mortality cost (or term cost) that the insurer must charge for the life insurance protection (the "net amount at risk") it is providing on the insured's life under the policy.] In addition, there may be an annual (or periodic) *administrative charge* to cover the insurer's general administration costs in writing and maintaining the policy, which may be a fixed dollar amount per policy or a percentage of premiums or values, and there may be a further charge for premium taxes. These various annual (or periodic) expense loadings (i.e., investment management fees, mortality and expense risk charges, and administrative charges and other fees) vary among insurers, but they may range, say, from 1.5 percent to 2.5 percent or more per year of the assets standing behind a variable life policy.[8]

Since these expense loadings can be significant, and vary among insurance companies, the consumer should evaluate them in relation to those of

---

[7] In the case of regular (nonqualified) deferred annuities, a loan secured by the annuity cash value is considered to be a taxable distribution for federal income tax purposes. Hence, loans are not a tax-free method of getting funds from a nonqualified annuity as they are from life insurance policies (other than modified endowment contracts as explained on p. 86).

[8] This percentage of assets is somewhat analogous to the expense ratio (mutual fund annual administration fees—including investment management fees—divided by the fund's net assets) of mutual funds, which will be discussed in more detail in Chap. 9. The comparison is not completely appropriate, however, because mutual funds themselves do not provide life insurance protection, and some of the periodic expense loadings of variable life policies are for the creation or administration of the life insurance coverage (although not for the actual term cost in this analysis). Recognizing that there are limitations on the comparison, the expense ratios of comparable mutual funds probably are generally lower than these expense loadings as a percentage of plan assets for variable life insurance.

other variable life policies and in relation to the expenses of other kinds of managed investment arrangements. In making this latter comparison, however, the consumer should recognize that variable life policies are a combination of a managed investment arrangement (the separate accounts) and life insurance protection and that some of the loadings are due to the life insurance element.

In addition to the expense loadings just described, variable life policies also must charge for the *mortality cost or term cost* of the pure life insurance protection they are providing. This would be part of the fixed premium for variable life (VL) insurance or a periodic mortality charge that varies with the insured's attained age and is applied to the net amount at risk under the policy for universal variable life (UVL) insurance. Thus, either way, the consumer must pay for the life insurance element in variable life insurance. This may limit its rate of return if *only* a capital accumulation vehicle is desired. Of course, when a *combination* of insurance protection and managed investment options is desired, then variable life comes into its own and is a logical financial instrument to use.

Variable life policies are of two general types: variable life (VL) insurance and universal variable life (UVL) insurance. These types are described next.

Variable Life (VL) Insurance.   This kind of variable life policy is a fixed-premium contract that is similar in some ways to traditional fixed-premium (nonvariable) whole life insurance. However, the cash values and death benefits under VL vary with the investment experience of the separate accounts to which the premiums are allocated. Thus, if the investment experience is good, the cash values and death benefits will increase, but if the investment experience is bad, the reverse will be true. Thus, *both* the cash values and death benefits may fluctuate, up and down, under these policies. If the investment experience were really bad, theoretically the cash value could be entirely depleted, but VL policies have a guaranteed minimum death benefit that is set when the policy is written, below which the actual death benefit cannot go, no matter how bad the investment experience under the contract may be. This guaranteed minimum death benefit is intended to protect the insured's beneficiaries against possible adverse investment results under these policies. Some VL policies are participating, while others are nonparticipating.

Universal Variable Life (UVL) Insurance.   This is the more popular form of variable life insurance. It is unbundled universal life insurance combined with the policyowner investment choices (and risks) of the variable life concept. The policyowner can decide into which separate account or accounts provided under the policy his or her flexible premiums will go. The cash value then will be determined by the investment experience of the separate account or accounts chosen. The death benefit will depend on whether UL option A (level death benefit) or option B (stated amount plus the cash value at death) is initially selected by the policyowner (see p. 77). In UVL, there are no guarantees by the insurance company of the principal amount of the cash value or of any minimum rate of return on the cash value as would be true for regular (guaranteed principal) UL insurance described on pp. 76–78 of this chapter.

Joint Survivorship Life Insurance ("Second-to-Die Policies")

All the previously discussed forms of life insurance covered only one person's life as the insured. Joint survivorship life insurance (also called second-to-die, joint last survivor, survivorship, and joint life[9] insurance) is a life insurance contract that normally insures *two lives* in the same policy and where the policy proceeds are payable to the beneficiary at the death of the second insured to die. The two lives insured are usually a husband and wife. Particularly since the unlimited federal estate tax marital deduction was adopted in 1981, second-to-die policies have become quite popular as a way to provide for estate liquidity needs and estate conservation needs for larger estates (as explained in Chap. 15), because now the federal estate tax bite does not really come until the second-spouse-to-die's death. These policies may also be useful in making up the loss of wealth for a family when charitable remainder unitrusts or annuity trusts have been used (see pp. 321–324 of Chap. 11 for a description of these trusts). They may also be useful in other business and estate planning situations.

Joint survivorship policies can be written in a number of ways. They can use permanent (cash-value) life insurance plans such as traditional whole life (participating or nonparticipating), interest-sensitive whole life, or universal life, or the policy can be some composite of permanent insurance, term insurance, and perhaps paid-up additional amounts of insurance. Thus, many newer plans can be tailored to fit the needs of policyowners. The premiums on joint survivorship life insurance normally are considerably less than the premiums for comparable policies on a single life of the same age, sex, and amount. This is because two lives are insured and the proceeds are not payable until the second death. However, the mix of permanent and term insurance also affects such comparisons.

One thing to consider in purchasing joint survivorship life insurance is whether the policy (or a rider added to the policy for an extra premium)

---

[9] Technically, some writers refer to joint life insurance as a policy that insures two lives and where the policy proceeds are payable on the first death. As a practical matter, however, this is not the way these policies are written in the marketplace, and we shall use the term here only to refer to second-to-die policies.

allows the owner(s) to *split it* into two single life plans, one for each joint life insured, in an amount on each equal to the joint policy benefit or some other amount, or to change it into a single life plan on only one of the joint insureds. Most second-to-die policies allow such a split. This right to split the policy (or to change it) may be valuable for spouses in the event of divorce or other family discord, possible changes in the estate tax law or estate tax rates, or changes in their estate situation or plans. For joint insureds other than spouses, there may be many reasons for desiring to split the coverage. Some policies allow the split or change without any new evidence of insurability (new underwriting); others require new underwriting; while still others will allow the split without new underwriting only when there is some specified independent event involved (such as divorce, repeal of the unlimited marital deduction, or a 50 percent reduction in estate tax rates). This right to split or change may be important to policyowner(s), particularly in the event one or both of the insureds should become uninsurable or be in impaired health.

Definitions of Life Insurance for Income Tax Purposes

Life insurance contracts have a number of income tax advantages for the policyowner and beneficiary. Some of these advantages have already been noted in the preceding discussion in that life insurance proceeds paid by reason of the insured's *death* normally are received entirely income tax–free by the policy beneficiary [Section 101(a) of the Internal Revenue Code] and the periodic increase (or changes in separate accounts in variable products) of the policy cash values are not taxed currently as income (i.e., the so-called inside buildup of life insurance policy cash values are income tax–deferred). It was also noted that loans secured by life insurance policies are treated for tax purposes as loans and not as potentially taxable distributions; there is no 10 percent penalty tax on "premature distributions" (i.e., distributions before age 59½ with some exceptions) from life insurance policies; and partial surrenders (withdrawals), where permitted, *may* be viewed as first coming from the policyowner's investment in the contract (income tax basis) and then, when that tax basis is recovered, coming from potentially taxable investment earnings inside the policy.[10]

General Tax Definition of Life Insurance (Section 7702).   However, in order to get these rather substantial tax advantages of life insurance, a policy issued after December 13, 1984, must be a life insurance contract under state law and must meet one of two alternative tests under Section

---

[10] The income tax status of life insurance policies is discussed further in Chap. 16. Also, as noted on pp. 86–87, some of these tax advantages do not apply to modified endowment contracts.

7702 of the Internal Revenue Code. These tests are a cash-value accumulation test or a guideline premium and corridor test. This tax law definition of life insurance does not apply to contracts (other than flexible-premium contracts) issued before January 1, 1985. As a practical matter, while it is very important that any life insurance policy purchased by a consumer meet this tax law definition of a life insurance contract, the policies sold by life insurance companies are designed to meet it. Therefore, it generally is not a problem for consumers.

Modified Endowment Contracts (MECs). The Technical and Miscellaneous Revenue Act of 1988 (TAMRA) created a new kind of life insurance contract (within the general tax law definition of life insurance just explained) for income tax purposes—the modified endowment contract (or MEC). An MEC is a policy that meets the general tax law definition of life insurance, was entered into on or after June 21, 1988, and does not meet a special seven-pay test given in the law. A policy will not meet this seven-pay test if the accumulated premiums at any time during the first seven years of the policy are more than what would have been the sum of the net level premiums for a paid-up policy at the end of seven years. In essence, this rather complicated definition means that if the premiums on a life insurance contract are paid faster than those for a hypothetical seven-pay life policy, it is an MEC.

An MEC loses some, but not all, of the income tax benefits from being a life insurance contract. Loans secured by an MEC are treated as taxable distributions for income tax purposes, there is a 10 percent penalty tax on "premature distributions" (before age 59½ with some exceptions), and distributions from MECs are viewed as first coming from the investment earnings inside the policy (and hence are taxable) and then as a tax-free return of the policyowner's investment in the contract (income tax basis).[11]

These new rules regarding MECs apply only to life insurance contracts entered into on or after June 21, 1988, unless there have been material changes to the contract on or after that date. Thus, policies that otherwise would be an MEC entered into before June 21, 1988, generally are "grandfathered" for this purpose, and the regular tax rules applying to life insurance contracts apply to them unless they are materially changed. Of course, life insurance contracts whose premium-payment patterns meet the TAMRA seven-pay test are not MECs regardless of when they were entered into, and so all the regular (and generally favorable) income tax rules applying to life insurance contracts continue to apply to them.

---

[11] It may be noted that these income tax rules also apply to regular (nonqualified) annuity contracts as explained in Chap. 13. Thus, in effect, the tax writers applied some of the nonqualified annuity income tax rules to life insurance contracts *when they are MECs.*

The practical effect for consumers of these rather techni
tions of life insurance is that single-premium life insurance
very popular primarily as investment-type contracts, now a
MECs if entered into (or materially changed) on or after June 21, 1988.
This means that some of the formerly very attractive income tax dynamics
of these policies have been taken away by the more restrictive income tax
rules applying to nongrandfathered MECs. That has made these single-
premium or essentially single-premium life products much less attractive
than before 1988.

Single-Premium Whole Life Insurance (SPWL). As just noted, this represents primarily an investment-type life insurance product. The policyowner pays a single premium, such as $10,000, $25,000, $50,000, or more,
and receives a life insurance contract. The full premium normally goes into
the policy's cash or accumulation value, which value is credited with a current interest rate that may change periodically but on which is credited at
least a minimum guaranteed rate of interest. Insurers normally charge
annual fees against the accumulated values to cover administration costs
and mortality risks. There frequently is a surrender charge if the policy is
surrendered during its early years. Single-premium life policies also have
been written as variable life, universal life, and universal variable life plans.
As just explained, they now are taxed as MECs (unless grandfathered) and
so are much less popular than formerly.

Some Important Life
Insurance Policy Provisions

Most people buy individual life insurance contracts as part of their personal
financial planning. Thus, an understanding of some important policy provisions will be helpful.

Assignment

A life insurance contract is personal property and, as such, is freely transferable (assignable) by the owner in the absence of a policy provision to the
contrary. There are two types of assignments of life insurance contracts.
One is the *absolute assignment,* under which all ownership rights in the
contract are transferred to another. An absolute assignment may be used,
for example, when an existing policy is given to another person or to an
irrevocable trust to avoid federal estate taxation (see Chap. 16). The second type is the *collateral assignment,* whereby only certain rights are transferred to another when the policy is to serve as security for a loan or in

other debtor-creditor situations. The right to assign a life insurance policy can be a valuable one in both personal and business transactions.

Grace Period

The grace period, commonly 31 days, is a period after the premium for a life insurance policy is due during which the policy remains in full force even though the premium has not been paid. This provision is designed to protect the policyholder against inadvertent lapse of the policy.

Incontestability

This provision states that after a life insurance contract has been in force a certain length of time (called the "contestable period"), which normally is two years, the insurer agrees not to deny a claim because of any error, concealment, or misstatement (generally including even fraud) on the part of the insured. From the standpoint of the insured and the beneficiary, such a clause alleviates the fear of lawsuits, especially at a time, after the insured's death, when it may be very difficult for the beneficiary to combat successfully a charge by the insurer of a violation in securing the contract.

Delay

The delay clause is included in life insurance to permit an insurance company to postpone payment of the cash surrender (or loan) value for a period of six months after requested by the policyholder. Insurers by law must include this provision in their contracts. It is designed to protect the insurer against losses that might develop from excessive demands for cash in times of economic crisis. It is expected that only under the most severe economic circumstances would this clause be invoked by insurers. However, it must be recognized that use of this provision potentially could restrict the liquidity of life insurance cash (or loan) values.

Suicide

Life insurance contracts contain a suicide provision stating that if the insured commits suicide during a certain period of time after the policy is issued, generally two years, the insurer is liable only to return to the beneficiary the premiums paid, either with or without interest. After the two-year period, suicide becomes a covered risk and is treated like any other cause of death.

Reinstatement

The reinstatement provision is designed to help a policyholder who has failed to pay a premium within the time allowed, including the grace period. This clause usually gives the insured the right to reinstate the policy within a specified period, usually three years of any default in premium payment, subject to furnishing evidence of insurability satisfactory to the insurer and the payment of back premiums.

This clause may be helpful to a policyholder for several reasons. For example, it may be advantageous to use the reinstatement clause of a current policy, instead of purchasing a new policy, because a new policy generally will involve a higher premium (because of the insured's higher age); the contestable and suicide periods may have run their course under the current policy; a new contract may have no cash value for one or two years; and some older life insurance policies may have more liberal provisions with regard to policy loan interest rates and perhaps other provisions. On the other hand, it may be that some newer policies currently being offered by life insurance companies are more attractive than an existing contract. In that case, it may be better to surrender or exchange the older policy for a newer one. This decision should be made only after a careful analysis of the alternatives.

Policy Loan Provision

The policy loan provision in a life insurance contract allows the policyowner to take a loan (technically an "advance" because it does not have to be repaid) on the sole security of the policy up to an amount that, with interest on the loan, will not exceed the cash (loan) value of the policy as of the next policy anniversary. The rate of interest that can be charged on a policy loan may be stated in the contract, or it may vary periodically according to some standard such as corporate bond yields. Policy loans on older life insurance policies may have a 5 or 6 percent guaranteed interest rate and on some more recent policies an 8 percent guaranteed rate. These guaranteed policy loan interest rates can be advantageous to a policyowner during periods of high interest rates and/or "tight" money. Under these circumstances, policy loans can be a low-cost, readily available source of credit.

The policy loan provision is a valuable right of the policyowner. It enables the policyowner to draw upon policy cash values to meet temporary financial needs without surrendering the contract. It also enables the policyowner to take money out of his or her life insurance policy (except for an MEC) without any income tax liability. The main disadvantage of policy loans is that when a policyowner borrows against his or her life insurance and does not repay the loan, the death proceeds going to the beneficiaries will be reduced by the amount of the loan. Further, interest paid by individuals on policy loans generally is not deductible for federal income tax purposes, since it usually is consumer interest. Finally, many insurance companies include in their more recently issued participating policies a *direct recognition provision* under which policy dividends are less for policies with policy loans against them than for comparable policies without such loans.

Automatic Premium Loan Provision

Closely akin to the policy loan provision is the automatic premium loan provision. This provision operates when a policyowner fails to pay a premium when due. In this event, the premium is paid out of the policy loan value. Thus, through use of an automatic premium loan, a life insurance policy can be protected against lapse if the policyowner fails to pay a premium, as long as the policy has sufficient loan value to cover the premium payment.

In many companies, the automatic premium loan provision is not included automatically in the policy but can be included at the request of the policyowner. It is a feature that should be included in policies, since it is possible for anyone to overlook making a premium payment. Also, there is no extra cost for the provision.

Beneficiary Designation

A life insurance contract allows the policyowner to select the person or persons (beneficiaries) who will receive the proceeds of the contract in the event of the insured's death. When the owner reserves the right to change the beneficiary, the beneficiary designation is called "revocable." When the owner does not reserve the right to change the beneficiary, the designation is called "irrevocable." An irrevocable beneficiary in effect becomes a joint owner of the policy rights. This means his or her signature is necessary for such things as assignments and policy loans. Revocable beneficiary designations are used in most cases.

It usually is advisable to name a second beneficiary to receive life insurance proceeds in case the first (primary) beneficiary predeceases the insured. This contingent or secondary beneficiary can then receive the proceeds directly according to the insured's wishes. If no contingent beneficiary is named in the policy, the proceeds normally would go to the insured's estate if the primary beneficiary predeceases the insured and the insured dies without naming another primary beneficiary.

Aviation Clause or Exclusion

The aviation hazard at one time was either excluded from coverage or subject to an extra premium. Now, however, travel as a passenger in any type of aircraft, except military aircraft, is no longer considered an extra hazard. Additionally, many insurers are ignoring aviation restrictions previously written into existing policies if the insured currently would qualify under the new underwriting rules.

War

Insurers may add so-called war clauses to their new contracts issued during periods of war or impending war. This is particularly true of policies to young men of draft age.

Cash Values and Nonforfeiture Options

Life insurance companies are required to include certain nonforfeiture options in life insurance contracts. These provisions are designed to protect a policyowner who has accumulated a value in his or her life insurance policy but who for one reason or another wishes either to stop paying premiums or to surrender the contract. Nonforfeiture options (values) normally can take one of three forms: (1) a cash surrender value, (2) reduced paid-up life insurance, or (3) extended term life insurance.

Cash Surrender Value

Under state nonforfeiture laws, a cash value generally is required, at the latest, after premiums have been paid for three years and the policy produces a nonforfeiture value. Many traditional whole life policies today, however, provide for a cash value at the end of the first or second year. Also, for universal life and interest-sensitive whole life with no or a small front-end load, there will be a cash value the first year.

When the cash-value option is elected by a policyowner, life insurance protection ceases and the insurer has no further obligation under the policy. Consequently, although this option provides a ready source of cash for emergencies or other needs, careful consideration should be given to this alternative before a policy is surrendered. Also, the surrender of a life insurance contract will produce gross income for the policyowner to the extent that the cash surrender value received exceeds the net premiums paid for the contract. A policy loan from a life insurance contract, however, is not considered a surrender or distribution for tax purposes (except for an

MEC) and hence does not result in any current taxable income. Essentially the same amount of cash can be obtained through a policy loan (described above), and so the policy loan alternative should be considered before surrendering a policy for cash. However, interest must be paid by the policyowner on a policy loan.

But if the insured no longer needs all the life insurance protection (as at retirement, for example), surrendering some policies for cash may be a logical move. Remember, too, that when a policy is surrendered for cash, the amount of insurance protection lost is not the face amount of the policy but rather the so-called net amount at risk. Generally speaking, this is the face amount less the cash surrender value. Suppose, for example, that a person has a traditional $30,000 life paid-up-at-age-65 policy with a current cash value of $12,000. If this policy is surrendered for cash, the insurance protection will decline by $18,000 ($30,000 face minus the $12,000 cash value). This is so because there is now a $12,000 cash value (less any income tax payable) to invest in some other form and which will go to the policyowner's heirs in the event of his or her death. However, in the case of a universal life policy with an option B death benefit, the lost insurance protection will be the original face amount.

Reduced Paid-up Insurance

The reduced paid-up insurance option permits the policyowner to elect to take the cash value as paid-up insurance of the same type as the original policy but for a reduced face amount. This option would be appropriate where a smaller amount of permanent insurance is satisfactory and it is desirable to discontinue premium payments, such as when the policyowner approaches retirement. However, if the policy is participating, policy dividends will continue to be paid under one of the dividend options discussed next even though the reduced policy is now paid up and premiums are no longer being paid.

Extended Term Insurance

The nonforfeiture option of extended term insurance allows the policyowner to exchange the cash value for paid-up term insurance for the full face amount of the original insurance contract. The duration of the term coverage is that which can be purchased with the net cash value applied as a single premium at the insured's attained age. This option is useful when the need for the full amount of insurance protection continues but the insured cannot, or does not wish to, continue premium payments.

Uses of Policy Dividends

Policyowners who have participating life insurance contracts, i.e., those under which the policyowners are entitled to policy dividends as declared by the insurer, may use such dividends in various ways.

Types of Dividend Options

Participating policies contain several options available to policyowners as to how their dividends may be taken. These options usually include to (1) take dividends in cash; (2) apply dividends toward payment of future premiums; (3) leave dividends with the insurance company to accumulate at interest; (4) use dividends to buy additional amounts of paid-up whole life insurance, called "paid-up additions," or additional variable life insurance in variable life policies; and (5) use dividends to purchase one-year term insurance.

Cash dividends most frequently are taken when a policy is paid up. This may be done, for example, during retirement under a paid-up policy or when the reduced paid-up nonforfeiture option is elected to provide an additional source of retirement income. The use of *dividends toward the payment of future premiums* is a convenient and simple way to handle dividends. In order to afford a reasonably adequate life insurance program, many families depend on policy dividends to help meet their premium obligations.

Dividends also may be left with the insurer to *accumulate at a minimum guaranteed rate of interest (dividend accumulations)*. If the insurer earns more than the guaranteed rate, dividend accumulations may participate in the excess earnings. This dividend option essentially is like a savings account held with the insurance company. However, the policyowner or his or her advisors might want to check the interest rate being paid on them by the insurance company as compared with comparable rates elsewhere. Also, the interest earnings on dividend accumulations constitute current gross income for federal income tax purposes to the policyowner.

Another dividend option is *paid-up additions*. This option provides paid-up insurance at net single-premium rates (i.e., no charge for expenses is added to the rate). This is a popular option because the paid-up additions purchased in this way have cash values of their own and are themselves participating. Further, the growth in the cash values of the paid-up additions is not subject to current income taxation, as also is true of other policy cash values.

One-year term insurance (the so-called fifth dividend option) is another option offered by many insurance companies. The amount of one-year term insurance that can be purchased with dividends generally is limited to the cash value of the policy. This option provides for the purchase of term insurance at net rates.

Vanishing Premiums

A recent and popular concept for participating life insurance policies is the use of policy dividends and possibly the cash values of surrendered previously existing paid-up additions to pay the current policy premiums. In this sense, the premiums, when paid in this way, are said to "vanish." In fact, of course, they do not "vanish" or go away in any fashion. Instead, at the point in the policy's duration when the premiums are said to vanish, they are being paid by the current year's policy dividend and, in case that dividend is not sufficient to pay the whole premium, by the cash value from the surrender of just enough previously purchased paid-up additions to make up the difference between the premium and that year's policy dividend. Thus, the time when a policy's future premiums *may* "vanish" depends on the insurance company's dividend scale for the policy and is not guaranteed. In their proposals or projections, insurance companies may indicate that the particular policy's premiums will vanish in, say, 10 years, 15 years, and so forth, based on the insurer's current dividend scale for the policy. However, if the dividend scale changes (and dividend scales for participating life insurance cannot be guaranteed by the insurers), so will when, if ever, the policy premiums will vanish. If the dividend scale increases, the vanishing point will decrease. On the other hand, if the insurer's dividend scale is cut (or even eliminated), the vanishing point will increase or even vanish itself.

Vanishing-premium policies have been popular with consumers because they expect a stopping point to when they must continue to pay premiums. However, it must be emphasized that they are *not the same as paid-up life insurance policies.* When a life insurance policy is paid up, it means that the accumulated values under the policy are equal to the net single premium for the face amount of insurance involved and so it is guaranteed that no further premium payments are required to keep the policy in force until the insured's death. Both participating and nonparticipating policies can be or become paid up. As just noted, this is not the case with vanishing-premium policies, for which the premiums continue to be paid by policy dividends and surrender of paid-up additions.

The vanishing-premium approach can be attractive to policyowners as a way to use their policy dividends and paid-up additions. Consumers should be aware, however, that any vanishing point or duration is not guaranteed by the insurance company because the insurer's dividend scale cannot be guaranteed for the future. Both regular participating policies and participating joint survivorship policies can be on a vanishing-premium basis.

Settlement Options

Life insurance policies provide that when the proceeds become payable, the insured or the beneficiary may elect to have such proceeds paid in some form other than a lump sum. These forms of settlement, other than lump sum, are called "settlement options." The various settlement options include the (1) interest option, (2) fixed-amount option, (3) fixed-period option, and (4) life income options.

Interest Option

The proceeds of a life insurance policy may be left with the insurer at a guaranteed rate of interest, such as 2½ or 3 percent, for example. In addition to this guaranteed interest rate, most life insurers pay an additional, nonguaranteed rate of interest consistent with the earnings on their investments (called "excess interest"). For example, an insurer may guarantee 3 percent but actually be paying 6½ percent (i.e., 3½ percent excess interest).

Proceeds left under the interest option may carry a limited or unlimited right of withdrawal by the beneficiary. The beneficiary also may be given the right to change to another option or options. The interest option provides a great deal of flexibility in that the principal can be retained intact until such time as it is needed. In essence, it is like holding the proceeds in a savings account with the insurance company.

Fixed-Amount Option

The fixed-amount option provides a stated amount of income each month until the proceeds are exhausted. For example, the insured or beneficiary may desire that the proceeds be paid out at the rate of, say, $1000 a month for as long as the proceeds last. Each payment is partly interest and partly a return of principal. Again, the insurer usually guarantees a minimum rate of interest but actually pays a rate closer to that being earned on its investments.

Fixed-Period Option

The fixed-period option is similar to the fixed-amount option except that the period of time over which payments are made is fixed and the amount of each monthly installment varies accordingly. For example, $100,000 of proceeds at 2½ percent interest (guaranteed) payable in 120 monthly installments would be $940.70 per month. Again, most insurers pay a higher rate than that guaranteed, and such excess interest increases the amount of each installment.

Life Income Options

Under a life income option, the insured or beneficiary elects to have the proceeds paid for the rest of his or her life or for the life of one or more beneficiaries. This option amounts to using the proceeds to buy a life annuity of some sort. Several types of life income options may be available. They include (1) pure or straight life income, (2) life income with a period certain, (3) refund life income, and (4) joint and last survivor life income.

Pure Life Income.   This option permits the policyowner to have the proceeds paid out over the lifetime of the recipient. There are no guarantees as to the return of the entire amount of the original life insurance proceeds. Among the life income options, this option provides the highest monthly income for a given dollar amount of proceeds, primarily because of the absence of any refund feature. But the entire proceeds are considered "used up" at the recipient's death, and therefore people tend to shy away from this option.

Life Income with Period Certain.   Under this option, payments are guaranteed for as long as the recipient lives; however, if the recipient should die before the end of a specified period, such as 10 or 20 years, for example, payments continue for the remainder of that period to a second payee. Thus, if a surviving spouse is left $100,000 of life insurance proceeds under a life income option with 10 years certain, and the surviving spouse lives for 18 years, he or she would receive the monthly income for 18 years. However, if the spouse should die after 4 years, monthly income payments would continue to a second payee (perhaps the children) for an additional 6 years.

Refund Life Income.   This type of option provides a life income with the additional guarantee that in the event the recipient dies before receiving the full amount of the original life insurance proceeds, the difference (original proceeds less the amount paid to date) will be paid to a second payee. The difference can be paid either in a lump sum (cash refund option) or in installments (installment refund option) until the full proceeds are paid.

Joint and Last Survivor Life Income.   Under these options, the policyowner or beneficiary may elect to have the proceeds paid during the lifetimes of two or more recipients. For example, a husband and wife may wish to use this type of settlement arrangement. Income can be paid while both live and then continue for the lifetime of the survivor. A joint and last survivor option can be set up to have the same income continue to the second person (joint and survivor option), or the payments can be reduced upon the death of the first payee (such as joint and two-thirds or joint and one-half options). The lower the percentage of income to the survivor, the larger will be the life income payments while both recipients are alive.

Use of Life Income Settlement Options. These options, like annuities, can be used to provide the insured or a beneficiary with a secure life income that the recipient cannot outlive. The beneficiary also generally cannot "get at" the proceeds once they are placed under a life income settlement arrangement. Thus, the option can be used to protect the beneficiary against himself or herself.

However, whether to use life income options should be considered carefully by consumers or their advisors. First, once the option begins, it cannot be changed. The funds are committed once the recipient begins to receive the life income payments. Second, use of life income options for relatively young beneficiaries, who have longer life expectancies, often is questionable. The extra income resulting from the annuity aspect (i.e., the scientific using up of principal) may be relatively small for them, particularly in the case of women who have longer life expectancies than men. Also, one should consider how much the life insurance proceeds could earn in alternative, secure investments, such as insured certificates of deposit and high-grade bonds, where the principal would remain intact, and then decide whether any extra income from a life income option is worth the expending of principal and the loss of flexibility. Naturally, it generally is unwise to elect a life income option for beneficiaries who are in poor health.

Riders to Individual Life Insurance Contracts

Riders are a way of adding additional amounts and/or types of insurance benefits to a basic life insurance contract. For example, if a person owns or is buying a $100,000 whole life policy and needs additional protection until his or her children are self-sufficient, the person might obtain a $200,000 decreasing term insurance rider added to the whole life contract for increased protection during the child-rearing years.

Decreasing term insurance and some of the forms of special life insurance contracts previously described (i.e., family income and family maintenance benefits) may be provided through riders to basic contracts. In addition, some of the other types of riders frequently purchased include (1) guaranteed insurability, (2) double indemnity, and (3) waiver of premium. Further, some insurers are now offering long-term care (LTC) insurance as a rider to some of their life insurance policies.

Guaranteed Insurability Option

The guaranteed insurability option, for an additional premium, permits the policyholder to purchase additional amounts of insurance at stated intervals without additional proof of insurability. For example, Maria Hernandez might purchase a $50,000 whole life policy at age 27 with a guaranteed insurability rider added. The rider might permit her, beginning at age 30, to purchase additional amounts of insurance (up to $50,000) every three years until she is, say, age 40 without any proof of insurability for the subsequent purchases. This rider often is used by persons who feel they will have increasing future insurance needs.

Double Indemnity

The double-indemnity clause or rider, often referred to as an *accidental death benefit,* provides that double (or sometimes triple or more) the face amount of life insurance is payable if the insured's death is caused by accidental means. From an economic standpoint, there seems little justification for double indemnity. The loss to the insured's dependents is just as great if death is caused by means other than accidental. Furthermore, the risk of death from disease, for most persons, is much greater than the risk of death by accident.

Waiver of Premium

The waiver-of-premium rider also may be added to life insurance contracts for an extra premium. It provides that in the event the insured becomes totally disabled before a certain age, typically 60 or 65, premiums on the life insurance policy will be waived (i.e., not required to be paid by the insured) during the continuance of disability after six months. In addition, premiums are normally waived retroactively for this six months. The operation of, and values in, the basic life insurance policy continue just as if the disabled insured actually were paying the premiums. Some life insurance companies include waiver of premium automatically in their life insurance contracts and include its cost in their basic rates. Others, however, write it as an extra benefit which the insured must elect and for which the insured must pay an extra premium. Waiver of premium really is disability income insurance, where the amount of insurance equals the life insurance premium that would be waived in the event of disability.

Disability Income Rider

Some life insurance companies have allowed disability income benefits, based on the face amount of life insurance, to be added to permanent life insurance policies for an extra premium. Such disability income riders often provided a disability benefit of 1 percent of the face amount of life insurance per month (or $10 per $1000 of life insurance). Disability income insurance written in this fashion is not common today but may exist under older policies.

Long-Term Care (LTC) Riders

Some life insurers are now offering riders to individual life insurance contracts for an additional premium that provide long-term care (LTC) benefits for skilled or intermediate nursing home care and also for custodial care and home health care. Benefits are often paid when the insured person is unable to perform a specified number (such as any two) of a list of activities of daily living (such as eating, bathing, dressing, general mobility, toileting, and taking medication). LTC riders on life policies may be so-called *dependent riders,* under which the death benefit and cash value of the life policy are reduced by any LTC benefits paid, or *independent riders,* under which those life policy benefits are not so reduced. As an example, one such LTC rider will pay 2 percent of the life policy's face amount per month for skilled or intermediate nursing home care and 1 percent per month for custodial care or home health care. These benefits are subject to maximums of $10,000 per month and 50 percent of the life insurance face amount. This example is a dependent rider.

These LTC riders to life contracts are still in the developmental stages and, as of this writing, their income tax status is unclear. However, they do represent a possible approach for consumers to cover the increasingly important custodial care exposure to which they may be subject, provided the consumers also need life insurance protection. As will be noted in Chap. 5, individual LTC policies also are available from insurers without the need for an underlying life insurance policy. These may be referred to as "stand-alone contracts." Further, LTC coverage may be available on a group or association group basis without any underlying life insurance.

Accelerated Death Benefit Life Insurance Policies

As still another approach to the final care issue, some life insurance contracts or riders provide that the discounted value of usually a portion (such as 50 percent) of the policy death benefit will be paid to the policyowner in the event the insured contracts a dread disease, or at the onset of a terminal illness (such as an illness expected to result in death within one year), or perhaps in the event of permanent residence in a nursing home. These events may be referred to as "benefit triggers."

Such accelerated death benefits reduce the cash value and death benefits of the underlying life policy. There may be no initial premium charged for this benefit. While this accelerated death benefit concept may not be a policy rider in all cases, it is another kind of effort to help meet the potential pre-death care need under individual life insurance policies. Such benefits sometimes are referred to as "living benefits" from life insurance policies.

Other Riders on Life Policies

In addition to those just described, there can be a variety of other kinds of riders or options on life insurance contracts. These might include: options to provide additional amounts of life insurance and cash values through increased premiums, options to make one-time payments ("dump-ins") into life policies, children's insurance riders, payor's benefit riders, term insurance riders, options to change premium patterns, and transfer-of-insureds riders.

Substandard Risks

Most applicants who cannot qualify for individual life insurance at standard rates can still obtain insurance through the issuance of life insurance on a so-called substandard ("rated") basis. While a number of factors may cause a person to be classified as "substandard" for life insurance purposes, about 80 percent of these cases concern such physical defects as heart conditions, overweight, albumin in the urine, and high blood pressure. The other 20 percent are accounted for by occupational hazard, moral hazard, extensive foreign travel or residence, and less common medical impairments.

An insured who has been issued insurance on a substandard basis may subsequently learn that he or she is eligible for new insurance at standard rates or at least under better terms than those governing the existing substandard insurance. Such an insured should appeal to the insurer issuing the original insurance for a reconsideration of the original substandard rating. An insurer generally will consider a premium reduction for an insured who demonstrates an improved condition; otherwise, the insured could get insurance from a competing company.

Also, if an applicant has been told he or she can get insurance only on a rated basis, the applicant or his or her advisors may want to check with some other life companies to see what kind of offer of insurance coverage may be available from them. Reputable life companies can differ in their underwriting of certain conditions, and so a lower rating or perhaps even none at all may be secured by shopping around a little.

Nonmedical Life Insurance

"Nonmedical insurance" typically refers to regular life insurance issued without requiring the applicant to submit to a medical examination. Many life insurers will provide $100,000 or more to younger people on a non-medical basis. This nonmedical limit varies by age groups, with the largest amounts being permitted at the younger ages. Additionally, there is typically an age limit, such as 45 or 50, beyond which nonmedical insurance is not available. There is no disadvantage to the insured in buying nonmedical life insurance. The cost is the same as for medically examined business, except that some plans may not be available on a nonmedical basis.

What Actions Can an Uninsurable Person Take?

Although only about 3 percent of the applications for ordinary life insurance are rejected entirely, this nevertheless causes a severe problem for this group who desire and need life insurance. The following are some steps that uninsurable persons may take. First, they can see if it is possible to remove or reduce the reason for the uninsurability. Second, they should check with several different insurers. As we said before, underwriting standards vary, and a person who may be considered uninsurable by one insurer may be regarded as insurable on a substandard basis by another company. Also, the life insurance industry has made considerable progress in making insurance available to previously uninsurable people. Therefore, even if a person has been uninsurable, he or she may be able to get insurance on some basis now.

In addition, look for sources of insurance that do not require the showing of individual evidence of insurability. Group insurance, for example, may be available through the place of employment, and typically no individual evidence of insurability is needed; or, other groups or associations to which the person belongs may be checked to see if he or she can get association group insurance through them. However, association group coverage often requires at least some individual underwriting. Also, nonmedical life insurance may be available on an individual basis. Remember, though, that nonmedical life insurance does involve individual underwriting, and the applicant must answer questions about previous medical history on an application that becomes part of the policy. Also, an insurer can require a medical examination or additional underwriting information in nonmedical cases if it seems warranted. Finally, persons can sometimes qualify for life insurance on a so-called guaranteed-issue basis, where members of a group cannot be denied coverage by the insurer. Some examples may be individual policy pension trusts and group universal life policies (GULP).

Group Life Insurance Coverages

Most people who are eligible for group life insurance obtain such coverage through their place of employment. From the standpoint of many insureds and their families, employer-employee group life insurance is a very important form of life insurance available to them. However, as we said at the beginning of this chapter, group life insurance can be provided through other means as well.

Group life insurance for employer-employee groups may be provided on either a term or a permanent basis. Most, however, is term insurance.

Group Term Life Insurance

Under group term life plans, the insurance protection has the same basic characteristics as individual term life insurance. The employee has the insurance protection (with no cash values) while he or she is working for the employer. If the employee leaves the employer, the group term coverage terminates 31 days after employment ceases, subject to the right of the employee to convert the group insurance to an individual permanent life insurance contract. This conversion privilege is discussed below.

Permanent Forms of Group Life Insurance

Several types of group life plans providing permanent life insurance have been devised and are provided by some employer-employee groups.

Group Paid-up Plans.   These plans are basically a combination of accumulating units of single-premium whole life insurance and decreasing amounts of group term life insurance. While they were once sometimes used, they are not common today.

Level-Premium Group Permanent Plans.   Under this type of plan, the distinguishing characteristic is that some form of permanent life insurance is purchased on a level-premium basis, with premiums payable for life or to a specified age. Upon termination of employment, the employee will have certain cash or paid-up insurance privileges and also may have the option of continuing the full amount of insurance in force. For tax and other reasons, this kind of group product also is not commonly used today as purely group life insurance.

Group Universal Life Insurance.   When permanent life insurance is desired for employees, group universal life plans (GULP) are the vehicle being used now. These plans have already been described on pp. 66–67 of this chapter.

Other Group Plans

Survivor Income Plans.   Another type of employer-employee group plan is one designed to provide a monthly income that becomes payable to surviving dependents upon the death of an employee. There generally are three characteristics that distinguish this type of plan from other kinds of group life insurance: (1) The benefits are payable only in the form of a monthly income; (2) the covered employee does not name his or her beneficiary, benefits being payable only to specified beneficiaries; and (3) benefits usually are payable only as long as there is a living, surviving beneficiary. (See Chap. 13 for more on survivor income plans.)

Group Credit Life Insurance.   This is a special form of group term insurance issued to creditors covering the lives of their debtors in the amount of their outstanding loans.

Elective Group Coverages

Employers often make several group life insurance plans available to their employees. Such arrangements may specify that an employee must sign up for a "basic" group term life insurance plan to be eligible to elect coverage under one or more of the other group life plans. Such *elective plans* often include additional levels of group term insurance. If coverage is needed, employees should consider electing one or more of these plans if available, because they may be a convenient way of supplementing an individual insurance program at a favorable cost and with little or no individual underwriting. Such additional levels or layers of group term life insurance on employees (or their dependents) also usually are available under flexible-benefits (cafeteria compensation) employee benefit plans.

Conversion Rights

An insured employee has the right to convert up to the face amount of his or her group term life insurance to an individual policy of permanent insurance under certain conditions. Typically, the employee may convert, within 31 days after termination of employment, to one of the insurer's regular permanent forms at standard rates for his or her attained age *without evidence of insurability*. For employees who are in poor health or even uninsurable, this can be a very valuable provision, allowing such individuals to obtain life insurance at standard rates.

Group policies also may give a terminating employee the right to continue the amount of his or her group life insurance as term insurance for one year following termination of employment and then to convert to a permanent form of life insurance if the insured so elects. This gives the employee more time to make a final decision.

Coverage After Retirement

In the past, whenever an employee terminated employment, whether for retirement or otherwise, his or her group term life insurance ceased unless the employee exercised the conversion privilege. At advanced ages, however, many people feel that it is too expensive to utilize the conversion right. Nowadays, a number of group life plans continue at least some life insurance coverage after retirement.

Social Security

Some people consider the social security system to be one of the most complex and perplexing concepts ever designed, yet the basic philosophy of the program is quite simple. This basic concept is that during one's working years, employees, employers, and self-employed individuals pay social security taxes (FICA taxes), which are pooled in special trust funds. Then, when a covered worker retires, dies, or becomes totally disabled, monthly benefits are paid to the worker and/or his or her dependents to replace part of the earnings lost as a result of these events or risks. There also is an HI [Hospital Insurance (Part A) of Medicare] tax on a separate wage base that goes into a separate Hospital Insurance Trust Fund so that when workers and their dependents reach age 65 (and for certain other groups), they will have coverage for their hospital bills. Voluntary medical insurance also is available to persons age 65 or over to help pay physicians' bills and other medical expenses. This voluntary program is financed out of premiums shared equally by covered persons and the federal government. To better understand the social security system, the following sections will analyze the coverage, eligibility, and benefits provided by the system.

Eligibility for Benefits

Eligibility for various benefits under social security depends on the "insured" status of the worker. Eligibility for retirement benefits requires that a worker be *fully insured*. Eligibility for survivorship benefits generally requires that a worker, depending on the benefits sought, be *fully insured or currently insured*.

Fully Insured.   Although there are several ways in which workers can achieve fully insured status, two basic ones are noted here. First, workers are considered fully insured if they are credited with 40 quarters of coverage earned at any time since 1936. Second, from a minimum of 6 up to 40 quarters of coverage, they can attain fully insured status by earning specified numbers of quarters of coverage (defined as certain covered earnings during a calendar year, up to four quarters in any one year), with the specified numbers of quarters required depending on the worker's date of birth and the type of benefit involved. A minimum of six quarters is required in any case.

Currently Insured.   To achieve currently insured status, a worker must be credited with a minimum of 6 quarters of coverage during the 13-quarter period ending with the quarter in which he or she died.

Benefits

The basic types of benefits provided by the social security system are retirement, survivorship, disability, and medical.

Retirement Benefits.   The basic retirement benefit provides a *monthly income* which begins as a full benefit at a specified retirement age, between age 65 and 67 (depending on the year the retired worker reaches age 62), and continues from the specified full-benefit retirement age for the remainder of the retired worker's lifetime. There also are reduced retirement benefits for early retirements at ages from age 62 to the full-benefit retirement age. The amount of the monthly benefit is determined by a formula based on the worker's covered earnings over his or her working years. (There are benefit deductions for early retirements.)

The spouse (or a divorced spouse, provided the marriage existed for at least 10 years immediately preceding the divorce) of a retired worker is entitled to a benefit, called the "spouse's benefit," equal to 50 percent of the worker's retirement benefit if the spouse is 65 (the present full-benefit age) or over (or is age 62 through 64 at reduced benefits). Or, regardless of age, a spouse is entitled to this benefit, referred to as the "parent's benefit," if he or she is caring for an unmarried child of the worker under age 16 or a child who is disabled and has been so since age 22. In addition, each unmarried child under 18 (or under 19 if a full-time high school student) is entitled to a benefit, called the "child's benefit," equal to 50 percent of the retired worker's retirement benefit.

Depending on a person's or married couple's other income, social security benefits will be at least partially, and may be fully, income tax–free and normally are important in a person's retirement planning. However, the total of all social security retirement benefits is subject to an overall family maximum.

Survivorship Benefits.   These may be in the following forms:

1. Monthly payments to a deceased worker's:
   a. Widow, widower, or eligible surviving divorced spouse, who has reached the survivor's full-benefit retirement age (now age 65) (or ages 60 through 64 at reduced benefits), or a disabled widow or widower age 50 or older
   b. Widow, widower, or surviving divorced spouse (regardless of age) if caring for a child who is under age 16 or is disabled before age 22
   c. Surviving children under age 18, or disabled prior to age 22 and still disabled, or ages 18 through 19 if a high school student
   d. Dependent parents age 62 or over
2. Lump-sum benefit ($255)

Disability Benefits.   A disabled worker and his or her eligible dependents may be entitled to monthly cash disability benefits under social security if the disabled worker meets the requirements of the law. The requirements and benefits are explained further in Chap. 5.

Health Insurance Benefits.   The health insurance portion of the social security system, popularly called Medicare, comprises two major programs, Hospital Insurance (HI) and Supplementary Medical Insurance (SMI). Both programs generally are for persons age 65 or over and for disability beneficiaries. These programs also are described in greater detail in Chap. 5. The preceding discussion merely provides a framework of the provisions and various benefits of the social security system.

Planning and Using Life Insurance

Paying Life Insurance Premiums

Premiums on life insurance contracts can be paid at different intervals and in several different ways.

Annual or Fractional Premiums.   A policyowner normally may pay life insurance premiums on an annual, semiannual, quarterly, or monthly basis. When paid other than annually, the annual premium is modified by adding a percentage amount to the annual premium and then dividing the result into the requisite number of parts. It generally is more economical to pay life insurance premiums annually.

Preauthorized Check Plans.   If a policyowner so desires, he or she may authorize the life insurer to collect the premiums as they come due from the policyowner's bank. This may be more convenient for the policyowner.

Prepayment of Premiums.   Subject to certain limitations, most life insurance companies permit policyowners to prepay premiums, either in the form of so-called premium deposits or through the discounting of future premiums. If the insured dies, the balance of any prepaid premiums is paid to the insured's estate or designated beneficiary in addition to the face of the policy.

Premiums Graded (Reduced) by Size of Policy.   Most life insurers follow the practice of grading premium rates by size of policy issued. That is, the larger the face amount of the policy, the lower will be the premium rate per $1000 of insurance.

As a practical matter, another way of giving lower rates per $1000 for larger policies is by offering certain policies only in minimum face amounts, such as $100,000, $250,000, $500,000, or more. Such contracts often have a lower rate per $1000 of insurance than applies to reasonably comparable coverage of lesser face amounts.

The practical effect of grading premium rates by size of policy is that life insurance has become "cheaper by the dozen." Thus, it is relatively less expensive to buy one larger policy than several smaller ones. So in buying life insurance, consider the various ranges at which the cost per $1000 decreases. Also, look for the availability of lower-cost contracts of a minimum face amount.

Lower Cost for Women.   Women generally have lower mortality rates than men. For many years life insurance rating did not reflect this fact, but today most companies have lower premium rates for women than for men, and sometimes the difference can be substantial.

Life Insurance Policy Dividends.   One of the basic decisions in buying life insurance is whether to buy participating or nonparticipating insurance. Unfortunately, there is no pat answer to this question, but the following information may be helpful in making this choice.

Participating life insurance refunds a portion of the gross premium to the policyholder in the form of policy dividends that are based on the insurer's actual mortality experience, investment earnings, and administrative expenses. Such policy dividends cannot be guaranteed by the insurer and depend upon its actual experience.

Nonparticipating (*nonpar*) policies are sold at definite, fixed premiums that do not provide for any dividends. Thus, the policyholder knows in advance what his or her life insurance cost will be under a nonpar policy, while under a participating contract the final premium will depend on (1) the gross premium and (2) the policy dividends actually paid by the insurer. Of course, depending on the insurer's actual experience under a participating policy, the policyholder's final premium may be lower or higher than under a comparable nonpar contract.

Participating life insurance is sold by both mutual and stock life insurance companies. Nonparticipating policies normally are sold only by stock companies.

For most plans of life insurance, a given dividend scale will produce dividends that generally increase each year with policy duration. This assumes that the dividend scale itself does not change. However, an insurer may either increase or decrease its whole dividend scale, depending on its experience and its management policies.

Beneficiary Designations

The right to name a beneficiary or beneficiaries is vested in the policy-owner. The insured usually is the owner of a policy, but there are many policies outstanding today that have been applied for and are owned by someone other than the insured (or a trust), or in which ownership has been transferred by the insured to another (or a trust) after the policy was issued. The insured generally reserves the right to designate and change the beneficiary, and the rule prevailing in most states is that the insured can exercise the rights under a policy without a revocable beneficiary's consent.

Consider this beneficiary designation: "Sue Smith, wife of the insured, if living at the death of the insured, otherwise to such of the lawful children of the insured as may be living at the death of the insured." Here Sue Smith is the primary beneficiary and the children are contingent beneficiaries. Also, second contingent beneficiaries may be designated in the event none of the primary or contingent beneficiaries survive the insured. It is considered good practice to designate more than one beneficiary.

Probably the most commonly used designation is one that names the insured's wife or husband as primary beneficiary, with the children as contingent beneficiaries. It is customary to describe the beneficiary by his or her family relationship to the insured, or as a "friend," "business associate," "fiancée," and the like.

The insured may want to designate a group of persons without identifying the individual members of the group. This is known as a "class designation." For example, in the illustration cited above, the designation "lawful children of the insured" is an example of a class designation. The beneficiaries actually entitled to receive the proceeds in the event of the insured's death will be determined by the members of the class at that time. Such a class designation automatically includes members of the class who may be born or otherwise join the class after the date of the beneficiary designation but before the insured's death.

When all children of the insured are desired to be named as beneficiaries, usually the safest way is to designate "children of the insured" as a class. If the children are designated by name, such as "John Smith and Doris Smith, children of the insured," then unnamed children or children born after the date of the beneficiary designation will be excluded. If this result is not desired, then "children of the insured," or "children of the insured, including John Smith and Doris Smith," should be used.

If there are children by a former marriage of the insured's wife or husband, these children must be named specifically to be included under the beneficiary designation. This can be done by some designation such as "children of the insured, and George Baker and Carol Baker, children of the insured's wife (husband)."

With regard to adopted children, until the adoption proceedings are completed, such children would not be included in a class designation "children of the insured." To share in the proceeds, their names would have to be specifically included in the beneficiary designation, as was done above.

An insured may wish to have the death proceeds of his or her life insurance paid to a trustee, with the fund to be administered for the beneficiaries as a trust. A trust may be established under an agreement signed by the insured during his or her lifetime or under the insured's will. A typical lifetime trustee beneficiary designation might read: "The XYZ Trust Company, trustee, or its successor or successors in trust, under trust agreement dated ———." Of course, an individual can be named as trustee or as cotrustee if the insured wishes. (See Chap. 16 for a discussion of the uses of insurance trusts.)

Sometimes insureds name an individual (e.g., wife or husband) as primary beneficiary and a trustee as contingent beneficiary. This is referred to as a "contingent life insurance trust." In this case, the proceeds may be paid to the primary beneficiary in one sum or under one or more of the settlement options discussed earlier.

There may be some legal complications in naming minors, say minor children, as beneficiaries of life insurance. If a minor is named beneficiary and becomes entitled to the policy proceeds, the minor may not be able to give a legally valid release for receipt of the life insurance proceeds because a minor may not be legally competent to enter into contracts. Today, of course, many states have lowered the age at which a person attains majority to 18. Other states have adopted special enabling statutes applicable to insurance which authorize minors of a designated age, such as 15, to contract for insurance, give a valid receipt for benefits payable, and otherwise deal with policies as though the minor had attained majority. Other state statutes permit payment of a modest amount directly to a minor. But if such a statute does not apply, and if proceeds are payable to a minor, it would be necessary to have a guardian appointed to receive payment of the proceeds on behalf of the minor. This normally involves legal formality, expense, and restrictions as to who may be guardian and what the guardian can do without specific court approval.

There are several possibilities for handling any problems that may arise out of naming minor beneficiaries.

1. *An insurance trust* can be used and the trustee named as beneficiary of the life insurance. The trust then would be administered for the benefit of the insured's family, including any minor beneficiaries. (See Chap. 16 for the other advantages and the disadvantages of using a living insurance trust.)

2. An adult (say, the insured's spouse) could be named as primary beneficiary and then a *contingent life insurance trust* could be used for the children (i.e., the minors), as described above.

3. In the case of some insurance companies, this problem can be simplified by allowing the proceeds to be retained at interest by the insurer with the full right reserved to withdraw the principal or to elect any other settlement option(s). The minor is named beneficiary, but it is provided that if he or she is still a minor when the proceeds are paid, a trustee named in the policy, rather than a guardian, will receive the payments on behalf of the minor and may exercise the privileges specified in the policy.

Providing for Simultaneous Death Situations

An insured and his or her spouse rarely die in a common accident or disaster. But it does happen, and so this contingency should be considered in life insurance planning. For example, as mentioned previously, a beneficiary arrangement might provide, in substance: "Sue Smith, wife of the insured, if living at the death of the insured, otherwise equally to such of the children of the insured as may be living at the death of the insured." Under such a designation, assuming the proceeds are payable in a lump sum, if Sue survives her husband for only a few moments, her estate will be entitled to all the proceeds. In this event, the proceeds will be exposed to probate costs in her estate and to possible claims of her creditors and will pass in accordance with the terms of her will or according to the applicable intestate law if she left no valid will.

This result can be avoided by making all or a portion of the proceeds payable to Sue under the interest option subject to her full right of withdrawal, and naming the children (or a trust) as second beneficiaries to receive any remaining proceeds whether Sue dies before or after the insured. If Sue survives her husband, the proceeds are subject to her complete control. But if she dies before, simultaneously with, or shortly after the insured, the proceeds will be paid to the second beneficiary or beneficiaries rather than being tied up in the estate of the insured or his wife.

Another procedure for handling the common-disaster situation is to provide that the proceeds will be paid to the beneficiary only if he or she is living on, say, the thirtieth day after the insured's death. However, this procedure has some potential disadvantages that are avoided by using the interest option with the proceeds subject to withdrawal, as just described.

An insurance trust also can be arranged to avoid the simultaneous death situation.

How Much Life Insurance Is Needed?

Depends on the Purpose of the Life Insurance

This question often perplexes consumers. They want to know how much life insurance they need to protect their families adequately, but they do not want to overinsure needlessly. Unfortunately, there probably is no one answer to this question; but as far as family protection is concerned, two approaches traditionally have been suggested for attempting to measure the amount of life insurance a person should have—the human life value approach and the needs (or programming) approach.

It is a different question with regard to estate liquidity and conservation needs and business life insurance needs. For estate liquidity and conservation purposes, the amount of life insurance needed depends on the size of the estate or estates involved, the potential estate shrinkage, any other liquid assets or arrangements available, and the person's estate plan, as explained in Chap. 15. For business life insurance needs, it depends on the owners' goals for their business, on the business values involved, and on the particular business plans adopted, as explained in Chap. 17. The remainder of this discussion will focus only on family protection needs.

Human Life Value Approach

The human life value approach attempts to measure the economic worth of an individual to his or her family or to others dependent on that individual's income. This approach seeks to measure the economic loss, defined as the loss of earnings devoted to an individual's dependents over his or her working lifetime, if the individual were to die today. This value is commonly computed by using the following five steps.

1. Estimate the person's average annual earnings from future personal efforts over the remaining years of his or her productive lifetime. This period normally is the difference between the person's contemplated retirement age and present age.

2. Deduct from the average annual earnings estimated federal, state, and other income taxes; personal life and health insurance premiums; social security (FICA) taxes; and the individual's personal living expenses. The difference represents the amount of the person's earned income devoted to his or her family.

3. Determine the remaining years of his or her productive lifetime as explained above.

4. Select an appropriate interest rate at which the estimated future earnings devoted to the person's family can be discounted (for capitalization purposes).

5. Multiply the amount of annual earned income devoted to the family by the present value of $1 per year for the period of the remaining years of the person's productive lifetime, assuming the interest rate selected in item 4 above.

An example will help explain this procedure. Let us take the fairly typical case of a rising young executive, Harry Smart, and his wife, Alice. Harry is age 34 and Alice is 30. They have three young children, ages 6, 4, and 1. Harry now earns about $35,000 per year in base salary. He and Alice jointly own their home, which is worth about $140,000 and has a $60,000 mortgage outstanding on it. They also jointly own about $10,000 worth of common stocks, $4000 in mutual fund shares, and $2000 in savings and checking accounts. Harry owns individually purchased life insurance on his life having total death benefits of about $110,000. Alice is primary beneficiary of this insurance. Through his employer, Harry has group term life insurance equal to two times his base salary (or $70,000) and a deferred profit-sharing plan with about $16,000 currently credited to Harry's account; the benefits of both these plans are payable to Harry's estate at his death. Alice owns only a modest amount of property in her own name.

For purposes of calculating Harry's human life value for insurance purposes, let us assume (for the sake of simplicity in illustrating the concept) that Harry's $35,000 annual salary will remain level over his working lifetime and that $21,000 per year is devoted to his family.[12] Thus, we can calculate Harry's present estimated human life value by multiplying $21,000 by the present value of $1 per year for 31 years (65 − 34), discounted at an

---

[12] This figure can be estimated from the information given in the family income statement. (See Table 1.2 in Chap. 1).

interest rate of, say, 5 percent, or a present value factor of 15.59. This product gives us an estimated human life value for Harry Smart of $327,390 ($21,000 × 15.59). This human life value will diminish as Harry grows older, assuming no changes in income, retirement age, taxes, cost of self-maintenance, etc. Of course, if any of these factors change, as they likely will, this will affect Harry's economic worth to his family.

In practice, the human life value approach generally has not been used in the sale of life insurance as much as the needs approach, which is described next. However, the human life value is a factor to consider in determining how much life insurance a person may want to carry.

Needs, or Programming, Approach

Another main method for estimating how much life insurance is needed to protect a person's dependents is the "needs," or "programming," approach. This approach attempts to analyze the various needs of a family in the event an income earner dies. Such needs vary, of course, from family to family, but the following categories of needs normally would apply to most families.

1. Final lump-sum expenses (last illness expenses, burial expenses, probate costs, and the like)
2. Readjustment income (an income sufficient to allow the family to make any adjustment that may be necessary in living standards gradually)
3. Income for the family until the children are self-supporting (referred to as the "dependency period" or "child-rearing period")
4. Life income for the widow or widower after the children are self-supporting
5. Special needs (such as mortgage redemption, emergency fund, educational funds, and other specific needs)
6. Retirement needs

Once the family's needs are identified, the next step is to determine what income or benefits are available from sources other than life insurance to meet those needs. The difference between the funds required to meet the family's "needs" and those available from other sources represents the amount of life insurance a person needs.

The following is an illustration of the needs, or programming, approach. Assume the following facts as given above:

Husband—Harry Smart, age 34

Wife—Alice Smart, age 30

Son—John Smart, age 6

Daughter—Susan Smart, age 4

Daughter—Cindy Smart, age 1

Needs of the Smart family:

Lump-sum needs:

Funds for estate settlement at Harry Smart's death: $18,000 (estimated funeral expenses, debts, estate and inheritance taxes, and other estate settlement costs)

Emergency fund: $4000

Mortgage cancellation fund: $60,000

Educational needs: $72,000 (assuming four years of college for each child at $6000 per year for each child)

Income needs: Harry Smart would like his family to have the following approximate monthly income if he were to die today:

$2200 per month until his son (John) and daughter (Susan) reach age 18 (total of 14 years)

$1600 per month from the time John and Susan reach 18 until Cindy reaches 18 (3 more years)

Thereafter, a life income of $1200 per month to his widow (Alice)

A first step in the programming process often is to plot out in a simple graph what the family income needs are and to what extent those needs would be met by social security and other benefits should the income earner die now.[13] Social security benefits may be increased by automatic cost-of-living increases and, of course, by future changes in the law. The social security benefits used in the following programming illustration assume that Harry Smart has a primary insurance amount (PIA) of approximately $850.

Social security survivorship benefits will provide about $1480 per month until Susan reaches age 18. For the next year, until Cindy becomes 16, social security benefits will decrease to about $1275 per month. Then, for the next two years after that, they will decline again to about $637 per month until Cindy becomes 18. At that time, social security benefits will cease until

---

[13] This is an illustration of the "regular" programming approach. Another approach, called the "capitalization and discount" method, also is commonly used. While these programming methods may differ in technique, they have the same objectives, and the results are essentially the same. Naturally, the results of any such illustration depend on the assumptions used in planning.

Alice reaches age 65 (or ages 60 through 64 at reduced benefits), at which time she will receive a life income of about $850 per month. The period during which no social security benefits are paid is called the social security "gap" or "blackout period."

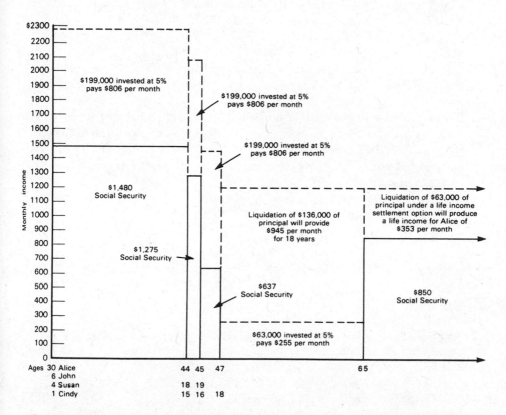

Assume that life insurance is needed to make up the deficits in the amounts of monthly income desired. By a combination of the various settlement options described earlier in the chapter, and using the rates of a major life insurance company, approximately $199,000 of life insurance will be needed to meet the desired monthly income figures. The $199,000 of proceeds invested at 5 percent (a conservative assumed interest rate on settlement options) would yield $806 of interest each month. Added to social security of $1480, a total monthly income of $2286 could be provided until both John and Susan reached age 18. The proceeds still could be left at interest, yielding $806 per month, until Cindy reached age 18. The $806 added to the levels of social security benefits for this period would give the family a total monthly income that would average out to more than the $1600 desired for this period. When Cindy reaches 18 three years later, the monthly income desired is reduced to $1200. Thus, at this point it would be necessary to plan to liquidate some of the life insurance proceeds (principal). To provide for the 18-year social security gap, or "blackout period" (Alice's ages 47 to 65), $136,000 of proceeds would provide $945 per month under a fixed-period option. The balance of the life insurance, $63,000, still would remain at interest and would yield $255 per month, making a total monthly payment of $1200.

When Alice Smart reaches age 65, social security will pay her a monthly life income of about $850. The remainder of the desired $1200 per month could be obtained by liquidating the remaining $63,000 of proceeds through a life income settlement option which would provide $353 per month. Of course, it could be decided that a life income option would not afford the best yield available and that other, equally secure investment instruments should be considered. This would depend on the circumstances. The life income option is used here only for planning purposes. The dashed lines on the preceding graph illustrate the amounts and settlement arrangements for the life insurance described here.

If all these needs are to be handled through life insurance, Harry Smart will need the following:

Estate settlement	$ 18,000
Emergency fund	4,000
Mortgage cancellation fund	60,000
Education	72,000
Family income	199,000
Total	$353,000

Part of the needs, or programming, approach is to consider other resources available. Social security already has been considered. Harry Smart's other current benefits and assets in the event of his death are as follows:

Group life insurance and profit-sharing death benefits from his employer	$ 86,000
Whole life policy with ABC Insurance Company	20,000
10-year level term life policy (renewable and convertible) with XYZ Insurance Company	30,000
Decreasing term (mortgage protection) life policy with RST Insurance Company (present benefit)	60,000
Other investable assets	16,000
Total	$212,000

Therefore, Harry Smart has a need for additional life insurance of about $141,000 under these assumptions.[14]

Of course, depending on the amount involved and the person's age, his or her ability to pay premiums for additional life insurance and also the general strategy to be followed in purchasing life insurance must be evaluated carefully. The person, for example, may want to purchase a lower-premium form of life insurance now, such as term insurance, or perhaps graded-premium whole life or modified life (which have lower initial premiums), or universal life insurance with lower premiums being paid during the early years. Later, some or all of any term insurance could be converted to a permanent form of life insurance, if this proves desirable and fits into the person's insurance-buying strategy. Or the flexible premium payments can be increased under a universal life plan. Naturally, it is important that any life insurance program be reviewed periodically in light of inevitable changes in the person's or his or her family's needs or goals.

How can consumers make these calculations to determine how much life insurance they need? Normally, it is not necessary for them to do so, because competent life insurance agents and financial planners usually are more than willing to perform this service.

Other Approaches

Aside from these two traditional approaches, as a practical matter other approaches also are used today. They include a multiple of earnings approach (where the amount of insurance is equal to, say, six to ten times the insured's annual earnings); a simple capitalization of earnings to be replaced approach (where, for example, if $20,000 per year of earnings are to be replaced and 5 percent interest is assumed, $400,000 of life insurance is needed—$20,000 ÷ 0.05 = $400,000); and just buying an arbitrary amount of insurance.

---

[14] Other assumptions and techniques could properly be used in programming for these needs. However, while they might vary in detail, the basic ideas are the same. The above example illustrates the needs approach to determining how much life insurance a person should own. One important modification that might be made to this approach is to consider the effects of inflation on the family's needs in the future. This would increase considerably the amount of life insurance needed.

5
Health Insurance

There are two traditional types of health losses against which people should protect themselves and their families—*disability income losses* and *medical care expenses*. Either type can result in financial catastrophe and hence should be provided for in overall financial planning. Another type of related loss—*custodial care expenses*—has been receiving increased attention in recent years and also should be provided for in the financial planning process.

Health Insurance Coverages

Health insurance is insurance against loss by sickness or injury. It can provide coverage for disability income and medical expense losses caused by accident only or by accident and sickness. Correspondingly, long-term care (LTC) insurance provides coverage for various custodial care expenses in the event the insured person becomes incapacitated as defined in the policy.

The following are the major sources of health insurance coverages that may be available. Social insurance and group insurance are discussed first because they have become so important and because they usually are made available more or less automatically and so provide a basic level of protection which can then be supplemented.

Social Insurance

The main social insurance programs that provide health benefits are:

1. The disability portion of the federal social security system (i.e., the "D" of OASDHI)

2. The "Medicare" portion (Hospital Insurance and Supplementary Medical Insurance) of the federal social security system (i.e., the "H" of OASDHI)

3. State (and federal) workers' compensation laws

4. The nonoccupational temporary disability benefits laws of California, Hawaii, New Jersey, New York, Puerto Rico, and Rhode Island

5. While not social insurance as such, the Medicaid program of medical assistance, which may provide benefits under certain circumstances

Group Insurance

Group insurance is the predominant way of providing private health insurance in the United States. Thus, group coverages represent the backbone of health insurance planning for most people. As in the case of group life insurance, group health insurance is a contract made with an employer, or sometimes with another entity, that provides protection to a definitely identified group of persons.

Individual Insurance

Individual health insurance policies are contracts made with an individual to cover the individual and perhaps some specified members of his or her family (usually spouse and children). When the insured and specified family members are covered, the policy may be referred to as a "family health insurance policy."

Franchise and Association
Group Insurance

Franchise health insurance is a mixture of the individual and group approaches. It involves the issuance of individual policies to employees, or members of other groups, under an arrangement with the employer or other entity. Even though individual policies are issued, certain group underwriting standards may be used, such as the guaranteed issue of policies (without individual underwriting) if the number of covered lives is sufficiently large. There also may be premium discounts for franchise cases. Franchise insurance is the health insurance product that is comparable to wholesale life insurance.

Association group insurance is similar to franchise insurance except that it is typically issued to members of professional or trade association groups, covered persons usually pay their premiums directly to the insurer, and covered persons may receive certificates of insurance rather than individual policies. The premium rates for association group insurance may be less than for individual insurance but more than for regular group insurance. However, this depends on the circumstances, and the consumer should compare association group (and franchise) rates with those of comparable good-quality individual insurance before buying.

Other Insurance Coverages

Health insurance benefits also may be provided under a variety of other insurance coverages. Some of the more important are:

1. Disability benefits under group life insurance
2. Disability benefits and perhaps medical expense benefits under pension plans
3. Disability benefits under individual life insurance policies
4. Medical payments under liability insurance policies (and benefits under automobile "no-fault" plans)
5. Blanket health insurance and miscellaneous health coverages

Disability Income (Loss of Time) Coverages

In this section we shall describe the various kinds of disability income coverages that people may use to protect themselves against this important, and often neglected, risk. However, first let us review a few basic features that will be encountered in buying or dealing with these coverages.

Features Affecting Disability Income Coverage

Maximum Benefit Period.   This is the maximum period of time disability benefits will be paid to a disabled person. It represents a maximum limit of liability expressed in weeks or months or extending to a specified age or in some cases even for life. Lifetime benefits for disabilities caused by accident are common, and increasingly lifetime benefits are also provided for disabilities caused by sickness. Generally speaking, the longer the maximum benefit period, the better is the coverage for the insured.

Perils Insured Against.   These perils normally are either *accident alone* or *accident and sickness.* Coverage of disability caused by accident only is limited in scope and normally should be avoided in buying health insurance. Coverage generally should be purchased for both accident and sickness.

Waiting (Elimination) Period.   This is the period of time that must elapse after a covered disability starts before disability income benefits begin.

Suppose, for example, a plan has a 30-day elimination period for accident and sickness. If an insured person becomes disabled as defined by the plan, he or she must wait 30 days after the start of disability before beginning to collect benefits. In health insurance, benefits normally are not paid retroactively to the start of a disability once such an elimination period has been satisfied.

Definition of Disability.   This important provision describes when a person is considered to be disabled for purposes of collecting benefits. There are essentially three varieties of definitions of disability in common use today when disability is defined in terms of the insured's inability to perform occupational duties—the "any occupation" type, the "own occupation" type, and the so-called split definition.

As it was originally conceived, the "any occupation" type defines disability as the complete inability of the covered person to engage in any occupation whatsoever. This is a very strict approach. So the modern tendency is to phrase an "any occupation" definition in a way that will consider total disability as the "complete inability of the insured to engage in any gainful occupation for which he (or she) is or becomes reasonably fitted by education, training, or experience," or some similar wording. The "any occupation" approach is the least liberal from the consumer's viewpoint.

The "own occupation" type defines disability so that the covered person is considered disabled when he or she is "prevented by such disability from performing any and every duty pertaining to the employee's (or insured's, in the case of an individual policy) occupation." In some more modern policies, this may be phrased as the insured's inability to engage in the substantial and material duties of his or her regular occupation or specialty, or some similar broader wording. This general "own occupation" (or "own-occ") approach is the most liberal from the consumer's viewpoint. It is best for the consumer to have an "own occ" definition apply to the full maximum benefit period.

The "split definition" is a combination of these two approaches. An example is as follows:

> "Total disability" means complete inability of the insured to engage in *any* [emphasis added] gainful occupation for which he (or she) is reasonably fitted by education, training or experience; however, during the first 60 months of any period of disability, the Company (insurer) will deem the insured to be totally disabled if he (or she) is completely unable to engage in *his* (or *her*) [emphasis added] regular occupation and is not engaged in any form of gainful occupation.

This definition, in effect, applies an "own occ" definition for a specified period—five years in this example—and then applies an "any occupation for which the insured is reasonably fitted" definition for the remainder of the benefit period. From the consumer's viewpoint, it is better to have as long an "own occ" period under a split definition as possible. How long a period of "own occ" coverage is available varies among insurers and with the circumstances, but it often is two to five years and may run to 10 years or to age 65, depending on the circumstances.

Another general approach to defining disability is in terms of the loss of a certain percentage of the insured's earned income due to accident or sickness. This is termed a loss-of-income approach.

Social Security Disability Benefits

Benefits Provided.   There are two basic kinds of social security disability benefits: cash disability income benefits and the "freezing" of a disabled worker's wage position for purposes of determining his or her future retirement or survivorship benefits. Most workers (and their dependents) in covered employment under the social security system would be eligible for social security disability benefits. Thus, they may consider these benefits as their base layer of protection against disability income losses.

An eligible worker is considered disabled for the purpose of receiving these benefits when he or she has a medically determinable physical or mental impairment which is so severe that the worker is unable to engage in *any substantially gainful work or employment*. This amounts to an "any occupation" definition of disability and is strict by health insurance standards. In addition, the *disability must last five months before benefits can begin*. After five months of disability, benefits are payable if the impairment can be expected to last for at least 12 months from when the disability began or to result in death or if it has actually lasted 12 months. This amounts to a five-month waiting (elimination) period. The combined effect of the strict definition of disability and the long waiting period is largely to restrict social security disability benefits to total and severe (probably permanent) long-term disabilities.

The amount of the monthly social security cash disability benefits payable to a disabled worker and his or her dependents is based on the worker's wages subject to social security taxes.[1] Let us take an example to help clarify these benefits. Consider again the case of Harry Smart (age 34), who makes about $35,000 per year. You will recall that his wife, Alice, is age 30 and that they have three children, John, age 6, Susan, age 4, and Cindy, age 1. One day, Harry is involved in a serious automobile accident (not work-connected) and as a result becomes totally disabled and unable to earn a living. After five months of disability, Harry and his family will be entitled to the social security cash disability benefits listed below, regardless of any private insurance benefits he also may have. For illustrative purposes, assume that Harry's basic social security disability benefit is $825 per month.

---

[1] The same general approach to calculating earnings applies to social security retirement, survivors, and disability benefits.

Harry	$825 per month, until he recovers, dies, or reaches age 65
Alice	$412 per month, until Cindy (the youngest) reaches age 16 (or for 15 years)
John	$412 per month, until he reaches age 18 (or for 12 years)
Susan	$412 per month, until she reaches age 18 (or for 14 years)
Cindy	$412 per month, until she reaches age 18 (or for 17 years)

But because of the maximum family benefit, this is reduced to about $1237 per month.

Thus, as long as Harry remains disabled as defined in the law, his family will receive $1237 per month for 17 years (by which time Alice, John, Susan, and Cindy will no longer be eligible), and then $825 per month for the next 14 years, by which time Harry will be 65 (and his wife, Alice, will be 61). When Harry reaches 65, his social security retirement benefits will begin.

Taxation of Benefits.   Beginning in 1984, social security benefits are subject to federal income tax if the sum of (1) the taxpayer's income (i.e., adjusted gross income for federal income tax purposes plus any tax-exempt income) and (2) one-half of the taxpayer's and his or her spouse's social security benefit(s) exceeds $25,000 for a single taxpayer and $32,000 for a married couple. The amount then included in income is the smaller of (1) the excess amount over the $25,000 or $32,000 base described above, or (2) one-half the social security benefits. Thus, social security disability income benefits, like other social security benefits, may or may not be taxable income for federal income tax purposes, depending on the person's or couple's other income. Therefore, assuming Harry's taxes averaged about 15 percent of his earned income prior to his disability and his social security disability benefits are not taxable, the $1237 per month of tax-free disability benefits is equivalent to about $1455 per month (or $17,464 per year) of taxable income. But it is clear that even this $17,464 of equivalent benefits is a far cry from the $35,000 per year Harry earned prior to his disability. Also, the social security disability benefits will decline as Harry's children reach age 18 (or age 19 if they are still in high school). Thus, Harry's disability protection needs to be supplemented by private insurance and/or other sources, or else his family will have to make drastic changes in their living standards.

Workers' Compensation Disability Benefits

For persons injured or suffering covered diseases from their employment, some coverage usually is provided under workers' compensation laws. These laws are intended to provide benefits only for work injuries and diseases, and so they really cannot be relied upon in health insurance planning.

Group Health Insurance
(Disability Income)

Group health insurance is a common method of providing disability income protection for the public. The two basic kinds of plans are (1) short-term group disability income insurance, and (2) long-term group disability income insurance.

Benefits Provided.   *Short-term plans* are widely written on a group basis and are characterized by a schedule of weekly benefits based on earnings categories but with a relatively low maximum benefit, such as $500 per week; a short elimination period of from 3 to 14 days (or none for accident benefits); an "own occupation" definition of disability; and relatively short maximum benefit periods of, say, 13, 26, or 52 weeks. These plans generally are intended to provide relatively modest benefits for a short period of time. They do not attempt to meet the need for protection against more serious, prolonged disabilities that can be financially catastrophic for the family.

Long-term group disability income plans are designed to take care of the more serious, long-term disabilities. They are characterized by benefits stated as a percentage of earnings (such as 60 percent of base salary) with a relatively high maximum monthly benefit of $2000, $3000, $5000, or more; a longer elimination period, such as 90 days or 6 months; a "split" definition of disability; and payment of disability benefits for longer maximum benefit periods, such as 5 years, 10 years, to a certain age such as 65 or 70, or in some cases even for life. These plans usually try to avoid, at least in part, duplication with other disability benefits. To be eligible for coverage, it is common for employees to have to be employed by the employer for a substantial period, one year or more in some cases.

Thus, as an example, a group long-term plan might provide benefits equal to 60 percent of the covered employee's base salary, but subject to a maximum monthly benefit of $5000 and with a six-month elimination period for accident and sickness. The maximum benefit period is to age 65 for both accident and sickness. A full-time employee becomes eligible for the plan after being continuously employed for one year, and the plan is noncontributory (i.e., the full cost is paid by the employer). The plan covers occupational as well as nonoccupational disabilities (so-called 24-hour coverage).

Coordination of Benefits.   Most group long-term plans have *coordination-of-benefits* provisions that indicate how other disability income benefits available to the covered person will affect the benefits payable under the group policy. Such provisions are important in planning disability protection. These

provisions are not uniform, but a fairly typical coordination-of-benefits provision in a group long-term plan might provide that the maximum benefit
otherwise payable will be reduced by any benefits paid or payable under:

1. Any workers' compensation or similar law
2. The federal Social Security Act (based on the "maximum family benefit")[2]
3. Any disability or early-retirement benefits actually received under the
   employer's pension plan
4. Any state disability benefits law or similar governmental legislation
5. Any other *employer-sponsored* (emphasis added) disability plan
6. Any full or partial wage or salary payments by the employer

In disability income planning, the coordination-of-benefits provision in any
such group contract should be reviewed. Most group plans, for example, do
not reduce their benefits on account of individual disability income insurance that is not provided by the employer (as in the example above).

Let us see how the particular group long-term disability plan outlined
above would affect our hypothetical case of Harry Smart. Harry's base salary
is $35,000 per year, or about $2917 per month. Sixty percent of $2917 is
$1750 per month, which is less than the plan's maximum monthly benefit.
Therefore, after the six-month elimination period, Harry could recover up
to $1750 per month from the group plan. However, under the coordination-
of-benefits provision cited above, the social security benefit of $1237 per
month would be deducted from the maximum benefit otherwise payable by
the group plan. Thus, the group plan benefits would become $513 per
month ($1750 – $1237) for the first 17 years of Harry's disability. Note that
if Harry had a personally owned disability income policy, the benefits under
that policy would not reduce his group benefit under the above-cited
coordination-of-benefits provision.

Termination of Coverage. A covered employee's group disability
income coverage typically terminates when (1) the employee leaves his or
her employment, (2) the employee retires, (3) the group policy is terminated by the employer, or (4) the employer fails to pay the premium for the
employee, except through error. Thus, the employee's *group disability
income insurance* normally terminates when the employee terminates his
or her employment, and, contrary to the case with group life insurance, the
terminating employee normally does not have the right to convert the
group disability coverage to an individual disability income policy.

---

[2] Sometimes only the disabled employee's basic social security benefit is taken as a deduction.

Therefore, when an employee leaves one job to take another, he or she normally will lose any group long-term disability coverage from the time of leaving the former employer until meeting the eligibility-period requirement of the group plan of the new employer. In the group long-term plan described above, for example, this eligibility period is one year.

The terminating employee might deal with the above problem in either of two ways: (1) Some insurers or plans will waive the eligibility period requirement for a new employee if the employer consents and the new employee provides at least some evidence of insurability, or the new employee was covered under a comparable plan with a previous employer; or (2) the employee could buy his or her own disability insurance for the period of time he or she is not covered by a group policy. It is also possible that a terminating employee may find that his or her new employer does not provide as good a group disability plan as the former employer or, in fact, may not provide any such plan at all. Under these conditions, the terminating employee probably would need to carry (or increase) his or her own disability income coverage.

Taxation of Benefits.   The income tax status of disability income benefits obviously is of importance in disability income planning. The tax status of social security benefits was noted previously.

The tax code provides that amounts received through accident or health insurance for personal injuries or sickness are not considered gross income for federal income tax purposes, *except* for amounts received as an employee to the extent that such amounts are attributable to employer contributions that were not includible in the employee's gross income. Thus, disability income benefits from personally purchased disability income insurance are not gross income; nor are disability benefits received as an employee from an employment-related plan to the extent that the employee contributed to the cost of the benefits. However, to the extent that disability income benefits for an employee are attributable to employer contributions that are not includible in the employee's gross income (as normally would be the situation for employer-provided disability income benefits), they constitute gross income to the disabled employee. Thus, in the hypothetical case of Harry Smart, the group long-term disability benefits (presently $513 per month) would be gross income to Harry, since his employer paid the full cost of the disability plan (i.e., the plan is noncontributory).

Individual Health Insurance (Disability Income)

Despite the importance and growth of group disability income insurance, individual policies remain an important way for people to protect themselves against the critical disability risk.

Need for Coverage.   There are several reasons why people might need individual coverage in their financial planning despite the growth of group insurance.

1. Many people are not members of groups that provide such group insurance.

2. Others may be members of insured groups but for one reason or another are not eligible, or not yet eligible, to participate in the group plan.

3. Group disability income benefits may be inadequate, either in amount or in duration (as in the case of group short-term disability income benefits, for example).

4. Some people may feel it necessary to provide short-term individual disability income protection for themselves during the elimination (waiting) period of a group plan when this period is relatively long, such as six months or even a year.

5. Others may not want to rely entirely on their employer's group insurance or other employee benefits for their financial security in this important area. They may want to purchase additional individual coverage to the extent that it is available under insurer underwriting rules and limits.

6. Individual policies may be used in situations where business health insurance is needed, such as buy-sell agreements or "key employee" situations.

Benefits Provided.   Like group coverage, individual policies provide weekly or monthly benefits for a specified period (maximum benefit period) during the continuance of the insured's total (and sometimes partial) disability. Individual disability income insurance should be analyzed mainly in terms of the *perils covered, maximum benefit period, definition of disability, elimination period,* and *amount of coverage.* Any individual health insurance policy should also be analyzed in terms of its *renewal or continuance provision.* Renewal provisions for all forms of health insurance are discussed later in this chapter. Naturally, *cost* also is an important consideration and is related directly to the above factors. Moreover, the premium cost for basically the same coverage can vary among insurers, and, therefore, consumers or their advisors should "shop around" for coverage with several insurers before buying.

Individual disability income policies provide benefits for disability either (1) resulting from accidental bodily injury (accident-only coverage) or (2) resulting from accidental bodily injury or from sickness (accident and sickness coverage). As we said before, *it is important to protect against both accident and sickness, as opposed to accident only, if at all possible.* Of course, accident-only coverage costs considerably less because the insured gets much less protection.

Today, there usually is a wide choice of maximum benefit periods in buying individual disability income policies, ranging from a period as short as six months to a period as long as the insured's reaching age 65 or 70 or for the insured's lifetime.

The maximum benefit period selected should depend on the person's needs. However, assuming that permanent protection is needed, *consider buying or recommending coverage with longer maximum benefit periods, such as to age 65 or 70, or for life, for both accident and sickness.* To buy shorter benefit periods (usually to reduce the cost) of, say, two or five years may result in the disability benefits running out before the person reaches retirement age (when, presumably, his or her retirement benefits will start). This is false economy; there are better ways to save premium dollars.

When insurers use a "split" definition of disability in individual contracts, in general the longer the "own occupation" period, the better for the consumer. Of course, an "own occupation" definition for the entire maximum benefit period is better yet for the consumer.

There normally is a fairly wide choice of elimination periods in buying individual disability income insurance. They may range, for example, from none for accident and seven days for sickness up to one year or more for accident and sickness. There are several factors that may be considered in choosing an appropriate elimination period.

1. *Coordination with other disability coverage.* Other disability benefits may be available during the initial period of a disability. For example, the employer may have a noninsured salary-continuation ("sick-pay") plan or perhaps a group short-term disability income plan. Thus, the elimination period of an individual policy could be structured so the benefits will start after such other benefits are exhausted.

2. *Other resources.* For example, an emergency fund could be maintained to take care of short periods of disability, among other purposes.

3. *Cost saving.* A relatively small increase in the elimination period will normally produce considerable saving in premium.

Amount of Coverage. Within limits, applicants can choose the *amount of coverage* in individual health insurance for which they want to apply. This, of course, depends on the amount of weekly or monthly benefits they need, want, and can afford to buy. It also may depend, however, on the amount of insurance that insurers are willing to write on a given individual.

In underwriting individual disability income insurance, insurers have issue and participation limits that may affect the amount of insurance that can be purchased. An *issue limit* is the maximum amount of monthly benefit an insurer will write on any one individual. A *participation limit* is the maximum amount of monthly benefits from all sources in which an insurer will "participate" (i.e., write a portion of the coverage). Issue and participation limits vary among insurers, but they have increased considerably in recent years. Depending on insurer underwriting policy, companies that are active in the individual disability income market may be willing to write or participate in coverage of $10,000, $20,000, $25,000, or more per month for persons who otherwise meet the insurer's earned income and other financial underwriting rules.

In addition, to try to avoid overinsurance, insurers limit the amount of disability income insurance they will issue to a person so that the monthly benefits from all sources will not exceed a specified percentage of the person's earned income. The percentages used for this underwriting rule vary among insurers, but they might be from 60 to 75 percent of earned income for persons with lower incomes and then be graded downward to from 50 to 60 percent for earned income in excess of certain levels. For example, using the facts of the illustrative case of Harry Smart given earlier (with social security and the group long-term disability plan described), one insurer would write an additional $600 per month of individual noncancellable disability income insurance on Harry.

These underwriting rules may limit the amount of coverage available to the consumer. However, since they vary among insurers, consumers or their advisors may be able to get the amount of coverage desired by "shopping around" a little.

Supplementary Benefits.   A wide variety of *supplementary benefits* may be included in, or added to, a basic individual disability income policy. Some of the more important include the following:

1. *Waiver of premium.*   This provision is included automatically in most individual disability income policies and is comparable with the similar benefit in life insurance.

2. *Residual disability (partial disability) benefit.*   This benefit may be an integral part of the disability contract but is often written as an optional rider for an extra premium. The residual disability benefit normally pays a proportionate part of the total disability benefit when the insured suffers at least a specified percentage reduction in his or her earned income (such as at least a 20 percent reduction). Loss of income often is the coverage "trigger" for this benefit. Many policies will pay this benefit only after a period of total disability.

3. *Guaranteed insurability provisions.*   These are similar to the corresponding provisions in life insurance policies. They commonly provide that on stated policy anniversary dates the insured may purchase specified additional amounts of disability income benefits as of his or her attained age and at the insurer's rates then in effect, with no evidence of insurability being required.

4. *Cost-of-living adjustment coverage.* This benefit provides specified cost-of-living increases in disability benefits after a total disability has lasted a certain period, such as one year. The increases often are tied to a cost-of-living index, such as the Consumer Price Index, subject to minimum and maximum annual percentage increases. Cost-of-living adjustment coverage that applies to disability income benefit limits prior to a disability also may be purchased.

5. *Social security supplement coverage.* This provides additional benefits when the insured is disabled and receives no social security benefits. This may be helpful because the social security definition of disability generally is considerably stricter than the definition in many individual policies, and so benefits may be payable under an individual policy but not by social security.

6. *Accidental death or accidental death and dismemberment (AD&D) coverage.* This is similar to "double indemnity" in life insurance. And, as with life insurance, the logic of buying this kind of coverage is highly questionable.

7. *Accident medical reimbursement, hospital income, or other medical expense benefits.* These medical expense–type benefits usually can be added to disability income policies.

8. *Benefits that increase the amount of the basic disability income coverage.* One such benefit is a family income-type benefit that provides for a decreasing amount of disability income insurance. Another is a variable disability income benefit that allows the amount of monthly income to vary during an initial period of disability (such as during the first six months or year of disability) so as to coordinate with other disability benefits.

Coordination of Benefits. In general, individual disability income policies pay their benefits regardless of whether other disability benefits also are payable. However, health insurers *may* place certain policy provisions relating to other insurance in their disability income contracts. There are basically two such provisions: the "insurance with other insurers" provision, and the "relation of earnings to insurance" provision.

The "insurance with other insurers" provision may be used by insurers in policies where the insurer retains at least some right to refuse policy renewal. It is not widely used today.

The "relation of earnings to insurance" provision (sometimes called the "average earnings" clause) can be used only in guaranteed renewable or noncancelable policies (see later in this chapter for a discussion of these terms). It provides that if the total amount of "valid loss of time coverage" exceeds the insured's monthly earnings at the time of disability or his or her average monthly earnings over the two years immediately preceding the disability, whichever is greater, the policy benefit will be reduced proportionately. This provision is less used by insurers than formerly.

Most individual disability income policies are written on a "24-hour basis." This means that they pay their benefits for both occupational and nonoccupational disabilities. In some cases, however, individual policies will exclude disability arising out of the insured's employment. Such "nonoccupational" coverage is, of course, less favorable to the consumer than "24-hour" coverage.

Termination of Coverage.   Policies that are noncancelable or guaranteed renewable typically provide that coverage will continue, if the insured continues to pay the premiums, until a specified age, such as age 65. Some policies, however, allow the insured to continue the coverage beyond age 65 on a guaranteed renewable basis, on a conditionally renewable basis, or at the option of the insurer, usually provided that the insured continues to be gainfully employed. This kind of extension of coverage allows insureds to continue their protection (in fact, gives them the right to do so if the extension is on a guaranteed renewable basis) if they continue working beyond normal retirement age. Many people do continue working past 65. Thus, it is advantageous for the consumer to have such a provision in the policy. Policies may have a terminal age, such as 70 or older, beyond which the coverage cannot be continued in any event.

Taxation of Benefits.   The benefits paid during disability from personally purchased individual (or group) disability income insurance are not gross income for federal income tax purposes. In effect, the premiums (or contributions) were all paid by the insured with after-tax dollars, and so any benefits are received income tax-free.

Thus, for example, if Harry Smart in our previous example purchases an individual disability income policy providing an additional $600 per month of coverage (as permitted by the financial underwriting rules of the insurer just mentioned), and then unfortunately suffers our previous hypothetical auto accident and is totally disabled, the disability income benefits payable and their respective tax statuses would be as follows:

- *Social security disability income benefit:* $1237 per month (up to one-half is potentially taxable, but none is taxable in this case because the Smarts' income during disability is less than the $32,000 limit noted previously)
- *Group long-term disability income benefit:* $513 per month (fully taxable because the employer paid the full cost of the plan)
- *Individual disability income benefit:* $600 per month (not taxable because it was paid for by the insured)

Franchise and Association Group Disability Insurance

The benefits provided under franchise or association group disability insurance are much the same as under individual policies, except that the insured person has less flexibility in choice of plan, benefits, and optional coverages. There usually are limitations on the amount of disability income insurance that can be applied for under these plans, similar to, but often lower than, those used in underwriting individual policies. Under these plans, the insurer usually waives its right to discontinue or modify any individual policy unless all policies in the group also are discontinued or modified. The consumer should look for such a protective provision.

Premiums for association group coverage usually apply to an insured as of his or her attained age at each annual renewal, frequently on the basis of 5- or 10-year age brackets. These are referred to as "step-rate premiums," and they increase as the insured grows older. This is different from "level-premium policies," where premiums vary with the insured's age at the time the policy is issued but then remain the same (level) for the duration of the coverage. Individual policies often are sold on a level-premium basis.

If disability coverage is needed, consumers or their advisors should check out any association group plan available. The rates may be lower than for individual policies, and there often is less extensive underwriting. But be careful about how the rates are quoted, and remember that step-rate premiums can increase markedly as the insured grows older. Also note the circumstances under which association group coverage can be terminated (as compared with an individual policy, for example). Association group coverage may be terminated:

1. If the whole plan is discontinued for the group (either by the association or by the insurer)
2. If the covered person ceases to be a member of the association or franchise unit
3. If the insured person fails to pay his or her premium within the grace period
4. At the attainment of some age, such as 65

Other Insurance Benefits

Various other kinds of coverages may provide disability income benefits. Here are some of the more important.

Disability Benefits under Individual Life Insurance Policies. As we saw in Chap. 4, individual life insurance policies can contain disability coverage in the form of (1) waiver-of-premium benefits and (2) perhaps disability income riders.

The *waiver-of-premium benefit* is modest in cost when a separate premium is charged for it, and consumers generally should include it in their life insurance programs. It also can provide substantial benefits. If a person is paying, say, $1200 per year in premiums for individual life insurance, the waiver of these premiums is the equivalent of $100 per month of tax-free disability income benefits.

Disability income riders are not common today. They are really a kind of individual disability income benefit tied to a life insurance policy.

Group Life Insurance Disability Benefits.   Three basic types of disability provisions are used in group term life insurance plans. The *maturity value type* provides for the payment of the face amount of a disabled employee's group term life insurance, usually in monthly installments over a fixed period of time such as 10, 20, 60, or 120 months.

The *waiver-of-premium type* provides for the continuation of a disabled employee's group term life insurance coverage after termination of employment.

The *extended death benefit (or one-year extension) type* is the least common and least liberal. It extends a disabled employee's group term coverage for only one year after termination of employment.

Disability Benefits under Pension Plans.   While pension plans are intended primarily to provide retirement benefits, they may contain some disability benefits, such as the following:

1. A number of plans allow an employee who has become totally and permanently disabled to take early retirement under certain conditions.

2. Some pension plans provide a separate disability benefit for a totally and permanently disabled employee who has met specified requirements.

3. Many plans allow full vesting (see Chap. 12 for an explanation of vesting in general) of an employee's pension benefits in the event of total and permanent disability.

4. Some private pension plans provide a disability benefit akin to waiver of premium or the "disability freeze" in the social security system. This benefit allows a disabled employee's pension credits to continue to accumulate during his or her disability.

Medical Expense
Insurance Coverage

Another broad category of health losses against which people seek to protect themselves and their dependents is medical expenses. People usually are well aware of the need for protection in this area.

Services versus Indemnity Benefits

Medical expense coverage can be provided in two different ways: on a *service basis* or on an *indemnity basis*, depending to some degree on the type of insuring organization involved. Which of these ways is used can be important to the consumer.

The main types of insuring organizations writing private medical expense benefits are the insurance companies, the Blue Cross–Blue Shield associations, and health maintenance organizations—HMOs. A fundamental distinction between Blue Cross–Blue Shield plans and insurance company plans is the basis on which benefits are provided. Blue Cross plans normally provide service benefits to the subscriber (insured), such as, for example, 365 days of semiprivate care in a member hospital with other specified hospital services included. With some exceptions, the subscriber is entitled to receive the specified service benefits in a member hospital without additional cost, regardless of what the hospital might have charged the patient if he or she had not been covered by Blue Cross. On the other hand, insured plans may agree to indemnify (reimburse) an insured person for covered hospital (or medical) expenses up to specified maximum dollar amounts. However, it is common today for insured plans to pay for covered hospital care up to the reasonable and customary (R&C) charges for semiprivate care for a specified period of time. HMOs also provide service benefits, but their benefits typically are comprehensive in scope and tend to emphasize prevention of illness. The trade-off with HMOs is that the services usually must be provided by physicians who participate in the particular HMO, and hence choice of physician normally is restricted.

Kinds of Medical Expense Benefits

On either a service or an indemnity basis, a wide variety of medical expense benefits are available to the public. Medical expense coverages, however, can be divided into two broad categories: the so-called basic coverages, and coverages under major medical–type policies or comprehensive services from HMOs.

By "*basic*" *coverages* we generally mean the traditional hospital, surgical, and regular medical expense coverages that provide benefits for specified kinds of care, usually starting with the first dollar of expense incurred, with relatively low maximum benefits.

The limitations of these "basic" coverages for the consumer led to the development of major medical expense insurance around 1950. Since then, major medical–type policies have shown rapid growth. Briefly, *major medical–type policies* provide broad coverage for most types of medical expenses, make use of deductibles, require the covered person to bear at least a portion of his or her covered expenses through a so-called coinsurance provision, and pay covered expenses up to a relatively high (or unlimited) maximum limit of liability. On the other hand, HMO coverage also is broad in scope (often referred to as comprehensive), but it normally does not make extensive use of deductibles, coinsurance, and other cost-sharing provisions.

Types of "Basic" Benefits.   Although there are a great many different kinds of basic medical expense benefits, written on either a group or individual basis, the following are the most common.

Hospital Expense Benefits.   These benefits are designed to cover the expenses of hospital confinement. The specific benefits provided by hospital expense coverage include:

1. The hospital daily room-and-board benefit, which covers the per-diem charges made by hospitals for room, board, and general nursing services.

2. The hospital services ("extras") benefit, which covers hospital services other than those included in the daily room-and-board charge, including use of operating or delivery rooms, diagnostic services (such as laboratory and X-ray), anesthetics, drugs, use of medical equipment and supplies during confinement, and the like.

3. Other benefits may also be added, such as an emergency outpatient accident benefit, outpatient diagnostic benefits, and supplementary nursing benefits.

While deductibles traditionally were not used for hospital expense insurance, it has been increasingly common to use deductibles for basic hospital expense insurance. Using such deductibles can reduce substantially the cost of hospital insurance for the consumer.

Hospital Income Benefits.   This kind of hospital insurance differs from the coverages described above in that, instead of reimbursing the insured for hospital expenses that the insured or his or her family have actually incurred, hospital income policies (or riders to other contracts) agree to pay stated amounts of daily, weekly, or monthly benefits while a covered person is confined in a hospital. These stated amounts are paid regardless of any other health insurance.

Surgical Benefits.   This type of benefit customarily provides reimbursement for the charges of operating surgeons (and sometimes anesthesiologists) and may be subject to a series of limits for various common surgical procedures set forth in a surgical schedule included in the policy. Surgical schedules are commonly described on the basis of the "schedule limit," which is the highest fee provided for in the schedule. Thus, a "1000 surgical schedule" means simply that the highest amount paid for any procedure(s) in the schedule is $1000. Other amounts paid will be scaled down from this figure, depending on the nature of the procedure. Many surgical plans, however, now provide their benefits up to the reasonable and customary charges for the covered services without any scheduled limits in the policy.

Regular Medical (Doctors' Expense) Benefits. These benefits cover physicians' charges for other than surgical procedures. Regular medical benefits generally pay so many dollars (or R&C charges) per day for doctors' visits for a specified number of days.

Other "Basic" Benefits. A great many other kinds of specified medical expense benefits are available. Space does not permit their description here.

Limitations of Basic Coverages. "Basic" medical expense coverages have been important ways of insuring against certain types of medical expenses, but they have become less important than formerly. When planning for complete health insurance needs, the following limitations of basic coverages should be noted.

1. Many types of important medical expenses may not be covered.

2. In relation to how large medical expenses can get today, the maximum benefits may be quite low.

3. In a period of rapidly rising medical costs, "basic" plans can easily become out of date.

4. There are many different "basic" coverages that the consumer must piece together to develop a complete insurance program.

Major Medical–Type Benefits. Major medical and comprehensive medical expense coverages (as well as comprehensive HMO coverage) represent the backbone of protection for the insuring public against catastrophic medical expenses.

Types of Plans. There are two broad types of major medical plans: major medical expense insurance and comprehensive medical expense insurance. *Major medical expense insurance* covers most types of medical expenses up to a high overall maximum limit of liability and uses a deductible and a so-called coinsurance provision. These policies contain relatively few exclusions and internal limits. They are often used to supplement basic hospital-medical-surgical coverages.

Comprehensive medical expense insurance is similar in concept to regular major medical coverage except that comprehensive plans usually provide, after a small deductible, a certain amount of basic hospital-medical-surgical coverage without applying any coinsurance provision, and then cover these expenses above this amount, as well as all other covered expenses, up to the policy's overall maximum limit of liability, with a coinsurance percentage applying to these expenses. In essence, the comprehensive approach combines some basic hospital-medical-surgical coverage with major medical coverage in the same policy.

Covered Expenses. Major medical plans cover most types of medical care expenses whether the covered person is confined in a hospital or not.

Covered expenses are specifically listed in the policy and most are covered subject only to the overall maximum limit of the policy. Some expenses, however, may have special limits applying only to them. These are called "inside limits." Inside limits may apply to daily room-and-board charges for private hospital accommodations, private-duty nursing, mental and nervous diseases (especially when the patient is not hospital-confined), nursing home or extended-care facility coverage, and sometimes surgical charges. Generally speaking, *the fewer and higher such inside limits are, the more valuable is the major medical coverage for the consumer.*

Major medical policies almost always specify that only "reasonable and necessary" or "reasonable and customary" charges will be paid. Thus, on this basis, insurers may reduce covered charges that they feel do not fall within the prevailing pattern of charges in a community. But this is an administrative matter, and a covered person can contest what he or she may feel is an unjustified reduction in a claim made by the insurer on this basis.[3]

Maximum Limit.   Major medical policies usually contain an overall maximum limit of liability that may range from as low as $10,000 to $1,000,000 or more, and some plans now have no maximum limit at all.

Major medical maximum limits can be applied in several ways, including on a *per-cause* basis, on a *calendar year* or *benefit-year* basis, on an *aggregate lifetime* basis, or using some *combination* of these, such as on a calendar-year basis but subject to an aggregate lifetime limit. Maximum limits can usually be reinstated after a specified amount of benefits, such as $1000, have been paid and the covered person submits evidence of insurability or returns to work for a specified period of time. Some policies, however, provide for an automatic restoration of the maximum, such as a 10 percent restoration each year, for example. It is wise for a covered person to maintain his or her major medical coverage by reinstating the maximum limit if this is necessary.

Deductibles.   There are several types of major medical deductibles, such as an *initial deductible,* a *corridor deductible,* and an *integrated deductible.* As in the case of the maximum limit, deductibles can be applied on a per-cause or on a calendar- or benefit-year basis. Sometimes, particularly in group plans, deductibles are not applied to certain kinds of covered expenses, such as hospital charges. Use of a reasonably large deductible can result in considerable premium savings for the consumer.

Coinsurance.   After the deductible is satisfied, most major medical policies require the covered person to bear a certain portion, commonly 20 or 25 percent, of covered expenses, with the insurer paying the remainder. This usually is referred to as a "coinsurance" provision. A few major medical plans do not use coinsurance provisions at all. Further, many major medical plans today have so-called *stop-loss provisions,* which limit the

---

[3] Insurers may have review procedures for such contested claims.

unreimbursed, covered expenses for a person or sickness to a maximum amount, such as $1500 per year. After this unreimbursed stop-loss limit is reached in a year (normally due to the operation of the deductible and coinsurance provisions), the plan pays 100 percent of covered expenses up to a maximum limit. Clearly, the consumer benefits from provisions that limit the rigor of a "pure" coinsurance provision, particularly for larger claims. (As noted previously, HMO plans typically do not apply significant cost-sharing provisions, i.e., deductibles and coinsurance, to their service benefits. They seek to control costs through their control over, or arrangements with, their participating physicians and other providers of health care.)

A simple illustration will demonstrate the effect of the various provisions just discussed on a claim. Suppose that a person and his or her family are covered by a major medical policy with a $200 deductible (on a per-cause basis), a $100,000 maximum limit, an 80/20 coinsurance provision, and a $1500-per-person ($3000-per-family) stop-loss provision per year. Further suppose that the person's spouse (who is covered) suffers a serious illness, is confined to a hospital, and incurs other covered expenses. Total covered expenses (charges) for the year on a reasonable and customary basis are $25,000. In this situation, the above policy would pay as follows:

Total covered charges	$25,000	
Deductible	− 200	
	$24,800	(effect of deductible)
Coinsurance	0.80	(80 percent of covered charges payable)
	$19,840	(effect of coinsurance)

Therefore, tentative cost sharing by the insured would be $5160 ($200 deductible and $4960 coinsurance). However, the stop-loss provision limits annual cost sharing per person to $1500, and so the recovery is $25,000 − $1500, or $23,500.

Thus, the value to the consumer of a major medical stop-loss provision is made clear by this example.

Excess Major Medical.   Some insurance companies write excess major medical coverage on an association group basis or as an individual policy. Excess major medical applies after other medical expense coverage has paid its benefits and thus is intended to cover catastrophe-type situations. While such excess coverage has its limitations, it can add to the consumer's protection against very large medical expenses.

Medicare

Persons age 65 and over who are not currently employed may rely primarily on Medicare for their medical expense protection, although many also have retiree health coverage from their former employer and/or use individual plans to supplement Medicare. Private health insurance plans are generally coordinated with Medicare so that their benefits will not overlap.[4] Medicare comprises two major programs. Hospital Insurance (HI) and Supplementary Medical Insurance (SMI).

Hospital Insurance.   Nearly everyone age 65 or over is eligible for HI, which provides several types of benefits. Among the major ones are the following (as of 1991):

1. HI covers up to 90 days of inpatient care in any participating hospital for each benefit period. For the first 60 days, HI pays for all covered services except for a $628 deductible. For the 61st through the 90th day, it pays for all covered services except for a deductible of $157 per day.

2. There is an additional "lifetime reserve" of 60 hospital days. For each of these days used, HI pays for all covered services except for a $314-per-day deductible.

3. After hospital confinement, HI covers up to 100 days of care in a participating extended care facility (nursing home). It pays for all covered services for the first 20 days, and all but a $78.50-per-day deductible for up to 80 additional days.[5]

4. Further, HI covers unlimited home health "visits" by a participating home health agency (e.g., a participating visiting nurse service) on a part-time, intermittent basis.

5. HI also covers certain hospice care services.

Supplementary Medical Insurance.   The SMI portion of Medicare is voluntary, although persons eligible for HI are covered automatically unless they decline the SMI coverage. SMI is financed by individuals age 65 and over who participate and by contributions from the federal government. It generally will pay 80 percent of the reasonable charges for covered medical services after a $100 deductible in each calendar year. The following are some of the major services covered by SMI:

---

[4] Under federal law, for *active workers* and their spouses over age 65, their employer's health plan is primary over Medicare unless the worker elects otherwise. For *retired* workers and their spouses, Medicare can be made primary, and usually is made so, by any employer's health plan for retirees.

[5] All these deductibles or cost-sharing provisions are adjusted periodically to reflect changes in hospital costs.

1. Physicians' and surgeons' services, no matter where such services are rendered

2. Home health services on an unlimited basis

3. Other medical and health services, such as diagnostic tests, surgical dressings, and rental or purchase of medical equipment

4. Outpatient physical therapy services

5. All outpatient services of participating hospitals, including diagnostic tests or treatment

Medicare Supplements

Since there are "gaps" or limits to the coverage of Medicare for eligible persons, many people seek to supplement their Medicare coverage with individual or association group policies.[6] At one time, insurers offered the public a very broad array of policies intended to supplement Medicare. Critics suggested that some of these policies offered relatively low benefits for the premiums charged and that the sale of some of these policies was duplicative and hence unnecessary. As a result, federal legislation (the Omnibus Budget Reconciliation Act of 1990) and implementing state legislation and regulations [the National Association of Insurance Commissioners (NAIC) Medicare Supplement Model Act and Regulation] have made substantial changes in the regulation of policies sold by insurance companies to supplement Medicare—called Medicare supplement policies or "Medigap" policies.

Standard Medicare Supplement ("Medigap") Policies.   A task force of the National Association of Insurance Commissioners (NAIC) has approved 10 standard "Medigap" policies that can be sold by insurance companies to the public. In effect, if insurers are in the Medicare supplement market, these are the only plans (with a few exceptions) they can offer once the states adopt the appropriate enabling legislation.

All these standard plans must contain a basic "core" of benefits, which include: the 20 percent SMI coinsurance, the HI daily copayment for the 61st through the 90th days of hospitalization, coverage for 365 additional days of hospitalization beyond the 90 days provided by HI, and coverage of

---

[6] An employer may provide continuing medical expense coverage for its retired, former employees and often their spouses (retiree health coverage). When the retired, former employees and their spouses (if covered) are age 65 or over and hence are covered by Medicare, this retiree health coverage is secondary to Medicare and thus supplements Medicare. Whether a retired, former employee and his or her spouse in this situation with reasonable retiree health coverage needs to supplement Medicare further with individual coverage may be questionable, depending on the circumstances.

the patient's charges for the first three pints of blood each year. One standard plan provides only these "core" benefits.

The other nine standard plans provide these "core" benefits and one or more of the following optional benefits: the HI deductible for the first 60 days of hospitalization, posthospital skilled nursing home daily copayment for the 21st through the 100th days, the SMI deductible, covered doctors' charges in excess of those reimbursed by Medicare, charges for treatment of medical emergencies during foreign travel, at-home recovery nursing care for eight weeks beyond Medicare coverage, prescription drug coverage, and certain preventive health tests and shots. The most extensive standard plan includes all these optional benefits. The others include combinations of some but not all of the optional benefits. Naturally, the cost of the standard plans reflect the benefits they provide.

Thus, for the consumer with Medicare coverage, the planning issues in this area become:

- Whether the person wants to supplement Medicare in light of his or her other resources and other possible needs

- If so, whether the person needs to purchase a standard "Medigap" policy in light of any other benefits that may be available (such as retiree health coverage)

- If a standard Medicare supplement policy is desired, which of the standard policies (i.e., which of the optional benefits, if any) should be selected, considering the cost and other possible needs [such as the need for long-term care (LTC) insurance, which is described later in this chapter].

Other Regulatory Requirements for Medicare Supplement Policies. In addition to the standard policy requirement just described, federal law and implementing state action now also mandate additional consumer safeguards regarding "Medigap" policies. First, persons enrolling in Medicare Part B (SMI) after November 1, 1991, are given a *six-month open enrollment period* starting from their enrollment in Part B, during which insurers writing Medicare supplement policies may not deny the person a "Medigap" policy, nor discriminate against them in pricing such coverage, due to the person's health status, claims experience, or medical condition. This open-window enrollment period can provide valuable protection for Medicare enrollees who are in poor health and desire "Medigap" coverage.

Another protection is that insurance companies and their agents are *not permitted to provide duplicate "Medigap" coverage* by selling a "Medigap" policy to someone who already has one. However, insured persons can still replace one "Medigap" policy with another if they wish. Further, there is a six-month limit after issue of a "Medigap" policy on any exclusion of preexisting conditions.

Finally, federal law sets a *minimum loss ratio* (the percentage of policy premiums that are paid out to claimants in benefits) for individual "Medigap" policies of 65 percent and for group "Medigap" policies of 75 percent. The law also requires premium rebates and credits when policies fail to meet these minimum loss ratio standards. These standards are intended to make sure that these policies provide adequate "value" to consumers.

Workers' Compensation

In addition to the disability income benefits discussed previously, all workers' compensation laws provide medical benefits to employees injured on the job. The laws generally provide unlimited medical benefits. Health insurance policies providing medical expense benefits normally specifically exclude expenses of any injury or sickness for which a covered person is entitled to workers' compensation benefits.

Group Health Insurance

The lion's share of medical expense benefits in the United States now is provided under group medical expense coverage. Therefore, the beginning point in medical expense coverage planning is to determine and analyze what group insurance protection applies.

Who Is Covered?   Group medical expense plans cover the insured employee and the employee's "dependents." The definition of these "dependents" is important because it indicates, in effect, the scope of the group protection and perhaps will point out some dependents for whom other arrangements for medical expense coverage need to be made.

Definitions of "dependents" vary among group plans, but they often include any unmarried, dependent child of the employee who has not attained a certain age (such as 19, or 23 or 25 if a full-time student); handicapped or disabled children; and the employee's spouse. In some contracts, this definition is extended to include certain other family members, such as dependent parents.

Benefits Provided.   Group plans can provide any of the types of benefits previously described. The group technique generally makes possible the provision of broader benefits at lower cost than would be provided under individual policies.

Coordination of Benefits.   Most group medical expense contracts include a "coordination of benefits" (COB) provision, which has the effect of setting a priority of payment among plans and limiting the total amount recoverable from group contracts (and certain other coverages) in effect for a person to 100 percent (or some other percentage, such as 80 percent) of the expenses covered under any of the contracts. This serves to avoid duplication of benefits when a person is covered under more than one group contract, such as might occur, for example, when a husband and wife are both employed and each is covered as an insured employee under his or her own employer's group policy and the spouse also is covered as a dependent. Their children also might be covered as dependents under both group contracts.

In most cases, however, group medical expense policies do not coordinate their benefits with individual medical expense policies. Therefore, a group policy's benefits normally will not be reduced because a covered person also may have individual coverage.

Termination of Coverage.   Since group coverage often is the backbone of a family's medical expense protection, it is important to consider the alternatives in case this coverage is terminated. An employee's group medical expense coverage may terminate when the employee terminates his or her employment with the group policyholder. Dependents' coverage also may terminate when the insured employee's coverage terminates or when their dependency status changes, as, for example, when a child reaches age 19 or 23 or when a wife and husband get a divorce.

COBRA Continuation Rights.   The rights of employees and their covered dependents have been significantly broadened in this area by the Consolidated Omnibus Budget Reconciliation Act of 1985 (popularly called COBRA). This law requires most employers to provide continued coverage under group health plans to covered employees and other "qualified beneficiaries" (spouse and dependent children) in case of certain "qualifying events," such as termination of employment or reduction of hours, death of the employee, divorce or legal separation, and a child's reaching the maximum age for coverage, without the qualified beneficiary's needing to show any evidence of insurability. The continued coverage is the same as under the group health plan and must be available for 18 or 36 months, depending on the nature of the "qualifying event." The eligible person must elect this continuation of coverage, and a premium may be charged for it up to 102 percent of the cost of the coverage to the plan. Such continuation is not available when there is coverage under another group plan whether as an employee or otherwise, except that continuation is not stopped when the other group health plan contains a preexisting-condition exclusion or limitation affecting the beneficiary. When a qualified beneficiary's continuation coverage expires (generally at the end of the 18 or 36 months, whichever is applicable), the qualified beneficiary must be given the option of enrolling in any conversion health plan that otherwise would have been available under the group health plan during the 180-day period ending with the expiration of the COBRA coverage. COBRA continuation coverage also ends when a qualified beneficiary becomes covered by Medicare.

Thus, there are several possibilities for a person whose group medical expense coverage may be terminated.

1. The person may be eligible immediately for other group insurance.

2. The person may be eligible for Medicare upon reaching age 65.

3. The person may elect continuation of the group coverage under COBRA as just described.

4. The person may elect to convert his or her terminating group insurance to an individual policy without showing individual evidence of insurability. This right of conversion, where it exists, can be important to an individual who is uninsurable or who is insurable only at higher rates or for restricted coverage under individual insurance. In addition to the conversion privilege provided the insured employee, his or her dependents may have a right to convert their terminating insurance. For example, such a privilege may be extended to a surviving spouse in the event of the insured employee's death and may be granted to a dependent child whose group coverage terminates. As just noted, if a plan otherwise has a conversion right, it must also be made available at the end of a COBRA continuation period (through election during the preceding 180 days).

5. The person may purchase new individual insurance to replace the terminated group coverage or to supplement any new group coverage for which the person may be eligible that is not as liberal as his or her former coverage.

Retiree Health Coverage. Employers may continue medical expense coverage under their employee benefit plan for their retirees and often the retirees' dependents—referred to as *retiree health benefits* or *postretirement medical expense benefits.* When these benefits are provided, there normally are some age and/or service requirements to qualify. Thus, one of the factors employees should consider in deciding on their retirement age (or whether to accept an early retirement offer) is how it will affect their eligibility for retiree benefits under their employer's plan.

Depending on the plan, retiree health coverage can be quite valuable for retired, former employees and usually also their spouses. Some plans simply continue the employer's regular medical benefits that cover active employees for the retirees, while in other cases retiree benefits are reduced. Some plans require contributions to the cost from retirees, while others do not. Once retired, former employees and their spouses become eligible for Medicare. Retiree health coverage is coordinated with

Medicare so there is not duplicate coverage, with Medicare being the primary coverage. In effect, these plans can supplement Medicare.

One point for retirees and employees to consider is whether an employer that now has retiree health coverage as part of its benefit plan may at some time in the future attempt to modify or terminate those benefits. Employers often attempt to reserve the right to modify (most likely reduce) or terminate retiree health coverage. Whether they can do so legally, particularly for those already retired, depends on the terms of the plan and the circumstances. It is always possible that some employers may find themselves in a situation where they might want to modify or terminate this retiree coverage due to rising costs or economic difficulties for the employer. On the other hand, many employers, particularly larger employers, have maintained, and even improved upon, rather generous retiree health coverage for many years and apparently will continue to do so for the foreseeable future. Thus, in planning in this area, the consumer simply must evaluate the situation in light of his or her other resources and other possible insurance needs (such as for LTC insurance, for example). Normally, employer-provided retiree health coverage is a rather good deal for retired employees and usually their spouses.

Individual Health Insurance

A great many different individual and family medical expense policies are available to the public from many different insurance companies. These policies often offer consumers broad coverage for their medical expense insurance needs, but some offer only limited coverage. Therefore, such policies should be evaluated carefully.

Blue Cross–Blue Shield associations and some HMO plans also offer individual medical expense contracts. Subscription charges for nongroup subscribers normally are higher than for the plans' group subscribers. Blue Cross–Blue Shield tends to solicit its nongroup subscribers at the time they leave a group covered by Blue Cross, in periodic open-enrollment campaigns, and to some extent through advertising and continuous enrollment.

Who Is Covered?   Individual medical expense insurance can be written to cover the insured person, the insured's spouse, and the dependent unmarried children of the insured. The persons covered normally are listed in the policy, and each must be acceptable to the insurance company according to its underwriting standards. A separate premium often is charged for each covered person in insured plans.

Blue Cross–Blue Shield plans often have one rate for individuals, another rate for husband and wife (or a covered person with one dependent), and a third rate for families, or some similar rating system.

Benefits Provided. The same basic kinds of medical expense benefits can be provided under individual policies as under group coverages. Individual policies may offer somewhat less liberal benefits than could be purchased under comparable group coverages, but this is largely a matter of degree. People generally can select the coverages they want and feel they need when buying individual coverage.

Coordination of Benefits. Since people are free to buy individual medical expense policies from a number of different insurers, may have group coverage as well, and may also be covered by other medical expense benefits (such as automobile or homeowner's medical payments coverage), they may find themselves with several sources of recovery for medical expenses. This is not necessarily bad, and in fact people often buy individual policies to supplement other coverage. But it is an area that can be analyzed to see if premium dollars can be saved by dropping any unnecessary coverage.

Individual hospital-medical-surgical policies usually do not contain provisions that would coordinate or prorate their benefits with other medical expense insurance. Insurers generally try to avoid overinsurance here by their underwriting requirements.

In the case of individual major medical coverages, the deductible is used to coordinate that coverage with other medical expense benefits. The effect of such a deductible is that the major medical policy picks up coverage only after other medical expense coverage has been exhausted. Thus, if a person has only some form of relatively limited "basic" hospital-medical-surgical coverage—either group or individual—he or she can supplement this "basic" coverage with a more comprehensive individual major medical policy. However, insurers usually will not issue such a major medical policy if the person is covered by another major medical plan or by a "basic" plan with benefit limits above certain levels.

Termination of Coverage. Most individual medical expense policies terminate the insured's or the spouse's coverage when he or she reaches age 65 or first becomes eligible for Medicare, whichever is earlier. Of course, policies designed to supplement Medicare are not so terminated or reduced.

At one time it was customary for individual medical expense policies to terminate upon the insured's death. Now, however, it is common for policies to provide that a surviving spouse automatically becomes the insured upon the original insured's death. Some policies also provide that when no spouse survives the insured, coverage is continued for minor dependents up to the policy's limiting age for such dependents. Another advantageous feature commonly provided in family medical expense policies is a conversion privilege for dependents whose coverage terminates.

Other Insurance Benefits

An injured person may be entitled to other medical expense insurance benefits. These may include (1) medical payments benefits under various kinds of liability insurance, (2) automobile no-fault benefits, and (3) blanket accident medical reimbursement benefits under individual or group policies.

Benefits from such sources normally are payable only if a covered person is injured in an accident or a specified kind of accident. Therefore, this is not coverage that can be relied upon for full protection.

Individual Health Insurance Policy Provisions

Several kinds of individual health insurance policy provisions may be important in making policy purchase decisions. These include (1) renewal or continuance provisions, (2) provisions concerning preexisting conditions, and (3) certain general provisions.

Renewal or Continuance Provisions

Renewal provisions relate to the insured's rights to continue his or her individual health insurance coverage in effect from one policy period to another. These provisions are significant to the consumer since they may determine his or her ability to retain health insurance protection. They generally can be classified as provisions that make policies (1) guaranteed renewable, (2) noncancelable and guaranteed renewable (noncancelable), (3) conditionally renewable, or (4) renewable at the option of the insurer.

Starting with the last category, policies that are *renewable at the option of the insurer* specify that the insurer has the right to refuse renewal as of any premium due date or policy anniversary. This approach is much less common today than formerly.[7] It is the least liberal for the insured.

Another approach is that policies may be *conditionally renewable,* in that there are restrictions on the insurer's right of nonrenewal. An example of this is in franchise or association group coverages, where the insurer may not be able to refuse renewal unless the insured person ceases to be a member of the association, the insured person ceases to be actively engaged in the occupation, or the insurer refuses to renew all policies issued to members of the particular group.

The term "guaranteed renewable" (or guaranteed continuable) is reasonably descriptive of the nature of this type of renewal provision. The pol-

---

[7] Some states have adopted regulatory restrictions on the rights of insurers to refuse renewal under such contracts.

icy provides that the insured will have the right to renew the coverage for a specified period of time, such as to age 65, or in some cases for life. Also, during this period, the insurer cannot by itself make any change in the policy, *except that the insurer retains the right to make changes in premium rates for whole classes of policies.* This means that the insurer cannot change the premium or classification for an individual policy by itself but may change the rates for whole rating classifications. Individual medical expense policies that guarantee the right of renewal normally are written on a guaranteed renewable basis because of the generally rising and unpredictable nature of medical costs. Some insurers also write disability income coverages on this basis.

The final category of renewal provision is the *noncancelable and guaranteed renewable (noncancelable)* type. When the term "noncancelable," or "noncan," is used alone to describe a type of renewal provision, it means the noncancelable and guaranteed renewable type. This provision gives the insured the right to continue the policy in force by the timely payment of premiums *as specified in the policy,* usually for a specified period of time, such as to age 65. Also, the insurer retains no right by itself to make *any* change in *any* policy provision during this period. The distinction between this and a guaranteed renewable policy is that the insurer guarantees the premium rates for noncancelable and guaranteed renewable contracts but reserves the right to change premiums for whole classes of insureds under guaranteed renewable contracts.

Not surprisingly, the greater the renewal guarantees contained in a policy, the higher the premium will tend to be, all other things being equal. Thus, assuming that the consumer has a choice among renewal provisions, the question becomes: How much is he or she willing to pay for renewal protection? In general, it probably is better for the consumer to try to purchase noncancelable and guaranteed renewable coverage if it is available; otherwise, he or she should purchase guaranteed renewable coverage. The added continuance security in these policies probably is worth the added premium cost in most cases. Sometimes, however, consumers can get good value from association group plans with reasonable continuance protection, and this possibility should be evaluated when it is available.

Preexisting Conditions

Individual health insurance policies normally cover only losses that begin during the policy period. Thus, accidents sustained or sickness existing prior to the effective date of coverage are not covered. These are preexisting conditions. Group health insurance, on the other hand, normally covers preexisting conditions, except in certain cases, such as smaller groups.

However, a section of the "time limit on certain defenses" provision, which is a required provision in individual health insurance policies, in effect provides that after a policy has been in force for two (or three) years, coverage cannot be denied by the insurer on the ground that a loss was caused by a preexisting condition, unless the condition is specifically excluded in the policy. This provision can be a valuable protection to the insured, because after the two or three years, the insured does not need to worry about conditions that might have existed before he or she purchased the policy. Further, some policies deny coverage only for a specified period of time (such as six months) after issue of the policy for preexisting conditions for which treatment was provided or recommended within another stated period of time (such as six months) prior to the effective date of the policy. This is an even more liberal preexisting conditions provision.

General Provisions

Here are some other required policy provisions which are important as far as the consumer is concerned.

Time Limit on Certain Defenses.   In addition to the part of this provision dealing with preexisting conditions noted above, this important provision specifies that after a policy has been in force for two (or three) years, no misstatements, except fraudulent misstatements, made by the applicant in securing the policy can be used to void the policy or to deny liability for a loss commencing after the two- (or three-) year period. It is similar in concept to the incontestable clause used in life insurance.

Grace Period.   Like life insurance policies, individual health insurance contracts allow a grace period for the payment of premiums.

Notice and Proof Requirements.   The policy indicates certain time limits for the insured to give the insurance company written notice of a claim and to furnish the insurer with completed proofs of loss. The insured should try to comply strictly with these notice and proof requirements to avoid any possible complications with claims.

Long-Term Care (LTC) Insurance

As indicated in Chap. 2 (pp. 26–27), long-term care (LTC) insurance is the main source of protection at the present time for the custodial care expense exposure. As also indicated there, this is an important exposure (largely uncovered as of this writing) that will ultimately affect many persons, particularly in their later years. It is also an exposure to loss whose cost increases dramatically with age (analogous to that of life insurance) and which, therefore, can logically be prefunded through level premiums over a reasonably long period of time before the actual loss occurs (again in a manner analogous to life insurance as explained in Chap. 4.) A difference between the custodial care expense exposure and the premature death exposure, however, is that while death is sure to occur, some persons will not incur custodial care expenses. Also, LTC insurance is now in its infancy and undoubtedly will change over the years as it develops, while the nature of life insurance is well established. There of course are other important differences between the two kinds of insurance.

Sources of LTC Insurance

Several sources may be available for acquiring LTC insurance. They currently include:

- Group LTC insurance purchased by employees through their employers
- Individual LTC insurance purchased by consumers (sometimes called "stand-alone" policies)
- Individual LTC riders to life insurance contracts
- LTC insurance purchased by individuals through association group plans (such as from professional societies, universities, fraternal orders, and other associations and groups)

Besides these sources of advance-purchased LTC insurance as such, as noted in Chap. 2 (p. 27) and explained in Chap. 4 (pp. 99–100), some life insurance companies provide accelerated death benefit provisions (sometimes called "living needs" benefits) that may meet some last-illness or custodial care needs. Further, again as noted in Chap. 2 (p. 27) and explained here and in Chap. 15 (pp. 456–458), some persons may engage in "Medicaid estate planning" by making lifetime gifts or taking other actions so that they may become eligible for Medicaid coverage of custodial care in nursing homes. However, these actions are usually taken after the need for custodial care arises. This section is concerned with preparing in advance for the custodial care need through the purchase of LTC insurance.

Nature of Coverage

LTC insurance customarily provides a specified reimbursement or an indemnity benefit per day (a per diem benefit) for covered custodial care after an initial waiting period of a stated number of days up to certain maximum benefits. Under present contracts, benefits generally are payable when the insured person becomes unable to perform a certain number (usually two or three) of a list of *activities of daily living (ADLs)* that are stated in the policy. Examples of such ADLs are eating, bathing, dressing, taking medication, toileting, and transferring and walking. Thus, the so-called coverage trigger for these contracts is generally defined in terms of the insured person's being unable to perform two or three of the stated ADLs.

The kinds of *covered services* that may be covered under LTC policies include: skilled nursing facility care, intermediate nursing facility care, custodial nursing facility care, other custodial facility care, home health care, adult day care, and respite care. Many commentators have suggested that consumers are better protected by purchasing coverage with a relatively broad range of covered services that includes not only custodial care in a nursing home but also home health care and probably adult day care. This is because many people will want to receive custodial care other than in an institutional format when possible.

In the past, some LTC insurance plans required prior hospitalization or other kinds of care before plan benefits would be paid. State laws and insurance company practices generally have limited or eliminated such provisions, and so many plans today do not require any prior care before an insured person can receive any LTC benefit. From the consumer's viewpoint, it is much better not to have any prior care requirements before LTC benefits are payable, because in many cases covered persons may not need or receive such prior hospitalization or other care before covered custodial care is needed.

Insured persons normally can select from a range of waiting periods, maximum daily benefits, and maximum lifetime benefits, depending on their perceived coverage needs and how much they want to spend for LTC coverage. Like all insurance policies, LTC contracts contain certain exclusions. An exclusion to check carefully is any for nervous or mental disorders. While nervous or mental disorders may be excluded in general, an LTC policy definitely should cover organic brain disorders including Alzheimer's disease and similar forms of senility. Unfortunately, Alzheimer's disease and related conditions are important reasons for the need for custodial care. LTC policies now generally cover them.

LTC policies often provide optional inflation-protection benefits and frequently have waiver-of-premium provisions. The policies usually exclude preexisting conditions, but such restrictions normally are limited.

When LTC benefits are offered on a group basis as an employee benefit, coverage normally is voluntary and employees generally must pay the full cost of the insurance if they elect to buy the group LTC coverage. When LTC coverage is purchased as a rider to a life insurance contract, the benefits may be a function of the face amount of life insurance. LTC riders on life insurance contracts have already been described on p. 99 of Chap. 4.

Premiums

The premiums for LTC insurance depend on such factors as the insured's age, daily benefit amount, maximum aggregate benefit period, waiting period, any inflation-protection benefit, and perhaps the state where the policy was issued. LTC premium rates often are *level or issue-age rates* which means that they are based on the insured's age when the policy was originally issued and do not increase as the insured ages, except for possible general rate increases applied to whole classes of insureds under guaranteed renewable policies and some conditionally renewable association group policies. Such an issue-age rate structure tends to make it relatively attractive for an insured to retain his or her coverage, since it will be more expensive to purchase new or replacement coverage as the insured becomes older, assuming that the existing policy is reasonably competitive with newer policies. Also, LTC policies now may have certain nonforfeiture values. However, some LTC policies use *attained-age rates,* which increase as the insured becomes older. The issue-age approach generally seems more desirable for the consumer, since LTC premiums increase dramatically with age and hence the attained-age cost will be rising rapidly just when the insured (and his or her family) may need the coverage most.

As an example of LTC coverage and premiums, let us assume that a 60-year-old person buys an association group LTC insurance plan with an $80-per-day benefit limit, a 60-day waiting period, a 6-year maximum lifetime benefit period, and no prior confinement requirements. This plan covers the following kinds of expenses: skilled nursing facility care (up to the $80 daily maximum limit), intermediate nursing facility care (up to the $80 daily maximum limit), custodial nursing facility care (up to the $80 daily maximum limit), respite care (up to the $80 daily maximum limit), home health care (up to 50% of the $80 daily maximum limit), and adult day care (up to 50% of the $80 daily maximum limit). The reduction of benefit amount for home health care and adult day care is fairly common in these policies. The coverage "trigger" for this plan is the insured's inability to perform either two or three (depending on the kind of covered expense) of the list of ADLs noted previously in this discussion. At age 60, the annual level (issue-age) premium for this particular plan is $608. Naturally, premiums can and do differ among insurers and plans. By contrast, if the person in the previous example had waited 10 years until age 70 to buy this same plan (as many people are tempted to do), the annual level (issue-age) premium would increase to $1785 (or almost three times greater). Also, as one grows older, there may be a question of continued insurability for LTC insurance.

Continuance (or Renewal) Provisions

Continuance, or renewal, provisions are an important aspect for the consumer to consider in buying LTC insurance, just as they are in buying other types of health insurance. In general, the consumer probably should seek to buy a guaranteed renewable policy when possible (noncancelable or "noncan" policies are not available for LTC coverage). Sometimes, the consumer might consider association group coverage that is conditionally renewable, or where the insurer and the association have the right together to change the coverage; however, this is not as much continuance protection for the individual insured as guaranteed renewable coverage.

Medicaid Eligibility

Medicaid is a federal-state public-assistance (welfare) program designed to provide broad medical expense benefits (including some custodial care benefits) to certain categories of the needy, such as the aged (65 or older), blind, or disabled. Thus, persons in these eligible categories must meet certain financial requirements for need. These financial requirements include an *income limit* and a *resource limit* which are quite low. For example, the resource limit generally is $1500 for a single person and $2000 for a married couple. However, certain income and resource items are excluded in determining whether a person meets these financial requirements for eligibility, and persons also can "spend down" their resources to the point where they may ultimately become eligible for Medicaid.

The medical services covered by Medicaid are very broad and include certain custodial care (such as intermediate nursing home care) that is not covered by Medicare or most regular private health insurance. Thus, persons facing heavy nursing home custodial care expenses may look to becoming eligible for Medicaid as a way out of their or their family's financial problems in meeting such expenses. This has given rise to a new area of planning known as *Medicaid estate planning*, which is discussed in greater detail on pp. 456–458 of Chap. 15.

6
Property and Liability Insurance

Buying property and liability insurance is important in planning for personal financial security. A person can be very successful in his or her job or profession; have a good life and health insurance program; be successful with investments; have a nice home, cars, perhaps a boat, and other valuable personal property; and yet be destroyed financially by an accident or lawsuit for which adequate property and liability insurance is not available. This is particularly true today for liability insurance, because people in general have become so litigous and claims-conscious.

Property Insurance

Most people face risks of loss or damage to their real and personal property. To many, the purchase of a home represents the largest single investment they make. Even those who rent face the chance of suffering a severe financial loss through damage to their personal property. The questions that should be asked in this area include the following:

What can possibly happen to cause loss or damage to property?

What kind(s) of insurance coverage would best meet these risks?

What amount(s) of insurance should be carried?

Which insurer or insurers should be selected to provide the coverage?

There are two basic approaches to insuring property: (1) specified perils coverage and (2) "all risks" coverage (or all causes of physical loss coverage). *Specified perils coverage* protects against the specific perils (causes of loss) named in the policy. It does not cover against loss by other perils. Some common examples of specified perils coverages include fire insurance, theft insurance, extended coverage, homeowners policies 1, 2, 3 (for personal property), and 4, and the dwelling buildings and contents—broad form. Some of these coverages, such as homeowners policies, and dwelling buildings and contents—broad form, cover a number of specified perils in one contract and may offer quite broad protection.

"All risks"-type coverage protects against all the risks or perils that may cause loss to the covered property, *except* those specifically excluded in the policy. Thus, the exclusions stated in the policy or form are important in determining the real extent of "all risks"-type coverage. Remember that no insurance policy or form covers everything. There are always exclusions. However, "all risks" coverage frequently is broader than specified perils coverage, but it also usually costs more. So insureds or their advisors have to decide whether "all risks" coverage is worth the extra cost. Some common examples of "all risks"-type coverage are homeowners policy 3 (for dwellings and other structures), dwelling buildings special form, personal articles floater coverage (e.g., on furs, jewels, fine arts, stamp collections, and cameras), and automobile comprehensive physical damage insurance.

Historically, probably the most planned-for risk of loss to real or personal property is by fire and related perils. The fire insurance policy is perhaps the most standardized in the insurance industry. The perils covered by the basic policy are fire, lightning, and removal of covered property from the premises to escape damage. The policy can be tailored to cover various types of property, including, of course, a dwelling and its contents. The standard fire policy is included automatically in the homeowners forms that are so commonly used today to cover residential risks. To the standard fire policy is attached at least one form or endorsement further describing covered property and/or perils. The fire policy frequently has been broadened by endorsement to include the "extended coverage" perils, which are:

Windstorm

Hail

Damage by aircraft and vehicles

Riot, riot attending a strike, and civil commotion

Explosion

Smoke

Additionally, other endorsements can be added to the standard fire policy to include such coverages as:

Vandalism and malicious mischief

Additional extended coverage (e.g., weight of ice, sleet, and snow; collapse of buildings; limited water damage; falling objects; damage by burglars; glass breakage; and freezing of plumbing and heating systems)

"All risks" coverage

The insuring clause of an "all risks" contract typically states that the policy covers "all risks" (written in quotation marks to indicate the conditional nature of the term) of direct physical loss or damage, except as hereinafter provided. Some of the commonly used exclusions in "all risks" contracts are the following:

Wear and tear, deterioration, rust, mechanical breakdown, and the like. These are gradual, inevitable causes of loss which are uninsurable because the occurrence is certain.

Flood, surface water, water backing up through drains, water below the surface of the ground, etc. Many private insurance contracts do not provide flood coverage because of its catastrophic nature and because of the limited regions of exposure. However, many flood-prone areas have been designated as eligible for flood insurance through the governmental flood insurance program.

Earthquake, landslide, and other earth movement. In most states, this coverage can be "bought back" by the insured upon payment of an additional premium.

To many homeowners and apartment dwellers, the detailed conditions, exclusions, and extensions that seemingly characterize property insurance policies may appear like more trouble than they are worth. In reality, however, they are not difficult and can be analyzed in a "building-up" pattern as follows:

1. *Basic specified perils coverage.* Fire, lightning, and extended coverage
2. *Broader specified perils coverage.* All the above plus vandalism and malicious mischief, theft, and additional extended coverage
3. *"All risks"-type coverage.* All the above plus anything not specifically excluded

Which Coverage and in What Amount?

The question then becomes "Which policy should be purchased?" A cost-benefit type of analysis can provide the answer. By comparing the additional coverage provided with the additional premium, the insured can decide on the coverage that best suits his or her needs. Sometimes the cost differential for broader coverage may be so little as to make it a worthwhile purchase.

Once a decision has been made as to the type of coverage, the amount of insurance must be determined. Most homeowners policies (to be discussed later in the chapter) are written with a *replacement-cost provision* that applies to the dwelling and related structures, and may be endorsed to apply to personal property. The insured should be sure to have enough insurance to meet the requirements of this provision, as explained later in the section on homeowners insurance. Of course, the insured also wants to *be sure that property insurance policy limits are adequate to cover the maximum loss that is likely to be suffered* as a result of damage or loss to the various kinds of property at risk. In most cases, these will be limits equal to the full value of the covered property. But different kinds of property can be insured in different ways, and we shall point out some kinds of property that may present special coverage considerations when we discuss homeowners policies.

In the case of personal property valuation, an additional problem confronts the insurance buyer. This problem is all too familiar to those who have suffered a loss of this nature; it centers around the difficulty of recalling the articles destroyed and their description, purchase price, and date of purchase. To alleviate this kind of situation, insured persons or their advisors might take periodic inventories of personal property. Many insurers and agents provide inventory checklists that include all pertinent information. When completed properly, this inventory should present a fairly accurate basis for setting the amount of insurance, and, of course, it should be stored *away from the insured premises,* preferably in a safe deposit box.

What May Suspend or Reduce Coverage?

There are a few things that may suspend or reduce property insurance coverage. Therefore, the insured should watch out for them so that the insurance protection will not be impaired.

For example, coverage for certain perils may be suspended if a covered building had been vacant (or unoccupied) beyond a stated period of time immediately preceding a loss. In homeowners policy 2 (HO-2), for example, such a suspension of coverage applies to loss caused by vandalism or malicious mischief, breakage of glass, and accidental discharge or overflow of water or steam if the covered building had been vacant beyond a period of 30 consecutive days immediately preceding a loss. If the insured plans to leave property vacant beyond such a time limit, the insurance agent or broker should be notified so he or she can take appropriate action to maintain coverage.

Also, fire insurance policies provide that the insurance company will not be liable for a loss occurring while the hazard is increased within the control or knowledge of the insured. The policy does not spell out exactly what constitutes an increase in hazard within the insured's control or knowledge. Suppose, though, that the insured stores in the garage an amount of gasoline that is far in excess of normal household needs. Not only is this unwise from the standpoint of physical safety, but it also *might* constitute an increase in hazard that would suspend the fire insurance coverage.

Finally, remember that property and liability insurance premiums must be paid by the due date or coverage will expire. Property and liability insurance policies do not contain a provision similar to the grace period found in life and health insurance policies. Of course, property and liability insurance agents may extend credit for a short period to their customers for their premium payments.

Personal Liability

The risk of loss of assets is by no means limited to the physical destruction of the assets. A potentially greater risk is the loss of assets or earnings through the judicial process as a result of one's negligence or other legal liability. Large liability judgments and settlements are common, and awards of a million dollars or more are quite common today. As in the case of property coverages, a careful review of exposures to loss, coverages, policy limits, and differences among insurers will be helpful in developing a comprehensive insurance program at the lowest practical cost.

When consumers look at their diverse personal liability exposures, the following general *categories of exposures* come to mind:

1. Ownership, rental, and/or use of automobiles

2. Ownership and/or rental of premises

3. Professional or business activities

4. Directorships or officerships in corporations, credit unions, school boards, and other organizations

5. Employment of others (workers' compensation and employer's liability exposures)

6. Ownership, rental, or use of watercraft or aircraft

7. Personal activities

These exposures can be covered by a variety of liability insurance coverages. We shall consider first the so-called comprehensive personal liability coverage which can be purchased separately but usually is bought as a part of a homeowners policy.

Comprehensive Personal Liability Coverage

Daily nonbusiness activities include a host of exposures to loss through legal liability. A person's dog bites a neighbor, a visitor trips and falls on the front walk, or a tee shot on the eighth hole slices and hits another golfer—all these accidents could result in liability losses, as well as put the person involved to great expense and trouble in defending against liability claims even if they are groundless. This widespread exposure to liability losses stresses the need for comprehensive personal liability (CPL) insurance protection.

CPL insurance (using the Liability Coverages-Section II of the homeowners policy for illustrative purposes) agrees to pay on behalf of an insured[1] all sums up to the policy limit that the insured becomes legally obligated to pay as damages because of bodily injury and property damage. The insurance company also agrees to defend the insured in any suit that would be covered by the policy, even if the suit is groundless, false, or fraudulent. However, the insurer's duty to defend ends when the amount the insurer pays for damages resulting from an occurrence equals the policy's limit of liability. This is another important reason for a person to carry adequate limits of liability.

The insuring agreement is quite broad but still is limited by certain exclusions. Coverage, for example, does not apply to:

1. Business or professional pursuits (Separate liability insurance is available for such exposures.)

2. The ownership, maintenance, or use of automobiles, larger watercraft, and aircraft (Each of these exposures presents special needs, and policies exist to cover each of them.)

3. Injury or damage caused intentionally by the insured (Some forms of intentional torts can be covered by personal injury coverage that can be purchased through umbrella liability policies discussed on pp. 173–174 of this chapter.)

4. Benefits payable under any workers' compensation law (to avoid duplication of coverage)

5. Injury or damage due to war, revolution, etc., or nuclear energy

6. Liability assumed by the insured under any unwritten contract or agreement or under any business contract or agreement

7. Damage to property rented to, used by, or in the care of the insured, except for property damage caused by fire, smoke, or explosion (in effect, giving fire legal liability coverage)

---

[1] The word "insured" includes the named insured and, if residents of his or her household, his or her relatives, and any other person under the age of 21 in the care of an insured.

In addition to the basic liability coverage, CPL insurance contains two additional coverages: (1) medical payments and (2) damage to property of others. Medical payments coverage agrees to pay all reasonable expenses incurred within three years from the date of an accident for necessary medical, surgical, dental, and similar services for each person who sustains bodily injury caused by an accident (*a*) while on the insured's premises with permission, and (*b*) elsewhere, if the accident is caused by an insured, a resident employee, or an animal owned by the insured. Note that this provision is not based on the insured's legal liability; that is, eligible medical expenses are paid under medical payments coverage (up to the medical payments limit), whether or not the insured was at fault. For example, if a neighbor is injured on the insured's premises and incurs medical expenses as a result of the injury, there is medical payments coverage without the necessity of determining who was at fault. Damage to property of others coverage promises to pay under certain conditions for a loss of property belonging to others caused by an insured up to a $250 policy limit, again without regard to the legal liability of the insured.

Limits of Liability and Cost

Comprehensive personal liability insurance provides bodily injury liability and property damage liability coverage on a so-called single-limit basis—which means that one limit of liability, such as $50,000, $100,000, $300,000, or more, applies to each occurrence regardless of the number of persons injured or the amount of separate property damage. In other words, there are no separate per-person or property damage liability limits.

Medical payments coverage is written subject to a per-person limit for each accident. As noted previously, the damage to property of others coverage has a $250 limit. Thus, an illustrative set of policy limits for CPL coverage under a homeowners policy might look like this:

Personal liability (bodily injury and property damage)	$300,000 each occurrence
Medical payments to others	$1000 each person (for each accident)
Damage to property of others (an additional coverage)	$250 each occurrence

Cost of protection is dependent chiefly on the number and uses of properties owned or used by the insured. Many individuals, however, are surprised at the reasonableness of the premiums for a person who owns or rents one home or apartment. The following are examples of CPL premiums for various limits of liability based on a single residence.

CPL limit of liability	Annual premium
$ 50,000	$18
100,000	20
200,000	23
300,000	26

Perhaps as important as the absolute cost of the policy shown above is the relatively small cost of doubling or even quadrupling the coverage. For example, a doubling of coverage from $50,000 to $100,000 costs only $2 additional; for four times as much coverage, a $200,000 limit costs only $5 more than a $50,000 limit. This is an example of sound insurance buying—getting a great deal of additional protection against potentially catastrophic losses for a relatively small cost.

Homeowners Insurance

Earlier in this chapter, the basic fire policy with endorsements was discussed, as well as CPL insurance. When these basic coverages (with CPL coverage) are added to other coverages (such as personal theft insurance), or in some cases written on an "all risks" basis, the resulting package is called a "homeowners" policy. They are an example of what the insurance industry calls "package policies." Developed and refined through the years, the various homeowners policies generally provide broader coverage than the separate policies discussed above, and at a lower cost—hence their wide popularity.

Types of Policies

There are basically six variations of homeowners policies, as follows:

Homeowners 1 (HO-1) (Basic)	Fire, lightning, extended coverage, vandalism and malicious mischief, theft, glass breakage on dwelling buildings and personal property (contents), and comprehensive personal liability
Homeowners 2 (HO-2) (Broad Form)	All the above, and additional extended coverage which provides coverage for other specified causes of loss
Homeowners 3 (HO-3)	"All Risks" on buildings and Broad Form on personal property
Homeowners 4 (HO-4)	Personal property coverage only (Broad Form); for tenants

| Homeowners 6 (HO-6) | Personal property and loss of use coverage (Broad Form), and certain dwelling coverage within the unit and for which the unit owner may have insurance responsibility under an association agreement, for condominium unit owners |
| Homeowners 8 (HO-8) | Coverage on buildings and personal property somewhat more limited than HO-1; used to provide coverage on homes that may not meet the insurer's underwriting requirements for other homeowners forms |

All homeowners policies contain a set of standard coverages (including CPL) that may be altered by endorsements which increase the amount of insurance, broaden the coverage, or modify the conditions or restrictions. An example of the coverages and limits under an HO-2 is as follows:[2]

Section I Property Coverages

Coverage A	Dwelling	$150,000 (selected by the insured or recommended by the insurer)
Coverage B	Other structures	$15,000 (10% of dwelling amount, but may be increased)
Coverage C	Personal property (unscheduled[3]) that is anywhere in the world	$75,000 (50% of dwelling amount, but may be increased, or reduced to 40%)
	Personal property, usually at a residence of an insured other than the residence premises described in the policy	$7500 (10% of the Coverage C limit, but not less than $1,000)
Coverage D	Loss of use (including additional living expenses)	$20,000 (20% of dwelling amount)

---

[2] Homeowners policies generally follow this basic pattern, but some variations exist in certain states and under the forms used by some insurers.

[3] "Unscheduled" means property that is not specifically named or listed in a schedule in the policy. As we shall see later, a person sometimes needs to list certain valuable property in a separate schedule for full coverage.

Section II Liability Coverages

Coverage E	Personal liability	$300,000 each occurrence
Coverage F	Medical payments to others	$1000 each person
	Damage to property of others	$250 each occurrence

It is readily apparent that this "package" provides a combination of coverages that fits the needs of many homeowners. A tenant's homeowners policy (HO-4) simply deletes Coverages A and B. Another form (HO-6) is designed specially for condominium and cooperative unit owners. Also, an endorsement to HO-3 for an additional premium can be used to provide "all risks" coverage on contents.

To appreciate fully the extent and limitations of the homeowners policy, consider the protection provided by each division of coverage.

Coverage A	The dwelling amount includes the dwelling and materials and supplies located on the residence premises used to construct, alter, or repair the dwelling and related structures. Trees, plants, shrubs, and lawns are covered only for certain perils and with an aggregate limit of 5 percent of the dwelling amount and not more than $500 on any one tree, shrub, or plant.
Coverage B	Private structures (garages, sheds, etc.) separated from the dwelling by clear spaces are covered in an amount as shown above in addition to the dwelling amount.
Coverage C	Personal property owned or used by the named insured and his or her family is covered against the policy perils (including theft). However, among the property items specifically excluded from coverage are motorized vehicles, aircraft, business property while away from the premises, salespersons' samples, automobile sound recording equipment and tape decks, and property which is specifically insured elsewhere (a painting insured under a fine arts floater, for example).
Coverage D	Loss of use coverage provides, at the insured's option, either: (1) additional living expenses incurred by the family while the dwelling is uninhabitable because of damage due to an insured peril; or (2) if the dwelling is the insured's principal place of residence, the fair rental value of that part where the insured resides. Such additional living expenses might include hotel bills, meals, and the like, but only to the extent they are in addition to normal living expenses. Coverage D also covers the fair rental value of any portion of the residence premises that may be rented to others.

The remaining coverages apply to the liability portion of the policy. This is the comprehensive personal liability coverage which was discussed previously.

Replacement Cost Provision
or Endorsement

There are several "additional conditions" in homeowners policies that consumers or their advisors should watch for. One is the replacement cost provision that applies to Coverages A and B (the dwelling and other structures). This provision is advantageous to the insured because if the proper amount of insurance is maintained on the dwelling, the insured can recover any loss to the dwelling and private structures (but not personal property, unless the insured purchases additional coverage providing replacement cost coverage on replaceable personal contents) on the basis of the full cost to repair or replace the damaged or destroyed property *without any deduction for depreciation*. Without such a replacement cost provision, the homeowners policy (and the standard fire policy) would pay only the actual cash value at the time of a loss of lost or damaged property. Actual cash value (ACV) normally means the replacement cost new of the property at the time of a loss minus the amount the property has physically depreciated since it was built or was new. *Note that property still physically depreciates (i.e., wears out), even though its market value,* which basically depends on the supply and demand for real estate or other property, *may be rising or falling.*

But under the standard loss settlement condition of homeowners policies, the insured must carry enough insurance in relation to the value of his or her dwelling to get the benefit of the replacement cost provision. Specifically, the policy provides that if the insured carries insurance on a building equal to at least 80 percent of its replacement cost new, any covered loss to the building will be paid to the extent of the full cost to repair or replace the damage without deducting depreciation, up to the policy limit. What if insurance of less than 80 percent of replacement cost is carried? Then, in case of a loss to the building, the insurance company would pay only (1) the actual cash value of the loss or (2) the amount produced by the following formula:

$$\frac{\text{Amount of insurance carried on the building}}{80\% \text{ of the building's replacement cost new}}$$

$$\times \text{cost to repair or replace the damage}$$

whichever is greater. In either case, though, this would be less than what the insured would have to pay to repair or replace the damaged building in the event of a loss. Therefore, it is important to buy enough insurance to meet the 80 percent requirement and to keep the coverage up to date with rising construction costs.

In addition to this standard replacement cost provision, however, homeowners policies may have added to them a replacement or repair cost protection endorsement that substantially modifies the previously cited standard replacement cost provision. Under the endorsement, if the insured allows the insurance company to adjust the Coverage A dwelling limit (and the premium) in accordance with a property evaluation the insurer makes and with increases in property values due to inflation, the form will automatically increase the limit of liability on the dwelling (Coverage A) to the current replacement cost of the dwelling if there is a loss that exceeds the limit stated in the policy for the dwelling. (There are also corresponding proportionate increases in the limits for Coverages B, C, and D under these circumstances.) In addition, if the insured conforms to the terms of this endorsement, losses to the dwelling and other structures (Coverages A and B) will be paid on a replacement cost basis without application of the 80 percent provision in the standard provision noted previously. This endorsement would seem to be valuable to the insured since it relieves him or her of the problem of estimating the right amount of insurance to meet the requirements of the standard loss settlement (replacement cost) condition.

Further, in most states the insured can buy a special endorsement on homeowners policies, called an "inflation guard endorsement," that automatically increases the coverage limits periodically by small percentage amounts. However, use of this endorsement does not necessarily mean that there is enough coverage.

Finally, the insured may be able to purchase for an additional premium a personal property replacement cost endorsement that extends replacement cost coverage to personal property (Coverage C) and damage to the property of others coverage (in Section II) under certain conditions. There also are some limits on this coverage, such as 400 percent of the actual cash value of the personal property at the time of the loss.

Internal Limits (Sublimits)

Another thing to consider in property and liability insurance planning is the smaller internal limits (called "sublimits") that apply to certain kinds of property under homeowners policies. The following are some of the more important of these sublimits under homeowners policies.

1. $200 aggregate limit on money, bank notes, bullion, gold other than goldware, silver other than silverware, platinum, coins, and medals

2. $1000 aggregate limit on securities, accounts, deeds, and similar property, or stamps, including philatelic property (stamp collections)

3. $1000 aggregate limit on watercraft, including their trailers, furnishings, equipment, and outboard motors

4. $1000 aggregate limit on trailers not used with watercraft

5. $1000 aggregate limit on grave markers

6. $1000 aggregate limit for loss by theft of jewelry, watches, precious and semiprecious stones, and furs

7. $2000 aggregate limit for loss by theft of firearms

8. $2500 aggregate limit for loss by theft of silverware, silver-plated ware, goldware, gold-plated ware, and pewterware

The effect of these internal limits may be to make it necessary to schedule specifically additional amounts of insurance on certain property items. Let us take a specific example. Suppose an insured has a Homeowners 3 policy with $100,000 of insurance on the dwelling. He also owns a coin collection worth about $3000, and has recently given his wife a fur coat worth about $4000. In this case, the basic homeowners policy would provide only specified perils coverage of $200 on the coin collection. And on the fur coat, the policy's theft coverage would be limited to only $1000. So in this situation the insured might want to insure specifically on an "all risks" basis the coin collection for $3000 and the fur coat for $4000 to get full coverage on these items. The insured could do this under a Scheduled Personal Property Endorsement added to the homeowners policy or under a separate Personal Articles Floater. Kinds of property that often are separately scheduled and insured in this way include jewelry, furs, cameras, musical instruments, silverware, golfers' equipment, guns, fine arts, stamps, and coins.

Liability Exclusions

Proper planning for personal liability requires the analysis of the liability exclusions under homeowners policies and making sure that there are no uncovered liability exposures. Specifically, the following are some of the potential liability exposure areas, usually excluded under homeowners personal liability insurance, that should be reviewed and evaluated:

1. Any watercraft owned by an insured with inboard or inboard-outdrive motor power, or rented to an insured if it has inboard-outdrive motor power of more than 50 horsepower, or a sailing vessel of 26 feet or more in length owned by an insured, or if it is powered by outboard motor(s) of more than 25 horsepower and owned by any insured under certain conditions. (In other words, homeowners policies provide liability coverage for smaller boats, but not larger ones. For excluded watercraft, boat or yacht insurance may be needed.)

2. Arising out of aircraft or various aircraft exposures.

3. Any motor vehicle owned or operated by, or rented or loaned to, an insured.

4. Rendering or failing to render professional services.

5. Most business pursuits of an insured.

6. Any premises, other than an insured premises, owned by or rented to any insured.

7. Cases where the insured is liable to provide workers' compensation benefits or does provide such benefits.

8. For damage to property occupied by, used by, rented to, or in the care of the insured. (This is the "care, custody, and control" exclusion in liability policies.) However, this exclusion does not apply to property damage caused by fire, smoke, or explosion; therefore, the "fire legal liability" exposure is covered.

9. Bodily injury or property damage that is expected or intended by the insured.

Eligibility

For those who are eligible, homeowners policies generally provide broad coverage at a reasonable price. To be eligible, a dwelling must be owner-occupied. Seasonal dwellings, not rented to others, are considered to be owner-occupied, but a common problem in this regard is the two- or three-family house bought for investment purposes which is rented to others. In many states, the liability coverage for such a rental property may be added to the liability portion of the homeowners policy, but a separate fire policy must be purchased to protect the building and contents values.

Cost

Homeowners premiums reflect many factors, and accordingly, rates can vary considerably. They can also vary among insurers, and so here again savings may be secured by shopping around for homeowners coverage.

Cost also depends on which homeowners form is used. The following chart presents an example of the relative cost differentials among three homeowners forms:

Homeowners 1	$255 annually
Homeowners 2	$274 annually
Homeowners 3	$321 annually

Homeowners policies usually have a deductible, applying to losses under the Section I (property damage) coverages. This deductible may be increased in return for a reduced premium. The use of a higher deductible may be attractive because of the reduction in premium.

Automobile Insurance

Perhaps no product has been at once so creative and yet so destructive as the automobile. Modern society has been shaped by the influence of the automobile, and along with it has evolved automobile insurance.

Coverage and Persons Insured

Personal automobile insurance policies typically provide coverage for automobile liability, automobile medical payments, uninsured motorists, physical damage to the automobile, and related exposures, each of which can be further subdivided as follows.[4]

Part A   Liability coverage (including bodily injury and property damage liability)

Part B   Medical payments coverage

Part C   Uninsured motorists coverage (or uninsured/underinsured motorists coverage)

Part D   Damage to covered autos (including comprehensive, collision, towing and labor, and transportation expenses)

The insuring agreement of the automobile liability policy covers the insured's liability arising out of the ownership, maintenance, or use of owned and nonowned automobiles. At one time, automobile liability coverage generally was written with "split limits," that is, with separate limits applying to each person and each occurrence for bodily injury liability, and a further limit applying to each occurrence for property damage liability. However, in modern policies, such as the Personal Auto Policy, it is common to have a single limit of liability that applies to all covered liability losses arising out of an accident, regardless of the number of persons injured or the amount of separate property damage. This is the same concept as is applied for comprehensive personal liability coverage under all types of homeowners policies.

For example, some sample limits for a Personal Auto Policy (PAP) might be as follows:

---

[4] Certain states have enacted "no-fault" auto insurance statutes which remove at least some auto accidents from the realm of negligence liability. Auto policies issued to residents of these states also contain the appropriate no-fault endorsement or coverage for that state. These no-fault benefits may be called personal injury protection (PIP), basic reparations benefits, or other names. They basically are payable to injured, covered persons without their having to show that anyone was negligent in causing their injuries.

$300,000 each accident	Liability (bodily injury and property damage)
$5,000 each person in any one accident	Medical payments
$30,000 each accident	Uninsured motorists
Actual cash value	Collision and/or comprehensive (subject to a $100 deductible)
Personal injury protection per endorsement	Statutory

Under the above limits, the policy would pay all liability claims against any covered person arising out of an auto accident up to an overall limit of $300,000. The medical payments portion will pay up to $5000 for medical expenses of each person, including the insured and any occupants of his or her auto, without regard to legal liability. Uninsured motorist coverage generally provides a minimum limit (normally the state financial responsibility law limits) for bodily injury from uninsured and hit-and-run motorists. (An insured may also purchase "underinsured" motorists coverage, which covers the insured in the event another motorist's liability insurance limits are not sufficient to pay the full amount of the insured's legally recoverable damages against the other motorist.)

The next coverages refer to property insurance (technically called "physical damage" coverage) on the insured's own car. Comprehensive provides broad "all risks" coverage, except for collision, which is written as a separate coverage. Recovery is made on an actual cash-value basis. Collision is the other major automobile physical damage coverage and also is written on an actual cash-value basis. A stated deductible(s) normally applies to both collision and comprehensive coverages. Finally, in the illustrative limits cited above, the policy contains a mandatory state no-fault endorsement (called Personal Injury Protection in this case) providing certain statutory benefits for covered persons injured in automobile accidents without regard for who was legally liable (i.e., negligent) for the accident. A number of states, however, do not have automobile no-fault laws, and so the automobile policies written in those states would not have such a no-fault endorsement.

Under the PAP, the following are considered to be a "covered person" as far as policy liability coverage is concerned:

1. The "named insured" (i.e., the person named in the policy declarations), his or her spouse if a resident of the same household, and any family member (i.e., a person who is related to the named insured or spouse by blood, marriage, or adoption and is a resident of the insured's household) with respect to the ownership, maintenance, or use of any auto or trailer

2. Any person using the insured's covered auto

3. Any other person or organization with regard to the insured's covered auto but only for their legal responsibility for the acts or omissions of a person for whom coverage otherwise is provided under the liability part of the policy

4. Any other person or organization with regard to any auto other than the insured's covered auto but only for their legal responsibility for the acts or omissions of the named insured, his or her spouse, and any family member covered under the liability part of the policy

Accordingly, the named insured is covered by his or her PAP for anyone using his or her car, and further, if he or she, his or her spouse, or a family member (as defined above) borrows someone else's car. This can be summed up by saying that the auto insurance follows the named insured and a covered auto.

As always, the exclusions are important in defining the coverage of an insurance contract. The following are some of the important liability exclusions of the PAP. For example, the policy does not provide liability coverage for the following:

1. Damage to property owned or being transported by a covered person.

2. Damage to property rented to, used by, or in the care of a covered person.

3. Bodily injury to an employee of a covered person during the course of employment; however, this exclusion does not apply to a *domestic employee* unless workers' compensation benefits are required for or made available for that employee. (This is an important exception to the exclusion if domestic workers are employed.)

4. Liability arising out of the ownership or operation of a vehicle while it is being used to carry persons or property for a fee; however, this exclusion does not apply to normal share-the-expense car pools.

5. The ownership, maintenance, or use of a motorcycle or other self-propelled vehicle having less than four wheels. (Additional liability coverage is needed for this kind of exposure.)

6. The ownership, maintenance, or use of any vehicle, other than the insured's covered autos, that is owned by or furnished or available for the regular use of the named insured or his or her spouse.

7. The ownership, maintenance, or use of any vehicle, other than the insured's covered autos, that is owned by or furnished or available for the regular use of any family member; however, this exclusion does not apply to the named insured or his or her spouse.

8. Any person using a vehicle without a reasonable belief that the person is entitled to do so.

Cost

The fact that automobile insurance often is costly is brought home to the consumer every time he or she gets a premium notice. Although it appears to be quite complex, the rating of automobile liability insurance generally is based on four factors: (1) age and perhaps sex of drivers, (2) use of the auto, (3) territory where the car is garaged, and (4) the operators' driving records.

Similarly, auto physical damage insurance rates generally are affected by such factors as (1) the cost (new) of the car and (2) its age. Since comprehensive and collision coverages promise to pay for the repair costs of a damaged vehicle, it follows that a more expensive car will have a higher premium than a less expensive one. Additionally, as the years go by, the actual cash value of a car diminishes through depreciation, and thus the premium also declines. However, at some point in the life of a car it normally is economical for the insured to consider dropping his or her collision (and perhaps comprehensive) coverage. The value left to insure simply is not worth even a reduced premium. This point is discussed further below.

The following table illustrates the additional cost associated with increasing the basic automobile liability limit of $35,000 per accident.

Liability limit	Premium
$ 35,000	$ 92
50,000	105
75,000	111
100,000	118
200,000	132
300,000	140
500,000	149
1,000,000	168

It can be seen from these figures that it costs very little to increase liability limits to a more adequate level. In this regard, there is no simple formula to determine the "correct" limit of liability an insured should carry. The problem, however, generally is best solved by incurring the small cost differential for the higher limits. Of course, the problem also can be solved by carrying an adequate excess or umbrella liability policy, described later in this chapter.

The cost of automobile liability insurance can vary considerably among insurance companies for the same coverage in the same territory. In a study conducted by the New York State Insurance Department, it was shown that the basic rates for auto liability policies of different companies could vary by as much as 50 percent in certain territories of the state. Thus, consumers or their advisors may secure significant savings by shopping around for their automobile insurance. Of course, premium cost is not the only factor that should be considered. Other important factors include the service provided by the particular insurance agent or broker; insurer claims, underwriting, and renewal policies; insurer financial strength; and any dividends that may be paid by some companies.

In the area of physical damage insurance, one major cost-cutting technique that often is not utilized fully is the use of higher deductibles. For example, increasing a collision deductible from, say, $100 to $200 may involve a premium saving of $25 to $30 per year, depending on the rating factors involved.

A question often asked is "For how many years should I carry collision coverage?" The answer, of course, varies with the type of car, whether it is financed, the financial position of the consumer, his or her risk-taking philosophy, and the like. However, many consumers do not purchase collision coverage after an auto is, say, three to five years old.

Types of Policies

Up to this point, we have been talking about the Personal Auto Policy (PAP). This policy is intended to cover the personal automobile exposures of most individuals and families. A distinguishing characteristic of this policy is that it is written in language that is meant to be more readable and understandable for the consumer than insurance contracts generally have been in the past. Most individuals and families are covered by the PAP. However, some insurers (including some large ones) use their own forms of automobile insurance policies.

In addition, there are other kinds of automobile policies used, each serving its own purpose, that might be briefly mentioned. A Basic Automobile Form is used to insure commercial vehicles as well as some private passenger automobiles. This form is limited in that it is essentially designed to insure only automobiles described in the policy. A Comprehensive Automobile Policy (CAP) also may be used by businesses or individuals to cover their exposures arising out of the ownership, maintenance, or use of any automobile (owned or nonowned) that is not specifically excluded.

Other Property and Liability Insurance Policies to Consider

We now have introduced the basic core of most people's property and liability insurance programs—the homeowners and automobile insurance policies. In keeping with the personal risk management approach, the next logical step is an analysis and evaluation of additional, but less frequent, risks of loss and the available methods for dealing with them.

Excess (Umbrella) Liability

Less than a decade ago, the public began to read, with considerable interest, newspaper articles concerning jury awards of $1 million or more in some negligence liability cases. Professionals, businesspeople, and other people of means (who would be "target risks" for liability claims) began to examine the extent of the liability protection afforded by their automobile and homeowners policies. Also of importance were the claims which would not be covered under most standard policies. Thus, demands for higher liability limits and broader protection inspired the creation of the personal "excess liability," catastrophe liability, or "umbrella" contract, so called because, like an umbrella, it is designed to cover everything under it. However, there are required underlying liability policies, such as automobile and homeowners policies. Most personal umbrella policies are issued with a minimum limit of $1 million, and higher limits are available at relatively modest increases in cost.

Personal excess policies are issued by many insurers, but they are not standardized. Therefore, care must be taken when comparing the contracts of different companies. Basically, the umbrella policy is designed to pay and defend liability claims after the limits of underlying liability policies are exhausted. For example, John Doe is involved in an auto accident and, as the result of his negligence, Richard Roe is seriously injured. A jury finds John liable to Richard for damages of $500,000. John's automobile policy, written with a single limit of $300,000, which John thought was "more than adequate" when he bought the policy, pays its limit of $300,000. Unfortunately for him, John remains personally liable for the remaining $200,000 of damages, unless he had the foresight to buy a personal umbrella policy that would pay this amount on his behalf. Similarly, an umbrella policy takes over and provides additional protection up to its limits after other forms of liability insurance are exhausted, such as the CPL or watercraft policies.

In response to the demand for broader coverage as well as higher limits, the personal excess liability contract is written on a basis similar to the "all risks" approach in property insurance; that is, all liability losses are included unless specifically excluded. Some important extensions of coverage follow:

1. Property damage liability for loss to property of others in the insured's care, custody, or control

2. Worldwide coverage (no territorial restriction)

3. Coverage of "personal injury" claims, which might include libel, slander, false arrest, wrongful entry, invasion of privacy, and the like

These extensions, which normally are not covered by "underlying" liability policies, are subject to a deductible (called a self-insured retention or SIR) that might be $250 or more.

Most people with any significant liability exposures, whether they think of themselves as "well off" or not, should consider buying personal excess liability insurance. While the likelihood of a "jumbo" or catastrophic liability loss is quite small, if it did happen, it would destroy the person involved financially. That is not a risk people can afford to take. Furthermore, the premium is not unduly burdensome. Also, a personal excess policy may require underlying liability insurance with lower limits of liability than the insured now is carrying. Thus, the insured may be able to reduce some of his or her present liability limits and save some premium dollars, which would reduce somewhat the cost of buying the personal excess policy.

Directors' and Officers' Liability

A trend by the courts to require additional responsibility of officers and directors of corporations (and other organizations) in conjunction with their duties therein has created a need for insurance to meet this risk. The Directors' and Officers' Liability (D&O) policy covers any "wrongful act," which generally is defined as a breach of duty, neglect, error, misstatement, misleading statement, or omission. For those persons serving on various kinds of boards of directors or otherwise subject to this exposure, it has the potential for catastrophic financial loss and is important from the individual's viewpoint. Thus, persons so exposed or invited to serve on boards should inquire into what protection they are afforded by the corporations or organizations involved. Sometimes the organization agrees to indemnify its directors, and then it carries D&O coverage to protect itself, while other times the organization carries D&O coverage that covers its directors directly.

Professional Liability

Many professionals and businesspeople need liability coverage to protect themselves against claims and suits arising out of possible or alleged negligence or errors or omissions in the practice of their professions or business pursuits. Such claims and suits are not covered under other personal liability coverages. Specialized professional liability forms for the various professions and businesses are needed to cover this exposure. Such professional liability policies often are written on a *claims-made* basis. This means that the event or incident covered must occur after a retroactive date stated in the policy, and a claim arising out of the event or incident must be made and reported to the insurance company during the policy period.

The other kinds of liability insurance policies discussed in this chapter are *occurrence* forms. This means that the covered injury or event must occur during the policy period, but claim can be made for it and reported to the insurance company after the policy period ends as well as during the policy period.

Coverage under Business Liability Policies

Sometimes executive officers or employees can be sued personally for their activities on behalf of their employer (say, a corporation). It may be alleged that they caused bodily injury, property damage, or personal injury to others. Business liability policies (such as the commercial general liability form) normally define who is insured broadly so as to generally include as an insured under the policy executive officers and employees so long as they are acting within the limits of their employment or duties with the employer. If a person feels that he or she may have a business liability exposure, the person or his or her advisors may want to check into his or her employer's liability coverage.

Workers' Compensation

The states, the District of Columbia, and the federal government have workers' compensation laws which set forth the benefits payable to employees who suffer on-the-job injuries and occupational diseases. The relevance of this risk may seem somewhat remote from the realm of personal risk management, but certain states include domestic and/or casual employees under their workers' compensation act. Therefore, depending on the particular state law, a person may need workers' compensation insurance.

Investment Properties

Investment properties a person may own or manage present similar risks of loss, as does personally used property, and all the risk management steps taken in connection with the individual's own property can be applied successfully here. On the property side, insurance to value must be dealt with, and decisions must be made regarding type of policy, deductibles, and the like. Because homeowners policies are limited to owner-occupants, a commercial package policy or perhaps a fire policy with appropriate endorsements may be used to provide the necessary property protection. Similar considerations apply in the liability insurance area. A competent insurance agent or broker can be of great help in designing and placing the proper coverage for such commercial-type risks. In some cases, it may be valuable to retain an independent risk management consultant.

Insurance Companies and Premiums

A common misconception is that most property and liability insurance companies are alike and that their rates for insurance are "about the same."

This is not the case. Although rates often are regulated, the *final cost to the consumer can vary considerably among insurers.* Therefore, as indicated previously, consumers or their advisors often can save money on property and liability insurance by shopping for coverage.

In this connection, two basic ideas are helpful—rate deviations and dividends. A "rate deviation" is a discount from the standard premium given in advance. For example, some insurers offer rate deviations on automobile insurance and/or homeowners policies because of favorable loss experience, lower expenses, or both.

A "dividend," on the other hand, is a refund usually paid by a mutual insurer at the end of the policy term. Some mutual insurers do not pay dividends but rather charge a lower initial premium, while others have traditionally paid a fairly constant percentage of the premium, ranging from 5 to 30 percent. These factors, of course, reflect only one element to be considered in selecting an insurer.

Insurer Selection

Security, service, and cost are the three yardsticks against which insurers should be measured. These criteria for selecting an insurer were discussed in Chap. 3.

Types of Property and Liability Insurers

The debate concerning which type of insurer is best probably will continue as long as there are different types. No attempt is made here to evaluate the performance of each, but let us at least mention the different types. First, in terms of how they sell their products, property and liability insurers are (1) independent agency companies (distribution is made through independent insurance agents), (2) so-called exclusive agency companies (which distribute their products through agents representing only the one company), and (3) direct writers (distribution is through company-employed salespeople or no salespeople). Additionally, insurers can be further subdivided on the basis of their organizational form (as described in Chap. 3) as stock insurers, mutual insurers, reciprocal exchanges, and so forth.

Personal Risk Management Process and Conclusion

In this chapter, we have attempted to describe the basic elements of property and liability insurance as they apply to nonbusiness risks. In a somewhat oversimplified way, the technique that should be followed to formulate or evaluate a personal insurance program is as follows:

1. *Discover the risks.*   Ask the question, "What can possibly happen?" Look for loss-producing hazards. Analyze and evaluate each risk particularly from a potential loss severity standpoint.

2. *Determine which risk management method(s) should be used for each risk.* That is, determine which risks can be transferred and which should be retained. Plan and implement any possible loss-prevention activities, like using smoke detectors in the home. Insurers may give premium discounts for the use of such devices.

3. *Select the insurance policies and coverages needed.*   Determine the coverages, amounts of insurance, and any endorsements needed to prevent gaps or overlaps in the insurance program.

   Also, consider ways to reduce property and liability insurance premium costs by using or increasing deductibles, dropping marginal coverages, and the like.

4. *Obtain competitive quotations.*   As we said before, too few consumers "shop" for their insurance. Having done so, select your insurer on the basis of coverage, service, and cost. The quality of service received from insurance agents or brokers is also a factor in making this choice.

5. *Evaluate and update the insurance program periodically.*   Even a perfect program of insurance coverages can quickly become outdated, possibly causing disappointment at the time of a loss. A periodic review of all policies and exposures, possibly in conjunction with an overall financial planning review, is desirable.

PART 3

Accumulating Capital and Income Tax Planning

7

Basic Investment
Principles

A basic financial objective of many people is to accumulate capital. They want capital for emergencies, various family purposes, a general investment fund, or retirement needs.

People can acquire capital in a variety of ways. Probably the most common is through an excess of family income over family outgo (that is, saving). Other important sources of capital include inheritances; gifts; growth or liquidation of business interests; growth of other investments; and receipt of distributions from pension, profit-sharing, and similar plans. Once capital not needed for more or less immediate family expenditures has been acquired, a person needs to consider how to invest his or her capital and make it grow.

The Basic
Investment Objective

The basic investment objective of most people is to *earn the maximum possible total, after-tax rate of return* on the funds available for investment, *consistent with the person's investment objectives and the investment limitations or constraints under which he or she must operate.* This statement does not mean that rate of return (yield) is the only investment consideration. There are a number of factors, other than yield, to be considered in the choice of investments. However, it does mean that, after all these factors are taken into account, most people want the highest total, after-tax rate of return they can get, given the choices open to them. We saw in Chap. 2, for example, that even a 1- or 2-percentage-point difference in yield can result in a substantial difference in the amount of capital that can be accumulated over a period of years.

Forms of Investment

People with capital usually have a wide choice of investments open to them. In Chap. 2 we classified these forms of investment into fixed-dollar investments and variable-dollar investments, depending on whether the principal and/or income are guaranteed in advance.

Therefore, in this part of the book, Chaps. 8 and 9 deal largely with variable-dollar investments, including common stock, mutual funds, real estate, other tax shelters, and other equity investments. Chapter 10 covers fixed-dollar investments, including corporate bonds and preferred stock, U.S. government securities, municipal bonds, mutual funds that invest in these kinds of assets, and other savings instruments.

Investment Directly or through Financial Intermediaries

People can invest by holding and selecting assets directly themselves in their own names or in joint names with their spouse or someone else. Then, the responsibility for investment selection, management, and performance falls on the person or persons themselves, but correspondingly they do not have to pay any direct or indirect investment management charges or fees and administrative fees.

On the other hand, people can invest through financial (investment) intermediaries, such as mutual funds, which will perform investment selection and management functions and will render certain administrative services for the person. For performing these investment management and administrative functions, the financial intermediary must levy a fee or charge in some fashion, either directly or indirectly. Some important financial intermediaries in the management of the public's investments, and the way they charge for their investment management services, and perhaps other administrative services, include the following:[1]

---

[1] There may be other costs for some of these financial intermediaries, such as sales costs (marketing loads or costs), other administrative charges, and insurance-type fees. These also must be evaluated when considering a particular intermediary in terms of what, if any, value they provide to the consumer. It also may be argued that investment options under some kinds of employee-benefit plans, such as qualified savings plans and profit-sharing plans, can also be considered like financial intermediaries in this sense. These plans are covered in Chap. 12.

Financial intermediary	Way of charging for investment management services
Investment companies (e.g., mutual funds)	Annual percentage charge against the assets in the fund (called the *expense ratio*)
Variable annuities	Annual percentage charge against the assets in the separate account
Variable life insurance	Annual percentage charge against the assets in the separate account
Revocable trusts (through banks or trust companies, either as separately administered trusts or through common trust funds)	Annual trustees' fees (usually with a minimum annual fee that is higher for separately administered trusts than for trusts invested in the bank's common trust funds)
Investment management accounts	Annual management fees (usually with a minimum annual fee)

There are, of course, other financial intermediaries that provide essentially guaranteed principal and interest assets for the public, including CDs from banks and thrift institutions, traditional or universal (nonvariable) life insurance from life insurance companies, nonvariable annuities from life insurance companies, and others. These investment media, however, do not provide separate investment management to the public for a fee. The cost of their investment management really is reflected in the interest rates they pay to the public on their respective financial instruments.

The classical arguments for investing through financial intermediaries include some or all of the following:

- Professional management
- Diversification
- Relief from the burdens of investment management
- Convenience for investments of small amounts

Balanced against these advantages is the inevitable cost of securing the services of these financial intermediaries. Thus, the real questions for the consumer in deciding whether to invest directly or through one or more financial intermediaries are: (1) Are these advantages worth the cost, and (2) does the consumer feel that he or she can do about as well, or perhaps even better, on his or her own than through the intermediary?

In answering these questions, it appears that in today's investment environment many consumers choose to place some or all of their investment assets in one or more such intermediaries, as evidenced by their tremendous growth (particularly mutual funds) in recent years. Of course, investors can diversify their decisions in this area too, and invest some part of their assets directly themselves and another part through one or more financial intermediaries. Many seem to do so. Naturally, the actual past and present investment performance of the financial intermediaries being considered as compared with other competing intermediaries and perhaps also with that of the person himself or herself with their direct investments is an important factor in this decision.

It should also be noted in discussing this subject that when an investor invests through one of these financial intermediaries, the investor really is investing in the particular kind or pool of assets being invested in by the particular intermediary. This might be common stocks (possibly of a particular type), corporate bonds, U.S. Treasury bonds, municipal bonds, other government obligations, real estate, or a balanced (diversified) portfolio. The investment risks and rewards inherent in each of these categories of assets remain, whether they are purchased directly or through a financial intermediary such as a mutual fund. Thus, in the process of asset allocation (discussed later in this chapter), either direct investments or investments through financial intermediaries can be used for each of the asset categories being considered in the asset allocation (e.g., common stocks, corporate bonds, municipal bonds, etc.).[2]

Investment and Speculation

At one time it was common to draw a rather sharp distinction between "investment" on the one hand and "speculation" on the other. For example, high-grade bonds were considered "investments," while common stocks were viewed as "speculative."

Now, however, such distinctions often are blurred. Good-grade common stocks generally are looked upon today as investment-grade securities, while low-quality ("junk") bonds generally are not. Also, many people today invest for capital gains as well as for dividends or interest income.

In general, however, the term "speculation" probably can be used to mean the purchase of securities or other assets where it is hoped that their fluctuations in value will produce relatively large profits over a comparatively short period of time. In other words, the "speculator" takes large risks in the hope of large gains.

Is speculation, as we just defined it, to be avoided by prudent investors? The answer seems to be that it depends. It depends on such things as how much of the total investment portfolio the investor wants to risk in speculation, what other kinds of assets are available for the family, how good the

---

[2] Balanced mutual funds are themselves a diversified portfolio of common stocks, preferred stocks, and bonds and so have already been allocated into these asset categories based on the fund's objectives.

investor or his or her advisors are at speculating, and whether the investor has the temperament to take speculative losses as well as speculative gains. Of course, a considerably higher rate of return should be expected on speculations than on more conservative investments to justify the greater risks inherent in speculation.

Thus, while speculation is not necessarily bad, and in fact some persons are successful speculators, it seems reasonable to say that most people are not really prepared to speculate successfully. They generally are much better off investing more conservatively for the long pull. However, this is a matter of individual choice, once the facts have been considered realistically.

Factors in the Choice of Investments

A number of factors or investment characteristics may be considered in choosing among different categories of investments or individual investments. Authorities differ somewhat on the exact number and what they are called, but the following commonly are included:

Security of principal and income
Rate of return (yield)
Marketability and liquidity
Diversification
Tax status
Size of investment units or denominations
Use as collateral for loans
Protection against creditor's claims
Callability
Freedom from care
Legality

Some of these clearly are more important than others, and their importance also varies among individual investors.

No single kind of investment is superior to all others in every one of these characteristics. In other words, there is no "perfect investment." Investments will be relatively strong in some of these characteristics but weak in others. For example, to earn a high rate of return, it is usually necessary to sacrifice security of principal and income (i.e., to take greater risks). Thus, when any investment is considered in relation to these factors, investors should do so in terms of (1) *their needs and objectives* and (2) *the characteristics of alternative investments that are available.*

Security of Principal and Income

For many investors, security of principal and income is of paramount importance. They want to be able to "get their money back" or "not lose money" on their investments. This is perfectly natural.

But when this factor is analyzed more closely, a fundamental question arises: Does "security" mean in terms of *dollars* or in terms of *purchasing power?* In the best of all worlds, we all naturally would like both. In the real world, however, the decline in the purchasing power of the dollar, caused by inflation, has become a major consideration for investors in seeking security of principal and income.

Thus, when different investments are analyzed in terms of security of principal and income, investors or their advisors really need to keep in mind five different types of risks to investment values. These are (1) financial risk, (2) market risk, (3) interest rate risk to values of existing investments, (4) interest rate risk to income from investments, and (5) purchasing power risk.

Financial Risk. This risk arises because the issuers of investments may run into financial difficulties and not be able to live up to their promises or expectations. For example, a person who buys a corporate bond runs the financial risk that the issuing corporation will default on the periodic interest payments and/or the payment of the principal amount at maturity. The buyer of common stock runs the financial risk that the corporation will reduce or eliminate its regular dividend payments in the future.

Market Risk. This is the risk arising out of price fluctuations for a whole securities market, for an industrial group, or for an individual security, regardless of the financial ability of particular issuers to pay the promised or expected investment returns. Thus, an investor may buy the common stock of a company whose earnings and financial position are good (and perhaps even are improving), only to find that the market price of the stock is falling because the investor misjudged the timing of his or her purchases and the market in general is falling (i.e., it is a "bear" market). Of course, the price of a given stock may also fall because of financial risk or some combination of financial and market risks.

But the point to remember is that even if an investor selects a high-quality stock that has prospects for good earnings growth and has low financial risk, the stock still may experience substantial price declines if the investor's market timing is bad. However, the theory of investing for the long term is that, over several such market cycles, the price (and probably also the dividends) of such a stock will show very satisfactory average annual rates of return.

Interest Rate Risk to Values of Existing Investments. This risk is a little complex and involves the price changes of *existing* investments because of changes in the general level of interest rates in the capital markets. In general, a *rise* in general market interest rates tends to cause a *decline* in market prices for existing securities, and, conversely, a *decline* in interest rates tends to cause an *increase* in market prices for existing securities. Thus, market prices for existing securities tend to move *inversely* with changes in the general level of interest rates.

It is not difficult to see why this is true. Assume, for example, that 10 years ago an investor purchased a newly issued, high-grade corporate bond with a 7 percent interest rate for $1000 (at par). The bond was to come due (mature) in 30 years. Therefore, the investor receives interest of $70 per year from the bond. At the time he or she bought the bond (10 years ago), the prevailing level of interest rates in the capital markets for bonds of this type, grade, and duration was around 7 percent; otherwise this bond issue could not have been sold successfully to the public. But in the meantime the general level of interest rates in the capital markets for bonds of this type, grade, and remaining duration has risen, and now (10 years later) let us say the prevailing interest rate for comparable bonds with a 20-year duration is about 9 percent.

What effect does this have on the existing bond? First of all, the 7 percent interest rate (coupon rate) on the bond does not change, because this was set by the terms of the bond indenture when it was originally issued. So the investor still will get interest of $70 per year until the bond matures 20 years from now. Also, when the bond matures in 20 years, he or she will get the full $1000 maturity value from the issuing corporation. Unfortunately, however, the current market price of the bond in the bond markets will have declined to somewhere in the vicinity of $816.[3] This is about what the investor would get if he or she sold it today. Why is this so if it's a $1000 bond? Because at about this price the yield to maturity (in 20 years) of this bond would be 9 percent, and this is the prevailing market interest rate. Therefore, since we assume investors can buy newly issued bonds at around 9 percent, the prices of existing bonds carrying lower interest rates must decline in the market to the point where they will offer generally comparable yields to maturity for a buyer. When the market price of bonds declines in this manner below their maturity value, they are said to be selling "at a discount" and are called "discount bonds."[4]

[3] A bond table shows that a 20-year bond with a 7 percent coupon rate will yield 9 percent to maturity if it is priced at 81.60 ($816).

[4] Bonds also may be originally issued at a discount from their ultimate maturity value, so that some or all of their "annual interest return" comes from the gradually accruing increase in their value as the bond approaches maturity. These may be called zero-coupon bonds or original-issue discount bonds and are of a different nature than the point being made in this section. However, as a practical matter, the prices of zero-coupon bonds also will fluctuate with changes in market interest rates as described in this section. In fact, their market prices will fluctuate quite drastically, because they have no coupon rate at all. Zero-coupon bonds are described in more detail on pp. 282–283 of Chap. 10.

Now, what will happen if interest rates in the capital markets should decline? Assume, for example, that one year passes and during that time the prevailing interest rate in the capital markets for comparable bonds moves from 9 to 8 percent. This would mean that the current market price of the existing 7 percent bond would rise to somewhere around $903. Again, why? Because at about this price the yield to maturity (in 19 years) of this bond would be 8 percent, and this is now the prevailing market interest rate.

The basic point here is that the market prices of existing bonds will fluctuate as the general level of interest rates changes so that their yields will be competitive with those of more recent issues.

We have illustrated the interest rate risk in terms of a 30-year corporate bond. Does the interest rate risk also apply to other types of securities? Yes, changes in the general level of interest rates in the economy have some influence on the prices of all securities. For example, when interest rates generally rise, bonds may become more attractive than common stocks for some investors, thus exerting a downward pressure on the stock market. Of course, the reverse is also true when general market interest rates fall.

In general, prices of securities that are of high quality because of their low degree of financial risk tend to be the *most* affected by changes in interest rates. This is so because the financial risk factor has relatively little impact on their market prices. Thus, the interest rate risk for securities tends to vary *inversely* with their quality in terms of financial risk. High-grade securities (in financial risk), whose prices are affected mainly by changes in interest rates, often are called *money rate securities. High-grade bonds* normally fall in this category. However, the prices of other securities, such as *high-quality preferred stocks* and *certain types of common stocks* (*such as high-grade utility, insurance, and bank stocks*), also are considerably influenced by changes in interest rates.

Further, the longer the duration or remaining duration of bonds, the more influenced their prices will tend to be by changes in market interest rates. That is because, once a bond matures, it will be paid off by the issuer at par (its maturity value), regardless of the prevailing level of interest rates. Thus, for example, a 30-year U.S. Treasury bond will be much more affected by this interest rate risk than will, say, a 5-year U.S. Treasury note.

Interest Rate Risk to Income from Investments.   From the viewpoint of maintaining the income from an investment portfolio, however, changes in interest rates may present a different kind of investment risk—that of declining interest (or dividend) income from (1) bonds and preferred stocks that are "called" (redeemed) prior to maturity by their issuers and (2) securities that mature when interest rates are lower than when they were issued or purchased.

With respect to the "call risk," the issuers of callable bonds and preferred stocks may redeem them when comparable market interest rates fall significantly below the coupon rates being paid on the securities. Thus, when securities are callable, the issuers (e.g., corporations or municipalities) can pay them off (redeem them) before maturity under certain conditions. While this may save interest expense for the issuer of the called security, it clearly is disadvantageous for the holder of the called security, because the holder now must reinvest the principal from the called security at the present lower market yields. Thus, for example, suppose that Ms. Hernandez invested $40,000 in investment-grade, 30-year municipal bonds that paid 9 percent interest (i.e., the coupon rate on the bonds was 9 percent). Thus, her interest income from the bonds was $3600 per year. Assume further that the bonds are callable at par (i.e., they can be redeemed by the municipality for the $1000 face amount of each bond) any time after 10 years from when they were issued. Suppose now that 10 years after these bonds were issued, interest rates for comparable bonds (i.e., 20-year, investment-grade, callable municipal bonds) have fallen to 6 percent. Under these conditions, it is very likely that the state or municipality will call these bonds and pay Ms. Hernandez their $40,000 face amount in return for her surrendering the bonds to the state or municipality. Now Ms. Hernandez has her $40,000 back, but if she wants to invest in similar bonds, she can only secure 6 percent interest (or interest income of $2400 per year), rather than the $3600 per year she enjoyed before her former bonds were called.

It can be seen that this "call risk" is important when investors would like to "lock-in" relatively high current interest rates or yields for a reasonably long period of time, such as during their retirement years or in saving for a child's education. Thus, the "call risk" tends to be more significant for longer-term bonds than for shorter-term bonds.

The only real protection for investors from this "call risk" is to buy securities with call protection or at least partial call protection. How to secure such *call protection* is discussed in greater detail on pp. 203–204 of this chapter.

The other aspect of this kind of interest rate risk is from securities and other investments that mature or come due when interest rates are lower than when they were issued or purchased. The investor then must reinvest the proceeds at lower yields. This "reinvestment risk" really arises from investing in or holding shorter-term securities and other investments. Thus, for example, suppose that Mr. and Mrs. Wilson placed $50,000 of their retirement savings in three-year insured CDs (certificates of deposit) with a local bank that then paid 8 percent interest. Thus, their annual interest income from these CDs was $4000. However, at the end of the three-year period when the CDs have come due and the Wilsons are ready to "roll them over" into new CDs, assume that the economy is in recession, the Federal Reserve has pushed shorter-term interest rates down to try to stimulate a recovery, and the interest rates currently being paid on comparable CDs and other similarly secure investments are around 4½ percent. Thus, if the Wilsons place their $50,000 into comparable new CDs, their annual interest income from the CDs will drop from $4000 to $2250, or about a 44 percent decline. Of course, if shorter-term interest rates should rise, the reverse of the above situation would be true, and the Wilsons would be better off with their shorter-term investments. Unfortunately, as with the stock market, no one can really foretell the future course of interest rates.

A protection for investors from this "reinvestment risk" is to buy longer-term bonds or other securities with full call protection or at least partial call protection so as to lock in current interest rates for a reasonable period of time. In this way, the investor at least can be sure of the present interest rates for a significant period of time (say, 15 to 30 years), regardless of what market rates may do. Also, if market rates should fall, the market values of the long-term bonds would rise, giving the investor a capital gain. Of course, the downsides of this strategy are that if market interest rates should rise, (1) the market prices of the investor's long-term bonds would fall (sometimes dramatically) and the investor would suffer capital losses prior to the bonds' maturities (i.e., suffer the effects of the previously described interest rate risk to the values of existing investments), and (2) the investor would lose his or her opportunity to invest at the higher interest rates until the long-term investments matured or came due.

Thus, there is no perfect answer to this interest rate risk dilemma. If one expects market interest rates to rise, it is better to be in shorter-term bonds and other investments (i.e., to shorten maturities). On the other hand, if one expects market interest rates to fall, it is better to be in longer-term bonds and other investments with adequate call protection (i.e., to lengthen maturities). The problem is, of course, that no one knows for sure which way interest rates in the economy will go in the future and what the relationship between short-term rates and long-term rates will be (i.e., what the yield curve will look like).

A Diversification Strategy to Deal with Interest Rate Risk.   In view of the uncertainties concerning interest rates just noted, one possible approach for the risk-averse investor is to diversify the bond or bond and CD portion (i.e., the fixed-income portion) of his or her overall investment portfolio according to the maturity of the instruments in the bond portfolio. Thus, just as an example, the bond and CD portion of an investor's overall portfolio (asset allocation) might be allocated with regard to maturity as follows:

Maturity range	Percentage of bond and CD portion of the overall portfolio
1–5 years (short-term bonds)	33⅓%
5–15 years (intermediate-term bonds)	33⅓%
15–30 years (long-term bonds)	33⅓%

With this kind of allocation, there would be some protection for the investor no matter which way interest rates went. If market rates declined, the investor would benefit at the long end of his or her portfolio and be harmed only at the short end. Further, the portion of the portfolio with longer maturities could provide a locked-in interest income stream for the investor for a long period of time. On the other hand, if market interest rates rose, the investor would not be greatly harmed at the short end of his or her portfolio and significantly harmed in terms of price only at the long end, although there would be at least some bond price declines at all maturity levels. Further, at the short end of the portfolio, there would be at least some bonds or CDs maturing each year whose maturity values then could be reinvested at the current higher interest rates.

Finally, the allocation of maturities in the bond portion of the portfolio could be periodically reviewed and possibly changed by the investor, possibly with the advice of his or her advisers, in light of their expectations for future changes in interest rates. If rates are expected to rise, relatively greater weight can be given to shorter maturities, with the reverse being the case if rates are expected to decline. Or the investor can simply stick with his or her initial allocation and not try to "outguess" the economy. This is a matter of judgment and is up to the individual and his or her advisers.

Purchasing Power Risk.   This is uncertainty over the future purchasing power of the income and principal from an investment. The purchasing power of income and principal depends on changes in the general price level in the economy. When prices rise, purchasing power declines; and when prices decline, purchasing power rises. Since around 1940, the United States has experienced a rather steady inflationary trend, given some periods of general price stability, with a consequent generally consistent decline in the purchasing power of the dollar. This has made inflation, and hence purchasing power risk, a matter of great concern to investors and financial planners.

The economic fact of persistent price inflation over such a long period has led many investors to seek investments that they believe will protect them against severe declines in purchasing power. Thus, investors seek investments whose principal and income they hope will increase during an inflationary period, so that the purchasing power of their investment dollars at least will not decline. Such investments are often called "hedges against inflation" or "inflation hedges."

The purchasing power risk to investment values is a very real and important one, but the concept of some investments being good "hedges against inflation" must be considered with care. First, no investment is a perfect "hedge against inflation." That is, no investment currently available in the United States can be counted upon to fluctuate at all times so that its purchasing power will be maintained. Second, while some types of investments, such as common stocks, *may* increase in value (both market price and dividends) at the same time that the general price level is rising, there is no assurance that this will be true for an individual stock, or several stocks, or the stocks of a whole industry group. Third, no "sure" relationship has been proved between movements in consumer prices and movements in, say, common stock prices. The only thing that can be said is that economic studies have shown that over a long period of years, broad indexes of common stock prices have *tended* to move in the same general direction as consumer prices. There have been a number of times, however, during which common stock prices and consumer prices did *not* move together. Finally, *an investor's goal is not really to "hedge against inflation," but rather to obtain the best investment returns possible, consistent with other objectives.* What is really important is whether an investment can be expected to produce an attractive total rate of return relative to other available investment opportunities. Common stocks as a group generally have done that over substantial periods of time.

It is true, however, that certain equity-type investments, such as common stocks, real estate, business ventures, commodities, collectibles, and others, *may* increase in value during an inflationary period and thus preserve the purchasing power of the returns from the investment. On the other hand, fixed-dollar-type investments, such as bonds, CDs, savings accounts, savings bonds, nonvariable life insurance cash values, and nonvariable annuity cash values, normally will not increase in value during an inflationary period. But in investment decision making, investors or their advisors are probably better off to consider how a given investment is expected to perform in the future, the other investment opportunities, and what the investors' needs are, rather than worrying about whether the investment is called a "hedge against inflation" or not.

Also, it is important to remember that while, in the past, consumer prices generally have been rising (inflation), there have been periods during which prices were stable and even declined, and that it is possible for them to decline in the future (deflation or depression). While fixed-dollar assets will *lose* purchasing power during an *inflationary period,* they will *gain* purchasing power during a *deflationary period.* Therefore, *investors or their advisors should never ignore the possibility of a deflationary economic period in personal financial planning.* Proper planning considers all possible general economic environments.

No one kind of investment should be considered capable of successfully meeting all these investment risks. An investment considered "low risk" with respect to one or more of these risks will almost invariably be considered "high risk" with respect to others. To illustrate this important point, various types of investment media have been graded in Table 7.1 as "low," "average," or "high" in terms of how they are affected by the basic investment risks. Of course, any such classification is partly a matter of opinion, and all investment media are not shown in the table. However, what is important is the recognition that no single investment vehicle can be "low"

Table 7.1. Classification of Selected Investment Vehicles in Terms of the Degree of "Risk" They Have in the Face of Different Kinds of Investment Risks

Investment vehicle	Financial risk	Market risk	Interest rate risk: value of existing investments	Interest rate risk: income from investments	Purchasing power risk
Savings accounts (Insured by FDIC)	Low	Low	Low	High	High
Certificates of deposit (insured by FDIC)	Low	Low	Low	Medium	High
Money market funds or accounts	Low	Low	Low	High	High
Annuity cash values (nonvariable)	Low	Low	Low	High (or medium)	High
High-grade corporate bonds (with some call protection)	Low	Low	High	Low	High
High-grade common stocks	Low	High (or medium)	Medium	Low	Low (assuming a broadly diversified portfolio)
Speculative common stocks	High	High	Medium	Low (or medium)	Low (or medium)

risk in terms of all these investment risks. This clearly suggests *the need for diversification* in an investment portfolio.

Rate of Return

The primary purpose of investing is to earn a return on one's capital. This return can take a variety of forms, including interest, dividends, rents, business profits, and capital gains. Investors normally want to maximize *their total after-tax investment returns* (investment income and capital gains combined). But to increase expected total investment return at any given time, an investor normally must take greater investment risks. Thus, yield and degree of investment risk are directly related—*the higher the yield, the greater the risk*. Unhappily, investors cannot have their cake and eat it, too.

Since an investor wants to maximize total investment returns, it is important to know what those returns are. For this purpose, it is helpful to divide investment returns into investment income and capital gains. We should also distinguish between before-tax and after-tax returns.

Annual Rates of Return (Yield).   There are several ways of measuring the annual rates of return represented by the periodic income from an investment. They include (1) the *nominal yield,* (2) the *current yield,* and (3) the *yield to maturity.*

Nominal Yield.   This is the annual amount of interest or dividends paid compared with a security's par or face value, shown as follows:

$$\text{Nominal yield} = \frac{\text{annual interest or dividends}}{\text{investment's par or face value}}$$

The nominal yield is often called the "coupon rate" when applied to bonds and the "dividend rate" when applied to preferred stocks with a par value. For example, a bond with a maturity value (face amount) of $1000 that pays interest of $70 per year has a nominal yield (coupon rate) of 7 percent, and a $100 par value preferred stock that pays dividends of $6.50 per year has a nominal yield (dividend rate) of 6½ percent. Nominal yield really has no meaning in connection with common stocks and other forms of investment.

Current Yield.   This measure of investment return generally is more significant to an investor than the nominal yield, and the current yield normally is expressed as the annual amount of income received from an investment compared with its current market price or value. This is the measure of yield normally used for common and preferred stocks and frequently used for bonds as well. It can be calculated as follows:

$$\text{Current yield} = \frac{\text{annual investment income}}{\text{investment's current price or value}}$$

An investment's current yield normally will change over time because its market price will fluctuate and its annual investment income may change.

As examples of current yield, a common stock selling at $50 per share with an annual dividend rate of $2.00 has a current yield of 4 percent, and a 6 percent bond (coupon rate) that is selling for $700 (quoted as 70 in the bond markets) has a current yield of about 8.6 percent.[5]

Yield to Maturity.   Another measure of yield commonly applied to bonds is the yield to maturity, sometimes called the "net yield," "effective yield," or "true yield." Bonds have a definite maturity date when their par or face amount (usually $1000 per bond) is to be paid off by the issuer. However, investors can purchase bonds for less than their maturity value (at a discount) or for more than their maturity value (at a premium). Thus, the concept of yield to maturity for a bond can be illustrated by adding the annual gain (discount) or deducting the annual loss (premium) that will be realized if the bond is held to maturity from the bond's annual interest income. The result is then divided by the average investment in the bond. To illustrate the principle involved, *approximate* formulas for calculating yield to maturity can be shown as follows.

For a bond selling at a discount:

Yield to maturity

$$= \frac{\text{annual coupon interest} + (\text{discount} \div \text{number of years to maturity})}{(\text{current market price of bond} + \text{par value}) \div 2}$$

For a bond selling at a premium:

Yield to maturity

$$= \frac{\text{annual coupon interest} - (\text{premium} \div \text{number of years to maturity})}{(\text{current market price of bond} + \text{par value}) \div 2}$$

Thus, for bonds selling at a discount, the yield to maturity is greater than either the current yield or the coupon rate. For bonds selling at a premium, the opposite is true: The yield to maturity is less than either the current yield or the coupon rate. Some examples will illustrate this. (These yields to maturity are taken from a bond table and not from the approximate formulas given above.)

First, assume an 8 percent bond maturing in 10 years that currently is selling for $920. For this bond, the

Coupon rate = 8%

Current yield = 8.69%

Yield to maturity = 9.25%

---

[5] Annual bond interest of $60 ($1000 maturity value × 6%) divided by $700 equals 0.0857, or about 8.6%.

On the other hand, assume a 12 percent bond maturing in 10 years that currently is selling for $1159. For this bond, the

$$\text{Coupon rate} = 12\%$$

$$\text{Current yield} = 10.35\%$$

$$\text{Yield to maturity} = 9.50\%$$

When a bond is selling at or near par, the coupon rate, current yield, and yield to maturity will be essentially the same. In most cases, when an investor plans to hold a bond until maturity, the yield to maturity is considered the most accurate measure of annual investment return.

The current yields for stocks and bonds are often shown in financial newspapers and similar sources. Bond yields to maturity for different coupon rates, bond prices, and remaining periods to maturity are available from "bond yield tables" like the one used for the calculations just given. Investment houses also supply information on the yields to maturity for bonds they have for sale, and other financial publications may contain this information for the bonds whose prices they report.

Capital Gains Rates of Return. People may invest for capital gains as well as regular annual income. In fact, in the past some investors, particularly those in the higher income tax brackets, were interested primarily in capital gains. The Tax Reform Act of 1986, as amended by the Revenue Reconciliation Act of 1990, has diminished the attractiveness from a tax standpoint of taking investment returns as long-term capital gains. This is because for 1991 and thereafter, net capital gains will be taxed at a maximum income tax rate of 28 percent, as compared with a maximum 31 percent tax rate for ordinary income. See Chap. 11 for a more detailed discussion.

However, despite this relatively small spread in income tax rates, there still may be good reasons for a policy of investing for capital gains. Capital gains are not taxed until actually realized (and recognized for tax purposes). Therefore, an investor can determine when, if ever, the gain is to be taxed. Second, if an investor does not sell and realize a capital gain on appreciated property, but instead holds the property until his or her death, the estate or heirs will get a stepped-up income tax basis in the property equal to its value for estate tax purposes (e.g., the date of death value), and the capital gain prior to death will forever escape capital gains taxation. Third, well-selected investments and good investment planning often will produce capital gains in any event. Finally, an individual may have adequate earnings or income from other sources and not need investment income currently, and so may be able to make investments for relatively higher hoped-for capital gains.

But the rates of return from capital gains are difficult to measure. First, no one can know what, if any, capital gain there may be in the future on an investment. If the investment is successful, such a return can be very handsome. But if the investment turns sour, a loss may be suffered. Thus, an investor really can reason only from past experience with similar investments and from an analysis of future developments to estimate what the hoped-for capital gains might be.

Second, even measuring past capital gains rates of return can be difficult and confusing. A friend may proudly remark, for example, "Boy, I really made a killing in the stock market. I bought XYZ Company at $20, and now it's worth $40 per share." But the listener does not know how long it took him to double his money, and this makes quite a difference. Also, the investor should compare such capital growth with, for example, what could have been earned, or can currently be earned, by simply putting the same investment dollars in an insured certificate of deposit, or by investing in high-quality corporate bonds, or by investing in investment-grade tax-free municipal bonds that involve less financial and market risk. Finally, most investors suffer some capital losses as well as realize capital gains. It sometimes is easy psychologically for an investor to remember successes but to forget losses when mentally calculating how well he or she has done with capital gains.

One approach to measuring capital gains rates of return is to estimate an *average annual compound rate of gain* from capital gains for the period of time an investment has been held. Then, the *total annual investment return* may be determined by adding the yield from investment income to the rate of gain (or loss) from capital gains (or losses). An approximate *average annual compound rate of gain* for a security that will be satisfactory for the purposes of most individual investors can be estimated by referring to a compound interest table.[6] Thus, if it is known *how much* an investment has grown over *how many years*, one can estimate roughly what the annual compound rate of gain (interest) has been over those years to produce the given capital growth. For example, let us say that the friend who bought XYZ Company common expands a little on his previous statement and indicates that he bought the stock 10 years ago at $20 per share and now it is worth $40 per share. In other words, his capital growth has been 100 percent in 10 years, or his investment has doubled over this period. If we look at a compound interest table (or use a calculator), we can see that he has had about a 7 percent average annual rate of capital gain from this particular stock over the 10 years. The so-called *rule of 72* can also be used to estimate an average annual rate of gain. This is done by dividing the number of years it takes an investment to double in value into 72. The result (quo-

---

[6] A compound interest table shows the amount $1 will accumulate to at various rates of interest over various time periods.

tient) is approximately the annual rate of return over those years. In this situation, for example, $72 \div 10 = 7.2$ percent per year. Properly programmed calculators and personal computers also can be used to develop such data. Using such a calculator, the average annual rate of gain in the above illustration is determined to be 7.18 percent.

If in addition, during this 10-year period, the current yield from the dividends paid on XYZ Company common has averaged, say, 5 percent, the *total annual investment return* on the stock for this time period would be roughly 12 percent. Of course, there is no assurance this return will be repeated in the future, but at least the investor can know how he has done in the past to help him make intelligent investment decisions for the future. He now would be in a much better position to compare this stock's total yield with that of alternative investments, such as bonds, CDs, and real estate.

After-Tax Yields.   Up to this point, we have not considered the effect of income taxes on investment returns. As a practical matter, however, investors want to know what their investment returns are after taxes. This is what they get to keep. Seeking this information complicates comparing investment yields because different kinds of investments are taxed in different ways and individual investors can be in varying income tax brackets. For purposes of estimating after-tax yields, we can view the returns from investments as (1) income that is taxable currently as ordinary income, (2) income that is entirely tax-exempt, and (3) returns that are taxable when realized (and recognized) as capital gains.[7]

Investment income that is fully taxable as ordinary income, such as interest on savings accounts, certificates of deposit, taxable money market funds or accounts, and corporate bonds, as well as dividends from common stocks, is easy to express on an after-tax basis. The *after-tax yield* can be determined by multiplying the current yield by 1 minus the investor's highest marginal income tax rate. Thus, if a married taxpayer's highest tax bracket is 28 percent, a CD paying 6 percent interest would provide the following after-tax yield.

$$\text{After-tax yield} = \text{current yield } (1 - \text{tax rate})$$

$$= 0.06 \ (1 - 0.28)$$

$$= 0.06 \ (0.72)$$

$$= 0.0432 \text{ or } 4.32\%$$

---

[7] This is intentionally a somewhat simplified classification. Some forms of investment income, for example, are entirely tax-exempt for regular income tax purposes but are a tax-preference item for Alternative Minimum Tax (AMT) purposes. See Chap. 11 for a discussion of the income taxation of different kinds of investments.

The after-tax yield for a fully tax-exempt investment equals the current yield. Thus, the after-tax yield for a 6 percent municipal bond is 6 percent. It is common practice in investment literature also to express what a fully taxable security would have to earn to equal the yield from a tax-free security at different income tax rates. For example, a 6 percent tax-free yield received by a married investor in a 28 percent tax bracket really is worth 8.33 percent to him or her on a fully taxable basis.[8]

It becomes more complicated to determine after-tax yields when investment returns are in the form of capital gains (or losses) or are partly ordinary income and partly capital gains (or losses). Some examples are when an investor purchases common stock or real estate that appreciates (or depreciates) in value or a corporate or U.S. government bond at a discount and holds it until maturity. The impact of capital gains taxation on investment decisions can be quite complex, depending on the circumstances, and this subject is covered in greater detail in Chap. 11.

Marketability and Liquidity

Marketability and liquidity are important factors in choosing investments for many people. Life is uncertain, and people want to know how readily they can dispose of their investments and how much they can get for them if they do.

Sometimes the terms "marketability" and "liquidity" are used to mean almost the same thing, but they do have an important difference in meaning. *Marketability* means the ability of an investor to find a ready market should he or she wish to sell or otherwise dispose of the investment. *Liquidity* means that an investment is not only marketable but also highly stable in price. In other words, an asset is liquid when an investor feels reasonably sure he or she can dispose of it quickly *and also* can receive for it approximately the amount put into it.

Some investments are neither marketable nor liquid, others are marketable but not very liquid, while still others are both marketable and liquid. In Table 7.2 various types of assets are graded for both marketability and liquidity. Of course, these classifications are somewhat subjective, but they do give a general idea of the relative positions of these types of assets with respect to these investment characteristics. Naturally, the degree of marketability or liquidity of some of these assets depends on the particular circumstances.

---

[8] Any similar equivalent yields can be calculated by dividing the tax-free yield by 1 minus the investor's highest marginal income tax rate. In this case, $6\% \div (1 - 0.28, \text{ or } 0.72) = 8.33\%$. These are sometimes referred to as the taxable equivalent yields. The highest marginal income tax rate used also can include state and local top marginal income tax rates if the income from the security also is exempt from these taxes as well as from the federal income tax.

Table 7.2. Classification of Assets in Terms
of Marketability and Liquidity

Asset	Marketability	Liquidity
Savings accounts	Good	Good
Money market funds or accounts	Good	Good
Life insurance cash values (through policy loans)	Good	Good
Corporate bonds (actively traded)	Good	Average
Municipal bonds (actively traded)	Good (or average)	Average
U.S. government securities:		
Short term (including T-bills)	Good	Good
Long term	Good	Average
Savings bonds (e.g., Series EE)	Good	Good
Common stock (actively traded)	Good	Poor
Real estate	Average (or poor)	Poor
Annuity cash values	Good	Poor
Business interests (proprietorships, partnerships, stock in close corporations)	Poor	Poor

It is clearly preferable to hold highly marketable or liquid investments rather than less marketable or liquid ones. But the investor normally has to "trade" some yield for marketability and liquidity. That is, highly marketable or liquid assets usually yield less than less marketable or liquid ones. So an important question in investment planning becomes: "Is marketability or liquidity important enough to give up some yield?" This, of course, depends on the investor's overall circumstances and objectives, as well as on his or her overall liquid position.

Investors normally desire to keep some percentage (or amount) of their overall investment portfolio in liquid assets (also called cash equivalents). The percentage to be so held depends on the investor's current asset allocation strategy, as described on pp. 209–214 of this chapter.

Diversification

Diversification is an important investment policy to consider in constructing an investment portfolio, as well as in other aspects of financial planning. The basic purpose of diversification is to reduce or minimize an investor's risk of loss. It is primarily a defensive type of policy.

Investment diversification can take a number of forms. One is to *diversify an investment portfolio among the various types of investment media*—such as common stocks, bonds, CDs, money market funds and other liquid assets, life insurance and annuities, real estate, and perhaps other tax shelters. The prices or values of all types of investment media do not go up or down at the same time or in the same magnitude, and so investors can protect themselves against economic fluctuations in this way.

An example of this is the way the prices of common stocks and high-grade bonds may move in opposite directions over a business cycle. During periods of economic prosperity, the stock market generally rises because of increasing business and higher corporate profits and dividends. However, the prices of high-grade bonds often decline during prosperity because interest rates generally are rising (the interest rate risk) as the result of increasing demands for capital at that time. During recession or depression, the opposite occurs: Stock prices fall because of declining business, but high-grade bond prices tend to rise because of falling interest rates, because the demand for capital diminishes then. This traditionally has been known as the *contracyclical price movement of high-grade bonds.*

This traditional relationship between the movement of stock prices and investment-grade bond prices has held true during some time periods but not others. For example, during the Depression years of the 1930s, the average annual rate of total return on high-grade bonds was substantially higher than that for common stocks (which was actually negative for that decade). Correspondingly, during the generally prosperous 1950s and 1960s, the average annual rates of total return on common stocks far outpaced those of high-grade bonds. However, during the 1980s, both common stocks and high-grade bonds had substantial average annual rates of total return, although the return from stocks was better than the return for bonds.[9]

An investor may also want to diversify among types of investment media to balance the portfolio between marketable and less marketable investments and between fixed-dollar and variable-dollar investments. It is normally considered sound practice to diversify investments among several types of investment media.

Another form is *diversification within a particular class or type of investment.* For example, the investor may invest in the common stocks of several companies, may buy some "growth"-type stocks and some stocks to be held primarily for income, may purchase some "speculative" issues but generally invest in more stable stocks, and so on. Use of financial intermediaries for this form of diversification can be quite effective.

A third form is *diversification of investments according to maturity.* For securities with a fixed maturity date (such as bonds or CDs), maturities can be spaced so that there will be securities of various durations coming due periodically. This way new principal will be available to invest periodically,

---

[9] Just to complete the picture, during the war and readjustment years of the 1940s, stocks performed much better than bonds; and during the 1970s, they performed about the same, with high-grade bonds doing somewhat better than stocks.

during periods of high and low interest rates, thus reducing the interest rate risks. This form of diversification was discussed and illustrated earlier in this chapter on pp. 190–191. Investors may also want to buy other securities, such as common stocks, from time to time rather than all at once, so that the market risk can be spread over both good and bad markets.

Another aspect of investment diversification is to reduce the overall risk level of inherently highly risky investments. Examples of this arise in connection with the purchase of units of certain tax-sheltered investments (such as oil and gas limited partnerships, for example) and in buying high-risk ("junk") bonds. The whole concept behind an individual's placing a percentage (probably a relatively small percentage) of his or her overall investment portfolio in these inherently very risky forms of investment is that the losses on some of them will be more than offset by the higher returns on others, with the result that the overall return on the total investment in these risky asset categories will be quite satisfactory relative to other investment categories. But to do this, there must be a broad enough spread or number of these investments so that the good will have a chance to outweigh the bad. Thus, regardless of any other merits or demerits of this investment philosophy, there must be a broad enough spread of risk (diversification) to give it a chance to work. This makes diversification particularly important for these highly risky categories of assets. Thus, in junk bond investing, for example, use of mutual funds or other financial intermediaries providing diversification can be particularly valuable for many individual investors.

How can diversification be secured in an investment portfolio? Here are several ways.

1. Investments can be made through financial institutions (intermediaries) that themselves diversify their investments. Such institutions include:
   a. Investment companies (including mutual funds)
   b. Life insurance companies, in connection with variable life insurance, variable annuities, and the like
   c. Real estate investment trusts (REITs)
2. One or more securities or units can be purchased periodically over a long period of time (for example, dollar cost averaging in buying common stocks, as discussed in Chap. 8).
3. A personal trust (or advisory account) can be established with authority for the trustee to invest in a bank's common trust fund(s).

Tax Status

As we saw above, an investment's tax status can have an important bearing on its attractiveness. This factor is discussed more fully in Chap. 11.

Size of Investment Units (or Denominations)

In some cases, an investment may be made only in certain minimum amounts. For example, municipal bonds frequently are sold in lots of $5000 or more, and participations in certain tax-sheltered investments often are limited to some minimum amount, such as $5000, $10,000, or substantially more in some cases. Also, direct investments in real estate require a down payment and payment of closing costs, as well as adequate mortgage financing. These minimum size constraints may make diversification difficult for direct investments in some cases.

Use as Collateral for Loans

Many forms of property can be used as collateral for loans. Some kinds are more readily available than others, however. Good-quality securities (other than municipal bonds), life insurance policies, and improved real estate may serve well in this regard. However, some types of property, such as speculative common stocks, unimproved real estate, and closely held business interests, may be relatively poor for collateral purposes. Also, tax-free municipal bonds can involve tax pitfalls when used as collateral for loans, or even when they are owned and other property is used as collateral for loans, as is discussed in greater detail in Chap. 11.

Creditor Protection

Some assets can be arranged to provide their owners and/or their owners' heirs with protection against the claims of creditors in the event of bankruptcy or financial difficulties. So-called spendthrift clauses in life insurance settlement options and personal trust agreements are examples.

Callability

As discussed earlier in this chapter on pp. 188–189, callability (or redeemability) can be an important factor when investing in bonds and preferred stocks. Many issuers of corporate and municipal bonds have reserved the right to call or redeem (i.e., pay off) the bonds before maturity, usually subject to certain conditions. Use of such call provisions by these issuers of bonds varies with economic conditions. They tend to be used more often when market interest rates are high and for longer-term bonds. Most issues of preferred stock also are callable. On the other hand, most U.S. government bonds and some general-obligation municipal bonds and corporate bonds are not callable prior to maturity.

Callable bonds and preferred stocks are usually redeemed by their issuers when market interest rates are below the coupon rates of the callable securities. The issuing corporation can then refinance the called securities in the capital market at the lower, prevailing interest rates and thus save money. However, as explained earlier in this chapter, this is disadvantageous to the holder of the called securities. *Thus, other things being equal, securities that are not callable, or that have limited callability, are more attractive to investors than are callable securities.* But, as is so often true, other things may not be equal because callable bonds and preferreds normally provide investors with higher yields than comparable noncallable securities. Thus, it is really a trade-off between call protection and higher yield. However, as noted earlier, call protection often is important for individual investors who need to be assured of a certain income stream from their investment portfolio (i.e., they need to lock in a certain yield).

What can investors do to protect themselves against the threat of callability? Here are some ideas.

1. They can buy noncallable securities (such as U.S. Treasury bonds). However, municipal bonds, corporate bonds and preferreds may be callable, and callable securities normally provide higher yields.

2. They can buy securities with strong "call protection."[10] However, they will probably have to pay a "price" in terms of lower yields for strong call protection.

3. They can buy bonds or preferreds selling at a "deep discount" from their maturity or par value. (See Chap. 10 for a discussion of "deep discount" bonds.) However, sometimes such "deep discount" securities are scarce in the bond markets, and again the investor normally must accept a lower yield on them than for comparable securities selling around par.

4. They may be able to diversify their purchases over time so that only a small portion of the portfolio will be called at any one time.

5. They may purchase high-quality, high-yielding common stocks which, of course, have no maturity date and are not subject to any callability. However, the dividends on any common stocks conceivably could be cut or eliminated by the corporation.

Freedom from Care

Freedom from care really has two dimensions: (1) freedom from the time and work involved in managing investments, and (2) freedom from worry and concern over investment results. These freedoms are quite important to some people but of little or no concern to others. Much depends on the

---

[10] The types of call protection used in bonds and preferred stocks are covered in Chap. 10.

investor's interests, financial position, experience, education, time available from business or professional pursuits, personal situation, and psycho-
logical makeup.

Personal Investment Management

Having outlined some general factors to consider in choosing investments,
we now come to the overall question: How can personal investment management be carried out? In this regard, personal investment management
can be broken down into the following fundamental areas: (1) considering
investment constraints or limitations and *investor attitudes*, (2) defining
investment objectives, (3) establishing *investment policies* (including an *asset
allocation* strategy) in light of the constraints and objectives, and (4) *implementing those policies.*

Investment Constraints and Investor Attitudes

Every investor has certain personal factors that govern or limit how he or
she should invest. As we said at the beginning of the chapter, the basic
investment problem is to maximize investment returns within the framework of these personal financial constraints. Here are some of the common
investment constraints that might be considered in the process of personal
investment management.

1. The investor's *ability to risk loss of investment income and principal.* This
   in turn is influenced by a number of personal factors, such as:
   a. Earnings and the nature and stability of his or her employment
   b. Other sources of income
   c. Age, health, family responsibilities, and other obligations
   d. The person's overall assets, liabilities, and net worth position (i.e., the
      personal balance sheet)
   e. Ownership of closely held business interests or other relatively non-
      marketable assets
   f. Any likely (or possible) inheritances
   g. Plans to use investment principal for particular purposes, such as edu-
      cation expenses, retirement, travel, other large expenditures, future
      gifts, and estate settlement costs
   h. The extent to which current investment income is needed for current
      living expenses
   i. The degree and duration of price inflation (or deflation) the person
      feels are being risked, and how other assets and sources of income will
      be affected by inflation (or deflation)

2. The *degree of liquidity and marketability* needed in the portfolio.
3. How well the investor is *able to weather the ups and particularly the downs in the securities markets.* In other words, can he or she afford to hold onto securities during a bear market and wait for better times?
4. The investor's *overall tax and estate status,* including consideration of his or her spouse's income and estate tax positions.
5. The *quality of available investment management services.*
6. The investor's *attitudes and emotional tolerance for risk.*

Investment Objectives

Making investment decisions without defining the person's objectives is like trying to steer a ship without a rudder. Consistent investment decisions probably will not be made in the absence of a clear understanding of the desired investment objectives. While this seems obvious, many investors, in fact, do make their investment decisions on such tenuous grounds as "A golfing buddy told me confidentially that this stock is bound to 'go,' " or "A broker called me and told me I should get in on this one," or "This stock just looks good," without any consistent idea of their objectives in mind. Of course, investment objectives are just one part of overall financial objectives.

Investment objectives are shaped by a person's investment constraints and are influenced by many personal factors that vary among individuals and families. In turn, they tend to shape the asset allocation strategy to be considered later in this chapter. Further, people's investment objectives normally change over their life cycles and as circumstances change. There are, however, certain common patterns of investment objectives into which people frequently fall. The following can be listed as typical of these.

Maximum Current Income. This objective emphasizes current yield over other factors. It is typical of people who must rely on investment income for part or all of their livelihood, such as retired persons.

Preservation of Capital. This is a commonly heard objective, and in its purest form means that the dollar value of the portfolio should not fall. This rather rigorous form of this objective would serve to limit considerably the investment vehicles that are used in the portfolio to those with guaranteed principal. And, in fact, some people mean just that. However, in a more flexible form it means investing so that the potential for declines in the overall value of the portfolio is minimized. In this form, this is a common and quite logical objective. It also is consistent with some of the other objectives stated here.

Reasonable Current Income with Moderate Capital Growth.   This modifies the first objective in that current investment income is not the predominant aim. While current income is important, capital gains also are sought.

Long-Term Capital Growth.   This objective aims primarily at capital gains over a relatively long period of time. It implies investment in securities and other assets that are expected to produce relatively consistent capital growth over the long pull. This kind of objective is typical of younger business and professional men and women who do not need current investment income to meet their living expenses.

Aggressive Capital Growth.   This objective seeks maximum capital growth and implies making riskier investments with considerable investment analysis and management. Current income is of minor importance.

Tax-Sheltered Investments.   In some cases, a person's income tax bracket makes tax-free or tax-sheltered investments attractive, assuming that these investments are also economically attractive purely as investments.

These objectives are, of course, not mutually exclusive, and an investor often will have some combination of them. The investor might, for example, seek relatively conservative long-term capital growth for the bulk of his or her securities portfolio but hold another portion for more aggressive capital growth. Or an investor in a higher income tax bracket may place, say, one-half of his or her portfolio in municipal bonds (or tax-sheltered investments) and the other half in growth-type securities. Or the objective of preservation of capital normally might be quite consistent with the objectives of maximum current income or reasonable current income with moderate capital growth. There are many possible combinations depending on individual circumstances. What is important, however, is for investors to understand what their objectives are and to follow them.

Investment Policies

Investors should establish their investment policies to meet their objectives within the framework of their investment constraints. But in setting investment policies, the following kinds of questions should be considered:

1. To what extent should *aggressive* or *defensive* investment policies be followed?
2. How much liquidity and marketability should be built into the portfolio?
3. To what extent, and in what manner, should the portfolio be diversified?
4. What *kinds and grades* of securities should be included in the portfolio?
5. How should the investor react to changing market prices of securities? That is, what policy or policies should be followed with respect to *investment timing?*

Aggressive versus Defensive Investment Policies.   There are investment risks (financial, interest rate, market, or purchasing power) inherent
in any kind of investment policy, but some approaches or attitudes toward
investment policy clearly imply more risk taking than others. Thus, we can
broadly categorize investment policies as being aggressive or defensive in
nature. *Aggressive policies* generally seek to maximize investment profits
and, thus, accept above-average investment risks. On the other hand, *defensive policies* seek to minimize investment risks and, thus, accept correspondingly lower profits.

In general terms, aggressive and defensive investment policies can be distinguished on the basis of the following characteristics.

Quality of Securities Purchased.   To maximize returns, an aggressive
portfolio includes securities of greater financial risk than would be true of
a defensive portfolio. Thus, the aggressive investor is willing to take more
financial risk.

Attitude toward Investment Timing.   Again, to earn maximum returns,
an aggressive investor tries to make profits by timing purchases and sales of
securities according to his or her views on how the market will go. He or she
tries to predict market movements and profit from them. A defensive
investor, on the other hand, tends to use more or less automatic methods of
timing purchases and sales, such as formula plans or a "buy-and-hold" philosophy, and usually does not try to "outguess the market."

Frequency of Investment Transactions.   The aggressive investor tends to
buy and sell more frequently, while the defensive counterpart tends to follow a "buy-and-hold" policy. The aggressive investor wants to hold a security
only during periods of rapid appreciation in its price.

Variety of Investment Vehicles Used.   In the search for greater profits
from available investment capital, an aggressive investor may use many
techniques and investment media, such as stock warrants, puts and calls,
initial public offerings (IPOs), and short sales, that are not commonly used
in more defensive portfolios.

Use of Credit.   An aggressive investment policy may involve borrowing,
such as purchases of stock on margin, to increase the profit potential from
available investment funds. A defensive policy generally does not contem-
plate the use of credit in this way. In other words, an aggressive policy tends
to be highly leveraged.

Attitude toward Diversification.   An aggressive policy normally *concentrates* its purchases in a relatively small number of securities at any given
time to maximize the investor's (or the advisor's) skill at selection and,
hence, to maximize the profit from good selections. Risk is increased, however, because this approach loses the advantages of diversification.

Probably few people consistently follow only aggressive policies or only
defensive policies in all respects. In fact, they employ some combination of

the two; however, investors with medium-sized or small portfolios probably tend more toward defensive-type policies in general.

Liquidity and Marketability. The degree of liquidity needed in a portfolio is an important investment constraint. The following are some personal factors that can affect this decision:

1. The nature and immediacy of financial obligations
2. The nature of other assets
3. The person's age and the potential liquidity needs of the estate
4. What credit facilities may be available
5. Availability of adequate health insurance, long-term care (LTC) insurance, and other insurance coverages to meet emergencies

Setting the proper degree of liquidity in a portfolio is largely a matter of judgment. It can be done by deciding to hold a certain number of dollars, say $10,000, in liquid assets; or to hold a certain percentage of assets, say 10 percent, in liquid form; or to hold some combination of the two, such as 10 percent of assets but no more than $20,000, in liquid form. In the asset allocation decision, liquid assets are often stated as a percentage of the overall portfolio, as is done on pp. 212–214 of this chapter.

Diversification versus Concentration. The investor's policy here depends partly on whether he or she wants to follow a more defensive or aggressive policy at a particular time. Diversification is basically a defensive policy.

The opposite of diversification is a policy of concentration. As just noted, *concentration* involves investing in only a few issues at any one time in hope of higher profit. People really are speaking of a policy of concentration (usually without using that term) when they say, "If I had put my money in Coca Cola, or Merck, or selected others 20 years ago, I'd be rich today." That probably is true. On the other hand, if they had put the bulk of their assets in declining stocks, they would be far from rich today. The problem in applying a policy of concentration is to find the *next spectacular growth stock now.* As indicated previously in this chapter, many people believe a policy of diversification (perhaps in several ways) of an investment portfolio is the better policy for most people.

Asset Allocation Strategy. This policy issue comes down to the question of what kinds and grades of investments should be included in the portfolio. It is the "$64,000 question."

As indicated previously, the asset allocation (composition) of an investment portfolio should be based mainly on the person's investment objectives and constraints. However, it also depends on yield differentials among different kinds of securities or assets at a given time and over time. Current economic conditions also are very important. One normally would not invest in common stocks at the start of a recession or depression, for example, *provided* one could identify when one was starting.

The normal way to define the asset allocation of a portfolio is in terms of the proportions or percentages that various assets or types of assets represent in the total portfolio. This is frequently done in terms of percentages of securities or other investments with different characteristics. For example, one such classification of investments might be:

1. Liquid assets (cash equivalents)
2. Fixed-income securities (investment-grade)
   a. Corporate bonds
   b. Municipal bonds
   c. U.S. government bonds and notes
   d. Other fixed-income securities (e.g., foreign bonds)
3. Convertible bonds and preferred stocks
4. High-yield (high-risk or "junk") bonds
5. Certificates of deposit (CDs)
6. Common stocks in mature companies (domestic or foreign)
   a. Growth stocks
   b. Cyclical stocks
   c. Defensive stocks
7. Common stocks in special situations or small-growth companies
8. Speculative common stocks or initial public offerings (IPOs)
9. Investment companies (e.g., mutual funds) that themselves invest in a diversified portfolio (i.e., balanced mutual funds)
10. Investment real estate
11. Oil and gas participations and other tax-sheltered investments
12. Commodities
13. Gold and other precious metals
14. Annuities and life insurance (fixed-dollar)
15. Guaranteed investment contracts (GICs)
16. Other assets

The idea behind any such classification is to help construct a portfolio of different types and grades of securities than can reflect the individual's investment objectives, attitudes, needs, and limitations. For the sake of completeness, this list is far more exhaustive than will be found in the asset allocations of most people. There is, of course, no "proper" or "right" asset allocation. It naturally will vary among individuals. Also, a portfolio may change over time and with market conditions.

As a practical matter, it is also interesting to observe how greatly the general asset allocation models recommended by brokerage houses and other financial institutions can differ from one another at any given time. Obviously, given the same general economic conditions, even the experts cannot agree on this matter. This just underscores the subjective nature of the asset allocation decision.

Two other ways in which investors or their advisors can subdivide an investment portfolio for purposes of analysis are according to:

1. The percentages of *liquid* and *marketable* assets to total assets

2. The percentages of *fixed-dollar-type* assets and *variable-dollar-type* assets

Investors may have assets in the various categories for asset allocation purposes directly, through financial intermediaries, through IRA investments, or through employee benefit plan investments. Thus, directly owned investments, mutual fund shares, variable life insurance and annuity accounts, IRA accounts, and qualified savings and profit-sharing plans, among others, all should be considered in this asset allocating analysis.

Illustrations of Asset Allocation Strategies.   As just noted, there can be wide differences of opinion concerning asset allocation strategies, even with a given factual situation. Thus, the two case situations given here are meant simply to be illustrations of the general asset allocation technique in personal investment planning.

First, let us assume that Harry and Susan Modern are married; both have careers outside the home; and they have two children, ages 5 and 3. Harry, age 35, is a lawyer and had been with a major law firm but five years ago started his own practice (as a sole proprietor). Susan, age 34, has an MBA degree and is an executive with a large pharmaceutical company. They each earn approximately $70,000 per year in their respective careers. Harry has a retirement plan for the self-employed (an HR-10 plan), and Susan has a qualified pension plan and a qualified savings plan (with five separate investment options among which she can select) from her corporate employer.[11] Harry has an individual noncancelable and guaranteed renewable disability income policy, while Susan's employer provides her with a group long-term disability (LTD) plan. Susan's employer also provides her with group medical expense insurance under which she also covers Harry and her children as dependents. Harry carries $500,000 face amount of life

[11] See Chap. 12 for a description of these kinds of qualified retirement plans.

insurance on his life, with $100,000 from a universal variable life (UVL) policy and $400,000 as term insurance. Susan also carries $500,000 face amount of life insurance on her life, with $100,000 from a traditional, fixed-premium, nonvariable whole life policy and the remainder as group and individual term insurance. Susan's qualified savings plan account balance and Harry's variable life insurance cash value are both allocated to the common stock accounts under these plans. From an employee stock purchase plan at Susan's employer, their personal savings, and a small inheritance from Harry's mother, they have accumulated other investible assets of $100,000. They also own their own home, on which there is a mortgage, but they have decided not to use their investible assets at this time to pay off the mortgage.

As investment objectives, and considering their personal situations and insurance coverages, Harry and Susan would like to follow mainly a long-term capital growth investment strategy, but also to maintain a reasonable degree of liquidity and diversification. Therefore, considering their directly

Asset category	Percentage of portfolio	Reasons
Liquid assets	5%	For emergencies. To provide some investment flexibility.
Common stocks in mature companies (growth stocks):		
Directly held growth common stocks	35%	To meet primary investment objective. Low income-tax basis stock of Susan's employer already held. Regard Susan's employer's stock as a good investment.
Mutual fund shares in growth-stock fund	25%	To meet primary investment objective. For diversification.
Common stocks in small growth companies (through mutual fund shares)	10%	To meet primary investment objective. For diversification.
Corporate bonds (through Harry's UVL policy)	10%	For diversification. Good, tax-deferred yield. Potential liquidity. Insurance needed.
Guaranteed investment contracts (GICs) (from a top-rated life insurance company) under Susan's qualified savings plan	10%	For diversification. Good, tax-deferred yield. Guaranteed principal.
Life insurance guaranteed (fixed-dollar) cash values (from Susan's whole life policy)	5%	Reasonable, tax-deferred yield. Guaranteed principal. Potential liquidity. Insurance needed.

owned assets, the account balance in Susan's qualified savings plan, the cash value of Harry's UVL policy, and the cash value of Susan's whole life policy, they have decided (with the help of their advisors) on the asset allocation strategy, shown on the previous page, for the present time. Thus, with this asset allocation, Harry and Susan would have about 70 percent of their investment assets in equity (variable-dollar-type) investments and 30 percent in fixed-dollar-type investments.

Now, let us consider an entirely different case situation. Assume that John and Martha Senior are married, their three children are out of their home and are self-supporting, and the Seniors are retired. John, age 67, had been employed as an engineer for most of his working life by a large industrial corporation from which he retired two years ago at age 65. Martha, age 64, worked as a teacher early in their marriage, but during most of their married years she worked in the home. John receives monthly social security retirement benefits and a monthly pension for his and Martha's lifetime (with a 50 percent survivor's benefit for Martha if he should predecease her) from his former employer. Martha has not yet begun to receive social security retirement benefits, but she will elect to begin to do so next year when she reaches age 65. Martha does receive a small amount of trust income from a trust established for her under her mother's will. John is covered by Medicare, and presently Martha has COBRA continuation coverage under John's former employer's medical expense plan. Martha will be eligible for Medicare when she reaches age 65. John's former employer does not provide retiree health coverage, and John does not have any Medicare supplement coverage. John also carries $100,000 face amount of traditional, fixed-premium, nonvariable whole life insurance. Neither John nor Martha has long-term care (LTC) insurance. At John's retirement, he took a lump-sum distribution of his entire account balance from his former employer's qualified savings plan and rolled the taxable portion into a rollover IRA. He now has $200,000 in this rollover IRA that is invested in insured CDs. From their personal savings and the nontaxable part of John's savings plan lump-sum distribution, John and Martha have another $150,000 in personal savings that also is mostly in insured CDs.

As investment objectives, and considering their situation, John and Martha would like to preserve their capital as much as possible, receive reasonable current income with moderate capital growth (to help protect them against possible future inflation), protect their income against declines in interest rates as much as possible, maintain reasonable liquidity, and have reasonable diversification. Therefore, considering their directly owned assets, the rollover IRA, and the cash value of John's whole life policy, they have decided (with the help of their advisors) on the asset allocation strategy on the following page for the present time.

Asset category	Percentage of portfolio	Reasons
Liquid assets	10%	For emergencies. To provide some investment flexibility.
U.S. Treasury bonds and notes (owned directly or through IRA)	30%	For income. For call protection. Maximum safety. Tax-deferred if through IRA.
Corporate bonds (owned directly or through IRA)	20%	For higher yield (income). Investment grade. Tax-deferred if through IRA. Possible call protection.
Common stocks in mature companies (defensive):		
Held directly	10%	For income and growth.
Mutual fund shares in income and growth mutual fund	20%	For income and growth. For diversification.
Life insurance guaranteed (fixed-dollar) cash values (from John's whole life policy)	10%	Guaranteed principal. Reasonable, tax-deferred yield. Potential liquidity. Insurance needed for Martha.

Thus, with this asset allocation, John and Martha would have about 30 percent of their investment assets in equity (variable-dollar-type) investments and 70 percent in fixed-dollar-type investments.

Investment Timing.   As we saw before, an aggressive investment policy aims at making profits by successfully forecasting future price changes of securities and buying and selling accordingly. A defensive policy involves buying and selling from time to time without consciously trying to forecast how securities prices will change in the future.

There are a variety of *techniques or plans an investor can use in applying a defensive policy with respect to investment timing.* Among them are the following:

1. *Dollar cost averaging.*   This has been a widely used defensive policy toward price changes. It is an application of time diversification and can be defined briefly as a policy of periodically investing equal dollar amounts in securities, usually common stocks.[12]

2. *Formula plans.*   There are a variety of so-called formula plans for the timing of investment purchases and sales. Some of the more common

---

[12] Dollar cost averaging as applied to common stocks is discussed in Chap. 8.

are (*a*) constant-ratio plans, (*b*) variable-ratio plans, and (*c*) norm-type plans. In general, they all attempt automatically, through a formula, to time purchases when stock prices are low and sales when stock prices are high.

3. *Buying and holding a well-diversified group of common stocks for long-term investment.* This can be characterized as a "buy and hold" or "sock 'em away" approach. It assumes that a policy of investing in a diversified list of common stocks of the more successful, leading companies in a number of major industries, purchased over a period of years, and held for the long pull, will provide a satisfactory rate of return when compared with other investments.

4. *Buying and holding growth stocks.* This has been a popular policy, but it assumes that an investor will be able to identify and purchase the "growth stocks" of the future. These, of course, may not be the same as the growth stocks of the past.

There are also a number of *techniques used by investors who want to follow an aggressive policy with regard to investment timing.* Many of these are aimed at forecasting cyclical swings in the stock market. There are many such techniques used, but they generally fall into three main classifications.

1. *Forecasting overall stock prices by forecasting cyclical fluctuations in business activity (forecasting the business cycle).* This is a common approach, but it obviously relies on predicting—or, at least, following others who predict—changes in the business cycle. This is no small feat, even for trained economists. Also, while there clearly is a positive correlation between stock prices and business activity, they are not perfectly related. For example, overall cyclical changes in stock prices generally precede—or "lead," as economists would say—changes in the business cycle.

2. *Forecasting overall stock prices by use of monetary statistics.* This approach seeks to forecast stock prices by studying changes in the money supply (or "liquidity") in the economy. The theory is that when the money supply expands, stock prices (and business activity generally) will rise, and when the money supply contracts, so will stock prices.

3. *Forecasting overall stock prices by use of the statistics of the stock market itself.* The theory here is that basic patterns exist in the stock market which tend to repeat themselves. Therefore, if students of the market can determine what these patterns are, their fortunes will be made. Those who follow this general approach are called "chartists" or "technicians" in the securities industry.

There are a great many of these so-called technical methods for predicting stock price movements. However, some of the more widely known are:

1. The Dow theory

2. Advance-decline series

3. Odd-lot studies

4. Volume studies

5. Breadth-of-market studies

6. Data on the market's short position[13]

Objective studies have not shown that any of the many technical methods for predicting stock market behavior can be completely relied upon. However, many market analysts believe such technical data are valuable as indicators of stock market behavior when used with each other and with other basic economic data.

Unhappily, none of the techniques or methods for investment timing is sure to yield the desired results. They can, of course, give clues to changes in the investment climate; however, that indescribable, undefinable factor called "judgment on the part of the investor" remains the key to successful investment timing.

Implementation of Policies

The final step in personal investment management is the implementation of the plan by selecting and purchasing the appropriate securities and making whatever changes are necessary in the portfolio from time to time. The selection and purchasing of specific securities will be discussed further in the following chapters.

---

[13] Detailed descriptions of the reasoning behind the techniques used in these methods are beyond the scope of this book. Descriptions of them often can be found in standard texts on investments.

8

Common Stock and Other Equity Investments

Once there is adequate insurance protection and an appropriate emergency fund, a person may be ready to think about establishing an investment program for any discretionary income or capital he or she may have. As we said before, when such a point is reached, there are a number of possible investment outlets. This chapter concentrates on investments in common stocks and certain other equity-type investment media; later chapters focus on other types of investments.

Investment Characteristics of Common Stocks

To develop a sound common stock investment policy, it is necessary to understand the fundamental characteristics of common stocks. "Common stock" may be defined as the residual ownership of a corporation that is entitled to all assets and earnings after other claims have been paid and that generally has basic voting control. In short, common stock is the fundamental ownership equity. Common stockholders bear the main burden of the risks in a business enterprise and also receive the lion's share of any success.

The selection of common stock investments requires care and competence, but a careful investor should not fear investing in common stocks. In fact, many people may need stocks to have a diversified investment program. Therefore, people should either learn to select common stocks themselves, or place that function in the hands of a financial intermediary or an investment advisor.

The Arithmetic
of Common Stocks

Once the decision is made to allocate part of an investment fund to common stock investments, investors or their advisors need to understand the "arithmetic of common stocks" in order to evaluate a particular stock or stocks. Four basic calculations may serve as convenient preliminary indicators of the worth of a common stock. These are (1) earnings per share, (2) price-earnings ratio, (3) net asset value per share, and (4) yield. These indicators, along with a general knowledge of the industry and company, should give sufficient background information to determine whether further investigation of the particular stock is warranted.

Earnings per Share   *profit — Dividends*
                                 #shares

Since common stock is the residual claimant to the earnings of a corporation, it usually is possible to compute its earnings per share by taking net corporate profits after taxes, subtracting any preferred dividends, and dividing the remainder by the number of common shares outstanding. This may be illustrated by the following example: Over the most recent 12 months in which it reported earnings, the XYZ Company had a profit of $2,300,000 after deduction of expenses, interest, and taxes. Preferred dividend requirements for the year were $200,000. The remaining $2,100,000 amounted to $3 per share on the 700,000 shares outstanding ($2,100,000 ÷ 700,000 = $3). Earnings per share are computed in the same way for quarterly or semiannual periods when the data are available. Nonrecurring items contained in current income are generally excluded when computing earnings per share. Decisions based on trends or growth rates of earnings per share would otherwise be misleading.[1] The example just given is based on what are called "trailing earnings" because the earnings figure used is for the most recent *past actual earnings* of the corporation. This measure has the almost unique merit of reality. However, sometimes analysts will *estimate* future earnings per share and then base their calculations (such as the price-earnings ratio to be considered next) in whole or in part on estimated future earnings rather than on the actual "trailing earnings." There is nothing wrong in doing this so long as the investor remembers that some part of the analysis is based on future estimates, not actual earnings.

Investors generally place great emphasis on earnings per share and the trend of earnings per share in evaluating common stocks. It can be argued that both present and future dividends are dependent on earn-

---

[1] Two earnings-per-share figures are sometimes reported. One is based on the number of common shares outstanding (as in the XYZ Company example), and the other is adjusted to reflect potential dilution from warrants, convertible securities, stock options, and the like.

ings and that a stock's market price ultimately tends to keep pace with the growth (or decline) of its earnings per share.

Analysts will also sometimes calculate a figure called *cash flow per share.* This figure is derived by adding back depreciation expense (which is a non-cash expense) to net profit less preferred dividends and then dividing by the number of common shares outstanding. The idea is to be able to better compare companies with varying depreciation policies.

Price-Earnings Ratio

The price-earnings (P/E) ratio of a common stock is simply the market price of the stock divided by the current earnings per share of the corporation. Thus, if XYZ Company common stock sold for $42 per share at a time when its reported earnings over the latest 12 months amounted to $3 per share, its P/E ratio (on a "trailing earnings" basis) would be 14 ($42 ÷ $3).

The price-earnings ratio is a conventional and highly regarded measure of stock value because it gives an indication of stock price measured against the earning power of the stock. A high P/E ratio normally can be justified only if the company's earnings are expected to grow. Thus, a high multiple for a stock normally indicates that the stock market expects the stock's future earnings to be higher than its current earnings.

An investor may find a review of the past price-earnings ratios of a stock a helpful means for estimating its current value relative to the past. Assume, for example, that over a 10-year period, XYZ Company common stock has shown consistent growth in earnings per share and market price, and that its P/E ratios have ranged from around 10 on the low side to the high 20s on the high side. Therefore, since this stock currently is selling for $42, and the earnings per share for the latest 12 months are $3, a potential investor would know that the stock now is selling for a price-earnings ratio (14) that is historically low and thus might be a "good buy" at this time. On the other hand, if XYZ common currently were selling for $78, its P/E ratio (26) would be on the high side historically.[2] Of course, investors must consider other factors about the stock in making a final decision. They also must evaluate the stock's current P/E ratio in light of present economic and stock market conditions and what those conditions are expected to be in the future.

However, the P/E ratios for stocks of small or speculative companies, or of companies with erratic earnings records, often do not provide dependable data on which to base valuation estimates.

The financial sections of newspapers and financial periodicals often indicate the P/E ratios of the stocks whose prices they report.

---

[2] Historical data on price-earnings ratios for common stocks are readily available to investors. For example, the Standard & Poor's Corporation Standard Stock Reports gives this information for many stocks.

Net Asset Value
(Book Value) per Share

assets − debt & stock (Preferred) / *# shares*

The net asset value per share, commonly referred to as the *book value* per share, attempts to measure the amount of assets a corporation has working for each share of common stock. It is arrived at by taking the net balance sheet value of the corporate assets, subtracting the face value of creditors' and preferred stockholders' claims, and dividing the remainder by the number of outstanding common shares. For example, the XYZ Company at the end of its last fiscal year had total assets of $33 million and debts and preferred stock totaling $12 million. The remaining $21 million indicated a net asset value of $30 for each of its 700,000 common shares.

For businesses whose assets are a good measure of earning power, net asset value per share may be significant for investment purposes. However, it must be noted that corporate book values usually are based on cost, not earning power, and intangible assets that are not on the books may be more significant than book value in determining earning power.

In most cases, the net asset value per share of common stock is of much less importance than the ability of these assets to generate a stream of earnings. The market value of the common stock of so-called growth companies frequently will be many times the net asset value per share. On the other hand, for firms in a stagnant or declining industry, market value may be much less than net asset value. In some cases, the book value of a firm's assets might reasonably approximate their market or liquidating value. In such cases, the net asset value may keep the price of the firm's stock at a higher level than might be justified by the firm's earning potential. On the whole, however, net asset value per share for a publicly held corporation is not a very useful measure for evaluating the investment merits of its common stock. However, the investment community does tend to measure the current market price level of a stock, an industry group, or the whole market in relation to past price levels by a measure often called "price to book" (the market price divided by the book value).

Another measure sometimes used is *liquidating value per share.* This is determined by using the market or liquidating value of a corporation's assets rather than the balance sheet values (which generally are based on historical cost) in the calculation noted previously.

Yield

As we saw in Chap. 7, the *yield for common stocks* typically refers to the percentage that the annual cash dividend bears to the current market price of the stock (i.e., the current yield). Thus, if XYZ Company common stock pays dividends at a current indicated annual rate of $1.50, and sells for $42, the dividend yield is about 3.6 percent.

The yield can be an indicator of the reasonableness of a stock's market price. This can be particularly true if the dividend used is a normal prospective annual rate and the company is expected to have stable, rather than rapidly increasing, decreasing, or erratic earnings. The common stocks of many utilities may be examples of stocks that might be appropriate for this kind of evaluation. As in the case of price-earnings ratios, the principal purpose in studying dividend yield history is to obtain a basis for stock valuation. If the dividend to be paid by a stock is reasonably certain, and if a "normal" yield that investors generally expect to receive on stocks of its type can be determined, an evaluation can be made on this basis. If, for example, a stable utility pays a $1.80-per-share annual dividend, and if a stock of this quality normally might yield about 8 percent, dividing $1.80 by 0.08 results in a valuation estimate of around $22 per share. If, however, this utility is selling for $26 per share, the current yield would be about 7 percent, and an investor may feel this is too low in terms of the yield expectations for a stable utility. Naturally, the yields investors expect from different kinds of securities change as economic conditions change. Also, if the utility's earnings and dividends are expected to grow at a moderate but reasonable rate in the future, this would affect its stock valuation positively.

Information about Common Stocks

Once a decision to invest in common stocks has been made, an investor is ready to acquire information about industries and companies that may be of investment interest. There are many potential sources of information about common stocks. Only some are discussed here.

One of the first sources is the financial pages of a good newspaper. In a newspaper can be found the stock tables, where daily price changes are reported. For example, on a particular day, here is how the record for the common stock of a hypothetical firm called "Typical Manufacturing Company" might appear in the New York Stock Exchange tables:

| 52 weeks | | Stock and div. | | Sales in | | | | | Net |
High	Low	in dollars	P/E	100s	Open	High	Low	Close	chg.
32¼	20¾	Typ. Mfg. 1.20	13	29	25	26	25	25½	+½

Reading from left to right, this shows that the price range for Typical Manufacturing common on the New York Stock Exchange during the current year has been from a low of 20¾ ($20.75) to a high of 32¼ ($32.25). The stock currently is paying an annual dividend rate of $1.20 per share, it has a price-earnings ratio (P/E) of 13, and 2900 shares were bought and sold during the day in question. The first sale of the day was at 25¼ ($25.25) a share; the highest price for the day was 26; the lowest was 25; and the last sale for the day was at 25½, half a point (50 cents a share) above the previous closing price (which must have been 25).

There are a number of stock market barometers (market averages) that are useful. Among the best known probably are the Dow Jones Averages, Standard & Poor's 500 Stock Index, the New York Times Index, the New York Stock Exchange indexes, the NASDAQ over-the-counter indexes, the Value-Line index, the Russell 2000, and the Wilshire 5000. The Dow Jones Averages include four averages: (1) 30 industrials, (2) 20 transportations, (3) 15 utilities, and (4) a composite of the 65 stocks. The Dow Jones Industrial Average (DJIA) probably is the most widely followed of the four and is the one usually referred to in summaries of daily stock market activity.

A number of financial newspapers and periodicals carry news of interest to investors and prospective investors. Some of these are *The Wall Street Journal, Barron's, Financial Daily, Commercial and Financial Chronicle, Standard & Poor's Outlook, Forbes,* and *The Magazine of Wall Street,* plus such business news magazines as *Fortune, Business Week,* and *Nation's Business.* In addition, daily newspapers usually have a financial section that reports such news. Investors also may subscribe to many different investment advisory newsletters and technical charting services of varying quality and price.

These sources are useful for obtaining current information on developments in the economy and the stock market and for individual industries and companies. If an investor wants to know more than can be gained from reading these sources, he or she can simply write to any company and ask for a copy of its latest annual report, from which much can be learned about that company's financial situation and its business.

Another way of getting information on a specific company is to look it up in one of the major reference works of financial information, such as *Standard & Poor's, Moody's,* or *Value-Line.* One of these services is almost certain to be available in any large library or through banks or stockbrokers.

Another important source of information on common stocks is from stockbrokers. Brokers are not infallible, of course, but most of them make a point of being well informed and of making their information available for the benefit of investors and prospective investors. Depending on their investment research facilities, brokerage houses frequently have reports containing brief summaries of pertinent investment information on a great many companies. Some brokerage houses issue periodic reports that analyze the effect of current and anticipated developments on individual securities, companies, and industries. Brokers may also maintain lists of "recommended" stocks for various investment objectives. These lists are constantly revised on the basis of current developments. Again, depending on the extent and quality of a broker's research facilities, such lists can be helpful in selecting industries and stocks to consider for investment.

The Investment Process

So far, we have touched on some basic essentials of common stock investment. But there still remains the important problem of selecting appropriate stocks for investment.

Investing is an art, not a science. Many helpful tools and techniques are available to help analyze a particular stock, but no one can say that, given a certain set of conditions, such-and-such will happen in the stock market. What will happen depends at least partially on human nature, and nothing is less predictable. Stock prices are subject to constant change, and a stock is worth only what somebody is willing to pay for it at a given time. "Buy low and sell high" certainly is good advice, but so far no one has been able to devise a way of determining exactly where the high and low will be. Money is not made through hindsight. Successful investing in common stocks cannot intelligently be based on hunch, hope, or hearsay; it must be founded on a study of the particular company and industry involved.

The first step in choosing a stock is evaluating the industry. The following are some of the important questions to consider in evaluating different industries:

1. Does the industry provide products or services widely used and needed and for which the demand is substantial or the growth steady?
2. Is the industry cyclical, i.e., subject to major ups and downs, or is it relatively stable?
3. Is the industry likely to be adversely affected by new developments or technological changes? For example, is its source of raw materials in an area where crises are frequent, or is it strongly subject to government orders?
4. What is the industry's labor situation?
5. Is the use of the industry's products growing rapidly (i.e., is it a "growth" industry), growing at a more stable rate, or perhaps declining relative to other industries?
6. Is the industry dependent largely on one or a few products, or is it diversified?

After answers to such questions have been secured, the competitive positions of the various companies within the industry can be analyzed. In doing this, the investment analyst must consider such questions as the following:

1. What is the company's relative position in its industry?
2. Is this position improving, stable, or declining?
3. How good does the company's management appear to be?
4. Does the company seem to work hard to expand its market and grow?

The answers to these and other pertinent questions about the company's fundamental position will help the analyst to *estimate the company's future earning power, and that generally is the key to its quality as an investment.* The size of a company, in itself, is not necessarily a major consideration, but many investors tend to buy securities of large, well-known companies.

As a practical matter, it is difficult, if not impossible, for most individual investors personally to research and analyze such factors as industry characteristics, competitive positions of companies, and the fundamental position of any given company. However, various professional investment concerns, investment services, stockbrokers, and other investment advisors are in a position to do such research, and this type of investigation frequently is readily available to individual investors. Investors normally should make it a practice not to buy a stock unless they have determined its fundamental business position from such sources or perhaps from their own personal research.

One of the advantages of owning securities in companies listed on one of the major stock exchanges is that information about them is readily available. Another is that such listed stocks generally can be sold without difficulty (i.e., they are marketable). On the other hand, there are likely to be some attractive investment opportunities—particularly in the case of smaller growth stocks—in companies whose stocks are traded over the counter. Also, some other types of stocks such as those of banks and insurance companies, often are traded over the counter.

As we saw before, most experienced investors like to know the price-earnings ratio for a stock before they invest. Price-earnings (P/E) ratios vary from industry to industry and from company to company within an industry. The P/E ratio for a particular stock also will vary as the economic outlook for the company, the industry, or the whole economy is favorable or unfavorable. And, of course, the ratio is higher for a "growth stock" than for others. By and large, however, if a stock is selling at a ratio very much higher or very much lower than the average for the stocks of other companies in the same industry, it is wise for the investor to find out why before making an investment.

Decisions Concerning Diversifying a Common Stock Portfolio

As we saw in Chap. 7, diversification is a sound investment principle designed to minimize the risks of investing by dividing holdings among various industries and companies, as well as among different kinds of securities or other investments and by maturities for bonds and CDs. However, investment diversification in common stocks does not mean that if one is investing, say, $100,000, one should try to split it too many ways and arbitrarily buy stock in, say, 40 different companies. Investors normally should not own stock in more companies than they or their investment advisors can keep track of. In fact, some studies of diversification have shown that after a certain point, more diversification provides very little spreading of risk. It probably would be more sensible to put the $100,000 investment fund into, say, 10 to 12 stocks.

As we noted in the previous chapter, concentration is the opposite of diversification. Concentration is typical of a more aggressive type of investment policy, while diversification represents a more defensive approach to investments. For most investors, however, a reasonable program of investment diversification probably is superior to alternative investment strategies.

Periodic Review

Investors or their advisors should reexamine the investment situation periodically and adjust the investors' commitments accordingly. Also, any major change in personal or family circumstances or in the general economic situation may call for a review of the whole financial plan, including their common stock investments.

When to Sell

Although much of the emphasis expressed in the past concerning common stock investment has been on buying, the question of when to sell can be equally important. There are many *reasons for selling stocks.* Obviously, one is the *need for cash* for a variety of reasons. An investor who has to sell when the price of a stock is down may be forced to realize a loss. That is why people are urged to invest in common stocks only if they have surplus cash beyond the needs of their daily life.

Another reason for selling is to *take a profit* (or reduce a loss) when an individual thinks a stock has reached its upper limit. Or, one may sell who believes the *money can earn a higher rate of return if invested elsewhere.* It should be remembered, however, that there are transfer costs (i.e., brokerage commissions) and capital gains taxes on any profits when a stock is sold. Therefore, only the net proceeds of a sale can be invested elsewhere. This means that the attractiveness of the alternative investment must outweigh over time the costs of selling the existing stock or other investment.

Still another reason for selling a stock is if its *performance has not been up to expectations* and it shows no sign of improving in the future. In general, it is unwise to stay with an unprofitable stock for too long. It normally is better to take a small loss now and make a change to something better.

Do not consider any investment decision permanent or irrevocable. Keep track of the current performance of the stocks in the investment portfolio and change its composition as conditions and prices dictate. And, as a rule of thumb, whenever the price of any security in the portfolio is so high that it would not be considered a good buy now, consider selling the security (again, recognizing the costs of a sale).

On the other hand, do not panic into selling without good reason. If investments have been made with care and for the long term, do not let every change in the price of stocks be a signal for gaiety or gloom. Remember that the nature of the stock market is fluctuation.

Dollar Cost Averaging

One timing technique for long-term investing is dollar cost averaging. *Dollar cost averaging* is the investment of a certain sum of money in the same common stock or stocks at regular intervals. It is an application of time diversification and may enable investors to capitalize on price fluctuations instead of just worrying about them. The method normally results in a lower average cost per share than the average market price per share during the period in question because the investor buys more shares of the stock with the fixed amount of money—say, $500 a quarter—when the stock is low in price than when it is comparatively high. Then, when the stock rises again (if it does), the investor shows a profit on the greater number of shares purchased at the lower prices.

Table 8.1 shows how the principle of dollar cost averaging could work.

Dollar cost averaging frequently works, unless the stock goes into a persistent decline. It works better if the stock has had an early decline and a later rise than if the reverse is the case. It takes a certain amount of strength of conviction. The investor must be convinced that, whatever happens from time to time, the stock is a good long-term investment. The investor also must be prepared to invest at regular intervals regardless of the price of the stock. Further, he or she must have the ready cash to stick to a regular program of buying even in periods when stock prices are down. Finally, the investor must remember that dollar cost averaging does not protect against loss of stock values in declining markets and that a loss will result if he or she must sell when the market price of the stock is below the average cost of the shares purchased.

Thus, dollar cost averaging may be particularly well suited for investors with more or less uniform amounts of money periodically available for investment, who tend to follow a general investment policy of "buying and holding" securities, and who generally do not want to try to forecast stock

Table 8.1. Illustration of Dollar Cost Averaging

Date	Amount invested	Market price paid	Number of shares purchased
1st Period	$ 500	$20	25
2d Period	500	12½	40
3d Period	500	10	50
4th Period	500	12½	40
5th Period	500	25	20
	$2500		175

Total amount invested over 5 periods	$2500
Number of shares purchased	175
Average market price	$ 16.00 per share
Average cost ($2500 ÷ 175 shares)	$ 14.29 per share

prices. As noted in the previous chapter, dollar cost averaging is a defensive investment policy with respect to price changes of securities, particularly common stocks. Mutual fund shares and individual common stocks are common vehicles for dollar cost averaging.

The Mechanics of Buying and Selling Common Stocks

Buy and Sell Orders

Various kinds of buy and sell orders may be used in common stock transactions. Some of the more common are described below.

Market Orders.   The most common type of order is the *market order,* an order to buy or sell securities at the best price obtainable in the market at the moment. It is expressed to the broker as an order to buy or sell "at the market," that is, at whatever the market price happens to be.

Limit Orders.   For many stock transactions, a market order is a reasonable one to use. However, when market prices are uncertain or are fluctuating rapidly, it may be better for an investor to enter a *limit order* that specifies the maximum price the investor is willing to pay, or, if selling, the minimum price the investor is willing to accept. For example, the broker might be instructed to buy 100 shares of a certain stock at 50 but no more.

The opposite is true when selling. For example, a broker might be given a limit order to sell 100 shares of a certain stock at 53. Here, the broker may sell the shares at 53 or, if possible, at a greater price, but not at *less* than 53.

Orders Based on Time.   Most types of orders to buy and sell common stocks include a time reference. Such orders can take several forms. *Open* *orders* are good until canceled and are designed as GTC orders ("Good Till Canceled"). Another type is the *day order,* which is good only for the day on which it is ordered.

Stop Loss Orders.   Another common type of order is a *stop loss order.* It is generally used as a basis for selling a stock once its price reaches a certain point, usually below the current market price. The reason a stop loss order might be used can best be explained by an example. Suppose a stock's current market price is 100. Assume further that the investor feels the condition of the stock market is so uncertain that the price of the stock could fluctuate markedly in either direction. To minimize any potential loss from the 100 level, the investor might enter a stop order at, say, 90. If the market price declines, the stock will be sold when the market price reaches 90. A stop loss order becomes a market order once the specified price is reached, and the stock will be sold immediately at whatever price the broker can secure. Of course, if the market price goes up and never declines to the stop loss price, the investor would have lost nothing by placing this order.

An investor who wishes to use a stop order for a stock only at a specific price would enter a *stop limit order.* In the above illustration, for example, this order could instruct the broker to sell out at, for example, 90 and 90 only. If the transaction cannot be executed at 90, it will not be executed at all.

Margin Accounts

Most individual investors open *cash accounts* with their brokerage firms. As the name implies, all transactions in this type of account are for the full amount of the trade in cash. That is, a $5000 trade requires a $5000 cash settlement within five full business days after the trade was made.

Many investors, however, are interested in buying securities "on margin." A *margin account* is used to allow investors to assume a larger position in a security than they could if they used only their own funds. Investors put up some of their own money and borrow the remainder. Margin accounts frequently are used by investors following more aggressive policies who want to lever their investment position and thereby magnify their return. They typically hold a security for relatively short periods of time, and they do not intend to pay off their margin account. In a few cases, margin accounts are used to finance long-term holdings of a security that currently is considered by the investor to be underpriced. In this situation, margin is used to purchase as many shares (or bonds) as possible, and the investor eventually intends to pay for the securities in full.

Margin accounts for listed securities can be opened through either a brokerage house or a commercial bank. The minimum "down payment," or *margin requirement,* is set by the board of governors of the Federal Reserve System. Let us consider a specific example. Suppose the margin requirement is 50 percent, and Mr. A buys 100 shares of ABC Corporation common stock at $70 per share. If this is a margin trade, Mr. A is required to come up with only $3500 in cash (or its equivalent in other securities). He then borrows the rest ($3500) from a bank or broker at the interest rate for this type of loan from the lender. (Incidentally, it may be noted that the margin interest rates charged by different brokers can vary considerably. They also often are less for larger loan balances.) The entire $7000 worth of securities is then put up as collateral for the $3500 loan. Federal Reserve requirements specify only the *initial margin,* the minimum margin required at the time a loan is made. The minimum margin required *after* loans are made is discussed below.

But if the price of ABC common declines, so that Mr. A's equity in the account decreases, he may get a "maintenance margin" call. *Maintenance margin* is the minimum equity position investors can have in their accounts before they are asked to put up additional funds. In the above illustration, for example, assuming maintenance margin at 30 percent, ABC common could fall to a price as low as 50 without a margin call.[3]

However, by borrowing to buy securities, investors stand a chance of magnifying their losses, just as they do of magnifying their gains. Also, aside from the risks involved, other factors may discourage an investor from buying on margin. First, member firms of the New York Stock Exchange are required to establish a minimum margin account requirement. Also, a number of brokerage houses have a house policy concerning the minimum size of margin accounts. The idea behind these requirements, aside from trying to discourage speculative excesses, is to dissuade smaller investors from becoming overly committed in the stock market, to their potential detriment.

Brokerage firms can also make securities loans on eligible unlisted or over-the-counter (OTC) stocks that have been approved for margin trading by the board of governors of the Federal Reserve System.

Selling Short

"Selling short" means selling securities that the investor either (1) does not possess, and therefore must borrow to settle the account for them; or (2) does possess but does not wish to deliver.[4] The former is the typical

---

[3] Since Mr. A must maintain an equity position of 30 percent in his margin account, he can borrow up to 70 percent of the value of the securities. His present loan is $3500. Therefore, $3500 divided by 0.70 (70 percent) equals the minimum value of securities Mr. A can have in his margin account without having to add more margin (cash or securities). In this case, the amount is $5000 ($3500 ÷ 0.70), or $50 per share.

[4] In the common sequence of transactions, where investors buy a security which they hope eventually to sell at a higher price, they have assumed what is called a "long position." When the order of these transactions is reversed—sell first, and hope to cover the sale later by buying at a lower price—the investor has taken a "short position." In either case, the overall objective is to buy low/sell high.

short sale arrangement used when the investor expects the stock to decline in price. The latter is called "selling short against the box" and is not used as frequently. "Selling short against the box" can be used to lock in a profit on a stock and postpone paying taxes on the capital gain. (See Chap. 11.)

To understand the technique of the short sale, let us first consider how an account is settled once an ordinary trade is made. Most settlements take place by regular-way delivery. This requires settlement by the fifth full business day after a trade has taken place. In other words, an investor who buys shares must pay for them by the fifth business day after the day the trade was made (the trade date). Similarly, when an investor is selling shares, the brokerage house must come up with the cash payable to its customer by the fifth full business day after the trade date, and the investor must make actual delivery of the shares sold.

Since investors must make regular-way delivery by five full business days after a trade is made, a short seller must borrow the necessary securities within that time to make delivery. Usually, the securities can be borrowed directly from the short seller's broker, or the broker can arrange for such borrowing. Short sellers are responsible for making up any dividends, rights, etc., that are declared on stock they have borrowed.

The most obvious reason for selling short is that the investor anticipates a declining market price for the security.[5] A typical example would be selling today at 100 with the hope of "covering," say, a month from now, at a lower price, say, 80 or less. Covering involves buying securities to replace the borrowed ones and, thus, delivering the securities originally sold short.

Of course, the reverse of the above situation may occur, and therein lies the danger of the short sale. That is, the price of the stock may not decline—it may even rise, thereby making it necessary to buy the stock later at a higher price than that at which it was sold. Thus, selling short involves considerable investment risk. It is normally considered an aggressive investment policy.

Securities Investor Protection Corporation

Following several sizable brokerage house failures, the federal government passed the Securities Investor Protection Act of 1970, which created the Securities Investor Protection Corporation (SIPC). SIPC is intended to provide funds, if necessary, to protect customers of an SIPC member firm in the event the firm is liquidated under the provisions of the act. If a member firm

---

[5] To prevent accumulating selling pressures in a downward market, short sales are permitted only if the last price change between successive round-lot transactions for a stock was *up* ⅛ of a point or more.

is to be liquidated, a trustee is appointed to supervise the liquidation. The trustee attempts to return to customers out of the liquidated firm's available assets the securities that can be "specifically identified" as theirs (generally, these are fully paid securities in cash accounts and excess margin securities in margin accounts that have been set aside as the property of customers). SIPC pays any remaining claims of each customer up to $500,000, except that claims for cash are limited to $100,000. In general, customers' securities and cash held by SIPC member firms are covered by the act. Other kinds of property, such as commodities accounts, are not covered.

Thus, the SIPC provides protection to investors who wish to leave securities or cash with member firms against the risk of the insolvency of such firms, up to the $500,000/$100,000 limits.[6] The SIPC, of course, is not intended to provide any protection to investors against losses resulting from everyday fluctuations in securities prices.

Investment Categories of Common Stocks

In determining what type or types of common stocks (or financial intermediaries investing in common stocks) to consider buying, it is important to understand the various investment categories of common stocks. Many different classification systems are used by securities firms and investment analysts. The basic system we shall follow is to classify stocks as (1) growth, (2) income, (3) growth (moderate) and income, (4) defensive, (5) cyclical, (6) blue chip, (7) speculative, (8) special situations, (9) small company, and (10) foreign. Of course, these categories are not necessarily mutually exclusive.

Growth Stocks

A growth stock is hard to define, but it is usually considered to be the stock of a company whose sales and earnings are expanding faster than the general economy and faster than those of most stocks. The company usually is aggressive, is research- or innovation-oriented, and plows back most or all of its earnings into the company for future expansion. For this reason, growth companies, intent on financing their expansion from retained earnings, often pay relatively small dividends, and their current yield generally is low. Over time, however, investors hope that substantial capital gains will accrue from the appreciation of the value of their stock as a result of this plow-back and expansion.

---

[6] Some firms also provide private insurance protection for their customers up to higher limits.

The market price of growth stocks can be volatile, particularly over the short run. They often go up in price faster than other stocks, but at the first hint that the *rate of increase* in their earnings is not being sustained, their prices can come tumbling down. And when the earnings of a "growth" stock actually falter, the result on its market price can be disastrous. Smaller or newer "growth companies" may be especially vulnerable when their earnings fail to live up to investors' expectations.

In an effort to define a "growth" stock with more precision, several investment services have developed statistical tests to identify and select growth stocks. Standard & Poor's, for example, has developed a list of "200 Rapid Growth Stocks" by screening over 6000 issues by computer.

However they are defined, growth stock investing has been a popular common stock investment strategy. Many claim that it has yielded handsome investment results over a period of years.

Income Stocks

Sometimes people buy or own common stocks for current income. While in recent years common stocks, on the average, have had lower current yields than bonds, there are stocks that may be classified as income stocks because they pay a higher-than-average return. Income stocks are those that yield generous current returns as compared with common stocks generally.

Some care is needed in selecting income stocks. A stock may be paying a high current return because its price has fallen as the result of uncertainty about whether the company can continue to maintain its present dividend rate in light of declining earnings. Or the stock may be of a lackluster company in an unpopular industry with little future.

On the other hand, there are many sound stocks that are paying higher-than-average current yields because of the nature of their products or industries. When general economic conditions become more uncertain, investors often become more interested in the current income from stocks. Possible future capital growth seems less attractive then.

Growth (Moderate) and Income Stocks

The category we call growth (moderate) and income stocks really just represents a combination of the previous two groupings. These common stocks pay dividends which are equal to or hopefully somewhat above the dividend yield from common stocks in general and also offer reasonable growth potential. They often are in seasoned but moderately growing industries. It is also hoped that the dividend rates paid on these stocks will be increased periodically in the future.

Defensive Stocks

Some stocks are characterized as "defensive." Such stocks are regarded as stable and comparatively safe, especially in periods of declining business activity. During such periods, these stocks tend to decline less than others, and some may actually rise.

Defensive issues are often found among companies whose products suffer relatively little during recessions or depressions. Also, companies that provide the essentials of life tend to hold up well. The shares of utilities and food companies are examples of defensive issues.

In many cases, defensive stocks can also be classified as income stocks. For example, utilities generally are an example of both.

Cyclical Stocks

Considerably different from defensive stocks are cyclical shares. A *cyclical company* is one whose earnings tend to fluctuate sharply with the business cycle (or with a cycle peculiar to its own industry). When business conditions are good, the company's profitability is high and the price of its common stock rises. But when business conditions deteriorate, the cyclical company's sales fall off sharply and its profits are greatly diminished. Automobile manufacturers and machine tool companies are good examples of cyclical companies. Thus, cyclical stocks are often viewed as good investments at the start of an economic recovery (providing that start can be properly identified).

Blue Chip Stocks

"Blue chip" stocks generally are considered to be high-grade, investment-quality issues of major, well-established companies that have long records of earnings growth and dividend payments in good times as well as bad. Stocks such as IBM, Du Pont, General Electric, and Procter and Gamble are generally considered "blue chip."

The ability to pay steady dividends over bad years as well as good for a long period is, of course, a strong indication of financial stability. Some "blue chips" of previous eras, such as the railroads, are no longer considered such now. On the other hand, some stocks that were not previously considered "blue chip" probably are today. "Blue chip" is a rather vague term that is not very helpful in investment analysis.

Speculative Stocks

In one sense, all common stock investment is "speculative" in that common stocks provide a variable- rather than a fixed-dollar outcome. However, this view of common stock investment is no longer commonly held (although it yet may return), and what are "speculative common stocks" has a more limited meaning to most investors. Some high-flying glamor stocks are speculative. Likewise, hot new issues and penny mining stocks are speculative. Other types could be identified from time to time as they come and go. Some are easy to identify; some are more difficult. Speculative high-flying glamor stocks can usually be identified by their *very* high price-earnings ratios. For example, at one time in the past when the Dow Jones Industrials were selling at an average of about 18.5 times earnings, some leading "runaway" stocks were selling at multiples of 50 to 100 times earnings.

Also, there usually comes a point in a bull market when small, hitherto unknown companies go public or new small companies are formed. The offering of their shares finds a fierce speculative demand at this stage of the economic cycle, and their prices often rise precipitously. Unfortunately for the uninitiated buyers of such issues, a day of reckoning often follows.

Special Situations

There are stocks that may show very rapid price appreciation due to some special and unique development that will affect the company positively. There might be a new process or invention, a natural resource discovery, a new product, a dramatic management change, a turnaround situation, and so forth. Companies normally in other categories can become a special situation in the face of such a special development. It often is very difficult for the average investor to become aware of such special situations in advance. Of course, once it is common knowledge, most of the advantage normally is gone. Some recognized investment services publish information for their subscribers on possible special situation stocks.

Small Company Stocks

As the name indicates, small company stocks are stocks of smaller corporations—sometimes called small "cap" (capitalization) stocks. They often are traded over the counter. They may also be growth stocks. Some observers argue that, on average, the performance of small company stocks has been better than that of their larger counterparts. Sometimes this has been true, but at other times large "cap" stocks have outperformed smaller company stocks.

Foreign Stocks

Americans can buy the stocks of foreign companies through American Depository Receipts (ADRs). There has been increasing interest in such stocks in recent years.

Some Theories of Common Stock Investment

There are many theories of how to invest in common stocks. They tend to rise and fall in popularity depending on market and economic conditions. Clearly, everyone does not agree on any one theory. This probably is so because no one theory has consistently proved to be *the* answer to investment success. If one were, those who knew the theory would be rich. Much depends on the needs and objectives of investors, their financial and tax positions, the investment policies they have elected to follow, the yields on alternative investments, the general economic outlook, and so forth. Some examples of such theories follow:

Growth Theory

The growth theory has been a popular one and is followed by those who hope to secure greater capital appreciation than is evidenced by the Dow Jones averages or some other indicator of trends in common stock prices. The theory now advocates careful analysis of corporate and industry records to select those "quality" issues that show continuing growth from one business cycle to another and a growth rate equal to some multiple of the growth rate for the overall economy. Implicit in this growth theory approach is that the investor is seeking returns primarily in the form of capital growth (or gains) rather than as current dividend income.

There can be no doubt that some investors who have made long-term commitments to industries which have had a strong, continuous, and above-average growth trend of earnings have had considerable investment success. They may have bought common stock in companies in such industries—sometimes in only one company—and then simply held these securities over the years.

If an investor can identify and purchase the stock of such companies in an industry in its early growth stages, and the companies go on to be leaders in a growing field, the investor probably will accumulate substantial capital. However, the odds against selecting the right company or companies that will survive this initial stage are considerable.

Thus, in many cases the most likely course for the growth theory investor to follow is to wait until an industry has passed through its initial, competitive crises, and then attempt to select several of the strongest companies that have emerged from the struggle. [The investor may also purchase mutual funds (or assets through other financial intermediaries) that specialize in certain industries that the investor considers to be "growth industries" or in funds with growth or aggressive growth as investment objectives. This way the investor gets (and pays for) professional management in selecting the particular stocks.] If the investor makes the correct selection or selections when the industry still has a significant period of growth ahead of it, and the investing public has not already pushed the stock prices up to discount future growth for too many years in the future, the investor can do well at this stage as well.

What may happen, however, is that investors substantially overprice stocks in such favored "growth" industries. Either they may buy in too late or they may stay with the securities too long, or both. Many investors buy into such growth stocks after a long rise. The higher the stock prices go, the more popular and fashionable the industry appears. Yet the higher the market price goes, the greater the market risk becomes, and at some point the former growth stock no longer "grows."

There are no pat answers with respect to growth stocks. Properly selected, they can produce substantial profits for investors over the long run. But they are no investment panacea, and investors who purchase "growth stocks" when they are most popular and high-priced often are not psychologically conditioned for any substantial decline in the market prices of such stocks. And as fashions change, these popular stocks may go out of fashion, at least temporarily. While this situation may be temporary, some investors do not have the required patience to hold securities under such circumstances. Also, of course, the decline (or lack of growth) may not be temporary. This can be a difficult situation for investors to judge accurately.

Moderately Growing Industries and Income Approach

Many investors prefer a policy of purchasing common stocks of good-quality companies in moderately growing industries. This is particularly true if they are seeking income and stability along with moderate capital appreciation. Such stocks may sell at reasonable price-earnings ratios and provide good yields most of the time. While investors in such stocks may not stand to make spectacular capital gains, neither are they likely to be exposed to substantial capital losses. Certain food and utility stocks may be cited as examples of this category.

Depressed-Industry Approach

Almost the opposite of the popular growth stock approach is the depressed-industry approach, where the investor endeavors to select "comeback" industries and companies. As just noted, certain stocks labeled as growth stocks may be very popular and selling at high prices that may overdiscount their future growth. Similarly, stocks in depressed industries may be selling at prices that substantially overdiscount their troubles.

Note, however, that this theory does *not* mean that investors should purchase a stock just because it is low in price. Stocks should be purchased only on the basis of careful analysis of expected future earnings. To follow the depressed-industry approach, investors should have the time and experience to analyze securities carefully to make sure they are not purchasing stocks of companies that are likely to go bankrupt or in an industry that is going out of existence. In fact, for the most part, investors probably are best advised to select the highest-grade, or at least one of the highest-grade, securities in a depressed industry.

The "Value Investing" Approach

The "value investing" theory of common stock investment now generally calls for investing in the stocks of good companies that have strong balance sheets and whose stock is selling at a discount in relation to the company's net asset value or the net value of only some of its assets (e.g., its current assets). This theory requires careful security analysis and considerable patience. In a more rigid form than is generally applied today, it was popularized by Benjamin Graham during the Great Depression of the 1930s (when there were a number of such stocks to be found in the market). Some investment advisory services publish lists of such stocks for their subscribers. Since the end of World War II, this theory has been substantially less popular than, say, the growth stock theory. However, in the face of another experience like the 1930s, it may return to prominence.

Other Theories

This listing of theories of common stock investment is not meant to be exhaustive. Others could be given, but the ones mentioned here are probably the most widely followed today.

Common Stocks and Market Cycles

Investors in common stocks need to be aware of and to evaluate stock market cycles. When carried very far in either direction, stock market price movements are exaggerated and irrational in retrospect, no matter how logical they may have appeared at the time they were taking place. Investor psychology toward common stocks can change swiftly, and attitudes toward different companies and industries can follow a similar pattern. Thus, investors should try not to be in a financial position where they will *have to liquidate* their common stocks to secure cash. As noted in Chap. 7, emergency funds in money market funds or accounts, other cash equivalents, life insurance cash values, and the like should be maintained at reasonable levels to avoid just such an eventuality. As also noted in Chap. 7, investors should consider what their investment policy should be with respect to stock market cycles (i.e., with respect to investment timing).

Common Stock Warrants

Common stock purchase warrants are certificates that give the holder the option to purchase the common stock of a corporation at a stated price, which normally is higher than the market price at the time the warrant is issued. Some warrants are perpetual, but most expire 5 to 10 years after being issued.

Warrants represent a call on the future earnings of a corporation. Their value is speculative and depends on the terms of the contract, the current and estimated future price range of the common stock, and the relationship between the number of warrants outstanding and the number of common shares outstanding. The price of warrants may fluctuate widely. Thus, they provide a vehicle for speculation. Like other options, warrants give the buyer greater leverage to magnify the return, and thus they tend to be used by investors following more aggressive policies.

How Good Are Common Stock Investments?

To many people, "investment" has almost come to mean buying common stock. There have been several reasons for this. First has been the decrease in the purchasing power of the dollar (the purchasing power risk). Second, generally rising stock markets during much of the 1950s, 1960s, 1980s, and early 1990s have provided substantial capital gains for many people who were "in the market." This has fostered the idea that the purchase of common stock is a good way to keep abreast of declining purchasing power. In fact, during these periods, common stocks in general did far better than just keeping pace with inflation.

This is all well and good for these periods, but have there been any extensive research studies on how well common stocks have done over long periods of time? The answer is yes! The Center for Research in Security Prices of the University of Chicago has conducted several such studies. The first study contained rates of return on all common stocks listed on the New York Stock Exchange for 22 periods between January 1926 and December

1960.[7] If, for example, a married man who had an income of $10,000 in 1960, and its equivalent in earlier years, had bought an equal dollar amount of every common stock listed on the New York Stock Exchange starting in 1926, and if he had reinvested the dividends in all the stocks listed there year after year through 1960, his total return would have equaled 8.2 percent compounded annually (after paying commissions and applicable income and capital gains taxes). Of course, if he had bought at the high in 1929 and sold at the low in 1932, he would have shown a loss—a whopping loss, at that.[8] But in almost all the 22 selected time periods covering boom and bust and war and peace from 1926 through 1960, he would have earned a good return—often better than could have been earned on most other investment media.

While the first study from the Center for Research in Security Prices showed what average rates of return an investor would have earned from common stocks in the various time periods under the assumptions used, it did not answer the question of what risk (i.e., variability of rates of return) might have been encountered.

Another study from the center bears on this point. It covers all possible combinations of month-end purchase and sale dates for all common stocks listed on the New York Stock Exchange from January 1926 through December 1969—56,557,538 transactions. Among the conclusions are these:

An investor in all common stocks would have made a profit 78.3 percent of the time.

Over two-thirds of the time the rate of return would have exceeded 5 percent per year compounded annually.

Almost one-fifth of the time the rate of return would have exceeded 20 percent per year compounded annually.

Losses of 20 percent per year occurred only about once in 13 times, and losses exceeding 50 percent per year only once in 50 times.

The median rate of return was 9.8 percent.

It should be remembered, however, that the overall purpose of investing is to earn the best possible after-tax total return on capital. In some time periods, inflation has continued strongly while most stock prices have declined. Also, at various times yields on other kinds of investment media, such as corporate bonds, marketable U.S. Treasury bonds, municipal bonds, and even CDs have climbed dramatically (such as during the early 1980s, for example, when interest rates on high-grade municipal bonds

---

[7] Lawrence Fisher and James H. Lorie, "Rates of Return on Investments in Common Stocks," *Journal of Business,* University of Chicago, January 1964.

[8] Just for historical interest, the Dow Jones Industrials fell approximately 84 percent during this period.

reached 12 percent and on 30-year Treasury bonds exceeded 15 percent). At these times, investments in other media (such as long-term bonds with reasonable call protection) would have been better than those in common stocks. Further, at other times well-selected real estate has produced very good long-term investment results. These phenomena just stress the idea presented in Chap. 7 that, before investing, the investor should decide on specific investment objectives and policies and then invest accordingly. This may or may not involve investing in common stocks. In most cases, common stocks (either directly owned or held through financial intermediaries) should be one part of a *diversified* asset allocation strategy (as illustrated in Chap. 7).

Thus, the fact that common stocks generally have been good investments over extended periods of time in the past does not necessarily mean that they are good investments now or that they will be in the immediate future. An investor's analysis should always be based on current and anticipated future economic conditions as they may relate to stock prices and yields, as well as the prices and yields of other investment media.

Other Equity Investments

Real Estate

Historically, real estate has been a widely used investment medium for income and capital gains. A great many people have, in a sense, an investment in real estate in that they own their home, condominium, or cooperative apartment. Many people also own a second or vacation home. Some others may own smaller, income-producing properties that they hold as an investment, while a few have larger real estate interests of various kinds.

Should Real Estate Be Included in an Investment Portfolio?   This is a hard question, for the answer depends on such factors as the investor's personal circumstances; the kind of real estate involved; the state of the local real estate market; the tax status of real estate investments; and general economic conditions, including interest rates.

Advantages of Real Estate as an Investment.   To help answer this question, let us first consider the advantages cited for real estate investments.

1. The possibility exists of earning a higher-than-average total *yield* on well-selected real estate investments. This may result from the inherent advantages of owning well-selected real estate (i.e., the idea that real estate is a good investment), the use of financial leverage, and some tax advantages. But one difficulty in comparing the yields on real estate investments with those of other investments is that there are several concepts and techniques used for measuring real estate rates of return, and

some of them are quite complex for most people to apply. However, to give a point of reference, here is a simple formula that often is used by real estate brokers and individual investors as a rough rule of thumb for comparing the yields on different investment properties:

Rate of return

$$= \frac{\text{net income from property before interest and depreciation}}{\text{purchase price for property}}$$

Thus, if a small apartment house produced a net annual income, after allowances for property taxes and expenses, but before interest on a mortgage note, depreciation, and income taxes, of $15,000, and its purchase price is $160,000, the rate of return under this formula is:

$$\text{Rate of return} = \frac{\$15,000}{\$160,000} = 9.4\%$$

Now, how does *financial leverage* enter the picture? "Leverage" is simply the use of borrowed funds (normally under a long-term mortgage note in real estate) by an investor to try to increase the rate of return the investor can earn on his or her own funds invested in the project.[9] In general, when the cost of borrowing is less than what can be earned on the investment, it is considered "favorable" leverage, but when the reverse is true, it is called "unfavorable" leverage.

2. Some consider real estate, like other equity investments, as a *hedge against inflation.*

3. Good-quality income property normally will produce a *favorable cash flow.* This results from the fact that soundly selected and managed income real estate should produce a reasonable net rental income and because depreciation, which is a substantial expense factor in improved real estate, is a noncash expense that will diminish taxable income but will not reduce the cash flow from the property.

4. There are certain *tax advantages.* As noted above, the main tax advantage of investing in improved real estate is the opportunity to take depreciation (i.e., writing off the cost of buildings and other physical property, but not land, over a specified period of years) as an income tax deduction against the income from the real estate. However, under the Tax Reform Act of 1986 the write-off period has been substantially increased, to 31.5 years for commercial real estate and 27.5 years for res-

---

[9] Sometimes leverage is also viewed as the use of borrowed funds with the *hope* that the *value* of the real estate will increase at a faster rate than the cost of borrowing the funds. This has turned out to be a risky view of leverage.

idential real estate, with the straight-line depreciation method to be used in both cases. This has considerably lessened the tax advantage of depreciation in real estate investing. Further, costs to operate and maintain property, such as property taxes, insurance, and repairs, are deductible. Also, real estate can be traded or exchanged for like-kind property on a tax-free basis under Section 1031 of the Internal Revenue Code. Such like-kind exchanges are an important way for real estate investors to avoid the current recognition of capital gains on the proper exchange of one parcel of real estate for another. Further, on the sale of investment real estate, any gain normally is a capital gain. Finally, since borrowing against real estate as security for a loan is not considered a sale or exchange for capital gains tax purposes, refinancing real estate traditionally has been viewed as a way of taking appreciation out of a real estate project without incurring current capital gains taxation.

The Tax Reform Act of 1986 dealt some severe blows to the former considerable tax advantages of investing in many forms of real estate. First, *passive activity rules* were adopted, without excluding ("grandfathering") activities entered into before 1986 from their effect. For purposes of these rules, a *passive activity* is: (1) a trade or business in which the taxpayer does not "materially participate" on a regular, continuous, and substantial basis;[10] and (2) an activity primarily involving the rental of property, whether the taxpayer "materially participates" or not. Thus, a rental activity (including rental real estate) can be termed passive per se, regardless of material participation by the owners. Taxpayers to whom these passive activity rules apply include: individuals (acting as an individual, a partner in a partnership, or a stockholder in an S corporation); estates; trusts; and certain closely held C corporations. When there is a passive activity, the tax law provides that expense deductions in excess of income (i.e., passive activity losses, or PALs) generally may be used only to offset passive activity income from other passive activities. Thus, PALs may not be used currently to offset (or "shelter") income from other sources, such as salary, taxable interest and dividends (referred to as portfolio income), and taxable income from active business pursuits (i.e., a trade or business in which the taxpayer does materially participate). However, the unused PALs are not lost entirely but are merely suspended until the taxpayer can use them against passive activity income in the future (if any), or until the taxpayer sells the passive activity in a fully taxable transaction (at which time they can be taken against other income), or to a certain extent at the death of the taxpayer. These passive activity loss rules have had a considerable impact on many tax-sheltered investment programs (since the limited partners in such tax-shelter limited partnerships, for example,

---

[10] There are also some objective tests in the income tax regulations as to what the statutory term, "materially participates," means.

normally do not participate at all and hence would be passive) and on investment real estate which generally would be passive.

There is, however, a special exemption from these rules that allows an individual taxpayer who "actively participates" in rental activity to deduct up to $25,000 of losses on the rental real estate each year from his or her taxable income from other sources, provided the taxpayer's adjusted gross income (AGI) is less than $100,000. For taxpayers with AGIs over $100,000, this $25,000 special exemption is phased out by reducing it by 50 percent of the amount the taxpayer's AGI exceeds $100,000. Thus, for example, if a taxpayer's AGI is $125,000, the special exemption would be reduced to $12,500 for the year [$25,000 − 0.50 ($125,000 − $100,000)]. Similarly, if the taxpayer's AGI were $150,000, the special exemption would be entirely eliminated.[11] This special exemption may be important for some investors who manage to some extent (i.e., enough to qualify as "actively participating," which is a lesser requirement than "materially participating") a relatively small amount of rental real estate. However, it will not help individuals who invest in real estate as limited partners of real estate limited partnerships, since they normally would not participate in the activity at all.

Second, the longer depreciation periods for commercial (31.5 years) and residential (27.5 years) real estate, noted above, will considerably lessen the early tax write-offs that had been so popular in real estate investing. Third, under the Tax Reform Act of 1986, construction-period interest and taxes for real property must be treated as a cost of the property and hence depreciated over 31.5 or 27.5 years (rather than amortized over 10 years as formerly). Finally, prior to the Tax Reform Act of 1986, the so-called at-risk rules (which limit the current deductibility of losses from tax shelters and certain other activities to the amount that the taxpayer economically has "at risk" in the activity—i.e., the amount the taxpayer actually invested and borrowed amounts used to finance the activity to the extent the taxpayer is personally liable for the debt) did not apply to real estate. However, the Tax Reform Act applies the at-risk rules to real estate investments, except that third-party nonrecourse debt (called "qualified nonrecourse lending") is treated as "at risk."

5. As noted earlier, a real estate owner may be in a position, in effect, to take his or her gains from the real estate through refinancing the property without having to sell the property and take a taxable capital gain. Real estate is particularly advantageous in this regard because good-quality property normally can be used to secure a mortgage loan up to a relatively high percentage of its current value.

---

[11] It can be seen from these examples that the phaseout of this special exemption occurs between AGIs of $100,000 and $150,000. There are different phaseout rules for another $25,000 exemption resulting from the use of low-income housing and rehabilitation credits.

Disadvantages of Real Estate as an Investment.   Now let us look at some of the possible disadvantages of real estate as an investment.

1. There is relatively *slow marketability* in real estate (depending on the nature of the property), as compared with other investment media, and the expenses of buying and selling are relatively high. Similarly, there is a *lack of liquidity* in real estate.

2. A relatively *large initial investment* often is required to buy real estate.

3. It may be difficult to determine the proper value for real estate, particularly for the uninitiated. Real estate is not uniform, and there are definite *cycles in the real estate market*. All real estate does not go up, even in times of economic prosperity. On the other hand, real estate prices can fall precipitously during the down phase of the cycle. Then, the very financial leverage that was so attractive when real estate prices (and rents) were rising begins to work against the investor.

4. Real estate is considered by many to be an *inherently risky* form of investment. It is basically fixed in location and character. Also, it is an equity-type investment, and real estate values will fall during a period of economic depression as rapidly as, or perhaps even more rapidly than, other kinds of equity investments. Also, high interest rates may adversely affect real estate investments.

5. As noted previously, the Tax Reform Act of 1986 substantially reduced the tax advantages of real estate investments. Investing in real estate primarily or even wholly for tax benefits was eliminated. However, depreciation still remains a tax benefit, and buying real estate having sound economic worth as an investment should continue to be an attractive investment medium for many people.

How Can Investments in Real Estate Be Made?   There are several ways to invest in real estate. First of all, investors can simply buy property in their own names or as joint tenants or tenants in common with someone else. This is the traditional way of holding real estate, but it limits the size of the investment that can be made to the amount of capital the investor and perhaps a few others can raise. Real estate, of course, can also be owned by corporations and partnerships.

Many individuals invest in real estate by buying units in a *limited partnership* that holds real estate. The limited partnership has been a commonly used vehicle for real estate investment where the investors are the limited partners and the promoter, builder, or developer is the general partner. In this way, the limited partners can invest their capital with only limited liability for partnership debts, and the earnings (or losses) from the real estate can be "passed through" the partnership form of organization to the individual limited partners without being taxed to the partnership. The earnings (or losses) are taxable to (or, to the extent permitted by the tax law, deductible by) the individual partners. The general partners can manage the real estate investment, which usually is their business. But note the importance of the character, ability, and experience of the general partners in any such deal, because the general partners are in control.

Another method of real estate investment for the public is through a *real estate investment trust* (*REIT*). A REIT is similar in concept to a closed-end investment company (see Chap. 9, "Mutual Funds"), but it is organized to invest in real estate. A REIT can give the real estate investor many of the investment advantages of corporate ownership, including centralized management, limited liability, continuity of interests, and transferability of ownership.

The main advantage of a REIT over a public real estate corporation is the REIT's unique tax status. Taxable corporations are subject to the corporate income tax (i.e., they are taxable entities), while a REIT (like an investment company) can avoid, or largely avoid, the corporate income tax by distributing its earnings to its shareholders. The distribution is then taxed to the shareholder as ordinary income or capital gains.

REITs vary considerably in size, origin, and types of real estate investments made. Some are speculative and others are more conservative in their investments. Therefore, investors or their advisors should take care to find out the investment objective of any REIT that is being considered. Also, the *management of a REIT is critical.* The public generally is not able to judge the investments a REIT makes, so a major concern should be the quality of its management. This makes careful selection a particularly important factor in this kind of investment. Shares in REITs are traded on organized stock exchanges and over the counter.

Kinds of Investment Real Estate.   Not all real estate investments are the same. Some are very speculative, while others are relatively conservative. As far as tax and investment considerations are concerned, real estate probably can be classified as the following:

1. Unimproved land investments ("bare land")

2. Improved real estate
   New and used residential property (apartment houses and the like)
   Vacation homes
   Low-income housing[12]
   Old buildings and certified historic structures[12]
   Other income-producing real estate (such as office buildings, shopping centers, and various industrial and commercial properties)

3. Mortgages (such as through government-guaranteed Ginnie Mae pass-throughs, for example—see Chap. 10)

---

[12] Certain special tax incentives still apply to these types of real estate investments.

Oil and Gas (Natural Resource) Ventures

Oil and gas ventures are inherently risky investments, but by the same token they can yield handsome returns if successful. It has been estimated, for example, that about 1 in 15 wildcat wells results in a small oil field, 1 in 200 results in a medium-sized field, and only 1 in 1000 results in a large field.

Some basic tax incentives have existed, and may continue to exist after the Tax Reform Act of 1986, for oil- and gas-drilling investments. For example, the tax law permits:

1. The deduction from income of intangible drilling costs (IDCs), which could be up to 80 or 90 percent of the cost of a productive well. The Tax Reform Act of 1986 still permits persons with a "working interest" in oil and gas drilling operations (i.e., the person generally has unlimited liability for his or her own share of the costs) to deduct their losses from these operations against their other taxable income. However, a limited partnership interest would not constitute such a "working interest."

2. A percentage depletion allowance, whereby taxpayers can deduct this allowance from their gross incomes from oil and gas investments.

People can, of course, invest directly in oil and gas operations. However, in the past many oil and gas limited partnerships, registered with the SEC, have been offered to the public as a way of investing in oil and gas.

Other Tax Shelters

Aside from real estate and oil and gas ventures, there are other kinds of tax-sheltered equity-type investments that may be mentioned. They include cattle feeding and other farming enterprises, horse and cattle breeding, timber, minerals and mining operations, equipment leasing, movies, and research and development (R&D) ventures, among others. They all have their particular characteristics, tax features, and advantages and limitations for the investor. Space does not permit full discussion of each of them in this book, but interested persons can get information on them from other sources and from professional advisors in this field. As noted above in connection with the discussion of the tax aspects of real estate, the Tax Reform Act of 1986 has prohibited the use of "passive losses" from tax-sheltered investments generally to offset or "shelter" other taxable income. Such "passive losses" generally may be used only to offset "passive income" from tax shelters and other passive activities.

Put and Call Options

Trading in options to buy or sell common stocks ("calls" or "puts") has become a significant investment or speculative technique for many investors in recent years. While options have been purchased and sold in this country for many years, large-scale activity in this field really did not begin until 1973 when the Chicago Board Options Exchange (CBOE), a nationally registered securities exchange, began trading in listed options with standardized exercise prices and expiration dates. Listed options now also are traded on other national exchanges, including the American, Philadelphia, Pacific, and Midwest Stock Exchanges. The trading of options on these organized exchanges has provided investors with open trading, continuous reporting of prices and quantities of option transactions, and the ability to close out or offset their original option positions at any time prior to the expiration of their options (i.e., has provided liquidity in option trading). The prices of options listed on the organized exchanges are quoted daily in the listed options quotations section of financial newspapers or the financial pages of other newspapers. This trading of standardized options on organized securities exchanges that provide liquidity for investors has made the older over-the-counter options market virtually obsolete.

Now let us briefly describe how investors can deal in options. Calls and puts are options to buy and sell securities within a specified time period. A "call" is an option allowing the buyer of the call *to purchase* from someone a certain stock at a set price (called the exercise or "striking" price) at any time within a specified period. On the other hand, a "put" is an option allowing the buyer of the put *to sell* to someone a certain stock at a set price at any time within a specified period. These options normally are for round lots (100 shares) of common stock. The expiration date is the last day on which the holder of an option can exercise it and purchase or sell 100 shares of the underlying stock. Listed options have standardized quarterly expiration dates, such as the Saturday following the third Friday of January, April, July, and October.

Buying Options. People normally buy options (either calls or puts or both) when they want *to speculate* on whether a stock is going up or down or is going to fluctuate beyond certain limits. The price paid for the option is called the premium.

Let us see how buying options might work. Suppose a person thinks XYZ Common is too low and the price soon will go up substantially. In this case, he or she might buy a *call option* for XYZ Common. Suppose, for example, that on June 1, XYZ Common (the underlying stock) is selling at $62 a share and that a listed XYZ Common October 60 call option is purchased for a premium of $7 per share, or $700 for the 100-share option. This means that for $700 (exclusive of commissions for the sake of simplicity) the person has purchased a standardized contract allowing him or her to buy (call) 100 shares of XYZ Common stock at $60 per share (the exercise price) at any time prior to the end of October (the expiration date), or in this example about five months away. Now, if the person's judgment is correct, and, let us say, XYZ Common stock climbs to $72 a share by September 1, the October 60 call option obviously will have become more valuable in the listed options market. How much more valuable will depend on the open market factors affecting the option's price, but let us say that the premium for this call option has been bid up to $13 per share by September 1. If the person decides to close out the option position in XYZ Common on September 1 (prior to the expiration date), he or she would sell the call option on the options exchange for $13 per share (less commissions). In this case, the profit from this transaction (exclusive of commissions and other charges) would be:

June 1—Purchased call option for	$ 700
September 1—Sold call option for	1300
Profit on the 3-month transaction	$ 600

It can be seen that the above profit would be an 85 percent increase over the $700 "investment" in the option, while the price of the underlying stock (XYZ Common) rose only 16 percent (from $62 to $72 per share). It is this greater *speculative leverage* that generally is the attraction of buying options. But if the option buyer is wrong, and the price of XYZ Common stays around $62 or declines during the five-month period prior to the expiration date of the option, he or she will lose all the $700 premium or suffer a 100 percent loss. However, the option buyer's risk of loss will be limited to the premium paid for the call option, or $700 in this case. Thus the chance of profit can be high but the loss will be limited in dollar amount.

The person could, of course, simply have bought XYZ Common outright or on margin if he or she had thought the price was going up. But because of the speculative leverage involved, a much bigger "swing" out of a dollar "invested" can be secured with options than even with buying on margin.

While leveraged speculation is the main reason for buying calls, there are some other possible reasons, such as to sell some existing investments to release cash while still maintaining a short-term market position, to protect against short-term market uncertainty, and to have a hedge against short sales.

On the other hand, if the person thinks XYZ Common is overpriced and soon will fall substantially, he or she might buy a *put option*. It would work basically the same way as a call, except in the opposite direction. The option buyer now wants the stock to fall substantially to make a speculative profit. Another reason for buying puts may be to protect an investment position for the short term in a declining market.

The *amount of the premium* paid for an option naturally varies with market factors, but as a generalization, premiums (i.e., option prices) are influenced by the general trend of stock market prices, the current market price of the underlying stock in relation to the exercise price of the option, the time to the option's expiration date, and the volatility of the price of the underlying stock. To make a profit on options (puts or calls), the price of the underlying stock must fluctuate rapidly and substantially (and, of course, in the right direction). Thus, options may prove to be unprofitable for speculators if the underlying stock prices do not fluctuate enough over the relatively short option periods to offset the premiums paid for the options.

More sophisticated traders can engage in a variety of option techniques. One is the straddle, in which a put and a call on the same stock is purchased with the same exercise price and expiration month. Here the speculator will profit if the underlying stock's price moves far enough in either direction to more than offset the premiums on both options.

Buying options is an *aggressive, speculative* investment strategy. Therefore, even persons who want to follow this kind of strategy normally should commit only a relatively small percentage of their investable assets to buying options, as is true for risky, speculative investments in general.

Selling (Writing) Options.   Now we are on the other side of the fence. We are selling options (calls or puts) to others.

The motivation for selling options normally is entirely different from the motivation for buying them. The option writer (an individual or an institution with portfolios of stock or cash) normally wants to secure an attractive yield on his or her existing investment. This increased yield comes from the premiums received by the option writer on the options granted to buyers. For example, it has been estimated that, based on past experience, an option-writing program can yield a return of about 15 percent per year on existing stock investments. The option writer also is entitled to all the cash dividends paid on the stock on which he or she has written options. However, the option writer may pay commissions and other transaction charges on the option and any related securities transactions. Depending on the circumstances, the commissions on the one hand and the cash dividends on the other may just about cancel each other out in actual option-writing programs.

The option writer, however, gives up the opportunity for capital appreciation on stock he or she owns that is called away. But if the price of the stock declines, the option writer bears this risk (except, of course, that the writer has the premium on any call written on the stock). Thus, it can be seen from this brief description that option writing on existing stock investments really is closer to a defensive investment strategy than to an aggressive one. The objective is yield rather than quick capital appreciation.

But there are some warnings that may be given to the conservative option writer. Writing so-called "naked" call options is highly speculative. These are options where the writer does not own the underlying security. Generally, calls should be sold only on securities in the option writer's portfolio or on securities purchased for this purpose. Also, puts should be sold only against cash and only on stock the writer would otherwise want in his or her portfolio. However, some pure speculators do write options with the objective of profiting from price changes.

New Issues or Initial Public Offerings (IPOs)

Stocks and bonds offered by corporations for the first time are called "new issues" or initial public offerings (IPOs). Some new issues have been offered by corporate giants, such as Campbell's Soup, Exxon, General Motors, and American Telephone and Telegraph, either to raise money or to "go public." Such corporations often are of the "blue-chip" variety, and the investment merits of their new issues can be judged by an investor accordingly. In many cases, the market price of these new issues rose substantially immediately after they were sold, and there was considerable interest in them at the time.

However, most new issues are made by smaller, relatively unknown, or newly formed corporations. Many of them do not have an established "track record" of operations and earnings. Hence, they are often speculative. Some investors, however, like to buy such new issues as speculations. Those, such as the Kentucky Fried Chicken Corporation or Microsoft Corporation, that prove successful offer phenomenal gains for their original buyers. But a great many such new issues do not prove successful in the long run, and so the chance of loss in such speculative investments is high.

Another aspect of investing in new issues, however, is that some studies have shown that the prices of new issues *during the first year of their life* have outperformed already existing stocks. This may be because of the speculative interest at that time in such new issues.

Commodity Futures Trading

Persons usually engage in commodity futures trading in hopes of profiting from price changes in one or more of a number of basic commodities. These commodities include wheat, corn, oats, soybeans, potatoes, platinum, copper, silver, orange juice (frozen concentrated), cocoa, eggs, frozen pork bellies, lumber, iced broilers, and many more. One can speculate on price changes in these commodities by buying and selling futures contracts in the particular commodity.

A *futures contract* is an agreement to buy or sell a commodity at a price stated in the agreement on a specified future date. While futures contracts call for the delivery of the commodity (unless the contract is liquidated before it matures), this is rarely done, and the speculator in commodity futures almost always "closes out" his or her position in a futures contract before the contract matures. This way the commodity itself never actually changes hands among speculators. On the other hand, contracts to buy or sell the physical commodities are made in the cash (or "spot") market. The listing of the prices of commodity futures and cash (spot) commodity prices is shown in the financial pages of many daily newspapers and in various financial newspapers.

Let us see how trades are made in commodity futures. Suppose a person thinks the price of, say, corn is going up. He or she might back up that opinion by entering into a futures contract *to buy* 5000 bushels of corn (a full contract in corn) for delivery in December at a price of $3 per bushel, which would be the market price for December corn at the time the buy order was executed (assuming it was a market order). This is referred to as being "long" in the commodity.

Now suppose that the person is correct and in a month the price of December corn futures rises 20 cents per bushel to $3.20. The speculator now might decide to close out the transaction by selling 5000 bushels of December corn and taking a 20 cents per bushel profit, or a total of $1000 (5000 × 0.20 = $1000), exclusive of commissions and other costs. However, the speculator in the above example could have effectively magnified this profit through the leverage of trading on margin. Margin requirements in commodities are relatively low—usually 5 to 10 percent of the value of the commodity traded. If the margin requirement in this example had been 10 percent (for purposes of illustration), the speculator would have had to deposit with the broker only $1500 as security for the original futures contract with a value of $15,000. Thus, such leverage can magnify a speculator's potential profits (and losses) in terms of the amount the speculator actually puts up. Of course, if the price of December corn futures had declined and the speculator had closed out the transaction, he or she would have suffered similar speculative, leveraged losses. As in other areas, *leverage works both ways*.

Suppose, instead, that the speculator thinks the price of corn is too high and is going down. In this case he or she would *sell short* and might, for example, enter into a futures contract *to sell* 5000 bushels of corn for delivery in December at a price of $3 per bushel. But here the speculator hopes to close out the transaction (cover the short position) when the price of December corn has fallen below $3 per bushel, and then the profit (exclusive of commissions and other costs) would be the difference between the original selling price ($3 in this example) and the eventual (ideally lower) purchase price. Of course, if the price of December corn futures rises, and the speculator covers the short position, he or she will lose on the transaction. There are, of course, many other techniques for dealing in commodity futures that are not discussed here.

A word of caution is in order. While the opportunities for speculative profits in commodity futures trading can be enormous and quick, the risks are equally so. Trading in commodity futures is inherently speculative and risky. Authorities in the field estimate, for example, that speculators lose 75 to 80 percent of the time. Therefore, investors generally should not get involved unless they have substantial risk capital in liquid form, adequate other resources, and the ability to control their emotions—mainly fear and greed. Also, as we said above with respect to puts and calls, investors normally should not commit more than a relatively small percentage of their total resources to speculation. In other words, if they cannot afford to lose, they should not get involved. But by following these cautions, they will have a much better chance to be successful speculators.

Art, Antiques, Coins, Stamps, Gold, and Other Precious Metals

Some people are interested in investing in more unusual items. In the past, properly selected items in some areas have shown substantial increases in price. This has led some to regard buying such items as a "hedge against inflation." As we have said before, however, this is true only if their prices keep rising, and there is no necessary connection between the prices of such items and inflation. This is not to say that these items may not be good investments for some people under the right circumstances. It is just that inflation does not have much to do with it.

Some of these items are unique and specialized, and so buying them successfully requires a knowledge of what one is doing. Also, they produce no investment income—only possible price appreciation. Of course, many people have a collector's interest in such property anyway, and so it may be quite logical for them to acquire these items.

9

Mutual Funds

Mutual funds are, in effect, large portfolios that are formed by many individual investors collectively pooling their resources. Many different types of funds exist, with varied investment objectives. Individual mutual funds also differ in the degree of success they achieve in meeting their stated objectives. Investing in mutual funds and how this may affect personal financial planning are discussed in this chapter.

In popular usage, the term "mutual fund" often is meant to refer to any kind of investment company. Actually, however, there are three basic kinds of investment companies: (1) those that sell face-amount certificates, (2) unit investment trusts (where the fund invests in a fixed portfolio of securities), and (3) so-called management companies. The most important of these are the management companies, which, in turn, can be classified as (1) closed-end funds and (2) open-end or *mutual funds*. Again, the open-end or mutual fund is by far the most important variety of investment company and, hence, we devote most of our attention to it in this chapter. However, it must be recognized that many funds are sold today as unit investment trusts, under which the fund invests in a fixed portfolio of assets which are not managed further by the fund or added to by investors. There are many municipal bond and corporate bond unit investment trusts. There are also some common stock unit investment trusts.

Why Invest in Mutual Funds?

A number of advantages are frequently given for investing in mutual funds. First, by pooling their investible capital, smaller investors are able to enjoy a degree of *diversification* they could never achieve on their own. Second, a mutual fund offers *experienced professional management* to select the securities to which the fund's resources will be allocated. And, third, a mutual fund offers *convenience* and *ready marketability* through the fund's obligation to redeem its shares. Further, mutual funds offer investors *reasonable investment unit size* so that many persons can invest through them. Thus, individual investors in a mutual fund do not have to keep on top of individual securities; investors do not have to be constantly on the alert for new investment opportunities; tax statements concerning fund distributions are prepared by the fund and sent to all investors; if the investors wish, fund distributions can normally be reinvested systematically; the investors' holdings in the fund usually can be liquidated systematically if they want to supplement current income; and the like.

Given these advantages, it is not surprising that mutual funds, as financial intermediaries, can play a major role in one's investment planning. Today, hundreds of mutual funds compete actively for the public's investment dollars so investors have a wide choice among funds. As discussed in Chap. 7, however, investors should consider whether mutual funds or other investment intermediaries are best for accomplishing their objectives, and whether the services provided by a mutual fund are worth the expense. If the decision is made that mutual funds should be used, investors still must find those funds whose investment objectives are consistent with their own and then choose from among them. To obtain meaningful answers, investors should be familiar with the different types and structures of mutual funds, know where to secure relevant information about mutual funds, and know how to evaluate such information.

Types of Funds

As just noted, investment companies can be classified in several ways. However, one of the major distinctions is between open-end and closed-end funds.

Open-End Funds

A mutual fund is, by definition, an open-end investment company. Open-end companies represent the dominant type of investment company. They are called "open-end" because the number of outstanding shares—or capitalization—is not fixed. Instead, the number of shares is continually changing as investors purchase new shares or redeem old ones. Thus, when people want to buy shares in an open-end fund, they, in effect, buy them from the fund itself. And when they want to redeem such shares, the fund must stand ready to buy them back.

The price for purchase or sale of open-end fund shares is based on the most recently computed net asset value (NAV) of the fund. Net asset value per share is the total value of all securities and other assets held by the fund, less any fund liabilities, divided by the number of outstanding shares. It is calculated daily.

Closed-End Funds

A closed-end investment company is similar in many respects to a typical corporation. It issues a fixed number of shares, which normally does not fluctuate except as new stock may be issued. It can issue bonds and preferred stock so as to leverage the position of the common shareholders. The closed-end fund uses its capital and other resources primarily to invest in the securities of other corporations. There are many more open-end funds than closed-end funds.

The shares of closed-end funds are bought and sold in the market just like the stock of other corporations. The stock of closed-end funds can be listed on stock exchanges or traded over the counter. The price quotations for the stock are given daily in the same manner as for other traded common stocks (see Chap. 8). The seller or buyer contacts his or her stockbroker, who handles the transaction and charges the usual commission for the broker's services. The total number of outstanding shares is not affected by transactions in a stock, because both buyers and sellers are outside investors and not the fund itself.

Unlike open-end shares, the price for purchases and sales of closed-end fund shares is determined by the supply and demand for the shares in the market—just as with any other common stock—and is not tied directly to a fund's net asset value (NAV) per share. When the stock market price of a fund's shares exceeds its NAV, the fund is said to sell *at a premium* (over its NAV). On the other hand, when the stock market price is less than a fund's NAV, it is said to sell *at a discount* (from its NAV). Thus, at any given time, some closed-end funds may sell at a *premium* while others sell at a *discount.*

Open-End versus Closed-End Funds

In buying a fund, should the investor consider an open-end or a closed-end fund? This is a debatable question, and there are no pat answers. But here are some things to consider. First, both types provide professional investment management, diversification, and periodic distributions of investment income and capital gains to investors. They both also are readily marketable, but in different ways—an open-end fund through redemption of its shares by the fund itself and a closed-end fund by sale of its shares on the open market. There are more open-end funds from which to choose, and they often are sold by sales representatives who handle mutual funds. Therefore, when one is solicited to buy a fund, it will almost certainly be an open-end fund. Thus, people tend to be more aware of open-end funds than closed-end funds. When an investor buys or sells a closed-end fund, he or she pays regular (or discount) stock market commissions and other costs. What sales charge is paid for mutual fund shares depends on whether it is a "load" or "no-load" fund, as described next.

What fund shares are worth at any given time is not guaranteed for either type, but their value is determined differently. In the case of a mutual fund, it is the NAV of the fund shares at that time; for a closed-end fund, it is the price of the fund shares on the stock market at that time. But in both cases investors can make money, break even, or lose money on the fund shares, depending largely on how the particular fund's investments do. Investors cannot buy a mutual fund for less than its NAV per share but they frequently can buy a closed-end fund at a discount or at a premium. Sometimes closed-end funds sell at substantial discounts, particularly during downturns in the stock market ("bear" markets).

In the final analysis, of course, a person's investment success with a fund will depend on the investment performance of the particular fund rather than on what type it is. There are good funds with good performance records of both types.

Load and No-Load Mutual Funds

As we said above, the price of an open-end fund is based on the net asset value (NAV) per share. However, two significantly different pricing arrangements are used for open-end funds. Open-end funds are sold on either a load or a no-load basis. A "load" refers to the sales charge levied on an investor by a fund for executing a transaction with the investor. The most common arrangement is where the investor pays the full charge when purchasing shares but then pays no charge when redeeming them.

Typical loads would range from 4 to 8½ percent of the public offering price.[1] Thus, when a load fund is purchased, the investor pays the net asset value plus the load. But if the shares are redeemed, the investor normally receives the net asset value. For example, suppose the L Fund, which charges a load of 8½ percent, has an NAV per share of $10. The load for an investor wanting to purchase shares of the L Fund would be 93 cents per share or 8½ percent of $10.93. So the investor would pay the sum of the

---

[1] Note that this results in a slightly higher percentage load based on the net amount actually invested (i.e., the offering price less the sales load, or the NAV per share). An 8½ percent load, for example, is equal to 9.3 percent of the amount actually invested.

NAV and the load, or a total of $10.93 per share. However, if he or she wants to redeem the shares in the future, and the NAV at that time is, say, $10.50, the investor would receive the NAV, or $10.50 per share.

No-load funds traditionally do not charge a sales commission (load) when the shares are purchased or redeemed. Thus, both transactions would occur at the fund's NAV per share.

In considering the costs of investing in a mutual fund, investors also should note that some funds may levy what are called *12 b-1 fees* (named after the 1980 SEC rule that first permitted them). These are annual sales fees taken against fund assets to reimburse the fund for distribution costs such as brokers' commissions and advertising expenses. These 12 b-1 fees may go as high as 1.25 percent of fund net assets per year. Such funds may also charge a declining contingent-deferred sales fee if shares are redeemed within a few years of their purchase by the investor. Such contingent fees on redemption are also called a "back-end load." Finally, some funds are known as "low-load" funds since they charge relatively lower loads at purchase, such as 3½ percent or less.

Open-end fund values and prices are given daily in the financial pages of most newspapers in a special section on mutual funds. Prices are quoted on a net asset value (NAV) basis and an offering price (offer) basis. These prices for the L Fund (a load fund), mentioned above, would be NAV—$10 and offering price—$10.93. The spread between the NAV and the offering price is the load. For a no-load fund, the quoted NAV and the offering price would be the same.

To illustrate the differences in these funds, and to help identify closed-end funds, load-type mutual funds, and no-load-type mutual funds, the following examples may be helpful.

First is a daily quotation for a *closed-end investment company* that is listed on the New York Stock Exchange (the Big Board):

52 weeks		Stocks	Div.	P/E ratio	Sales in 100s	High	Low	Close	Net chg.
High	Low								
29⅝	23⅞	XYZ Corp.	2.53e	—	87	29⅝	29⅜	29½	+⅛

This basically is the same quotation as for any stock listed on the exchange, except that no price-earnings (P/E) ratio is given and the dividends of $2.53 are those declared or paid in the preceding 12 months. Note that the net asset value is not given in this quotation. However, an interested investor can find out the NAV of closed-end funds from various sources. For example, each Monday *The Wall Street Journal* publishes a weekly listing of net asset values of closed-end investment company shares as of the previous Friday's close. By referring to this listing or a similar one in other sources, we can find that this corporation's shares had a NAV of $31.88 as of the date of the above quotation. Thus, this closed-end investment company's stock was selling at a 7.5 percent discount on that date.

Now, let us take two mutual funds—one a load fund and the other a no-load fund. The daily quotation for the load fund as listed in the mutual funds section of daily newspapers would be as follows:

NAV (sell)	Offer price (buy)	NAV change
19.72	21.55	+.03

From other sources, the investor could find out what the payments (from income and/or capital gains) by the fund have been for the latest 12-month period.[2] The difference between the quoted NAV and the offer price is, of course, the sales load ($1.83 per share in this example).

A similar quotation for a no-load fund that also is listed in the mutual funds section of daily newspapers would be as follows:

NAV (sell)	Offer price (buy)	NAV change
15.58	NL (or 15.58)	+.04

Here the no-load fund can be distinguished from the load fund in that its NAV and offer price are the same. Again, the investor can find the recent investment income and/or capital gains payments made by no-load funds from other sources.

Reducing the Sales Load

For load funds, the percentage load is normally reduced as an investor makes larger dollar purchases. The minimum initial investment is usually specified in dollar amounts, such as $2500, for example, rather than in numbers of shares. A typical schedule of reducing load charges is given below.

---

[2] Such payments are listed weekly in the mutual funds section of *Barron's*, for example.

Amount of investment	Sales charge as percent of offering price
Less than $10,000	8.5%
$ 10,000 but less than $ 25,000	7.5%
$ 25,000 but less than $ 50,000	6%
$ 50,000 but less than $ 100,000	5%
$ 100,000 but less than $ 250,000	4%
$ 250,000 but less than $ 500,000	3%
$ 500,000 but less than $1,000,000	2%
$1,000,000 or more	1%

The amounts at which the percentage sales charge declines (e.g., $10,000, $25,000, etc., as shown above) are called "discounts" or "breakpoints." Obviously it is to the investor's advantage to be in the highest breakpoint bracket possible because the reduced sales charge applies to the entire investment the investor makes.

There are some *ways an investor can save money by taking maximum advantage of the reduced sales load applicable to larger investments in a load fund.* First of all, the investor, his or her spouse, and all the couple's children under age 21 are considered as one "person" in determining how much is being or has been invested in a fund's shares. The trustee or other fiduciary of a single trust or other fiduciary account also is considered a single "person" for this purpose, even though the trust or account may have a number of beneficiaries.

Second, the investor may be entitled to an "accumulation discount" or "right of accumulation" on the basis of previous fund purchases. In calculating a person's total investment in a fund's shares, the aggregate value (usually at the current offering price) of *all* the fund's shares held at the time an additional purchase is made is taken into account in determining the sales load to be applied to the additional purchase. Suppose, for example, an investor (or his or her spouse or children under 21) owns shares in our hypothetical L Fund that currently are worth $5000. If the investor now buys another $9000 worth of L Fund shares, he or she would have crossed the $10,000 breakpoint, and the sales load applicable to the $9000 purchase (but not retroactive to the first $5000 worth of fund shares) would be 7.5 percent, according to the above schedule. This would save $90 in sales charges in this example (8.5% − 7.5% = 1% × $9000). There is no time limit on when additional shares must be purchased to take advantage of this right of accumulation.

Third, investors can use a "letter of intent" to save on mutual fund sales charges. Suppose an investor is planning to buy enough of a mutual fund to reach a certain breakpoint but does not have the cash to do it all at once. In this case, he or she can sign a "letter of intent" indicating that the investor (or the spouse or children under 21) intends to invest a stated amount in the fund within a specified period—usually 13 months. Then the sales load on all purchases during the 13-month period is at the rate applicable to the total amount indicated in the letter of intent. For example, an investor might sign a letter of intent indicating an intention to invest $25,000 in a fund over 13 months. If the investor actually does this by buying, say, $5000 worth of the fund's shares on each of five occasions during the 13-month period, only a 6 percent, rather than a higher, sales charge will be made on each purchase. A letter of intent costs nothing, and it does not obligate the investor actually to buy the fund shares (a sales charge adjustment is made if the investor does not). An investor can also decide at any time up to 90 days after having made an initial purchase of fund shares whether he or she wants to sign a letter of intent for the future and have those shares included in it. Furthermore, many management companies that have several funds under their management will allow letters of intent and rights of accumulation to apply to purchases of one or a combination of their mutual funds.

In addition to the sales load of load funds, and any annual 12 b-1 sales fees, both load and no-load funds charge *investment management fees* and *administrative fees and other expenses* on an annual basis against the fund's net assets. These annual investment management and administrative fees are expressed as a percentage of the fund's average net assets. While they vary widely among different mutual funds, and among funds within a single family of mutual funds, investment management fees might start at ½ of 1 percent per year of the fund's assets and range up from there to 1.5 percent of net assets or even more, depending on the particular mutual fund. Administrative fees and other expenses (if any) also might start at around ½ of 1 percent per year and go up from there, depending on the particular fund.

Load versus No-Load Funds

Assuming that an investor has decided to invest in a mutual fund, he or she should consider whether to buy a load fund or a no-load fund. Prospective investors often are uncertain whether load or no-load funds are best for them. This is a controversial question, and again there are no pat answers. However, here are some things to think about in making a decision. Load funds have been more numerous, but some funds have changed from a load to a no-load (or "low-load") status, or funds that previously had only a load status have set up no-load funds as well. Also, while investors historically have put more money into load funds than into no-load funds, in recent years the proportion of total mutual fund assets held by no-load funds has been increasing. This has been particularly true with the growth of no-load bond and other fixed-income funds.

The greater part of the load paid by investors when they purchase load fund shares is received as a commission by the sales representative or broker. No-load funds ordinarily are not sold through sales representatives. Their shares normally are purchased and redeemed directly through the fund itself.[3]

Thus, no-load funds avoid the sales representative's commission. On the other hand, the mutual fund purchaser loses the advice and sales efforts of the representative. There also is no sales charge to switch from one fund to another fund in the same "family" of funds in the case of no-load funds.

As a group, load funds historically have probably performed no better or no worse than no-load funds. Of course, some load funds can justifiably claim to have outperformed particular no-load funds, or even the average performance of all no-load funds, over an extended period of time. On the other hand, some no-load funds also can show better results than most other no-load funds as well as the average results of load funds. It is very difficult to draw the conclusion that either type of fund is inherently superior to the other in terms of investment performance—so much depends on the individual fund.

Investors should be relatively sure when buying a load fund that they will not have to liquidate their position in the fund in the near future. If there is a possibility that some shares will have to be redeemed to meet other needs, this is a factor in favor of a no-load fund. If, on the other hand, an investment can be committed for a long period of time, the initial sales load itself becomes relatively less important over time.

How to Invest in Mutual Funds

There are a number of ways to invest in mutual funds, including outright purchase, voluntary accumulation plans, contractual periodic payment plans (so-called "contractual" plans), single-payment plans, and the reinvestment of dividends and realized capital gains payable from the fund.

The outright purchase of mutual fund shares is similar to such a purchase of any other kind of security. The investor receives a stock certificate for the number of shares purchased.

Acquisition plans are available for the investor who wants to make mutual fund purchases on a regular, periodic basis. Thus, an investor may seek to accumulate fund shares by making periodic, say monthly, payments to the fund.

A popular kind of periodic mutual fund investment plan is the "voluntary accumulation" plan. Under this plan, investors indicate, without any bind-

---

[3] Brokerage houses through which load funds channel their business are generally willing to handle transactions for affiliated no-load funds.

ing commitment on their part, that they will periodically invest additional amounts of money in the fund. However, investors do not agree to make these periodic investments for a specified time period or to invest a certain total dollar amount. An investor, for example, might start such a plan with an initial investment of $2000 with subsequent investments of $200 per month.

Any sales charge (load) under a voluntary accumulation plan is level for each purchase made. The investors fill out an application to start this kind of plan, and the shares and fractional shares they acquire under the plan are often held for them by the fund's custodian. Fund distributions are often automatically reinvested in fund shares. Investors can terminate the plan any time they choose without penalty. Some plans also make available decreasing term life insurance as an optional feature.

Another kind of periodic investment approach is the "contractual" plan, whereby the investor agrees to invest a certain amount in periodic payments over a specified period of time, perhaps 10 or 15 years. Such a plan provides for the reinvestment of capital gains and dividend distributions at no charge (i.e., at the fund's NAV). Loans secured by the accumulated shares can be conveniently arranged. Decreasing term life insurance coverage can be added to ensure completion of the plan in the event of the purchaser's death. Finally, despite the term "contractual" used to identify these plans, the investor is under no legal obligation to make the regular payment each month, or even to complete the plan. The investor may request at any time that the shares for which he or she has paid be redeemed.

Contractual plans have been subject to criticism, and they are not permitted to be sold by the securities laws of some states. The bulk of this criticism has been directed at the practice of deducting the total sales charges (load) that would be made if the plan were completed from the periodic payments made by the investor in the first few years of the plan. For this reason, these plans generally are called "front-end-load" plans. Up to 50 percent of the payments made during the first year of a contractual plan may be deducted as sales charges.[4] Thus, the amount of the actual investment made by an investor during the first few years of a contractual plan is substantially reduced. This practice exacts a particularly heavy burden on those investors who, for whatever reason, are unable to complete the plan.

A *single-payment plan* for buying mutual fund shares is essentially an outright purchase under a contractual-type arrangement. The shares are held by a bank as custodian, and the owner can name a beneficiary to receive them directly in the event of his or her death. Thus, the shares do not have to pass through the owner's probate estate. (See Chap. 14 for the advan-

---

[4] The portion of the first 12 monthly payments that can be deducted as a sales load is legally limited to a maximum of 50 percent.

tages of bypassing the probate estate.) Dividends are reinvested at net asset value under this plan.

Mutual funds (and some closed-end investment companies) have *automatic reinvestment plans* whereby investors can reinvest dividends and capital gains distributions from the fund in additional fund shares. Depending on the method of investing in the fund, and on the fund's prospectus, the automatic reinvestment may be at the fund's offering price or the net asset value at the time of reinvestment. Of course, reinvestment at net asset value is more advantageous to the investor.

Mutual funds may also offer a *systematic withdrawal plan* to investors whose shares are worth a certain minimum amount, such as $5000 or $10,000. The investor may establish a withdrawal plan to pay a specified, periodic amount to him or her, such as $2000 per month. The investor may want to do this during his or her retirement years, for example. Remember, however, that such a systematic withdrawal plan is not the same as a life annuity sold by an insurance company. To the extent that the periodic payments under a withdrawal plan involve the use of the capital invested in the fund (as opposed to the income and/or capital gains), the share balance in the fund may become depleted over time, particularly in a declining stock market. Thus, the periodic payments are not guaranteed for the investor's and/or the spouse's lifetime(s). If an investor wants such a life annuity guarantee, coupled with a common stock or balanced investment program, he or she might consider redeeming the fund shares and buying an individual variable annuity. (See Chap. 13 for a discussion of variable annuities.) Of course, if the investor cashes in the fund shares (either for periodic payments under a withdrawal plan or otherwise), he or she may have a capital gain or loss for income tax purposes, depending on whether the fund shares have appreciated or depreciated in value. Remember, too, that withdrawals under a systematic withdrawal plan made at the same time as an investor is buying mutual fund shares in the same or another load fund normally are disadvantageous because the investor is, in effect, paying duplicate sales charges.

Management companies that handle several mutual funds (a "family" of funds) often permit investors to *exchange* all or part of their shares in one fund for those in another fund or funds they manage at net asset value. Thus, an investor who may have purchased shares in a growth fund during his or her working years might exchange them for shares in an income fund at retirement. Such an exchange, however, will be considered a sale or exchange of a capital asset for federal income tax purposes and hence may result in the investor's realizing and recognizing a capital gain or loss at that time. Further, load funds usually require the investor to pay any difference (increase) in the sales loads between the fund the investor had and the one into which the investor is exchanging his or her shares at the time of the exchange. There may also be exchange fees charged by the fund for making such exchanges. Finally, funds often place restrictions on this exchange privilege (usually in terms of a limit on the number of permitted exchanges each year) to avoid excessive trading by investors in the fund's shares.

Mutual Funds and Their Investment Objectives

There are mutual funds available to meet just about any investment goal. Recognizing these different goals is very important for the mutual fund investor because, after all, the investor really is indirectly investing in the underlying assets held by the fund. It is also by noting carefully these different investment objectives that investors can use mutual funds to meet or help meet their needs for investments in certain categories of an asset allocation strategy (see pp. 209–214 of Chap. 7). A fund's investment objective and policies are described in its prospectus.

Common Stock Funds

Common stock funds are mutual funds that invest their assets in common stocks (and corresponding assets), with the possible exception of some cash reserves. However, they still can differ markedly in their investment objectives as explained below. Thus, these funds may include the following categories.

Growth Funds. The primary investment objective of these funds is capital appreciation rather than current dividend income. Growth funds tend to hold the common stocks of the more established, larger growth-type companies. These funds fit the growth theory of common stock investment quite well.

Aggressive Growth Funds. Again, the primary investment objective is capital appreciation rather than current dividend income. However, the investment policies and approaches used tend to be more aggressive and risky than for growth funds. These funds may hold common stocks in startup companies, newer industries, and turnaround situations, as well as regular growth-type stocks. These funds also may use other investment techniques, such as option writing. Thus the risks taken are greater than for growth funds, and so, logically, also greater should be the rewards for investors (i.e., the fund performance). These funds may fit the growth theory of common stock investing, but with a more speculative orientation.

Growth and Income Funds. These funds invest in the common stocks of well-established companies that are expected to show reasonable but moderate growth of principal and income (dividends) and that also pay reasonable current dividends. Hence, they have the dual investment objectives of reasonable growth and market or above-market dividend yield. Thus their risk level is moderate, as is their performance potential. They fit well the moderately growing industries and income theory of common stock investing.

Income-Equity Funds.   These mutual funds tend to invest primarily in common stocks of companies with stable and good dividend returns. The emphasis is on secure and reasonable dividend yields. Risk tends to be relatively low.

Option-Income Funds.   These funds also invest in dividend-paying common stocks, but they seek to maximize current return by writing call options on the stock they hold.

International Stock Funds.   These funds invest in the stocks of foreign companies.

Global Equity Funds.   In this case, the mutual funds invest in the common stocks of both foreign and U.S. companies.

Small Stock (Small "Cap") Funds.   As the name implies, the objective of these funds is to invest in the common stocks of smaller, lesser-known companies. These stocks frequently are traded over the counter. Some analysts argue that over the years these small "cap" stocks have generally performed even better than their larger "cap" breathren. These funds may also fit into one of the other categories, such as aggressive growth funds. Mutual funds are a particularly appropriate vehicle for investing in such smaller stocks because most investors probably do not have the time, knowledge, or resources necessary to evaluate a large number of smaller, lesser-known companies.

Precious Metals Funds.   The investment objective here is to invest primarily in the common stocks of gold mining companies and companies that produce other precious metals. These stocks may be viewed as surrogates for holding gold or other precious metals directly (since the prices of these stocks tend to move with the market prices of the precious metals they produce, rather than with the stock market in general). In this sense, the prices of these stocks historically have tended to move in a counter-cyclical fashion—rising during depressions (when the demand for precious metals increases due to their perceived security) and falling during periods of prosperity. In recent years, however, this historical theory has often not held up. In any event, these funds can be used by investors for any gold or other precious metals component of an asset allocation strategy, if they desire such a component.

Bond Funds

Bond funds are mutual funds that invest primarily in bonds of various kinds, depending on the investment objective of the particular fund. They may provide one or more bond components, either in whole or in part, of asset allocation strategies where such a bond component is desired. There may be many different kinds of bond funds, however, with some being very secure while others are very risky.

U.S. Treasury Bond Funds.   These funds invest primarily in U.S. Treasury bonds, which are backed by the full faith and credit of the U.S. government. They are therefore viewed as completely safe in terms of financial risk, while their interest rate risk depends on their average duration. As noted earlier, U.S. Treasuries normally are not callable prior to maturity. In terms of duration, some mutual funds make available U.S. Treasury bond funds of varying maturities, such as short-term, intermediate-term, and long-term. Such funds can be used to diversify a bond portfolio by duration.

U.S. Government Income Funds.   These funds seek a somewhat higher yield by investing in a variety of U.S. Treasury bonds, federally guaranteed securities, and other government securities.

Ginnie Mae (Government National Mortgage Association) Funds.   As the name implies, these funds are invested mainly in these government-backed mortgage-backed securities.

Corporate Bond Funds.   These funds invest mainly in corporate bonds. The objective of some corporate bond funds is to invest in a diversified portfolio of high-quality (investment-grade) corporate bonds. In this case, the fund's financial risk is low and its interest rate risk depends on the bonds' maturity and call protection. In terms of duration, some mutual funds make available corporate bond funds of varying maturities, such as short-term, intermediate-term, and long-term.

High-Yield (High-Risk or "Junk") Bond Funds.   There are corporate bond funds whose investment objective is to invest mainly in a diversified portfolio of lower-than-investment-grade bonds (i.e., normally lower than the first four quality ratings by Moody's or Standard & Poor's, see pp. 294–295 in Chap. 10). Thus, the objective is to attempt to secure a higher yield than from investment-grade securities by accepting the greater financial risk of buying lower-quality bonds. These funds came to prominence during the

1980s. However, not all high-yield corporate bond funds are equally risky. They vary in the average quality levels of the bonds in their portfolios and in the levels of their cash reserves. There are also high-yield municipal bond funds. As stated in Chap. 7 (see p. 202), use of investment companies (e.g., mutual funds) seems particularly desirable for investment (when desired) in "junk bonds" because of the diversification and professional management secured.

Income-Bond Funds.   These funds invest in a combination of corporate bonds and government bonds for greater yield.

International Bond Funds.   These funds invest in the bonds of foreign companies, foreign governments, or both. The market prices of the bonds (assets) held by these funds are expressed in the currencies of the foreign countries whose bonds (assets) are held by the fund. Thus, as the value of these countries' currencies changes in the world currency markets in relation to the dollar, so will the share value of these funds expressed in dollars. When the value of the dollar falls relative to the currencies of the countries in which the bonds (assets) in the fund are stated, the share value of the fund in dollars will rise (because the foreign currencies are now worth more in dollars), and when the value of the dollar rises relative to foreign currencies, the reverse will be true. As a result, there can be three kinds of risks or exposures in these funds: (1) the financial risk, depending on the credit quality of the bonds held by the fund (with international government bond funds generally regarded as being more secure); (2) the interest rate risk, depending on the average maturity of the bonds in the fund; and (3) the currency risk, depending on which countries' bonds are held, as just described. Thus, purchase of shares in these mutual funds enables investors to take an indirect investment position in foreign currencies and thus also diversify their portfolios in terms of currencies. (Of course, a person could buy directly one or more foreign currencies, or purchase some mutual funds that invest in foreign currencies.) This currency exposure is also present in international stock funds and in varying degrees in global equity funds and global bond funds. Some international bond funds seek to hedge against this currency risk in various ways.

Global Bond Funds.   These funds invest in the bonds of foreign companies and countries as well as in bonds originating in the United States.

Municipal Bond Funds.   These mutual funds invest in the bonds and other securities issued by states, cities, and other municipalities. The interest on such bonds and securities generally is free of federal income taxation (see pp. 313–314 of Chap. 11 for a discussion of the tax-free status of different types of municipal securities), and may be free of state and local income taxation. Because mutual funds pass through their income to their shareholders for tax purposes (see pp. 274–277 for a discussion of the tax aspects of mutual funds), this income generally is tax-free for federal income tax purposes and may be tax-free for state and local income tax purposes to the shareholders. The investment objectives of municipal bond funds vary. In terms of duration, there are long-term, intermediate-term, and short-term funds. There are also funds that invest only in investment-grade municipal securities, while others may buy lower-quality ("junk") municipals. Finally, there are *state* municipal bond funds that invest only in the municipal securities of a particular state. This enables the residents of that state (usually only the more populous states) to buy a municipal bond fund for their state only and thus have tax-free interest income from the fund for *both* federal and state and local income tax purposes.

Diversified Mutual Funds

Diversified mutual funds are funds whose own investment objectives are or may be to have a diversified portfolio in terms of types of investment media. Thus, in buying these funds the investor already has or may have some diversification by asset types in his or her portfolio, depending on what the asset allocation strategy of the particular fund may be.

Balanced Funds.   The investment approach of these funds is to have a diversified portfolio of common stocks, preferred stocks, and bonds. The asset allocation by the fund of these various investment media will be indicated in its prospectus or elsewhere and, of course, may change over time depending on the investment policies of the fund's management. The investment objectives of these funds often are to conserve principal to a reasonable degree, to pay reasonable current income, and to achieve long-term growth in principal and income consistent with the prior two objectives. As might be expected given the diversified asset allocation of balanced funds, they generally may be expected to grow less in share value (than, say, growth stock funds) during periods of prosperity; but, correspondingly, they generally will decline less in share value during recessions or depressions. As stated earlier, they generally are a diversified investment medium (by asset allocation) in themselves, and so an investor who wants a diversified portfolio but does not want to make the asset allocation decisions himself or herself can simply buy one or more good balanced mutual funds and let the fund management(s) make the asset allocation decisions and the investment selection decisions. Naturally, balanced funds differ in their asset allocations and investment policies. Sometimes they use quantitative asset allocation models. Some funds allocate their portfolios by using combinations of other mutual funds (as, of course, individual investors can do).

Flexible Portfolio Funds. These funds differ from balanced funds mainly in that they may change their asset allocation more rapidly based on perceived market conditions and may hold up to 100 percent of their assets in only one type of asset (e.g., common stocks or bonds) at any given time— hence the use of the term "flexible" in their name. Thus, they are probably less conservative (and diversified) than balanced funds.

Income-Mixed Funds. The investment objective of these funds is high current income. This is achieved by investing in good-dividend-paying common stocks and also possibly corporate and government bonds.

Money Market Mutual Funds

Money market mutual funds are highly secure, liquid investments that frequently are used by individual investors for the liquid portion of their portfolios. They are generally viewed as cash equivalents in that the mutual fund management companies selling their shares expect and intend to be able to redeem them at all times at a certain fixed value, often $1 per share. Thus it is intended that investors will always be able to get their money back immediately upon demand. This is done by redeeming the money market mutual fund's shares at $1 per share (or some other fixed value). Many money market funds also offer their investors check-writing privileges, which are called negotiable order of withdrawal (NOW) accounts. Thus these funds are intended to be safe, liquid, and convenient. They also generally have provided higher yields than have bank money market accounts. However, there is no guarantee or assurance that the shares of money market mutual funds will be redeemed at the fixed value or par (e.g., $1). Technically, a fund could make bad investments in its short-term money market instruments that would make it unable to redeem its shares at par. Thus investors should pay attention to the nature and quality of the underlying short-term assets in money market mutual funds. Bank money market accounts, on the other hand, technically are accounts in the bank that may be insured up to $100,000 per eligible account by the FDIC.

A variety of short-term investment vehicles may be used by money market mutual funds, but the underlying rationale is that the vehicles should be safe, short-term, and liquid so that they will be maturing regularly or can be sold quickly at face value to meet any share redemptions from the fund. Thus, two measuring standards for money market mutual funds are (1) the average duration in days of the fund's underlying investments (with shorter average durations considered safer), and (2) the fund's yield.

The investment vehicles or portfolios that may be used by money market mutual funds might include:

- Short-term commercial instruments (CDs, bankers' acceptances, and commercial paper)

- Short-term securities that are guaranteed or backed by the U.S. government or its agencies

- Short-term direct U.S. government securities (e.g., Treasury bills) that are backed by the full faith and credit of the U.S. government

- Short-term municipal securities

- Short-term municipal securities of a particular state

The yields on these funds will decline as the quality of the underlying assets in the fund improves. Correspondingly, the yields on tax-free municipal funds will be lower than for taxable funds. Money market funds do not have sales loads, but the funds do normally charge relatively low annual investment management and expense fees that are a percentage of the net assets of the fund.

Other Types of Funds

There are a variety of other kinds of mutual funds, but space does not permit discussing them all here. For example, *specialty funds* concentrate on the common stock of firms in particular industries or in a given geographic area. These are sometimes called industry or sector funds. For example, funds have specialized in the drug, airline, chemical, energy, and biotechnology industries. Some funds make heavy use of options, while others are interested primarily in new issues.

Another specialized type of fund is the *dual fund*. A dual fund actually is organized as a closed-end investment company and is really two funds in one. Dual funds are based on the fact that some investors are interested exclusively in capital gains while others are interested only in income. Thus, half of a dual fund's shares are sold as capital shares and the other half as income shares. The capital shares benefit from any capital appreciation of the entire fund, while the income shares receive all the income. Capital gains are not distributed annually. Rather, the fund is organized for a specific period of time, typically 10 to 15 years, after which the income shares are retired at a fixed price. All capital growth of the fund then goes to the growth shareholders at that time.

Leverage and hedge funds generally utilize the same concepts and strategies but give them different labels. Their investment objective is maximum capital appreciation, but at the expense of substantially increased risk. Thus, they can be considered inherently speculative. In their quest for maximum capital appreciation, hedge funds may use such aggressive investment techniques as financial leverage, short sales, and options, in addition to the more conventional investment methods. At one time, there were also some *tax-free exchange funds,* but because of an adverse tax ruling, no new offerings of these funds have been made since 1967.

Getting Information about Mutual Funds

Several sources of information on mutual funds are readily available. From these sources an investor can determine a fund's investment objectives and philosophy, study the current composition and changes in its portfolio, and see how the fund has performed historically as compared with other funds with similar objectives. The intelligent use of available information can help investors select appropriate funds for their objectives and circumstances. It can also help determine which funds have had better performance records over a reasonably long period of time.

Probably the most commonly used source of information is the *prospectus* prepared by mutual funds. While a fund naturally will attempt to present itself as attractively as possible, its prospectus must be accredited by an outside auditor and approved by the Securities and Exchange Commission (SEC). It must also be prepared in accordance with SEC guidelines regarding form and content. The prospectus, for example, gives information on the fund's investment objectives and program; how to purchase, redeem, and transfer shares; minimum initial and periodic investments; periodic purchase and systematic withdrawal plans; the officers and directors of the fund; recent purchases and sales of securities; the current composition of the fund's portfolio; the fund's financial statements; and so on. In addition to the prospectus, funds prepare less comprehensive quarterly reports for shareholders.

Closed-end funds prepare annual reports similar to those of most other publicly held corporations. Moody's and Standard & Poor's financial manuals also provide comprehensive information on closed-end funds.

Forbes magazine, *Money* magazine, and *Barron's* publish periodic reviews of the performance of many funds. They also may compare the funds' performance with several of the better-known stock market indexes.

Wiesenberger Investment Companies Services publishes a comprehensive summary of essential information and performance records. This annual volume, entitled *Investment Companies,* covers all leading open- and closed-end funds. Other recognized sources of information include *Mutual Fund Performance Analysis,* published by Lipper Analytical Distributors; *Johnson's Charts,* published by Hugh Johnson and Company; *Mutual Fund Guide,* published by Kalb, Voorhis and Company, and *Fundscope* magazine.

Mutual Fund Performance

Anyone interested in investing in a particular mutual fund will certainly want to know how that fund has performed historically relative to other, comparable funds and perhaps to the market as a whole. It is difficult to devise a widely acceptable, reliable, and understandable measure of performance, however. Actually, several areas of performance might be of interest.

One might be to measure administrative efficiency or the investment management fees and other administrative fees to the investor. These are generally evaluated by expressing total operating expenses as a percentage of a funds's net assets (the *expense ratio*) or as a percentage of fund income (the *income ratio*).

Another is the assessment of the investment performance of a fund. One commonly used measure of performance is simply to analyze the annual income dividends paid, realized capital gain distributions, and price fluctuations of the fund's shares over a period of time. But such "performance" data should be used by an investor with care. First, comparisons should be made based on a number of years of performance, such as 5 to 10 years. The results of any one year can be misleading or unique. Also the investor should be sure to use similar time periods. Be careful, too, about evaluating mutual fund performance only during "good times" (years of business prosperity). Second, it is important in analyzing performance to consider the investment objectives of a fund. For example, a balanced fund should do better than a growth fund in a declining market, while the opposite should be true in a sharply advancing market. Also, consider the risks involved. For example, since investors in, say, an aggressive growth fund normally would be exposed to far greater investment risks than would investors in, say, a balanced fund—given the nature of the investments of the two types of fund—the aggressive growth fund shareholders should expect to be rewarded with a higher average rate of return over a period of years.

Mutual Fund Expenses

As was noted in Chap. 7, the investor naturally must pay for the investment management and other services and costs of any financial intermediary—including mutual funds. These costs have been explained elsewhere in this chapter (and in Chap. 7), but since they are one of the factors that investors should consider in selecting a fund or funds, they will be briefly summarized and illustrated here. Fund expenses are required to be summarized and illustrated at the beginning of each fund's prospectus, and so this information is readily available to potential purchasers of fund shares.

The following summary of fund expenses is for a no-load intermediate corporate bond fund that generally invests in investment-grade corporate obligations. This summary is given here only as an illustration.

Summary of Fund Expenses

A. *Shareholder transaction expenses:*

Sales load imposed on purchases (the front-end load for a load mutual fund)	None
Sales load imposed on reinvested dividends	None
Deferred sales load imposed on redemptions (the back-end load used by some funds)	None
Exchange fees (imposed by some funds for the privilege of exchanging one fund for another within a "family" of mutual funds)	None

B. *Annual fund operating expenses (as a percentage of average net assets):*

Management fees (investment management fees generally charged by mutual funds)	0.33%
12 b-1 fees (sales and marketing fees charged by some mutual funds in addition to any sales load)	None
Other expenses (such as administrative or servicing fees)	0.33%
Total fund operating expenses	0.66%

Naturally, as explained earlier in this chapter, these fund expenses can vary considerably among funds. They should be evaluated only in conjunction with a fund's overall investment performance over a significant period of time. For example, one of the best-performing stock mutual funds for the last decade or more is a load fund.

The expense ratio of the fund illustrated is 0.66 percent (about ⅔ of 1 percent). This expense ratio can vary considerably among funds, including those within the same "family" of funds managed by the same investment management company. Expense ratios tend to be lower for money market funds (and the yields normally are quoted net of expenses) and higher for funds whose assets require more management or specialized knowledge. However, no general conclusions on expense levels are really possible. The actual expenses charged by each fund being considered for purchase should be evaluated by the investor.

Selecting a Fund

Suppose, after considering all the preceding factors, an investor has decided to invest in mutual funds. But which one? And when is the right time? These are not easy questions, and there are no "sure" answers, but here are some ideas that may be helpful in this important choice.

1. *Do the fund's objectives and investment policies* generally coincide with the investor's objectives and asset allocation strategy? As we saw above, funds have a wide variety of investment objectives, and one can normally find a fund or funds to meet most objectives. So it is largely a matter of finding the right fund or funds to meet the desired objectives. A mutual fund's investment objectives and how it seeks to attain those objectives (its investment policy) are described in its prospectus.

2. Consider *the fund's past performance* in light of its objectives. Information in this regard is given in a mutual fund's prospectus and is published periodically in the financial press.

3. Determine *the qualifications and experience of the people in management* who are managing the fund's portfolio. Information on the officers and directors of a mutual fund is included in the prospectus.

4. Briefly look over *the securities in the fund's portfolio* to see how well selected they seem to be.

5. If it is a load fund, *consider its sales charges* to see how they compare with those of similar funds.

6. Consider the fund's annual operating expenses (expense ratio) in comparison with those of other similar funds and in light of fund performance.

7. Consider the *various shareholder services* the fund will make available to investors, including the right of accumulation, available investment plans, a systematic withdrawal plan, and any exchange privilege.

8. Remember that *funds normally are considered long-term investments.* Therefore, do not be too concerned with strictly short-term changes in fund values.

9. However, *investment timing* is as important in buying fund shares as in investing in individual stocks or bonds. Therefore, an investor should consider the investment climate and his or her own strategy with respect to investment timing (see Chap. 7) before buying fund shares.

Tax Aspects of Mutual Funds

Assuming that they qualify, mutual funds are taxed as regulated investment companies. As far as the fund's income is concerned, they and their shareholders are taxed essentially on a pass-through basis. Thus the mutual fund pays out its investment income to its shareholders as various kinds of dividends, and then the shareholders report those dividends on their own tax returns as taxable or nontaxable depending on the nature of the dividends. There are three kinds of such dividends: (1) ordinary income dividends from the fund's net investment income (interest and dividends); (2) tax-exempt-interest dividends (provided that at least 50 percent of the fund's assets are in tax-exempt securities); and (3) capital gains dividends (as long-term capital gains to the fund regardless of how long the shareholder owned the fund's shares). Ordinary income dividends are taxed as dividend income to the shareholder; tax-exempt-interest dividends are not included in the shareholder's gross income for federal income tax purposes [except possibly for alternative minimum tax (AMT) purposes in the case of certain private activity municipal bonds as discussed in Chap. 11]; and capital gains dividends are taxed as capital gains of the shareholder in the year they are received.

Dividends that are automatically reinvested in additional fund shares under a reinvestment program are treated as constructively received by the shareholder and are taxed currently to the shareholder, depending on the nature of the dividend. Mutual fund shares are not *in themselves* a tax-sheltered investment program. However, if mutual fund shares are used as the investment medium for a plan or program that itself is tax-sheltered under the tax law (e.g., a qualified retirement plan; a retirement plan for the self-employed, or HR-10 plan; or an IRA), then the net investment income and capital gains dividends from the mutual fund are not taxable until paid out from the tax-sheltered plan to its beneficiaries. The same, of course, would be true for any other kinds of investments used in such tax-sheltered plans. (See Chap. 12 for a description of the tax advantages of qualified retirement plans, HR-10 plans, IRAs, and other tax-sheltered plans.)

The preceding discussion dealt with the taxation of the investment income of the funds themselves. However, a mutual fund shareholder may have a taxable capital gain or a capital loss in the event he or she sells, exchanges, or redeems his or her mutual fund shares. Mutual fund shares are capital assets, and so any gain or loss on the sale, exchange, or redemption of shares held by the shareholder for more than one year is a long-term capital gain or loss, and any gain or loss on shares held for one year or less is a short-term capital gain or loss and is taxed accordingly. (See Chap. 11 for a discussion of the income taxation of capital gains and losses.) To illustrate, suppose that Harry Wilson had invested $10,000 in a load growth stock mutual fund 15 years ago and that all dividends had been automatically reinvested in additional fund shares. The mutual fund shares are now worth $55,000, and Harry's income tax basis in them (the initial $10,000 purchase price plus the dollar amount of the reinvested dividends) is $17,000. Harry is planning to retire and would now like to pursue a more conservative asset allocation approach. Therefore, he is planning to exchange his load growth stock mutual fund for shares in the load growth and income fund maintained in the same "family" of funds. The mutual fund management company permits such exchanges without another sales load and with no exchange fees. (Assume that the sales loads of the two funds are the same, so no additional charge is due on that score.) However, this exchange of one fund for another is a *sale or exchange* of a capital asset for capital gains tax purposes and thus results in a long-term capital gain in this case. Therefore, Harry has an amount realized of $55,000 and an adjusted income tax basis in the mutual fund shares of $17,000, which results in a long-term capital gain realized and recognized to him in the year of the exchange of $38,000 ($55,000 − $17,000 = $38,000). At a federal income tax rate of 28 percent, this would mean a capital gains tax of $10,640. The result would be the same had Harry exchanged his growth stock fund for any other mutual fund or if he had redeemed his shares from the fund. Again, if the growth stock mutual fund had been used by Harry as the investment medium inside a plan or program that itself is tax-sheltered—say, an HR-10 plan or a rollover IRA—then the exchange (or a redemption) of the fund when the assets are still in the plan would not result in any capital gains tax. Instead, the assets would be taxable as ordinary income when they are finally distributed from the tax-sheltered plan. Again, this is true of any tax-sheltered plan investments.

When a mutual fund shareholder sells, redeems, or exchanges all the shares he or she owns, the total income tax basis of the shares is used to calculate any capital gain or loss as just illustrated. Also, if a shareholder acquired all his or her shares at the same time and with the same basis, the sale, redemption, or exchange of only a part of the shares he or she owns will be at the shareholder's basis and holding period for that part of the shares. However, if the mutual fund shares were acquired over a period of time and for different prices (bases), as in an automatic dividend reinvestment plan, for example, the taxpayer has some flexibility in determining the income tax basis in the case of a sale, redemption, or exchange of only part of the shares owned. If the shareholder can adequately identify the group from which the shares sold, redeemed, or exchanged came, that basis and holding period can be used (as is true of securities in general, as noted in Chap. 11 on p. 335). If not so adequately identified, however, the shareholder may have an election in determining the basis and holding period for the shares disposed of. The shareholder may assume that the earliest acquired shares were those that were sold (which would tend to have a lower cost or basis if the value of the shares is increasing, or a higher cost or basis if the value of the shares is declining), applying a *first-in, first-out (FIFO) concept,* or, if the shareholder qualifies, he or she may elect to use either one of two *average basis methods* for determining basis and holding period for the shares. The two alternative averaging methods are a double-category method and a single-category method. The shareholder qualifies to elect to use one of these averaging methods if the shares are held in a custodial account maintained for the acquisition or redemption of fund shares and the shareholder purchased or acquired the shares at different bases. Thus, for sales, redemptions, or exchanges of only a part of the shares owned, a shareholder may have some planning options in determining the income tax bases and holding periods for the shares disposed of under these rules.

With regard to closed-end investment companies, if the company elects to be taxed as a regulated investment company, its shareholders will be taxed as described previously in this section with regard to mutual fund shareholders. On the other hand, if the company does not elect to be taxed as a regulated investment company, it and its shareholders will be taxed under regular corporation tax rules.

10
Investing in Fixed-Income Securities

Two earlier chapters—Chap. 2, "Setting Financial Planning Objectives," and Chap. 7, "Basic Investment Principles"—covered many of the essentials needed for making investment decisions as a key part of personal financial planning. These earlier chapters, which stressed the need to look objectively at an investor's attitude toward taking risks and his or her basic investment objectives, presented several ways of determining before-tax and after-tax yields on investments, discussed the very important concept of investment diversification, and presented the fundamental factors to consider in evaluating many different kinds of investments. These points then culminated in Chap. 7 in the discussion and illustration of the commonly used investment management technique of asset allocation.

The previous two chapters have dealt with various equity-type investments and mutual funds. Yet, for most individuals, equity-type investments should form only part of their overall asset allocation strategy. Many types of "fixed-income" securities or investments also are available. In fact, the variety of these fixed-income investment outlets has increased in recent years. This chapter examines many of these fixed-income securities and investments to see how they might fit into an investor's asset allocation and financial planning.

What Are Fixed-Income Investments?

Simply stated, fixed-income investments promise the investor a stated amount of income periodically. As examples as of 1992, taxable money market funds may pay 3 percent a year, CDs, 3 to 6 percent, 30-year U.S. Treasury bonds 7½ percent, 20-year investment grade municipal bonds 6 percent, and so forth. Naturally, such rates will vary over time.

The buying and selling of fixed-income securities after their initial offering create a public market in many of these securities. Dealings in short-term securities—those sold to satisfy short-term money needs—create the money market. Dealings in long-term securities—those sold to finance long-term capital needs—create the capital market. Both markets are large, broad, and active.

A number of different kinds of securities are traded in the money and capital markets. The kinds of securities available can satisfy a variety of investment goals. For example, investors can obtain current income with maximum safety by buying Treasury bills, or maximum income over a period of time by buying long-term corporate bonds, or a tax-free return by buying municipal bonds. Also, opportunities for at least some capital growth may be provided by convertible bonds and preferred stocks, "deep-discount" bonds, and "zero-coupon" bonds. Thus, the markets for fixed-income securities offer investors a variety of possibilities for meeting at least some of their investment objectives.

In the following sections of this chapter, the various kinds of fixed-income investments, the influences that affect their market prices, and some strategies for investing in fixed-income securities are discussed.

Types of Fixed-Income Investments

Many varieties of fixed-income securities and investments are available to the individual investor. They include the following:

Preferred stocks and convertible preferred stocks

Corporate bonds and convertible corporate bonds

Deep-discount bonds and zero coupon bonds

Municipal bonds

U.S. government obligations, including Treasury bills, Treasury notes, Treasury bonds, and savings bonds

U.S. government agency securities

"Guaranteed principal" fixed-income securities

Liquid assets ("cash equivalents")

Financial intermediaries that invest in bonds and other fixed-income securities

Preferred Stocks

Preferred stocks ("preferreds") represent equity capital of a corporation, and the claim that preferred stockholders have against the assets of the corporation follows the claim of bondholders but precedes that of common stockholders. In almost all cases, a company must pay dividends on its preferred stock before paying anything on its common. But a corporation can pass (omit) its preferred dividends without becoming insolvent.

The dividend rate on preferred stock is usually fixed, and when dividends are cumulative, any arrears of preferred dividends must be paid before dividends can be paid on the common stock. Although preferred stocks typically do not have fixed maturities, they may be subject to call. They may also have sinking-fund provisions, but preferred stockholders normally do not have voting rights. Some preferreds are convertible into common stock.

Corporations generally have considerably lessened their use of preferred stocks as a means of raising new capital. Also, a steady decline in the gross-yield advantage provided by preferred stocks in relation to high-quality bonds has occurred in recent years. Thus, preferred stocks may be less attractive than formerly to individual investors.

Corporate Bonds

Bonds are usually promises to pay interest at a stated rate (the coupon rate) or, in some cases, at a "floating" rate adjusted periodically to some market interest rate measure (such as the rate currently being paid on Treasury securities), and to repay the principal at a specified maturity date. They differ mainly in their terms concerning security pledged, their provisions for repayment of principal, their provisions for redemption by their issuers prior to maturity (call provisions), and various other technical features.

Kinds of Corporate Bonds.   Public utilities offer a significant percentage of corporate bond issues. Most utility bonds are *mortgage bonds,* bonds secured by a lien on all or a portion of the fixed property of the company. Most bonds offered by industrial corporations are *debentures*—bonds backed by the full credit of the issuing corporation but with no special lien on the corporation's property. Debentures generally have first claim on all assets not specifically pledged under mortgage bond indentures. *Subordinated debentures* have a claim on assets only after the claims of senior debt are satisfied. A few bonds are called *income bonds or debentures,* and on which interest is payable only if it is earned.

Various kinds of *equipment trust certificates* (such as railroad equipment trust certificates) rank among top-quality corporate securities because of their direct claim on specific property that can be used by other corporations (e.g., other railroads) if the issuer should default on its obligation. A trust certificate can be issued against various kinds of equipment that a trustee, usually a bank, buys from an equipment manufacturer and then leases to the user.

Call Provisions. Many corporate bonds can be redeemed or "called" before maturity, and periods of declining interest rates historically have provided opportunities for corporations to re-fund their bond issues at a lower interest cost. However, many corporations now issue securities that offer investors protection for a specified period of time against call or re-funding (the redemption of an entire issue by the sale of a new issue) at lower interest rates. This period of call protection varies but may be from 5 to 10 years. Investors are willing to accept lower yields in exchange for some call protection or for bonds that are not callable at all. This assures them that their interest income will be maintained at a certain level for at least a given time, even if interest rates should decline in the future (i.e., gives them protection against the interest rate risk of maintaining income from investments).

In recent years, many new issues have either been noncallable or have provided some protection against early call or re-funding. However, this situation has varied with economic conditions. When corporate bond issuers believe that interest rates are likely to be stable or to increase in the future, they tend to be more willing to issue noncallable bonds and bonds with call protection in order to get the lower interest rates that go with restrictions on the right to call. But when such issuers believe that interest rates will decline significantly in the future, they usually want to issue callable bonds or bonds with more limited call protection even though they may have to pay higher current interest rates on the bonds in order to sell them (sometimes called a "call premium"). Bond investors, of course, have the opposite motivations. Unfortunately, no one really knows how interest rates will move in the future.

Sinking-Fund Provisions. Many bond issues also have sinking-fund provisions designed to retire a substantial portion of the bonds before maturity. Bonds in a designated amount are selected by lot for retirement at fixed intervals; in that way, the issuer repays the debt gradually. Some companies may also satisfy sinking-fund provisions by buying their own bonds that are to be retired in the open market. Sinking funds have been thought to strengthen the fundamental position of a bond issue; however, in recent years such provisions have become less popular with investors who are seeking to preserve liberal returns for as long as possible. For that reason, sinking-fund provisions may be deferred.

Deep-Discount Bonds and Zero-Coupon Bonds

Deep-discount bonds sell in the market for less than their face amount (*par value*) because they were issued at a time when interest rates were lower. For example, consider a bond with a 6⅛ percent coupon rate that is to mature in 11 years. Assume that the current market price of this bond is 82. This means that a $1000-face-amount bond is selling in the market for $820, or at an 18 percent discount from par. Investors may like such bonds for several reasons.

1. They provide *automatic call protection* because their coupon rates are relatively low compared with current market interest rates.

2. They provide, in effect, a *built-in gain upon maturity*—18 percentage points (or 22 percent on the $820 purchase price) in 11 years in the above example—coupled with a reasonably good current yield in the meantime. [However, any such gain at maturity (or sale) is a capital gain (long-term or short-term, depending on the investor's holding period for the bond) for federal income tax purposes. This capital gain also applies to municipal bonds, even though their coupon interest rate is federal income tax–free. Therefore, such bonds also have a built-in capital gains tax liability at maturity.]

But because of these advantages, investors tend to bid up the prices of these bonds, and deep-discount bonds normally sell in the market at somewhat lower yields than comparable bonds with higher coupon rates. Nevertheless, deep-discount bonds are still attractive to many investors. Any kind of bond—corporate, municipal, or U.S. government—may sell at a discount in the open market.

Zero-coupon bonds (or "zeros") are *original-issue* discount bonds sold without any stated coupon rate and hence without current annual interest income payable in cash. They are sold originally at usually substantial discounts from par, and their return to the investor is measured by their yield to maturity from issue to maturity. For example, a 20-year "zero" backed by U.S. government bonds issued at $185 per bond and with a par (maturity) value of $1000 would have a yield to maturity over its 20-year term of 8.80 percent. The main advantage to investors is that "zeros" lock in current interest rates for the duration of the bond (unless the bonds possibly are callable at some accrued values). However, since these bonds are originally issued at a discount, in contrast to most bonds purchased in the open market at a discount after being originally issued at par, for taxable bonds an annual amount of estimated appreciation (calculated by applying the bond's yield to maturity to an adjusted issue price) is currently taxable to the owner as ordinary income for federal income tax purposes, even though the investor currently receives no cash income from the bonds.

Therefore, taxable "zeros" normally are used to fund tax-favored retirement plans, such as IRAs and pension plans, where the investment income is not taxed currently anyway. Municipal bonds are also issued as "zeros," with the annual appreciation being tax-free.

Municipal Bonds

Interest that is exempt from federal income tax, and perhaps state and local income taxes as well, is the most important feature of municipal bonds (see Chap. 11). Municipals are particularly attractive to persons whose income tax brackets enable them to realize a greater after-tax net return from tax-free interest than from interest that is fully taxable. Columns 2, 3, and 4 of Table 10.1 illustrate the relationship between the effective after-tax returns on municipal bonds and those of certain other fixed-income investments. Column 5 of Table 10.1 shows the equivalent taxable yields to a 7 percent tax-free yield at the various marginal federal income tax rates applicable in 1992.

For example, a husband and wife who file a joint return and are in a 28 percent federal income tax bracket, such as George and Mary Able, whom we met in Chap. 1, would keep on an after-tax basis all the income from a tax-free municipal bond (or 7 percent after taxes in the example shown in Table 10.1). But this same couple could keep only 3.6 percent from a savings account paying 5 percent (taxable) and 6.48 percent from a 9 percent corporate bond (taxable). Based on these figures, this couple probably should consider municipals. Note that while the above-quoted yields will change over time, it is the *investor's tax rate (or rates)* combined with *the relationship* between municipal bond yields and generally comparable taxable yields that are the basic points for the investor to consider in this analysis.

Investors in municipal securities also need to be aware of the possible effect of the Alternative Minimum Tax (AMT) on certain municipal bonds.

Table 10.1*

(1) Federal tax bracket	(2) After-tax return from a municipal bond paying a tax-free yield of 7%	(3) After-tax return from a bank paying 5% taxable	(4) After-tax return from a corporate bond paying 9% taxable	(5) For the investor to keep 7% (tax-free) from a taxable investment, it would have to pay an equivalent taxable yield of
15	7	4.25	7.65	8.23
28	7	3.60	6.48	9.72
31	7	3.45	6.21	10.14

*All values are in terms of percentages. These yields do not consider the possible effects of state or local government income taxation, which can vary considerably among the states.

While the interest on most municipal bonds continues to be free of the regular federal income tax, the interest on certain private activity municipals issued after August 7, 1986, is considered to be a tax preference item for purposes of the federal AMT. Thus, the interest on these bonds potentially could be subject to the 24 percent individual alternative minimum tax rate. (See Chap. 11 for a more extensive discussion of the AMT.) Further, the interest on some private-activity municipals is subject to regular federal income taxation. Therefore, after the Tax Reform Act of 1986, interest on all municipal bonds issued prior to August 8, 1986, generally is exempt from all federal income taxation. For municipal bonds issued after August 7, 1986 (or other applicable dates), there is a three-tiered system of federal income taxation as follows: (1) interest on so-called public-purpose municipals remains free of all federal income taxation; (2) interest on tax-exempt private-activity municipals (i.e., "qualified bonds") is exempt from regular income taxation, but generally is a preference item for AMT purposes; and (3) interest on taxable private-activity municipals (i.e., other than "qualified bonds") is fully taxable for federal income tax purposes. To date, relatively few fully taxable municipals have been issued.

Kinds of Municipal Bonds.   There are several kinds of municipal bonds in terms of the security behind them. This is important for the investor in terms of their financial risk. The following are some examples of these kinds of municipal bonds.

General-Obligation Bonds.   This is the largest category of municipal bonds; they are secured by the full faith, credit, and taxing power of the issuing municipality. The principal and interest on state obligations, for example, are payable from the state's many and varied sources of revenue. The principal and interest on general-obligation bonds of local governments usually are payable from unlimited *ad valorem* taxes on all taxable property within the area. General-obligation bonds are normally considered to offer a high level of security for the investor, consistent, of course, with their credit rating.

Sometimes an issuer borrows funds and pledges only a limited portion of its taxing power for the payment of principal and interest. Under these conditions, the bonds still are considered general-obligation bonds but are referred to as *limited tax bonds.*

Special Tax Bonds.   These bonds are payable only from the proceeds of a single tax, a series of taxes, or some other specific source of revenue. Such bonds are not secured by the full faith and credit of the state or municipality.

Revenue Bonds.   Revenue bonds are issued to finance many different kinds of projects, such as water, sewage, gas, and electrical facilities; hospitals; dormitories; student-union halls and stadiums; hydroelectric power projects; and bridges, tunnels, turnpikes, and expressways. The principal and interest on such bonds are payable solely from the revenues produced by the project. A well-known kind of agency that may issue revenue bonds is a turnpike authority, which raises funds by means of bond issues and pays interest and principal out of the net earnings from the particular toll road. Thus, the kind of project involved and its long-term viability as a source of revenue to stand behind these bonds are critical matters for investors to consider in evaluating the financial risk of particular revenue bonds.

Housing Authority Bonds. These bonds are issued by local authorities to finance the construction of low-rent housing projects and are secured by the pledge of unconditional, annual contributions by the Housing Assistance Administration, a federal agency. Housing authority bonds are considered top-quality investments because they are backed by the full faith and credit of the United States government.

Industrial Development Bonds (IDBs). These bonds are issued by a municipality or authority but are secured by lease payments made by industrial corporations that occupy or use the facilities financed by the bond issue. The rules concerning IDBs were further tightened and the amounts of government bonds that can be used for private purposes were further limited by the Tax Reform Act of 1986.

Insured Municipal Bonds. Some municipal bonds carry insurance to protect investors in the bonds against the risk of default on the bonds (i.e., against financial risk in buying the bonds). Such insurance enhances the creditworthiness of the bonds and either enhances or gives them a quality rating (see below for a discussion of quality ratings on municipal bonds). However, municipal bond insurance does not protect investors against market fluctuations in the prices of their bonds prior to maturity (i.e., against market risk). Three large insurers of municipal bonds are: the Financial Guarantee Insurance Company (FGIC), Municipal Bond Investors Assurance (MBIA), and AMBAC. It is the considerable financial strength of these private insurers that stands behind their insurance of a municipal bond issue. While municipal bond insurance is a comparatively recent financial technique, bonds insured by these companies are generally considered very secure and are normally given the highest quality ratings.

Municipal Bond Ratings. Quality ratings on municipal bonds are provided by Moody's and Standard & Poor's, the financial services that also rate corporate bonds (see the later section in this chapter, "Bond Ratings and Their Investment Quality"). The ratings are objective because these rating services conduct no security transactions. In general, high-grade municipal bonds rank second in quality only to securities issued by the U.S. government and government agencies. During the Depression of the 1930s, for example, payments on more than 98 percent of all municipals were met without fail. In recent years, however, the quality ratings on some municipals have declined. As just noted, the highest ratings are normally accorded to insured municipal bonds.

Other Basic Facts about Municipal Bonds.   Many municipal bonds *mature serially;* that is, a certain number of bonds in each issue reach maturity in each year over a period that may range from one month to 30 years or longer. Such a range of maturities offers investors a great deal of flexibility in selecting maturities according to their needs.

Short-Term Tax-Free Notes.   These are notes of local issuing agencies, states, municipalities, or other political subdivisions in denominations of $5000 or more. They are issued to mature in one month to one year. These notes normally are secured by the full faith and credit of the issuer. Interest is paid at maturity. Some investors in high tax brackets use these tax-free notes as liquid assets.

U.S. Government Obligations

Because the federal government generally is considered as having the highest possible credit rating, yields on government obligations are basic for all maturity ranges throughout the capital markets. Rates on other securities tend to follow the rate structure set by government obligations but are generally higher.

Treasury Bills.   Treasury bills are issued on a discount basis and redeemed at face value at maturity. Treasury bills are issued in minimum denominations of $10,000. At present, the Treasury offers two new issues of bills each week for competitive bids; one issue matures in three months, the other in six months. Noncompetitive tenders from $10,000 to $500,000 of each issue can be submitted without a stated price. Such bids are allotted in full at the average price of accepted competitive bids.

Each month the Treasury offers, under the same general rules that apply to three- and six-month bills, a series of bills that mature in 12 months. From time to time the Treasury also offers *tax-anticipation bills* for bids on a competitive basis.

Treasury Notes.   Treasury notes have maturities of from 1 to 10 years. The notes are issued at or near par, and their interest is paid semiannually.

Treasury Bonds.   Treasury bonds mature in more than 10 years. They also are issued at or near par, and their interest is paid semiannually. Some of the outstanding bonds are callable at par 5 years before maturity on interest payment dates, but otherwise Treasury bonds are not callable. This can be a distinct advantage of longer-term Treasuries, since most other long-term, fixed-income securities are callable at some point.

Savings Bonds.   U.S. savings bonds are registered, noncallable, and non-transferable securities. They also are not acceptable as collateral for loans. Two kinds of savings bonds are now being issued—Series EE and Series HH.

Series EE bonds are sold in face-value denominations of $50 to $10,000; denominations of $100,000 are available for employees' savings plans. Except for employees' savings plans, the maximum purchase in any one calendar year is $30,000 for one person and up to $60,000 face amount for bonds registered in co-ownership form. Series EE bonds pay no current interest; instead, they are issued at a discount and are redeemable at face value on the maturity date. For bonds purchased after October 31, 1982, and held for five years, the effective interest rate is the higher of 85 percent of the average return on certain marketable Treasury securities or 6 percent. Series EE bonds are redeemable at any time starting six months after the issue date, but redemption before maturity usually reduces the effective yield. With these higher yields, EE bonds have proved more attractive to individual investors than formerly was the case. Further, there may be some income tax advantages for these savings bonds for individuals as explained on pp. 334–335 of Chap. 11.

Series HH bonds can be secured at par in exchange for EE bonds. Interest is paid every six months, and denominations range from $500 to $10,000. HH bonds may be redeemed six months after the issue date.

Other U.S. Government and Agency Securities

U.S. Government Agency Securities.   These securities are not issued directly by the federal government, but some have government guarantees. They typically carry yields somewhat higher than for comparable U.S. government securities. Some of the governmental agencies that issue these types of securities are the *Federal Intermediate Credit Banks,* the *District Banks for Cooperatives,* the *Federal Land Banks,* the *Federal Home Loan Banks,* the *Federal National Mortgage Association* (Fanny Mae), the *Government National Mortgage Association* (Ginnie Mae), the *International Bank for Reconstruction and Development* (World Bank), and the *Inter-American Development Bank.*

Flower Bonds.   These are U.S. government bonds with a special feature. The federal government will accept them at full par value in payment of federal estate taxes. Although no longer issued, and with relatively few still outstanding, they still may be purchased at a discount in the secondary market until 1998. While an estate can realize a gain if they are purchased at a discount and then used to pay estate taxes at par, they normally are attractive only in situations where death is considered to be reasonably imminent.

Pass-through (Participation) Securities.   This type of investment is a participation in a pool of assets (e.g., federally insured mortgages) where the investor receives a certificate evidencing his or her interest in the underlying assets. Probably the most important of these securities are those issued by the Government National Mortgage Association or the so-called Ginnie Mae pass-throughs. These certificates permit investors to earn high mortgage yields with both principal and interest payments guaranteed by the federal government. These securities feature an average life of 10 to 12 years with a typical minimum investment in individual Ginnie Maes of $25,000. However, investors can buy units of Ginnie Mae mutual funds for as little as $1000.

A special feature of these securities is that part of the principal is returned with the interest each month as the underlying mortgages in the pool are amortized and paid off by the borrowers (mortgagors). Thus they may be useful for such purposes as providing a retirement income with guaranteed, higher-yielding securities. On the other hand, there is an interest rate risk inherent in these pass-throughs in that if interest rates generally decline significantly, mortgage borrowers will tend to pay off and refinance their loans at the lower rates. This will cause higher principal payments to the pass-through investors, who then must reinvest these payments at the currently lower available interest rates.

In this general area, it may be briefly noted that there are several categories of securities. *Mortgage-backed securities* are participations in pools of mortgages; *asset-backed securities* are similar participations in pools of consumer loans; and *collateralized mortgage obligations* (CMOs) are a form of mortgage-backed security but which may consist of portions with different investment characteristics.

"Guaranteed Principal" Fixed-Income Securities

The types of fixed-income investments we have discussed so far provide guaranteed investment income and/or a promised value at maturity, but during the term of the investment (e.g., until a bond matures), the market value of the security can fluctuate depending on economic conditions. Thus, if an investor sells before maturity, the investor may suffer a capital loss or realize a capital gain. In other words, prior to maturity there is market risk regarding the principal value of these investments.

The category of fixed-income investments we are now considering has both a *guaranteed principal value* and a *stated or guaranteed investment income,* at least for a specified period of time. Such fixed-income investments do not have any market risk and do not have any interest rate risk to their principal value. They may, however, have some financial risk in that the security of these investments (in the absence of government insurance) depends on the ability of the issuer to meet its financial commitments. Thus, the financial strength of the issuer (with the possible exception of deposits insured through the FDIC) is of critical importance to the investor in this area.

Certificates of Deposit.   Certificates of deposit (CDs) have been mentioned previously in this book (see Chap. 7) and are interest-bearing, negotiable, and redeemable evidences of time deposits at banks and at savings and loan associations. They are sold in varying amounts (usually with some modest minimum amount) and with maturities varying from a few months to 10 years. There usually is an interest penalty for early withdrawal of savings if they are redeemed by the purchaser prior to their maturity. (This interest penalty, however, is deductible by the investor for federal income tax purposes from gross income to arrive at adjusted gross income.)

In most cases, CDs are insured up to $100,000 per eligible account through the FDIC. Thus, insured CDs have the protection of the FDIC behind them regardless of the financial strength of the issuing bank or S&L, and this has been an important factor in their popularity over the years. However, if a CD is purchased in excess of this insured amount, the investor should evaluate whether the bank or S&L is financially sound. Banks and S&Ls may sell so-called jumbo CDs in certain minimum amounts, such as $100,000, that carry higher interest rates for investors than the bank's or S&L's regular CDs in lower denominations.

CDs have been popular investments for many persons seeking guaranteed principal and guaranteed interest for the life of the CD. At maturity, however, the investor must reinvest the principal in another CD at the then-prevailing interest rates or in other investments at current yields. Thus, there is an interest rate risk to the level of investment income inherent in CDs.

Commercial Paper.   These are short-term promissory notes issued periodically by well-known corporate borrowers. They are normally issued in reasonably high minimum amounts, such as $10,000. The only security behind this paper is the financial strength of the issuing corporation, which typically has been quite good. They are considered money market instruments (i.e., shorter-term, high-quality instruments) and are often purchased by money market mutual funds and other lenders interested in short-term, liquid investments.

Guaranteed Investment Contracts (GICs).   These are popular investment options for employees under certain kinds of qualified retirement
plans (often savings plans) provided by their employer. (See Chap. 12 for a
more complete description of qualified retirement plans as employee benefits.) As such, they are contracts between the employer (as the qualified
retirement plan sponsor) and an insurance company, under which the
insurance company accepts funds for investment for a specified duration at
a guaranteed interest rate or rates.

The insurance company guarantees the principal and interest of the GIC
for the specified period of time. The participating employee, in effect, may
elect to place part or all of his or her savings plan dollars, to the extent
permitted by the terms of the employee benefit plan, in a fixed-dollar or
guaranteed-dollar investment option under the plan (which is provided
through the GIC) and have a guaranteed principal and interest investment
at all times for as long as the GIC continues. Of course, when one GIC
matures, the insurance company and the employer may negotiate another
one for a new term but perhaps at a different guaranteed interest rate
(either higher or lower), depending on market conditions then for GICs.
Representative current interest rates for GICs of certain amounts and for
certain durations (such as three, five, and seven years) are quoted in the
financial pages of certain publications.

Even though GICs arise from qualified retirement plans as a part of
employee benefit plans (usually savings plans), they are discussed here
because they really represent for participating employees an opportunity to
allocate savings plan funds to a guaranteed principal–guaranteed interest
investment vehicle. Of course, those who do not have qualified savings
plans that offer GICs as an investment option available to them through
their employers cannot do so. However, for many employees who do have
GICs available to them, the GIC has proven to be a popular investment
choice.

The employee must remember, however, that the security behind a
GIC is the financial soundness of the insurance company that is providing
it. While there are state guaranty funds covering insurance companies,
there is no direct federal government insurance covering GICs comparable to that through the FDIC with respect to bank and savings and loan
deposits. Therefore, employees considering placing their savings plan
assets in GICs should evaluate carefully the financial soundness of
the insurance company providing the GIC, in much the same way as he or
she would if the employee were purchasing insurance directly from the
insurer.[1]

---

[1] See pp. 53–57 of Chap. 3 for a discussion of evaluating the financial soundness of insurance companies.

In the final analysis, then, investors who want a part of their asset allocation to be in longer-term, guaranteed principal/guaranteed interest types of instruments that are not intended to be liquid assets (with presumably lower yields) might consider the following:

- Insured certificates of deposit (CDs) from banks or savings and loans
- Guaranteed investment contracts (GICs) through the person's employee benefit plan
- U.S. government savings bonds (Series EE or HH)

Liquid Assets ("Cash Equivalents")

Liquid assets or cash equivalents should be *highly liquid* (convertible into cash immediately with no loss of principal) and *financially secure* (low or no financial risk). On the other hand, to achieve such investment characteristics, these assets are *short-term* and tend to offer a *lower yield* than other fixed-income securities.[2] Thus, it often is necessary to trade safety and liquidity for yield in the liquid assets portion of an investor's portfolio. Investors may want this liquid portion for possible emergencies (as noted in Chap. 2), for flexibility to be able to take advantage of unforseen investment opportunities, as an investment strategy if interest rates are expected to rise significantly, and as a repository for cash while deciding on an investment or other large expenditure.

The types of liquid assets that may be held in a portfolio were noted in Chap. 2 and Chap. 7. However, since generally they are really types of short-term, fixed-income securities, they are outlined here for the sake of completeness.

Money Market Mutual Funds. These are commonly used and were described in Chap. 9.

Bank Money Market Accounts. These also are commonly used and also were noted in Chap. 9.

---

[2] This statement reflects the general principle that for a given quality of fixed-income investment, the yield will rise with duration. This may be referred to as the *yield curve* for fixed-income securities. However, under certain economic conditions this yield curve can be quite flat (with little or no difference in yields between shorter-term and longer-term securities of the same type), or can even be inverted (with shorter-term yields higher than longer-term yields). A flat or inverted yield curve may occur, for example, when investors generally believe that interest rates will fall significantly in the future and thus are seeking to lock in the present rates by buying (and hence bidding up the prices of) longer-term securities with adequate call protection (such as longer-term Treasuries).

Directly Owned Liquid Assets.   In this case the investor owns directly such assets as Treasury bills, short-term tax-free municipal notes, commercial paper, short-term high-quality bonds, and other similar liquid assets. The advantage of doing this as compared with investing in money market funds or accounts is that the investor may be able to improve his or her yield by direct ownership and the avoidance of the management expenses of mutual funds or banks. However, this may be feasible only or mainly for larger investors.

Savings Accounts.   These are accounts in banks or savings and loan associations that pay interest and generally are immediately withdrawable with no interest penalty for early withdrawal. They have no fixed term or maturity. They also may be insured through the FDIC, which adds to their safety. Thus, they are highly secure (if insured by the FDIC), highly liquid, and very convenient for the depositor. However, their yield tends to be lower than that of other liquid assets.

Other Liquid Assets.   Other kinds of assets that may be considered as liquid, such as life insurance cash values, have been mentioned in previous chapters.

Financial Intermediaries that Invest in Bonds and Other Fixed-Income Securities

Financial intermediaries may invest in bonds and other fixed-income securities. These vehicles include mutual funds, closed-end investment companies, variable life insurance policy separate accounts, variable annuity policy separate accounts, and investment options under certain types of qualified retirement plans that are invested in whole or in part in bonds or other fixed-income securities.

Probably the most extensive of these intermediaries are mutual funds. The various types of bond, money market, and diversified mutual funds were described in Chap. 9, and that discussion will not be repeated here. As with other types of investments, with mutual funds the investor needs to decide whether to invest through a financial intermediary or directly. The factors involved in that decision have been discussed previously.

Before leaving the discussion of investment companies, it should be noted that many bond funds are unit investment trusts in which a portfolio of securities is selected at the time the trust is organized and is not subsequently changed. The sponsor of the trust (say, a broker, investment banker, or mutual fund) then sells units in the trust to investors. There may be no management or redemption fees in connection with these trusts, and the units may be redeemable by the trust for an amount depending on the value of the bonds in the trust at the time of redemption.

Conversion Privileges in Fixed-Income Securities

Investors may consider whether to buy *convertible bonds* or *convertible preferred stocks,* which provide the security of a bond or a preferred, but also provide an opportunity for capital appreciation through hoped-for appreciation of the underlying common stock. Convertible bonds and preferreds contain a provision that gives the holder the right (in effect, the option) to convert the security into a certain number of shares of the company's common stock at a predetermined price for the common. The purpose, operation, and significance of this provision to investors is the same whether the provision appears in a corporate bond or a preferred stock. This section presents the factors to evaluate in considering securities with a conversion feature.

The purpose of a conversion privilege is to make a bond issue (we shall use bonds for our illustrations) more attractive to investors. But this opportunity is not free. The conversion privilege, in effect, is an option to buy stock at a predetermined price, and as an option, it has a price. The price is the difference between the yield on a convertible bond and the yield on a nonconvertible bond with the same investment merits. This difference varies with economic conditions, market conditions, and with the relationship between the current market price of the common stock and its conversion rate in the bond, but it might be, say, as much as a full percentage point. That is, a bond selling at a 9 percent yield as a straight bond might sell at an 8 percent yield on a convertible basis. The price of the conversion privilege depends on the terms of conversion and estimates of the possibility that the common stock obtainable by conversion will significantly exceed its conversion price in the future.

Convertible bonds generally are callable. Although callability of securities was discussed earlier, it deserves special mention with respect to convertible securities. The callability feature allows the issuer to call convertible bonds whenever the market value of the stock obtainable by conversion is greater than the call price of the bonds, and thus, in effect, to force conversion. To illustrate, a bond callable by the issuer at 105 may be convertible into 50 shares of common stock at $20 per share. Whenever the market price of the common stock exceeds $21 per share, the issuer can force conversion by calling the bonds for redemption. The bondholders then have a choice of receiving $1050 per bond in cash or converting the bond to 50 shares of stock (worth $50 \times \$21$, or $1050). The importance of the callability feature combined with the conversion privilege is that it may be used to shorten the maturity of convertible bonds.

Bond Ratings and Investment Quality

One of the first things the individual investor should realize is that all bonds are not created equal. The ability of the issuer of a bond to meet its obligations can vary considerably. Bonds issued or guaranteed by the U.S. government generally are considered to be the safest of investments. As for other bonds, the probabilities that all bond provisions will be met range from virtually certain to questionable.

Bond Rating Systems

To aid investors in assessing the investment quality (in terms of financial risk) of large numbers of corporate and municipal bonds, bond ratings are published and periodically reviewed (and revised when needed) by independent rating agencies. The two main rating agencies in this field are Moody's and Standard & Poor's.[3] The corporate and municipal debt rating systems of these two agencies are outlined in Table 10.2. These ratings are of the creditworthiness or financial ability to meet the specific obligations of the issuer on the bond involved. They are not, of course, guarantees of the bonds, nor do they measure any market or interest rate risks of bonds. Thus, for example, the market prices of even the highest-quality bonds may fluctuate widely with changes in interest rates.

As can be seen from Table 10.2, bonds with one of the top four ratings from one or both agencies are often considered to be "investment grade."[4] Bonds with lower ratings than the top four are considered by the rating agencies as having speculative elements, and those elements become more and more dominant as their quality ratings decline, until the lowest ratings include bonds that are in default of their principal or interest.

High-yield (or "junk") bonds generally could be considered those with ratings below investment grade. As can be seen from the rating systems in Table 10.2, however, this can embrace a fairly wide range of degrees of financial risk. Therefore, in evaluating high-yield bond mutual funds or other investments in such bonds, the investor probably should consider the

---

[3] These agencies also rate many insurance companies for financial soundness or claims-paying ability, as described in Chap. 3 on pp. 54–55. They also rate commercial paper.

[4] Moody's judges bonds in its top two ratings to be of "high quality."

Table 10.2. Bond Rating Systems

	Standard & Poor's	Moody's
Investment grade:		
Highest quality*	AAA	Aaa
High quality	AA	Aa
Upper medium grade	A	A
Medium grade	BBB	Baa
Below investment grade:		
Moderately speculative*	BB	Ba
Speculative	B	B
Highly speculative	CCC	Caa
Lowest quality (including in default)	C, D	C

*These are abbreviated terms used to describe these rating systems and are not the complete descriptions used by the rating agencies themselves to describe their ratings.

relative degrees of financial risk involved (e.g., the percentages of a portfolio in the various rating grades). In other words, some bonds are "junkier" than others.

Some bonds and other fixed-income securities are not rated by outside rating agencies.

Bond Ratings and Yield

As a general principle, the yields for lower-rated bonds should be higher than those for higher-rated bonds of the same general type, to compensate investors for the increased financial risk. This is clear and rather obvious. A major question, however, is the degree to which this is true. In other words, do the higher yields on lower-quality bonds make up or more than make up for the higher default rates on such bonds? Part of this question, of course, is what are the real, long-term, average annual default rates on bonds of lower quality. While a review of all the research on this issue is well beyond the scope of this book, it appears at this writing that no one really knows.

During the 1980s and even 1990s, a theory that was advanced in favor of investing in high-yield ("junk") bonds was that the yields in such securities would more than make up for their average annual default rates, and hence they were superior in overall performance to higher-rated bonds. Economic studies were cited to support this idea. The problem is, however, that as of this writing no one seems to be sure what the long-term effect will be on junk bond experience of the vast amounts of newly issued low-quality corporate debt floated during the 1980s. Unfortunately, some financial institutions have run into difficulties due to their excessive investments in junk bonds, and many people believe that some undesirable economic consequences for issuers and the investing public flowed from certain uses of junk bonds, particularly during the 1980s. However, there presently is an active market in high-yield (junk) bonds, and many people have invested in them either directly or through mutual funds or other financial intermediaries. It just appears that as of this writing "the jury is still out" on whether the long-term average annual net rate of return on junk bonds is superior to that on investment-grade bonds or U.S. Treasury bonds (which have the highest credit rating). The answer probably lies in the combination of good timing and broad diversification in the purchase of high-yield, high-risk bonds.

Strategies for Investing in Fixed-Income Securities

As the discussion in this chapter has unfolded, it can be seen that there are several areas where investors need to develop investment strategies with respect to the fixed-income portions of their overall asset allocation.

Investment Duration Considerations

One area where investors need to develop a strategy is with regard to the durations or maturity structure of their fixed-income portfolio. One part of this strategy is to determine what portion of the overall portfolio is to be kept liquid.

For the remainder of the fixed-income portfolio, one approach would be to adjust maturities at least some degree with regard to expected changes in interest rates. As a general rule with this approach, *maturities should be lengthened when interest rates are expected to decline and should be shortened when interest rates are expected to rise.* In this way, investors will have committed their funds at the present high rates when future rates are expected to be lower, and will have their funds available to commit later at the expected higher rates when it is anticipated that interest rates will be higher in the future. Of course, judging future moves in interest rates is not easy and is far from certain. It is like trying to judge which way the stock market will go. But, as in buying stocks, the investor really has to make some kind of judgment.

On the other hand, investors can follow a *diversified approach* toward the maturity structure of their fixed-income investments. Such a diversification strategy was illustrated on pp. 190–191 of Chap. 7 with regard to planning for the various kinds of interest rate risk.

Taxable versus Nontaxable Considerations

Investors need to evaluate their tax situation to determine the relative attractiveness of taxable as compared to municipal securities. This should be done considering both federal and state and local income taxes, particularly in high-income-tax states. The factors involved in this analysis were discussed on pp. 283–284 of this chapter and will be developed further in Chap. 11.

Strategies for Call Protection and Interest Rate Risk

Investors also need to evaluate their exposure to the two kinds of interest rate risk (including the possible need for call protection) and to plan their fixed-income investments accordingly. Some strategies for doing this were discussed in Chap. 7 and, as just noted with regard to the diversified approach toward maturities, on pp. 190–191. Particularly in the case of investors who need to have an assured flow of investment income at certain levels regardless of economic conditions, call protection and related interest rate risk are important issues to address in structuring the fixed-income portion of their portfolio.

Investment Quality Considerations

Investors should develop a specific strategy with regard to the quality they seek in their fixed-income portfolio (we shall use bond ratings as an example). We have already discussed the relationship between yield and bond ratings in this chapter, and have noted that there do not seem to be any "pat" answers. Much depends on an investor's personal circumstances, investment objectives, and tolerance for investment risk. There is no question that lower quality in fixed-income investments means greater financial risk. The issue then really becomes whether that greater risk is worth the potentially greater returns to the investor. That is the issue the investor should consider in formulating his or her strategy in this area.

There can be a variety of strategies regarding investment quality in general and with respect to fixed-income securities in particular. Very risk-averse investors, for example, may decide to purchase only bonds rated in the top two or three grades according to Moody's or Standard & Poor's, and U.S. Treasuries or U.S. government-guaranteed or -backed bonds (or invest only in mutual funds or other financial intermediaries that have essentially these investment objectives). On the other hand, other investors may decide to allocate the bulk of their portfolio—say, 75 to 80 percent—only to investment-grade (or high-grade) fixed-income securities, while allowing the balance to be in below-investment-grade bonds if market conditions and yield spreads (between high-grade and "junk" bonds, for example) seem propitious. At the other end of the scale, more aggressive (and much less risk-averse) investors may be willing to allocate a much larger portion of their fixed-income portfolio to higher-yield ("junk") bonds when they think market conditions and yield spreads warrant it, and then change the allocation when market conditions and yield spreads are no longer viewed as favorable to low-quality issues. The point is that investors should consciously set their own strategy in light of their personal circumstances and attitudes toward risk.

Diversification Strategies

Investors should decide when and how they wish to diversify their investments. It has been suggested throughout this book that in investments, as well as in other areas of financial planning, diversification probably is the best strategy for most persons in planning their affairs. That idea is continued here.

With respect to fixed-income investments, the following areas of possible diversification have been suggested in this chapter and elsewhere (see, for example, Chap. 7):

- By maturity
- By call protection
- With regard to taxable and nontaxable securities
- By types of fixed-income investments
- With regard to investment quality

Thus, investors should at least consider diversification in these areas within their personal investment and asset allocation strategies.

11
Income Tax Planning

Most people are concerned about saving on their income taxes. Income taxes must be paid each year, and the total tax burden takes a significant portion of the income of most families. Also, many states (and cities and other local government units) have enacted income taxes on top of the federal levy.

The landmark Tax Reform Act of 1986 and subsequent tax legislation have made substantial changes in the federal income tax structure. Some of the more important changes include lowering and flattening individual and corporate income tax rates; reducing substantially the favorable treatment of long-term capital gains; reducing the tax advantages of tax-sheltered investments (discussed in Chapter 8); eliminating or reducing certain formerly available deductions, such as for most consumer interest; curtailing those eligible to take tax deductions for contributions to individual retirement accounts and annuities (IRAs); reducing the allowable amount of before-tax employee contributions to Section 401(k) plans; eliminating the Clifford trust; and a number of other important changes. These legislative changes have had a significant effect on financial planning. This chapter covers briefly the structure of the federal income tax system and then discusses the principles of income tax planning.

The Federal Income Tax

Basic Individual Income Tax Structure

The federal income tax law is detailed and complex. Obviously, all its rules, provisions, and exceptions cannot be discussed here. But the basic formula for determining an individual's tax can be shown briefly as follows.[1]

---

[1] The basic income tax structure presented here is not meant to be exhaustive. There are a number of excellent income tax publications that taxpayers can consult to obtain more detailed information on the deductions, exemptions, etc., due them.

GI
(Ded)
AGI

Gross Income (meaning all income from whatever source derived, unless specifically excluded by a provision of the tax code—this is described as gross income's being an "all inclusive concept")

Less: Deductions to arrive at adjusted gross income

Including:

Trade and business expenses (not incurred as an employee)

Expenses of producing rents and royalties

Losses from sale or exchange of nonpersonal property

Contributions to retirement plans for the self-employed (HR-10 or Keogh plans) and SEP plans

Contributions to individual retirement accounts or annuities (IRAs) for eligible persons (i.e., contributions that are tax deductible, but not the non-tax-deductible contributions that may be permitted)

Alimony paid

Interest penalty on early withdrawal from time savings accounts

Twenty-five percent of amounts paid by self-employed persons for health insurance on themselves and their dependents, subject to a "sunset" provision

Certain other deductions

Equals: Adjusted gross income (AGI)

Less: Itemized deductions[2] (or the standard deduction)

Including (as itemized deductions):

Medical and dental expenses (in excess of 7½ percent of AGI)

Taxes (other than state and local sales taxes)

Charitable contributions

Certain interest expense [including "qualified residence interest," which is mortgage interest on the taxpayer's principal residence and a second residence to the extent the mortgage loan(s) does (do) not exceed the "cost basis" (generally the purchase price plus the cost of any improvements) or the fair market value of the property, whichever is less. Mortgage interest still may be deducted on loan balances over this limit if the indebtedness is for medical or educational expenses. This limit also does not apply to interest on mortgage debts incurred on or before August 16, 1986. Effective in 1988 and thereafter, there are additional dollar limitations on the deductibility of personal mortgage interest. First, when the interest is on *aggregate residence indebtedness,* which is indebtedness incurred in acquiring, constructing, or substantially

---

[2] The overall amount of certain itemized deductions now may be phased out in the case of higher-income taxpayers until January 1, 1996.

improving a taxpayer's residence, it is deductible only to the extent that the indebtedness does not exceed $1,000,000. Second, when the interest is on *home equity indebtedness,* it is deductible only to the extent that the indebtedness does not exceed the smaller of (1) $100,000, or (2) the taxpayer's equity in the residence. The $1,000,000 limitation does not apply to interest on indebtedness incurred prior to October 14, 1987. However, *consumer interest expense* (other than qualifying residence interest just described) is no longer deductible by individuals for federal income tax purposes. On the other hand, personal interest expense for loans on personal investments—*investment interest or portfolio interest*—is deductible to the extent of investment income (if the taxpayer itemizes).

Casualty losses (in excess of $100 for each loss and 10 percent of AGI for all losses)

Miscellaneous deductions (in excess of 2 percent of AGI with certain exceptions)

Less: Personal exemptions[3]
Equals: Taxable income
Federal income tax (determined by applying income tax rates to taxable income)
Less: Credits (i.e., amounts deducted from the tax itself)
Including:

Credit for the elderly or permanently and totally disabled

Child and dependent care credit

Equals: Federal income tax payable
Plus: Other Taxes Payable
Including:

 Alternative minimum tax (AMT) to the extent it exceeds the regular income tax

Self-employment tax (social security tax paid by the self-employed on their earnings subject to social security taxes)

Equals: Total federal taxes payable

Federal Income Tax Rates

Perhaps the most significant part of the Tax Reform Act of 1986 was the dramatic lowering (and flattening) of individual income tax rates. Income tax rates and brackets were again changed to some extent by the Revenue

---

[3] As with itemized deductions, the overall amount of a taxpayer's personal exemptions now may be phased out for certain higher-income taxpayers until January 1, 1996.

Reconciliation Act of 1990.[4] The federal income tax rates as of 1991 for various filing statuses (see discussion of filing status next) are shown in Table 11.1. This table shows the three-bracket individual federal income tax rate system of 15 percent, 28 percent, and 31 percent. Thus, the top *marginal* individual federal income tax rate is 31 percent. The *average* income tax rate for a taxpayer is the tax payable divided by the taxpayer's taxable income, and for individuals and trusts and estates the average rate will always be less than the marginal rate.

Individual income tax rates under the law existing prior to the Tax Reform Act of 1986 ranged from a low of 11 percent to a high of 50 percent over 14 progressive tax brackets. Thus, the current rates are generally lower and considerably less progressive, or "flatter," than were the rates under prior law. These rate changes have had significant implications for income tax planning. They generally make income shifting to lower-bracket taxpayers and deferral of income relatively less attractive than before the 1986 tax law, although these are still viable techniques in the proper circumstances. They (along with other changes discussed in Chap. 8) generally have made tax-sheltered investments less attractive than formerly, but such investments still may retain some tax advantages, depending on the type of shelter, and they may remain viable investments for their investment characteristics themselves. Finally, the lower and flatter rates generally have had an effect on the relative after-tax attractiveness of taxable investment income as compared with tax-free income.

Filing Status

There are separate federal income tax rate schedules for various categories of taxpayers. These include married individuals filing joint returns (and also a qualified surviving spouse during the first two years after the year in which the other spouse died); heads of households; single individuals; married individuals who elect to file separate returns; and estates and trusts.[5] This is referred to as the taxpayer's filing status. Determining the appropriate filing status is one aspect of income tax planning.

---

[4] This law also eliminated the so-called "bubble" in individual income tax rates, whereby a 5 percent surtax was added to the 28 percent regular tax to take back the tax benefits of the 15 percent bracket and personal exemptions for higher-income taxpayers. However, a "bubble" still exists in the corporate income tax system (see Chap. 17).

[5] There also are separate federal income tax rates applying to corporations, which are not discussed here. See Chap. 17.

Table 11.1. Individual Federal Income Tax Rates as of 1991 for Various Filing Statuses

Married individuals filing jointly		Single individuals		Head of household		Trusts and estates*	
Taxable income†	Tax rates	Taxable income†	Tax rates	Taxable income†	Tax rates	Taxable income†	Tax rates
$0–$34,000	15%	$0–$20,350	15%	$0–$27,300	15%	$0–$ 3,450	15%
$34,000–$82,150	28%	$20,350–$49,300	28%	$27,300–$70,450	28%	$3,450–$10,350	28%
Over $82,150	31%	Over $49,300	31%	Over $70,450	31%	Over $10,350	31%

*These rates are for trusts (as tax-paying entities) and for estates beyond the second taxable year of the estate after the decedent's death. During the first 2 taxable years after the decedent's death, an estate uses the tax rates for married persons filing separate returns which are not shown in this table.

†These tax brackets (ranges of taxable income) are adjusted (increased) annually to reflect changes in the Consumer Price Index (CPI) in accordance with Section 1 (f) (entitled "Adjustments in Tax Tables So That Inflation Will Not Result in Tax Increases") of the Internal Revenue Code. As noted in this chapter, this is often referred to as being indexed for inflation. The brackets and rates shown in this table are after the inflation adjustments for 1991.

Indexing for Inflation

The tax law now adjusts annually for the effects of inflation the individual tax bracket schedules, the standard deduction amounts, the amount of the personal exemption, and certain other limits or features in the tax law. This is referred to as "indexing" the tax schedules and other amounts and is intended to help make up for what has come to be known as "bracket creep." Bracket creep exists because, during an inflationary period, increases in income that solely or largely just keep up with inflated living costs result nevertheless in moving taxpayers into higher income tax brackets, with consequent higher tax rates on the increased income.

Alternative Minimum Tax (AMT)

An alternative minimum tax (AMT) may be imposed on individual taxpayers and estates and trusts (corporations also are subject to a corporate AMT) with so-called tax preference items (or adjustments) under certain circumstances. This minimum tax applies if it exceeds the amount of a taxpayer's regular income tax.

The AMT is calculated by starting with the taxpayer's regular taxable income. To this amount are added back certain "tax preference" items, and certain "adjustments" are made. These include tax-free interest on certain private-activity municipal bonds issued after August 7, 1986 (see pp. 283–284 of Chapter 10), the untaxed appreciation on charitable contributions of appreciated capital gain property (see pp. 320–321 this chapter), income deferred by use of the installment method by individuals, the amount by which the value of stock purchased under incentive stock option plans (ISOs) (see pp. 404–405 of Chap. 13) exceeds its option price, certain excess depreciation and depletion, certain excess intangible drilling costs, and certain other items. Also, other adjustments are made because certain itemized deductions (such as taxes) and personal exemptions are allowable for purposes of the regular tax but not for the AMT. An AMT exemption amount then is deducted, which is $40,000 for married taxpayers filing jointly, $30,000 for single taxpayers, and $20,000 for married taxpayers filing separate returns and for trusts and estates. This exemption amount is phased out when alternative minimum taxable income (AMTI) reaches certain levels. For example, for married taxpayers filing jointly, the $40,000 exemption amount is reduced by 25 percent of the amount by which AMTI exceeds $150,000 (i.e., it is completely phased out when AMTI reaches $310,000).

The result of these calculations is the taxpayer's alternative minimum taxable income, to which a flat 24 percent tax rate is applied to produce the alternative minimum tax (AMT). The taxpayer must pay any excess of the AMT over his or her regular tax (less certain credits). Thus, in tax planning, it may be desirable for a taxpayer to avoid or defer certain tax preference items (such as exercising an ISO), if possible, in a year in which such items will produce an alternative minimum tax that exceeds the taxpayer's regular tax.

Capital Gains Taxation

General Considerations. Capital gains and losses are realized from the sale or exchange of capital assets. With some exceptions, capital assets include the property taxpayers own. Some examples of capital assets are common stocks, bonds, preferred stocks, investment real estate, collectibles, generally partnership interests, personal residences, other personal assets, and others. These gains and losses also are recognized in the year of the sale or exchange unless there is some specific nonrecognition provision in the Internal Revenue Code that defers recognition, as discussed in the next section. The difference between the *amount realized* from the sale or exchange and the *adjusted basis* of the asset in the hands of the taxpayer is the amount of the *capital gain or loss.*

The amount realized generally is the value received from the sale or exchange of the capital asset. The adjusted basis for income tax purposes generally depends on how the taxpayer acquired the property. It can be a rather complicated concept. In general, adjusted basis can be identified in certain common situations as follows:

- If the taxpayer originally *purchased the property,* its adjusted basis is its cost plus any purchase commissions.

- If the taxpayer acquired the property as a *lifetime gift* from another, its adjusted basis is its basis in the hands of the donor (plus any gift tax on the unrealized appreciation of the gift property). (See pp. 453–455 in Chap. 15, on making lifetime gifts.)

- If the taxpayer *inherited the property* from a decedent, its adjusted basis is the property's fair market value at the date of death (or alternative valuation date for federal estate tax purposes). This is often referred to as the step-up in income tax basis at death.

(A taxpayer may increase his or her adjusted basis in the above categories of property by the cost of any improvements and reduce it by any depreciation, depletion, or amortization.)

- If the taxpayer receives new stock or securities in a *tax-free reorganization or merger* (as one of those tax-free reorganizations defined in the Internal Revenue Code), the new stock's or security's basis will be the former basis of the stock or securities the taxpayer exchanged for the new stock or securities (called a carryover basis).

- If a person acquires a partnership interest by a *contribution of property* (including money) to the partnership, the basis of the person's interest in the partnership generally is the money contributed plus the adjusted basis to the contributing partner of the property contributed (i.e., a carryover basis from the property contributed), under the rules of Section 722 of the IRC.

- If a person or persons *transfer property to a corporation solely in exchange for stock in such corporation and immediately after the exchange the person or persons have control of the corporation* (at least 80 percent ownership), the basis of the person's stock in such a corporation generally is the same as the basis of the property the person transfered to the corporation in exchange for the stock, under the rules of Section 351 and Section 358 of the IRC.

These statements do not include all the situations or rules for determining basis. They are intended only to be representative of fairly common situations, and other rules for determining basis will be discussed elsewhere in this book as appropriate.[6] In this regard, the reader should also note the discussion of nonrecognition provisions in the following section of this chapter. Finally, a taxpayer may increase his or her basis at sale or exchange by any expenses of sale (such as brokers' fees, commissions, transfer taxes, and the like), unless these expenses were taken from the amount realized as reported on the tax return.

The federal income tax rates that apply to net capital gains have changed dramatically in recent years. *Net capital gains* are net long-term capital gains (long-term capital gains less long-term capital losses) less any net short-term capital losses (short-term capital losses less short-term capital gains). For this purpose, short-term capital gains and losses are those on capital assets held for one year or less (and the taxpayer first determines any *net* short-term capital gain or loss for the year). Long-term capital gains and losses are those on capital assets held for more than one year (and the taxpayer also determines any *net* long-term capital gain or loss for the year).[7] Thus, under this system capital losses will offset capital gains and, to the extent of $3000 per year, other ordinary income of the taxpayer. As an example of determining net capital gains, assume that a taxpayer had the following gains and losses during a taxable year:

$12,000 long-term capital gains

3,000 long-term capital losses

---

[6] While they generally are not subject to capital gains tax rules, it may also be useful to note at this point that the net investment in the contract (or income tax basis) for life insurance policies and nonqualified annuity policies for purposes of determining any taxable income from them is the net premiums paid for the policy. Similarly, the net investment in the contract (or income tax basis) for qualified retirement plans is the participant's after-tax contribution to the plan plus certain other items.

[7] The disposition (sale or exchange) of inherited property is assumed to give rise to a *long-term* gain or loss, regardless of how long the person inheriting the property actually held it.

1,000 short-term capital gains

2,500 short-term capital losses

Thus, this taxpayer has *net long-term capital gains* of $9000 ($12,000 – $3000), *net short-term capital losses* of $1500 ($2500 – $1000), and *net capital gains* of $7500 ($9000 – $1500). (As we shall see next, the importance of this calculation is that the tax rate on net capital gains now is capped at 28 percent, while the rate on ordinary income and net short-term capital gains can be as high as 31 percent.)

Prior to the Tax Reform Act of 1986, net capital gains (as just defined) in effect were taxed at only 40 percent of the income tax rate applying to ordinary income, which meant that the highest possible marginal rate on capital gains was 20 percent since the highest marginal rate on ordinary income at that time was 50 percent. However, this was changed drastically by the Tax Reform Act of 1986, which, from 1988 through 1990, taxed all net capital gains at the same rates as the taxpayer's ordinary income. The Revenue Reconciliation Act of 1990 again changed the direction of federal tax policy with respect to the tax rates applying to net capital gains (as just defined). Thus, effective for tax years beginning after 1990, there is a maximum tax rate of 28 percent on net capital gains, which is somewhat lower than the maximum rate of 31 percent on other income.

To give an example of the present system (as of 1992), assume that Ms. Smith owned 200 shares of ABC Biotech common, which she purchased three years ago for $20 per share and which was selling for $70 per share in 1991. Ms. Smith and her husband both work outside the home, file a joint return, and together have taxable (ordinary) income of $90,000. Ms. Smith was concerned about the level of ABC's stock price in terms of its current earnings and realistic future prospects, and so she decided to sell her 200 shares in 1991. Assuming that the Smiths have no other income or capital gains or losses for 1991, their income tax situation would be as follows:

Ordinary income		$90,000
Capital gain:		
Amount realized (200 shares × $70 per share)	$14,000	
Adjusted basis in stock (200 shares × $20 per share purchase price)	–4,000	
Long-term capital gain realized and recognized on sale	$10,000	10,000
Federal income tax payable (using 1991 tax rates indexed for inflation—see Table 11.1):		
On $90,000 of ordinary income:		
		Tax
$0–$34,000 at 15%		$ 5,100
$34,000–$82,150 at 28%		13,482
Over 82,150 at 31%		2,434
		$21,016

On $10,000 of net capital gain ($10,000 long-term capital
gain less 0 long-term capital loss and less 0 net short-
term capital loss in this case):
$10,000 at the maximum rate of 28% $2,800
Total income tax payable $23,816

(If, however, a taxpayer's other taxable income is less than the upper 15 percent tax bracket limit (e.g., less than $34,000 for a married couple filing a
joint return in 1991), the tax would be 15 percent times the total amount in
the 15 percent bracket (including part of the net capital gains) plus 28 percent times the remainder of the net capital gains. Thus, under the present
system, net capital gains may be taxed at 15 percent and/or at 28 percent.)

On the other hand, capital losses are first used to offset capital gains of the
same type and then any net capital loss (short-term or long-term) can be used
to reduce the taxpayer's other ordinary income dollar for dollar up to a maximum of $3000 in any one year. Any unused net capital losses may be carried
forward by the taxpayer indefinitely and used in future years, first to offset
any capital gains, and then to offset ordinary income up to $3000 per year.

As an illustration of the use of capital losses, suppose, for example, that
Mr. Baker had the following capital gains and losses on his stock and bond
transactions in 1991:

Long-term capital gains	$1000
Short-term capital gains	$2000
Short-term capital losses	$6500

In addition, Mr. Baker and his wife had other ordinary taxable income of
$45,000. Mr. Baker first can offset his capital gains against his capital losses
so that he has a net capital loss for the year of $3500. He then can use up to
$3000 of this net capital loss to reduce the other ordinary taxable income,
or by $3000 in this case to $42,000. Thus, since Mr. and Mrs. Baker file a
joint return and are in a 28 percent top marginal tax bracket, this would be
worth $840 in income tax saving this year. Mr. and Mrs. Baker can carry the
remaining $500 of net capital loss forward to the next and subsequent tax
years. Thus, a taxpayer with capital losses can use these losses to save on
income taxes by planning for realizing them at the proper time. This is
sometimes called tax loss selling with regard to securities.

Nonrecognition Provisions.   It was noted at the beginning of this discussion that capital gains are *realized* as a result of the sale or exchange or a
capital asset and also are *recognized* for tax purposes in the year of the sale
or exchange *unless* there is a specific provision in the tax code that defers
recognition. Such provisions are often called nonrecognition provisions.
The effect of a nonrecognition provision is to defer income tax on any gain

to some future transaction or event when, depending on the property involved and the circumstances, there may or may not be an income tax due. When a nonrecognition provision applies, there normally is a carryover of income tax basis from the property sold or exchanged to the new property acquired, so in effect the new property takes the old property's basis. In this way, the nonrecognized gain is not forgiven; it is simply potentially deferred until some future transaction or event. It can be seen that such nonrecognition provisions can be very important in income tax planning. Some of the more commonly used nonrecognition provisions are briefly listed here to illustrate the concept. A more in-depth discussion of nonrecognition provisions is beyond the scope of this book.

- Section 1034: Rollover of Gain in Sale of Principal Residence. (This provision applies to the sale of a person's principal residence when a new principal residence is acquired by the person within the period of two years before to two years after the sale.)

- Section 1031: Exchange of Property Held for Productive Use or Investment. [These exchanges are referred to as *like-kind exchanges* and are used for property held in a trade or business or for investment with certain exceptions (such exceptions include the important categories of stocks, bonds, notes, and other securities or evidences of indebtedness). Like-kind exchanges under this provision are commonly used for investment real estate to defer gain.]

- Section 1035: Certain Exchanges of Insurance Policies. (While it does not involve capital gains, this important provision states that no gain or loss shall be recognized on the exchange of certain life insurance policies or the exchange of certain annuity contracts.)

- Section 354: Exchanges of Stock and Securities in Certain Reorganizations. (This and other code provisions allow stockholders to exchange their stock for other stock with no gain or loss being recognized in the case of certain corporate reorganizations and mergers as specified in the IRC. It permits tax-free reorganizations and mergers in these cases.)

- Section 351: Transfer to Corporation Controlled by Transferor. (As noted previously, this provision permits a tax-free exchange of appreciated property for corporate stock if the combined transferors are in control of the corporation immediately thereafter. This nonrecognition provision can be important in the formation of corporations.)

- Section 721: Nonrecognition of Gain or Loss on Contribution. (Again as noted previously, this provision permits a tax-free exchange of appreciated property for a partnership interest upon contribution of the property to the partnership. This provision can be important in the formation of and in adding partners to partnerships.)

■ Section 1041: Transfers of Property between Spouses or Incident to Divorce. (This provision specifies that no gain or loss shall be recognized on a transfer of property from an individual to his or her spouse or to his or her former spouse, provided in the case of a former spouse that the transfer is incident to a divorce. This nonrecognition provision permits the tax-free sale of property between spouses and the tax-free transfer of property from one spouse to another as part of a divorce settlement.)

As stated earlier, this is not a complete listing of all possible nonrecognition provisions.

Phaseout of Personal Exemptions and Itemized Deductions

The Revenue Reconciliation Act of 1990 placed certain phaseouts and limitations on otherwise available deductions for personal exemptions and certain itemized deductions (the standard deduction for those who do not itemize was unaffected) for higher-income taxpayers. These phaseouts apply to tax years after December 31, 1990 and before January 1, 1996 (or is subject to a so-called "sunset" provision).

Under this law, the taxpayer's personal exemptions are reduced until they are eliminated once the taxpayer's adjusted gross income (AGI) exceeds certain threshold amounts (indexed for inflation) based on the taxpayer's filing status. For example, in 1991 this threshold amount for the AGI of married persons filing a joint return was $150,000.

For certain itemized deductions, an individual whose AGI exceeds $100,000 (indexed for inflation) will have his or her itemized deductions reduced according to the *smaller* of two limitations. The first is that the total amount of itemized deductions will be reduced by 3 percent of the amount by which the taxpayer's AGI exceeds the $100,000 (indexed for inflation) threshold amount. However, the second limitation provides that in no event may the reduction in otherwise deductible itemized deductions exceed 80 percent of the allowable itemized deductions, but *not counting* for purposes of this second limitation itemized deductions for *medical expenses, investment interest, casualty losses,* and wagering losses to the extent of wagering gains. For planning purposes, the importance of the exceptions to this second limitation is that, in effect, these itemized deductions are not subject to any phaseout or limitation. Thus, for example, if a taxpayer pays interest on debt incurred to carry a portfolio of securities (e.g., margin interest, see pp. 228–229 of Chap. 8), which would be investment interest or portfolio interest, and if the investor itemizes his or her deductions, the investment interest in effect would be fully deductible (but always limited to the extent of the investor's investment income) as an itemized deduction in arriving at the taxpayer's taxable income.

It can also be seen that these phaseout rules may result in higher effective income tax rates when they apply.

State Income Taxes

In addition to the federal income tax system just outlined, many states and some cities and other localities levy personal income taxes or wage taxes on individuals. These taxes should also be considered in overall income tax planning. For example, in investment planning, the top effective state (and perhaps also local) income tax rate(s) should be added to the top effective federal rate in evaluating the relative attractiveness of the yield on municipal securities of the state (assuming the municipals are tax-free for federal, state, and perhaps local tax purposes) as compared with taxable investments. Such municipal securities are sometimes referred to as "double tax-free municipals" (free of federal and state taxes) or "triple tax-free municipals" (free of federal, state, and local taxes).

State personal income taxes vary greatly. Most states have graduated income tax rates like the federal system, but some have flat rates on all taxable income with few deductions. Some permit federal income taxes paid to be deducted in determining the state tax payable, but most do not. The top effective personal income tax rate among the states varies from as low as somewhat more than 2 percent to as high as 10 percent (without counting local income or wage taxes). Thus, effectively, there are high-income-tax states and relatively lower-income-tax states. As was noted previously, persons in higher-income-tax states may be more likely to be exposed to the federal AMT (see pp. 304–305), because state income taxes are not deductible in determining alternative minimum taxable income (AMTI) as they are in determining regular federal taxable income if the taxpayer itemizes.

The various state and local income tax systems will not be discussed further here, because there is considerable diversity among them. Naturally, taxpayers should consider the effects of their own state's tax system on their financial and tax planning.

Basic Tax-Saving Techniques

We turn now to some specific ways in which taxpayers may be able to eliminate, reduce, shift, shelter, or postpone their income taxes. These basic tax-saving techniques can be broken down into those that essentially involve (1) tax elimination or reduction, (2) shifting the tax burden to others, (3) allowing wealth to accumulate without current income taxation and postponing taxation, and (4) taking returns as capital gains. Some plans involve a combination of these ideas. This kind of classification helps evaluate properly what might be accomplished by a given tax-saving plan. The Tax Reform Act of 1986 and subsequent tax legislation have eliminated or changed some of the formerly popular income tax–saving techniques that existed under prior law. However, a number of viable tax-saving techniques still remain.

Tax Elimination or Reduction

Tax-saving techniques aimed at producing income tax deductions, exemptions, and credits that reduce otherwise taxable income (or the tax itself) and techniques that result in nontaxable income or in economic benefits that are not taxable are perhaps the most desirable tax-saving techniques because they avoid tax altogether. Here are some such techniques.

Use of Checklists of Income Tax Deductions, Exemptions, and Credits

A great many specific income tax deductions, exemptions, and credits are available to taxpayers. Space does not permit discussion of all of them here, but some are mentioned in this and other chapters. Also, there are checklists of the following: items included in gross income; income (and other items) that are not taxable; deductions to arrive at adjusted gross income; itemized deductions; nondeductible items; other taxes (federal, state, and local); and various taxable or deductible items that apply particularly to certain occupations or businesses, all available from the government and from commercial publishers. In addition, banks, accounting firms, financial planners, stockbrokers, insurance agents, and other businesses may make available to the public pamphlets and other information on how to save income taxes with regard to their special areas of activity. Taxpayers (or their advisors) can often save taxes by finding deductions, exemptions, and the like that they had not considered previously by going through one or more of these checklists when they prepare their returns.

Use of the Proper Filing Status

A related matter is the choice of the most advantageous filing status. For example, a taxpayer should be sure to claim the *head of household status* or the *special surviving spouse status* if he or she qualifies. Also, while married persons usually file joint returns, they can elect to *file separate returns*.

Receipt of Nontaxable Income

There are various forms of nontaxable income. However, from the view-point of taxpayer decision making, perhaps the most important is interest paid on most state and local government bonds—municipal bonds. Investment in municipals is a popular way to avoid federal, and often state and local,[8] income taxes.

But it is only the interest paid on the municipal (i.e., the coupon rate times the par value) that is income tax-free. When a municipal is bought in the open market at a price less than par, the difference between the pur-chase price and the par value of the bond (the "discount") is taxable as a capital gain at the time the bond comes due. If the bond is sold before maturity, the difference between the purchase price and the net sales price also is taxable as a capital gain or loss. Unhappily for taxpayers, when bonds are purchased at a "premium" (purchase price in excess of par), the differ-ence between the purchase price and par value at maturity is *not* consid-ered a capital loss.

However, in order to safeguard their tax break on municipal bonds, investors must watch their borrowing policies. If taxpayers borrow money "to purchase *or carry* tax-exempts" (emphasis added), they cannot deduct the investment interest on the loan. (Aside from this rule, as noted previ-ously, taxpayers normally can deduct interest incurred in connection with investments to the extent of their investment income.) But when is a tax-payer borrowing to buy or carry municipals? In general, if a taxpayer has debt outstanding which is not (1) incurred for purposes of a personal nature (such as a mortgage on real estate held for personal use) or (2) incurred in connection with the active conduct of a trade or business, *and* if the taxpayer also owns tax-exempt bonds, the IRS may *presume* the pur-pose of the indebtedness was to carry the tax-exempt bonds and thus deny an income tax deduction for the interest on the indebtedness (the interest on the tax-exempts, however, remains tax-free). Of course, this presump-tion may be rebutted by the taxpayer, but the taxpayer may not win. Suppose, for example, a taxpayer owns debt-free municipal bonds but bor-rows money from a bank or on margin to buy taxable common stock. Under these circumstances, the IRS may deny part of the investment inter-est deduction on the loan, even though the common stock dividends are taxable income.

Finally, as noted in Chap. 10 in the discussion of municipal securities, and in this chapter, the interest from certain tax-exempt "private-activity" municipal bonds issued after August 7, 1986, may be subject to the alterna-

---

[8] States generally give preferential tax treatment to their own municipal bonds, but they may tax bonds issued by other states. However, the states cannot tax the interest on U.S. govern-ment obligations, even though such interest is subject to federal income taxation.

tive minimum tax (AMT). Also, the interest from some other private-activity municipals is fully taxable for federal income tax purposes.

Nontaxable Employee Benefits

One of the great advantages of many kinds of employee benefits is that they provide real economic benefits for the covered persons, but in many cases there is no taxable income to the employee on the value of these benefits. In other cases income taxation is deferred, and these plans are considered later in this chapter under "Allowing Wealth to Accumulate without Current Taxation and Postponing Taxation."

Among the more popular employee benefits that provide protection for employees and their families but may involve no taxable income for the employee are:

1. Group term life insurance (up to $50,000 of insurance)

2. Group medical expense coverage (except that benefits may reduce otherwise deductible medical and dental expenses if deductions are itemized)

3. Group disability income insurance (except that benefits provided through employer contributions are taxable)

4. Noninsured sick-pay plans (again except that benefits are taxable)

5. Group accidental death and dismemberment, travel accident, and related plans

6. Dependent care assistance plans (up to $5000 per year), educational assistance plans (up to $5250 per year), and group legal services plans[9]

If such benefits were not provided for employees, in many cases employees would have to purchase similar benefits for themselves and their families with after-tax dollars.

Employers get an income tax deduction for the premiums or contributions they pay toward such benefits for their employees. Thus, the cost of the benefits is deductible by the employer but generally not taxable to the employees—an advantageous tax situation.

Planning Sales of Securities for Tax Losses

Investors can often save taxes by selling (or holding) securities at the right time. This involves using the capital gain and loss rules to the taxpayer's

---

[9] The tax advantages of educational assistance plans and group legal services plans are currently scheduled to expire, unless they are extended as similar expiration dates for them have been in the past.

best advantage. We should state at the outset, however, that tax considerations should not be permitted to outweigh sound investment decisions in buying or selling securities. The tax "tail" should not wag the investment "dog." But in many cases astute investors can plan their securities transactions so as to realize tax savings and yet not significantly affect their basic investment decision making.

Such tax savings also can take some of the sting out of unrealized investment losses ("paper losses") that investors really have even though they have not actually sold the security. Psychologically, this is hard for some investors to accept. If an investor buys a stock at $90 per share and over time it rises to, say, $180 per share, the stock has doubled in value, and at the time it is quoted on the stock exchange at 180, each share actually is worth $180 in cash (less selling expenses), not $90. Investors, of course, readily accept this concept. Similarly, if the stock is purchased at $90 per share and over time it falls to, say, $45 per share, the stock has declined 50 percent in value, and at the time it is quoted on the stock exchange at 45, each share actually is worth only $45 in cash (less selling expenses), not $90. It may never again rise to 90. Understandably, some investors find it harder to accept this concept. They somehow feel they have not really had a loss unless they sell the stock. But this is not true; they really do have the loss—the only question is whether or not they realize and recognize the loss by selling the stock. From an investment standpoint, investors must consider the investment merits of their securities *at the current prices,* not at what they paid for them.

Thus, investors who already have an unrealized loss on a security and are lukewarm on the future investment performance of the security anyway, or who can make a satisfactory "tax exchange" (explained below), should seriously consider selling the security, realizing the loss, and taking an income tax deduction for it now. For example, assume that Mrs. Bailey, who is in the 31 percent income tax bracket, owns a stock she purchased for $4000 and which now is worth $3000 in the market. If she has no capital gains for the year, and she sells this stock now, she will realize a $1000 capital loss, which she can deduct from her other ordinary income and save $310 in taxes (less selling expenses). Her actual after-tax loss then is $690. Viewed in another way, if Mrs. Bailey holds the original stock, she has an investment worth $3000, but if she sells the stock and gets her tax deduction, she has $3310 (less selling and any buying expenses) to reinvest ($3000 from the sale of the original investment plus $310 in income tax saving).

The above example illustrates the general concept of *tax-loss selling* of securities (it works with bonds as well as stocks). The following are some specific ideas on how to maximize tax savings in this area.

1. If investors already have taken capital gains on securities or other property, they can *offset* these *gains by taking losses on other securities* they

may own. Thus, investors can plan the purchase and sales of securities or other capital assets they own so as to minimize or even eliminate any taxable capital gains for a given year. Of course, it must be remembered that net capital gains will be taxed at a maximum rate of 28 percent while other income (which might be offset by capital losses up to $3000 per year) may be subject to a 31 percent top income tax rate. However, currently this difference seems relatively small.

2. Investors can use "tax exchanges" to enable them to sell a security for a tax loss and yet still keep an investment position in the same field or industry.

In connection with item (2) above, suppose, for example, that Mr. Brown owns a stock in which he has a capital loss that he would like to take now for tax purposes, but he also feels the stock has investment merit for the future and he would like to retain it or one like it. So he asks himself, "Why not sell the stock, take my tax loss, and then immediately buy it back again?" The reason is that this would be a "wash sale," and the loss would be disallowed for tax purposes. The tax law does not recognize losses taken on the sale of securities if the taxpayer acquires, or has entered into an option or contract to acquire, substantially identical securities within 30 days before or after the sale. Therefore, Mr. Brown would have to wait at least 30 days after the sale or else run afoul of the "wash sale" rule.

Undaunted, Mr. Brown then says, "Why not sell the stock to my wife (or other family member), take my tax loss, but still keep the stock within the family?" Unhappily, this will not work either. The tax law disallows all losses on sales within the family (that is, those made directly or indirectly between husband and wife, brothers and sisters, and ancestors and lineal descendants).

Mr. Brown, however, can maintain approximately the same investment position in the field or industry, even for the 30-day period before or after the tax sale, by selling the stock in which he has the loss and then immediately purchasing a different stock of about the same (or perhaps even greater) investment attractiveness. This often is referred to as a "tax exchange." Many stock brokerage houses each year maintain lists of suggested tax exchanges to aid investors in this regard. The same technique can be used with bonds and other securities.

Note that the "wash sale" rule applies only with respect to losses, not gains. Therefore, if an investor has an unrealized gain in a security, he or she could sell the security, realize the capital gain for tax purposes, and then immediately repurchase the same security. It is possible that some investors might want to do this, for example, to establish a higher income tax basis in the security (the cost of the repurchased security) if they expect income tax rates to rise in the future.

3. An investor who has substantial net capital losses and wants to take them now but has no gains with which to offset the losses[10] might consider selling the securities, taking the tax loss, and replacing them with good-quality bonds selling at a discount. As the bonds mature—and some or all of them could be purchased with only a relatively short time to maturity—the difference between the bonds' purchase price and maturity value would be a capital gain (for taxable bonds issued on or before July 18, 1984, and for tax-exempt obligations) which can be reduced or eliminated by the capital loss carried over.

4. An investor who wants to "lock in" a capital gain that is already in a stock, but for any of several reasons does not want to take it yet for tax purposes, can use the technique of "selling short against the box." Here the investor borrows an equal amount of stock from a broker and sells the stock short. This locks in the gain on the stock owned. Then, when the investor is ready to take the gain, the stock owned can be used to close out the short position.

Tax Benefits on Sales of Principal Residences

For tax purposes, a personal residence is considered a capital asset, but one held for personal use. Therefore, while a gain on the sale of a personal residence is taxable (unless postponed or excluded, as explained below), a loss on the sale of such a residence is not deductible because the loss was not incurred in a trade or business or in connection with a transaction entered into for profit. The same is also true, incidentally, for other assets held strictly for personal use, such as cars, boats, airplanes, or furniture. In effect, the gain is taxable, but the loss is the taxpayer's.

However, the tax law does allow some relief from the rigor of these rules in connection with gains on the sale or exchange of a residence (including sale of ownership in a cooperative apartment or a condominium) which is the taxpayer's principal place of abode. In this case, there are two tax-saving provisions of the Internal Revenue Code: (1) the mandatory "rollover"-of-gain provision under Section 1034 (a nonrecognition provision—see p. 309 of this chapter); and (2) the optional, one-time $125,000 exclusion-of-gain provision under Section 121 for taxpayers age 55 or older (an exclusion provision). Under the rollover-of-gain provision, if taxpayers buy and occupy or build another principal residence within the period from two years before to two years after the sale of their former home, any gain

[10] The losses could of course be offset against ordinary income to the extent of $3000 per year, but perhaps the investor wants to get tax benefits more rapidly from these losses.

on the sale of the former residence is not taxed at that time, except to the extent that the sales price exceeds the cost of the new residence (under the rules of Section 1034). But technically the capital gains tax is only postponed, not forgiven (except for the one-time $125,000 exclusion of gain under Section 121 with respect to sales of a principal residence by persons age 55 or older), because any gain not taxed at the time of a sale reduces the tax basis of the new residence.

Let us briefly illustrate this. Assume that a taxpayer (age 52) sells a principal residence for $180,000; has broker's commissions, legal fees, and other expenses of the sale of $9000; and incurred "fix-up" expenses[11] prior to the sale of $3000. The residence originally cost $30,000 (the adjusted tax basis). A month after the sale, the taxpayer buys another home as a principal residence for $185,000. The taxpayer's tax status with respect to this sale is as follows:

Gross sales price for former residence	$180,000
Less:	
Expenses of sale	−9,000
Amount realized for former residence	$171,000
Less:	
Adjusted tax basis of former residence	−30,000
Gain *realized* on sale	$141,000

But since the purchase price of the new residence equals $185,000, which exceeds the adjusted sale price of $168,000 ($171,000 less the $3000 of fix-up expenses) of the former residence, no current gain is *recognized* on the sale.

Further, the tax basis of the newly acquired residence now is:

Cost of new residence	$185,000
Less:	
Gain on sale of former residence not	
taxed currently	141,000
Adjusted tax basis of new residence	$ 44,000

Since this is a mandatory provision, it must be used if the taxpayer qualifies for it. However, there is no limit on the number of times it can be used, and the taxpayer can be of any age.

---

[11] These are expenses such as painting, repairs, and replacement of shrubs incurred to make the residence more attractive for sale. Such work must be performed within the period of 90 days prior to the date of the contract of sale.

In addition, under the Section 121 exclusion-of-gain provision, there is an exclusion of gain on the sale of a principal residence by a taxpayer or spouse over age 55 under certain conditions. This is a one-time *exclusion* of gain up to $125,000. Thus, in our example above, if the taxpayer subsequently sells the "new" principal residence at age 56 for $190,000, elects to use the Section 121 exclusion-of-gain provision, and does not replace it within a four-year period (so there is no further rollover of gain to another new principal residence), the taxable gain on the sale will be $21,000 ($190,000 sales price minus the $44,000 adjusted basis and also minus the $125,000 exclusion). This exclusion can be quite valuable to taxpayers, but it is available only once during an individual's lifetime and is available only to owners age 55 or over who have owned and used the residence as their principal residence for at least three years in the five-year period ending on the date of the sale. A married couple can use the $125,000 exclusion-of-gain provision even if only one of them meets the age 55, ownership, and time-of-use requirements of the law, provided they file a joint return and own the residence jointly as of the date of the sale. However, if an election to use the exclusion is made during marriage (which must then be joined in by both spouses), neither spouse (nor any future spouse of either spouse) can ever again elect to use the exclusion. Thus, careful planning for the use of this exclusion can be important.

If, however, property held for personal use is converted to property used for the production of income, as when a residence is rented to others, depreciation is allowed as a tax deduction from rental income, and at least part of a capital loss on a subsequent sale of the property is deductible. Thus, if owners of a residence actually rent it, they can treat a loss on its sale as at least a partially deductible capital loss.

The tax status of an inherited residence depends on the use made of it by the person inheriting it. If the new owner does not use it as a residence but immediately attempts to sell or rent it, the property then is considered held for profit, and a loss on its sale is a potentially deductible capital loss. The same also is true even though two persons own the residence jointly and use it as a personal asset, and one of them dies. The tax status of the residence in the hands of the survivor depends on how the survivor then uses it.

Making Charitable Contributions

Another way to reduce taxable income and save taxes is by making charitable contributions which are itemized deductions. Such contributions often are expected of taxpayers anyway, and so they might as well make them in the most tax-advantageous way possible. Most charitable gifts are relatively simple and straightforward gifts of money. However, there also are a number of more sophisticated techniques for charitable giving that may give the charitably inclined substantial tax and other benefits in addition to the satisfaction of knowing they have helped others. Many of these techniques will be discussed briefly here.

While charitable gifts generally are deductible for federal income tax purposes, there are annual limits on such deductibility.[12] These limits can be quite complex, but in general a taxpayer can deduct up to 50 percent of his or her "contribution base," which is the taxpayer's adjusted gross income (AGI) without allowance for any net operating loss carryback, for contributions to charities defined as "public charities," and up to 30 percent for contributions to other charities (semipublic charities and private charities). However, there is a special rule for contributions of appreciated long-term capital gain assets under which if the deduction is taken at 100 percent of the appreciated property's fair market value, the annual deductible limits are 30 percent of the contribution base for gifts to public charities and 20 percent for gifts to other charities. But if the taxpayer makes a special tax election to reduce the value of the charitable deduction by the unrealized appreciation on the gift property (i.e., to limit the charitable deduction to the income tax basis of the property), then the annual deductible limits are 50 percent to public charities and 20 percent to other charities. Thus, the taxpayer must decide whether to contribute appreciated property at fair market value but with a lower contribution limit to public charities or to elect to contribute the property at its basis with a higher contribution limit. In general, any unused ("excess") charitable deductions for a year can be carried forward for deduction purposes for up to five additional years. There are other rules and limits on charitable contributions that are not discussed here.

Giving Appreciated Property. One interesting technique for making charitable contributions that actually may be available to many persons is the giving of appreciated long-term capital-gain property, such as common stock, with a sizable "paper gain." Here the gift generally would be deductible at its fair market value on the date of the gift and no capital gain would be realized by the donor.[13]

Suppose, for example, that Mr. Whitcomb has owned common stock in a growth company for a long time and has a sizable "paper gain" on it. He would like to dispose of some of this stock but has no offsetting losses. He also customarily gives about $1000 per year to his church. If he were to

---

[12] While there are annual limits on the deductibility of charitable contributions for federal income tax purposes, there are no such limits on federal gift tax and federal estate tax charitable deductions. For these taxes, gifts to any eligible charities are deductible in full.

[13] As just noted, the annual limit on such contributions to public charities is 30 percent and to other charities is 20 percent of essentially the taxpayer's AGI. However, if the election to limit the deduction to basis is made, the applicable limits are 50 percent and 20 percent, respectively, of essentially AGI.

give $1000 worth of this stock (rather than his customary cash donation) to his church, he would be better off taxwise and the church would get the same dollar donation (less any selling expenses on the stock).

Let us see why. Assume that Mr. Whitcomb's cost basis in the $1000 of stock is $100 and he and his wife are in a 31 percent federal income tax bracket. We shall compare the tax results of a gift to charity of the stock itself with the results of a sale of the stock, retaining the after-tax proceeds of the sale, and making the investor's customary $1000 cash contribution to charity.

	Sale of stock and gift of cash	Gift of stock
Market value of stock (fair market value)	$1000	$1000
Sale of stock		
Cost basis	100	—
Capital gain	$ 900	—
Charitable contribution	$1000 (cash)	$1000 (stock)
Tax deduction	−310	−310
	$ 690	$ 690
Capital gains tax (from above at the maximum 28% rate)	252	—
After-tax cost of transaction to taxpayer	$ 942	$ 690

The net effect of this illustration, under the assumptions given, is a tax saving equal to the capital gains tax on the sale of the appreciated property. But this works only if the taxpayer is going to make a charitable contribution anyway.

Also note that the unrealized appreciation on contributions of appreciated property to charity is a tax preference item for purposes of the alternative minimum tax (AMT). Therefore, persons may want to use this technique only in years when they will not be subject to the AMT. For many persons, however, this will not be a major problem in making such gifts.

On the other hand, if a person is holding property on which he or she has a potentially deductible loss, the reverse is true. The contributor then is better off taxwise first to sell the property and take the tax loss, then to give the proceeds to charity in cash. That way the contributor gets both the capital loss on the sale and the charitable deduction.

Making "Split" Gifts to Charity. An increasingly popular approach to more sophisticated charitable giving is to make a gift now of a future interest in property to charity while retaining a present interest in the property for the donor and/or the donor's family. This is commonly done by giving a remainder interest in property to a charity, under which the charity will get the property sometime in the future (see p. 416 of Chap. 14 for a definition of a remainder interest), while retaining an intervening income interest in the property for a period of years or for someone's lifetime for noncharitable beneficiaries (e.g., the donor, the donor and his or her spouse, or perhaps other family members). This approach can be very useful in retirement or estate planning in many situations. However, the tax law permits this approach to be used only in certain ways. These are: (1) gift of a remainder interest in a personal residence or farm; (2) use of a charitable remainder unitrust; (3) use of a charitable remainder annuity trust; and (4) use of pooled income funds.

Gift of Remainder Interest in Personal Residence or Farm. A taxpayer-donor may give these types of real property to charity but reserve the right to live in or use the property for the remaining lifetime of the donor or the donor and his or her spouse. The donor then gets a current income tax charitable deduction for the present value of the charity's remainder interest in the depreciated value of the residence or farm. This type of future gift to charity does not require a formal trust.

Charitable Remainder Unitrust. The concept behind this technique often is that the donor will create, and place highly appreciated property into, an irrevocable charitable remainder unitrust under which the donor (or perhaps the donor and another income beneficiary or beneficiaries after the donor's death) will receive a *specified percentage* (but not less than 5 percent) of each year's current value of the trust assets annually for the income beneficiary's lifetime or for a fixed period of years that do not exceed 20 years. This income interest can also be expressed as the lesser of the stated percentage (say, 7 percent) of trust assets or that year's actual trust income (a net income unitrust) or that year's actual trust income with a provision to make up any difference in later years when trust income may exceed the stated percentage (a net income with make-up unitrust). Naturally, at the income beneficiary's (or beneficiaries') death, the trust corpus will go to the charity, but in the meantime the income beneficiary or beneficiaries is (are) being provided for.

The potential advantages of this technique for the donor and his or her family are: (1) a current income tax deduction equal to the present value of the charity's future remainder interest as of the date the unitrust is created; (2) avoidance of any capital gains tax on the appreciated property used to fund the unitrust (thus avoiding the "capital gains lock-in problem" for this property as explained on pp. 337–339 of this chapter); (3) the possibility of greater current income from the unitrust depending on how the corpus is invested (such as if the original, perhaps lower yield, property is sold by the trust without capital gains tax and the proceeds are reinvested in higher-yielding investments); (4) the possibility of even greater future income at the sacrifice of current income under a make-up provision in the unitrust's terms; and (5) a life income for, say, the donor (or perhaps for the donor and his or her spouse).

Charitable Remainder Annuity Trust. This vehicle uses essentially the same general concept as the charitable remainder unitrust, except that the return to the noncharitable income beneficiary must be a fixed or determined amount (again, not less than 5 percent) calculated on the basis of the *initial value* of the property originally transferred to the irrevocable trust.

Thus, as an example of the operation of this concept and of the difference between these trusts, suppose that Mr. Martinez is an executive of Growth Corporation, is planning to retire soon, and has a large part of his investment portfolio in highly appreciated Growth Corporation common stock (with a 2 percent current yield) that he acquired over many years through the exercise of stock options and through an employee stock purchase plan. Mr. Martinez would also like to make a meaningful contribution to the university from which he graduated many years ago, mainly with the help of scholarship money. He would like to help other students as he was helped years ago. One possibility in this situation is that Mr. Martinez could transfer, say, $350,000 of his highly appreciated Growth Corporation stock to a charitable remainder annuity trust with a 7 percent payout rate to Mr. Martinez and his wife for as long as either of them lives (i.e., a life estate over both their lifetimes). As a result, Mr. and Mrs. Martinez would receive a fixed annual distribution of $24,500 from the trust ($350,000 × 0.07) as long as either of them lives, and this amount would not change even if the corpus of the trust should rise or fall in value. If trust income is not sufficient to pay out this fixed amount, trust principal (corpus) would have to be used to make up the difference. Then, upon the last of their deaths, the value at that time of the trust corpus would go outright to the charity (the university) as the remainder interest. The Martinezes also would get a current income tax charitable deduction for the actuarial value (considering their ages and the applicable interest rate, which changes monthly) of the charity's remainder interest.[14] Thus, the investment income on the tax saving from this deduction also would be available to the Martinezes. Finally, the Martinezes would realize no capital gain from the appreciated stock transferred to the irrevocable charitable trust (thus avoiding their capital gains lock-in problem) and, of course, neither would the charity because it is tax-exempt.

On the other hand, if Mr. Martinez had used a charitable remainder unitrust with the same general terms instead, he and his wife would receive an annual distribution from the trust for their lifetimes of 7 percent of each year's current value of the trust assets. Thus, if the trust assets grow in value, their annual income correspondingly will grow, but if the trust assets decline in value, the reverse also will be true. Thus, to make an admittedly

---

[14] However, since this is a gift of appreciated long-term capital gain property to a public charity, the 30 percent of essentially AGI charitable deduction annual limit described previously would apply. Also, the appreciation is a tax preference item for individual AMT purposes.

overly simplistic comparison, the unitrust may be better for donors and their families in the event of capital growth (or inflation), while the annuity trust will be structured to provide the donor or his or her family with a stable income in the face of recession or depression (or other declines in trust asset values). There also are other important differences, such as the use of a net income with make-up provision unitrust to build greater future income, and the fact that after the trust is established, additional contributions can be made to a unitrust but not to an annuity trust.

It can be seen that the establishment of either a charitable remainder unitrust or an annuity trust is a complicated legal and financial transaction that normally requires the aid of the donor's professional advisers. These arrangements also are normally practical only for larger estates and gifts. Further, it must be remembered that the gift property ultimately will go to the charity and not to the donor's heirs. As a solution to this estate reduction problem, some donors have purchased life insurance on their lives or joint life (survivorship life) insurance on their and their spouses' lives to make up the value of the gift property to their heirs. This life insurance often is arranged so that it is owned by an unfunded irrevocable life insurance trust, so the life insurance proceeds also will escape federal estate taxation in the donor's estate and in his or her spouse's estate (see pp. 470–472 of Chap. 16 for a discussion of the unfunded irrevocable life insurance trust).

Pooled Income Fund.   The final way to make "split" gifts to charity is through pooled income funds maintained by many larger charities. These are pooled funds maintained by some individual charities in which the contributions of a number of donors are combined for investment purposes. In this sense, they are like mutual funds run by charities, and, in fact, some larger charities maintain several pooled income funds with different investment objectives to meet the investment needs of their donors.

Like the previously described charitable remainder unitrusts and annuity trusts, the donor can make a gift of appreciated property and escape capital gains tax on the appreciation, get an immediate income tax deduction for the actuarial value of the charity's remainder interest, and receive an income from the fund for life or for a period of years. In the case of pooled income funds, however, the donor receives a certain number of units (the number depending on their current value and the amount contributed) in a particular pooled income fund (again, like an open-end mutual fund). In addition, the donor gets the advantage of investment diversification through contributions to a well-managed pooled income fund or funds.

The annual income received by the donor or others is determined each year by the pooled income fund's investment return. Thus, before contributing to such a fund, a potential donor, or his or her advisors, should check into the fund's current and past investment returns as well as its investment objectives, again much like one would before investing in a mutual fund or other financial intermediary.

To contribute to a pooled income fund, a donor does not have to create an individual trust (as he or she would for a unitrust or annuity trust). Thus, a carefully selected pooled income fund can be a practical charitable giving technique even for donors with more modest estates. Of course, after the noncharitable income interest or interests expire, the property will go to the charity that maintains the pooled income fund.

Other Forms of Lifetime Charitable Contributions. As stated at the beginning of this section, a number of charitable giving techniques are being used, and they cannot all be described in detail here. One other fairly common technique is the *charitable gift annuity*. This is essentially the sale of an annuity (usually a life annuity) by a charity to the donor-annuitant for a price in excess of what would be charged for the same annuity income by a commercial life insurance company. The difference (excess price) determines the amount of the income tax charitable deduction for the donor-annuitant. If a donor transfers appreciated property to a charity for such an annuity, he or she will realize taxable gain. As with any annuity, the donor-annuitant should evaluate carefully the financial soundness of the charity guaranteeing the annuity income.

Another technique that may be used for larger estates is the *charitable lead trust*. This technique conceptually is the reverse of the charitable remainder unitrust or annuity trust in that an income interest is given to charity for a period of time and then a future remainder interest goes to noncharitable beneficiaries (e.g., the donor's family) at the end of the charity's income interest. Such a trust may be established during a donor's lifetime or at death. Its purpose is not income tax saving but rather to get a gift tax or estate tax charitable deduction for the actuarial value of the income interest going to charity.

Other charitable giving techniques may include *conservation easements* for real estate given to some communities, *bargain sales to charities, gifts of life insurance to charities,* gifts to charities *involving closely held corporation stock,* and gifts of other *partial interests* to charity.

When to Make Charitable Contributions. Charitable contributions can be made during a potential donor's lifetime or at death under his or her will. From just a tax perspective, it normally is better to make charitable gifts during life (perhaps using one of the techniques just described), because the donor gets an income tax deduction for the value of the gift, and, effectively, the gift amount is removed from his or her gross estate for federal estate tax purposes. Gifts at death get only a federal estate tax charitable deduction. Of course, tax factors are not the only considerations in this decision. Naturally, the donor should be very careful that he or she (or his or her family) can afford to make the lifetime gift.

Shifting the Tax Burden to Others

Because of the progressive federal income tax structure, it may be attractive taxwise to use plans that are intended to shift income or capital gains from persons in higher tax brackets to those in lower brackets. This is normally done within the family so that the economic benefits remain "at home." However, the Tax Reform Act of 1986 (and subsequent tax legislation) have imposed some important restrictions on income shifting for income tax purposes.

First, since income tax rates now are less progressive (i.e., from 15 percent to 31 percent), shifting the income tax burden simply saves less tax than formerly. Second, some formerly popular tax shifting techniques, such as "Clifford trusts" and spousal remainder trusts, have been eliminated, except for some existing arrangements protected by "grandfather" provisions in the tax law. Further, the taxing of unearned income in excess of a certain amount per year of children under age 14 at their parents' top tax rate (the "kiddie tax" described on pp. 328–329 this chapter) will inhibit some tax shifting through gifts of income-earning property to children. Despite these restrictions, however, some techniques resulting in the shifting of income remain important financial planning devices in the proper circumstances. Thus, while the tax advantages from income shifting may be smaller than formerly, they still can be significant. In addition, there often are mixed motives for making gifts that also result in income shifting, such as motivations arising from estate planning considerations. These other motives basically have not been changed. Finally, many people want to make gifts in any event for family or other reasons.

The following are some of the methods for shifting income.

Outright Gifts of Income-Producing Property

One of the simplest and most obvious ways of shifting income to others is the outright gift to them of income-producing property. Father gives stock to his adult children; grandmother gives mutual fund shares to her grandchildren; mother registers Series EE savings bonds in her children's names; and so on. In general, when a donor gives a donee property, future income from the property is taxable to the donee, not the donor.[15] However, to escape income tax liability, the donor must give away the property as well as the future income from it. Gifts of only the income from property will not shift the income tax to the donee.

For capital gain purposes, the donee of a capital asset takes the donor's income tax basis in the property plus the amount of any gift tax paid on the transfer by the donor that is attributable to the net appreciation in the gift property at the time of the gift. Thus, if a father paid $1000 ten years ago for common stock which is now worth $3000, and gives the stock to his son, the son's tax basis is $1000. If the son later sells the stock for $3200, he will have a capital gain of $2200. Thus, the donor (father) can transfer a potential capital gain to his presumably lower-tax-bracket son, provided the son is age 14 or over when the stock is sold (so the "kiddie tax" does not apply).

On the other hand, if the owner (father) holds the stock until his death, it acquires a new (stepped-up) income tax basis in the hands of the decedent's executor or heirs as inherited property. This new stepped-up basis is generally equal to the fair market value of the stock (or other property) as of the deceased, former owner's death. Thus, if the common stock in our previous example had a market value of $4000 as of the owner's (father's) death, and the stock was inherited by his son, the stock's income tax basis in the son's hands would become $4000. Now, if the son later sells the stock for $4200, he will have a capital gain of only $200. Thus, the potential capital gain in the stock prior to the father's death is, in effect, wiped out and will never be taxed to anyone. This still remains a tax advantage of capital gains–type property.

For capital loss purposes for property given during the donor's lifetime, however, different rules apply. In this case, the donee's tax basis is either the donor's basis or the fair market value of the property at the date of the gift, whichever is lower. This means capital losses cannot be transferred to the donee. Therefore, *property in which the owner has a sizable "paper" loss is not desirable gift property from an income tax–saving standpoint*. Here, it would be better for the owner to sell the property, take the capital loss, and then give away other assets.

Property on which the donor's cost basis is about the same as its current market value does not present a built-in capital gains tax for either the donor or the donee. Therefore, some argue that it is generally the most desirable gift property; however, this would seem to depend on the circumstances.

---

[15] Lifetime gifts can have other advantages as well, such as saving state death taxes, reducing probate costs, and saving federal estate taxes. However, lifetime gifts can result in gift taxes, which may mean that estate taxes are saved only on any appreciation in the gift property after the gift. These concepts are discussed further in Chaps. 15 and 16.

Gifts of Income-Producing Property in Trust

Rather than being given outright, property can be given in trust—an irrevocable lifetime trust. The creator of an irrevocable lifetime trust establishes it during his or her lifetime and does not retain the power to alter or terminate the trust. The nature, uses, and advantages of trusts in estate planning are described in Chaps. 14, 15, and 16. In this chapter, we are concerned with how trusts can be used to save income taxes.

First, let us briefly describe how the income from property in irrevocable trusts is taxed. The taxation of trusts is a complex area of tax law, but the basic concept of the taxation of trust income is that the trust serves as a conduit for such income—somewhat similar to the concept applied to mutual funds. Thus, the tax initially falls on either the trust or the trust beneficiaries, depending on the trust's terms, and ultimately may fall on the beneficiaries to whom the income is distributed. Tax-exempt trust income (such as interest on most municipal bonds) is received by the trust or trust beneficiaries tax-free.

Gifts to Minors

People frequently want to make gifts of income-producing property to minors—children or grandchildren, for example.

Reasons for Making Gifts to Minors

One of the hoped-for advantages in making such gifts has been for the income from the property to be taxed to the minor at the minor's lower tax bracket. This hoped-for result, however, has been made more difficult to achieve by the Tax Reform Act of 1986, as explained below. Another reason is the desire to help minors get a good financial start in life and perhaps help provide some of their education expenses. Further, the gift property will be removed from the donor's gross estate for federal estate tax purposes, and, if the $10,000 per donee per year gift tax annual exclusion can be utilized (as is normally planned for), there may be no taxable gifts either.

Taxation of Unearned Income of Minor Children

As a general income tax principle, the income from property is taxed to the owner of the property at the owner's tax rate, regardless of whether the owner is a minor or an adult and whether the property was acquired by the owner by gift or otherwise. However, the Tax Reform Act of 1986 introduced a novel concept with respect to the unearned income of children under age 14. Such net unearned income of a child under age 14 is taxed to the child but at the child's *parents'* top marginal federal income tax rate. However, this special rule can only apply when a child has unearned income in excess of a specified amount ($1200 for 1992), which is indexed for inflation. This has been dubbed the "kiddie tax." Therefore, there normally would be no income tax advantage in shifting unearned income that will be subject to this "kiddie tax."

The tax law also provides that an individual who is eligible to be claimed as a dependent on another taxpayer's return may not take a personal exemption on his or her own return. Further, such a dependent's standard deduction generally may not exceed the larger of (1) a specified amount which is indexed for inflation ($600 for 1992), or (2) the dependent's earned income, subject to the regular standard deduction limits.

These rules, and the reduced tax rates generally, have lessened the ability of taxpayers and their advisors to save income taxes through shifting income to minors. However, as noted previously in this section, there are other reasons for making gifts to minors.

Methods for Making Gifts to Minors

At this point, it will be helpful to discuss the basic methods that are used in making gifts to minors. These general methods themselves have not been changed by the Tax Reform Act of 1986, but it must be remembered that the "kiddie tax" may apply to a minor's unearned income which might arise from such gifts, whether they have been made in the past or are made in the future.

Outright Gifts.   Some kinds of property may be conveniently given outright to minors—such as savings accounts, U.S. Series EE savings bonds, and life insurance on the minor's life. Income from such property also may be shifted to the minor. Interest from a savings account opened for a child is taxable to the child, provided that under state law the *account belongs to the child,* and the child's parents may not use any of the funds in the account to support the child. Also, interest on U.S. savings bonds bought in a *child's name* is taxable to the child, even though the child's parent(s) may be named as beneficiary(ies) in the event of the child's death. But interest on U.S. savings bonds bought by a parent who names the child only as co-owner is taxable to the parent.

However, outright gifts to minors of other kinds of property, such as securities or real estate, may cause problems because outsiders may not be willing to deal with minors in managing the property since minors are not generally considered legally competent to contract. Of course, a legal guardian could be appointed for minors to manage property they own, but guardianship tends to be inflexible, it ends when the person comes of age, and donors generally prefer other ways of giving property to minors.

Other than outright gifts, there are several methods for making gifts to minors that may meet the objectives of the donor in making such gifts. One of these objectives is to secure management and control of the gift property until the minor-donee comes of age and in many cases beyond that. These methods include (1) use of regular trusts [sometimes called Section 2503(b) trusts], often with a so-called "Crummey power" to take best possible advantage of the federal gift tax annual exclusion (described on pp. 453–454 of Chap. 15), (2) gifts to minors in trust under the special Internal Revenue Code section [Section 2503(c)] enacted for this purpose, and (3) gifts under a Uniform Gifts to Minors Act (UGMA) or Uniform Transfers to Minors Act (UTMA).

Uniform Gifts (Transfers) to Minors Acts.   The Uniform Gifts to Minors Act (or the more modern Uniform Transfers to Minors Act) is a popular way to make smaller gifts of securities and other property to minors. Laws of this type have been enacted in all states. Briefly, they provide for the registration of securities, and, depending on the law, other kinds of property, by a donor in the donor's own name, or in the name of any adult member of the minor's family, to act as "custodian" of the property for the minor. As an example, a grandfather might give stock to his grandson with the boy's father named as custodian.

This arrangement technically creates a custodianship, not a trust. The custodianship operates only under the terms of the state law under which it is created, and the donor cannot change these terms. The gift property is held by the custodian, who manages, invests, and reinvests it for the minor's benefit. The custodian can apply the property or the income from it for the benefit of the minor at the custodian's sole discretion. But to the extent the property and income are not expended for the minor's benefit, they must be delivered or paid over to the minor when he or she reaches majority. If the minor dies before attaining majority, the property and income must go to his or her estate. Thus, a possible disadvantage of this method is the forced distribution of the gift property and accumulated income to the former minor at majority (at age 18 or 21), depending on the particular state's law.

The UGMA or UTMA simplifies making smaller gifts to minors. No formal trust agreement is required. Income from property transferred in this way is taxable to the minor, unless the income is used to satisfy a legal obligation to support the minor. Also, the donor gets full use of the gift tax annual exclusion, even though the custodian may accumulate income for the minor. Thus, to continue the previous example, if a grandfather gave $10,000 worth of stock to his grandson in one year under his state's UGMA or UTMA, it would all qualify for the gift tax annual exclusion and no taxable gift would result.

Use of Regular Trusts.   Gifts can be made to minors through *regular irrevocable trusts* the same as they can to anyone else. Trusts enable the donor to set the terms of the gift (as grantor or creator of the trust) within the generally much more liberal and flexible rules of the state's trust law. A trust [other than a Section 2503(c) trust described below] does not have to be terminated when a minor-beneficiary reaches majority or even, in many cases, for many years (or even generations) thereafter. Thus, donors often want to use the trust mechanism when they are planning for a long-term lifetime giving program to minors or are planning for other substantial gifts.

The practical problems are that a formal trust must be established, and, depending on the size of the gift and the terms of the trust, the donor may not be able to take advantage, or full advantage, of the $10,000 federal gift tax annual exclusion when making gifts to the trust. This is because without a so-called Crummey power (discussed next), only a part or none of each gift to the trust will be considered a gift of a present interest to the donee (the trust beneficiary or beneficiaries), and only a present interest (entitling the donee to the immediate use, possession, or enjoyment of the interest given) will qualify as a gift for the annual exclusion. That is, gifts of future interests do not qualify for the annual exclusion. If the terms of a trust call for the accumulation in the trust of trust income or for discretion on the part of the trustee to pay trust income to or for one or more beneficiaries (e.g., a sprinkle or spray power), then *no part* of a gift to the trust would be a present interest to any specific beneficiary, and no annual exclusion would be allowed. If the trust requires the current distribution of its income to the trust beneficiary or beneficiaries, then *only a part* of each gift to the trust would be a gift of a present interest (measured by the part of each gift representing the mandatory income interest). However, such a mandatory income distribution requirement at all times may not be suitable for a long-term trust for minors.

The famous Crummey case and its eventual acceptance by the IRS gave estate and tax planners at least one solution to these complex problems regarding making gifts to trusts, so that the *whole gift* (up to certain limits) would be a gift of a present interest and hence would qualify for the gift tax annual exclusion. This solution involves having a *Crummey power* in these trusts to get the annual exclusion, as explained next.

Regular [or Section 2503(b)] Trusts with Crummey Powers.   When regular irrevocable trusts are used as the vehicle for making periodic gifts to minors or others, with the idea that the gifts will be covered by the gift tax annual exclusion so no taxable gifts will be made, the terms of the trust often give the trust beneficiary or beneficiaries the noncumulative power each year to withdraw that year's gift to the trust up to some dollar limit, such as $5000. This withdrawal right is the Crummey power, after the case of that name, and assures a gift tax annual exclusion for each year's gift to the trust up to the dollar limit for each trust beneficiary with a Crummey power. This is because since each beneficiary has a Crummey withdrawal power over his or her share of each year's gift to the trust, each beneficiary is considered to have a present interest in the whole amount of his or her share of each year's gift (up to the dollar limit, say, $5000), because each beneficiary could get the immediate use, possession, or enjoyment of his or her share by withdrawing it. However, even though the trust beneficiary or beneficiaries actually possess this limited annual withdrawal right, and normally should be notified of it, its real purpose is to make the periodic gifts to the trust gifts of present interests (up to the sum of the dollar limits of the Crummey powers for all the beneficiaries) and hence to bring them within the gift tax annual exclusions for all the trust beneficiaries and avoid (or limit) the making of taxable gifts. Thus, it really is expected (and hoped) that the trust beneficiaries will never actually exercise their Crummey rights. They are meant to be for tax purposes only.

Thus, such trusts can result in the shifting (or accumulation) of income for income tax purposes, removing the trust property from the donor's estate for federal estate tax purposes, and normally in no taxable gifts being made because of the gift tax annual exclusion. The trustee can also be given discretionary power to distribute trust income and/or corpus to the beneficiaries for various needs or at the trustee's sole discretion. The trust may also continue for many years after the beneficiaries reach majority or even for the beneficiaries' lifetimes, depending on the desires of the creator of the trust (the donor). There are several ways that Crummey powers can be structured, and this basic concept is very useful to estate planners in making periodic lifetime gifts in trust.

Trusts for Minors under Section 2503(c).   Under Section 2503(c) of the Internal Revenue Code, a donor can have full use of the gift tax annual exclusion for a gift in trust if it meets the requirements of the law. The law provides that the trust income and principal may be expended by the trustee for, or on behalf of, the minor beneficiary. Any amounts remaining in the trust when the beneficiary becomes 21 must be distributed to the beneficiary then. As noted previously in this section, this may be a disadvantage because many donors prefer to postpone the distribution of trust property to a beneficiary until after age 21, or perhaps in installments, such as one-third at 25, one-third at 30, and the final third at 35. If the beneficiary dies prior to age 21, the trust property must go to the beneficiary's estate or as the beneficiary designates. If the donor is not the trustee or one of the trustees under this kind of trust, the trust property will be removed from the donor's gross estate for federal estate tax purposes.

There is an additional potential income tax problem that can be involved in gifts of income-producing property to minors which should be mentioned. Trust income or income from property held for a minor under a UGMA or UTMA that is used to discharge a parent's or guardian's *legal* obligation to support the minor will be taxed to the parent or guardian. Thus, parents cannot use these arrangements to discharge their own legal obligations to support their children at favorable tax rates. However, just what a parent's legal support obligation is in a given case may not be entirely clear. The obligation is limited by the duties imposed on parents by the law of the state in which they live.

Allowing Wealth to Accumulate without Current Taxation and Postponing Taxation

A number of important tax-saving techniques involve postponing taxation until the future rather than reducing or eliminating taxes now. Postponing taxes can be advantageous to taxpayers for several reasons. Taxpayers may be in a lower tax bracket in the future; their financial circumstances may be better known then; they get the investment return on the postponed tax while it is postponed (i.e., a tax-deferred or tax-free buildup of investment values); they may not be in a financial position to pay the tax now; and, under some circumstances, the tax may never have to be paid. However, when reviewing a proposal involving tax saving, the taxpayer should recognize whether taxes are being permanently reduced or merely postponed. Also, some flexibility usually is lost when taxes are postponed and investment values are allowed to accumulate without being reduced by current taxation, because there are normally tax law rules to be met before this can be done.

Various kinds of employee benefit plans, executive compensation plans, and tax-sheltered annuity plans represent important ways by which many people postpone taxation until a presumably more favorable time for them. The nature of these plans is discussed in more detail in Chaps. 12 and 13. Among the more important are:

Qualified pension, profit-sharing, and employee savings plans

Employee stock purchase plans

Nonqualified deferred compensation plans

Retirement plans for the self-employed (HR-10 plans)

Individual retirement accounts and annuities (IRA plans)

Tax-sheltered annuity plans for employees of nonprofit organizations and public school systems (TSA plans)

Other approaches to postponing taxation have already been mentioned in this chapter, including:

Postponing the sale of appreciated securities or other investments

Selling stock "short against the box" to lock in a capital gain

Postponing capital gains taxation on the sale of a taxpayer's principal residence

In addition, the following are other commonly used ways of postponing the impact of income taxation.

Postponing Income Taxation on Series EE Savings Bonds

Series EE U.S. savings bonds are issued on a discount basis, and the interest they earn is represented by the periodic increase in their redemption value over time. Other U.S. savings bonds, such as Series HH bonds, pay their interest periodically to the owner in cash.

Owners of Series EE bonds have a choice as to when they want to be taxed on the increase in value of their bonds. They may (1) elect to report and pay tax on the increase in redemption value as interest each year, or (2) take no action and thus postpone paying tax on the increase in value until the bonds mature or are redeemed. Interest on Series EE bonds held beyond their maturity date, where taxation is postponed, does not need to be reported until the bonds are actually redeemed or the period of extension ends.

Series EE bonds on which the owners postponed taxation can be exchanged for Series HH bonds without the owners' being taxed in the year of the exchange, except to the extent that they receive cash on the exchange. Thus, a person can buy Series EE bonds during working years, postpone taxation, and then exchange the EE bonds for HH bonds upon retirement to receive a periodic retirement income. The increase in value of this taxpayer's EE bonds (which were exchanged tax-free for the HH bonds) will not be taxed until the HH bonds mature or are disposed of by the taxpayer.

Another possible tax advantage for Series EE bonds issued after December 31, 1989, is that for tax years beginning after that date, the accrued interest on such bonds redeemed to finance qualified higher education expenses for the taxpayer, the taxpayer's spouse, or the taxpayer's dependents is *excluded* from the taxpayer's gross income for federal income tax purposes. Thus, such income becomes tax-free, not just tax-deferred as is normally the case. To qualify, the bonds must be redeemed in the year the qualified higher education expenses are paid; the bonds must be issued in the taxpayer's or the taxpayer's and his or her spouse's name; the taxpayer was age 24 or older before the bonds were issued; and the taxpayer's filing status is single, married filing a joint return, head of household, or a qualifying surviving spouse with dependent child. This accrued interest exclusion is phased out between certain income levels (e.g., from $60,000 to $90,000 of modified adjusted gross income for married taxpayers filing a joint return and from $40,000 to $55,000 of income for single taxpayers and heads of households, indexed for inflation). This rather interesting tax provision (the first real tax subsidy for people trying to save for their children's education) may help make Series EE bonds relatively attractive for lower- and middle-income families with children to educate and for others saving for higher education.

Selecting the Particular Stock Certificates to Be Sold

The tax law permits investors to select the particular stock certificates they want to sell, assuming they are going to sell only part of their holdings of a stock.

Suppose an investor owns 300 shares of a common stock with a present market value of $50 per share. The stock was acquired over the years as indicated below, and the investor now wishes to sell 100 shares.

Purchased 100 shares 10 years ago at $20 per share

Purchased 100 shares 5 years ago at $50 per share

Purchased 100 shares 2 years ago at $60 per share

Thus, depending on which certificates the investor decides to sell, he or she could have a capital gain, no gain or loss, or a capital loss. In the absence of identification as to which certificates are sold, the tax law assumes the first purchased are the first sold (a first-in, first-out concept).

Tax-Deferred ("Tax-Free") Buildup of Life Insurance and Deferred Annuity Policy Values

Life insurance cash values normally increase over time. In addition, policy dividends based in part on an "excess interest" factor are paid on participating policies. These amounts are not subject to income taxation as they increase year by year, but generally only when the policy matures, is surrendered, or when partial cash withdrawals are made from it. This commonly is referred to as the "income tax–free buildup" in life insurance. This feature of life insurance contracts has become even more important in recent years with the advent of many investment-oriented policies and variable life policies as described in Chap. 4.

In a sense, however, this may only be a postponement of income taxation, because if a policy matures; is surrendered; or, depending on the circumstances, partial withdrawals are taken from it for more than the net premiums paid, the gain is taxable as ordinary income. But if the insured dies, the "gain" permanently escapes taxation since it is paid out tax-free in the form of life insurance proceeds paid by reason of the insured's death.

Similarly, the growth in the policy value of nonqualified deferred annuity contracts is not taxed currently to the owner of the annuity. The income tax is deferred until the owner begins receiving periodic payments from the annuity; surrenders it for cash; makes nonperiodic withdrawals from it; secures loans on it; or until the value of the annuity is paid to a beneficiary upon the owner's death. This tax-deferred feature is one of the attractions of deferred annuities. However, a distribution (cash payment or policy loan) from an annuity will result in current ordinary income taxation and may result in a 10 percent penalty tax if it is a premature distribution (i.e., generally a distribution before the owner is age 59½, with some exceptions).

Installment Sales

For various kinds of property (other than publicly traded stocks or securities), when the selling price is paid to the seller in a tax year after the year of the sale (e.g., in installments), the seller generally pays the tax on any gain arising from the sale as the installments are collected (i.e., on the installment method) rather than in the year the sale is made, unless the seller elects otherwise. This in effect defers the tax on the uncollected installments or selling price.

Taking Returns as Capital Gains

Despite the changes made in capital gains taxation by the Tax Reform Act of 1986 and subsequent tax legislation, taking returns on property as capital gains still offers some distinct tax advantages. First, the taxpayer has the option of deciding when, if ever, he or she will realize, and perhaps recognize, a capital gain through the sale or exchange of an appreciated capital asset. This allows planning flexibility by the taxpayer. Second, capital assets will receive a step-up in income tax basis upon the owner's death equal to their value for federal estate tax purposes, and so an unrealized or unrecognized capital gain inherent in such property may escape taxation entirely at the owner's death. This should be considered by those making lifetime gifts or sales of such property. Third, any capital gain also can be avoided by making lifetime gifts of such appreciated property to charity as described previously in this chapter (subject to certain limits and a possible AMT tax).

Finally, the maximum tax rate on net capital gains again is somewhat lower than for ordinary income and, if history repeats itself, may go even lower.

People can plan for capital gains in a variety of ways. Some of the ways are mentioned below.

Ownership of Investments (or Property) That May Appreciate in Value

This is one of the cornerstones of the investment policy of many people. Purchase of so-called growth stocks, for example, is aimed at reaping capital gains, rather than dividend income.

But investors should not feel that common stocks are the only vehicle for securing capital gains. Other equity-type investments also may grow with the economy in the future. Also, marketable bonds, such as corporate and U.S. government bonds, may result in capital gains.

Bonds Purchased at a "Discount"

As has been pointed out, when bonds are purchased in the open market at a price less than their par (maturity) value, the difference between a bond's purchase price and its par value at maturity often is a capital gain (i.e., for taxable bonds issued on or before July 18, 1984, and for tax-exempt municipals). This really is a built-in capital gain, since the bond will eventually mature at par. Of course, the bond may also be sold prior to maturity at a capital gain (or loss).

For deep-discount municipals, however, whose current interest return is not taxable, any such "discount" still is taxable as a capital gain. Therefore, this is not a desirable tax feature for municipals.

Note also that the "discount" on Treasury bills, which customarily are purchased by investors at a discount from their maturity value to provide a given yield, is ordinary income, not capital gains, for federal income tax purposes.

Taxation and the Capital Gains Tax "Lock-in" Problem

The capital gains tax can produce a situation in which investors feel "locked in" to a stock or other property because of their investment success. For example, investors may have made the "right" investment decision on a "growth stock" many years ago; they may have been buying a stock, or several stocks, right along under a dollar-cost averaging scheme; or they may have acquired stock many years ago, or periodically, under employee stock options, a stock purchase plan, an employee stock ownership plan (ESOP), or a profit-sharing or savings plan. Other possibilities could be named. They basically involve a situation in which investors find themselves (happily, of course) with a large "paper gain" in a stock (or other appreciated property) and are afraid to sell because they will have to pay taxes on the capital gain.

This kind of lock-in problem can have several bad effects for investors and their families. The investor's portfolio may become heavily "lopsided" in favor of the locked-in stock or appreciated property, and diversification may be badly lacking. What goes up can also come down, and in a declining market the investor may suffer losses in the locked-in stock or property. In addition, there may be better investments around now than the locked-in stock—another stock in the same industry or a different industry, mutual funds for diversification, stocks with different investment characteristics, high-yielding corporate bonds, municipal bonds for those in higher tax brackets, and so forth. Further, while the investors' personal situations may have changed and they could use the money, they may be afraid to sell the stock and pay the tax for fear of depriving their children and other heirs of part of their inheritances.

Assuming a lock-in problem, let us briefly review what investors' choices are. (Assume that the appreciated property is common stock just for convenience of explanation, recognizing that it could be other appreciated capital assets as well.)

1. They can simply hold the appreciated stock—never sell it during their lifetime—and upon their death, it would get a stepped-up income tax basis equal to its fair market value on that date. Thus investors could plan on passing the appreciated stock(s) on to their heirs free of capital gains tax as of the date of death.

2. They can give away the appreciated stock to someone in their family during their lifetime. The donee will take the donor's income tax basis in the stock; but if the donee is in a lower tax bracket than the donor, the capital gains tax on a subsequent sale by the donee will not hurt so much.

3. Investors can give some or all of the appreciated stock to charity. As noted previously (see pp. 320–321), they can then get a current income tax deduction for the value of the charitable gift and not realize any of the appreciation in the stock's value as a capital gain. If the investor is charitably inclined anyway, gifts of appreciated securities and other property are an attractive alternative. Of course, the appreciation on such gift property is a tax preference item for AMT purposes.

4. Investors can sell some or all of their appreciated stock, pay the tax (or offset the gain with capital losses), and reinvest the net (after capital gains tax) proceeds elsewhere. The investor must decide whether an

alternative investment is sufficiently better than the appreciated stock to justify paying a capital gains tax and transaction costs now.

5. Investors can seek some nonrecognition provision that will allow them to escape current recognition of gain and yet also give them some of the economic advantages of changing their portfolios. Some such non-recognition provisions might be for like-kind exchanges (other than for securities) or for tax-free reorganizations.

Of course, investors do not have to follow just one of these alternatives. They can mix them. They might, for example, sell some of their appreciated stock and reinvest the proceeds, use some to make their customary charitable donations, give some away within their family, and keep the rest. Further, if they happen to have acquired the stock at different times with different tax bases, they can sell the stock with the highest bases and give away to charity and/or keep the stock with the lowest bases.

Tax-Sheltered Investments

Tax-sheltered investments is a broad term that can apply to many kinds of investments, from the tax-deferred buildup of life insurance and annuity cash values and Series EE savings bonds to the interest on most municipal bonds. However, as the term generally has been applied, it means certain specialized kinds of investments, such as real estate, oil and gas businesses, and certain farming operations (see Chap. 8). Such tax-sheltered investments may involve one or more of the following tax benefits (as discussed more fully in Chap. 8).

1. Depreciation (or cost recovery) and amortization
2. Deferral of taxable income from the investment through current income tax deductions
3. Special statutory deductions, such as percentage depletion
4. Taking returns as capital gains

In addition, such investments often have relied on the investor's borrowing to finance the investment and taking an income tax deduction for the debt interest, subject to the at-risk rules. Further, if the tax shelter is a "passive activity," this interest is subject to the "passive activity" loss rules.

Reasons for Tax Shelters

In the past, tax-sheltered investments have been attractive to those in high income tax brackets who can afford to take considerable investment risks.

Such individuals have wanted to invest their money so as to "shelter" their returns as much as possible from income taxes. As noted previously, this aspect of tax shelters has been substantially diminished by the Tax Reform Act of 1986. However, some of these investments may be of interest primarily for their merits as investments, aside from possible tax advantages.

Passive Activity Loss (PAL) Rules and Other Tax Rules regarding Losses

Some important tax rules affect investments in a trade or business or rental property and so are very significant with regard to tax-sheltered investments, which typically are such investments. These tax rules were described on pp. 242–243 of Chap. 8 and so will not be repeated here.

Pitfalls of Tax-Sheltered Investments

Tax-sheltered investments should be made with great care and normally only after seeking competent professional advice. This is particularly necessary with respect to these investments for several reasons.

First, they are of a *specialized nature* in areas where the investor frequently is not knowledgeable. Thus, the investor really cannot judge the quality of such an investment without outside technical advice, which, of course, costs money. The investor also should have proper tax and legal advice on those important aspects of such an investment.

Second, *the ability, reputation, and character of the promoter and his or her possible financial stake in the deal* are of critical importance. Also, *consider the "load" or profit to the promoter.* This is shown in the prospectus of a public offering. If this load is too high, so little of the amount the investor actually pays will be available for investment that the chances for profit will be substantially diminished.

Many tax-sheltered investment deals have been sold as limited-partnership interests. While this usually means that the investor (as a limited partner) is not liable for the debts, obligations, or any losses of the partnership beyond the limited partner's original contribution to the partnership capital, it also means that the general partners (the promoters and/or their associates) have the exclusive right to manage and operate the partnership. The limited partners have no control. This again speaks to the need for evaluating the promoter.

Third, an investor should *be sure a tax shelter offers economic potential as an investment* before committing any funds to it. This is particularly true since the pure tax benefits of such investments have been so curtailed by the Tax Reform Act of 1986.

Fourth, *high interest rates may make some tax shelters questionable investments.* As we said above, many of these deals have been financed with borrowed funds and so high cost of money can make them impractical economically. Also, one of the investment alternatives of the high-bracket taxpayer is income tax–free municipal bonds.

Fifth, *tax shelters generally are high-risk, long-term investments with very limited marketability.* In a limited-partnership situation, for example, a limited partner may not be able to assign or sell his or her interest in the partnership without the consent of the general partner(s). Also, there are relatively few markets or price quotations for such interests, and it may be difficult for the investor to know whether any available price is a fair one for the economic value of his or her partnership interest. Further, a fairly sizable minimum investment usually is required.

Finally, *changes in the tax laws* over time, and particularly with the Tax Reform Act of 1986, have had the effect of making many tax shelters considerably less attractive in terms of income tax impact for high-bracket taxpayers than they once were.

However, with all these warnings, it should be recognized that certain tax-sheltered investments that are properly selected and evaluated for their investment merits may result in attractive after-tax yields, depending on the particular investment. Thus, investors may want to consider tax shelters *as a part of* their total investment portfolio. Also, *diversification* among tax-sheltered investments of the same type (a number of oil and gas participations, for example) and/or among several types of such investments (real estate and oil and gas participations, for example) will help reduce the inherent investment risk.

However, investors should make sure they have adequate liquid assets and life insurance protection before investing heavily in tax shelters. Also, they would be well advised to have impartial, outside experts evaluate a tax shelter before investing in it. Some banks, accounting firms, tax specialists, and other advisors will evaluate tax-sheltered investments on a fee basis.

Tax-Planning Caveats

While tax planning is important and can produce savings, it should not be overemphasized. Overemphasis on tax savings can result in unwise or uneconomical transactions in other respects. Therefore, in pursuing the legitimate objective of reducing his or her tax burden, the taxpayer should also keep in mind some tax-planning caveats or warnings so that the decisions made in this area will be sensible from all points of view.

Avoid "Sham" Transactions

Taxpayers sometimes undertake transactions that have no real economic significance other than the desire to save taxes. Such "sham" transactions will not work. A fundamental principle of tax law is that a transaction will not be recognized for tax purposes unless it makes sense aside from its tax consequences.

Also, a transaction must be in fact what it appears to be in form. Thus, if a father ostensibly gives property to his children but in fact continues to deal with the property as if he were the owner in accordance with an "understanding" with his children, the father will run a real risk that the "gift" will be regarded as a "sham" with no tax consequences.

In general, if a tax-saving plan makes no sense other than for tax purposes, it probably should not be adopted.

Do Not Let Tax Factors Outweigh Other Important Objectives

Most financial decisions involve a number of considerations, of which taxes are only one. The possibility of having to pay taxes, or of saving taxes, should be considered carefully but not to the exclusion of other nontax objectives. The capital gains tax "lock-in" problem, discussed above, is an example of this.

Consider What Must Be Given Up for the Tax Saving

A proposal that involves tax savings almost always also requires taxpayers to give up some flexibility, control, or other advantage that they would otherwise have. In other words, it is unlikely that you can "have your cake and eat it, too."

As an example of this, many people invest in municipal bonds because the interest is tax-exempt. But the "price" of this tax-free income is that the yields on municipals normally are lower than those on generally comparable taxable U.S. Treasury and corporate bonds.

Taxpayers should ask themselves, when confronted with a tax-saving proposition, "What will I have to give up to secure the expected tax saving?"

Be Sure the Tax Saving Is Enough to Justify the Transaction

In some cases there may be a real tax saving, but it may not be large enough to justify the transaction. Also, look at how long it takes to get the anticipated tax savings. Sometimes tax-saving proposals show promised savings at the end of 10 years, 15 years, 20 years, age 65, or some other lengthy period of time. But the promised tax savings really may not be very substantial when calculated on a per-year basis.

Keep Planning Flexible

The popular saying, "The times, they are a-changin'," is as true for financial plans as any other. Tax rates, laws, family circumstances, and the taxpayer's financial condition all may change over time. Therefore, a taxpayer should consider carefully any loss of flexibility that will result from a tax-saving proposal.

Be Sure the Analysis Is Complete

Before taxpayers undertake a financial plan that is based to any significant degree on expected tax savings, they should be sure they understand all the tax implications or dangers of the plan—not just the expected tax benefits. As part of such an analysis, they should consider how other types of taxes, such as estate, gift, and AMT taxes, will affect the plan.

PART 4

Planning for Retirement

12
Pension, Profit-Sharing, and Savings Plans

Earlier chapters have discussed the personal risks and potential solutions to the financial losses caused by premature death, disability, property and liability losses, and unemployment. The final personal risk, and one of growing importance, is that of "living too long," or outliving one's income. Thus, how to provide for retirement is a significant question.

Basic Retirement Principles

Economic Problems of Retirement Years

The assumption is often made that people's financial needs decrease after retirement. To some extent, this assumption may be valid. The retired individual's children probably are no longer dependent, and the family home and its furnishings have perhaps been paid for. There also are some income tax breaks available to persons when they retire.

However, the actual total reduction in the financial needs of a person upon retirement probably has been overstated. Social pressures may discourage any drastic change in standard of living at retirement. There is an increasing tendency for retired persons to remain active, particularly in civic, social, travel, and other recreational activities.

Some people also want to be able to make gifts to their grown children and grandchildren after they retire. Finally, individuals and their financial advisors cannot forget what economic forces, such as *inflation* or *deflation* (recession or depression), may do to a person's carefully planned retirement income. The trend in retirement planning seems to be in the direction of not expecting retired individuals to have to take a drastic reduction in their standard of living after retirement.

Some persons age 65 or over have some earnings from active employment, but the percentage of this age group for whom this is so has been declining. Many reasons account for the withdrawal of older persons from the labor force. A large number of older workers retire voluntarily, particularly if they can afford to do so. Others find it necessary to retire for reasons of health. Further, the OASDHI program and private pension plans, although not requiring retirement at age 65, have tended to "institutionalize" age 65 as the normal retirement age. The fact remains, however, that many workers may not want to count on employment opportunities during their retirement years.

Also, federal and state income taxes may reduce an individual's capacity to save. Thus, tax-favored retirement plans are attractive to many people. In addition, for many years inflation was and may continue to be an additional deterrent to increased levels of saving. Inflation is, of course, a particularly serious threat to the savings and retirement programs of persons who are already retired.

Another dimension to the problem is the increasing average life expectancy of people. Within the last 60 years, for example, the life expectancy at birth has increased from 47 years to approximately 74 years.

How to Provide for Retirement

The task of providing retirement income (other than earnings during retirement) seems to fall on (1) people's ability to accumulate their own retirement fund during their working years, (2) government retirement programs, and (3) employer-provided retirement plans. People frequently receive retirement benefits from all these sources. In fact, it seems prudent not to rely entirely on only one or even two of these sources. A balance (or diversification) of retirement income sources seems best in most cases.

Many people accumulate an investment fund, individual retirement accounts or annuities (IRAs), individual nonqualified annuities, life insurance cash values, and other funds during their working years to help provide for their retirement. In fact, as we said before, this seems only prudent so as not to be completely dependent on social security or an employer.

A second approach to the problem of financing old-age security is for the government to sponsor retirement programs. This has basically been accomplished through the Social Security Act of 1935 and its many subsequent amendments and expansions. It is generally felt that the essential purpose of social security is to provide a *guaranteed income floor* on which a more comfortable retirement income can be built by the individual and his or her employer.

The third main method of handling the problem of retirement financing is for the employer to assume some of the burden. And, in response to this need, as a result of inducements offered under federal tax laws and owing to other factors, employers generally have established tax-favored retirement plans. The remainder of this chapter will be devoted to these private pension, profit-sharing, and savings plans, while the next chapter will cover other types of private retirement programs.

Kinds of Employer-Provided Retirement Plans

General Considerations. As just noted, a major source of retirement income security in the United States is through various types of employer-provided retirement plans, which usually are part of the employer's overall employee benefit program. The most important of these employer-provided plans are qualified (defined on p. 350) pension plans, profit-sharing plans, and savings plans. To receive favorable income tax treatment (as explained next), these plans must be nondiscriminatory in the sense that they cannot "discriminate" in favor of the employer's "highly compensated employees," as defined in the tax law. These qualified plans are considered in this chapter.

Employers also may have other plans that directly or indirectly aid their employees or some of their employees in providing for retirement. Some of these include simplified employee pension plans (SEPs), tax-sheltered annuity plans (TSAs) for nonprofit and certain other employers, qualified stock bonus plans, nonqualified deferred-compensation plans, and supplemental executive retirement plans. The last two of these may be applied by the employer in a discriminatory fashion to benefit only some of its highly compensated employees, while the others must be "nondiscriminatory," as defined in the tax law.

Defined-Benefit Plans and Defined-Contribution Plans. In terms of how retirement benefits for employees are expressed in the plan, qualified retirement plans may be classified as *defined-benefit plans* or *defined-contribution plans.* In general, a *defined-benefit plan* is one in which the benefits are expressed as a specified, definite benefit (either a dollar amount or by a specified formula) at retirement. Thus, for a defined-benefit plan the retirement benefit is the stated or fixed factor, while the contributions needed to fund the plan are the variable factor, depending on the actuarial costs of the plan. A *defined-contribution plan,* on the other hand, is one that provides for an individual account for each plan participant, with specified or variable contributions being made into these accounts. A participant's retirement income, then, is based on whatever income his or her account balance will produce at retirement. Thus, for a defined-contribution plan the contributions to the plan are the stated factor, while the retirement income to the plan participants is the variable factor, depending on the amounts accumulated in their individual accounts when they retire or otherwise receive benefits from the plan. Pension plans may be defined-benefit plans or defined-contribution plans (called money purchase pension plans). Other types of qualified retirement plans, such as profit-sharing plans, savings plans, stock bonus plans, and employee stock ownership plans, are all defined-contribution plans.

Impact of Federal Tax Law on Employer-Provided Retirement Plans

As just noted, meeting the tax law requirements for a qualified retirement plan is very important in retirement planning. It also significantly affects the covered employees' rights and tax status under a plan.

Qualified versus Nonqualified Plans.   A nonqualified plan is one that does not meet the requirements for qualification set by the tax law. An employer using a nonqualified plan is willing to sacrifice the considerable federal income tax advantages, discussed in this section, accorded to qualified plans so the employer can retain greater freedom to establish coverage requirements, benefit structure, financing methods, and the like for the plan. To be qualified for tax purposes, a plan must meet certain requirements in these areas. The tax advantages of being a qualified plan usually are so great, however, that most retirement plans are designed to meet the tax law requirements for qualification. The essence of these requirements is that a qualified plan may not discriminate, as defined in the tax law, in favor of "highly compensated employees." However, there are many specific requirements established for qualified retirement plans, with some of the more important described in this chapter.

The types of retirement plans that the Internal Revenue Code specifies may be qualified retirement plans are pension plans, profit-sharing plans, and stock bonus plans. Savings plans also may be qualified plans because they are usually organized as a kind of profit-sharing plan.

Qualification Requirements.   Some of the important requirements of a qualified plan may be summarized as follows: (1) There must be a *legally binding arrangement* that is in writing and communicated to the employees, (2) the plan must be for the exclusive benefit of the employees or their beneficiaries, (3) it must be impossible for the principal or income of the plan to be *diverted* from these benefits for any other purpose, and (4) the plan must benefit a broad class of employees and not discriminate in favor of highly compensated employees.

Tax Advantages of Qualified Plans.   The tax advantages arising from qualified retirement plans are very significant. These advantages can be briefly summarized as follows:

1. A covered employee is not considered to be in receipt of taxable income from the plan until benefits are actually distributed to the employee.
2. Lump-sum distributions to covered employees may be accorded certain favorable income tax treatment, and most distributions (with some exceptions) can be rolled over or directly transferred on a tax-deferred basis to an IRA or certain other plans.
3. Contributions made by the employer, within certain limitations, are deductible by the employer for income tax purposes as a business expense.
4. Investment income on plan assets normally is not subject to federal income tax until paid out in the form of benefits.

Pension Plans

Private pension plans often are considered complex and confusing arrangements by participants. However, with an understanding of some basic concepts, pension plans can be understood by most people.

Basic Characteristics

Private pension plans today generally are formal, funded plans. With regard to the funding agency used to accumulate the funds, they may be classified as to whether they are insured or uninsured (trusteed). In addition, they may be classified by whether the funds paid in by the employer and/or employees are allocated to the individual participants at the time these funds are paid in, or whether these funds are held in an unallocated account and then used to provide retirement income for employees when they retire.

Funded Pension Plans.   When an employer puts aside money in excess of that required to pay current pension benefits to retired employees, and transfers this money to a trustee (usually a bank) or an insurance company, the plan is considered to be "advance funded." In the past, some employers paid retirement benefits out of current earnings directly to their employees as their pension benefits came due. This was referred to as a "current disbursement" or "pay-as-you-go" approach to pension financing. However, when the employer puts away enough each year to fund the accruing pension liability for the current service of covered employees, and in addition accumulates sufficient assets to offset the initial past-service liability (pension credits earned before the plan was installed), the plan is said to be fully funded. Pension plans today generally are funded, but they are not all fully funded. Certain minimum funding standards are required by the Employee Retirement Income Security Act of 1974 (ERISA) for pension plans covered by this law.

Insured versus Uninsured Plans.   Two agencies generally are available to fund pension plans: trust companies and insurance companies. When a trust is used as the funding agency, the plan is called a "trusteed" (or self-insured) plan. When an insurance company is used, the plan is called an "insured" plan. And when both funding agencies are used in connection with the same plan, it is said to be a "combination" or "split-funded" plan.

Allocated versus Unallocated Funding.   Pension-funding instruments may be classified as to whether the funds are allocated to each participant under the plan (allocated), or whether the allocation is deferred until the employee reaches retirement age or while retirement benefits are being paid out (unallocated). Trust fund plans are unallocated, while insured plans may be allocated or unallocated, depending on the funding instrument used.

When Are Retirement Benefits Payable?

Because the primary purpose of a pension plan is to provide a retirement income for covered employees, the usual requirement to qualify for benefits is attainment of a certain age. The plan generally will specify a normal retirement age. It may also provide for early retirement and will provide for late retirement as well.

Normal Retirement Age.   The normal retirement age, commonly 65, is the earliest age at which a covered employee is entitled to retire with full benefits under the plan's benefit formula. A minimum-service requirement also may be imposed.

Early Retirement.   Under many pension plans, employees who meet certain conditions, such as reaching at least age 55 and completing at least 10 years of service, may, at their option, retire early and receive a reduced benefit. The benefit may be scaled down from the normal retirement amount to reflect the difference in the actuarial cost of early retirement. For example, assume that normal retirement age is 65 and a pension formula produces a retirement income of $1000 a month at that age. The pension plan allows receipt of retirement benefits at age 55 at the option of the employee. At age 55, however, the pension formula produces a retirement income of only $600 a month (fewer years of service, lower average earnings, younger age at retirement, etc.). If early retirement is elected at age 60, the formula in our example will produce $800 a month of retirement income. However, in some cases early retirement may be conditioned not only on an employee's age and length of service but also on the employer's consent or the physical condition of the employee.

Obviously, the value to an employee of an early-retirement privilege depends on the amount of income, if any, that must be sacrificed to take advantage of it. When a plan permits early retirement at a certain age and/or length of service with no loss of pension income (or a reduction that is less than the full actuarial reduction that would be called for by the plan's regular benefit formula), the early retirement is referred to as "subsidized early retirement." Clearly, terms of this provision in a pension plan are one of the factors to consider in deciding whether to retire early.

Late Retirement.   Pension plans also provide for retirement after the normal retirement age. The law now requires plans to continue to accrue benefits or to make contributions and allocations for participants who work past normal retirement age under the regular provisions of the plan. This may be a factor to consider if an employee is trying to decide whether to continue working past normal retirement age.

Kinds of Pension Plan Benefits

Many people think that all they can receive under their employer's pension plan is a retirement pension when they reach age 65. While this is the primary purpose of pension plans, several types of benefits may be available to participating employees, as follows: (1) retirement income benefits for the employee, and, if married, also for his or her spouse (or only for the employee, provided that if the employee is married, his or her spouse consents in writing), (2) benefits in the event his or her employment is terminated prior to reaching the minimum retirement age (vested benefits), (3) death benefits, (4) a surviving spouse's pension (a preretirement survivorship benefit), and (5) possibly disability and medical benefits.

Retirement Benefits.   Pension plans are designed primarily to provide a life annuity (life income) for the covered employee or the covered employee and a joint annuitant. Thus, pension benefits normally are payable in the form of a life income.

Retirement Equity Act (REA) Requirements.   The Retirement Equity Act of 1984 (REA) requires that if an employee has been married for at least one year prior to retirement, the normal form of retirement benefit under qualified pension plans must be a joint and at least one-half survivor life annuity payable to the employee and his or her spouse. This is called a "qualified joint and survivor annuity" (QJSA). This QJSA form can produce an actuarially reduced retirement benefit from what would have been paid as a life income to the employee alone (a so-called pure life annuity). This is so because the joint and survivor form gives the employee's spouse greater security through the survivorship benefit, but naturally this added benefit has a cost. (See the discussion of joint and survivorship annuity forms in this chapter under "Death Benefits.") However, the law permits an employee and his or her spouse to elect any other form of retirement benefit (annuity form) provided by the plan, provided the employee's spouse consents to the other form in writing.

Other Forms of Retirement Benefits. Some plans give employees (and their spouses) the option to have their pension benefits converted (commuted) into a lump-sum payment at retirement. There also may be other available annuity forms that the employee (with the consent in the proper form of his or her spouse as required by REA if the employee is married) can choose.

Benefits upon Termination of Employment. Under a contributory pension plan, where the employees pay part of the cost, employees are always entitled to a refund (or the right to a deferred benefit) in the amount of their contributions to the plan upon termination of employment. The usual practice is to return these contributions supplemented by a modest rate of interest.

However, upon termination of employment the principal concern of most people lies in the disposition of benefits *attributable to employer contributions.* The disposition of these benefits depends on the vesting provisions of the plan. "Vesting" is defined as the employee's rights to benefits, *attributable to the employer's contributions,* that are not contingent on the employee's continuing in the specified employment. In other words, vested pension rights are those rights in the pension benefits paid for by the employer that a former employee can keep even if he or she should leave the employer. Vesting is important to the certainty of an employee's retirement income.

Vesting can take several forms. Immediate and full vesting of pension benefits is the most liberal form of vesting from the employee's standpoint. Only a few private pension plans have such a vesting provision. Under the tax law requirements for a qualified plan, a qualified retirement plan must provide for vesting at least as rapidly as under one of two alternative minimum vesting schedules. One alternative is for the plan participant to become fully vested after completing five years of service. This is sometimes called "cliff vesting." The other minimum vesting option allows for so-called graded vesting of at least 20 percent of employer-provided benefits after three years of service, 40 percent after four years, 60 percent after five years, 80 percent after six years, and 100 percent after seven years.

Of course, these *minimum* vesting standards do not prevent an employer from establishing more liberal vesting for its employees. In addition, if a plan is a "top-heavy plan," more rapid vesting is required. A plan is considered "top-heavy" if its accumulated benefits for so-called key employees exceed 60 percent of its benefits for all employees.

Death Benefits.   Pension plans can in effect provide death benefits in several ways. Contributory plans provide for a refund of the employee's contributions in the event of his or her death prior to retirement. If death follows retirement, contributory plans customarily refund to the participant's beneficiary at least the difference, if any, between the individual's contributions to the plan and the amount of retirement benefits paid by the plan to the individual prior to his or her death.

In addition, when an employee receives retirement income in the form of a joint life and last survivor annuity (or a refund annuity), benefits may become payable to a surviving annuitant or beneficiary upon the employee's death. As noted above, such benefits usually result from a "trade-off" of lower lifetime income payments to the retired employee in exchange for the survivorship or refund benefit after the retired employee's death.

Note that by providing a joint life and last survivor form of annuity, rather than a pure life annuity, a pension plan in effect is providing death protection for an employee's spouse in the event the employee predeceases his or her spouse. The "cost" to the employee of this death protection is the after-tax difference between the employee's pension benefit as a pure annuity and the reduced pension benefit payable on a joint life and last survivorship basis. Assume, for example, that a man who is retiring at age 65 has a wife age 63. Further assume that his pension benefit at age 65 on a pure annuity basis is $800 per month and that on a joint life and last survivorship basis with his wife it is $680. If the entire pension benefit is taxable as ordinary income in this case, and if our couple is going to be in a 15 percent income tax bracket after he retires, the "cost" of the guarantee of continuing the $680 monthly pension to the wife if the employee dies first would be $102 a month ($800 − $680 = $120 × 0.85 = $102). Remember, too, that if the retiring employee's wife in our example is not provided for in this way, he will have to do so in some other manner, such as by continuing (or even purchasing) life insurance coverage on his life for her benefit. Of course, her social security benefits will increase upon his death (she will be a surviving spouse rather than the wife of a retired worker), but this will not nearly make up for the loss of his pension benefit if they elect to take it on other than a joint life and last survivor basis [e.g., as a single life (pure) annuity].

As an example, Table 12.1 shows the changes in annuity income that result from the use of a joint life and two-thirds survivorship benefit or a joint life and full survivorship benefit rather than a single life annuity, under various age and sex assumptions.[1] These are based on the annuity rates used by one life insurance company. Other companies or plans employ different rates, and in employee pension plans, it is considered sex discrimination and therefore illegal to use different annuity rates for men and women in determining pension benefits. These rates, therefore, are only for the purpose of illustrating joint and survivor annuity forms. On this basis, assume a male retiring at age 65, his spouse is 63, and a joint-and-full-benefit-to-the-survivor annuity form is used. The illustration shows that these assumptions produce a monthly benefit equal to 85 percent of his single life (pure) annuity ($800 × 0.85 = $680 per month).

As explained previously, under REA the normal QJSA form is at least a joint life and one-half survivor annuity, unless the covered employee elects otherwise and his or her spouse consents to the election in writing. So if a retiring married employee wants a single life annuity form, for example, he or she must take the initiative to elect it under the rules of the pension plan and the spouse must consent in the proper form in writing. Any such REA waiver election and spousal consent out of the QJSA form must be made

Table 12.1. Joint-Life Options

Two-Thirds Benefit to Survivor with 10-Year Guaranteed Period (At death of either spouse, payments reduce to two-thirds benefit for the survivor for life)

Male retirement age				Spouse's age	Female retirement age			
62	65	68	70		62	65	68	70
94%	92%	89%	88%	60	101%	99%	97%	96%
96%	94%	92%	90%	63	103%	102%	100%	98%
97%	95%	93%	92%	65	105%	103%	102%	100%
100%	98%	96%	95%	68	108%	106%	105%	103%
102%	100%	98%	97%	70	110%	108%	107%	106%

Full Benefit to Survivor with 10-Year Guaranteed Period (Full benefit continues as long as either spouse lives)

Male retirement age				Spouse's age	Female retirement age			
62	65	68	70		62	65	68	70
86%	83%	80%	78%	60	94%	92%	89%	87%
88%	85%	82%	80%	63	95%	93%	91%	89%
89%	87%	84%	82%	65	96%	94%	92%	91%
91%	89%	87%	85%	68	97%	96%	94%	93%
93%	91%	88%	87%	70	97%	96%	95%	94%

[1] These rates are all based on the further assumption of a 10-year guaranteed period of annuity payments (called "10 years certain and continuous") in any event.

within 90 days prior to the married participant's annuity starting date. Such a waiver and spousal consent should be carefully evaluated by the retiring employee *and* his or her spouse. They should consider what protection the spouse will have in the event that he or she should predecease the participant spouse. (The REA rules are different for qualified profit-sharing, savings, and stock bonus plans. In the case of these plans, the REA requirements for annuity forms can be avoided if a married plan participant names his or her spouse as the beneficiary of the entire account balance under the plan in the event of the participant spouse's death and meets certain other requirements.)

Pension plans also may include preretirement death benefits. Such benefits may be in form of life insurance, for example, in the case of plans funded through individual life insurance policies. Preretirement survivor annuities, described next, are also an important kind of such benefits.

Qualified Preretirement Survivor Annuity (QPSA). This benefit commonly refers to the right of a surviving spouse to receive a pension benefit in the event the pension plan participant dies *prior to* his or her retirement age. It thus provides preretirement survivorship benefits to a surviving spouse under the pension plan. The joint life and last survivor annuity forms discussed under "Death Benefits" above relate to survivorship benefits *after* the pension plan participant reaches retirement age.

In addition to the surviving-spouse benefits (QJSA form) described above, REA also requires the provision of certain preretirement survivorship benefits for the surviving spouse of a participant who had a vested accrued benefit in the plan and who dies before his or her annuity starting date. In this case, the pension plan must provide for the payment to the participant's surviving spouse of a benefit that is not less than one-half the participant's actuarially reduced pension benefit as of the date of his or her death or the earliest retirement age under the plan. This is referred to as a qualified preretirement survivor annuity (QPSA). Of course, the "cost" of this QPSA benefit can be an actuarially reduced pension benefit for the participant and/or the spouse (as is also true of the QJSA form discussed previously). Also as with the QJSA form, the participant, with his or her spouse's written consent, may decline (or waive) this QPSA benefit under qualified pension plans. This REA election to waive the QPSA benefit and the required spousal consent must be given prior to the pension annuity starting date and subject to certain other requirements.

Here again, for qualified profit-sharing, savings, and stock bonus plans, the REA requirements for this QPSA benefit can be avoided if a married participant names his or her spouse as the beneficiary of the entire account balance under the plan in the event of the participant's death and meets certain other requirements. Thus, under these plans, if a married participant wants to name anyone or any entity (such as a trust for estate planning purposes, for example) other than his or her spouse as the beneficiary of the qualified retirement plan death benefits, the participant must elect to waive and his or her spouse must consent to a waiver of the REA QPSA benefit requirements.

Disability Income Benefits.   Workers on occasion are required to retire from a job because of permanent disability. Thus, a number of pension plans recognize the problem of permanent and total disability and make some provision for this risk.

In some pension plans, a form of permanent disability protection is afforded by allowing the disabled worker to retire early. Also, under some plans, pension credits continue to accumulate for a disabled participant, who then receives full retirement benefits at normal retirement age.

Other pension plans provide for a disability income benefit unrelated to retirement benefits and express this benefit as a percentage of earnings at the time of disability or as so much a month for each year of service.

Medical Expense Benefits.   Assets accumulated in pension funds may be used to provide specified medical expense benefits for retired employees, their spouses, and their dependents. Thus, some pension plans have incorporated provisions for accumulating funds for retiree medical benefits.

What Amounts of Pension Benefits Are Payable?

The size of the benefits to be paid upon retirement is an extremely important consideration in overall financial planning. Pension benefits usually are expressed in terms of a fixed number of dollars. However, some plans express benefits in terms of an annuity unit with a variable dollar value (so-called variable annuities). Some plans combine the fixed-dollar and variable-dollar features.

Benefit Formulas.   Pension plan benefit formulas establish either a defined benefit or a defined contribution to the plan. Defined-benefit formulas may be a flat amount, a flat percentage of earnings, a flat-amount-unit benefit, or a percentage-unit benefit. Defined-contribution formulas for pension plans are generally known as "money purchase" formulas.

Defined-Benefit Formulas.   Under a *flat-amount* formula, all participants upon retirement are given the same benefit, regardless of their earnings, their age, and, to some extent, their years of service. For example, all employees meeting some minimum credited service requirement, such as 15 years, might be given a monthly retirement benefit of, say, $500 a month. Employees who reach retirement age with less than 15 years of credited service may be given progressively reduced benefits.

A formula that relates pension benefits to earnings but not to years of service is the *flat-percentage formula*. Under this formula, a pension equal to a given percentage of the employee's average annual compensation may be paid at retirement to all employees completing a minimum number of years of credited service. Employees who fail to meet the minimum service requirement may be given a proportionately reduced pension. The percentage used varies among plans and might range from 20 to 50 percent. The average compensation to which the percentage applies may be the employees' average earnings over the full period of their participation in the plan or, more commonly, the average of their earnings over the final few years of their participation.

A formula that relates benefits to years of service but not to earnings is the *flat-amount-unit-benefit formula*. Here an employee is given a flat amount of benefit per month for each year of credited service. Thus, for example, an employee may be given $40 per month for each year of credited service. Under this formula, an employee with 15 years of service would receive a monthly pension of $600.

A widely used formula is the *percentage-unit-benefit formula*. Under this kind of formula, an employee may be given, say, 1½ percent of earnings for each year of credited service. Using this formula, an employee with 30 years of service would receive a monthly pension of 45 percent of earnings. The earnings to which the percentage is applied may be the earnings during each year in which the unit benefit is accumulated (career average) or the average annual earnings during, say, the last 5 or 10 years before retirement (final average). Many variations of the final-average compensation plan are in use, such as average annual compensation for the five consecutive years of highest pay.

Money-Purchase (Defined-Contribution) Formulas. Some business firms and other organizations use a money-purchase-type pension benefit formula. Under this plan, a percentage of an employee's pay (normally 5 to 10 percent) is set aside in a pension fund by the employer and sometimes is matched in whole or in part by the employee. The amount of an employee's retirement benefit will be determined by how much the accumulated contributions in the pension fund made on his or her behalf can buy at retirement age.

Integration (Permitted Disparity) with Social Security. Pension benefit formulas frequently take into consideration the old-age benefits payable under social security. This has been referred to as "integrating" the private pension plan with social security, but the term now used in the tax law is "permitted disparity." These terms will be used interchangeably in this book. Integrated defined-benefit pension plans usually either reduce the benefits otherwise provided under the formula by a percentage of the employee's social security benefit (the offset method) or provide a lower pension benefit on wages subject to social security than on wages above this amount (the excess method).

Level of Retirement Income.   In the past, many pension experts felt that the *minimum* pension, when combined with social security, should equal at least 50 percent of an employee's preretirement income to be considered adequate. But if a pension benefit is fixed at this level throughout retirement, the retired person is exposed to a purchasing-power risk because of inflation and is denied the opportunity to share in any increasing standard of living arising out of a growing economy.

The issue of inflation (or deflation) and retirement plan income is so important that a later section of this chapter, "Inflation and Pension Planning," will be devoted to it.

Maximum Benefit Limits.   ERISA originally set overall limits on the benefits or contributions allowed under qualified retirement plans. These limits (referred to as Section 415 limits) have been amended several times, with the most recent amendment by the Tax Reform Act of 1986. Under this law, annual employer-provided pensions under a defined-benefit plan may not exceed the lower of (1) $90,000 (adjusted for cost-of-living increases) or (2) 100 percent of the employee's average annual compensation for his or her three highest consecutive years under the plan. However, there is a $10,000 benefit exception, which generally permits an annual pension of $10,000 or less even though it exceeds 100 percent of compensation. The above limits are to be reduced proportionately if an employee has less than 10 years of participation or service, respectively, prior to retirement.

There are also limits on annual additions (including employer contributions, employee contributions, and any forfeitures allocated to an employee's account) to defined-contribution plans. Under the Tax Reform Act of 1986, the annual additions to a defined-contribution plan may not exceed the lesser of (1) $30,000 (adjusted for future cost-of-living increases when the defined benefit limit rises to the point where the $30,000 defined-contribution limit equals 25 percent of the defined benefit limit) or (2) 25 percent of the employee's annual compensation. Where an employer has both defined-benefit and defined-contribution-type plans, such as a defined-benefit pension plan and a savings plan, for example, the combination of annual benefits and contributions may not exceed 140 percent of the percentage limit and 125 percent of the dollar limit for the plans considered separately.

Most employees probably will not be affected by these maximum limitations on benefits and contributions. For more highly compensated employees, however, they may significantly affect pension and other retirement benefits. When this is case, employers often provide nonqualified "excess benefits plans" or supplemental executive retirement plans (SERPs) for these employees, as described later.

Inflation and Pension Planning

Over the years, there has been concern about the adverse effects of inflation in our economy and particularly about its impact on retired persons. The purpose of this section is to mention some of the approaches that are being used in pension planning to minimize the adverse effects of inflation on pension income. In the final analysis, however, perhaps the best defense against this problem is not to be completely dependent on an employer's pension plan. Try to have other sources of retirement income as well. This may be good advice in the face of *inflation* or *deflation*.

Inflation and Pension Income.   For many decades, the traditional concept of retirement security reflected the desire for an adequate income at retirement relative to the salary a person earned during his or her working lifetime. To this end, a "secure" pension plan often meant that the employer was willing and able to provide a fixed level of benefits to employees at retirement and that the plan was adequately funded. But with the emergence of inflation, pension planners recognized that planning only in terms of fixed-dollar levels might not be enough.

Approaches to Dealing with Inflation in Pension Planning.   Pension adjustment techniques are designed to give employees greater assurance that pensions, which were deemed adequate when created, will continue to prove adequate at, and even after, an employee's retirement.

Final-Pay Plans.   An employee's retirement benefit may be based either on the employee's *career earnings* or on his or her *final salary,* depending on the plan's benefit formula. In some plans utilizing a career-average formula, a possible approach to purchasing-power security consists of updating accrued benefits to reflect changing salary levels and to provide more reasonable benefit levels for longer-term employees.

As noted previously, benefit formulas also can be based on final average earnings, such as final earnings averaged over the last 5 to 10 years. This approach emphasizes levels of compensation just prior to retirement that may reflect more recent inflationary trends. Thus, final-pay defined-benefit pension benefit formulas are an indirect way in which preretirement inflation can be recognized in pension planning.

Cost-of-Living Plans.   An obvious vehicle for providing pension benefits with more secure purchasing power is a plan which stipulates that payments will be adjusted according to variations in some price index. For example, such a plan might provide for an upward adjustment in a year when the index exceeds a certain percentage, say, 105 percent, of a chosen base-period level, and downward adjustment when it drops below, say, 90 percent of that level.

This is often referred to as *indexing* retirement benefits for inflation. Unhappily for retirees, very few private pension plans have benefits that are *automatically* indexed for inflation. On the other hand, social security benefits, civil service retirement benefits, and a number of state and local retirement systems are automatically indexed for inflation.

Variable Annuities.   The variable annuity was developed to deal with the purchasing-power risk to pension security. Basically, variable annuities provide for the investment of pension contributions in a segregated portfolio of equity securities. The contributions are used to establish a fund or account which, with additional deposits and investment growth, is used to purchase a lifetime income (usually expressed in investment units rather than dollars) at retirement date. Thus, the account values under these contracts and the retirement income purchased with the proceeds reflect the performance of the invested funds, rising or falling as the market value of their underlying securities portfolio increases or decreases. The theoretical basis for the variable annuity concept is the long-range historical relationship between the cost of living and the investment performance of diversified portfolios of common stocks.

The claimed advantages of the variable annuity concept are (1) protection against long-term inflationary erosion of pension purchasing power, and (2) possible performance surpassing that of fixed-dollar annuities. The attendant disadvantages are the risk of loss of capital and fluctuating retirement income.

Discretionary (Ad-Hoc) Increases in Pension Benefits.   Some employers providing private pension plans have, as a matter of voluntary practice, been willing to make periodic increases in their already retired employees' pension benefits due to increases in the cost of living. While there is no assurance that these ad-hoc increases will be made in the future, to the extent that they are made as a practice of the employer, the retirees and their families clearly benefit.

Pension Benefit
Guaranty Corporation

Another development of ERISA was the establishment of a Pension Benefit Guaranty Corporation (PBGC), to be administered by the U.S. Department of Labor. This corporation, in effect, sets up an insurance program for employees and pensioners of companies that have gone out of business. The act insures vested benefits of defined-benefit pension plans up to a certain amount. Moreover, should a company go out of business, a portion of its net worth can be taken by the government and applied toward the pension program. This program provides an additional element of safety for plan participants and retirees in retirement planning.

Profit-Sharing Plans

The Concept of Profit Sharing

Some employers prefer to relate the amount of their contributions for employee retirement to profits rather than to payroll, especially if their profits fluctuate widely from year to year. Also, employers may use a profit-sharing plan to supplement a pension plan.

Much of what was previously discussed in this chapter concerning pension plans applies equally to profit-sharing plans. Therefore, this section will concentrate only on basic differences between these two approaches to retirement planning as they may affect personal financial planning.

Benefits under Profit-Sharing Plans

The primary objective of deferred profit-sharing plans is to help build financial security for employees and their families in the event of the employee's retirement, permanent disability, or death. However, severance benefits are an important by-product of these plans. While the principal functions of qualified profit-sharing plans are basically similar to those of qualified pension plans, deferred profit-sharing plans in practice usually have had more liberal vesting arrangements.

Withdrawal and *loan privileges* are other benefits provided by some deferred profit-sharing plans. These provisions may be useful in financial planning or in case of emergencies. However, loans to participants and beneficiaries that do not meet certain amount limitations and other conditions will be treated as taxable distributions from the plan.

Distributions are legally permitted under profit-sharing plans after two years. Thus, if a plan permits withdrawals, the maximum that can be allowed is the total amount in the fund less the contributions made and the interest earned on them during the previous two years. The plan itself, however, may not permit withdrawals up to the legal maximum. Furthermore, withdrawals may be allowed for hardship cases. Any amount withdrawn, less the participant's own after-tax prorata contributions, is taxable as income in the year received. However, an additional 10 percent excise tax (over and above the regular tax) will be applied to withdrawals from qualified retirement plans, tax-sheltered annuity (TSA) plans, and IRAs that are made before a participant's death, disability, or attainment of age 59½, subject to certain exceptions. This penalty tax on "premature" distributions from such plans inhibits the use of withdrawal rights under profit-sharing (and particularly savings) plans.

A participant may also have access to qualified retirement plan funds through a loan provision. A loan has an advantage over withdrawal in that the borrowed funds are not treated currently as taxable income to the par-

ticipant, provided the loan meets the amount limits and other requirements of the tax law. Further, the loan must be repaid in substantially level
installments made at least quarterly within five years, unless taken to
acquire the participant's personal residence (in which case it must be
repaid within a reasonable time).

A loan provision in a qualified retirement plan must include the terms
under which loans will be made. The tax law generally specifies that loans
from qualified plans must be limited to the smaller of (1) $50,000 (less
the highest loan balance during the preceding 12 months) or (2) one-
half the present value of the participant's vested accrued benefit, but not
less than $10,000. If a loan exceeds these limits, the excess will be treated
as a taxable distribution from the plan. The plan may restrict loans to specific purposes, such as home construction or repair, home mortgage payments, expenses of illness or death in the family, education of children, or
a sound purpose in keeping with the long-term objectives of the plan. A
loan waiting period also may be required. Further, the interest charged
plan participants on such loans must be reasonable (e.g., not unreason-
ably low).

There are limits on the contributions an employer can make to a profit-
sharing plan that will be currently deductible by the employer for federal
income tax purposes. The first limitation is that such currently tax-
deductible contributions cannot exceed 15 percent of the total annual
compensation of plan participants. Further, if an employer has covered its
employees under both a defined-benefit pension plan and a profit-sharing
plan (i.e., a defined-contribution plan), the currently tax-deductible contribution limit for both plans is (1) 25 percent of total annual compensation of all plan participants or (2) the contribution necessary to meet the
defined-benefit plan's minimum funding standard, whichever is larger.[2]
Excess nondeductible contributions in any year to qualified plans are subject to a 10 percent excise tax that is payable by the employer.

Retirement Equity Act (REA) Requirements for Profit-Sharing, Savings, and Stock Bonus Plans

Several types of qualified retirement plans are covered by REA, but a participant's account balance under one or more of these kinds of plans (but
not under a pension plan) can be excluded from the operation of the
REA rules if certain requirements are met. Thus, in general, to be
excluded, a participant's vested account balance must be payable in full

---

[2] However, to meet plan qualification requirements, the overall benefits and contributions
for each participant still must meet the IRC Section 415 limits.

upon the participant's death to his or her surviving spouse, the benefits must not be payable as a life annuity, and the plan must not have received a transfer from a pension plan. If the death benefits are payable to any other beneficiary (such as a trust or a child), the participant's spouse must consent on the proper form.

Retirement Plans for the Self-Employed (HR-10 or Keogh Plans)

Before 1963, sole proprietors and partnerships could have qualified pension and profit-sharing plans covering their employees, but the owners of these businesses could not get the tax benefits of these plans because they were not employees. This was true even though the sole proprietor or partner was actively engaged in the operation of the business. However, the *Self-Employed Individuals Tax Retirement Act of 1962* (also called HR-10 or the Keogh Act), and its subsequent amendments, made it possible for owner-employees of unincorporated businesses and other self-employed persons to be covered under qualified retirement plans. An HR-10 plan, therefore, is a formal arrangement whereby self-employed persons may establish a program to provide tax-favored retirement benefits for themselves and their eligible employees.

"Parity" with Corporate Retirement Plans

Prior to 1982, HR-10 plans were subject to a number of special restrictions and limits that did not apply to qualified corporate retirement plans (with the exception of some special limits on plans for S corporations). However, the Tax Equity and Fiscal Responsibility Act of 1982 (TEFRA) eliminated almost all these special requirements for HR-10 plans. This was referred to as establishing "parity" in qualified retirement plans, regardless of whether the plan is a corporate plan covering employees of a corporation or an HR-10 plan covering self-employed persons and their common law employees (if any). This "parity" also was extended to plans for S corporations (see pp. 499–502 of Chap. 17 for a discussion of S corporations). Therefore, HR-10 plans generally must meet the same eligibility and coverage requirements, contribution limits (except that such limits apply to net earnings from self-employment *after* reduction for contributions to the HR-10 plan for self-employed persons), vesting requirements, rules for integration with social security, and other plan requirements, as for qualified retirement plans covering corporate employees.

Another important exception to this "parity" concept is in connection with loans from qualified retirement plans. As noted above, qualified retirement plans generally may contain loan provisions allowing participants to borrow from the plan subject to certain conditions. However, loans to any owner-employee (i.e., a sole proprietor or a partner who owns more than 10 percent of a partnership), or a family member of an owner-employee, from an HR-10 plan or to a 50 percent or more shareholder of an S corporation from a plan maintained by the S corporation, would be a prohibited transaction for the plan (unless a special exemption is secured from the U.S. Department of Labor). Therefore, such loans generally have not been made to these persons, but would be available to stockholder-employees of regular corporations.

Advantages of Using Before-Tax Dollars to Save for Retirement

The advantages of using before-tax dollars to save for retirement (with an HR-10 plan used as an example) can be illustrated as follows. Assume that a self-employed woman, age 45, is in a 31 percent income tax bracket and that she wants to save $1000 of her earnings annually for retirement. Also suppose that she uses a deferred annuity contract (explained in Chap. 13) to fund an HR-10 plan.

Without plan		With HR-10 plan (deferred annuity)
$ 1,000	Savings out of gross income	$ 1,000
310	Federal income tax	—
690	Net after-tax contributions	1,000
21,711*	Cash accumulation at age 65	38,993*
	Monthly income (life	
210[†]	income, 10 years certain)	381[†]
This is income derived from funds accumulated with after-tax dollars. When applied to buy a single-premium annuity only a portion of the income is taxable.		This is income derived from funds accumulated with before-tax dollars. The entire amount of the income is taxable at retirement.

* Assumes 6% gross interest (4.14% net after taxes—interest on accumulations without plan is taxable each year, while interest on accumulations in the HR-10 plan is tax-deferred until taken as distributions from the plan).

[†] Figures involving life incomes are illustrations based on the experience of a major life insurance company.

Savings (or Thrift) Plans

An increasingly popular form of employee benefit plan is the qualified savings plan. Technically, tax-favored savings plans must be formulated as pension, profit-sharing, or stock bonus plans. They usually are established as a form of profit-sharing plan. These plans can be called by a variety of names, but probably the most common is *savings plan,* and this is the term we shall use in this book.

General Characteristics

The typical savings/thrift plan which has emerged in recent years has the following general characteristics:

1. The plan has been established either separately or in conjunction with a regular pension or profit-sharing plan for the purpose of encouraging thrift or investment savings on the part of employees.

2. Participation in the plan normally is voluntary on the part of eligible employees.

3. Contributions to the plan by participating employees are made through payroll withholding and are accumulated in separate, nonforfeitable trust accounts for their benefit; in most plans, employees have a prescribed choice with respect to how their contributions are to be invested by the trustee. Employee contributions usually may be made on a before-tax basis under a Section 401(k) option as described next.

4. Employer contributions usually are also made under the plan, and they are normally a percentage (such as 50 or 75 percent) of the amount elected to be contributed by each employee up to certain limits.

As just noted, savings plans normally are established as separate plans and involve at least some employer contributions, which generally are related to the amounts contributed by employees but may be determined, at least in part, by employer profits. In most plans, prescribed rates are established for employee contributions that are subject to employer matching contributions. Thus, employee contributions result in an employee's receiving a share of the matching employer contributions. The prescribed rate may be a set amount, such as 5 percent of pay, but more often it is based on an optional scale, with a prescribed minimum amount, such as 1 percent of pay, and then a set maximum amount, which usually does not exceed 6 percent of pay. In addition to such plan contribution limits, savings plans may permit additional, voluntary contributions by participating employees that are not matched by employer contributions.

Eligibility provisions are generally liberal, and vesting usually is rapid. Normally, employees are given the right to suspend participation at any time, and they may be permitted to make in-service withdrawals of at least some of their account balances within the limits of the tax law.

Cash or Deferred Arrangements
[Section 401(k) Options]

General Characteristics.   Many qualified savings plans permit participating employees to make contributions to the plan on a before-tax basis under a cash or deferred arrangement [a CODA, or as it is more popularly called, a "Section 401(k) plan," after the IRC provision dealing with CODAs]. These have become very popular options in plans for employees because they enable participants to save for retirement (or perhaps other purposes) on a before-tax basis, with all the advantages just illustrated for this concept (using an HR-10 plan as an example, see p. 366).

Section 401(k) options permit covered employees (participants) to authorize their employer to reduce their salary (i.e., salary reduction on a before-tax basis) and contribute the salary reduction on their behalf to a qualified savings plan, profit-sharing plan, stock bonus plan, or some money-purchase pension plans. Employees also may defer otherwise payable compensation for contribution to such plans. Thus, in effect, participants can elect whether to have wages or salary deferred (in the qualified plan) on a before-tax basis or paid to the participant as currently taxable cash compensation, hence the term "cash or deferred arrangements" (CODAs). The amounts that participants elect to defer under Section 401(k) are referred to as the employee's "elective contributions," "elective deferrals," or "before-tax elective contributions" and special tax law restrictions apply to such elective contributions.

As just noted, CODAs can be used with several kinds of qualified retirement plans. As a practical matter, however, employers very frequently use them with qualified savings plans (usually with matching employer contributions). Hence such savings plans sometimes are loosely called "Section 401(k) plans."

To qualify as a CODA under Section 401(k), an arrangement must meet certain nondiscrimination requirements. The plan must meet the normal coverage requirements for a qualified plan and, in addition, must meet a special "actual deferred percentage" (ADP) test with regard to average elective contributions as a percentage of compensation for highly compensated employees as compared with the average percentage for non–highly compensated employees.[3]

---

[3] There also is a similar actual contribution percentage (ACP) nondiscrimination requirement applying to *employer matching contributions* and *after-tax employee contributions* to qualified plans.

Limits on Contributions to CODAs. Because of the elective nature of Section 401(k) arrangements and other reasons, there are at least four separate kinds of limits on employee (and employer) contributions to qualified plans (say, savings plans) with a Section 401(k) option, as follows:

- There is a *$7000 (indexed for inflation) annual dollar cap* or limit on before-tax elective contributions from an employee to all CODAs covering the employee. (As of 1992, this indexed annual dollar cap was $8728.)

- There is the application of the special *ADP nondiscrimination tests for before-tax elective contributions* (just described), which, depending on the relative average contributions of highly compensated employees compared to those of non-highly compensated employees, may result in a limit on elective contributions for highly compensated employees for a year that will be lower than the annual dollar cap just noted. These ADP nondiscrimination tests apply each year, and so an employee's elective contribution status may change from year to year as a result.

- There also is the application of the *ACP nondiscrimination tests for combined after-tax employee contributions and employer matching contributions* (just described).

- In addition, the regular *Section 415 maximum limits* applying to any qualified plan (see p. 360) apply in this situation as well.

Restrictions on Distributions from CODAs. There also are special *restrictions on distributions* from plans with Section 401(k) options. In general, amounts in the plan attributable to before-tax elective contributions on behalf of an employee may not be distributed to the employee or his or her beneficiary(ies) earlier than: (1) attainment of age 59½; (2) separation from service (including retirement); (3) death; (4) disability; or (5) in the event of "hardship" for the employee (as defined in IRS regulations), without regard to the previous restrictions. Thus, the practical effect of these distribution rules is that, other than for hardship distributions, Section 401(k) arrangements cannot permit in-service withdrawals prior to age 59½ of amounts attributable to employee elective contributions (deferrals). Of course, plans can permit in-service withdrawals of other amounts, depending on the terms of the plan and other applicable tax rules (see p. 363).

As a planning point for participants in Section 401(k) arrangements (and other similar qualified plans for that matter), perhaps the preferred way to get money from the plan while in service in any event is through plan loans from the qualified retirement plan as described on pp. 363–364 (assuming that such loans are permitted by the terms of the particular plan). Such plan loans are not considered distributions and hence are permitted for elective contributions under Section 401(k) arrangements and also are not currently taxable for income tax purposes with regard to any qualified plan. Of course, the participant must pay interest on such loans at a reasonable rate, and must meet the other tax law requirements for non-taxable loans from qualified retirement plans (see p. 364).

Advantages of Savings Plans

As explained in the previous section, an employee's contributions to a savings plan may come out of after-tax dollars, but today they commonly are made on a before-tax salary-reduction basis under Section 401(k) arrangements. Savings plans also afford the other tax advantages of qualified plans in that investment returns increase on a before-tax basis, employer contributions are not currently taxed to the participants, lump-sum distributions may be accorded favorable income tax treatment, and most distributions can be rolled over or transferred directly tax-deferred to an IRA.

Another appeal of savings plans from an employee's standpoint is the opportunity they afford for systematic investment of small amounts through weekly or monthly payroll deductions on a comparatively low-cost basis. Employees attempting to set up a systematic investment program on their own may pay significant investment charges or commissions. But under most savings plans, these costs can be substantially reduced, or even eliminated when the employer pays the costs of investment administration. In addition, in savings plans with matching employer contributions (as is generally the case), the participating employees' accounts are credited with the employer's matching contributions as well as the employees' own contributions. Thus, participation in qualified savings plans, particularly when there are matching employer contributions, normally is a wise choice for eligible employees.

Another feature of qualified savings plans is that employees normally are given a choice among a prescribed number of different investment options for their contributions. These choices may include, for example, a common stock fund, a bond fund, a money market fund, a guaranteed investment contract (GIC) issued by an insurance company, and employer securities. Employees may also have such investment choices for employer matching contributions; however, employers also may direct these contributions themselves (say, into employer stock). When given investment choices, employees may direct how contributions are to go initially into the available investment outlets and also may move their savings plan money between or among accounts at reasonable intervals. Thus, in having such investment choices, employees may integrate their investment decision making with regard to their qualified savings plan accounts (and their other tax-deferred plan accounts) with their general asset allocation strategy as discussed in Chap. 7.

Further, with regard to changing their asset allocation strategy, qualified retirement plan (say, savings plan) account balances (as well as account balances in other tax-deferred and tax-favored plans, such as IRAs) present participants (or owners) with an inherent tax advantage in that asset allocation changes between or among available investment options *within the plan* can be made without there being a sale or exchange for capital gains tax (income tax) purposes. Thus, since such changes within the plan are income tax-free, there effectively is no capital gains tax lock-in problem (see pp. 337–339 of Chap. 11) with regard to assets in these plans. This is the same general concept as was discussed previously with regard to variable life insurance policies and variable annuity contracts.[4]

Thus, suppose that an investor would like to change his or her overall asset allocation strategy from 60 percent in common stocks and 20 percent in bonds to 20 percent in common stocks and 60 percent in bonds. In this event, *if the investor has unrealized gains* in the assets being reduced (common stocks in this example), it might make best tax sense at least to start with making the changes within one or more of these tax-deferred, tax-favored kinds of plans to avoid current capital gains taxation. On the other hand, *if the investor has unrealized losses* in the assets being reduced, it would be better taxwise to sell the assets outside these tax-deferred, tax-favored kinds of plans and realize the net capital loss to be used against any realized capital gains or against ordinary income to the extent of $3000 per year (as explained on pp. 314–317 of Chap. 11).

Stock Bonus and Employee Stock Ownership Plans

Stock bonus and employee stock ownership plans are the final kinds of qualified retirement plans defined in the Internal Revenue Code. They may exist in one form or another in a number of employee benefit plans.

Stock Bonus Plans

Stock bonus plans provide benefits to employees similar to those of profit-sharing plans. Under stock bonus plans, however, the employer's contributions to the plan do not necessarily depend on the employer's profits, and the benefits from stock bonus plans may be distributable to participating employees in the form of the stock of the employer. Employers may make contributions to stock bonus plans in cash or in their own stock.

---

[4] The kinds of tax-deferred and tax-favored plans to which the ability to change investment options within the plan without current tax consequences would include: qualified retirement plans (e.g., savings plans), variable life insurance, variable annuities, IRAs, and tax-sheltered annuities (TSAs).

Employee Stock Ownership Plans

In recent years, employee stock ownership plans (ESOPs) have attracted a great deal of publicity. An ESOP normally is a form of stock bonus qualified retirement plan. It enables employees to receive common stock of the employer as an employee benefit. As for stock bonus plans generally, ESOPs closely resemble profit-sharing plans, and the rules concerning vesting, eligibility, and the deductible limits by the employer are the same as for profit-sharing plans.

One key difference between ESOPs and regular stock bonus plans, however, is that an ESOP must invest primarily in the securities of the employer. Such plans are intended to give employees an interest in the ownership and growth of the employer's business. Another major difference is that an employer that establishes an ESOP may guarantee or make loans to the ESOP to enable the plan to acquire the employer's stock, while this normally is not permitted for regular stock bonus plans. This difference has resulted in ESOPs sometimes being called "leveraged ESOPs" and in their use as a purchaser of the employer through borrowing to buy the employer's stock.

Taxation of Distributions from Qualified Retirement Plans

Employee participants in qualified retirement plans can be affected by four types of federal taxation: (1) the income tax, (2) the estate tax, (3) possibly the gift tax, and (4) possibly the generation-skipping transfer tax. Planning for taking distributions from qualified retirement plans (and other tax-deferred, tax-favored plans) will require considerations of the income tax and perhaps one or more of the other taxes, depending on the circumstances.

In addition, there are now several possible "penalty" taxes that may apply to distributions from qualified retirement plans (and other tax-deferred, tax-favored plans). These are described in this section and must be considered in planning.

Federal Income Tax

In General.   A favorable federal income tax consideration of qualified plans is that participating employees do not have to report as current income contributions made on their behalf by their employer, except where life insurance is a part of the plan. Even in this case, the employee must report only the term insurance cost for the actual amount of life insurance at risk.

On the other hand, when funds are distributed to a participating employee (or to the employee's designated beneficiary upon the employee's death), an income tax liability may arise. The nature of this liability depends on whether the plan is contributory or noncontributory, the reason for the distribution, when the distribution is made or begins, the time period over which the distribution is made, and the nature of the distribution.

Under contributory plans, assuming that an employee's payments into the plan were made with after-tax dollars, the employee incurs no additional income tax liability when these funds are returned to him or her. The employee's total after-tax contributions to the plan are included in his or her investment in the plan (or income tax basis in the plan) and are returned to the employee or his or her designated beneficiary in the event of the employee's death income tax–free.

Distributions from qualified retirement plans may be made to participating employees at normal retirement, at early retirement, because of disability, upon termination of employment, or upon termination of the plan itself. Distributions also may be made to pay medical expenses of retired employees. In addition, distributions may still be permitted from deferred profit-sharing plans (and savings plans), other than from amounts attributable to elective contributions under Section 401(k) arrangements (except as noted on p. 369), to participating employees after a period of years, during periods of illness, on the occasion of layoffs, and perhaps in other events. However, there is a 10 percent penalty tax on "early" distributions from qualified retirement plans, as well as from certain other tax-advantaged retirement plans, as discussed on p. 383.

When the full amount credited to a participant's account is paid to the recipient within one taxable year under certain conditions, the distribution is called a "lump-sum" distribution; when the distribution is made as periodic payments over a person's lifetime or a period of years, it is called a periodic or an "annuity" distribution, and a nonperiodic distribution may be an "eligible rollover distribution."

Periodic (or Annuity) Distributions. Benefits payable to an employee participant or to his or her beneficiary as periodic payments are subject to the rules governing the taxation of annuities (in Section 72 of the IRC), with some special modifications applicable to employee benefit plans. In determining the income tax liability for annuity payments received from a qualified plan, under the *general annuity rule* of Section 72, the annuitant determines the ratio of his or her investment in the plan to the expected return from the plan and excludes a similar proportion of each annuity payment from his or her gross income.[5] Suppose, for example, that an employee receives a retirement income of $6000 a year for life, starting at age 65 (the annuity starting date in this case). Using an expected-return multiple of 15, which would be prescribed in the tax regulations, he or she would have an expected return of $90,000 ($6,000 × 15). If the employee has contributed $20,000 after-tax to the pension plan (this being his or her entire investment in the plan), the ratio of his or her investment in the plan to his or her expected return would be $20,000 to $90,000, or two-ninths (22.2 percent). Therefore, the employee would exclude two-ninths of each annuity payment from gross income and report as ordinary income only seven-ninths of the $6000, or $4667 a year, until the employee had recovered his or her $20,000 of after-tax contributions. Thereafter, the full $6000 per year would be gross income to the annuitant. If the annuitant should die before recovering his or her after-tax contributions tax-free, the remainder would be deductible on his final income tax return. If an employee's retirement income is guaranteed for a fixed number of years, the actuarial value of this guarantee would be deducted from the employee's investment in the plan, and this would increase the taxable portion of the pension payment.

In noncontributory plans, an employee usually does not have any investment in the plan (unless the plan includes life insurance coverage). The exclusion ratio, therefore, will be zero. Thus, the employee will have to report all the annuity payments as gross income.

These rules also apply to annuity benefits payable to the beneficiary of an employee participant following the employee's death. When a retirement income is paid to a retired employee and another annuitant under a joint and last survivor life annuity form, the survivor continues to use the same exclusion ratio, but the expected-return multiple is based on their combined life expectancies.

As noted in footnote 5, for life annuity payments from certain kinds of plans [i.e., qualified retirement plans, qualified employee annuity plans, and tax-sheltered annuity (TSA) plans], a *simplified general rule* may be available for determining the nontaxable part of life annuity payments when the annuity starting date is after July 1, 1986. Under this rule, the excluded amount (if any) is determined by simply dividing the annuitant's investment in the contract (plus any available $5000 employee death benefit exclusion) by a factor from IRS tables that is based only on the annui-

---

[5] Incidentally, this *general annuity rule* of Section 72 of the IRC also is the way periodic distributions (annuity payments) are taxed for other kinds of annuity plans, such as nonqualified annuities sold to the public by life insurance companies and described in Chap. 13. As will be noted next in this section, there also is a *simplified general rule* that may be used for determining the nontaxable portion of life annuity payments from qualified retirement plans, employee annuity plans, and tax-sheltered annuity (TSA) plans when the annuity starting date is after July 1, 1986.

tant's age as of the annuity starting date and then multiplying the quotient by the number of months that payments will be made in the year (normally 12). If an annuitant is eligible to use this simplified general rule, he or she can choose to use *either* the general rule (under Section 72) *or* the simplified general rule, and normally as a planning matter would use the one producing the lower gross income from the life annuity payments.

Lump-Sum Distributions.   Many pension plans and virtually all profit-sharing, savings, and stock bonus plans permit participating employees or their beneficiaries to take their plan benefits as a lump-sum distribution. Prior to the Tax Reform Act of 1986, lump-sum distributions from qualified retirement plans were accorded several substantial income tax advantages. Those advantages were significantly diminished by the Tax Reform Act of 1986, but some still remain for planning consideration. In addition, there are some special transition rules that may be helpful for some persons in planning for distributions from qualified retirement plans. It also seems possible that additional changes may occur in this area in the future, because there have been a number of tax simplification proposals presented to Congress for certain changes in these rules. As yet, however, none of these proposals has been adopted.

Definition of Lump-Sum Distributions.   A *lump-sum distribution* is a distribution made to a participating employee or his or her beneficiary *from a qualified retirement plan* of the employee's *entire account balance or interest in the plan* within *one taxable year* of the recipient. The distribution must be made on account of certain "*triggering events*," which are: (1) the employee's separation from service (including retirement); (2) after the employee's attaining age 59½; or (3) on account of the employee's death. (For self-employed persons, these "triggering events" are after age 59½, death, or becoming disabled.) In determining whether there has been a distribution of the entire account balance or interest in the plan of the employee, all qualified plans of the same type maintained by the employer must be considered together as one plan. For this purpose, all pension plans of the employer are one type of plan, all profit-sharing plans of the employer are another type of plan, and all stock bonus plans of the employer are still another type.

Thus, for example, if an employer maintains a defined-benefit pension plan and a savings plan for its employees, and Mr. Jones is covered by both plans and is retiring (separating from service), he could decide to receive a life annuity (periodic distribution) from the pension plan and still take his entire account balance under the savings plan as a lump-sum distribution [because it would constitute the entire balance to the credit of the employee (Mr. Jones) under the profit-sharing type of qualified plan]. (This assumes, of course, that the terms of the savings plan permit participants to take such lump-sum distributions, as they normally do.)

Taxable Amount of a Lump-Sum Distribution. The amount of a lump-sum distribution, as just defined, that is potentially subject to income taxation is the total amount of the distribution less the following items: (1) the employee's own net after-tax contributions; (2) the net unrealized appreciation on any employer securities included in the lump-sum distribution; (3) the term cost of any "incidental" life insurance protection which term cost the employee had previously included in his or her gross income; (4) repayments of any plan loans that previously were included in the employee's gross income (loans in excess of the tax law limits, for example); and (5) the actuarial value of any annuity contracts that were included in the distribution.

If a participant decides to take such a lump-sum distribution from a qualified retirement plan (such as Mr. Jones did with respect to the savings plan in the previous example), he or she still has to decide whether to pay the income tax currently on the distribution (perhaps with some favorable tax features), or to rollover (subject to 20 percent withholding) or directly transfer (not subject to withholding) part or all of the taxable portion of the distribution into an individual IRA or into another qualified plan that will accept such rollovers or transfers. This really is a decision of whether to pay the income tax now or to defer it further. Many people today opt to defer further through rollover or direct transfer. However, if the participant decides to pay the tax currently, there are several possible alternatives for taxing lump-sum distributions, depending on whether the employee was age 50 or older on January 1, 1986.

Alternatives for Taxing Lump-Sum Distributions for Employees Not Age 50 by January 1, 1986. This is the general rule, and for these employees the choices basically are: (1) use a one-time five-year averaging method at current income tax rates, provided the lump-sum distribution is received after the employee's age 59½; or (2) treat the entire taxable amount as ordinary gross income and pay the tax at current income tax rates (there really is no special tax attraction to this alternative).

As an illustration of five-year averaging, let us assume that at the end of 1995, Mr. Jones in our previous example is almost 60 (he was born on January 15, 1936), and there is an $80,000 total vested account balance in his qualified savings plan. Mr. Jones had made $20,000 in after-tax contributions to the plan [with the remainder of the account balance coming from before-tax elective contributions under a Section 401(k) option, employer matching contributions, and investment income on all contributions], and this $20,000 constitutes his entire investment (income tax basis) in the plan. The savings plan account balance had been invested 50 percent in a fixed-dollar fund through an insurance company–provided GIC and 50 percent in a diversified common stock fund. The account balance contains no employer securities. Mr. Jones has participated in the savings plan for 16 years.[6] Given these facts, the following shows the amount of income tax liability Mr. Jones will have in 1995 (assuming the same individual income tax rates as in 1991) on this lump-sum distribution using the one-time five-year averaging method.

Total lump-sum distribution	$80,000
Less: Employee's investment in the plan (employee's after-tax contributions)	−20,000
Taxable amount	$60,000
Less: Minimum distribution allowance*	− 2,000
Total taxable amount subject to averaging	$58,000
$58,000 ÷ 5	$11,600
Income tax on $11,600 at current (1995) single taxpayer rates (assume for the sake of this illustration that these current rates are the same as those shown in Chap. 11 for 1991)	$ 1,740
Tax on the lump-sum distribution (5 × $1,740)	8,700 (or about 15% of the taxable amount in this case)

*This *minimum distribution allowance* is the difference between (1) the smaller of $10,000 or 50 percent of the taxable amount and (2) 20 percent of the amount by which the taxable amount exceeds $20,000. In this case, this is (1) $10,000 minus (2) 0.20 ($60,000 − $20,000) or $10,000 − $8,000 = $2,000. It can be seen from this formula that this allowance will disappear once the taxable amount reaches $70,000 or more.

It can be seen from this illustration that five-year averaging (and also 10-year averaging, covered next) involves calculating the tax liability on the lump-sum distribution entirely separately from the taxpayer's other income and filing status for the year. This method can produce favorable tax treatment in some cases.

Alternatives for Taxing Lump-Sum Distributions for Employees Age 50 or over by January 1, 1986. This really is a transition rule adopted when the rules for taxing lump-sum distributions were made less liberal by the Tax Reform Act of 1986. Thus, the choices for these employees basically are: (1) use the one-time five-year averaging method using current income tax rates; (2) use a one-time 10-year averaging method using 1986 ordinary income tax rates; (3) pay a flat 20 percent capital gains tax on the pre-1974 portion of the taxable amount and use either the five-year or 10-year averaging method for the remainder; or (4) treat the entire taxable amount as

[6] For five-year averaging (and also for 10-year averaging discussed next), the employee must have participated in the plan for five or more years before the year of the lump-sum distribution. However, this five-year rule does not apply to averaging by a beneficiary of a deceased participant.

ordinary gross income and pay the tax at current income tax rates (again with really no special tax attraction to this alternative). It can be seen that there are more extensive and liberal choices here, and some analysis may be called for by those who are eligible for this transition rule (or by their advisers). Ten-year averaging involves basically the same concept as the previously illustrated five-year averaging, except that 10 years is used instead of five years and 1986 rates rather than current income tax rates are applied. Many persons who are now (as of 1992) retiring will be eligible for this more liberal rule. For example, if Mr. Jones in our previous example is assumed to be retiring at age 60 at the end of 1992 (rather than at the end of 1995, which we assumed just to illustrate the use of five-year averaging under the general rule), he would have been age 50 or older on January 1, 1986 [assuming now that he was born on January 15, 1932, he would have been age 53 (almost age 54) as of January 1, 1986].

Direct Transfers or Rollovers to an IRA or to Another Qualified Plan. An alternative to being taxed currently on certain distributions from qualified retirement plans (or tax-sheltered annuity plans) that are eligible to be rollover distributions is to defer part or all of the income tax on the distribution by either (1) having the participant's employer *transfer directly* all or part of the distribution to an individual retirement account or annuity (IRA) or to another employer's qualified retirement plan (that will accept such transfers), or (2) having the distribution paid to the participating employee who then *rolls over* all or part of the distribution to an IRA or to another employer's qualified plan (that will accept such rollovers) within 60 days of the receipt of the distribution. Thus, in the case of an *optional direct transfer,* there is a trustee-to-trustee transfer of part or all of the eligible rollover distribution to an eligible retirement plan (e.g., an IRA); while for the *rollover* alternative, the eligible rollover distribution is paid to the employee and then the employee transfers part or all of the distribution to an eligible retirement plan (e.g., an IRA) within 60 days of receiving it. While this distinction may seem technical, it makes considerable difference which approach is followed as far as the income tax effect is concerned.

For this purpose, an *eligible rollover distribution* is *any distribution* to an employee of *all or any portion* of the balance to the credit of the employee in a qualified retirement plan (or a tax-sheltered annuity), *except* that it does not include distributions made as substantially equal periodic payments over the lifetime (or life expectancy) of the employee or the lifetimes (or life expectancies) of the employee and his or her designated beneficiary, or distributions for a specified period of 10 years or more, or distributions required to satisfy the minimum distribution rules (a discussion of which follows). In effect, then, essentially any nonperiodic distribution can now be directly transferred to or rolled over to an IRA (or other eligible plan) and the income tax on the distribution can be further deferred. This is true regardless of the employee's age and is available for any number of distributions, provided they don't fall under the periodic payments (with exception to the definition of eligible rollover distributions just noted). There also is no longer any requirement for "triggering events" to be an eligible rollover distribution (as there still is to be considered a "lump-sum distribution," see p. 375). Also, *any part or all* of an employee's balance in the plan can be an eligible rollover distribution. (In effect, then, such a distribution includes, but is not limited to, a lump-sum distribution.)

The maximum amount of a distribution that can be rolled over or transferred is the amount which otherwise would have been included in the employee's gross income for federal income tax purposes. Thus, any part of a distribution which is excluded from the employee's gross income (like after-tax employee contributions and net unrealized appreciation on employer securities in a lump-sum distribution) cannot be rolled over or transferred. There is no dollar limit on the amount that can be rolled over or transferred to an IRA under these rules, as there is for regular IRAs (see pp. 398–399).

To the extent that an otherwise taxable distribution is directly transferred or rolled over to an IRA or another qualified plan, it is not currently taxable to the employee and will only be taxed in the future when paid out to the employee or his or her beneficiary, from the IRA or other plan. In other words, the tax is further deferred. However, effective for distributions after December 31, 1992, there now is a *mandatory 20 percent income tax withholding requirement* applicable to eligible rollover distributions, *except* where the distributee elects to have the distribution directly transferred to an eligible retirement plan (an IRA or other qualified plan). Thus, an employee rollover is subject to mandatory 20 percent withholding, while an employee optional direct transfer is not. This technical distinction can make quite a difference in planning for such distributions and will tend to strongly favor the use of optional direct transfers (which employers are required to provide under qualified retirement plans) over rollovers. In fact, it might be termed the "rollover withholding trap" for the unwary.

An example will help explain this important planning issue. Suppose that Susan Lewis, age 45, is leaving her present job to take another. She has vested benefits in her present employer's defined benefit pension plan and in its qualified savings plan under which she has made all her contributions under a Section 401(k) option, so she has no investment (income tax basis) in the plan. Her vested account balance in the savings plan is $100,000. Susan's present employer's plan permits her to leave her vested accrued pension benefits in the plan but does not allow this for the savings plan account balance. Any nonperiodic distribution to Susan from the savings plan would be an eligible rollover distribution as defined previously. In this situation, if Susan elects to have her present employer directly transfer all of her $100,000 savings plan account balance to an IRA for her or to her new employer's qualified plan, there will be no current income tax and no mandatory 20 percent withholding. On the other hand, if Susan decides to receive the distribution herself, her present employer must withhold 20 percent of the distribution (or $20,000 in this case if all the account balance is being distributed), and so she actually only receives $80,000. But to defer all taxes on this eligible rollover distribution, she must roll over to an IRA or another qualified plan the whole $100,000 distribution. As a practical matter, to do this she must come up with the $20,000 withheld from her other resources. (However, she presumably will get a refund of this withholding when she files her income tax return for the current year by April 15 of the next year, so this is really a cash flow problem.) If Susan only rolls over the $80,000 she actually receives, she will have received $20,000 in gross income for federal income tax purposes (which also will be subject to the 10 percent penalty tax on premature distributions because Susan is not yet age 59½).

In the event a *surviving spouse* of a deceased participant in a qualified retirement plan receives an eligible rollover distribution from the plan attributable to the deceased participant, the surviving spouse also may roll the distribution over to the spouse's own IRA (but not to the spouse's own qualified retirement plan) under generally the same conditions as the deceased participant could have. However, aside from a surviving spouse, no other beneficiary of qualified retirement plan death benefits can avail themselves of this rollover treatment.

Minimum Distribution Rules.   These are important rules in planning for distributions from certain tax-advantaged retirement plans. The plans covered by these rules are: qualified retirement plans, IRAs, tax-sheltered annuities (TSAs), and certain other plans. The basic purpose of these rules is to limit the time and extent to which participants and beneficiaries of these tax-advantaged retirement plans can defer the taking of benefits (and hence the taxation of those benefits) from the plans. For purposes of the minimum distribution rules, the *required beginning date* (RBD) for distributions to participants (or IRA owners) is no later than April 1 of the calendar year following the calendar year in which the person attains age 70½.

In the case of distributions *before a participant's (or IRA owner's) death,* the minimum distribution rules require that the entire interest of the participant or owner be distributed no later than the required beginning date (RBD) *or* that the entire interest will be distributed *beginning* no later than the RBD and will be distributed over no longer a period of time than over one of certain permissible periods. These *permissible periods* are: (1) the life of the participant or owner, (2) the joint and survivor lives of the participant or owner and his or her designated beneficiary, (3) a period of time not extending beyond the life expectancy of the participant or owner, or (4) a period of time not extending beyond the life expectancy of the participant or owner and his or her designated beneficiary. In effect, then, the minimum distribution must start by the RBD and be over no longer a period than the life or life expectancy of the participant (or owner) or of the participant (or owner) and his or her designated beneficiary. The designated beneficiary can be any identifiable individual (such as a spouse) or identifiable trust beneficiary (when the trust also meets certain other requirements) when the individual (or trust) is named by the participant or owner to receive any remaining plan benefits after the participant's or owner's death. In addition, there are other limits on the joint and last survivor life expectancies that can be used (other than in the case of a spouse as the only beneficiary), called the minimum distribution incidental benefits (MDIB) requirements, that are set forth in proposed IRS regulations.

In the case of *a participant's or IRA owner's death before the required beginning date (RBD)*, the general rule is that the decedent's entire interest in the plan must be distributed to the beneficiary (who is not a "designated beneficiary" as just defined) by the end of the fifth year following the year of death (called the "five-year rule"). However, there is an important exception to this five-year rule when a designated beneficiary (as just defined) has been named. This is called the *designated beneficiary exception,* and when it applies (as is often the case), the decedent's interest in the plan may be paid out in at least annual amounts over the lifetime or over a period of years not extending beyond the life expectancy of the designated beneficiary. Use of this exception can be important because it can extend the minimum payout period for death benefits in the case of death before the RBD for a much longer period than the five-year rule.

However, in the case of *a participant's or IRA owner's death after the RBD,* a different minimum distribution rule applies. In this situation, if periodic distributions have begun by the RBD (as they should), and if the participant or owner dies after the RBD, the undistributed amounts at the person's death must be distributed to the beneficiary at least as rapidly as under the method being used at the participant's or owner's death.

These minimum distribution rules can be complex, and they should be observed carefully so that substantial penalty taxes will not be incurred (as explained on p. 383–384).

Federal Estate Tax

The full value of any death benefits payable to a beneficiary of a deceased employee under a qualified retirement plan (or of a deceased owner of an IRA) is includable in the decedent's gross estate for federal estate tax purposes. (This includes benefits attributable to employer and any employee contributions.) The former exclusions of these death benefits for federal estate tax purposes have been repealed (except for a special transition rule that may apply in some cases). Of course, to the extent that such death benefits are payable to the decedent's surviving spouse as beneficiary (either directly or through a qualifying trust), they would qualify for the federal estate tax marital deduction and hence be deductible from the gross estate in arriving at the taxable estate (see pp. 433–439 for coverage of the federal estate tax in general and pp. 444–445 for a more complete discussion of the marital deduction).

Federal Gift Tax

If an employee designates a beneficiary irrevocably under a qualified retirement plan, the employee makes a taxable gift equal to the value attributable to his or her contributions to the plan (if any). Thus, participants in qualified retirement plans (and IRA owners) normally should not make such irrevocable beneficiary designations.

Federal Generation-Skipping Transfer Tax

The federal generation-skipping transfer tax (GST) is a tax applying to certain generation-skipping transfers from a transferor to certain "skip persons." A skip person is someone (or a trust for someone) who is assigned to a generation two or more generations below that of the transferor of the property potentially subject to the tax. This GST tax is described more fully on pp. 451–452 of Chap. 15. Transferors often seek to avoid this tax because the tax rate on transfers subject to the tax is at a flat rate equal to the highest federal estate tax rate (which is 55 percent as of this writing). Fortunately, however, every person has a $1,000,000 GST exemption allowable to transfers potentially subject to this tax and so the GST tax really applies only to sizable transfers.

Possible "Penalty" Taxes

Several potential additional "penalty" taxes have been enacted that may apply to distributions from qualified retirement plans, IRAs, and other tax-advantaged plans. They have been described as penalty taxes on taking distributions from covered plans "too soon" (the 10 percent tax on "early" or "premature" distributions), "too late" (the 50 percent tax on amounts not taken in conformance with the minimum distribution rules—see pp. 380–381), and "too much" (the 15 percent tax on "excess" retirement distributions or "excess" retirement accumulations). These additional taxes must be considered in planning distributions from affected plans. It would seem that the 50 percent tax should always be avoided by at least conforming to the minimum distribution rules, while the other two should be considered in planning and avoided or reduced if possible.

Excise Tax on "Premature" Distributions.   This is an additional 10 percent excise tax on the taxable portion of distributions from plans subject to the tax made prior to age 59½, with certain exceptions. Aside from reaching *age 59½*, the *other exceptions* for distributions from qualified retirement plans include: (1) distributions made on or after the participant's death; (2) distributions due to a participant's disability; (3) payments made as substantially equal periodic benefits for the lifetime or life expectancy of the participant or for the joint and survivor lives or joint and survivor life expectancy of the participant and his or her beneficiary (sometimes referred to as "annuitizing" the payments); (4) distributions to a participant after attaining age 55 upon separation from service; (5) distributions to a participant for deductible medical expenses; (6) distributions to persons under qualified domestic relations orders (QDROs); and (7) certain other distributions. Distributions from qualified retirement plans, tax-sheltered annuities (TSAs), and IRAs are potentially subject to this excise tax. (Note that only exceptions 1, 2, and 3 above apply to IRAs.) Further, distributions from nonqualified deferred annuities (discussed in Chap. 13) also are potentially covered by this excise tax [as are distributions from life insurance policies defined in the tax law as modified endowment contracts (MECs)—see pp. 86–87 of Chap. 4].

This excise tax on premature distributions is in addition to the regular income tax payable. Thus, for example, for a person in a 28 percent federal income tax bracket who is subject to this excise tax, the combined tax rate on premature distributions (assuming that they are taxed as ordinary income) would be 38 percent. This penalty tax, of course, would not apply to amounts transferred or rolled over to an IRA or another qualified plan, because these amounts would not be currently subject to regular income taxation.

Excise Tax on Insufficient Distributions.   In the event that the minimum distribution rules apply but are not complied with, the tax law imposes on the payee of any distributions a 50 percent nondeductible excise tax on the difference between the amount that should have been distributed under the minimum distribution rules and the amount (if any) actually distributed in the year. (There may be a waiver of this 50 percent tax in the case of "reasonable error.")

Thus, for example, if Mr. Johnson's RBD is April 1, 1992 (i.e., the April 1 of the year after the year in which he became age 70½), and he takes no distribution in 1992 from, say, his rollover IRA (assuming this is his only plan subject to the minimum distribution rules), he would be subject to the 50 percent excise tax (in addition to the regular income tax) on the minimum distribution he should have taken in 1992.

Excise Taxes on "Excess Retirement Distributions" and "Excess Retirement Accumulations." The tax on *excess retirement distributions* is a 15 percent excise tax, in addition to any other tax, on the amount by which the aggregate annual distributions received by an individual from certain tax-favored retirement plans exceed the larger of $150,000 or $112,500 (indexed for inflation) or the larger of $112,500 (indexed for inflation) or a grandfathered amount recovered for the year in the case of persons who had elected a special grandfather provision in 1987 or 1988. The plans whose distributions are subject to this 15 percent tax include qualified retirement plans, qualified annuity plans, IRAs, and tax-sheltered annuity (TSA) plans. The annual distributions from all these plans are aggregated for an individual to determine whether the limit has been exceeded. For persons receiving lump-sum distributions and electing averaging or capital gains treatment, the 15 percent tax applies separately to the lump-sum distribution, and the threshold limit is five times the annual limit.

As an example of these rules, suppose that Mary Harrison, age 71 and single, receives an annual life annuity from her former employer's noncontributory defined-benefit pension plan of $110,000 and this year took a distribution (as required by the minimum distribution rules) from her rollover IRA of $70,000. Assuming that the $150,000 annual threshold limit applies, the excess retirement distribution of $30,000 ($180,000 − $150,000) would be subject to the 15 percent excise tax (in addition to the regular income tax on the whole distribution). On the other hand, if Mary had taken a lump-sum distribution in the year of her retirement (say, at age 65) from all her qualified retirement plans of $1,200,000 (an assumption we make only to illustrate the operation of this tax), the excess retirement distribution of $450,000 [$1,200,000 − (5 × $150,000 annual limit or $750,000)] would be subject to the 15 percent excise tax.

There are certain *exceptions* to this tax on excess distributions, including: distributions with respect to an individual after his or her death (but here the excise tax on "excess retirement accumulations," described next, may apply); distributions attributable to an individual's investment in the plan; distributions not includible in gross income for tax purposes because they were the subjects of a tax-deferred rollover; and distributions payable to an alternate payee pursuant to a QDRO that are taxable to the alternate payee.

While only a comparatively few people will have retirement benefits large enough to subject them to this tax, it nevertheless is a significant planning factor for those who do. To some degree, this potential tax may have to be balanced against the desirability of income tax deferral in these tax-favored plans.

The companion tax is the 15 percent excise tax on the *excess retirement accumulations* of an individual at his or her death (also called the increase in estate tax). The excess retirement accumulation for this purpose is the amount by which the value of the decedent's interests in these covered retirement plans at his or her death exceeds the present value (using the appropriate monthly applicable federal interest rate) of the excess distributions annual limit ($150,000 or an indexed $112,500) payable as an annual term certain annuity for a period equal to the decedent's life expectancy immediately before his or her death (which depends on the decedent's age at his or her death). (Or, if the grandfather election was made in 1987 or 1988, this present value is the larger of any remaining grandfathered amount or the present value of a term certain annual annuity of an indexed $112,500.) In addition, this 15% increased estate tax cannot be reduced by the federal estate tax marital deduction, unified credit, or charitable deduction. In effect, it has to be paid at some point.

There is one planning opportunity for possible deferral of this tax that should be considered under the proper circumstances. The surviving spouse of a decedent with such excess retirement accumulations to whom essentially all the accumulations are payable can elect in the estate tax return not to have the additional estate tax apply at the decedent's death, but to have the decedent's accumulations aggregated with any retirement plan accumulations of the spouse for purposes of the 15 percent excise tax. The tax then would be paid when the surviving spouse had any taxable excess retirement distributions or accumulations.

Planning for Distributions from Qualified Retirement Plans (and IRAs)

It will come as no surprise to the reader, after reviewing the complex tax and other rules applying to qualified retirement plans outlined earlier in this chapter, that planning for distributions from these plans (and IRAs) can be a complicated matter. Yet it can also be quite important for a person's financial and estate planning, since in many cases the wealth accumulated in these plans over working lifetimes can be substantial and often is a major part of the person's total resources (particularly for retirement). Thus, in many cases, professional help may be advisable in helping the person and his or her spouse (if any) plan for the use of the benefits from such plans, depending on the circumstances.

Planning for these benefits is an extensive subject, and a complete discussion of it is beyond the scope of this book. Only an outline of the salient issues will be presented here. In doing so, we have divided up the planning issues into those applying while the employee-participant is still in service (working for the employer), at separation from service before retirement (as when the participant changes jobs or is laid off), at retirement, and at death.

While in Service

Plan participants may face several planning issues while in service, such as being able to choose among investment options under some plans and deciding whether to make voluntary contributions under some kinds of plans, such as savings plans. However, with regard to getting cash from qualified retirement plans while still in service, the choices generally may be:

- Use of plan loans (where permitted by the plan and subject to the tax law rules for such loans) as described on p. 364.

- Possible in-service withdrawals. While such withdrawals may be permitted in some cases by the tax law (and the plan provisions), they have lost much of their attraction. However, such withdrawals now may be eligible rollover distributions.

At Separation from Service
Prior to Retirement

A number of planning issues may face a terminating employee regarding qualified retirement plan benefits (and other employee benefits, such as medical expense benefits and group term life insurance) at this often very stressful time. Planning also is affected by whether the terminating employee is going to another job or career or is looking for employment. Further, the terminating employee only has rights in qualified retirement plan benefits for which he or she is *vested* at termination of service (see pp. 354–355 for a discussion of vesting).

With regard to vested qualified retirement plan benefits at separation from service prior to retirement, the logical choices generally may be:

- Leave the vested benefits in the former employer's plan.

- Take a lump-sum distribution and pay the income tax on the distribution currently (presumably using an averaging technique for the taxable amount).

- Elect to have a direct transfer made to an IRA or to a new employer's qualified plan.

- Make a rollover to an IRA or to a new employer's qualified plan.

At Retirement

Again, many planning issues face the former employee (and his or her spouse, if any) when he or she separates from service to retire. At this point, the retiree (and his or her spouse) must decide how, when, and in what amounts to take benefits from various retirement plans to provide an adequate retirement income and meet other financial planning goals. This really is the heart of retirement financial planning.

Thus, with regard to qualified retirement plan benefits at retirement, there generally may be the following choices:

- Take retirement benefits as a periodic life income for the retired person or the retired person and his or her spouse (or in periodic installments of fixed amounts or for a fixed period of years). This option essentially may involve taking benefits as a life annuity that the retiree or the retiree and his or her spouse cannot outlive (i.e., "annuitizing" the benefits). The retiree (and his or her spouse, if any) also must decide what annuity form to use (within the rules of REA).

- Take a lump-sum distribution and pay the income tax on the distribution currently (presumably using an averaging technique for the taxable amount). In some cases, this may be attractive, particularly where the lump-sum distribution is relatively small or where there may be a relatively large amount of highly appreciated employer securities in the distribution.

- Elect to have a tax-deferred direct transfer or possibly make a tax-deferred rollover to an IRA. This is a popular technique for at least the benefits from some kinds of qualified plans, such as savings plans or profit-sharing plans. The advantages frequently cited for this approach include: There is no current income tax on the amount transferred or (except for withholding) on the amount rolled over; the investment income and gains continue to accumulate income tax-deferred within the IRA; the IRA owner has flexibility in deciding how, when, and how much to take from the IRA for retirement income or other purposes, within the limits of the minimum distribution rules; the owner has control over his or her IRA and its investments within a very broad range of investment choices and/or investment intermediaries; if the owner wishes a life annuity, he or she can place or transfer the funds in a life insurance company individual retirement annuity; the retiree can diversify his or her choices and transfer or roll over some plan benefits but not others, or transfer or roll over only a portion of a distribution; and since the REA rules do not apply to IRAs, the IRA owner may have more flexible estate planning, but this may be controversial because correspondingly the IRA owner's spouse will have fewer rights and protections. On the other hand, some disadvantages might be: The benefits of a lifetime annuity income *from the plan* will not be available; the special advantages of the taxation of lump-sum distributions will be lost; and the investment flexibility argument can be a two-edged sword in that there may be investment losses as well as gains from the IRA.

With all of these choices, the participant or IRA owner can select a combination of them and thus diversify to some extent his or her sources of retirement income.

At Death

Since qualified retirement plans today generally provide preretirement and postretirement death benefits, a planning issue is to whom and how these death benefits should be payable. (IRAs also have death benefits.) In fact, in some cases these death benefits can be substantial and/or a major part of a person's estate. Planning for them can be complicated, and professional aid may be needed in some cases.

The logical beneficiaries for such qualified retirement plan (and IRA) death benefits may include:

- The participant's (or IRA owner's) spouse. This is a common choice.

- An individual other than the spouse (e.g., children or other family members).

- A trust. In this case, the spouse or others can be beneficiaries of the trust. Trusts may be used when trust administration for plan death benefits is desired (often when the benefits are substantial) and/or when trusts are desirable for estate planning reasons.

- Possibly the participant's (or IRA owner's) estate (but this seems to have few planning advantages).

- Possibly an eligible charity (assuming that the participant or IRA owner wants to make a charitable bequest or gift at death anyway).

It must be remembered, however, that if a participant in a qualified retirement plan is married, any of these beneficiary designations, other than the spouse, must meet the requirements of REA as explained on pp. 356–358 and 364–365.

The choice of a beneficiary or beneficiaries for these benefits really is part of a person's or couple's overall estate planning. However, these plans present special rules and problems in this area, and professional advice often is needed.

13

Other Retirement Plans and Other Employee Benefits

There is a wide range of employee benefits (sometimes called fringe benefits) beyond the group life insurance, group health insurance, and qualified retirement plans we have discussed before. Some of these additional employee benefits can include any or a combination of the following:

Nonqualified deferred compensation arrangements

Supplemental executive retirement plans

Dental insurance plans

Stock purchase plans

Stock option plans and other stock plans

Unemployment and severance pay arrangements

Vacation plans

Vision care plans

Dependent care assistance plans

Employee financial counseling

Others

The above programs constitute only some of the employee benefit plans that could be arranged. It is beyond the scope of this book to discuss all of these and other types of employee benefits. Only a sample of the more significant plans from a financial planning standpoint will be covered in this chapter.[1]

In addition to employee benefits, this chapter also covers some retirement plans other than employer-provided qualified retirement plans, which were covered in Chap. 12. We shall start with these plans.

Individual (Nonqualified) Annuities

The annuity can be an important instrument in planning for retirement. In its payout phase, a life annuity can be described as follows: An individual pays an insurance company a specified capital sum in exchange for a promise that the insurer will make a series of periodic payments to the individual (called the "annuitant") for as long as he or she lives. The periodic income collected under an annuity contract is composed of three parts: principal; interest; and a survivorship benefit, which arises from the fact that those who die release their investment to be spread among these survivors. However, modern individual annuity contracts permit the payout of accumulated annuity funds (cash value) in a variety of ways.

Objectives of Annuities

A basic purpose of a life annuity is to assure a person an income he or she cannot outlive, as well as one that is relatively large when compared with the amount paid for the annuity. The periodic income under a life annuity should be relatively large because the annuity principle involves the gradual consumption of the purchase price or cash value of the annuity.

The individual, in deciding whether to use his or her capital to purchase an annuity with a life income to begin currently (an immediate life annuity) or whether to use the cash values accumulated under a deferred annuity contract to provide a life income, should evaluate payments under the annuity as compared with the return from relatively safe certificates of deposit or high-grade municipal, corporate, or government bonds. In recent years, individual nonqualified deferred annuities have been widely used as investment vehicles because of the relatively high rates of return being paid on their cash values, the ability to purchase vari-

---

[1] A more complete discussion of employee benefits can be found in books on this subject, including: Jerry S. Rosenbloom and G. Victor Hallman, *Employee Benefit Planning*, 3d ed. (Englewood Cliffs, NJ: Prentice-Hall, 1991); and Jerry S. Rosenbloom, *The Handbook of Employee Benefits*, 3d ed. (Homewood, IL: Richard D. Irwin, 1992).

able annuities with their greater investment flexibility for the cash values, and the tax-deferred accumulation of those cash values.

Types of Individual Annuities

Annuities may be of several varieties. A key distinction in terms of an individual's personal financial planning is whether the annuity is of the fixed-dollar type or is a variable annuity.

Fixed-Dollar Annuities.   In these annuities, the cash value accumulation (or the annuity income) is a stated dollar amount that is guaranteed by the insurance company and on which (or with respect to the annuity income) the insurer pays a specified or determinable rate of interest. In effect, it is a fixed-dollar, guaranteed-principal kind of investment medium that is in some ways analogous to CDs. The investment authority and investment risk are on the insurance company because it is the insurer that guarantees the cash value (or annuity income) and specifies the interest rate currently being paid on cash value accumulations.

Variable Annuities.   A newer type of individual annuity being sold by insurance companies now usually is called a "variable annuity." Under this annuity, the annuity owner can choose from among several different investment funds with regard to where he or she wishes to place the annuity premiums. The annuity owner also usually has the option of moving the annuity contributions and/or cash values among the various investment funds offered at reasonable intervals. As long as the available annuity investment funds are not also offered to the general public, the annuitant is not regarded as the owner of these funds for income tax purposes. Therefore, the inside buildup of the annuity's accumulation or cash values remains currently not subject to income taxation, and the owner's changing the allocation of his or her cash values between or among the various investment funds does not constitute a sale or exchange for capital gains tax purposes. Thus, under this kind of annuity the annuity owner has considerable investment flexibility among the various annuity funds offered without any current tax liability as long as he or she does not take a distribution from the annuity. However, with variable annuities the investment risks also reside with the annuity owner. In other words, with the flexibility goes the risk.

  Variable annuities can also provide for a variable payout of annuity benefits. This is the same idea discussed in Chap. 12 with regard to protecting pension income from inflation.

Combination Plans.   Individual annuity contracts also may give annuity owners the choice of putting their annuity values in a fixed-dollar fund (like a fixed-dollar annuity), in one or more of a series of variable funds (like a variable annuity), or in a combination of fixed and one or more variable accounts. This gives annuity owners even more flexibility.

Flexible-Premium Annuities.   These contracts allow the annuity owner the discretion of paying periodic annuity premiums to build up an annuity cash value prior to retirement. The premium payments can be discontinued or changed at the owner's option. This approach necessarily applies to deferred annuities, and so they may be referred to as *flexible-premium deferred annuities*. They basically are a way to build up accumulated values over a period of time through flexible, periodic premiums.

Life insurance companies have also issued fixed-premium annuities, usually called retirement annuities, where the premiums were a stated amount each period (month, quarter, year, etc.), much like traditional life insurance policies. However, such retirement annuities are rarely issued today, generally having been replaced by flexible-premium deferred annuities.

Single-Premium Annuities.   Under these annuities, the contract is purchased with a single lump-sum payment. The single premium may be paid well in advance of when benefits are to be taken from the annuity (a *single-premium deferred annuity or SPDA*), or it may be paid just before annuity payments are to begin (a *single-premium immediate annuity*).

SPDAs are essentially investment arrangements for the growth of capital over a substantial period of time prior to retirement. They (as well as flexible-premium deferred annuities) also give the annuity owner various payout options (including life annuity options) for taking the accumulated value in the annuity. Single-premium immediate annuities are essentially a way of liquidating or paying out a capital sum to provide a life annuity for an annuitant or annuitants.

Both flexible-premium deferred annuities and SPDAs can be either fixed-dollar-type annuities or variable annuities as just defined.

Investment Returns on Annuities

Fixed-Dollar Annuities.   For this general type of annuity, the insurance company specifies an *initial credited interest rate* that it will pay on the cash accumulation under the contract. This rate (or perhaps several rates) often is guaranteed by the insurer for a specified period of time. This may be called the *yield guarantee.* This period can range widely among insurance companies and annuity contracts, from as little as one month to, say, as long as 10 years. After any yield guarantee period ends, the insurer then can set the interest rate it will pay in the future on the annuity's cash accumulation. This *current yield* can be increased or decreased by the insurer and may be more or less than the initial credited rate. However, many fixed-dollar annuities have a *minimum guaranteed interest rate* below which the insurance company cannot set its current interest rate. Finally, some annuities have a so-called *bailout escape rate* (or bailout provision), which provides that if the current rate declared by the insurer falls below a stated rate, the annuity owner may withdraw all funds from the annuity (or exchange the annuity) without a surrender charge (i.e., without a back-end load as described next). All these yield factors and guarantees can be important for the prospective purchaser of an annuity to consider. They also will vary in importance, depending on the general economic climate for interest rates (and the actual experience of the insurer issuing the annuity).

Variable Annuities. Here, the investment return realized in the cash value depends on the investment performance of the account or accounts to which the annuity funds are allocated. Therefore, the prospective purchaser should evaluate the past investment experience of the insurer writing the annuity, much as should be done when buying investment company shares (e.g., mutual funds) or variable life insurance.

Expense Charges on Annuities

Charges levied can be quite important in affecting the net yield from an annuity and so should be considered carefully by a prospective purchaser. There are two broad categories of charges: (1) sales charges (or sales "loads"); and (2) other, usually annual, charges.

Sales Charges. A sales charge may be deducted from the premium or premiums paid when the annuity is purchased. This is called a "front-end load." However, the trend in the life insurance industry with regard to individual annuities is not to impose a front-end load, but rather to impose a surrender charge (technically called a contingent deferred sales charge) if more than a certain percentage or amount (such as more than 10 percent of the accumulated value per year) is withdrawn from the annuity. This surrender charge generally declines over a specified period of time after purchase (such as 7 to 10 years), until it becomes zero at the end of that time. This common kind of sales charge is popularly called a "back-end load," and has the effect of tending to lock in the annuity purchaser for the period of time the load may be imposed, except for the operation of any bailout provision.

Other Fees. In addition to sales charges, there often are various kinds of annual or other fees for variable annuities. These may include: a mortality risk charge, an expense risk charge, investment management fees, administrative charges, and possibly others. Fixed-dollar annuities do not normally charge such fees separately, but rather they are handled indirectly through the level of interest rates currently being credited by the insurer. These annual charges are spelled out in the prospectus for the variable annuity.[2] They (and the sales charges) are similar in concept to some of the charges for variable life insurance.

Withdrawals, Loans, and Exchanges of Annuities

Individual deferred annuities normally permit withdrawals or policy loans from the cash value at any time. However, the income tax effects of such withdrawals or loans from annuities can be quite different than from life insurance policies (other than MECs) as discussed on pp. 86–87 of Chap. 4. The income taxation of nonqualified annuities is discussed in greater detail later in this chapter (see pp. 395–397).

Annuity contracts can also be exchanged tax-free for other annuity contracts under the terms of Section 1035 of the Internal Revenue Code (see pp. 57 and 308–309 concerning Section 1035). Thus, if an annuity owner is dissatisfied with the service, yield, or security of his or her individual deferred annuity, the owner can exchange the contract for another annuity contract with a life insurance company without current income tax consequences. This can be a valuable tax-free exchange provision for consumers.

However, the annuity owner must remember that withdrawals, surrenders, or exchanges of annuity contracts may give rise to a back-end load.

Annuity Payout Options

Individual deferred annuity contracts normally give the annuity owner a number of choices as to how the annuity values may be paid out to the annuity owner or others. The following are common payout options for the annuity owner: (1) cash surrender (or withdrawal) of the whole or a part of the accumulated value; (2) installment payments over a fixed period of time or in fixed amounts; (3) a straight life annuity; (4) joint and last survivor life annuities; and (5) life annuities with various kinds of guaranteed payments or refund features. Thus, the annuity owner is not limited to taking his or her annuity values as a life annuity at retirement, and, in fact, the value in a great many individual deferred annuities are actually paid out in other ways.

---

[2] While the annual or other fees for variable annuities can vary considerably among insurers and annuity contracts, they might *average* around 2 to 2½ percent of the annuity value per year. As noted previously, this can have a considerable impact on annuity investment yields to purchasers over a period of time.

Annuity Death Benefits

While individual annuities are primarily capital accumulation or capital liquidation vehicles, the owner does name a beneficiary or beneficiaries to receive the accumulated annuity cash value in the event of the owner's death before the annuity value is paid out. This produces a death benefit from the individual annuity; however, it should be noted that there are no life insurance proceeds involved in such an *annuity* death benefit. In fact, the difference between the deceased annuity owner's investment in the contract at death (his or her income tax basis in the annuity at death) and the death benefit payable to the beneficiary is taxable to the beneficiary as income in respect of a decedent (IRD). The tax will be paid by the beneficiary depending on how the beneficiary receives the annuity death benefit. Individual annuity contracts normally allow the annuity owner or the beneficiary to select one or more payout options for the annuity death benefit. It should be noted, however, that for individual nonqualified annuities there is no tax-free rollover provision for a surviving spouse (or anyone else) with regard to the annuity death benefit. However, the minimum distribution rules also do not apply to these annuities (see pp. 380–381 of Chap. 12).

Split-Funded Annuities

Split-funded annuities are a combination of an immediate annuity and a deferred annuity. This allows a part of the split-funded annuity to provide current income (from the immediate annuity part) for a fixed period of years or for life, while the remainder continues to grow tax-deferred (from the deferred annuity part). In this way, the deferred portion continues to grow while the annuitant still receives a current income which can be supplemented in the future by utilizing part or all of the deferred portion. Sometimes the immediate annuity income is paid out over a fixed period, at the end of which the deferred portion will have increased to about the same as the original annuity cash value.

Taxation of Nonqualified Annuities

The taxation of these nonqualified annuities can be complex. Therefore, only a brief outline of the basic principles will be presented here. However, this subject is becoming more and more important because of the increasing popularity of these contracts today.

Federal Income Taxation.   An annuity owner's *investment in the contract* (or income tax basis in the contract) is the owner's net premiums paid for the annuity. Since this amount (either as a single premium or as flexible premiums) has been paid for the policy with after-tax dollars, the owner (or his or her beneficiary at death) is entitled to this amount back tax-free when benefits are taken from the annuity.

During the accumulation phase of a deferred annuity, the investment earnings of the contract increase (or decrease) without current income taxation (or losses). This is the famous *tax-deferred* (sometimes erroneously called "tax-free") *buildup of annuity cash values* that is one of the main advantages of individual (nonqualified) deferred annuities over many other kinds of investment media. In the case of variable annuities, the owner of the contract can also elect to move the annuity cash value between or among the investment accounts within the annuity contract without this being considered a sale or exchange for capital gains tax purposes. This might be termed the *tax-deferred asset allocation change privilege* within variable annuities (or variable life insurance for that matter). (This concept was also discussed on pp. 80–81.)

When annuity benefits are taken as *periodic income* (in substantially equal installments or as a life income), they are taxed under the general annuity rules of IRC Section 72, as discussed on pp. 373–374 of Chap. 12. The investment in the contract for this purpose is the net premiums paid.

If an annuity contract is entirely *surrendered for cash,* the difference between the cash surrender value received and the investment in the contract is taxed as ordinary income in the year of the surrender.

However, if there are *partial* (nonperiodic) *withdrawals* from the contract, they are viewed for tax purposes as first coming from the potentially taxable investment earnings of the contract (the tax-deferred inside buildup) and are taxed as ordinary income until such investment earnings are exhausted. Once the inside buildup is exhausted, any further withdrawals are then viewed as a return of the investment in the contract and are income tax-free.[3] This can be termed a "last-in, first-out" or LIFO concept of taxation and is the opposite of that generally employed for partial withdrawals from life insurance contracts (that are not MECs).

Loans from annuities are considered for income tax purposes to be distributions from the contract and hence are taxable the same as just described for partial withdrawals. This is the opposite of the treatment of policy loans from life insurance policies (that are not MECs) (see pp. 81–82) and loans from qualified retirement plans (see pp. 363–364).

---

[3] There is a grandfather rule for annuities entered into before August 14, 1982, under which full or partial withdrawals of amounts allocated to the investment in the contract made before August 14, 1982, are assumed first to be a return of the owner's investment in the contract and hence are not taxable until that investment is recovered tax-free. This is really the former cost-recovery rule that generally no longer applies to annuities.

Further, for nonqualified annuity contracts issued after January 18, 1985, any taxable amount withdrawn (or taken as a loan) prior to age 59½ generally will be subject to a *10 percent excise tax on premature distributions* that is similar to the one described on p. 383 imposed on qualified retirement plans, TSAs, and IRAs. There are, however, certain exceptions to this 10 percent penalty tax (in addition to reaching age 59½) when applied to nonqualified annuities, such as the owner's disability or death, when payments are made in substantially equal periodic installments for the life or life expectancy of the annuitant or the joint lives or life expectancies of the annuitant and his or her beneficiary, and in the case of the purchase of an immediate annuity.

It may be noted that the general effects of these tax rules (as well as any back-end loads) are to make the purchase of deferred annuities a long-term proposition. However, as noted previously, there still can be *tax-free exchanges under Section 1035* of one annuity contract for another.

Federal Estate Taxation. The *total* accumulated cash value (death benefit) of a deferred annuity at the annuity owner's death will be included *in the owner's gross estate* for federal estate tax purposes at his or her death. It thus would be wealth "passing" from the annuity owner to the annuity beneficiary.

In addition, the difference between the annuity's death benefit and the deceased annuity owner's investment in the contract would be *income in respect of a decedent* (*IRD*) for federal income tax purposes and thus gross income taxable to the beneficiary depending on how the beneficiary takes the death benefit. Also, as noted previously, there are no tax-deferred rollover privileges with regard to nonqualified annuities.

Other Individual Annuity Arrangements

In addition to individual nonqualified annuity contracts sold to the public by life insurance companies as described in the previous section, there are also other kinds of nonqualified annuities. These are not nearly as widely used as those discussed previously, but they can be of significance in some cases.

Charitable-Gift Annuities. These are part charitable contribution and part annuity arrangements provided by some charities. They were described on p. 325 of Chap. 11.

Private Annuities. These really are an estate planning arrangement whereby one person (normally a family member—say, a child) promises to

pay a life annuity income to another person (the annuitant) as the purchase payment by the person providing the annuity for a business interest
or other property being sold by the annuitant. Under proper circumstances, private annuities can be useful wealth transfer devices within a family. However, the private annuity is secured only by the buyer's (annuity
provider's) personal promise to pay the life annuity.

Using Life Insurance Values
to Provide Retirement Income

Life insurance contracts contain a series of options concerning the disposition of life insurance proceeds and cash surrender values. These settlement
options were discussed in Chap. 4; however, they are mentioned again here
because of their relationship to annuities and retirement income.

Most life insurance companies make available by contract, or as a
matter of practice, settlement options providing a straight life income, a
life income with installments guaranteed, or a joint and last survivor life
income. Note that these life income settlement options are, in effect, simply immediate annuities purchased by applying the cash value or the proceeds of a life insurance policy as a single premium. Life insurance values
may also be paid out in installments or under an interest option. (See pp.
95–97 for a discussion of life insurance settlement options.) Persons at or
near retirement may choose to use some or all of their life insurance cash
values in this way, assuming they feel they no longer need the life insurance protection or all the life insurance protection.

Individual Retirement
Accounts and Annuities (IRAs)

A tax-favored retirement plan for individuals not covered by private qualified retirement plans was instituted in 1974 by ERISA. The IRA concept was
expanded considerably by the Economic Recovery Tax Act of 1981 (ERTA)
but was limited again by the Tax Reform Act of 1986.

The law provides that after 1986, *regular* (i.e., not transferred or
rollover) IRA contributions are tax-deductible up to the lesser of $2000 or
100 percent of compensation for each income earner (1) if the individual
and his or her spouse are not active participants in an employer-maintained
retirement plan, or (2) if the individual or his or her spouse is an active participant and his or her adjusted gross income (AGI) does not exceed certain amounts. For married taxpayers (where either spouse is an active
participant), the AGI must not exceed $40,000 for the full deduction, and
the deduction is phased out between $40,000 and $50,000 of AGI. For sin-

gle persons, the limit is $25,000 for full deduction, with the phaseout being between $25,000 and $35,000 of AGI.[4]

To the extent that IRA contributions are not deductible under these rules, it is still possible for an income earner to make *nondeductible* IRA contributions to a regular IRA equal to the difference between what could have been contributed on a tax-deductible basis had there been no income limits on contributions (generally either $2000 per income earner or $2250 when a spousal IRA is involved) and the amounts (if any) of tax-deductible IRA contributions actually permitted under the just-cited rules. The only advantage in making such nondeductible contributions is that their investment income accumulates without current income taxation (as is also true of the investment income of deductible contributions).

Many financial institutions offer IRAs to the public. An individual may initiate an *individual retirement account* with a brokerage firm, commercial bank, investment company (including a mutual fund), and a thrift institution (such as savings and loan associations and mutual savings banks). An individual may also have an *individual retirement annuity* with an insurance company (but not a life insurance policy). Thus, there can be a wide range of investments selected by the IRA owner for an IRA.

As noted on p. 383, individuals generally may not begin receiving IRA distributions prior to age 59½ without a 10 percent penalty tax, except in the case of death or disability.

Further, as explained on pp. 380–381, the minimum distribution rules apply to IRAs. Thus, an IRA owner must begin receiving payments by his or her required beginning date (the April 1 of the year following the year in which the owner becomes age 70½) and in certain prescribed amounts.

IRA distributions are taxed to the recipient as ordinary income. There is no capital gain treatment or special lump-sum distribution treatment for IRAs. Also, loans are not permitted from IRAs.

There may also be IRA-to-IRA rollovers and direct IRA transfers which permit IRA owners to make tax-free exchanges of one IRA for another. In an *IRA-to-IRA rollover,* part or all of the assets in one IRA are distributed to the owner and then the owner, within 60 days of the receipt of the assets, rolls over those same assets into another IRA. This can be done only *once* each year. On the other hand, a *direct IRA transfer* involves the transfer of IRA assets directly from one plan sponsor to another without those assets passing into the hands of the IRA owner. There is no limit on the number

---

[4] Eligible individuals can contribute a somewhat larger total dollar amount if they provide a part of the contribution for the benefit of their nonworking spouse (a spousal IRA). Thus, an eligible working individual can contribute up to $2250. If the spouse works and is also eligible under the above rules, an additional IRA can be set up with the same limits, that is, the lesser of $2000 or 100 percent of compensation.

of transfers that can be made in any one year. Thus, these techniques allow the tax-free movement of IRA assets from one IRA to another and give the IRA owner considerable flexibility in changing financial institutions and asset allocation for his or her IRAs.

In addition, as explained on pp. 378–380, there can be direct transfers or rollovers of eligible rollover distributions from qualified retirement plans (and TSAs) to IRAs. These transfers or rollovers are tax-deferred, and there are no earnings or amount limits for them.

Simplified Employee Pension (SEP) Plans

Since 1979, employers have been able to establish a SEP for their employees utilizing individual retirement accounts or annuities. Contributions to a SEP on a tax-deductible basis can be made up to the lesser of 15 percent of compensation or $30,000 (adjusted for inflation). The SEP is intended to reduce much of the paperwork required for HR-10 or qualified corporate retirement plans.

Under the Tax Reform Act of 1986, SEPs with 25 or fewer employees and which meet certain other requirements may permit participating employees to make elective before-tax contributions up to $7000 per year (adjusted for inflation) to the SEP or to receive a similar amount from the employer in cash. This is a cash or deferred arrangement similar to that permitted under Section 401(k), as described in Chap. 12.

Tax-Sheltered Annuity (TSA) Plans

A TSA plan [or Section 403(b) annuity] is an arrangement permitted under federal law whereby an employee of a "qualified organization" can enter into an agreement with his or her employer to have part of the employee's earnings set aside for retirement. No federal income tax is payable on the amount set aside each year to purchase retirement benefits, provided that (1) the amounts are used to buy an annuity contract, a retirement income insurance policy, or regulated investment company shares (e.g., mutual funds), and (2) the contribution amounts do not exceed the employee's "exclusion allowance." Thus, a TSA plan enables employees of qualified organizations to save for retirement with *before-tax* dollars.

Who Is Eligible?

Any employee who works for a public school system or a tax-exempt organization established and operated exclusively for charitable, religious, scientific, or educational purposes is eligible.

How Much Can an Eligible
Employee Contribute Each Year?

Assuming no current participation in a qualified retirement program, as much as 20 percent of an employee's salary can be put into a TSA plan, with additional amounts possible if the employee has had past service with the organization. However, under the Tax Reform Act of 1986, the maximum annual amount an employee can elect to defer under all TSA plans after 1986 is $9500 [indexed for inflation once the Section 401(k) dollar limit for elective deferrals reaches $9500], subject to a special catch-up election. The defined contribution Section 415 limits (discussed on p. 360) also apply to TSA plans, as well as to qualified plans.

There are two ways of approaching contributions to a TSA plan by eligible employees:

1. A salary increase for the employee, or

2. If the employer cannot afford to make contributions in addition to an employee's regular compensation, the employee can still do so by arranging for a salary reduction—in effect, a plan using before-tax dollars. (This probably is the more common approach.)

Example of Contribution via Salary Increase.   Assume that an eligible employee earns $30,000 per year, the employer will contribute to a TSA plan on the employee's behalf under the salary increase arrangement, and the employer has no other retirement plan for the employee and has made no past contributions. In this case, up to 20 percent per year of the employee's salary ($6000) could be invested this way. The 20 percent maximum is called the "exclusion allowance."

Example of Contribution via Salary Reduction.   Under a salary reduction arrangement, the exclusion allowance is 20 percent of salary *after* it has been reduced by the amount of the contribution to the TSA plan. The maximum annual contribution can be determined by taking ⅙ of the employee's unreduced salary, or ⅙ of $30,000 = $5,000, using the above facts. The resulting figure will be 20 percent of the employee's reduced salary (20% × $25,000 = $5,000).

The advantages of using *before-tax dollars* to save for retirement were illustrated on p. 366 of Chap. 12 and would also apply to TSA plans.

Effect of Contributions
to Qualified Retirement Plans

If a participant under a TSA program also participates in a qualified retirement plan or state retirement plan (in the case of public school teachers), any *employer* contributions to the plan reduce the employee's TSA exclusion allowance.

Past Service

An employee's annual exclusion allowance can be increased if he or she has past service with the organization. This would increase the employee's maximum exclusion allowance by giving him or her credit for past service with the employer.

Taxation of Distributions

Benefits from a TSA plan are taxed as ordinary income when received by a participant. However, tax-free rollovers from TSA plans to IRAs are allowed. TSA plans now also are subject to the minimum distribution rules (subject to a grandfather provision) and the 10 percent excise tax on premature distributions (subject to a grandfather provision), and they must be nondiscriminatory.

Nonqualified Deferred Compensation

A deferred compensation arrangement is an agreement whereby an employer promises to pay an employee in the future for services rendered today. The plan usually is set up to provide for salary continuation over a period of years following retirement or other termination of employment. Such payments are referred to as "deferred compensation" because they represent compensation earned currently but with payment postponed to the future. They are called "nonqualified" because they do not meet the requirements for a tax-favored "qualified" retirement plan. They are usually given to highly paid executives.

Why Deferred Compensation?

Some businesses do not have "qualified" retirement plans to offer their employees. But many others, which have such plans covering the bulk of their employees, may still want to provide additional benefits for certain key people that would not be permissible under "qualified" plans. Also, some highly paid executives would like to defer income from their peak earning years to some future date when they expect to be in a lower tax bracket—usually at retirement.

Deferred Compensation Arrangements

This is done by having the key executive enter into an employment contract with the employer stipulating that specific payments will be made to the executive or his or her beneficiaries in the event of the executive's death, disability, retirement, or other circumstances. The deferred compensation agreement may further provide that the key executive will continue in the employment of the company and may also obligate the executive, within limits, to refrain from engaging in a competitive business and/or to be available for consultation after retirement. However, such forfeiture provisions are no longer necessary to get the desired tax deferral in unfunded arrangements so long as the receipt of the benefits is subject to substantial limitations (such as the lapse of time).

Note, however, that from the executive's viewpoint, the benefits of such a plan are deferred into the future and the executive cannot get them in advance even if his or her circumstances should change. Also, the employer's obligation to provide the deferred benefits *cannot be secured in all events for the employee's protection* by any outside financial device (such as a life insurance policy) without adverse tax consequences (except for the use of so-called rabbi trusts, discussed next). However, the employer itself can informally fund its obligation by carrying life insurance on the employee's life, but here the policy becomes part of the general assets of the employer and cannot be earmarked specifically for the purpose of carrying out the employer's obligations under the deferred compensation agreement. Thus, the employee generally must rely on the employer's future financial strength and willingness to carry out its obligations under the deferred compensation agreement.

This security issue has caused employees covered by these and other kinds of nonqualified retirement benefits to seek certain limited security arrangements for their interests in nonqualified plans. As the economy has become more uncertain, interest in these arrangements seems to have intensified. The commonly used arrangement in this area is the so-called *rabbi trust*. This is an irrevocable trust set up by an employer to provide nonqualified retirement and other benefits to selected employees. However, the trust assets remain subject to the claims of the employer's general creditors in the event of the employer's bankruptcy or insolvency. This latter contingency results in no taxable income to the covered employees because it is viewed by the IRS as a substantial risk of forfeiture for income tax purposes.

Supplemental Executive Retirement Plans

In addition to the deferred compensation arrangements discussed in the previous section, supplemental executive retirement plans (SERPs) are also established for some executives. As noted on p. 360 of Chap. 12, there are maximum limits on the benefits any employee may receive from a company's qualified retirement plan (the Section 415 limits), but ERISA does allow so-called excess plans to pay the difference between this maximum and the employee's full benefit as determined by the plan's benefit formula. SERPs are set up to incorporate ERISA excess plans and/or to pay additional benefits on top of ERISA excess plans to increase the level of retirement income for executives beyond the level contemplated by the basic retirement plan benefit formula. Such plans also are nonqualified retirement plans and hence are offered only to selected employees on a discriminatory basis.

Employee Stock Plans

Although they are perhaps not as well known as other types of benefit programs, employee stock plans are important for a number of people in their personal financial planning. Since this can be a very complex subject, it is only briefly introduced here.

In general, the basic types of such plans that receive separate favorable tax treatment under the tax law are *employee stock purchase plans* (covered in Section 423 of the IRC) and *incentive stock options* (covered in Section 422 of the IRC). Thus, these are referred to as "statutory stock options" in this book, because as long as certain requirements of the tax law are met, their holders can receive various kinds of favorable federal income tax treatment with respect to the granting or exercise of these rights or options.

Employee Stock Purchase Plans

These are arrangements under which all full-time employees meeting certain eligibility requirements are allowed to buy stock in their employer corporation at a discount. The discount option price cannot be less than 85 percent of the value of the stock. The essence of employee stock purchase plans is that they are "nondiscriminatory," in that they do not favor just the highly paid executives of the corporation. In fact, no employee who owns 5 percent or more of the stock of the corporation can be granted such an option.

Incentive Stock Options (ISOs)

These options were created by the Economic Recovery Tax Act of 1981 (ERTA). They may be made available at the employer's choice to only some employees, normally certain highly compensated executives or employees of the corporation. Hence, these options are "discriminatory" in nature.

A number of requirements must be met under IRC Section 422 before a plan can qualify as an incentive stock option plan. For example, under such a plan the term of the option may not exceed 10 years, the option price must equal or exceed the value of the stock when the option was granted, no disposition can be made of the stock by the person within two years from the granting of the option or within one year from the transfer of the stock to him or her (after exercise of the option), the option must be nontransferable (except by will or by inheritance at death), and the maximum value of stock for which an employee may exercise options in any one year generally may not exceed $100,000, among other requirements.

The main tax advantage of ISOs to the recipient is that there is no regular income tax levied at the grant or at the exercise of the option by the employee. (However, as noted on pp. 304–305 of Chap. 11, the "bargain element" upon exercise of an ISO (i.e., the difference between the fair market value of the stock at exercise and the option price) is a tax preference for individual AMT purposes.) The employee is taxed only when he or she sells the stock purchased under the option plan, and then any gain is taxed as a capital gain. The capital gain would be the difference between the option price (the income tax basis of the option stock) and the stock's fair market value on the date of its sale. On the other hand, the employer gets no income tax deduction for a trade or business expense (i.e., compensation expense) arising out of an ISO (or an employee stock purchase plan).

While ISOs are still outstanding and being granted, their popularity as an executive compensation technique has declined in recent years. This may be because of the limitations imposed on their terms and use by the tax code, the fact that taking returns as capital gains is less attractive than it was before the 1986 tax law, and the lack of any income tax deduction for the employer from their use. Instead, nonqualified stock options (NQSO) have tended to become more popular.

Nonqualified Stock Options

Nonqualified stock options (NQSOs) are stock options that do not meet the tax law requirements for ISOs and so are taxed on the basis of general tax law principles concerning compensation. Correspondingly, NQSOs can have any terms decided upon by the parties and are not limited in the amount of stock subject to such options exercisable by an employee in any one year (as are ISOs). Hence, NQSOs are considerably more flexible for employers and selected employees as a compensation arrangement. Like ISOs, they are granted only to certain employees, who are usually highly compensated executives, and hence are inherently "discriminatory."

Since they are not special statutory plans meeting specific tax law requirements (like ISOs), the tax treatment of NQSOs differs considerably from that of ISOs. In the case of NQSOs, there usually would be no taxable event (i.e., gross income) upon grant of the option, but upon the exercise of the option by the employee (and transfer of the stock to the employee), the employee would receive gross ordinary income (as compensation) for regular federal income tax purposes equal to the difference between the fair market value of the stock at exercise and the option price (or the so-called bargain element noted previously). However, at exercise (when the employee realizes gross income), the employer correspondingly gets an income tax deduction as a trade or business expense equal to the gross ordinary income realized by the employee. The employee's income tax basis in the stock received at exercise then is its fair market value at exercise. Any future appreciation or depreciation in the stock's value upon sale or exchange is a capital gain or capital loss, just as for any other securities acquired by the person involved.

Restricted Stock and Other Plans

A wide variety of other kinds of stock and similar plans are used by employers to compensate their executives and other highly compensated employees. Like NQSOs, these plans must operate under the general principles of tax law relating to compensation.

Restricted stock plans are arrangements whereby a corporation grants stock (or stock options) to an employee (or someone rendering services to the corporation), but under which the grant of the stock is subject to a substantial risk of forfeiture (such as the grant's being contingent on the employee's staying with the employer for a certain number of years or on certain profit goals being met by the corporation). In this case, the employee receives gross ordinary income (as compensation) in the year in which the employee's rights to the stock are first not subject to the substantial risk of forfeiture or are transferable. The gross income to the employee is measured by the fair market value of the stock at that time (i.e., when the substantial risk of forfeiture ends or the employee's rights in the stock become transferable) less any cost to the employee.[5]

However, since it is possible that the value of the stock (or stock option) at the time of its grant under a restricted stock plan may be relatively low but may increase substantially in the future (which, in fact, may be the expectation of those involved in the plan), an election is allowed under Section 83 of the IRC to tax the value of the stock at the time of its grant to the employee. This is referred to as a Section 83(b) election and allows the person rendering the services to elect to include the then value of the stock (at the time of grant or transfer) less any amount paid for the stock in the person's gross income for federal income tax purposes. However, if the

---

[5] These tax principles are governed mainly by Section 83 of the IRC, which is entitled "Property Transferred in Connection with Performance of Services."

stock should subsequently be forfeited, the person gets no income tax deduction for the forfeiture. Thus, the person receiving such stock must make a planning decision with respect to this election. The election may be advantageous if the person can pay tax currently on a much lower value than it will be when the substantial risk of forfeiture ends. Of course, this assumes that the stock value will be much higher in the future. This option also may be attractive if tax rates on ordinary income (particularly for higher-income taxpayers) are expected to increase in the future. On the other hand, the risks of a Section 83(b) election are: the necessity of paying some tax now rather than deferring; the possibility that the stock will be forfeited, with the loss of the tax paid and no corresponding tax deduction; and the possibility that the value of the stock will go down in the future rather than up. The decision seems to rest with a balancing of these factors, given the facts and circumstances of the particular case.

The employer takes an income tax deduction with respect to restricted stock at the time and in the amount that the employee takes the value as gross income.

There are a number of other compensation plans involving stock, benefits based on stock or stock values, and similar arrangements. Examples include stock appreciation rights (SARs), phantom stock, and various kinds of performance units. This is a complex field, and a complete discussion of all these plans is beyond the scope of this book.

In recent years, there has been considerable interest in the various kinds of stock options and other stock plans as methods for compensating selected highly compensated executives and perhaps other high-income persons. These plans can be very attractive to such executives for tax and economic reasons, as noted in the preceding discussion.

Some companies also use nondiscriminatory employee stock purchase plans (noted on p. 404) to encourage their employees to buy company stock and thus become more closely identified with the company's goals. The plans normally are attractive for employees, because the stock option price is often 85 percent of the stock price at the beginning or at the end of the stock purchase period (whichever is lower), and at the end of the stock purchase period (often one or two years) the participant often can decide whether to exercise the option (perhaps at up to a 15 percent discount) or take his or her accumulated contributions to the plan in cash (often with interest). These plans (somewhat like qualified savings plans) also may provide many employees with a convenient (payroll deduction) method for saving and investment.

On the other hand, it must be recognized that while all these various kinds of employee stock plans and similar arrangements can be quite attractive when the price of a company's stock is rising, the reverse can be true when the price is falling. One danger in these plans is that employees can become too heavily concentrated in their employer's stock. Thus, the principles of investment diversification, particularly by kinds of investments, as discussed on pp. 209–214 of Chap. 7, can be particularly important with regard to acquiring stock or stock rights under these plans.

There may be a number of *financial planning issues* to consider with regard to these plans and options, including, among others:

- Whether or not employees should participate in their employer's employee stock purchase plan offerings (This, of course, depends on the terms of the plan and the employer stock, but, as just noted, these plans often are advantageous, and flexible as to whether to finally take the stock or not, for employees.)
- When to exercise stock options
- Whether to change an ISO into a NQSO by breaking an ISO requirement
- How to secure the funds with which to exercise options
- How to pay any taxes due on exercise or other events concerning these plans
- Whether to make a Section 83(b) election with regard to restricted stock or other plans
- How to maintain investment diversification in light of possibly favorable terms for acquiring more and more employer stock

Survivor Income Benefits

Survivor income benefit plans are distinguishable from traditional employer-sponsored group life insurance plans in that a benefit is payable only to certain specified dependents of the employee and only if these dependents survive the employee. Moreover, the benefit is payable in installments and, as a rule, only for the period that a dependency status continues to exist. While this approach may be logical in concept, it is not widely used in employee benefit plans today. Instead, the approach generally used to cover the exposure of the premature death of employees in employee benefit plans is group term life insurance.

PART 5
Estate and Tax Planning

14

Estate Planning Principles

Estate planning can be defined as arranging for the transfer of a person's property from one generation to the next so as to achieve, so far as possible, the person's objective for his or her family and perhaps others. In our tax-oriented economy, tax minimization often is an important motivator for estate planning. And, in fact, proper planning can reduce taxes substantially. Tax saving, however, is not the only goal of estate planning and should not be overemphasized.

Before we go on to talk about specific estate planning techniques, let us review briefly the basic objectives of estate planning for most people.

Objectives of Estate Planning

Estate owners should ask themselves, "What am I really trying to accomplish through estate planning, given my own circumstances?" This general question, in turn, can be broken down into a number of specific estate planning objectives, some or all of which apply to most people.

1. Determining who will be the estate owner's heirs or beneficiaries and how much each will receive. This depends mainly on the estate owner's family and personal situation.

2. Planning adequate financial support for the estate owner's dependents. This means providing adequate income (after taxes) for dependents to live on, as well as capital on which they can draw in emergencies.

3. Reducing estate transfer costs (i.e., death taxes, expenses of administration, and the like) to a minimum, consistent with the estate owner's other objectives.

4. Providing sufficient liquid assets for the estate to meet its obligations (i.e., adequate estate liquidity). This often becomes critical when an estate consists primarily of closely held business interests or similar unmarketable property.

5. Planning for the disposition of closely held business interests.

6. Deciding who is to settle the estate and how the property is to be administered. This involves selecting the executor or co-executors and deciding on investment and property management.

7. Planning how the estate owner's property is to be distributed. Property can be passed on to heirs through arrangements that take effect during a person's lifetime (called "living" or "inter vivos" transfers) or by transfers that take effect only at death. Most estate plans use several methods of transferring wealth—including both lifetime transfers and transfers at death.

These methods of estate transfer will be described later, but for now they can be outlined briefly as follows:

1. Lifetime methods of estate transfer
   a. Joint ownership of property with right of survivorship
   b. Lifetime gifts
   c. Life insurance proceeds paid to others
   d. Other beneficiary arrangements (e.g., death benefits payable under pension plans, profit-sharing plans, HR-10 plans, IRA plans, tax-sheltered annuities, deferred compensation agreements, and non-qualified individual annuities)
   e. Irrevocable living trusts
   f. Revocable living trusts
   g. Business buy-sell agreements
   h. Exercise of powers of appointment (and possibly powers of attorney)
2. Estate transfer at death
   a. Outright by will
   b. Testamentary trusts (i.e., trusts established under the will)
   c. Intestate distribution

Property and Property Interests

An estate can consist of a variety of different kinds of property and property interests. Therefore, let us review briefly what some of the more important of these are.

In general, *property* is anything that can be owned. Basically, there are two kinds of property—real property and personal property. *Real property* (or real estate) is land and everything attached to the land with the intention that it be part of the land. *Personal property* is all other kinds of property. Personal property can be *tangible*—property that has physical substance, such as a car, boat, or furniture—or it can be *intangible*—property that does not have physical substance, such as a stock certificate, bond, bank deposit, or life insurance policy.

Forms of Property Ownership

Property can be owned in various ways, and this can greatly affect a person's estate planning. Here are some of the common ways.

Outright Ownership. This is the highest form of ownership and is what people generally mean when they say that someone "owns" property. Outright owners of property hold it in their own names and can deal with it during their lifetimes. They can sell it, use it as collateral, or give it away. They can also pass it on to their heirs as they wish (within some broad limits that will be mentioned shortly). Examples of outright ownership are almost limitless—sole ownership of cars, furniture, boats, furs, jewelry, etc.; ownership in one's own name of stock, bonds, bank accounts, and other accounts; and ownership of a life insurance policy.

Joint Ownership. This exists when two or more persons have ownership rights in property. The more important kinds of joint ownership are as follows.

Joint Tenancy (with Right of Survivorship). The outstanding characteristic of joint tenancy with right of survivorship (WROS) is that if one of the joint owners dies, interest in the property passes automatically (by operation of law) to the other joint owner(s). This is the meaning of "with right of survivorship." Thus, if John and Mary own their residence as joint tenants and John dies, Mary automatically owns the residence (now in her own name) by right of survivorship. The same would be true if John and his brother Frank owned some investment real estate as joint tenants. Joint tenancy can exist between anyone—not just husband and wife.

During the lifetime of the joint tenants, the survivorship aspect of a joint tenancy can be destroyed by one of the joint tenants. Thus, if John and Frank own property as joint tenants, and John sells his interest to Harry, Frank and Harry then own the property as tenants in common (described below). Similarly, if John's creditors were to attach his interest in the property and have it sold to meet their claims, the purchaser and Frank would own the property as tenants in common.

Tenancy by the Entirety. In some states, this form of ownership exists when property is held jointly by a husband and wife only. It is similar to a joint tenancy, but there are some significant differences. First, tenancy by the entirety can exist only between husband and wife. Second, in many states the survivorship rights in it cannot be terminated except with the consent of both parties. Finally, depending on the law in the particular state, the husband may have full control over the property during their joint lives and be entitled to all the income from it.

It is a common error to assume that all the property owned by a husband or wife somehow is held "jointly" by them. This is not true. Except in community property states, where special rules apply, only property that is specifically titled or received as being held as joint tenants or tenants by the entirety is so held. Other property can be owned outright by the husband alone, by the wife alone, or even by either of them jointly with others. Survivorship rights apply only to joint tenants or tenants by the entirety. Thus, a wife may not automatically get all her husband's property at his death unless that is specifically planned for.

The mere fact that property is held as joint tenants or tenants by the entirety does not mean that it has to stay that way. The joint owners can agree to split up their interests if they want. Sometimes holding property as joint owners (WROS) is desirable, but in other cases it may not be. It all depends on the circumstances. The advantages and disadvantages of joint ownership are discussed in Chap. 16.

Other Joint Interests.   There are two common forms of joint ownership that involve the right of survivorship which are very similar to joint tenancy but are not quite the same.

1. *Joint bank accounts.* Many people have joint checking or savings accounts. Typically, either party can make deposits and either party can withdraw all or part of the account. When one party dies, the survivor becomes the sole owner of the account by operation of law. This is not exactly a joint tenancy, because a joint tenant can get at only his or her share of the property.

2. *Jointly owned government savings bonds.* Many persons have purchased government savings bonds (such as Series EE bonds) in a way that creates survivorship rights with another. Such bonds can be registered *in co-ownership form* and held in the name of "A or B." This means that either A or B can cash in the bonds during his or her lifetime, and if one of them dies, the other becomes sole owner. Such bonds can also be registered *in the name of "A payable on his (or her) death to B."* In this case, only A can cash in the bonds while he (or she) is living, but B becomes sole owner if he (or she) survives A and if A has not cashed them in previously.

The above forms of joint ownership—joint tenancy (WROS), tenancy by the entirety, joint bank accounts, and jointly owned government savings bonds—are common ways of holding property with family members. The survivorship feature makes this a natural and convenient method for transferring the property to the other owner(s) at one owner's death.

Tenancy in Common.   The main difference between this and the previous kinds of joint ownership is that tenants in common do not have the right of survivorship with respect to the property concerned. If John and his brother Frank own the investment real estate equally as tenants in common, and John dies, his half of the real estate goes to his heirs as if he had owned it outright. Frank, of course, retains his half interest. Tenants in common can have different proportionate interests in property. John and Frank could have 75 and 25 percent interests in the real estate, for example. Joint tenants and tenants by the entirety always have equal interests.

Community Property.   Some states (Arizona, California, Idaho, Louisiana, Nevada, New Mexico, Texas, and Washington) are community property states; the others are referred to as "common law states." In the so-called common law states, the forms of property ownership discussed above apply. But in the eight community property states the situation is quite different with respect to property owned by husbands and wives.

In community property states, husbands and wives can own separate property and community property. While the laws of the community property states are not uniform, *separate property* generally consists of property that a husband or wife owns at the time of marriage, property that each individually inherits or receives as a gift, and property purchased with individual funds. This property remains separate property after marriage, and the owner-spouse can deal with it as he or she chooses. Income from separate property may remain separate property or become community property, depending on the community property state involved.

Community property, on the other hand, generally consists of property that either or both spouses acquire during marriage. Each spouse has an undivided one-half interest in their community property. While the husband and wife are both alive, the applicable state community property law determines who has the rights of management and control over the community property. However, upon his or her death, each spouse can dispose of only his or her half of the community property by will. Since community property laws are not uniform, people should be advised as to how their state's law operates. However, even those living in non–community property states can have community property. This can happen if spouses once lived in a community property state and acquired property there that became community property. *Such property remains community property even after the owners move to a common law state.* However, property owned by spouses in a common law state does not become community property when they move to a community property state.

The new and controversial Uniform Marital Property Act (UMPA) also generally provides that property acquired during marriage, with certain exceptions, is owned one-half by each spouse. This basically is a community property system. To date, only Wisconsin has adopted the UMPA.

Other Property Interests

There are other interests in property that are commonly involved in estate planning. These include legal interests and equitable interests, life interests (or estates) and remainder interests, present interests and future interests, and powers of appointment. An example can help explain these concepts.

> By his will, A leaves his property to the XYZ Bank *in trust* to keep it invested and to distribute the net income from it to his wife, B, if she survives him, during her lifetime. At B's death, or at A's death if B does not survive him, the property is to go outright in equal shares to C and D (A's adult children) or their issue.

This example, incidentally, illustrates a will for the husband, with a trust for his wife for life and then distribution to his children—a reasonably common arrangement.

Legal Interests and Equitable Interests.   In this example, upon A's death, the XYZ Bank technically becomes legal owner of the property that passes into the trust. But the bank must exercise the ownership, as trustee, according to the terms of the trust agreement. B, C, and D have equitable (or beneficial) interests in the property, since it is held for their benefit.

Life Interests and Remainder Interests.   A *life interest in property* entitles the holder to the income from or the use of the property, or a portion of the property, for his or her lifetime. The *remainder interest* (or remainderman) is entitled to the property itself after a life interest has ended.

In the example above, B (A's wife) has a life interest in the trust property. But her interest will terminate upon her death, and then C and D (or their heirs if they are deceased) will get the property. Thus, C and D have remainder interests. Life interests often are created by trusts, but there can also be legal life estates without a trust.

Present Interests and Future Interests.   A *present interest* exists in property when the holder has a present or immediate right to the use, possession, or enjoyment of the property or property interest. In a *future interest,* on the other hand, the right to the use or enjoyment of the property or property interest is postponed to some future time or is in the hands of someone other than the holder.

In the above example, upon A's death, B has a present interest in the trust income because she has the immediate right to it for her lifetime. C and D have future interests because their rights to the property are postponed until B's death. As we shall see later, the concepts of present and future interests are important in connection with gift taxes.

Powers of Appointment.　Powers of appointment are commonly used in estate planning. In general, a "power of appointment" is a power or right given to a person (called the "donee of the power") that enables the donee to designate, sometimes within certain limits, who is to get certain property that is made subject to the power. In a nutshell, a power is the right to "appoint" property to someone.

The basic nontax purpose of powers of appointment is to postpone and delegate the decision as to who is to get property until a later time when the circumstances about people can be better known. This can result in better decision making in estate planning. Powers also can be used to achieve estate tax advantages, as is explained later.

There are several kinds of powers of appointment, including (1) general powers and nongeneral powers (also called special or limited powers), and (2) powers exercised by deed, by will, and by deed or will.

The difference between general and nongeneral powers is important for tax-saving purposes. A "general power" is a power to appoint property to the person having the power (i.e., the donee), the donee's estate, the donee's creditors, or the creditors of the donee's estate. In other words, a general power really means that donees can appoint the property to anyone they want, including themselves or their estate. It is close to owning the property. For federal estate tax purposes, the property will be included in the estate of someone who has a general power over it.

A nongeneral power of appointment allows donees to appoint the property only to certain persons who are not the donees themselves, their estate, their creditors, or the creditors of their estate. The possession of a nongeneral power over property at a person's death does *not* result in the property's being included in the estate for federal estate taxation. This is the big tax advantage of nongeneral powers.

When donees of either a general or nongeneral power can appoint the property only at their death, it is referred to as a power exercisable *by will* (or a *testamentary power*). A power exercisable *by deed* is one where donees can appoint the property only during their lifetime. The broadest power in this respect is one exercisable *by deed or will*, which is one exercisable both ways.

All these forms of property ownership and property interests can apply to an almost endless variety of kinds of estate assets. The general objective, then, is to plan for the transfer of this property to the estate owner's family so as to avoid the common pitfalls of estate planning.

Marital Rights in Property.   Almost all states have adopted equitable distribution statutes applying to so-called marital property in the event of divorce. (These statutes are incidental to the "no-fault divorce" concept.) Under such equitable distribution statutes, the appropriate court has the power to divide a divorcing couple's "marital property" between the parties in an "equitable manner" according to certain factors specified in state law, regardless of how title to the "marital property" is actually held.

What is defined as "marital property" can vary among the states, but—only as a generalization—it may include all property acquired during marriage from the earnings of either spouse, with certain exceptions. In order to avoid the effects of these equitable distribution statutes or other divorce laws, persons with property who are about to be married are increasingly entering into *prenuptial or antenuptial agreements* that specify how their property is to be divided in the event of divorce. Most states now recognize such prenuptial agreements, provided they meet certain standards.

What Is Meant by the "Estate"?

This sounds like a simple question, but there are several different ways of looking at an "estate." There is the *probate estate,* the *gross estate for federal estate taxation,* the *estate for state death tax purposes,* and the "*net*" *estate* that actually is available to the heirs. These "estates" often are not the same.

Probate Estate

The "probate estate" includes the property that is handled and distributed by a personal representative (executor if there is a will, or administrator if there is not) upon a person's death. Generally speaking, it is the property that can be disposed of by will, including:

1. Property owned outright in one's own name

2. Interest in property held as a tenant in common with others

3. Life insurance (or other death proceeds) payable to one's estate at death

4. The person's one-half of community property

It is sometimes argued that having property in a probate estate is bad. This is not necessarily true, and it really depends on the circumstances. There are, however, some disadvantages in leaving property so that it will be part of a person's probate estate, such as the following:

1. There will be *delay* in settling the estate and hence in the distribution of the property to the heirs.

2. The *costs* of administering the estate (executor's fees, attorney's fees, etc.) usually are based largely on the probate estate. These costs may not be levied, or at least not levied in the same amount, against assets that pass outside the probate estate.

3. *Creditors* can "get at" assets in the probate estate.

4. The probate estate can be made *public knowledge.*

5. Disgruntled heirs may seek to *contest* a will and hence "get at" probate assets.

6. Sometimes death taxes can be increased, depending on the property and/or the state involved.

Some common ways of arranging property so that it will go outside a person's probate estate are

1. Life insurance (or other death proceeds) made payable to a beneficiary other than the insured's estate (e.g., spouse, children, a trust)

2. Jointly owned property (WROS)

3. Joint bank accounts, government savings bonds, and the like

4. Living trusts with the trust property passing to the trust beneficiaries after the creator's death

5. Outright lifetime gifts

In all these cases, the property either goes, or has gone, directly to the beneficiary, joint owner, or other donee at the person's death without ever passing through an executor's hands.

But just having property bypass the probate estate is not an estate planning panacea. Most people have a probate estate. First of all, any property owned outright at death must pass through the probate estate. Many people do not want to part with ownership or control over property until they die. Also, estate owners usually want their executor to have adequate liquid assets to pay the claims, expenses, and taxes that will be owed by their estate.

Gross Estate for Federal Estate Tax Purposes

Since planning for the federal estate tax can be important for a number of persons, the "gross estate" for federal tax purposes is significant in estate planning. The gross estate is defined by the tax law and is the starting point for calculating how much federal estate tax the estate must pay.

It includes, among other items, the property in the probate estate; life insurance the insured owns on his or her own life; and one-half of property owned jointly (WROS) by a husband and wife and all the value of property owned jointly (WROS) by others than husband and wife, except to the extent that the survivor can show that he or she contributed to the purchase price of the property. Thus, a great deal of property can be in the gross estate that is not in the probate estate.

Naturally, there are deductions that can be taken from the gross estate to arrive at the taxable estate on which the tentative federal estate tax is calculated. Credits also are available against the estate tax itself. The calculation of the federal estate tax is illustrated in Chap. 15.

State Death Tax Value

All states except Nevada have some form of death tax. Some have inheritance taxes, which are levied on the right to *receive* property by inheritance; some have estate taxes; and some have both. An *inheritance tax* is different in concept from an *estate tax* (such as the federal estate tax), which is levied on the right to *give* property. While both are *death taxes,* there are some practical differences between them.

Inheritance tax laws vary considerably among the states, so it is necessary to check the state law of a person's residence (domicile) to see how it will apply. Banks, insurance companies, and others may have available brief pamphlets explaining the local inheritance tax law. As noted above, many states have estate taxes, and this is the trend in state death taxation.

Depending on the state, some property that will be included in a person's gross estate for federal estate tax purposes may not be taxable under the local inheritance tax. Some possible examples are life insurance, certain jointly owned property, employee benefits, and property subject to powers of appointment.

This means that generally both the federal estate tax and the state inheritance and/or estate tax must be considered in estate planning. State death taxes can be significant, particularly as a percentage of more moderate estates.

The "Net" Estate to One's Heirs

"Net" estate to one's heirs is what most people really are concerned about. They want to know what will be available to support their family. Basically, this "net" estate consists of the assets that will go to one's heirs after the payment of the costs of dying (debts, claims, administration expenses, and taxes).

An illustration may be helpful at this point. Let us return to our friends George and Mary Able, whom we first met in Chap. 1. Briefly, their asset picture looks like this:

Property George owns outright in his own name:	
His employer's common stock	$320,000
Other listed common stock	40,000
Mutual fund shares	10,000
Money market fund	40,000
Tangible personal property	30,000
	$440,000
Property George and Mary own jointly (WROS):	
Principal residence	180,000
Summer home	100,000
Bank accounts	30,000
	$310,000
Life insurance that George owns on his own life:	
Group term life insurance, payable to Mary in a lump sum	225,000
Individual life insurance, payable to Mary in a lump sum	200,000
	$425,000
Other employee benefits:	
Profit-sharing plan death benefit, payable to George's estate in one sum	300,000
Thrift plan death benefit, payable to George's estate in one sum	100,000
	$400,000
In addition, Mary owns some tangible personal property in her own name and expects a reasonably substantial inheritance from her parents.	

If George were to die today, his *probate estate* would be $840,000. This amount includes the $440,000 of property George owns in his own name and the $300,000 of profit-sharing funds and $100,000 of thrift plan funds payable to his estate. The rest of the assets pass to Mary or the children outside of George's probate estate.

Again assuming that George were to die today, his *gross estate for federal estate tax purposes* would be $1,420,000.[1] Because of the availability of the federal estate tax marital deduction and the unified transfer tax credit (both explained in Chap. 15), there would be no federal estate tax payable as George's estate now stands. However, better planning of

---

[1] This assumes that only one-half of the $310,000 in property that George and Mary own jointly would be included in his gross estate.

George's estate could result in lower estate taxes on *Mary's estate* upon her subsequent death.

Let us assume that George and Mary live in a state whose inheritance tax does not apply to property held jointly by husband and wife and to life insurance and employee benefits payable to a beneficiary other than the insured's estate. Under these assumptions, the amount of their property for *state inheritance tax purposes* upon George's death would be $840,000.

Now, let us see what George can transmit to his family—his net estate. This is estimated as follows:

Total assets (including jointly owned property)		$1,575,000
Less:		
George's debts (including the full amount of mortgages on homes)	$100,000	
Estimated funeral and estate administration expenses	45,000	
Estimated federal estate tax payable	—0—	
Estimated state death tax payable	47,000	
Total estate "shrinkage"	$192,000	−192,000
Net estate to George's family		$1,383,000

Of this $1,383,000, probably about $1,123,000 could produce investment income for the family and liquid assets for family needs, such as education expenses and emergency needs ($1,383,000 less the $230,000 of equity in the homes and the $30,000 of George's tangible personal property).

Settling the Estate

When a person dies, what happens to his (or her) property (estate)? This depends on whether the person died *intestate*—that is, without having made a valid will—or whether a *valid will* was made. Most people can make a valid will to dispose of their property if they want to do so.

If someone dies intestate, the probate estate is distributed according to the applicable state intestate law. In this case, an administrator, who is appointed by a court, handles the estate settlement. The estate owner has no voice in who will receive the property or who will be administrator; this depends on state law and the court. In essence, estate owners have an estate plan "created by the law," rather than themselves, when they die intestate.

People who leave valid wills, on the other hand, are the "captains" of their own estate plans. Through the will, they can determine who gets the property and can name an executor. Almost without exception, *people with property should execute wills* if they can.

Intestate Distribution

The laws of intestate distribution vary among the states. The surviving spouse first is entitled to his or her statutory share of the estate or the comparable common law rights of a surviving wife (dower) or husband (courtesy), depending upon the particular state's law. Then, a typical order of intestate distribution to persons other than the surviving spouse would be (1) lineal descendants (children, grandchildren, etc.), if any, then (2) parents, if any living, then (3) brothers and sisters and their descendants, if any, then (4) other collateral kindred (grandparents, uncles, aunts, etc.). If by chance a person leaves no one capable of inheriting, the property goes (escheats) to the state.

To take a simple example of intestate distribution according to one state's law, assume a family consisting of Husband; Wife; Son, age 24, with two minor children of his own; Daughter, age 16; and Son, age 12. Husband dies without a will and leaves a probate estate of $120,000 (consisting of personal property he owned outright and death benefits payable to his estate) after payment of claims against his estate. The intestate distribution would be as follows:

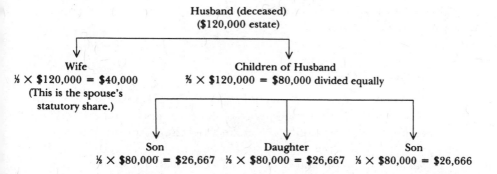

Suppose now that the 24-year-old son had died before his father. In this event, the deceased son's minor children would inherit their dead father's share equally ($13,334 each). Legal guardians would have to be appointed to manage property inherited by minor children.

Problems with Intestate Distribution

We noted above that people normally should make a will. The reason is that there are a number of problems that can arise when a person dies intestate.

1. Perhaps the most important is that intestate distribution is not specifically chosen by the estate owner. Thus, it may not be appropriate to the situation. For example, the wife's share often is inadequate (only one-third of the estate in the previous example). And other persons who may need support, such as daughters-in-law or stepchildren, are omitted completely.

2. Beneficiaries receive their inheritances outright, without regard to their individual capacities to manage the property. Guardians must be appointed for minor beneficiaries, and trusts cannot be used for the heirs.

3. The estate owner cannot select his or her executor. Also, in a will a person can excuse an executor from having to post bond with a commercial surety and thus save the estate the surety bond premiums.

4. Estate taxes may be increased because the surviving spouse's share probably will not be large enough to take full advantage of allowable estate tax deductions (see Chap. 15 for an explanation of the estate marital deduction).

5. Estate owners cannot delay distribution of property to their heirs even though they may be minors or otherwise not able to handle it, as they could through a trust under a will.

In view of these problems, it is indeed surprising to see the number of people who die intestate.

Distribution by Will

A "will" is a legally enforceable declaration of what people want done with their property and their instructions as to other matters when they die. The will does not take effect until the person's (testator's) death and may be changed or revoked at any time up to that death. Thus, a will is referred to as "ambulatory" until the maker's death. To be effective, a will must be executed in accordance with the legal requirements of a valid will. An estate owner's attorney will see that these requirements are met.

The importance of the will in an estate plan depends on how much of the estate is going to pass under the will (the probate estate) and how much will pass via lifetime-type transfers. In any event, however, it is important for both husband and wife to have wills for a complete estate plan.

Spouse's Elective Share

With certain limitations, people can leave their property by will to whomever they like. One important limitation, however, is that in many states a husband or wife cannot deprive his or her surviving spouse of the surviving spouse's so-called elective share of the estate under state law. This is referred to as the *spouse's right to elect against the will*. Taking against the will does not deny the will's validity but simply involves the spouse's taking his or her elective share allowed under state law rather than what is left to him or her under the will. To avoid the effect of a surviving spouse's elective share under state law, persons with property who are about to marry may enter into prenuptial agreements under which each party relinquishes in whole or in part his or her rights to the other's property at death. (Of course, a prenuptial agreement can also deal with property rights incident to divorce, as explained on p. 418.)

Steps in Estate Settlement

What does a deceased's personal representative (executor under a will or administrator of a person dying intestate) do in settling the estate? After the executor's or administrator's appointment, the following are the basic functions the personal representative performs. Performing these functions can be rather routine or very complex, depending on the circumstances of the estate.

1. Assembling of the property belonging to the estate
2. Safekeeping, safeguarding, and insuring of estate property during the period of estate settlement
3. Temporary management of estate property during the period of estate settlement, including carrying on or dealing with business interests
4. Payment of estate debts, taxes, and expenses
5. Accounting for the estate administration
6. Making distribution of the net estate to the proper heirs

In addition to these formal steps, we should also mention the valuable personal advice and services an executor can render to the deceased's family at this time which is particularly difficult for them. Estate owners should consider all these factors when selecting their executor(s).

For performing these functions, the executor is entitled to reasonable compensation, which is deducted from the estate. Executors' fees vary, but a reasonably typical commission schedule used by a commercial bank for normal services as an executor might be:

Calculated on the gross value
of the estate that passes
through the executor's hands
(i.e., the probate estate)

Gross value	Executor's commission
$25,000 or less	4%
$25,000 to $150,000	3½% plus $125
$150,000 to $300,000	3% plus $875
$300,000 or over	2% plus $3875
(Minimum commission is the full commission on assets of $200,000.)	

Therefore, on a probate estate of $200,000, for example, this bank would charge an executor's commission of $6875. Sometimes banks also may charge lower percentage fees on property not passing under the will if the bank must perform substantial services as executor with respect to such property.

An executor can be an individual (the testator's spouse, brother or sister, an adult son or daughter, a trusted friend, etc.); a corporate executor (a bank or trust company); or co-executors (such as the testator's spouse and a bank). An individual executor can waive any executor's compensation, or if he or she is an heir anyway, can receive this compensation from the estate and thus save paying a fee to a corporate executor. However, remember that an executor's duties can be complex, difficult, and technical, and the executor can be held personally liable for mistakes or omissions. Therefore, many people decide to name corporate executors or co-executors and pay the fee involved. Also, executors' fees are deductible in computing any federal estate tax due, or the estate's (or beneficiaries') income tax, whichever the executor elects. In effect, then, the estate pays only the after-tax fee.

Methods of Estate Transfer

We mentioned earlier that property can be passed on to others in a variety of ways. The estate owner must decide which methods of estate transfer to use.

In making these decisions, however, the estate owner frequently must decide whether to give or leave property outright or in trust. Therefore, we shall review briefly the nature of trusts at this point.

Trusts in Estate Planning

The famous jurist Oliver Wendell Holmes once said, "Don't put your trust in money; put your money in trust." Trusts have an important place in tax and estate planning today.

A "trust" is a fiduciary arrangement set up by someone, called the *grantor, creator,* or *settlor* of the trust, whereby a person, corporation, or other organization, called the *trustee,* has *legal* title to property placed in the trust by the grantor. The trustee holds and manages this property, which technically is called the trust *corpus* or *principal,* for the benefit of someone, called the *beneficiary* of the trust, who has *equitable* title to the trust property. Thus, the essence of the trust relationship is the placing of legal title to property with a trustee who is to administer the property, as a *fiduciary,*[2] for the benefit of the trust beneficiary or beneficiaries.

Kinds of Trusts.   There are various kinds of trusts; but as far as personal financial planning is concerned, the most important are (1) living (or inter vivos) trusts, (2) trusts under will (or testamentary trusts), and (3) insurance trusts. A *living trust* is a personal trust that individuals create during their lifetime to benefit themselves or someone else. A "testamentary trust" is a personal trust created under a person's will that, like the will, does not become effective until after the creator's death. An "insurance trust" is a particular kind of living trust whose corpus consists partly or wholly of life insurance policies during the insured's lifetime and/or life insurance proceeds after the insured's death.

Living trusts can be revocable or irrevocable. A "revocable trust" is one in which the creator reserves the right to revoke or amend the trust. In other words, the creator can change it or terminate it and get the property back. In an "irrevocable trust," the creator does not reserve any such right to revoke or alter it.

Insurance trusts can be funded or unfunded. A *funded insurance trust* is one in which the trust corpus consists of life insurance and other assets. The income and/or principal from these other assets is used by the trustee to pay the premiums on the life insurance policy(ies) in the trust. An *unfunded insurance trust* is one containing only life insurance policies or one that is named as beneficiary of life insurance policies. The trust does not contain any other assets (or perhaps minimal assets) that can be used to pay the insurance premiums; these premiums must be paid by the creator of the trust or from some other source.

Reasons for Creating Trusts.   There are a number of possible reasons for creating trusts. Some of the more common are

1. To place the burdens of *property and investment management* in the hands of an experienced trustee, rather than leaving them to the creator, his or her family, or heirs.
2. To allow the trustee to use his, her, or its *discretion* (as a fiduciary) in handling trust property for the benefit of the creator, his or her family, or dependents.

---

[2] A fiduciary is an individual or corporation that acts for the benefit of another with respect to things falling within the scope of the fiduciary relationship.

3. To protect the creator's family or dependents against demands and entreaties made by well-meaning, or perhaps not so well-meaning, family members, friends, spouses, spouses-to-be, and the like.

4. To provide a way of *giving or leaving property to minors* so that the trustee can manage it for them until they are old enough to handle the property themselves. This avoids the legal rigidities and practical problems of having to have a legal guardian appointed for a minor.

5. In some cases, to *protect trust beneficiaries against themselves* when they are physically, mentally, or emotionally unable to manage property themselves. Sometimes, for example, trusts are created to protect spendthrifts from themselves.

6. To provide *professional investment and property management for the creator himself or herself* during his or her lifetime. Also, investment diversification can be provided through the common trust funds set up by many banks.

7. To *manage a business interest* after the owner's death until it can be sold or one of his or her heirs can take over.

8. To provide an extremely useful device for *setting up tax-saving* plans.

Who Should Be Named Trustee?   A trustee can be an individual, a corporation, or any other group or organization legally capable of owning property. There can be one trustee or two or more co-trustees. These co-trustees, for example, can be two or more individuals or a corporate trustee and one or more individual trustees. The creator of a trust can be the trustee, but there may be tax problems in doing this.

Trustees, like executors, may receive compensation for their work. The fees charged by corporate trustees vary. It is common, however, for professional trustees to charge an annual fee based on the trust's gross income or the value of the trust corpus or both, with a minimum annual fee. Trustees also may charge a payout commission on all principal distributed from the trust. As an example, the following is the annual commission schedule for personal trusts of one company:

Calculated on the value of the trust principal	
Value of principal	Annual commission on principal
$500,000 or less	$5.00 per $1,000
$500,000 to $1,000,000	$4.50 per $1,000
$1,000,000 to $2,000,000	$3.50 per $1,000
Over $2,000,000	$2.50 per $1,000

Plus

A commission of 6% on all income earned.
(Minimum commission is $2,000. A 10% discount applies to these fees when the corpus is invested in the bank's common trust fund(s).)

Thus, if we assume a trust with $400,000 of principal and earning $20,000 per year in investment income, the trustee's annual fee under the above schedule would be $3,200 ($400,000 × .005 + $20,000 × .06). This equals .80 of 1 percent of the principal and 16 percent of the income for the trust in this example. However, trustees' fees may be deductible for federal income tax purposes. Thus, the after-tax cost could be less, depending on the trust's or the trust beneficiary's income tax situation and the terms of the trust.

Since the trustee can be so important to the functioning of a trust, the selection of a trustee is an important decision. This choice often boils down to an individual or a corporate trustee.

An individual trustee (or trustees) may be the creator, a member of the immediate family, a more distant relative, a trusted friend, an attorney, or someone else. The creator may want to continue to administer the property as trustee, despite possible adverse tax results. An individual trustee might decide not to charge any fee. It can also be argued that an individual trustee may be closer to the trust beneficiaries and more likely to be responsive to their needs than a corporate trustee. Finally, individual trustees can get professional help and guidance from attorneys, investment advisors, financial planners, and the like on administering the trust.

On the other hand, strong arguments can be made for the use of corporate trustees.

1. Corporate trustees are professional money and property managers and hence can provide technical expertise in this area.

2. Individual trustees may die, resign, or otherwise become incapacitated, while corporate trustees provide continuity of trust management.

3. Corporate trustees are unbiased and independent of family pressures.

4. Corporate trustees normally are financially able to respond to damages in the event of trust mismanagement.

5. If an individual trustee is given discretionary powers over trust income or corpus, and the exercise of these powers may be beneficial to him or her personally (e.g., he or she is a trust beneficiary), the trustee may be considered to be the owner of the trust corpus for federal estate and gift tax purposes and the recipient of trust income for income tax purposes. This would not be true of a corporate trustee.

6. A corporate trustee can serve as co-trustee with an individual trustee, thus combining at least some of the advantages of both. It should also be noted that it is possible to provide in a trust agreement that the corporate trustee can be removed and another corporate trustee substituted upon the demand of the trust beneficiaries (or someone else).

Estate Transfers at Death

We have already seen the problems of dying intestate and the desirability of having a will. An estate owner who leaves property to others by will must decide whether to leave it outright, under a testamentary trust, or perhaps some outright and some in trust.

To illustrate the use of a *will with a testamentary trust,* let us take the same family we did before in showing the intestate distribution of property. But this time let us assume that the husband has made a will with a testamentary trust for his family. Here is one way his $120,000 (probate) estate could be handled under this kind of arrangement.

Husband (deceased)
($120,000 net estate in trust)
↓
Wife receives:

1. Life income from $120,000
2. Limited right of withdrawal
3. Nongeneral power of appointment.
4. Trust principal for her or children's support or children's education at trustee's discretion

At wife's death
(Remaining trust principal divided into three equal shares, in trust, for the children or their issue)

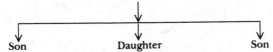

Son   Daughter   Son

Children receive:
1. Life income from his or her trust
2. Nongeneral power of appointment
3. Trust principal for his or her (or his or her issue's) support or education at trustee's discretion
4. Right to withdraw all or part of his or her trust at age 25 or 30

This kind of plan would meet virtually all the problems of intestate distribution. Of course, specific estate arrangements can take many different forms, depending on the circumstances. (See Chaps. 15 and 16, for example.)

Lifetime Transfers

As we saw before, there are many ways in which property can be transferred by estate owners during their lifetime without passing under a will. In fact, in many cases lifetime transfers are more important than transfers by will. Thus, these lifetime transfers should be coordinated with an estate owner's will in a well-designed estate plan.

Marital Agreements

We have seen in this chapter and elsewhere in the book that marriage can create certain rights in the property or qualified retirement plan benefits of each spouse. These marital rights, whether arising under state law (e.g., a surviving spouse's elective share at death or a spouse's right to "marital property" upon divorce) or federal law (e.g., a spouse's rights in the qualified retirement plan benefits of his or her spouse under the Retirement Equity Act of 1984), are based on certain ideas of social policy and generally are intended to protect the nonpropertied or nonparticipant spouse.

However, as has been noted previously, for estate planning, retirement planning, or other reasons, spouses may want to relinquish or modify some of these legal marital rights. This generally is legally acceptable, provided it is done in the proper manner. A rather "sticky" issue in this matter is whether both spouses truly understand what they are giving up and whether they have or need separate legal counsel to advise them since their interests may not be the same in making certain marital agreements. Sometimes the law specifies the requirements for a valid agreement (as under REA).

The kinds of such marital agreements that have been covered in this book are:

- Waiver of REA rights in certain qualified retirement plans by the participant spouse and written consent to the waiver in the proper form by the nonparticipant spouse (see pp. 353–354, 356–358, and 364–365).

- Prenuptial agreements concerning spousal rights in property at death (see p. 425).

- Prenuptial agreements concerning spousal rights in "marital property" incident to divorce (see p. 418).

15
Planning for Death Taxes

It is said that "nothing is certain except death and taxes." Here we are dealing with both. A great deal of estate planning is concerned with saving and planning for death taxes.

Death Taxes and Estate Settlement Costs

A person's estate may be subject to a number of claims that must be paid in cash. These frequently are discussed in estate planning and might be referred to as "cash demands on the estate," "total claims, expenses, and taxes," "estate shrinkage," and "estate liquidity needs," among other things. Estate planning seeks first to minimize these taxes and costs, and then to provide for their payment.

In a number of estates, the federal estate tax may represent an important part of this "shrinkage," and therefore, in this chapter we will review this tax and how to plan for it. We also will consider state death taxes and other estate settlement costs.

Unified Transfer Tax System

The Tax Reform Act of 1976 made many fundamental changes in the federal estate and gift tax structure. One of the most basic and pervasive changes was the adoption of a single, unified federal transfer tax system that applies to gifts a person makes during his or her lifetime (inter vivos gifts) and to gifts or transfers a person makes at his or her death (testamentary transfers). Formerly, the federal estate tax and the federal gift tax were separate. There was one set of tax rates and exemptions for the federal estate tax and another for the federal gift tax. Now, however, the gift and estate tax rates are combined into a single, progressive, unified transfer tax rate schedule—ranging from an effective rate (considering the application of the unified credit discussed on pp. 436–437) of 37 percent to 50 percent (a maximum rate of 55 percent applies through 1992) that applies alike to lifetime gifts and transfers made at death in a cumulative fashion.

An effect of this unified gift and estate tax system is a tendency to equalize the actual gift and estate taxes paid by persons who transfer a portion of their estates via the lifetime gift route as compared with those who retain all or most of their property and transfer it at death. Thus, lifetime gifts generally have lost some of their attractiveness as a tax-saving device under the unified transfer tax system. However, the Economic Recovery Tax Act of 1981 (ERTA) also made the fundamental change of allowing an unlimited federal gift (and estate) tax marital deduction for lifetime gifts between spouses. Thus, unlimited lifetime gifts that qualify for the marital deduction can be made between spouses without any gift tax liability. This tends to encourage such lifetime transfers between spouses. Also, the federal gift tax annual exclusion was increased from $3000 to $10,000 per donee per year by ERTA. This change may have stimulated gifts within the annual exclusion to save taxes.

Further, the tax law applies a single, unified credit of $192,800 for each person that can be applied to reduce or eliminate any gift taxes payable on gifts made during a person's lifetime, and then the credit, or the remainder of the credit if any part has been used to eliminate gift taxes, can be used to reduce or eliminate any estate tax payable at the person's death. This unified credit will allow a person to pass a substantial amount of assets to others (i.e., the equivalent of $600,000) by either lifetime gifts or gifts at death free of federal gift or estate taxes. However, effective for transfers after 1987, the advantages of this unified credit (as well as the lower, graduated transfer tax rates) are phased out by a 5 percent additional tax rate on transfers over $10,000,000.

In this chapter we are concerned primarily with planning for death taxes. Therefore, we shall start with an explanation of the federal estate tax. However, it is helpful to note at the outset that the estate tax is part of a unified transfer tax system, as mentioned above.

How to Estimate the Federal Estate Tax

The basic pattern for estimating a person's federal estate tax liability is as follows:

Gross estate

Less: certain estate settlement deductions (i.e., estate administration expenses, funeral expenses, and debts and claims against the estate)

Note: The gross estate less these deductions equals the *adjusted gross estate,* which is used to determine such things as eligibility for a Section 303 redemption of corporate stock (see Chap. 17).

Less: Marital deduction (which may be up to the full amount, that is, 100 percent, of property included in the gross estate that passes to a surviving spouse) and charitable deduction equals—

Taxable estate

Plus: Adjusted taxable (post-1976 lifetime) gifts (if any) equals—

Tentative tax base, to which the unified transfer tax rates are applied to produce—

Federal estate tax on the tentative tax base

Less: Credit for any gift taxes paid on post-1976 lifetime gifts[1] equals—

Federal estate tax before application of the unified credit

Less: Unified credit (and other credits) equals—

Federal estate tax payable

Gross Estate.   The gross estate for federal estate tax purposes is the starting point for determining how much estate tax an estate must pay. In general, it includes the following items:

1. All property the person owns in his or her own name and the person's interest in property held as a tenant in common with someone else

2. Proceeds of life insurance policies on the person's life if he or she has any ownership rights in the policy (incidents of ownership) or if the policy is payable to the person's estate

3. One-half the value of property held jointly (WROS) by a husband and wife, or the full value of property held jointly (WROS) with other than a husband or wife except to the extent the surviving owner(s) can show that he or she contributed to the purchase price of the property

4. The person's share of any community property

5. Property over which the person has a general power of appointment

---

[1] Note that the effect of adding any post-1976 taxable lifetime gifts to the taxable estate in order to arrive at the tentative tax base (to which the unified transfer tax rates are applied) and then deducting a credit equal to any post-1976 gift taxes paid during the person's lifetime from the federal estate tax calculated on the tentative tax base is to have the amount of any previous lifetime gifts serve to increase the unified transfer tax brackets applicable to the estate assets that pass at death. This makes the federal gift and estate taxes (the transfer taxes) both progressive and cumulative, as noted above.

6. Gifts of life insurance (and certain other interests in property) made within three years of death (as well as the gift tax paid on gifts made within three years of death)

7. Certain death benefits under IRAs, HR-10 plans, qualified retirement plans, nonqualified annuities, and similar plans.

8. Property transferred by gift during the person's lifetime while retaining certain prohibited rights or powers in the gift property

Using this list of items, people often can estimate their gross estate by using a family balance sheet and other pertinent information (or perhaps by using an asset inventory or estate survey form).

For purposes of estimating estate taxes, it normally is necessary only to approximate the values for property in the estate. However, for some kinds of property the estate tax value may not be clear, and valuation problems can arise. This can occur, for example, in the case of real estate, fine arts and collections, some kinds of tax-sheltered investments, and certain mortgages and loans. A particularly troublesome problem can be the valuation of closely held business interests, which may constitute a large portion of some estates. As we shall see in Chap. 17, this valuation problem can often be solved through a properly drafted buy-sell agreement for the business interest.

Deductions to Arrive at the Adjusted Gross Estate. These deductions also may be approximated for our purposes. Naturally, they vary among estates. The specific deductible items include

1. Estate administration expenses, including executor's commissions, attorney's fees, court costs, accounting and appraiser's fees, brokerage fees, costs of maintaining estate assets, and the like. These may be estimated at between 4 and 8 percent of the probate estate for planning purposes.

2. Current debts of the estate owner and any claims against the estate.

3. Accrued taxes, including real estate and nonwithheld income taxes.

4. Unpaid mortgages on property included in the gross estate.

5. Funeral and last-illness expenses. Funeral expenses can be estimated, but last-illness expenses are entirely uncertain. If the estate owner has adequate medical expense insurance, however, it can be assumed that this coverage will reimburse most of these last-illness expenses.

Estate planners sometimes make a rough approximation of these deductions at, say, 8 to 10 percent of the gross estate for planning purposes.

Adjusted Gross Estate. Prior to 1982, this figure was used to determine the maximum permissible marital deduction—which was one-half the adjusted gross estate (or $250,000 if greater). As of 1982, however, this has been changed by ERTA because of the introduction of the unlimited federal estate tax marital deduction (see below). However, in effect, the adjusted gross estate (AGE) still is used to measure whether the value of business interests in an estate is large enough to qualify for favorable installment payment of estate taxes on interests in closely held businesses (under Section 6166 of the Internal Revenue Code) or tax-protected stock redemptions under Section 303 of the code (see Chap. 17) and for certain other purposes. Thus, the AGE is defined for convenience at this point.

Federal Estate Tax Marital Deduction.   This often is a very important tax-saving device for married estate owners. This has become particularly so since the enactment of ERTA, which allows an estate owner to leave an entire estate without any dollar limit to the surviving spouse free of federal estate tax. In other words, there now is an unlimited federal estate (and gift) tax marital deduction. Planning for the proper use of the marital deduction to achieve maximum estate tax savings in the estates of *both* husband and wife will be considered in greater detail below.

Charitable Bequests.   Bequests for public, charitable, and religious uses are deductible in calculating the federal estate tax. Thus, such gifts are not taxed.

Tentative Tax Base.   The result of taking all these deductions from the gross estate is the "taxable estate" for federal estate tax purposes. To this taxable estate are added any "adjusted taxable lifetime gifts." These are the total of any taxable gifts, after the annual exclusion, the gift tax marital deduction, and the gift tax charitable deduction (which are explained later in this chapter), made by the deceased estate owner during his or her lifetime after 1976. The sum of the taxable estate and any adjusted taxable lifetime gifts is the "tentative tax base" (or the "estate tax computation base") to which the unified transfer tax rates are applied to produce the "tentative federal estate tax on the tentative tax base." These unified transfer tax rates are steeply progressive, ranging from 18 to 50 (or 55) percent of the tentative tax base. From this tentative federal estate tax are deducted with some adjustment any gift taxes paid on lifetime gifts made by the deceased estate owner after 1976 that have been included in the tentative tax base (as the adjusted taxable lifetime gifts, noted above). The result is the federal estate tax before the application of any credits (as described below).

Unified Credit.   The unified estate and gift tax credit, as well as any other applicable credits as explained below, are subtracted from the tentative tax as determined above to arrive at the actual federal estate tax payable. As explained previously, this unified credit applies to lifetime gifts as well as to property passing at the time of a person's death. Hence, it may be partially or wholly used up if a person makes taxable lifetime gifts. The unified credit was adopted by the Tax Reform Act of 1976 to replace both the former $30,000 gift tax lifetime exemption and the $60,000 estate tax specific exemption.[2] But note that as a *credit* against the estate (and gift) tax otherwise payable, rather than as an exemption or deduction from the gross estate or total gifts made, the unified credit may be worth considerably more to taxpayers than were the old gift and estate tax exemptions. The amount of the unified credit was substantially raised by ERTA, and under the law it increased in steps from 1982 to its present level of $192,800 for 1987 and thereafter.

Thus, in 1987 and thereafter, assuming that no taxable lifetime gifts have been made, any person could leave an estate (after deductions) of up to $600,000 without incurring any federal estate tax liability. This is referred to as the "exemption equivalent" of the $192,800 unified credit. Of course, with the unlimited marital deduction, a married estate owner who makes maximum use of the federal estate tax marital deduction could leave an estate of any size to the surviving spouse without paying any federal estate tax.

However, these new tax rules should not lull persons with reasonably significant estates or growing estates into a false sense of security with respect to their estate planning. First, full use of the marital deduction may not be possible or desirable in some cases. Also, use of the marital deduction by the estate of the first marital partner to die does not consider what happens when the surviving spouse subsequently dies and the marital deduction is no longer available (assuming no remarriage). In fact, the surviving spouse's subsequent death often is the time when the main estate tax bite comes. Further, conditions and property values can change, particularly in inflationary times, with the result that what previously would have been an untaxed estate may grow to one that will attract estate taxes when the owner or the owner's surviving spouse dies. Finally, to receive the full benefits of these provisions of the estate tax law, an estate owner frequently must plan carefully. Therefore, the federal estate tax is a significant factor to consider for many estate owners. It must be recognized, however, that the increase in the unified credit to an "exemption equivalent" of $600,000 will shield many smaller estates from any federal estate tax liability.

Other Credits.   Several other kinds of credits may be available to reduce the federal estate tax otherwise payable by an estate. Depending on the circumstances, these may include (1) a state death tax credit and (2) a credit for estate taxes paid on property taxed in a previous estate. Probably the most important of these for estates generally would be the credit for state death taxes paid. This credit equals the *smaller* of (1) the amount deter-

---

[2] Note, however, that the important $10,000 per donee annual gift tax exclusion still applies.

mined by applying the increasing rates contained in the federal estate tax law to the "adjusted taxable estate" or (2) the amount of state death taxes actually paid. Because state death taxes actually paid often equal or exceed the rate of credit allowed by the federal law, in practice the rates shown in the federal schedule often will determine the effective maximum credit.

Using the unified transfer tax rate schedule and unified credit that will apply in 1993 and thereafter, and assuming no taxable lifetime gifts, on a taxable estate of $600,000, there will be no federal estate tax payable because the $192,800 unified credit will entirely absorb the $192,800 of tentative tax on a taxable estate of $600,000. But on a corresponding taxable estate of $800,000, there will be a federal estate tax payable of $52,200 (a tentative tax of $267,800 less the unified credit of $192,800 and less a credit for state death taxes payable from the federal tax table of $22,800). Thus, an additional $200,000 of taxable estate attracts a federal estate tax payable of $52,200 and places the estate in a federal estate tax bracket of 39 percent. And on a corresponding taxable estate of $2,500,000, there will be a federal estate tax payable of $694,200 (a tentative tax of $1,025,800 less the unified credit of $192,800 and less a credit for state death taxes payable of $138,800). Thus, here an additional $1,900,000 of taxable estate (over the $600,000 "exemption equivalent") attracts a federal estate tax payable of $694,200 and places the estate in a federal estate tax bracket of 50 percent.

Thus, we can see the significance of the progressive nature of the federal estate tax. Also, the importance to estate owners and their heirs of seeking ways to reduce the estate tax burden on both the husband's and wife's estates, when they reach the point of being taxable, becomes clear.

Let us now illustrate these ideas by reviewing again the estate situation of George and Mary Able. We first met the Ables in Chap. 1 and then again in Chap. 14. As shown in Chap. 1, George's estate tax estimate is as follows:[3]

Gross estate		$1,420,000
Less:		
George's debts[4]	$75,000	
Estimated funeral and estate administration expenses	45,000	−120,000
Adjusted gross estate		$1,300,000
Less: Federal estate tax marital deduction (includes full amount of all property in gross estate that "passes" to the surviving spouse so as to qualify for the marital deduction)		−1,300,000
Taxable estate (and tentative tax base in this case)		—0—
Federal estate tax payable		—0—

---

[3] We also shall review later in this chapter what happens upon Mary's subsequent death.

[4] There also would be some income tax due from George's estate because of the profit-sharing and savings plan accounts which are payable to his estate.

It should be noted from these calculations that the $192,800 unified credit has generally not been used upon George's assumed death because of the availability of the unlimited marital deduction. [George's will leaves all his residuary estate outright to Mary, she receives all jointly owned property (WROS) as sole owner after George's death, and she is the beneficiary of all his life insurance.] So, one might ask, if there is no potential federal estate tax liability at George's death, why worry? The reason for concern is the potential substantial federal estate tax on Mary's estate upon her subsequent death, as is shown later in our analysis.

From a *tax standpoint,* George has actually qualified too much of his estate for the federal estate tax marital deduction, because the property so qualified normally will be in Mary's estate upon her death. This will result in paying unnecessary estate taxes. Technically speaking, it is referred to as the estate's being "overqualified" for the federal estate tax marital deduction. In this particular case, for example, it would be desirable from a tax standpoint to leave to Mary so as to qualify for the marital deduction only about $700,000 of George's estate. The remainder could be left in a way that would be for Mary's benefit, such as in trust with a life income and limited rights of withdrawal for Mary or for her benefit, but would *not* be in her gross estate at her subsequent death. If George's estate were arranged in this way, his taxable estate would be about $600,000 ($1,300,000 adjusted gross estate less $700,000 marital deduction), and the tentative estate tax on this amount would be more than absorbed by the $192,800 unified credit and the state death tax credit. (In fact, the part of George's estate that could be left so as not to qualify for the marital deduction and hence to escape estate tax on Mary's subsequent death could be further increased by the "exemption equivalent" of the state death tax credit for state death taxes payable in any event against the estate tax in George's estate.) This result can be achieved automatically by using a *formula clause* designed to make maximum use of the unified credit in the estate owner's will or other instrument of estate transfer. The proper use of the federal estate tax marital deduction is an important subject in estate planning and is considered in greater detail later in this chapter.

State Death Taxes

As noted in Chap. 14, state death taxes vary considerably among the states. State inheritance taxes, which are levied on the right to receive property, often have varying exemptions and rates for different classes of beneficiaries. One state, for example, levies a 6 percent inheritance tax on transfers to the spouse, children, grandchildren, other lineal descendants, adopted children and their descendants, stepchildren, spouse of a child, parents, and grandparents. The tax rate on transfers to others is 15 percent. There are no exemptions in this state.

Many states have a so-called credit estate tax designed to impose a state death tax at least equal to the federal estate tax credit for state death taxes paid. This allows the state to tax at least up to the full federal credit. The trend is for states to have only this type of estate tax.

Estimating an Estate's Liquidity (Cash) Needs

As we saw above, there are a number of claims and taxes an estate must pay shortly after the estate owner's death. These can be summarized for George Able's estate as follows:

Current debts	$ 10,000
Estimated funeral expenses	2,000
Estimated last-illness expenses (assumed covered by medical expense insurance)	—
Estimated costs of estate administration	43,000
Unpaid mortgages (assume that Mary decides to pay off the $20,000 mortgage on their principal residence and the $30,000 mortgage on their summer home after George's death)	$ 50,000
Other debts (bank loan)	40,000
State death tax	47,000
Federal estate tax	—
Any specific dollar bequests in the will (or widow's allowance)	—
Total cash needs	$192,000 (or 23% of George's $840,000 probate estate and about 14% of his $1,420,000 gross estate)

Providing Estate Liquidity

Liquidity can be an extremely serious problem for some estates but of minor importance for others. Much depends on the composition of the estate and what previous planning has been done. Estate liquidity often is a major problem when a large part of an estate consists of relatively unmarketable assets, such as closely held business interests, undeveloped real estate, or certain tax-sheltered investments.

Meeting the claims and taxes against an estate generally is the responsibility of the executor (or administrator), who does this using the probate assets. These are the only assets that are directly available to the executor. However, other assets, such as jointly owned property or life insurance payable to a third-party beneficiary, that pass outside the probate estate, *may* be made available to the executor by the person receiving them (such as a surviving spouse) as a loan to the estate or by a person purchasing assets from the estate. The executor, however, cannot normally use assets passing outside the probate estate to meet estate liquidity needs without the consent of the person (or trustee) controlling such assets.

Proper planning for estate liquidity often is necessary. Here are some of the common *sources of liquidity* for an estate.

1. Cash, bank accounts, and money market accounts or funds—owned outright or jointly with someone who will make them available to the estate.

2. Life insurance proceeds—payable to the estate or to a person (or trust) who will make them available.

3. Stocks and bonds that are actively traded. These can be sold to meet estate cash needs. Of course, in a declining market such securities may produce less than the estate owner would have liked. (There are some U.S. Treasury bonds, called "flower bonds," that can be used at par to pay the owner's estate taxes. However, such "flower bonds" are no longer being issued by the government, although some are still outstanding.)

4. U.S. government savings bonds—owned outright or jointly with someone who will make them available. These can be redeemed.

5. Mortgages or loans taken on estate assets.

6. Buy-sell agreements covering closely held business interests can produce substantial amounts of cash for the executor. In fact, a properly funded buy-sell agreement will usually solve the liquidity needs of an estate consisting largely of a closely held business interest (see Chap. 17).

7. Provisions of properly structured trusts—under which the trustee is *authorized* to make loans to, and/or buy property from, the creator's estate. Thus, the trustee can provide liquidity to the estate from trust assets if necessary.

8. Redemption of stock by the estate from a closely held corporation. This is the so-called Section 303 redemption to pay death taxes and funeral and estate administration expenses, which is discussed in Chap. 17.

Let us now analyze the sources of liquidity in George Able's estate as constituted at present.

Probate estate	
Money market fund	$ 40,000
Common stock	360,000
Mutual fund shares	10,000
Profit-sharing plan and savings plan death benefits	400,000
	$810,000

Passing outside the probate estate	
Bank accounts (owned jointly with Mary)	$ 30,000
Group life insurance proceeds (payable in a lump sum to Mary)	225,000
Individual life insurance proceeds (payable in a lump sum to Mary)	200,000
	$455,000

It is clear that there is more than enough liquidity in George's estate as it now stands.

Determining What Is Left for the Family (the "Net" Estate)

After estimated death taxes and estate settlement costs are paid, the estate owner wants to know how much "net" estate will pass to his or her family and how much income it will provide for them.

Again using George Able's estate as an example, we saw in Chap. 14 that his "net" estate for his family would be $1,383,000. Of this amount, about $1,123,000 could be put into income-producing investments or held for educational or emergency needs. If we assume that this amount can produce an average return of 8 percent over a long period of years before taxes, George's family would receive about $90,000 annually from this capital fund. However, this does not consider any possible invasion of the capital fund for purposes such as emergencies or the children's education.

What Happens When the Other Spouse Dies?

As we have said previously, what happens at George's death is only part of the story. It also is necessary to consider Mary's estate at her subsequent death. It is important to carry the analysis on through the estates of both spouses. This often discloses an unexpected estate tax liability.

Again using the estates of George and Mary Able as examples, we are assuming that George's "net estate" goes outright to Mary, and let us also assume that she does not "consume" any of the capital or make any gifts during her lifetime, she does not remarry, and she receives the expected $200,000 inheritance outright from her parents. Then, on Mary's subsequent death we would have

Property passing to Mary from George (through life insurance proceeds paid to her, from jointly owned property, and under George's will)	$1,383,000	
Property Mary received by inheritance	200,000	
Mary's gross estate	$1,583,000	
Less: Estimated funeral and estate administration expenses and current debts	−80,000	
Adjusted gross estate	$1,503,000	
Marital deduction	—0—	
Taxable estate (and tentative tax base in this case)	1,503,000	
Federal estate tax on tentative tax base	$ 557,150	
Less available credits:		
Unified credit	$192,800	
State death tax credit	64,592	−257,392
Federal estate tax payable	$ 299,758	(or about $300,000)

Assuming that Mary leaves her "net" estate to her children (and perhaps grandchildren), her state death tax is assumed to be about $90,000, although this can vary considerably among the states.

Therefore, Mary's "net" estate for her family (assuming George's prior death) would be $1,113,000, computed as follows:

Total assets		$1,583,000
Less:		
Current debts	$ 10,000	
Funeral and estate administration expenses	70,000	
State death tax payable	90,000	
Federal estate tax payable	300,000	
Total estate "shrinkage"	$470,000	−470,000
"Net" estate to heirs (e.g., children or grandchildren)		$1,113,000

Thus, after considering the "shrinkage" in both estates of $662,000 ($192,000 in George's estate—including the $50,000 unpaid mortgages—and $470,000 in Mary's estate), a "net" amount of about $1,113,000 will ultimately go to their children and grandchildren or other heirs. This "shrinkage" now represents about 37 percent of the $1,775,000 of estate assets which George and Mary had at the beginning (i.e., $1,575,000 in estate assets at George's death plus Mary's $200,000 inheritance). In the next part of this chapter, we shall look at some ways this fearful "shrinkage" can be reduced by proper planning.

Reversing the Order of Deaths

A final step that can be taken is to assume a reversed order of deaths and do the analysis again. That is, in this case assume that Mary dies first. This step may point up the problem of a wife with assets of her own, or possibly with a potential inheritance as in the case of the Ables, leaving all her assets to her husband, who already may have a sizable estate of his own. This problem is dealt with later in the section "Skipping Estates to Save Federal Estate Taxes."

How to Save on Death Taxes and Settlement Costs

We have seen how death taxes and estate settlement costs can be important "estate shrinkage" items. It is no wonder, then, that estate planning often is much concerned with saving taxes and estate settlement costs.

Using the Marital Deduction to Save Federal Estate Taxes

The basic idea of the federal estate tax marital deduction is to allow married estate owners to leave as much of their estate as they wish to their surviving spouse free of federal estate tax. The unlimited marital deduction for gift taxes and for estate taxes, introduced by ERTA, is intended to treat a husband and wife as a single economic unit and, hence, to allow transfer of property between spouses during their lifetimes or at the death of one of them free of gift or estate taxes. But this "marital" part must be left to the surviving spouse in such a way that it would be included in the gross estate at the surviving spouse's subsequent death. In tax language, these are referred to as transfers to the surviving spouse that "qualify" for the marital deduction. Thus, use of the marital deduction is not automatic; there must be enough property in the gross estate that qualifies for the deduction to take full advantage of it, if that is desired.

What Property Qualifies for the Deduction? Many kinds of transfers to a surviving spouse will qualify. The spouse does not have to have outright ownership of the property and, if the proper tax rules are followed, now does not even have to have complete control over the disposition of the property at death.

The following are among the more common kinds of transfers to a surviving spouse that will qualify for the federal estate tax marital deduction.

1. Outright bequests.

2. Property held jointly by the spouses (with right of survivorship) to the extent that the property is included in the deceased spouse's gross estate.

3. Property passing to surviving spouses in trust with the trust income payable at least annually to them for their lifetime and with the surviving spouse having a general power of appointment over the trust corpus. This is the "power of appointment trust" or "marital trust." It has frequently been used for qualifying property for the marital deduction, and we shall discuss it in greater detail later in the chapter.

4. Life insurance proceeds payable to the surviving spouse in a lump sum or under a settlement arrangement that will qualify or to a life insurance trust which itself meets the requirements for qualifying its corpus.

5. Other death benefits included in the deceased spouse's gross estate and payable to the surviving spouse in a lump sum or under an arrangement that will qualify.

6. Property that passes from a decedent to a spouse in such a way that it is "qualified terminable interest property." "Qualified terminable interest property" would be property passing to the surviving spouse in trust with the trust income payable at least annually to the surviving spouse for life, with no person having a power to appoint any part of the qualified terminable interest property to anyone other than the surviving spouse during the spouse's lifetime, but allowing another (including the decedent in his or her will) to create or retain powers over, or to control the ultimate disposition of, the trust property that will take effect after the surviving spouse's death. Such trusts have been popularly dubbed "Q-TIP trusts," and they were introduced by the Economic Recovery Tax Act of 1981 (ERTA). The essence of the concept of the Q-TIP trust is that while surviving spouses must be given the right to all trust income during their lifetime, and no one can deprive surviving spouses of the Q-TIP interest during their lifetime, the original estate owner (or someone else) can have the power to determine who will ultimately get the property after the surviving spouse's death.

How Much, if Any, of the Marital Deduction Should Be Used?   Since using the marital deduction can eliminate taxes in the estate of the first spouse to die, many married estate owners will want to plan to use the maximum allowable deduction in their estate planning. However, this can be a complicated question, and the maximum allowable deduction should not be used automatically without careful consideration of the facts in each case.

There will be cases in which the estate owner does not want to use the marital deduction or the full allowable deduction. For example, estate owners, for nontax reasons, may not want to give their spouses even the income from property for the surviving spouse's whole lifetime. In other cases, an estate may consist mainly of certain property, such as business interests or investment property, that the owner does not feel can conveniently be split up or left to the spouse.

In addition, when both spouses each have a large estate, use of the marital deduction or the full marital deduction actually may increase total estate taxes on *both* estates. This kind of estate situation may appear more frequently in the future as more women enter the business world or the professions and develop estates of their own and as more people are the recipients of inheritances in our affluent society. However, even in such cases it still may be desirable to use the marital deduction for estate liquidity, investment reasons, or other practical reasons.

Further, full use of the federal estate tax marital deduction may not be the most efficient *taxwise* even for those estates that otherwise would attract estate taxation (i.e., adjusted gross estates of one spouse of more than $600,000). This is true because overuse of the marital deduction in such estates may "waste" some of the unified credit (worth an estate "exemption equivalent" of $600,000) which would have been available to the estate anyway. As pointed out above, this problem can be seen in the present estate arrangements of George and Mary Able, whereby all of George's estate goes to Mary in a way that qualifies for the marital deduction, and so his estate naturally would take the full marital deduction in that case.

To illustrate how planning to use less than the full federal estate tax marital deduction in such estates can reduce the "shrinkage" in both estates, let us assume that, instead of his present estate arrangements, George plans to leave Mary only about $700,000 of his estate in a way that will qualify for the marital deduction. This amount is calculated to leave a taxable estate, and from this a tentative federal estate tax, that would be more than absorbed by the $192,800 unified credit and the state death tax credit. This "marital" bequest or transfer would be about equal to the difference between the adjusted gross estate and the $600,000 "exemption equivalent" of the unified credit ($1,300,000 − $600,000 = $700,000).[5] The remainder of George's estate could be left in trust with the trust income payable to Mary for her lifetime and with certain other trust powers provided for Mary's benefit, but without having the corpus of this trust (often called the "nonmarital" trust) included in Mary's gross estate upon her death. At Mary's death, the trust could provide that the corpus would go to George's and Mary's children or their issue. The "nonmarital" trust would thus bypass or "skip" Mary's estate.

---

[5] For the sake of simplicity, this calculation ignores the state death tax credit.

Now, let us see how this alternative plan would affect the estate shrinkage in both George's and Mary's estates. Assuming George predeceases Mary, George's estate situation would be as follows:

Gross estate		$1,420,000
Less deductions		−120,000
Adjusted gross estate		$1,300,000
Less marital deduction		−700,000
Taxable estate (and tentative tax base)		$ 600,000
Federal estate tax on tentative tax base		$ 192,800
Less credits:		
Unified credit	$192,800	
State death tax credit	14,000	−206,800
Federal estate tax payable		—0—

Total estate "shrinkage" at George's death can be estimated as

Debts (including the full amount of mortgages on homes)	$100,000
Funeral and estate administration expenses	45,000
Federal estate tax	—0—
State inheritance tax	47,000
Total estate "shrinkage"	$192,000

Then, Mary's estate situation would be as follows on her subsequent death:

Gross estate:		
From George's estate	$700,000	
Value of one-half of jointly owned property received at George's death (i.e., ½ × $310,000)	155,000	
Inheritance from her parents	200,000	$1,055,000
Less deductions		−55,000[6]
Adjusted gross estate		$1,000,000
Less marital deduction (assuming that Mary does not remarry)		—0—
Taxable estate (and tentative tax base)		$1,000,000
Federal estate tax on tentative tax base		$ 345,800

(continued)

---

[6] Estate administration expenses would be lower because Mary's probate estate has been reduced.

Less credits:		
Unified credit	$192,800	
State death tax credit	$ 33,200	−226,000
Federal estate tax payable		$ 119,800 (or about
		$120,000)

Total estate "shrinkage" at Mary's subsequent death can be estimated as

Debts	
$10,000	
Funeral and estate administration expenses	45,000
Federal estate tax	120,000
State inheritance tax	56,000[7]
Total estate "shrinkage"	$231,000

Thus, the "shrinkage" in both estates has been reduced to $423,000 ($192,000 in George's estate and $231,000 in Mary's estate) from the $662,000 of "shrinkage" under their present estate arrangements. This estimated reduction is due largely to more effective use *from a tax standpoint* of the marital deduction in George's estate plan.

"Qualifying" the Right Amount (Avoid "Overqualifying" the Estate). In the previous illustration dealing with the Ables' estates, we saw the tax disadvantage of qualifying too much property for the federal estate tax marital deduction. In that case, it actually would be better taxwise to qualify less than the maximum allowable deduction. This is because there is no particular tax advantage in an estate owner's qualifying that part of the estate that would be shielded from estate tax by the unified credit (and state death tax credit) in any event. However, when the surviving spouse dies, there is a tax *disadvantage* if the previous estate owner (i.e., the first spouse to die) qualified all of the estate for the deduction. This results because *all* the property that passes to the surviving spouse in a qualifying manner will be included in the spouse's gross estate at death unless the spouse consumes it or makes nontaxable gifts of it while alive. Thus, more property will be included in both estates than is necessary to avoid estate tax upon the first spouse's death.

As indicated above, this is referred to as an estate's being "overqualified" for the marital deduction. It is a common situation because so many husbands in their wills routinely leave everything outright to their wives. Or husbands and wives, probably in a spirit of togetherness, execute "recipro-

---

[7] The state inheritance tax on Mary's death also would be reduced.

cal" wills—he leaves everything to her and she leaves everything to him. While this may seem like the nice thing to do, it can be costly from an estate tax standpoint. Also, many husbands and wives hold property in joint names and/or have their life insurance payable to the other spouse.

The trick, then, in estates like those of the Ables, is to qualify only enough property so that, considering the unified credit, there will be no estate tax in the estate of the first spouse to die. At least this is a commonly followed approach in estate planning. It might be observed that by using this approach an estate owner could transfer an estate of up to $1,200,000 free of federal estate taxes in either the estate owner's estate or the surviving spouse's estate, assuming that the surviving spouse had only a minimal estate in his or her own right.

Methods of "Qualifying" the Right Amount.   One method of implementing the approach described above is for estate owners through their wills (or during lifetime in a revocable trust, for example) to leave an amount of property that equals or about equals the "exemption equivalent" of the unified credit to the surviving spouse for life in trust (a "nonmarital trust"), with the remainder to go to their children upon the surviving spouse's death. The property in this trust will not be in the surviving spouse's estate upon death. (All death taxes are paid from this nonmarital trust.) The remainder of the estate owner's estate is left to the surviving spouse in a "marital trust" (or outright). This method of using marital and nonmarital trusts (sometimes called "A" and "B" trusts) to qualify the right amount of an estate for the marital deduction is commonly used in estate planning. Let us see what these trusts for the surviving spouse are like.

The property in the marital trust, which could be a "power-of-appointment trust," or a "Q-TIP trust," depending on the estate owner's goals, qualifies for the marital deduction. For the property in a power-of-appointment trust to qualify, the trust must meet certain minimum requirements. Among these are that all the trust income must be payable to the surviving spouse at least annually, and the surviving spouse must have a general power of appointment over the trust corpus. The value of the property in this marital trust ultimately will be included in the surviving spouse's gross estate at death (because of the spouse's possession of the general power of appointment), unless it is consumed or given away free of gift taxes during life. The requirements for a "Q-TIP trust" were described earlier in this chapter.

The nonmarital trust is so named because it is arranged so that its corpus does not qualify for the marital deduction and hence is not includable in the surviving spouse's estate at death. This trust can have a great variety of provisions for the estate owner's spouse, children, or other heirs, provided the estate owner does *not* give the surviving spouse such powers (as a general power of appointment, for example) that would cause the trust property to be included in the survivor's gross estate.

Techniques for qualifying and amounts to be qualified for the federal estate tax marital deduction other than those described above also may be logical, depending on the circumstances. For example, in smaller estates (i.e., those of less than $600,000 in both the spouses' estates combined), the spouses' unified credits will protect their estates from federal estate tax anyway, and so use or nonuse of the marital deduction need not determine how those estates should be arranged, at least until they grow in size, which must always be considered. On the other hand, for larger estates, a spouse with a substantial estate logically could consider the technique of using a "nonmarital trust" or its equivalent for a share equal to the "exemption equivalent" of the unified credit and then qualifying the remainder of the estate for the marital deduction so that the estate would have no federal estate tax liability, assuming that the spouse is the first to die (as was described above for the Ables); or such spouses with larger estates could plan to approximately equalize their estates, either through lifetime trans- fers or at death, and so keep the federal estate taxes on both their estates at a minimum, again depending on the circumstances. In making such an analysis, however, one should always consider the net value (after income taxes) of investing any deferred estate taxes at the first death and the liquidity needs of the respective estates.

A marital trust (or marital gift), formula clause(s), and nonmarital trust can be included in the estate owner's will as *testamentary trusts,* or in a *liv- ing life insurance trust* which would be the beneficiary of life insurance policies, or under the terms of a *revocable living trust,* depending on the circumstances.

Marital Deduction of Community Property.   Community property in effect is owned one-half by the husband and one-half by the wife. Only a deceased spouse's half of community property would be included in the gross estate for federal estate tax purposes. To be consistent with the unlim- ited federal estate tax marital deduction, the tax law now permits commu- nity property included in the gross estate to be qualified for the marital deduction if the estate owner so desires.

"Skipping Estates" to Save Federal Estate Taxes

Some estate owners find themselves in the position where their natural instinct is to leave their property to family members who already have, or will have, a sizable estate in their own right. Several examples come to mind—the widow or widower with successful and increasingly affluent chil- dren, the brother or sister with a well-to-do sibling, or the wife whose hus- band has a sizable estate. Estate owners, however, should think twice before leaving a substantial amount of property outright to such family members, because by doing so they simply pile more property onto the family member's already sizable potential estate. This just increases federal estate taxes unnecessarily.

A technique for avoiding such an increase in taxes is to leave the relatively well-off loved one a life interest in the property in trust, rather than outright ownership. The property then can pass to someone else upon the life tenant's death. If the trust arrangement is set up properly, nothing will be in the life tenant's estate at death. Thus, the life tenant's estate is "skipped" for federal estate tax purposes. In addition, life tenants can be given many rights and benefits in this trust without having its corpus included in their gross estate.

Returning to the case of the Ables, for example, it might be desirable for Mary (who is expecting a $200,000 inheritance in the future) to use this trust technique to "skip" George's estate if she should predecease him. At George's subsequent death, the trust corpus could go to their children, either outright or in trust for them.

Generation-Skipping Transfer Tax

The technique of "skipping estates" to save federal estate taxes may be limited in certain cases by the generation-skipping transfer (GST) tax which was first imposed by the Tax Reform Act of 1976 and was substantially revised by the Tax Reform Act of 1986. The generation-skipping tax now applies to (1) "taxable terminations" and "taxable transfers" from generation-skipping trusts or their equivalent, and (2) "direct skips" between generations. These are referred to as generation-skipping transfers.

In essence, the tax applies in certain cases when a transfer of property misses or "skips" a generation in terms of the property's not being subject to estate taxation in that generation (i.e., the generation is "skipped" for federal estate tax purposes). In applying the tax, a "skip person" is defined as a person assigned to a generation that is two or more generations below that of the transferor of the property subject to the tax. Thus, a transferor's grandchildren and great-grandchildren would be examples of "skip persons."

There are some important exemptions to this tax. First, each person making generation-skipping transfers (the transferor) is allowed a $1,000,000 exemption which can be allocated to property transferred at any time. (In addition, there was a special exemption of $2,000,000 per grandchild for direct skips to grandchildren until 1990.) Thus, this tax generally will affect only the owners of larger estates. For amounts subject to this GST tax, the tax rate applied is the maximum federal estate tax rate (55 percent and 50 percent for 1993 and thereafter).

As an example of a generation-skipping trust, suppose that a widow with a sizable estate has two children, a son and a daughter, each of whom also has two children (the widow's grandchildren). Both the widow's son and daughter probably will have good-sized estates on their own; so the widow leaves her estate under her will in two equal trusts, one for each of her two children, with each child having a life income from his or her trust and with the property in each trust passing to each child's children (the widow's grandchildren) in equal shares upon their parent's death (i.e., with remainder interests to the widow's grandchildren). These would be generation-skipping trusts (assuming the widow's son and daughter are alive when the transfer is made, i.e. when the widow dies), and the grandchildren would be "skip persons." Upon the death of her son or daughter, there would be a "taxable termination" of his or her interest in the trust, and this would cause the then fair market value of the trust corpus to be a generation-skipping transfer subject to the applicable GST tax rate (which would be the maximum federal estate tax rate modified according to the widow's GST exemption allocated to each trust).

As an example of direct skips, if the widow in the above example had made gifts directly to her grandchildren, they would be "skip persons" and the transfers would be generation-skipping transfers (subject to the available exemptions). A planning point to note with respect to direct skips is that such skips which are not taxable gifts by reason of the federal gift tax annual exclusion (see pp. 453–454) are not subject to the GST tax. However, with respect to direct skip transfers made after March 31, 1988 in trust for an individual that are not taxable gifts, this rule applies only if, during the lifetime of the individual, no part of the trust income or corpus is distributed to, or for the benefit of, any other person, and if the trust corpus would be included in the individual's gross estate at his or her death (if the trust does not terminate before the individual's death).

The tax rules as to just what is a generation-skipping transfer and under what conditions it will be taxed are quite complex. They obviously cannot all be discussed here. However, it is important to note that many trust and other arrangements used to skip estates and save federal estate taxes are not generation-skipping transfers and hence are not taxable. A common example would be the traditional nonmarital trust with a life income to the estate owner's spouse and the remainder to their children. This is not a generation-skipping trust because estate owners and their spouses are of the same generation.

Thus, while the tax on generation-skipping transfers will be important in some cases, it by no means eliminates the technique of skipping estates to save federal estate taxes. Many transfers are not subject to the tax, but even when they are, there are the exemptions and exceptions noted above. However, planners generally try to avoid paying a GST tax because of its high rate.

Making Lifetime Gifts

Making completed lifetime gifts, either outright or in trust, traditionally has been an important way to save on death taxes and estate settlement costs. However, with the adoption of the unified transfer tax system, which has the same tax rates applying to lifetime gifts as to bequests at death and which applies a single unified credit to both, the potential estate tax savings from lifetime gifts have been diminished, particularly in the case of larger gifts. Nevertheless, there still may be significant advantages to a program of lifetime giving under the proper circumstances.

Federal Gift Taxation.   It comes as a surprise to many people that there is a federal gift tax. This tax applies to the act of transferring ownership or ownership rights in property. It is levied against the donor, who must file a gift tax return when required by law.

However, there are several tax breaks available, which, if used properly, can reduce or even eliminate any gift tax on a donor's gifts. They are the gift tax annual exclusion, the privilege of "splitting" gifts between spouses, and the unlimited gift tax marital deduction. Further, the unified credit applies to gift taxes otherwise payable as well as to estate taxes payable.

The "gift tax annual exclusion" allows every donor to make tax-free gifts *each year* of up to $10,000 each to however many persons the donor wishes. Gifts within the annual exclusion do not reduce the donor's unified credit. To take a rather extreme example, a donor might give $10,000 in money or securities outright to each of, say, 12 persons (perhaps his or her children and grandchildren), or total gifts of $120,000 in a given year without reducing his or her unified credit to all. For this reason, spacing out gifts to a single donee over several years sometimes can keep the amounts of the gift each year within the $10,000 annual exclusion. In addition, there is an unlimited gift tax annual exclusion for gifts made on behalf of a donee to an education organization for tuition or to a health care provider for medical services.

The annual exclusion, however, applies only to gifts of a present interest in property (i.e., where the donee has the immediate use and enjoyment of the gift); it does not apply to gifts of future interests (i.e., where the donee does *not* have immediate use and enjoyment of the gift). Since donors generally want full use of the annual exclusion, this can be a complicating factor in making some lifetime gifts in trust.

Married persons, in effect, can double the annual exclusion by "splitting" any gifts either makes while they are married. (They also each have their unified credit available for their share of any split gifts.) Thus, if either spouse makes a gift to a third person, the gift can be treated for tax purposes as if it were made one-half by the donor-spouse and one-half by the other spouse, provided the other spouse consents to the gift. Suppose, for example, that

Husband wants to give outright $20,000 of common stock he owns in his own name to his adult daughter in one year. If Wife consents to the gift, the $20,000 gift is treated as a $10,000 gift by Husband and a $10,000 gift by Wife. Both these gifts would be within their $10,000 annual exclusions. Finally, when married persons make gifts to each other, the gift tax marital deduction applies. This generally parallels the unlimited federal estate tax marital deduction and allows gifts between spouses free of federal gift tax, assuming that the gifts qualify for the federal gift tax marital deduction.

The federal gift tax is cumulative. Therefore, if donors make future taxable gifts, the gift tax will be computed on their total taxable gifts to date, less a credit for prior gift taxes paid. In addition, as was noted previously, the federal gift tax and the federal estate tax also are cumulative in a unified transfer tax system.

Gifts to charity are deductible in computing a person's federal gift tax. In effect, then, charitable gifts are not taxable.

Advantage and Dangers in Lifetime Gifts. Lifetime gifts still can be an attractive estate tax-saving technique *under the right conditions.* For example, grandparents, after a lifetime of hard work, may be comfortably fixed and have a significant estate. They have a grown son or daughter who is married, and they now have several grandchildren. It is entirely logical for grandparents to consider embarking on a careful and planned program of lifetime gifts to their children and/or grandchildren or perhaps others.

Such *lifetime gifts can have the following advantages* over bequeathing the property at death:

1. Amounts within the gift tax annual exclusion will escape gift taxation and will not be in the donor's estate as well.

2. Any future appreciation in the value of the gift property will escape gift taxation and estate taxation in the donor's estate.

3. Any income from the gift property will be transferred to the donee for income tax purposes (but note the effect of the "kiddie tax" described in Chap. 11).

4. Estate administration expenses, which generally are based on the probate estate, will be reduced.

5. Similarly, state death taxes can be saved, although some states also have gift taxes.

6. If the gift is made in trust with the proper trust provisions, federal estate taxes may also be saved on the donee's estate, subject, however, to the rules for the tax on generation-skipping trusts.

7. Finally, donors can enjoy all the personal and family advantages of their generosity during their lifetime.

But there also are *dangers in making lifetime gifts,* and the donor may want to consider the following warnings:

1. Donors should be very careful that they can do without the gift property. What if their health deteriorates? What if they find themselves in an expensive custodial care situation? What if the stock market plummets? What if interest rates decline or some present source(s) of income dry up in the event of economic recession or depression?

2. If donors are considering giving assets to their spouses, what would happen if they separated, divorced, or stayed together and had marital difficulties?

3. Donors should be careful about giving away cash, life insurance, marketable securities, or other liquid assets, if their estate may have liquidity problems.

4. Owners of closely held corporation stock should be careful not to impair their interest in, or control over, the corporation's affairs through gifts of its stock.

5. Some family members actually may be harmed by having control over too much property too soon.

6. Gift taxes may have to be paid by the donor, although substantial gift tax exclusions and deductions are available that frequently eliminate any actual taxable gift. Even if there is a taxable gift, the unified credit may be available to eliminate or reduce any actual gift tax (at the price, of course, of effectively reducing the unified credit for future transfers).

How to Save State Death Taxes

State death taxes vary considerably, so no universal rules can be given here. Each state's law must be considered individually by estate owners and their advisors.

Sometimes, however, state inheritance taxes can be saved by having the estate owner buy life insurance or by having life insurance proceeds payable in the proper manner. Also, jointly owned property may be favored for inheritance tax purposes—in some states only one-half the value is taxed, regardless of who contributed the purchase price, and in other states it is not taxed at all.

Saving Estate Settlement Costs

Estate administration expenses usually are based largely on the size of the decedent's probate estate. They also depend on the complexity of the particular estate situation. Thus, to a certain degree, these expenses can be reduced by minimizing the probate estate. The ways property can be arranged so as to go outside the probate estate have been discussed previously. However, this should not become "the tail that wags the dog." It may not be practical or desirable in many cases for additional property to pass outside the probate estate. But when this can be done conveniently, it often will save estate settlement costs.

Medicaid Estate Planning

A new dimension has been added to estate planning by the increasing concern of many persons and their families over the high costs of any potential custodial care that might be needed either currently or in the future. Of course, one approach to this problem is to purchase or to have long-term care (LTC) insurance to help meet this exposure and/or to have adequate other resources to do so. However, these other resources may be depleted by long-term custodial care expenses and thus lost to the person's family or other heirs.

The general nature of Medicaid [the federal-state program of medical assistance (welfare) for certain categories of persons who meet certain needs tests] was outlined on p. 153. The essence of *Medicaid estate planning* is to arrange a person's affairs (or transfers to other persons) so that their property or the bulk of their property can remain for the benefit of their families, but also so that they can meet the needs tests (normally an income limit and a resource limit) in order to qualify for Medicaid benefits in their state. Medicaid will then provide broad medical benefits for eligible persons, including paying for certain custodial care (e.g., intermediate nursing home care). As explained previously, at present neither Medicare (which is not based on need) nor private medical expense insurance (either group or individual) covers custodial care. (LTC insurance, of course, is the form of private insurance designed for the custodial care exposure.) Therefore, as a practical matter, for many persons (or their families) with some assets who are facing having to go into a nursing home for custodial care, their only real possibility of having a third-party payor pay for the custodial nursing home care is to qualify for Medicaid.

Medicaid estate planning is a complex, emerging, and controversial subject. Only some brief concepts are presented here. For those who must deal with these thorny issues, professional advice frequently is needed.

To be eligible for Medicaid, a person normally cannot have personal resources or income above certain quite low limits (i.e., must be needy) according to state and federal law. However, there are certain resource items (such as an occupied principal residence) and income items that are excluded in calculating these financial eligibility requirements.

Thus, one rather basic approach is to try to convert or change assets into excluded categories.

Further, federal law provides that assets transferred to another (other than the person's spouse) more than 30 months before application for Medicaid do not count as resources in determining financial eligibility for Medicaid. This does not include most assets transferred to a person's spouse, because a spouse's assets above certain limits (set by state law up to federal limits) are deemed to be those of the other spouse for Medicaid eligibility purposes. Thus, a possible planning technique for persons with assets who may face the need for extensive custodial nursing home care (and who do not have LTC insurance to help pay for it) is to give away much of their assets to other family members (presumably "trusted" family members), retain enough assets to pay for nursing home care for 30 months, pay for the nursing home care themselves for the 30 months, "spend down" their available resources to the point where they become eligible for Medicaid, and then apply for Medicaid and let it pay for the person's future nursing home and other covered medical expenses. The person also may have to "spend down" any excess income to qualify for Medicaid. It must be noted, however, that there often are significant practical, human relations, and perhaps legal problems with this kind of technique. After all, the person needing custodial care essentially must impoverish himself or herself to qualify for Medicaid. Thus, it is possible for there to be intergenerational conflict within families over this issue.

Another area of possible Medicaid estate planning is to draft trusts so that they can be for the benefit of the trust beneficiaries but also so that the trust corpus and/or income will not be counted as a disqualifying resource or source of income for the trust beneficiaries for purposes of their qualifying for Medicaid. A problem with this is that now federal law permits the states to count the corpus and income from certain trusts (oddly called "Medicaid qualifying trusts") as available resources or income for purposes of determining financial (needs) eligibility for Medicaid. In other words, the assets in or income from such trusts can *disqualify* the trust beneficiary from Medicaid eligibility. Such Medicaid qualifying trusts are trusts established (other than by will) by an individual or by his or her spouse under which the individual *may be* a beneficiary of the trust and the distribution of payments from the trust is determined by a trustee who has discretion with respect to making distributions to the individual. This rule generally seems to preclude the grantor (or the grantor's spouse) from keeping the corpus or income of such lifetime trusts that *may* benefit the grantor from counting as available resources or income in determining Medicaid eligibility. However, depending on state law and court decisions, trusts still may be established by other persons (i.e., other than the potential Medicaid applicant or his or her spouse) that may give the trustee discretion to make payments to or for the benefit of the individual but whose corpus and income nevertheless may not be counted in determining the individual's financial eligibility for Medicaid. Such trusts may also be established under a will (i.e., testamentary trusts) by anyone. These would not be Medicaid qualifying trusts. Thus, there still are planning opportunities to help preserve potential Medicaid eligibility for trust beneficiaries.

16

Will Substitutes in the Estate Plan

Jointly owned property, life insurance, and trusts that operate during a person's lifetime are so important in many estate plans that a separate chapter is devoted to them. As a practical matter, these are the major ways of transferring property to others at a person's death other than by will (i.e., outside the probate estate). Hence, they are referred to here as "will substitutes."

Joint Property

The characteristics of jointly owned property (with right of survivorship) were described in Chap. 14. This form of property ownership, particularly between husband and wife, is very common and can offer some advantages for many people. There are, however, pitfalls to joint ownership.

Advantages of Jointly Owned Property

1. Joint ownership is a *convenient,* and perhaps natural, way to hold property among family members. At one joint owner's death, the property passes automatically to the other.

2. Jointly owned property passes outside the probate estate of the first owner to die and hence avoids the costs and delays of probate. It will, however, be in the estate of the surviving owner unless the survivor otherwise disposes of it during his or her lifetime.

3. Holding property in joint names can avoid or reduce inheritance taxes in some states.

4. Jointly owned property generally passes to the survivor *free of the claims of creditors of the deceased joint owner.*

In many cases these are important advantages that justify holding at least some property jointly. But in other cases, particularly as estates grow larger, the estate owner should ask, "Is it really wise to hold so much property in joint names?"

Problems of Jointly Owned Property

One problem that may arise from too much jointly owned property is a possibly larger federal estate tax because of some possible overqualification of property for the marital deduction. The extra estate taxes that can result from overqualification were explained in Chap. 15.

For federal estate tax purposes, the general rule is that the *full value* of all property a person owns jointly with another with right of survivorship (including joint tenancies with right of survivorship, joint bank accounts, jointly owned government savings bonds, and savings accounts where one person makes a deposit in trust for another person) will be included in his or her gross estate at death, except to the extent that surviving joint owners can affirmatively demonstrate that they contributed to the purchase price of the property with their own funds or that a part or all of the property belonged to the survivor before the joint ownership was created.

However, the Economic Recovery Tax Act of 1981 (ERTA) made a very significant exception to the above "consideration furnished" rule for the federal estate taxation of joint tenancies in the case of joint tenancies *between husband and wife.* For these joint tenancies, only *one-half* the value of the property held in an eligible joint tenancy is includable in the gross estate of the first spouse to die, regardless of which joint tenant-spouse furnished the consideration to acquire the property. This may be referred to as the "fractional interest" rule.

There are no cut-and-dried rules on how much property should be held in joint names. In cases where the federal estate tax is not an important factor, the "overqualification" problem of joint ownership does not apply. Even where the federal estate tax is significant, the whole situation should be considered—perhaps *some* joint ownership still is acceptable. It may save state inheritance taxes, for example. Also, people often hold the family residence and perhaps small bank accounts in joint names for convenience. Furthermore, since property held jointly by spouses is subject to the fractional interest rule, the estate tax overqualification problem will be greatly reduced.

Some further problems with joint ownership also may arise. When joint ownership in property is created, and one of the joint owners contributes all or more than a proportionate share of the purchase price, a gift for federal gift tax purposes is made *if* the transfer to joint ownership is irrevocable. Thus, if Mother uses her earnings to buy corporate bonds in her and her daughter's joint names, she will have made a gift to Daughter of half the value of the bonds. She also will have surrendered some control over the bonds to Daughter.

Life Insurance in Estate Planning

Life insurance occupies an important place in many estates. It also has many uses in estate and business planning. Therefore, careful consideration should be given to how existing or any new life insurance should fit into the overall estate plan. Life insurance has some unique advantages in estate planning. However, before discussing the uses of life insurance in estate planning, we should say a few words about how life insurance benefits are taxed.

Taxation of Life Insurance

As was first noted in Chap. 4, life insurance has some interesting tax advantages. We shall consider these advantages in light of federal income, estate, and gift taxation.

Federal Income Taxation. The *face amount (or policy death benefit) of a life or accident insurance policy paid by reason of the insured's death* normally is not gross income for federal income tax purposes to the beneficiary. This is the important tax-free receipt of life insurance death proceeds.

When life insurance proceeds are held by the insurance company under a settlement option, the proceeds themselves remain income tax–free, but any interest earnings on the proceeds may be taxable income. How this "interest element" is taxed depends on the nature of the settlement option.[1] When proceeds are left under the *interest-only settlement option,* the total amount of the annual *interest* payable by the insurance company is taxable to the beneficiary as ordinary income. Payments to the beneficiary from life insurance proceeds left under the *fixed-amount, fixed-period,* or *life income settlement options* (the so-called liquidating options) are partly a return of the tax-free death proceeds and partly an "interest element" on the proceeds held by the insurance company. Therefore, for

---

[1] The various life insurance settlement options are described in Chap. 4.

income tax purposes, the periodic payments to the beneficiary are divided into two portions: (1) a portion of the death proceeds that is returned income tax–free, and (2) the interest earnings on the funds held by the insurance company (the "interest element"), which are taxable as ordinary income.

During the insured's lifetime, different tax rules apply. *Premiums paid for personally owned life or accident insurance,* or an employee's contribution to group life or accident insurance, normally are not deductible for income tax purposes. However, any *annual increases in the cash value* of a life insurance policy are not currently taxable to the policy owner. This can be referred to as the tax-deferred (or sometimes the "tax-free") buildup of life insurance cash values.

Similarly, *life insurance policy dividends* do not constitute taxable income to the policy owner (until they exceed the policy owner's income tax basis in the policy). Furthermore, when policy dividends are used to buy accumulated paid-up additional amounts of life insurance (paid-up additions), there is also a "tax-free buildup" of the cash value of these accumulated additions. But if the policy owner elects to let policy dividends accumulate with the insurance company at interest, the interest on the dividends, but not the dividends themselves, currently is taxable to the policy owner as ordinary income. Thus, a small tax advantage can be secured by using policy dividends to buy paid-up additions as compared with having them accumulate at interest.

If a life insurance contract is surrendered, is sold, or matures during the insured's lifetime, the policy owner will have taxable ordinary income to the extent that the amount received from the policy exceeds the policy owner's investment in the contract (or income tax basis in the policy). This investment in the contract normally is the sum of the net premiums paid for it. Life insurance companies can supply the figures needed to compute any such gain.

Life insurance policies normally allow the policy owner to leave the policy surrender value with the insurance company under one or more policy settlement options. How any gain is taxed in this case depends on the circumstances. If at any time prior to 60 days after the date of maturity or surrender the policy owner elects to receive the policy amount under the fixed-period, fixed-amount, or life income options, any taxable gain will be spread out over the period of time during which payments will be made under the settlement option. But note that the settlement option must be elected before the 60-day deadline after maturity or surrender, or else the entire gain is considered taxable income in that year. If the interest-only option is elected prior to maturity or surrender, and the policy owner does not reserve the right to invade the proceeds, any gain is again postponed, but the interest payments themselves are fully taxable. However, if the policy owner does reserve the right to withdraw the proceeds, as he or she probably would want to do, the entire gain is taxable in the year of maturity or surrender.

A policy owner does not have to surrender a whole life insurance policy before the insured's death. He or she can just continue it in force until the insured dies, at which time the death proceeds will be received by the beneficiary income tax–free. A policy owner also can decide to stop paying premiums for a policy and to take a reduced paid-up amount of life insurance without any current income taxation of the policy. If the policy is participating, the policy owner may allow the policy dividends to continue to accumulate and, say, be used to purchase paid-up additions (without any current income tax liability) or could take the policy dividends in cash (if, say, increased retirement income is desired) and pay income tax on the dividends only when they cumulatively have exceeded the policy owner's income tax basis in the policy.

For some policies (e.g., universal life contracts), policy owners can make *partial cash withdrawals.* In the case of policies that are not modified endowment contracts (MECs), as defined on p. 86, the general rule is that such cash distributions are not taxed until they exceed the policy owner's investment in the contract (a FIFO-type rule). However, if such cash distributions are received as a result of certain changes in the contract that reduce benefits under the contract and occur during the first 15 years after issue of the contract, different rules apply and such cash distributions may be initially taxable in whole or in part.

For life insurance policies that are not MECs, policy loans are not viewed as distributions from the policy for federal income tax purposes at all and hence are not gross income. Further, as discussed on pp. 80–82, changes in cash values among separate accounts in variable life insurance policies are not currently taxable sales or exchanges for capital gains tax purposes. Finally, different tax rules apply to MECs regarding partial withdrawals, policy loans, and the 10 percent penalty tax on premature taxable distributions before age 59½, as noted on pp. 86–87.

Federal Estate Taxation. Life insurance can be favorable property as far as federal estate taxation (and also state inheritance taxation) is concerned. Not only can life insurance provide the liquidity an estate may need to pay death taxes and other costs, but also the proceeds can often be removed from the insured's gross estate.

Life insurance death proceeds will be included in the insured's gross estate for federal estate tax purposes if (1) the insured's estate is named beneficiary, or another named beneficiary (such as a trust) is *required* to provide the proceeds to meet the estate's obligations; or (2) the insured at the time of death owned *any* "incidents of ownership" (i.e., ownership rights) in the life insurance policy. However, merely paying the insurance premiums, in itself, will no longer result in the policy proceeds being taxable in the insured's estate.[2] Thus, estate tax savings can result if the insured policyholder is willing to absolutely give away the insurance policy (or coverage) to someone else, with no strings attached.

The phrase "incidents of ownership" generally means any policy ownership rights, such as the right to change the beneficiary, borrow against the policy, surrender or assign the policy, elect settlement options, or receive policy dividends and other benefits. Therefore, the insured must not have *any* of these policy rights and benefits at the time of death in order for the proceeds to escape federal estate taxation.

However, if life insurance policies are given away within three years of the insured's death, the proceeds will automatically be included in the insured's gross estate. But if the policy is given away more than three years before the insured's death, the tax authorities cannot include *the proceeds* in the insured's estate.

Suppose that one person owns a life insurance policy on the life of another person and the policy owner (not the insured) dies. In this case, the then value of the insurance policy will be included in the deceased policy owner's gross estate, just like any other valuable property that he or she owns.

Federal Gift Taxation.   The gift of a life insurance policy, like the gift of other property, may be subjected to federal gift taxation. Thus, if policyholders absolutely assign a life insurance policy on their life to someone else (a child or a trust, for example), they have made a current gift to the donee of the then value of the insurance policy. The insurance company will supply this gift value upon request. If the insured continues to pay premiums on the gift policy, each such premium constitutes a gift to the new policyholder.

An unusual gift situation can arise when a life insurance policy on the life of one person is owned by another person and the beneficiary is still a third person. In this situation, upon the insured's death, the owner of the policy is considered to have made a taxable gift of the policy proceeds to the beneficiary. This sometimes is referred to as an "inadvertent gift" of the proceeds, because the policyholder usually has no idea that he or she is making a taxable gift. Suppose, for example, that Father previously had absolutely assigned a $100,000 life insurance policy on his life to his adult Son to avoid estate taxes in his estate. Son's children (rather than the Son) are named as beneficiaries. If Father then dies, the $100,000 of life insurance proceeds will be paid to Son's children as the policy beneficiaries, but the Son will have made a $100,000 gift to his children. The situation that can produce this kind of taxable gift can easily arise when policies are being given away to save estate taxes, but fortunately such "inadvertent gifts" can be avoided

---

[2] There was at one time a "premium payment test" for including life insurance proceeds in the gross estate, but this rule is no longer in effect.

by proper planning. *When the owner of a life insurance policy is other than the insured, the owner normally should name himself or herself as beneficiary.* In the above case, for example, this inadvertent gift could have been avoided if the Son had been named as beneficiary. Of course, an insurance trust also could have been made the owner and beneficiary of the policy, which would have avoided this problem and perhaps offered other advantages as well.

How to Arrange Life Insurance

When life insurance is purchased for family protection purposes, the insured often names his or her spouse as primary beneficiary and their children as contingent beneficiaries. This may be fine in many cases, but there are various other possibilities for arranging one's life insurance that should be considered. Since life insurance is an important part of many estates, particularly the more modest estates, decisions concerning how it is handled can be important.

A basic decision an insured needs to consider is whether he or she will be the owner of the insurance on his or her life, and thus have the proceeds included in his or her gross estate at death, or whether someone else, or a trust, will own the life insurance on his or her life and thus in most cases have the proceeds escape federal estate taxation at death. Another basic decision is whether to leave the insurance proceeds to his or her beneficiaries under the policy settlement options or to use an insurance trust. The pros and cons of both these questions will be covered here.

Now, let us briefly review the possibilities for arranging life insurance.

Policy Owned by the Insured. First, let us assume that the insured owns the policy, as is frequently the case. Individual life insurance policies customarily specify on their front page who owns the contract. The insured commonly is named as the owner. If this is the case, then the insured owns all rights and benefits (incidents of ownership) in the policy unless he or she takes specific steps to transfer ownership to another (such as absolutely assigning the policy to someone else, for example). Policies owned by the insured can be made payable in the following ways.

To the Insured's Estate. This usually is not done unless the insured wants to make sure that the proceeds will be available to his or her executor for estate settlement purposes.

To a Third-Party Beneficiary or Beneficiaries (i.e., Other than the Insured's Estate) in a Lump Sum. As we noted above, this is a common arrangement, frequently with the insured's spouse as primary beneficiary and the children as contingent (or secondary) beneficiaries. Upon the insured's death, however, this arrangement may leave the beneficiary with a sizable sum of money to manage, perhaps at the very time she or he is least able to manage it.

True, the beneficiary, herself or himself, normally can elect to leave lump-sum proceeds under policy settlement options, but this also involves management decisions on the beneficiary's part. In addition, there are some advantages in the insured's at least initially electing settlement options for a beneficiary, as discussed below.

To a Third-Party Beneficiary or Beneficiaries under Policy Settlement Options.   The settlement options generally included in life insurance policies are described in Chap. 4. Most insurance companies give the insured wide latitude in the settlement arrangements that he or she can make for the beneficiaries, or for himself or herself for policy surrender values, under settlement options.

If an insured is not going to use an insurance trust, it generally is preferable for him or her to leave policy proceeds under settlement options for his or her named beneficiary(ies), rather than to them in a lump sum, even though some or all of the proceeds may not remain under the settlement options that he or she elects. First of all, the insured can generally give his or her beneficiary what amounts to complete control over the proceeds held under settlement options by electing to have the proceeds placed under the interest option, and by also giving the beneficiary full right of withdrawal and the right to change to other settlement options. This can be referred to as the "interest option—all privileges" arrangement; it gives the beneficiary the opportunity to withdraw the proceeds and invest them elsewhere, or to elect other settlement options, as she or he wishes. Of course, the insured can elect a more restrictive settlement arrangement for the beneficiary if that is desired.

In addition, settlement options have the following advantages over lump-sum payments: (1) the insurance company provides immediate management of the proceeds and relieves the beneficiary of worry and concern in this regard; (2) full provision can be made for the contingency that the insured and beneficiary may die in a "common disaster" or within a short time of each other; and (3) a settlement option elected by the insured extends to the policy proceeds the protection allowed by the applicable state law against claims by the beneficiary's creditors (i.e., the protection afforded by the "spendthrift provision" in a settlement agreement).

To a Revocable Unfunded Life Insurance Trust.   As we noted above, this often is a basic decision the policyholder-insured must make. It boils down to the question, "Should life insurance proceeds be left with the insurance company under a settlement option arrangement, or with a bank or other trustee to be administered under a trust agreement?"

There are arguments on both sides, and insurance companies and banks compete with each other for this business. The tendency in recent years probably has been toward increasing use of life insurance trusts.

Here are the *main arguments made in favor of the use of settlement options.*

1. *Guarantee of principal and income.* A life insurance company *promises* to pay the full amount of the proceeds and at least a minimum rate of interest on proceeds left under settlement options. The insurance company legally owes the proceeds (and the guaranteed interest on them) to the beneficiary. A trustee, however, has only the duty to invest trust assets with due care under the terms of the trust. The trustee does not guarantee the security of, nor a minimum rate of return on, the trust principal. Of course, in the final analysis the real security and growth of capital are much affected by the investment skill of both insurance companies and banks. However, the guarantees provided by insurance settlement options could become important in the face of economic recession or depression. On the other hand, such guarantees are only as good as the financial strength of the particular life insurance company. (See pp. 53–57 for a discussion of evaluating the financial strength of insurance companies.)

2. *No direct fees for property management.* An insurance company charges no additional direct fees when policy proceeds are left under settlement options; this right is provided in the policy, and its cost is covered by the general expense "loading" in the life insurance premium. As we saw in Chap. 14, corporate trustees charge an annual fee for administering trusts. The minimum annual fees for personal trusts (as illustrated in Chap. 14) tend to make the use of trusts uneconomical for smaller amounts of life insurance.

3. *"Excess interest" usually is payable.* This is interest paid by the insurance company on funds left under most settlement options in "excess" of the rate guaranteed in the policy. "Excess" interest is payable at the discretion of the insurance company and can be increased or decreased depending on the insurer's investment results.

4. *Life income (annuity) options can be used.* Only insurance companies can directly provide a life annuity for policy values or proceeds.

On the other hand, the following are the *main arguments made for revocable unfunded insurance trusts.*

1. *Great flexibility can be provided in paying out and managing trust assets.* A trustee can be given *discretion* with respect to paying out trust corpus and/or income to the beneficiaries, while an insurance company cannot exercise such discretion with respect to policy proceeds under settlement options. The trustee, for example, can be given such discretionary powers as to pay out or accumulate trust income; to

"sprinkle" trust income in different amounts among trust beneficiaries, depending on the beneficiaries' needs and perhaps their income tax brackets; to distribute trust principal to the trust beneficiary or beneficiaries as the trustee, in its discretion, thinks desirable for the beneficiary or beneficiaries; and other similar powers. Of course, a trustee can be given lesser discretionary powers in the trust agreement, as the creator of the trust desires. The exercise of discretion by a trustee can be desirable to meet changing family needs and circumstances; to help deal with emergencies; to respond to changing economic conditions (such as inflation or depression); to meet the special needs of certain beneficiaries, such as a physically or mentally handicapped child; and perhaps to save taxes.

Settlement options can be arranged to provide considerable flexibility by giving the beneficiary limited or unlimited rights of withdrawal, the right to change to other options, powers of appointment, and the like. But the insurance company cannot exercise its own discretion in paying out policy proceeds held under settlement options, and this is the important difference in this regard.

2. *Trustees can be given broad investment powers.*   The trustee, for example, can be given the power "to invest in all forms of real and personal property." Naturally, the creator of the trust also can give the trustee lesser investment powers. In the past, as a practical matter, the availability of broad investment powers has meant that trustees could invest trust assets in common stocks, while life insurance companies remained largely fixed-dollar investors. During periods of business prosperity, this has favored trusts, but during a business depression the reverse could be true.

3. *Marital and nonmarital trusts can be set up under insurance trusts.* Thus, the insurance trust can become the main estate planning instrument. As we saw in Chap. 15, this may be desirable when life insurance and similar third-party beneficiary arrangements constitute the bulk of an estate.

Similarly, a trust can be used to unify the insured's estate. For example, a number of different life insurance policies can be made payable to one trust, and the estate owner's probate assets may be "poured over" into the insurance trust after death. Thus, all or most of the estate assets can be administered for the heirs under the terms of one instrument— the life insurance trust.

4. *Trustees can administer assets for minors and in other special cases.*   A trust can be used to administer assets for a minor when otherwise a guardian for the minor's property might have to be appointed. The same is true for other beneficiaries who may be physically or mentally incapacitated.

5. *Trust provisions can allow the trustees to save income taxes through proper planning of the distribution of trust income.* This can be done by giving the trustee the discretionary authority to pay out or accumulate trust income—to "sprinkle" trust income among beneficiaries with a view toward the income tax impact of the payments—and by creating multiple trusts.

Whether settlement options or a trust is used depends on the estate owner's wishes, needs, and the particular situation. There may be a tendency to use trusts for larger amounts and settlement options for smaller amounts of proceeds. Since the end of World War II, there has been a general trend toward greater use of insurance trusts.

However, the policyholder does not have to "put all his or her eggs in one basket." The policyholder could leave a portion of the life insurance proceeds under settlement options, perhaps viewed as a guaranteed fund for the beneficiary, and have the remainder payable to an insurance trust. The policyholder can, in effect, diversify the handling of the life insurance proceeds. In this way, his or her beneficiaries will not be entirely dependent on either an insurance company or a bank.

To a Testamentary Trust. Sometimes life insurance proceeds are made payable to the trustee of a testamentary trust, which is one set up at the insured's death under a will. Naming a testamentary trustee as beneficiary may be desirable in some estate situations. While some life insurance companies may not particularly like to have testamentary trustees named as beneficiaries, this normally can be done if proper safeguards are adopted.

Policy Owned by Someone Other than the Insured. We now turn to the less usual, but increasingly important, situation where life insurance is owned by someone other than the insured (i.e., by a third-party owner). This usually is done to keep the policy proceeds out of the insured's gross estate and save on estate taxes. Also, premiums can sometimes be paid with lower after-income-tax dollars when they are paid by someone other than the insured.

Ownership can be placed in a third party at the inception of the policy or after it has been issued. The placing of policy ownership in another can be effected by an *absolute assignment of the policy* (with proper notice to the insurance company) or by *use of an ownership clause* in the insurance policy. When an ownership clause is used, successive owner(s) of the policy can be designated in the clause in the event of the first owner's death prior to the insured's.

Policies owned by others on the insured's life can be held in various ways. Here are some of the more common ways.

Owned by Other Individuals Outright. Policies may be owned by various members of the insured's family—the insured's adult children, parents, etc.

When policies are owned by others outright, the proceeds normally *will not be in the insured's gross estate upon his or her death,* and so, depending on the circumstances, there may be an estate tax saving for the estate. Also, any policy premiums paid by the insured during his or her lifetime will be considered gifts of a present interest to the policyholder, and thus the $10,000 gift tax annual exclusion will apply each year.

A disadvantage in this approach, however, is that, assuming the insured dies before the policy owner, the policy proceeds will be paid to the policy owner as beneficiary and will be included in the policy owner's gross estate upon his or her subsequent death. If, for example, Mother absolutely assigns a $500,000 life insurance policy on her life to her adult son, the $500,000 proceeds will not be in her gross estate upon her death, but they will be in the son's gross estate upon his subsequent death, unless he makes lifetime gifts of the proceeds or consumes them in a way that removes them from his estate.

Owned by "Unfunded" Irrevocable Life Insurance Trusts. Rather than having life insurance owned by an individual other than the insured, the policies can be owned by and payable to an inter-vivos irrevocable life insurance trust. Upon the insured's death, the policy proceeds are paid to the trustee named as beneficiary and are administered according to the terms of the trust, usually for the benefit of the insured's family. The trust owns and administers the life insurance policy(ies) during the insured's lifetime, but it is otherwise "unfunded" in that no or very few income-producing assets are also placed in the trust (the income from which could be used to pay the life insurance premiums). The payment of premiums in this kind of trust is handled by the insured or someone else making periodic payments (gifts) to the trustee, who then can use the funds to pay the premiums.

An unfunded irrevocable trust as owner and beneficiary of life insurance offers the advantage, in addition to the general advantages of trusts, of making it possible to avoid including the insurance proceeds in the trust beneficiary's gross estate. Thus, both the insured's estate and the insured's spouse's estate normally would be skipped in these arrangements, and, if desired, other trust beneficiary's estates also can be "skipped" for federal estate tax purposes, provided the trust beneficiary (and the insured's spouse if he or she is also a trust beneficiary) is given only those powers over the trust that will *not* cause the corpus to be included in his or her gross estate. However, when the trust is arranged to skip the gross estates of nonspouse trust beneficiaries (say, children of the grantor), it will be a generation-skipping trust and so may be subject to the GST tax. In this event, the grantor may want to allocate part of his or her $1,000,000 lifetime GST exemption to each gift he or she makes to the trust to keep the trust exempt for GST tax purposes.

But a potential problem in this kind of arrangement is that the gift of the policy, and any subsequent gifts to the trust by the insured to continue the policy in force, may not be considered gifts of a present interest and hence not eligible for the $10,000 gift tax annual exclusion. However, if the trust is properly arranged to give the beneficiary(ies) a limited noncumulative annual right to withdraw that year's contributions to the trust by the insured (a so-called Crummey power), the annual exclusion then can be secured for those annual contributions up to the stated limits. Of course, it is not contemplated that the beneficiary(ies) actually will exercise such a "power."

The concept of the *Crummey power* (also described on pp. 331–332) normally is important to the success of most unfunded irrevocable life insurance trusts. The purpose of such a power is to gain the annual exclusion for gifts or most gifts made by the grantor to the trust, so that the trustee can pay the premiums and keep the life insurance (normally on the grantor's life) in force. The annual limits on Crummey withdrawal powers for each trust beneficiary with such powers normally are stated as the lesser of that year's contributions to the trust or some dollar limit.[3] There is some technical debate among practitioners as to the better approach to use in setting the dollar limits on annual Crummey withdrawal rights. This debate is beyond the scope of this book, but such annual limits often are set either as $5000 or 5 percent of the trust corpus (whichever is larger) for each beneficiary, or as $10,000 (or $20,000 if split gifts are involved) for each beneficiary. The power to withdraw generally should be available each year to the beneficiaries with such powers for a reasonable period of time (such as 60 days), and the beneficiaries should be notified of their Crummey withdrawal rights. Thus, even though the real purpose of Crummey powers is to get the benefit of the gift tax annual exclusion for periodic gifts to the trust by the grantor, the withdrawal right itself must be real (even though hopefully not actually exercised by the trust beneficiaries). To the extent that periodic gifts to the trust exceed the Crummey power limits used in the trust instrument, taxable gifts (future interests) will be made and the grantor's unified credit (to the extent it is still available) will have to be used to eliminate (or reduce) any actual gift tax payable.

It normally is considered desirable for the Crummey power to make all gifts to the trust excluded for gift tax purposes by the $10,000 per donee per year gift tax annual exclusion without using any of the grantor-donor's unified credit, *if this is possible.* That way, no gift tax is incurred in creating and maintaining the insurance in the trust, and no estate tax is incurred in the grantor-insured's estate or in his or her spouse's estate (if any) at their deaths. In effect, then, it is hoped that there will be no transfer taxation at

---

[3] There also may be so-called hanging Crummey powers, where the withdrawal rights are cumulative (rather than noncumulative as assumed in the discussion in the text). However, as of this writing the IRS has questioned hanging powers, and they probably are not as commonly used as the noncumulative powers assumed in this discussion.

all on the life insurance in these trusts upon creation of the trust, at the insured's death, and at the insured's spouse's death (if any). As noted previously, these trusts can also be used for generation-skipping purposes with proper planning.

These favorable transfer tax aspects, plus the general advantages of trust administration of life insurance proceeds, have led unfunded irrevocable life insurance trusts to be dubbed "supertrusts." They have become an important tool in the estate planner's arsenal of planning techniques. In fact, whenever a person and his or her spouse have combined estates sufficiently large so that they will attract federal estate taxation, and when the person owns life insurance on his or her life or is considering purchasing such life insurance, he or she should consider the use of an unfunded irrevocable life insurance trust (or perhaps someone else's owning the insurance, such as a child) as owner and beneficiary of the life insurance, so that it will escape federal estate taxation at least at the deaths of the insured and his or her spouse (if any). Such estate taxation on life insurance proceeds subject to the federal estate tax would start effectively at a 37 percent estate tax rate and currently could be taxed as high as 55 percent. This is a substantial transfer tax burden to have on life insurance proceeds, particularly when planning may help avoid it.

Most kinds of life insurance can be placed in, or purchased by, an unfunded irrevocable life insurance trust. Lower premium and lower (or no)-cash-value forms may be desirable to minimize the gift tax problems just noted. Also, since the insurance is being given away, the policy owner must be sure that he or she can or should part with the life insurance for other planning purposes. For example, a policy owner may not want to give away a high-cash-value policy that he or she is planning to use for retirement income purposes. In recent years, a popular kind of policy to have in unfunded irrevocable life insurance trusts has been the second-to-die (joint life) policies on husbands and wives as insureds.

Owned by Funded Irrevocable Life Insurance Trusts. This time the irrevocable trust not only owns and is the beneficiary of the life insurance but also contains income-producing assets which are used to pay some or all of the life insurance premiums. Thus, if this kind of trust is created, it must be given some income-producing assets to finance the life insurance owned by the trust.

Under the right kind of circumstances, use of a funded irrevocable insurance trust can be feasible. However, the income tax rules as to who is to be taxed on the trust income that is used to pay the life insurance premiums are important. The tax law provides that any income from a trust that can be applied to pay premiums on insurance on the life of the creator of the trust, or on the life of the spouse of the creator of the trust, will be taxable income *to the creator* rather than to the trustee. In other words, this is a kind of grantor trust for federal income tax purposes. Thus, for example, if a couple sets up such a trust to buy life insurance on one spouse's life, the trust income will be taxable to *the insured,* rather than to the trustee and ultimately to the trust beneficiaries. This considerably reduces the attractiveness of *funded* irrevocable insurance trusts unless someone other than the insured or the insured's spouse can fund the trust. Even then, it may be a generation-skipping transfer. Thus, these kinds of arrangements are not as popular as they once were.

Should Life Insurance Be Given Away?

The question of whether life insurance should be given away has become increasingly complex today as a result of the introduction of the unlimited marital deduction by ERTA. However, many persons have made gifts of their life insurance policies.

Advantages of Gifts of Life Insurance.   Life insurance is attractive as gift property, since life insurance normally can be removed from the insured's gross estate by giving away all incidents of ownership in the policy. Further, insureds can still continue to pay the premiums, *provided* they have made a *bona fide gift* of the policy. The gift tax value of insurance contracts normally is small, and in any event would be relatively less than the amount removed from the taxable estate (i.e., the policy face). In fact, there is normally little or no actual gift tax involved.

These transfer tax advantages of gifts of life insurance have already been explored in this chapter. Of course, if a person and his or her spouse do not have (or expect to have) estates large enough to attract federal estate taxation anyway, there seems to be little reason to give away his or her life insurance.

People also may be more willing to give away life insurance than, say, securities, because the life insurance usually is not producing income currently and is normally intended for the benefit of the policy beneficiaries anyway.

Pitfalls in Gifts of Life Insurance.   Despite the potential attractions in gifts of life insurance, there are some problem areas to consider. First, the unlimited federal estate tax marital deduction would seem to have eliminated any estate tax advantage that formerly may have existed in giving life insurance to one's spouse. However, gifts of life insurance to other family members or to trusts still may provide significant estate tax advantages, depending on the circumstances. Second, donors should be careful to divest themselves completely of all their interest and rights in the policy. Otherwise, they may directly or indirectly retain incidents of ownership in the policy and, as a result, the estate tax-saving purpose of the gift will be defeated.

In addition, the gift of life insurance must be a *bona fide gift* and not merely a sham transaction intended for tax-saving purposes only. The donee of the policy should be, and act like, the owner. For example, the donee should have possession of, and control over, the policy contract, and probably also should receive the premium notices and make the actual premium payments to the insurance company, even though the donor may supply the donee with the necessary funds.

Where gifts of life insurance are made to individuals, care should be taken not to have the policies return to the donor by inheritance if the donee should predecease the donor. This normally can be handled by having donees leave the policy to someone else in their wills or by naming a successive owner in a policy ownership clause.

Finally, a life insurance policy normally is valuable property. Therefore, insured persons should consider carefully whether they want to relinquish ownership and control over some or all of their insurance policies.

Gifts of Group Life Insurance.   Changes in the tax law have made it possible in most cases for employees to absolutely assign their group term life insurance to another and thus remove the proceeds from their gross estates for federal estate tax purposes. This can be an attractive tax benefit for many employees, because the face amounts of group term life insurance on individual lives may be quite substantial today (for example, two, three, or even more times annual salary). Also, since it generally is term insurance, employees themselves really are not giving away much in the way of policy values during their lifetimes. Thus, an employee's group term life insurance could be absolutely assigned, say, to a child or particularly to an unfunded irrevocable life insurance trust.

Historically, most group term life insurance policies (and certificates) prohibited assignment of the insurance by the covered employee. However, because the tax authorities now hold that group term life insurance can be removed from an employee's gross estate by a valid, irrevocable assignment of all his or her incidents of ownership in the insurance (i.e., by an absolute assignment), states have enacted statutes that specifically authorize or permit the assignment of all rights, benefits, privileges, and incidents of ownership in group life insurance. However, not all group life insurance master contracts may permit such assignments (although most do), and so the estate owner should check into the situation in his or her own case with professional advisors.

Other Death Benefits

Life insurance is a common and important kind of death benefit. Therefore, we have devoted considerable attention to life insurance arrangements in the estate plan. However, depending on the circumstances, estate owners may also have other kinds of death benefits that can be quite significant in their overall estates. These may include death benefits under qualified retirement plans, death benefits under tax-sheltered annuity plans, death benefits from HR-10 or IRA plans, survivors' benefits under nonqualified deferred compensation arrangements, death benefits under nonqualified individual annuities, and the like.

How these other benefits are to be arranged in an estate plan should be considered in the overall planning process. Planning for qualified retirement plan death benefits has already been briefly discussed on p. 388. An estate owner may want to coordinate these death benefits with life insurance arrangements, such as having them payable to a revocable unfunded life insurance trust. Naturally, the appropriate arrangement will depend on the circumstances of each case.

Revocable Trusts as a Will Substitute

An interesting and often advantageous way of managing an estate owner's property during his or her lifetime, and then transmitting the property to others at the estate owner's death, is the *living revocable trust*.[4] The idea of a revocable living trust as a way to transfer property to a person's heirs outside of his or her probate estate is not new, and yet it is a novel one to many people. This inter vivos (during lifetime) method of estate transfer has many advantages when compared with leaving property by will.

The essence of the plan is that estate owners during their lifetime create a revocable trust into which they place some or the major part of their property. The trustee administers and invests the trust property and pays the income from the trust to the creator or as the creator directs. Since creators can alter, amend, or revoke the trust at any time during their lifetime, they can get the trust property back whenever they wish. Upon the creator's death, however, the trust becomes irrevocable and the trust property is administered according to its terms for the benefit of the creator's beneficiaries.

If desired, such a trust can contain marital and nonmarital trust provisions to make proper use of the federal estate tax marital deduction. Life insurance on the estate owner's life and other death benefits can be made payable to the trust. Also, where permitted by law, property can be "poured over" from the estate owner's will into such a trust. Thus, a revocable trust can unify an estate so that it can be administered under one instrument.

---

[4] These are trusts that can be terminated or changed by the creator as he or she wishes during the creator's lifetime.

However, because a revocable trust can be terminated by its creator at will, the trust income will be taxable to the creator during his or her lifetime. (Thus, it is a kind of grantor trust for federal income tax purposes.) Also, the trust corpus will be included in his or her gross estate at death. No taxable gift is made when the trust is created. Thus, tax savings by the creator are not the primary motivation for setting up such trusts.

Let us take a specific example of such a revocable trust. Assume that John Mature, age 55, owns in his own name securities and other income-producing property worth approximately $800,000. This property yields about $50,000 per year in investment income. John is a busy, successful business executive who also is active in church and civic affairs. He is married and has two married children and four grandchildren.

John decides to transfer the $800,000 of securities and income-producing property to a revocable living trust with the XYZ Bank and Trust Company as trustee. The income from the trust is to be paid to John during his lifetime, and following his death the trust is to be continued for the benefit of John's wife, children, and grandchildren. The trust agreement contains marital and nonmarital trust provisions so that at John's death his estate can make proper use of the federal estate tax marital deduction without "overqualifying" his property for the deduction. John's will "pours over" the balance of his estate into this trust.

What might John hope to accomplish by the use of this revocable trust arrangement?

1. The XYZ Bank and Trust Company will manage and invest the trust property for John and pay him the income. (The bank also maintains several common trust funds in which some or all of the trust's assets can be invested.) Thus, John is relieved of these duties and has the benefit of the bank's expertise in these areas. However, if for any reason John becomes dissatisfied with the arrangement, he can revoke the trust and recover his property.

2. If John should become physically or mentally incapacitated or otherwise unable to manage his own affairs, the trustee will continue to manage and invest the trust property for John's benefit without interruption.

3. If the trust property is invested in the bank's common trust fund(s), the advantages of investment diversification can be secured.

4. Upon John's death, the trustee will continue to manage and invest the trust property for the surviving beneficiaries (John's family) and pay the trust income to them without interruption. John can also make special provisions in the trust for any family members who may have unusual needs or special problems, such as a disabled or mentally retarded child or grandchild, for example. Ultimately, the property will be distributed to the trust beneficiaries according to the terms of the trust. The revoca-

ble trust thus acts as a will substitute for the transmission of this part of John's estate at his death.

5. The use of a revocable trust may reduce the likelihood of a will's being contested with the attendant publicity. The importance of this factor, of course, depends on the particular circumstances.

6. A revocable trust may provide protection against the creditors of John's estate.

7. In some states, a revocable trust may be used to avoid a surviving spouse's elective share of the estate. However, the law generally is shifting against this use of the revocable living trust.

8. The revocable trust *may* be a less costly way for John to transfer his estate to his family, depending on the circumstances. The XYZ Bank and Trust Company will charge an annual trustee's fee, which in this case might be $6850 per year (see the illustrative fee scale in Chap. 14). However, because such trustee's fees may be income tax-deductible, the after-tax cost could be less. On the other hand, John's estate would save all or a part of the executor's and other fees that otherwise would have been levied on the $800,000 had it passed as a part of John's probate estate under his will. These probate costs (which are deductible for estate tax purposes) might run, say, 5 to 8 percent of the $800,000 principal amount. Thus, this kind of revocable trust results in annual trustee's fees but saves on probate costs at the time of the creator's death.

9. During his lifetime, if he wishes, John may name himself to be the trustee and then name a successor trustee in the event of his incapacity or death.

Property Management Arrangements to Deal with Physical or Mental Incapacity

Making arrangements to deal with possible physical or mental incapacity is a rapidly developing part of estate planning and planning for many elderly persons. The planning objectives and problems involved were outlined on pp. 24 and 40–41 of Chap. 2. This section will outline briefly some of the arrangements being used to meet these objectives. It should be noted that this also is a rapidly changing area of the law.

Durable Powers of Attorney

A *power of attorney* is a written instrument in which one person (called the principal) names another person or persons as his or her attorney-in-fact or agent to act in the principal's place and on the principal's behalf as provided for in the written instrument. In essence, it is an instrument creating an agency relationship. A *durable power of attorney* is one that continues in effect, or becomes effective, after the principal's incapacity. To be a durable power, the instrument must specifically so state. Powers of attorney may also be general or limited. A *general* power of attorney authorizes the agent to act for the principal generally in all matters, while a *limited* power applies only to certain specified matters.

One approach to planning for a person's potential physical or mental incapacity is to execute an *immediately effective durable general power of attorney* naming one or more highly trusted persons as attorney-in-fact to act for the person in all matters. The understanding among all involved should be that the durable power of attorney will not be used unless the person executing the power becomes incapacitated and unable to manage his or her own affairs.

Another approach is to execute a *"springing" durable general power of attorney.* A springing power becomes effective only in the event the principal becomes incapacitated as defined in the document. However, in this case a clear and workable definition of incapacity or disability is important. Also, the use of springing powers may not be permitted in a few states.

Durable Power of Attorney in Conjunction with Revocable Living Trusts

Still another approach is to have an existing (or springing) durable power of attorney under which the attorney-in-fact has the power to transfer some or all of the principal's assets to a previously existing revocable living trust. Thus, in the event of the principal's incapacity, the attorney-in-fact can use the power of attorney to fund or add assets to the revocable living trust and have those assets administered for the principal (and also beneficiary of the trust) during the person's incapacity. At the person's incapacity or disability, the formerly revocable trust becomes irrevocable. This technique combines the use of powers of attorney (an agency relationship) and revocable living trusts (a trust relationship) and also can give considerable flexibility to the attorney-in-fact.

Funded Revocable Living Trust

A funded revocable living trust can be set up generally as described previously in this chapter (see pp. 475–477). One of its advantages is to provide property management in the event of the creator's or grantor's physical or mental incapacity and inability to manage his or her own affairs. At this point, the trust becomes irrevocable.

Of course, these revocable living trusts have other purposes (as a will substitute, for example) and are created and funded before any possible incapacity of the grantor. The person may also execute a durable general power of attorney (either existing or springing) in addition to such a funded revocable living trust.

"Convenience" Joint Tenancies (Accounts)

Sometimes people will attempt to deal with the issue of property management in case of incapacity by creating joint bank accounts, CDs, or other accounts with another person, with the idea that should one of them (presumably the older one) become incapacitated (or die), the other joint owner would simply use the money or other assets to "take care of" the incapacitated joint owner and/or to distribute the assets in the event of his or her death. This seems quite simple, and it may be in some cases. However, the essential problem with this approach is that, assuming that both joint owners can withdraw freely from the account (as normally would be the case), the funds may be used other than as intended by the party placing them in the account (normally the older, propertied party), since they are held jointly and there is no power of attorney instrument or trust agreement to say otherwise. Thus, as a practical and legal matter, these convenience joint accounts are a questionable solution to the incapacity problem in most cases.

As indicated at the start of this section and in Chap. 2, this can be a complex and difficult financial planning problem with which to deal. Professional help often is advisable. Only a durable general power of attorney (either existing or springing) may be a satisfactory solution in many cases where there are relatively modest assets. On the other hand, when there are more extensive assets and perhaps other estate and family issues, a revocable living trust may be desirable. Frequently, both a revocable living trust (either unfunded or funded) and a durable power of attorney will be used. An overriding issue in all these arrangements is the selection of a person or persons (or institutional trustee) in which the property owner can have complete confidence (the highest trust) to be attorney-in-fact and/or trustee of a living trust. This is the really difficult part. After all, this person or persons (or institutional trustee) may be handling the property owner's affairs when the property owner is incapacitated and cannot. Of course, everyone hopes this will not happen, but in fact it often does.

Health Care Decision Making

The previous section dealt with the sensitive issue of how one can arrange for the management of his or her property in the event of physical or mental incapacity. Now we are dealing with the even more sensitive and controversial issue of health care decision making when the individual involved is no longer competent or able to make those decisions for himself or herself. It is generally recognized, of course, that competent persons have the right to accept or refuse medical care for themselves. Unfortunately, however, persons may reach the point where they are no longer competent or able to make such decisions for themselves, and persons may want to try to make advance arrangements for this unhappy contingency.

Durable Powers of Attorney for Health Care Decisions.   This essentially is an extension of the durable power of attorney idea to allow an attorney-in-fact to make health care decisions for the principal, within the limits of any applicable law and within any limits set by the principal in the power-of-attorney instrument, if the principal becomes incompetent to do so. This obviously can be a very important power. The health-care power of attorney can be a portion of one covering property management (as just discussed), or a separate health-care power of attorney. Of course, the power of attorney must be executed while the person involved is competent to do so.

The law in this area is new and emerging. The legal rules in a given state may not be entirely clear and, as a practical matter, some health care providers may refuse to honor such durable powers. Some states have enacted special statutes that specifically allow persons to execute durable powers of attorney for health care decisions. However, even in states without such specific authorizing statutes, many authorities believe that such durable powers can be legally effective for this purpose anyway. Nevertheless, persons generally should secure the advice of legal counsel as to the state of the law on these matters in their own jurisdiction.

Living Wills.   Most states now have statutes that permit persons to execute valid documents (so-called living wills) that can direct, in specified circumstances, how medical treatment should be rendered or withheld in terminal situations after the person has become incompetent to make his or her own health care decisions. Thus, persons living in those states may execute such living wills under the terms and subject to the conditions of their state's statute.

While living wills and durable powers of attorney for health care decisions have some similarities in purpose, they differ in several respects. First, living wills apply only in terminal situations. Second, not all kinds of care can be refused under the living will statutes of various states. Third, durable powers permit the principal, in drafting the instrument, to set such terms and conditions of the power as the principal may deem appropriate. Finally, only a durable power allows the principal to name a specific party (the attorney-in-fact) to make health care decisions if the principal is not competent to do so.

There is great interest in this exposure (issue) and in planning for it today. There also is great controversy surrounding it. In many cases, the law is unclear or is changing. Under these circumstances, legal, medical, and perhaps spiritual advice may be needed by many persons. Some persons who want to plan in advance for this unfortunate but possible situation have opted to execute both a living will and a durable power of attorney for health care decisions.

17
Planning for Business Interests

When an individual has an interest in a closely held business, whether it be as a sole proprietor, partner, or stockholder in a close corporation, it is of great importance that proper financial planning take place to develop and maintain a coordinated and smoothly functioning financial plan for the continuation of the business in the event of the death or disability of an owner. In these cases, proper planning is especially important, since a closely held business interest often is one of the owner's most important assets. Building such a business often represents a person's major lifetime work. Protecting its value and earning power should be one of the main purposes in constructing the owner's personal financial plan.

Anyone who owns such a business interest should have a definite plan to provide for either the perpetuation or the disposition of the business. Business owners face the following kinds of questions:

1. Who will control the business when I die?
2. Will there be a market for the business if it has to be sold?
3. Will the business provide adequate income for my heirs?
4. How will the value of the business affect the taxes and liquidity needs of my estate?
5. Will I be able to continue in business if one of my associates dies?
6. How can working capital be kept intact?
7. How can a business be transferred to a new owner without shrinkage in value?

8. What would happen to the business in the event of my disability or that of one of my associates?

9. What will become of my business interest if I retire?

10. What other actions should I and my co-owners take to enhance the worth of our business interests?

To answer these questions, the business owner should understand the various forms of business organization, the risks affecting personal financial planning involved in each form, and how to solve the potential problems created by these risks.

Types of Closely Held Business Entities

One important decision for a person or persons planning to start a business or already in business is what kind of business entity or entities to use in organizing their business venture. This decision can have legal, tax, and economic ramifications and can be quite important for the closely held business owner or owners.

The following is a brief outline of the various types of closely held business entities that could be used. Some, of course, are more common and popular than others. Also, some are so-called pass-through entities, in that their business profits and losses are not taxed at the entity level but are passed through directly to the owners, while others are taxable entities themselves. This can make a considerable difference in the type of business entity used because, as of this writing (1992), the top marginal income tax rate for individuals (31 percent) is lower than the top marginal corporate income tax rate (34 percent or 39 percent with the 5 percentage point phaseout rate added). This generally makes it more attractive in terms of income taxes for business profits to be taxed directly to the owners at their individual tax rates than to be taxed at corporate income tax rates. Hence, this factor in itself tends to favor use of pass-through-type business entities. Finally, some forms may provide limited liability for business obligations to their owners, while others do not (i.e., the owners have unlimited liability).

Outline of Forms of Business Entities

1. *Proprietorship:* one owner; pass-through entity; unlimited liability
2. *Partnership*
   a. *General partnership:* more than one partner; pass-through entity; unlimited liability

    b. Limited partnership: at least one general partner and one limited partner; pass-through entity; unlimited liability for general partner(s) and limited liability for limited partner(s)

3. *Corporation*
    a. C corporation: can have one or more than one stockholder; taxable entity; limited liability for stockholders
    b. S corporation: can have one or more than one stockholder (but not more than 35 stockholders); pass-through entity; limited liability for stockholders; only some corporations eligible
4. *Limited liability company:* newer concept; exists now in some states; generally has more than one member; pass-through entity; limited liability for members; generally does not have free transferability of interests and continuity of life

Deciding Which Type of Entity to Use

Deciding which type of entity to use can be a complex question, and a development of all the factors involved is beyond the scope of this book. The following is only a brief outline of some of these factors.

- The liability of the owners for business obligations
- Whether it is a pass-through entity for income tax purposes, and, if not, the comparative income tax rates of the owners and the entity
- The problem of double taxation of C corporations
- Organizational and operating requirements
- Flexibility for income tax purposes
- Recognition of gain in formation (see pp. 309–310 in Chap. 11)
- Recognition of gain upon liquidation
- Ease of governance (control)
- Ease of financing and bringing in other investors
- Ease of changing from one type of organization to another
- Income tax bases of owners in the business
- Ability to make gifts of business interests to family members
- Availability of employee benefits to owners
- Other factors

    These factors, of course, apply to business organizations for closely held businesses. Almost all publicly traded business entities are organized as C corporations.

Should a Business Interest Be Sold or Retained for the Family?

When business owners are planning their estates, they have two initial alternatives regarding the fate of the business. One plan may be to dispose of the business interest entirely upon the death or retirement of the owner; another may be to arrange for its retention in the family. Retention may be practical when the family owns a majority interest, when some member of the family is interested in the business and is capable of managing it successfully, when the future outlook for the business is promising, and when there are other assets in the owner's estate, including perhaps existing or new life insurance, so that the owner can arrange adequate liquidity for his or her estate and also equalize the distribution of the estate among those heirs who will receive a business interest and those who will not. If the above elements are missing, the business owner should carefully consider disposing of the interest in the most orderly and efficient way possible.

Partnerships

A partnership can be looked upon as a business marriage—two or more people (or organizations) joined together to conduct a business for profit. The partners are the business.

The Business Continuation Problem

The death of a partner legally dissolves the partnership, and the deceased partner's interest in the business must be settled. In the absence of an agreement to the contrary, the surviving partner or partners succeed to the ownership of the firm's assets *as a liquidating trustee.* The relationship between the surviving partner(s) and a deceased partner's estate is recognized as fiduciary in nature, particularly with respect to the remedies available if there is a breach of this trust. In this role, the surviving partner must make a fair and complete disclosure of all facts affecting those assets. Moreover, if anything goes wrong between the surviving partner and the heirs, who presumably are unfamiliar with partnership affairs, the surviving partner will have the burden of proving that his or her trusteeship was carried out in compliance with the high standards of responsibility required of trustees. Such a situation can bring the business to an abrupt standstill. It poses a dilemma both for the surviving partner(s) and for the heirs of a deceased partner that could result in severe financial loss to all concerned.

In the absence of an agreement entered into during the partners' lifetimes providing specifically for the continuation of the business, there are two alternatives at a partner's death: The business may be reorganized, or it may be terminated (i.e., liquidated or wound up). Either choice usually is extremely costly for everyone involved.

There are various possible approaches for surviving partners to continue a partnership on a reorganized basis, but generally none is completely satisfactory. Three of the more popular ones are discussed below.

1. The surviving partners might take in the deceased partner's heirs as new partners and, in effect, form a new partnership. However, even if the surviving partners are willing to consider the heirs as new partners, the heirs in most cases will be inexperienced and incapable of joining actively in the conduct of the business. Also, lack of liquidity for estate settlement costs might force the heirs to demand cash for the deceased's interest rather than the interest itself.

2. The survivors might take in as a new partner an outside party to whom the deceased partner's estate would sell the deceased's interest. However, even if a party willing to assume the risk could be found, and a selling price could be agreed upon, the outsider might be personally unsuitable to the survivors, incompetent, or even a competitor seeking control of the business.

3. The survivors might buy the deceased's interest from the heirs or estate and assume full ownership. However, the survivors and heirs may not be able to agree on a satisfactory selling price. In addition, the survivors still have the problem of raising sufficient cash to buy the deceased's interest.

The general inadequacy of reorganizing and continuing the business generally leads to *forced liquidation,* which, as noted above, usually is very costly. Accounts receivable may be collected for less than half their value. At the same time, creditors press their demands for full payment. All business activity, except as necessary for winding up the partnership affairs, must cease. Credit tends to vanish, and goodwill typically is lost entirely. In the end, a valuable business may be liquidated (or sold) for a fraction of its worth as a going concern. Also, by liquidating the going concern, the survivors have liquidated their own jobs.

Clearly, what the partners usually need is a plan that allows the surviving partners to obtain full ownership of the business and pay a deceased partner's estate a fair price for his or her interest. The plan should establish a fair price and produce the necessary cash.

The Plan—A Buy-Sell Agreement

This plan calls for a written agreement entered into during the partners' lifetimes, between the individual partners (cross-purchase type of agreement) or between the partnership and the partners (entity type of agreement), providing for the sale and purchase of a deceased partner's interest. The agreement establishes a mutually agreeable purchase price for each partner's interest and should contain a provision for adjusting the purchase price if the value of the business changes. Life insurance can be used to fund the agreement by providing, upon the death of a partner, the immediate cash necessary to purchase the deceased's interest.

As we said before, there are two main kinds of partnership buy-sell agreements—the *cross-purchase plan* and the *entity plan*. The partners, with the help and advice of their professional advisors, must make a choice as to which plan would be best for them considering their own circumstances and objectives. The factors involved in such a choice are complex and beyond the scope of this book. Table 17.1 illustrates the results of both the cross-purchase type and the entity type of buy-sell agreement for a partnership of three equal partners valued at $240,000.

Table 17.1. Partnership Value, $240,000

Partner A owns a ⅓ interest, $80,000	Partner B owns a ⅓ interest, $80,000	Partner C owns a ⅓ interest, $80,000

Cross-purchase agreement
The three partners agree in writing on (1) the value of their interests, and (2) that in the event of the death of a partner, the estate of the deceased will sell, *and the surviving partners will buy,* the interest of the deceased.

Life insurance to fund agreement

A insures:	B insures:	C insures:
B for $40,000	A for $40,000	A for $40,000
C for $40,000	C for $40,000	B for $40,000

Each partner is the applicant, owner, premium payor, and beneficiary of the policies on the other two partners.

At death
Each surviving partner utilizes the insurance proceeds on the deceased partner's life that he or she receives as beneficiary to purchase one-half of the deceased partner's interest from his or her estate according to the terms of the buy-sell agreement. (There may also be a disability provision in the buy-sell agreement to meet this risk as well.)

Entity agreement
The three partners agree in writing on (1) the value of their interests, and (2) that in the event of the death of a partner, the estate of the deceased will sell, *and the partnership will buy,* the interest of the deceased.

Life insurance to fund agreement
Partnership insures A for $80,000, B for $80,000, and C for $80,000.
The Partnership is the applicant, owner, premium payor, and beneficiary of all policies.

At death
The Partnership utilizes the insurance proceeds on the deceased partner's life that it receives as beneficiary to purchase the deceased partner's interest from his or her estate according to the terms of the buy-sell agreement. (There may also be a disability provision in the buy-sell agreement to meet this risk as well.)

Tax Aspects

The tax consequences of buy-sell arrangements are important and should be considered to evaluate their impact on the financial plans of the partners.

Income Taxation.   The income tax aspects of partnership buy-sell agreements can be complicated and are only summarized here.

Insurance Premiums.   Whether paid by the individual partners or the partnership, life insurance premiums are not deductible for income tax purposes since the premium payor(s) are either directly or indirectly beneficiaries under the life insurance policies. Such payments are considered personal rather than business expenses.

Death Proceeds.   Life insurance death proceeds are received by the beneficiary(ies) income tax–free. This is true whether the beneficiary is the partnership or the partners.

Purchase Payments.   The proceeds received by the partnership or the partners are used as payments to purchase the deceased partner's interest from the estate. The tax treatment of these payments depends on the particular partnership interest being purchased.

In typical commercial partnerships, tangible property, such as buildings, equipment and inventory, and perhaps goodwill, generally are the major items of value. These assets are considered capital assets.[1] Payments for capital assets are not deductible by the partnership or the partners and are not taxable as ordinary income to the estate of a deceased partner. Such purchase payments also normally would not result in a capital gain for the estate, because the estate would have a stepped-up income tax basis for the deceased partner's interest following his or her death.

In a professional or personal service partnership, tangible property normally represents only a minor portion of the total value of the partnership. A substantial portion of the firm's total value often consists of unrealized receivables and work in process.

In considering the total value of such a partnership, the value must be broken down into the portions allocable to tangible property and allocable to unrealized receivables, since different tax treatment is accorded to each. As in commercial partnerships, the payment(s) for capital assets (partnership property) is not deductible by the partnership and is not considered

---

[1] This assumes that (1) if an entity-type agreement is used, the agreement specifically provides for a payment for goodwill, and (2) for either type of agreement, the partnership does not have substantially appreciated inventory or unrealized receivables. On the other hand, in an entity-type agreement, if the agreement is silent as to goodwill (or states that the value does not include goodwill), the goodwill part of the value of the partnership interest is not considered a capital asset and any payment(s) attributable to it is (are) deductible by the partnership or partners and is (are) taxable as ordinary income to the selling partner or to his or her estate. This flexibility with regard to the income tax treatment of goodwill applies only to liquidations of a partner's interest by the partnership.

ordinary income to the decedent's estate. This amount generally is paid in a lump sum to the deceased partner's estate. On the other hand, payments of an agreed amount for unrealized receivables are taxable as ordinary income to the estate as income in respect of a decedent. The fact that these payments constitute ordinary income to the recipient may make it desirable to spread them over several years to cushion the tax impact.

As noted in footnote 1 on p. 488, when a partnership is liquidating a partner's interest in the partnership, the partners in effect may elect to treat an amount paid for goodwill as part of the purchase price for a capital asset or as ordinary income. This normally is a planning issue mainly upon retirement of a partner, but it also applies to an entity-type buy-sell agreement where the partnership technically liquidates a deceased partner's interest at his or her death.

Estate Taxation.   Upon a partner's death, the value of his or her partnership interest normally would be included in the deceased's gross estate, like any other asset he or she owns. A difficulty with closely held business interests, however, is that they may be difficult to value for estate tax purposes. There is, of course, no ready market for them. So the tax authorities may try to set a high value on such interests for tax purposes. But where there exists a properly drawn buy-sell agreement, normally only the purchase price actually paid for the interest will be included in the deceased partner's estate, provided the requirements of Chapter 14 (particularly Section 2703) and/or the common law regarding valuation are met. (See the discussion of the Chapter 14 special valuation rules on pp. 497–498 of this chapter.)

Both a lump-sum payment for capital assets and the commuted value of income continuation payments will be included in a deceased partner's gross estate for federal estate tax purposes. However, since income continuation payments are also taxable as ordinary income, the estate, when reporting this income, may claim a deduction for any estate tax attributable to its inclusion in the estate.

Close Corporations

In a close corporation (either a C corporation or an S corporation), stock ownership is limited to a small group of individuals, the stockholders usually are employees of the corporation in a management role, and the stock is, of course, not publicly traded. Unlike a partnership, which must by law be dissolved upon a partner's death, a corporation continues in existence. However, in practice, the death of a close-corporation stockholder usually has important and far-reaching consequences for the other stockholders and the corporation itself.

Effects of a Stockholder's Death

The effects of the death of a close-corporation stockholder are discussed below in terms of their impact on the corporation, the surviving stockholders, and a deceased stockholder's heirs.

On the Corporation.   The corporation itself may experience the following problems as the result of an executive stockholder's death:

1. Management disrupted.
2. Credit impaired.
3. Loss of business.
4. Impairment of employee morale—employees may worry about the future of the business and their own financial security. A decline in efficiency and perhaps an increase in turnover may result.

On Surviving Stockholders.   The following are some of the alternatives that may face the surviving stockholders:

1. They may continue in business with the heirs of the deceased stockholder as new stockholders. This often is undesirable, since the heirs frequently are not able or inclined to assume responsibility in management.
2. They may sell their stock. This often is undesirable or impractical, as they will sell themselves out of business, and there may be a real problem of finding an appropriate buyer who will pay a fair price for the stock.
3. They may buy the deceased's stock. Among the alternatives available after death, this probably is the best for all concerned. The surviving stockholders would acquire full control of the corporation, and the heirs could hope to receive a reasonable price for their stock interest. But there are several practical obstacles to this arrangement. Without a prior agreement, it is very difficult for all parties to agree on a selling price. Also, the surviving stockholders have the problem of raising the money needed for the purchase.

On the Deceased Stockholder's Heirs.   On the other hand, here are some of the alternatives that may face the heirs of a deceased stockholder as they survey their new situation as stockholders in a close corporation:

1. The heirs may retain their inherited stock as active or inactive stockholders. This approach often does not work because of the divergent interests of the heirs and the surviving stockholders. The survivors frequently are interested primarily in maintaining business growth, while the heirs usually are interested in income from the business.
2. The heirs may sell the stock to an outsider. However, it often is difficult for them to find a buyer who has the money, who will pay a fair price, and

who will risk entering a close corporation with the remaining stock-holders.

3. The heirs may sell their stock to the surviving stockholders. As we saw above, in the absence of a prior agreement, this probably is the best alternative for all concerned, if a fair price can be agreed upon and if the surviving stockholders can finance the purchase. But in practice these are big "ifs."

The Plan—A Buy-Sell Agreement

A prearranged written agreement between the individual stockholders (a cross-purchase agreement) or between the corporation and its stockholders (a stock retirement or stock redemption agreement) providing for the sale and purchase of the stock of a deceased stockholder often is the best solution to the problem of disposing of a business interest. The agreement would establish the purchase price for the stock and usually provides for periodic adjustments of the price as the value of the business changes over time.

Life insurance on the stockholders' lives is normally used to fund the agreement, so that upon a stockholder's death the cash necessary to purchase his or her stock will be available. As in partnership situations, two types of agreements are available—a cross-purchase type and a stock retirement type.

Once again, as with a partnership, the choice of the type of agreement is of importance to the stockholders and should be made with the help of their professional advisors.

Table 17.2 illustrates how a cross-purchase and a stock retirement buy-sell arrangement would operate for a typical close corporation with three equal stockholders.

Tax Aspects

Income Taxation.   Here again, the income tax aspects of buy-sell agreements can be complex. The basic rules are only summarized here.

Insurance Premiums.   Whether paid by the stockholders or by the corporation, life insurance premiums are not deductible for income tax purposes, since the premium payor(s) are either directly or indirectly beneficiaries under the policies.

Death Proceeds.   Life insurance death proceeds generally are received by beneficiaries free of federal income tax. This normally is true whether the beneficiary is the corporation or the individual stockholders.[2]

---

[2] When the individual stockholders are the beneficiaries (in a cross-purchase plan), a special rule—the "transfer for value" rule—may apply under certain circumstances and cause a portion of the proceeds to be taxed as income.

Table 17.2. Corporation Value, $300,000

Stockholder A owns ⅓ of the stock, $100,000	Stockholder B owns ⅓ of the stock, $100,000	Stockholder C owns ⅓ of the stock, $100,000

Cross-purchase agreement
The three stockholders agree in writing on (1) the value of the stock, and (2) that in the event of the death of a stockholder, the estate of the deceased will sell, *and the surviving stockholders will buy,* the stock of the deceased.

Life insurance to fund agreement

A insures:	B insures:	C insures:
B for $50,000	A for $50,000	A for $50,000
C for $50,000	C for $50,000	B for $50,000

Each stockholder is the applicant, owner, premium payor, and beneficiary of the policies on the other two stockholders.

At death
Each surviving stockholder uses the insurance proceeds to purchase one-half of the deceased stockholder's stock from his or her estate according to the terms of the buy-sell agreement. (There may also be a disability provision in the buy-sell agreement to meet this risk as well.)

Stock retirement agreement
The three stockholders and the Corporation agree in writing on (1) the value of the stock, and (2) that in the event of the death of a stockholder, the estate of the deceased will sell, *and the Corporation will buy,* the stock of the deceased.

Life insurance to fund agreement
   Corporation insures:
      A for $100,000
      B for $100,000
      C for $100,000
The Corporation is the applicant, premium payor, owner, and beneficiary of all policies.

At death
The Corporation uses the insurance proceeds to purchase the deceased stockholder's stock from his or her estate according to the terms of the buy-sell agreement. (There may also be a disability provision in the buy-sell agreement to meet this risk as well.)

However, for C corporations a complication is introduced in this area by the corporate alternative minimum tax (AMT). For C corporations, an amount that increases alternative minimum taxable income (AMTI) is 75 percent of the amount by which a corporation's adjusted current earnings (ACE) exceeds its AMTI (without regard to its ACE) for the year. The tax-deferred ("tax-free") investment growth of life insurance cash values would be included in ACE for this purpose, and so would the difference between life insurance death proceeds and the policy's basis for AMT purposes. As a practical matter, this means that 75 percent of these otherwise nontaxable items for regular tax purposes (i.e., the inside buildup of life insurance cash values and life insurance death proceeds less the policy's ACE basis) *may* be subject to the 20 percent corporate AMT rate. However, this will be true only for corporate-owned life insurance (COLI) by C corporations. There can be a number of reasons for corporate-owned life insurance, of which a stock retirement or redemption type of buy-sell agreement is one. Thus, this corporate AMT issue has made corporate-owned life insurance less attractive than formerly was the case.

Purchase Payment. A stock interest in a corporation is considered a capital asset. Thus, the purchase price for an interest is not deductible by the corporation or the stockholders, and it is not taxable income to the deceased stockholder's estate. This payment normally will not result in a capital gain for the estate because the estate would have a stepped-up income tax basis on the deceased's stock in the hands of his or her executor following the stockholder's death.

Estate Taxation. If the appropriate items are included in the buy-sell agreement (see pp. 497–498), normally only the purchase price actually paid for the stock will be included in a deceased stockholder's estate for federal estate tax purposes.

Sole Proprietors

A sole proprietorship is not a separate entity apart from the individual proprietor (as is a partnership or a corporation). Consequently, special problems arise in planning for the orderly disposition of the business at the sole proprietor's death.

The sole proprietor, in an economic sense, is the business, and unless plans are made during his or her lifetime, the business often will die with its owner. Business assets and liabilities pass into the proprietor's estate along with his or her other personal assets and liabilities. The proprietor's executor, lacking specific authorization in the proprietor's will, cannot legally continue the business without personal liability. Thus, the executor normally must dispose of the business immediately, pay estate obligations as quickly as possible, and distribute the remaining property to the heirs. This often results in severe financial loss to the family because of the forced liquidation of the business.

The Problem for the Business

The success of a sole proprietorship usually depends on the personal services and managerial ability of the proprietor. When the proprietor dies (or is totally and permanently disabled), and his or her family or a key employee is not capable of carrying on the business, the flow of income is cut off and, upon forced liquidation, the business may end up worth only a fraction of the value of its assets as carried on the books. Further, the "going concern value" of the proprietorship is lost to the proprietor's family at his or her death. The executor, unable to operate the business without prior authorization, will be forced to liquidate it, probably at a loss.

The Estate's Problem

Estate settlement costs may be even more significant than normal in the case of a sole proprietor because in many cases the business has substantial debts. Since no distinction is made between the proprietorship and the proprietor, all the proprietor's assets would be available to meet all his or her debts—business and personal.

In paying estate debts and obligations, the executor often discovers a cash-poor estate, since much of the proprietor's personal funds and business profits were invested in the proprietorship during his or her lifetime and, thereby, were converted into often nonliquid business assets. This also may force the executor to sell the business as quickly as possible to raise the necessary cash.

Possible Solutions

Clearly, what is needed is a plan that will enable the proprietor *during his or her lifetime* to (1) *set forth his or her objectives concerning the disposition of the business,* and (2) *make adequate financial plans to assure that these objectives can be carried out.*

The objectives set forth during the proprietor's lifetime will vary according to his or her desires and individual circumstances. However, three alternatives for disposing of the business generally are available: (1) orderly liquidation or sale, (2) family retention, and (3) sale to an employee.

Orderly Liquidation or Sale.   Many sole proprietors do not have family members or employees to whom they can transfer the business at their death. So they must plan to convert the business into cash in the most beneficial manner. If possible, this normally means selling the proprietorship as a going concern.

If this course is to be followed, the proprietor's will should authorize his or her executor to continue the business without personal liability until an advantageous sale can be made—if possible, as a going concern. The will may also provide the executor with related discretionary powers that enable the executor to carry out its functions.

The executor's ability to avoid a forced liquidation of the business hinges on the availability of liquid assets in the estate to satisfy estate creditors so that liquidation of the business is not necessary. Life insurance on the sole proprietor can provide the cash needed to pay estate settlement costs, including business debts. Thus, the executor can be given enough time to look around for the best deal in disposing of the business. Life insurance on the proprietor can also offset the diminishing value of the business if liquidation becomes necessary.

Family Retention.　In some cases, a sole proprietor will have a family member or members who can continue the business profitably. Perhaps it is a responsible son or daughter, or son-in-law or daughter-in-law, who has worked in the business and can retain the customers' goodwill. It may be the proprietor's wife or husband who has worked in the business. The proprietor in his or her will leaves the assets of the proprietorship, subject to its liabilities, to the family member, and then leaves the remainder of the estate to his or her other heirs. When a proprietorship is bequeathed to a family member in this manner, care must be taken to define carefully what is given as part of the business interest and what is to be considered as personal assets and liabilities apart from the business.

Life insurance on the sole proprietor can be used to supply cash to help pay estate settlement costs. The executor's ability to transfer the business as a going concern to the chosen heir depends on the ability to satisfy estate creditors from available liquid assets in the estate, rather than from the proceeds of liquidating the proprietorship. Thus, life insurance can be used to discharge estate obligations and help keep the business intact for the family member. Life insurance also can be used to provide those heirs who are not to inherit the business with equitable inheritances. Where a proprietor's estate consists of little property other than the business, as is so frequently the case, life insurance is an ideal means for creating such "inheritances."

Sale to an Employee.　The proprietor may have a key employee who is capable of continuing the business. In this case, a logical solution would be to have the key employee buy the business at the proprietor's death. This would enable the proprietor's estate to realize the going-concern value of the business, rather than a decreased, liquidated value.

Such a sale can be handled efficiently by having the proprietor and the key employee enter into a buy-sell agreement during their lifetimes providing for the sale by the proprietor's estate and the purchase by the key employee of the proprietor's business upon his or her death (and perhaps the proprietor's disability). Life insurance on the sole proprietor should be used to fund the agreement by providing, upon the proprietor's death, the immediate cash necessary for the employee to purchase the business.

Table 17.3 illustrates how these three alternatives might operate in planning for a proprietorship. Naturally, the particular circumstances of each

Table 17.3. Alternate Business Disposition Plans—Sole Proprietorship
Assumed Business Value, $100,000
Assumed Estate Settlement Costs, $25,000

Orderly liquidation or sale	Family retention	Sale to employee
The proprietor designates in his or her will that in the event of his or her death: (1) the business will be liquidated or sold in the most favorable way possible, and (2) the executor can continue the business without personal liability until the best sale can be obtained.	The proprietor designates in his or her will that in the event of his or her death: (1) the business will pass to a designated family member as his or her share of the estate, and (2) the remainder of the property will be divided among the other heirs.	The proprietor and a key employee agree in writing on (1) the value of the business, and (2) that in the event of the proprietor's death, the employee will buy, and the proprietor's estate will sell, the business.
Life insurance to fund plan	**Life insurance to fund plan**	**Life insurance to fund plan**
Proprietor is insured for $75,000.	Proprietor is insured for $125,000.	Employee insures proprietor for $100,000. Proprietor is insured for $25,000.
Proprietor is applicant, owner, and premium payor of the policy on his or her own life, with the executor, a family member, or a trustee designated as beneficiary.	Proprietor is applicant, owner, and premium payor of the policy on his or her own life, with the executor, a family member, or a trustee designated as beneficiary.	Employee is applicant, owner, premium payor, and beneficiary of the $100,000 policy on the proprietor. Proprietor is applicant, owner, and premium payor of the $25,000 policy on his or her life, with his or her executor, a family member, or a trustee, designated beneficiary.
At death	**At death**	**At death**
Executor can utilize part of the insurance proceeds to pay the assumed $25,000 in settlement costs. The remainder of the proceeds, $50,000, passes to the heirs to offset the shrinkage in the business value, assuming the executor can sell it as a going concern and realize 50% of its current value. If not, additional life insurance could be purchased to compensate for the loss.	Executor can utilize part of the insurance proceeds to pay the assumed $25,000 in settlement costs. The remainder of the proceeds, $100,000, passes to the other heirs according to the proprietor's desires. Additional life insurance could be purchased if larger inheritances are desired.	Employee utilizes the insurance proceeds he or she receives to purchase the deceased proprietor's business from the estate. Executor can utilize the $25,000 or proceeds to pay the assumed $25,000 of estate settlement costs.

business and estate situation would determine the particular plan appropriate for it. No "canned" solutions are possible in this field.

Tax Aspects

Income Taxation.   Premiums paid by a key employee for insurance to fund a sole proprietorship buy-sell agreement are not deductible by the employee. The death proceeds, however, are received by the beneficiary income tax–free.

Estate Taxation.   Under the orderly liquidation or sale alternative discussed above, the life insurance proceeds are included in the insured proprietor's gross estate if the proprietor has any incidents of ownership in the policy or names his or her estate as beneficiary. The liquidation value or sale price of the business also is included in the proprietor's estate as assets he or she owns.

In the case of family retention of the business interest, the insurance proceeds also are included in the proprietor's estate if the proprietor retains incidents of ownership in the policy or names his or her estate as beneficiary. The value of the business also is included.

When a properly drafted buy-sell agreement exists, only the value of the business as represented by the purchase price actually paid for it is included in the proprietor's estate.

Chapter 14 Special Valuation Rules

Chapter 14 was added to the Internal Revenue Code by the Revenue Reconciliation Act of 1990. Basically, it deals with certain special valuation rules for gift tax and estate tax purposes with regard to certain transfers of interests among family members. These valuation rules are quite complex and new, and a complete discussion of them is beyond the scope of this book. Chapter 14 replaced the controversial Section 2036(c) of the code, which was repealed retroactively to the date of its original enactment.

One section of Chapter 14 (Section 2703—Certain Rights and Restrictions Disregarded) provides certain requirements for valuation provisions in buy-sell agreements and so it is pertinent to the discussion here. This section provides that the value of any property (such as a business interest under a buy-sell agreement) shall be determined without regard to any option, agreement, or other right to acquire or use the property at a price less than the fair market value of the property, or any restriction on the right to sell or use the property, *unless* the option, agreement, right, or restriction meets each of three requirements. These requirements are that: (1) it is a bona fide business arrangement; (2) it is not a device to transfer such property to objects of the decedent's bounty for less than full and adequate consideration in money or money's worth; and (3) its terms are comparable to similar arrangements entered into by persons in an arms'-length transaction. By regulation, the IRS has ruled that these statutory requirements do not apply to agreements among unrelated parties. Further, agreements already in existence on October 8, 1990, are "grandfathered," and these statutory requirements do not apply to them unless they are "substantially modified" after October 8, 1990. However, the former common law (case law) rules still apply in these situations. These common law rules generally involved items (1) and (2) of the statutory rules.

Therefore, if the parties wish the value set for a business interest in a buy-sell agreement to fix the value of the interest for federal estate, gift, and generation-skipping tax purposes (as they normally do), the statutory requirements of Section 2703 of Chapter 14 must be met, unless the agreement is grandfathered or is among unrelated parties or is otherwise excepted, in which case the common law rules still must be met.[3]

Estate Liquidity through Section 303 Redemptions

When certain conditions are met, Section 303 of the Internal Revenue Code allows a corporation to redeem sufficient stock from a deceased stockholder's estate or heirs to pay death taxes, funeral costs, and estate administration expenses without creating a taxable dividend to the estate or heirs.

The proceeds received under a Section 303 redemption need not actually be used for meeting these death expenses. Section 303 merely sets a limit on the amount that can be received from a partial redemption of stock before it may be considered a taxable dividend. Thus, under the proper circumstances, Section 303 can be an attractive way to get cash out of a closely held corporation upon the death of a stockholder without danger of an income tax liability.

To qualify for a Section 303 redemption, the value of a deceased stockholder's stock in the corporation must comprise more than 35 percent of his or her adjusted gross estate. Assume, for example, the following estate situation for a divorced business owner:

---

[3] In addition to the above, Chapter 14 also deals with special valuation rules in case of transfers of certain interests in corporations or partnerships, special valuation rules in case of transfers of interests in trusts, and treatment of certain lapsing rights and restrictions.

Gross estate	$1,100,000
Less: Assumed debts, funeral and estate administration expenses	−100,000
Adjusted gross estate	$1,000,000

In this case, if the deceased stockholder owned stock in the corporation valued at $400,000, the estate would be eligible for a Section 303 redemption because 35 percent of the adjusted gross estate in this case is $350,000 and so the $400,000 stock interest qualifies.

So assuming $40,000 for funeral and estate administration expenses and combined federal and state death taxes of $203,000, this estate could offer for redemption a total of $243,000 of stock to the corporation without its being considered a taxable dividend.

However, stock qualifying for a Section 303 redemption, and hence protecting the proceeds of a redemption from tax treatment as ordinary dividend income, is limited to stock redeemed from a stockholder whose interest is reduced directly by the payment of death taxes, funeral expenses, or administration expenses. Hence, some stockholders may not be able to take advantage of Section 303.

S Corporations

What Is an S Corporation?

An S corporation is a corporation that meets certain qualification requirements and elects (under Subchapter S of the Internal Revenue Code) not to be taxed as a corporation. In other respects, except in the areas of corporate taxation and limits on the tax treatment of certain employee benefit plans, an S corporation operates like a regular corporation (called a C corporation).

An S corporation is taxed essentially as a partnership rather than a corporation. The taxable income of the corporation is taxed directly to the stockholders, whether the stockholders actually receive the profits as dividends or the profits are left in the business. The net profits are reported and taxed to the stockholder(s) of an S corporation as if they had been distributed.

Subchapter S Qualification Requirements

In order to elect Subchapter S treatment, a corporation must meet the following conditions:

1. It must be a domestic corporation.
2. It must have no more than 35 stockholders (with a husband and wife being viewed as only one stockholder).

3. It generally must have individuals or estates as stockholders; however, certain trusts [such as qualified Subchapter S trusts (QSSTs), grantor trusts, and voting trusts] may be S corporation stockholders.

4. It must have only one class of stock.

5. It must not have a nonresident alien as a stockholder.

6. It must not be a member of an affiliated group of corporations entitled to file a consolidated return (in effect, an S corporation cannot have an 80 percent or more owned subsidiary corporation).

Additionally, all stockholders initially must consent to the election. In general, once revoked or terminated, an election cannot be made again for five taxable years.

As an example of how an S election works, assume a sole stockholder of an incorporated drugstore whose annual income statement for the latest taxable year shows the following:

Gross sales		$500,000
Cost of sales		−300,000
Gross profit		$200,000
Expenses:		
Regular expenses	$130,000	
Stockholder employee's salary	40,000	−170,000
Net profit		$ 30,000

If the stockholder is considering making an S election, and none of the financial data change, the comparison might appear as follows:

Regular corporation status	S corporation status
Corporate income tax: $30,000 at 15% = $4500 corporate tax	Corporate income tax: None

Net corporate profits $30,000
  Corporate income tax   −4,500
  Corporate after-tax income $25,500	

If the entire $25,500 is paid as a dividend to the stockholder(assuming an average 28% individual income tax rate), his or her additional personal tax would be $7140 ($25,500 × 0.28) and after-tax income would be $18,360. If this amount is retained by the corporation, retained earnings would increase by $25,500.	The $30,000 net profit is reported and taxed to the stockholder as an individual. His or her additional personal tax would be $8400 ($30,000 × 0.28), and after-tax income would be $21,600.

In an S corporation, the entire $30,000 of net corporate profits would be taxed directly to the stockholder. If these profits, or a portion of them, are paid to the stockholder, it is considered a dividend. If these profits, or a portion of them, are left in the business, this "undistributed taxable income" still is taxed to the stockholder. If "undistributed taxable income" is not paid out to the stockholder within 2½ months after the close of the corporation's taxable year, it becomes "income previously taxed" and increases the stockholder's cost basis of his or her stock. If "income previously taxed" is withdrawn in a subsequent year, it may be received as a tax-free distribution and reduces the stockholder's cost basis by that amount.

Why Should an
S Election Be Made?

The previous example can help reveal the kind of situation where an S election might be advantageous. The data for the two corporations were identical until the disposition of the $30,000 in net corporate profits. In the nonelecting corporation, the profits were subjected to the corporate income tax before they could be paid to the stockholder or, as is frequently the case in closely held corporations, retained and accumulated in the corporation. In the electing corporation, the profits passed through directly to the stockholder without first being reduced by corporate income taxation.

The desirability of Subchapter S status generally depends on the nature of the business and the personal circumstances of the stockholder(s). A significant factor is the relative top income tax rates of the corporation and its stockholders. S corporations may well prove more popular after the Tax Reform Act of 1986 because the top average individual tax rate of 28 percent is less than the top corporate rate of 34 percent (on earnings over $75,000 per year).

Another possible advantage associated with an S corporation deserves mention. New corporations sometimes elect Subchapter S treatment and maintain this status during their early years in business. Normally, a net operating loss of a corporation for any taxable year is carried forward and used in subsequent profitable years to offset the corporation's taxable income. However, a net operating loss of an S corporation passes through the corporation directly to the stockholders, and may be available to them individually as a deduction from gross income (but subject to the passive activity loss rules). Thus, if a corporation sustains such losses during its early stages, an S election can provide a valuable personal tax-planning device for the stockholder-employees.

Other Aspects
of a Subchapter S Election

Employee Benefit Plans.   One advantage of incorporating a closely held business is that the owner who works in the business is an *employee* of the corporation. When the owner is an employee, a regular corporation can deduct contributions it makes on behalf of the owner to employee benefit plans along with contributions for other employees. These programs are available on a tax-favored basis only for employees; the owners of unincorporated businesses are not considered to be employees for tax purposes (although they can participate in HR-10 plans, as explained in Chap. 13).

S corporations, however, are subject to some special rules with respect to certain employee benefits for stockholder-employees of the corporation. At one time, there were special limitations on the amounts that could be contributed, on a tax-favored basis, by S corporations to qualified retirement plans for stockholder-employees who owned more than 5 percent of the corporation's outstanding stock. Effective in 1984, however, these special limitations on the qualified retirement plans of S corporations were repealed. Therefore, S corporations now generally are on a par with regular corporations (C corporations) with regard to qualified retirement plans. On the other hand, the Subchapter S Revision Act of 1982 provides that for purposes of certain "fringe benefits" (i.e., employee benefits), any shareholder of an S corporation who owns more than 2 percent of the corporation's outstanding stock shall be treated as if he or she were a partner in a partnership. This means that such 2 percent shareholder-employees of S corporations are not treated as employees with respect to such "fringe benefits," and, therefore, the S corporation cannot deduct, for tax purposes, the contributions it makes for them to such plans, and such contributions may be gross income to the shareholder-employees.

Accumulated Earnings Tax.   A regular corporation may have to pay a penalty tax, in addition to its regular corporate income tax, on any after-tax earnings that are retained and accumulated in the corporation beyond its reasonable business needs (in excess of a minimum amount of $250,000 or $150,000 in the case of certain service corporations). S corporations are exempt from this penalty because the corporate profits have already been taxed each year to the stockholders.

Buy-Sell Plans.   As in other corporations, the stockholders of S corporations often need a buy-sell agreement to dispose of a deceased (or disabled) stockholder's interest. In fact, the need may be even greater than it is in nonelecting corporations. Without such a plan, for example, a deceased stockholder's interest might possibly pass to a party not qualified under Subchapter S. This would end the election and disqualify the corporation from further Subchapter S treatment.

Personal Financial Planning Checklist for Decision Making

Consumers (and their advisors) can use this checklist to evaluate their insurance, investment, retirement, tax, and estate planning programs. The book itself provides needed information on the points raised in the checklist. The checklist also contains cross-references to the appropriate parts of the book.

I. OBJECTIVES

A. Generally identify your objectives in the following areas:

1. Protection for yourself and your family against the risks of death, disability, medical expenses, custodial care expenses, property losses, and liability losses

2. Capital accumulation and investments

3. Retirement

4. Estate planning

5. Property management in case of incapacity

6. Others

B. What other special concerns do you have?

1. Children or other dependents with special problems or needs

2. Economic or investment uncertainties

3. Employment uncertainties

4. Other

II. USING INSURANCE EFFECTIVELY

A. Life insurance (See Chap. 4.)

1. What kinds of death benefits do you now have (other than social security)?

Kind of Plan	Amount
Group life insurance (employer-provided)	
Individual policies *you own* on your life	
Individual policies *others own* on your life	
Association group life insurance	
Death benefits under pension, profit-sharing, and savings plans	
Death benefits under tax-sheltered annuity, IRA, and HR-10 plans	

Kind of Plan	Amount
Personal annuity contracts	
Death benefits under non-qualified deferred compensation plans and informal employer plans	
Other plans	

2. Do you have *enough life insurance,* along with other death benefits and assets available to your family, to meet your objectives?

3. If you need *additional life insurance,* how should you provide it?

4. Have you elected to take all the employer-provided group life insurance you are entitled to and want?

5. If you need additional life insurance, *what kind of policy should you buy?*

6. Should any new individual life insurance be on a *participating* or on a *nonparticipating basis?*

7. Should you *surrender for cash* (or terminate) any of your existing life insurance policies?

8. Should you place any of your existing life insurance policies under the *reduced paid-up* (or perhaps extended-term) nonforfeiture options and stop paying premiums on them?

9. Check whether you have *waiver of premium benefits* on all your individual policies. If not, can you add this benefit?

10. Do you have *accidental death benefits* (double indemnity) on your individual policies? If so, do you want these benefits, or would you rather drop them and save the premium?

11. Do you have *guaranteed insurability coverage* on your existing policies or any new policies? Do you need this coverage?

12. If you are carrying *decreasing term insurance* at a level annual premium, has the amount of insurance de-

creased to the point where you should consider dropping the insurance and saving the premium?

13. Do you have a *substandard premium rating* that the insurance company now will remove? Or, if the company will not remove it, can you now buy insurance at standard rates with another company?

14. How are you using any *policy dividends?* Are you making the best use of your policy dividends for *your needs?* Can you get a better interest return on this money than the insurance company is paying with equal safety?

15. What are your *policy loan values (cash values)?* What is the policy loan interest rate(s) in your policies? Should you consider borrowing on your life insurance rather than elsewhere?

16. Check your life insurance *beneficiary designations.*

    a. Are your primary beneficiaries the ones you now want (up to date)?

    b. Have you named contingent beneficiaries in all your policies? If not, why not? Are they up to date?

    c. Is your estate named as primary beneficiary on any policy(ies)? If so, why?

    d. Are minors named as beneficiaries? If so, have you made arrangements to avoid problems arising out of paying proceeds to minor beneficiaries?

    e. If there are any children of a former marriage, are they included in any beneficiary designations of children, if this is your wish?

    f. Are all your life insurance beneficiary designations consistent? If there are any differences among your policies, are they intentional?

17. Check the *beneficiary designations in any other plans* involving death benefits for your family. Are they

consistent with those under your life insurance policies? If not, why not?

18. Check how your *life insurance proceeds are to be paid.* (Also see "Estate Planning" later.)

    a. Lump sum

    b. Under *settlement options*

        (1) Do the options used meet your present needs?

        (2) Have you named second (or third, etc.) payees under the options where appropriate?

        (3) What flexibility do your beneficiaries have under the options? If no flexibility, why not?

        (4) Are any proceeds (other than National Service Life Insurance) payable under a life income option? Should this be changed?

    c. To an *insurance trust* as primary beneficiary

19. Have you provided for the *common-disaster or short-term-survivorship situations* in your life insurance? (Also see "Estate Planning.")

20. Do you own life insurance on others' lives? If so, you should be named beneficiary.

21. Do others (or a trust) own life insurance on your life? If so, the owner should be named beneficiary.

22. Have you been told you are uninsurable? If so,

    a. Have you checked with other insurance companies?

    b. Have you taken advantage of all the coverage you can get without having to show individual evidence of insurability?

B. Disability Income Insurance (See Chapter 5.)

    1. What kinds of disability income benefits do you now have (other than social security)?

| | Benefit Amount and |
Kind of Plan	Duration
Group short-term (employer-provided)	
Group long-term (employer-provided)	
Employer sick-pay plan (uninsured)	
Individual disability income policies	
Disability income riders added to life insurance policies	
Franchise (association group) plans	
Disability benefits under pension, profit-sharing, and group life plans	
Other plans	

8. If you have group long-term disability income coverage, check the *kinds of other disability benefits that will reduce the amount of insurance under the group plan*. In particular, will any individual disability policy you may buy serve to reduce your group plan benefits?

9. Does your employer have an uninsured sick-pay plan covering you (in addition to any group disability benefits)?

10. Check the *definition of disability* in existing or any new disability coverage you are considering.

11. What rights do you have to *continue your individual disability coverage* (i.e., *continuance provisions*)?

12. How much of your disability coverage is *franchise (association group) insurance* that can be discontinued if the franchise (group) plan is discontinued?

13. If you are considering buying an individual disability policy,

   a. Does it provide both *occupational and nonoccupational coverage* (so-called 24-hour coverage)?

   b. What *definition of disability* is used?

   c. Is it *noncancelable and guaranteed renewable* ("noncan")?

   d. Does it contain a *waiver of premium benefit*?

   e. Does it have a *guaranteed insurability provision*?

   f. Do you need any *supplementary disability income benefits* attached to it?

2. Do you have *enough disability insurance,* along with other disability benefits available to you and your family, to meet your objectives? Presume the worst—*total and permanent disability.*

3. If you need *additional disability insurance, how should you provide it?*

4. Should you *terminate* any of your existing disability insurance and save the premium?

5. Check the *maximum benefit period(s)* of your disability income benefits. Are the periods (durations) long enough to protect you against *long-term disability* (i.e., to age 65)?

6. Check the *elimination period(s)* of your disability income benefits. Should you increase the elimination period(s) to save premium and/or to coordinate your coverage with employer-provided or other benefits?

7. Do all your policies cover against *disability caused by both accident and sickness?* If not, consider dropping the "accident only" coverage and save the premium.

14. Do you have a *substandard premium rating* or *waiver of coverage* that the insurance company now may reconsider and perhaps remove? Or, if the company will not remove it, can you now buy insurance on a standard basis with another company?

15. Should you carry at least some *individual disability income insurance*

(that you control) to supplement your group insurance? (But note No. 8 above in this regard.)

C. Medical expense insurance (See Chap. 5.)

1. What kinds of medical expense benefits do you or your family now have?

Kind of Plan	Brief Summary of Benefits
Group insurance (employer-provided)	
Hospital, medical, surgical ("basic" coverages)	
Major medical (supplementary to "basic" coverages)	
Comprehensive medical expense	
Health maintenance (HMO) coverage	
Other	
Individual medical expense policies	
Hospital, medical, surgical	
Major medical	
Comprehensive medical expense	
Hospital income benefits	
Other	
Medicare	
Other	

2. Do you have *enough medical expense benefits* available to you and your family to meet your objectives with respect to

a. "Basic" hospital, medical, and surgical coverage

b. Major medical coverage

c. Catastrophic (excess) medical expenses

3. For which family members (or others) are you, or might you be, responsible for paying medical bills?

a. Wife or husband

b. Children

c. Aged, dependent parents

d. Other dependents

Does your or any other medical expense coverage apply to them? Do they need coverage or supplementary coverage?

4. If you have *major medical insurance,* do you need (or want) to *supplement this coverage—*

a. With "basic" coverage to take care of uncovered expenses due to the major medical's deductible, "inside limits," and coinsurance limitations?

b. With "excess" coverage to take care of catastrophic losses over the major medical's maximum limit?

5. If you or your dependents are covered by *Medicare,* do you need (or want) to *supplement it?*

6. If you or your dependents need *additional medical* expense benefits, how should you provide them?

7. Should you *terminate* any of your existing medical expense benefits and save the premium?

8. Do you have any dependents who have, or soon will have, terminated their coverage under group or family medical expense coverage? If so, what *conversion rights* do they have? What COBRA benefits may be elected?

9. What rights do you have *to continue your individual medical expense coverage* (i.e., *continuance provisions*)?

10. Does your medical expense insurance continue to protect your dependents in the event of your death?

11. Do you have a *substandard premium rating* or *waiver of coverage* that the insurance company now will reconsider and perhaps remove? Or, if the company will not remove it, can you now buy insurance on a standard basis with another company?

12. Do you have any *limited policies,* such as so-called dread disease policies, that you might want to drop and save the premium?

13. If you have any hospital income policies, do you need the supplementary coverage, or should you consider dropping it and saving the premium?

14. Do you have any "accident only" medical reimbursement coverage? If so, should you drop it and save the premium?

D. Accidental death and dismemberment (AD&D) insurance

1. If you have such coverage (group and/or individual), check the beneficiary designations to see if they are consistent with your life insurance. If they are not, why not?

2. If you have the choice, consider whether to keep AD&D coverage or drop it and save the premium. This is a good place to cut costs if you want to.

E. Long-term care (LTC) insurance

1. What kinds of LTC benefits do you or your family now have?

Kind of Plan	Brief Summary of Benefits
Group insurance (employer-sponsored)	
Association group insurance	
Individual policies	

2. For which family members (or others) are you, or might you be, responsible for paying custodial care expenses?

   a. Wife or husband

   b. Aged, dependent parents

   c. Others

3. If you are considering buying coverage,

   a. How long is the elimination period?

   b. What is the daily indemnity?

   c. How long is the benefit period?

   d. Does it cover home health care? Adult day care? Nursing home care? Other custodial care?

   e. Does it have any prior institutionalization requirements?

   f. Is it guaranteed renewable, and, if not, what are its continuance provisions?

4. Are (or will) you or any member of your family be eligible or potentially eligible for Medicaid? If not, should you consider Medicaid estate planning?

F. Property and liability insurance (See Chap. 6.)

1. What property and liability coverages do you now have?

Kind	Limit(s) of Liability
Homeowners (or fire and related coverages)	
Personal liability (e.g., Section II of Homeowners)	
Automobile	
Workers' compensation	
Watercraft	
Aircraft	
Professional liability	
Directors' and officers' liability	
Personal catastrophe (umbrella) liability	
Self-retained limit	
Personal articles coverage (or floater)	
Personal property floater (or Homeowners 5 coverage)	
Other	

2. Are you subject to the following *liability loss exposures* that may *not be covered* by your homeowners or automobile insurance?

a. Business or professional liability

b. Watercraft liability

c. Aircraft liability

d. Recreational motor vehicles

e. Workers' compensation

f. Liability arising out of premises, other than an insured premises, that you may own, rent, or control

g. Liability for property of others you have in your care, custody, or control

3. Are your *liability insurance limits high enough* and consistent in all coverages?

4. Do you have *personal catastrophe (umbrella) liability insurance?* Is its limit of liability high enough?

5. Do you have liability coverage for any *officerships and/or directorships* you may have?

6. Which *homeowners form* should you buy (if applicable) for your property loss exposures?

7. Do you have enough homeowners insurance (or the proper endorsements) to get *full replacement cost coverage* on your dwelling and private structures? On your personal property?

8. If you have homeowners insurance, do you need *extra coverage* for:

a. Money and *numismatic property* (coin collections)

b. Securities, deeds, etc., and *philatelic property* (stamp collections)

c. Jewelry, furs, and similar property

d. Watercraft

e. Other high-value property (e.g., fine arts, antiques, guns, cameras, musical instruments, silverware, golfer's equipment, and the like)

9. Do you have enough homeowners (or other) insurance to cover your *personal property on and away from your premises?*

10. Have you made an up-to-date *inventory of your personal property?*

11. Have you increased the hazard, or left your premises vacant, in a way that might possibly suspend your property insurance coverage?

12. Do you need *collision or comprehensive auto coverage,* or should you drop one or both and save the premium?

13. Do you need *automobile medical payments* coverage, or should you drop it and save the premium?

14. Do you need *federal flood or crime insurance, or earthquake insurance,* if you are eligible?

15. Have you shopped around with other insurers to see if you can buy your insurance at lower cost or with better coverage?

III. PLANNING INVESTMENT

A. What investments and assets do you now have?

1. Cash, bank accounts, etc.—include current balances and how owned (i.e., by yourself, your spouse, jointly, etc.)

a. Cash on hand

b. Checking accounts

c. Savings accounts, credit union shares, etc.—yield

d. Brokerage accounts, etc.

2. Money market accounts or funds

3. Bank savings certificates, etc.—yield, duration

4. U.S. savings bonds—maturity values

5. Life insurance and annuity cash values (net of policy loans)

6. Other liquid assets

7. Common stocks, including the stock's description and investment goal (e.g., growth, cyclical, defensive, income, etc.); cost (tax basis) and how long held; current market value; annual divided income; and how owned.

8. Mutual funds, including the fund's description and investment goal (e.g., growth stock, diversified common stock, balanced, income, etc.); cost (tax basis) and how long held; current market or net asset value; annual distribution from income and capital gains; and how owned.

9. Real estate

    a. Residential, including location and description; cost (including improvements); estimated market value; mortgage (including current balance, interest rate, prepayment privilege and termination date); and how owned.

    b. Income-producing, including location and description; when acquired; cost (including improvements); estimated market value; mortgage (including current balance, interest rate, and monthly payment); estimated annual net income (or loss); estimated annual cash flow; and how owned.

10. Bonds, including par value; coupon rate (annual income); cost (tax basis) and how long held; current market value; maturity date; investment rating; and how owned.

    a. Corporate

    b. Convertible

    c. Municipal

    d. U.S. government

11. Preferred stocks

12. Tax-sheltered investments (other than real estate)

13. Business interests (sole proprietorships, partnership interests, and close corporation stock)

14. Other investments and interests

B. How should you deal with your new and existing investments?

1. Review your *investment objectives*. Is your present program consistent with them? If not, what changes should be made?

2. Have you decided upon an *investment strategy* (*policies*) to follow?

3. Have you analyzed the *asset allocation of your investment portfolio?* Is it right for you?

4. Do you depend on your investment income for part or all of your livelihood?

5. Do you want, now or someday, an investment income to supplement your job earnings (to provide a "*second income*")? How much?

6. Are you earning as high an *after-tax total return* on your investments as you can in your circumstances? What can you do to improve your after-tax yield—current income and/or capital gains?

7. How large an *emergency fund* do you want?

8. How much capital do you need for your children's education, and how much time do you have to accumulate it?

9. What other personal or family capital needs—travel, weddings, gifts, etc.—do you have?

10. Do you have enough *liquidity and marketability* in your investment portfolio?

11. Is your portfolio adequately *diversified?* In what ways?

12. Do you have enough *security of principal and income* in your portfolio?

13. To what extent, if at all, do you want to *speculate?* In what ways? Can you afford to speculate?

14. In your investment planning, *are you ready for prosperity? Recession? Depression?*

15. What amount do you currently have available for investment?

16. How much do you have available annually for discretionary investments?

17. Which of the following *kinds of investment media* or speculations

would you consider for your program? (See Chaps. 7, 8, 9, and 10 for descriptions of these investment media.)

- Bank savings certificates or certificates of deposit
- Money market funds or accounts
- Corporate bonds
- "Deep-discount" bonds
- Corporate bond funds
- Convertible bonds
- U.S. government securities

  Treasury bills

  Treasury notes

  Treasury bonds

  U.S. government agency securities
- Ginnie Mae pass-throughs
- Municipal bonds
- Municipal bond funds
- Preferred stocks
- Convertible preferreds
- Common stocks
- Mutual funds
- Writing options
- Investment real estate

  Direct ownership (sole or joint)

  Limited partnership interests

  Real estate investment trusts (REITs)
- Fixed-dollar annuities
- Variable annuities
- Tax-sheltered investments
- Common stock warrants
- Selling stock short
- Buying puts and calls
- Trading in commodity futures
- Buying new issues

18. Have your *common stocks lived up to your investment expectations* for them? (Chap. 8)

If not, should you sell and invest elsewhere, switch to other stocks, or hold?

If so, should you buy more or hold?

19. Do you have stocks with *capital losses* you could sell?

20. Do you want to use *dollar cost averaging or formula plans* in buying common stocks?

21. Do you own stock acquired under stock option or stock purchase plans?

22. Do you have any *unexercised stock options* or *rights under stock purchase plans*?

23. Have your mutual funds lived up to your investment expectations for them? If not, what action should you take? (Chap. 9)

24. If you are going to buy funds (investment company shares), *should they be closed-end or open-end (mutual) funds*?

25. If you are going to buy mutual funds (open-end), should they be *load or no-load funds*?

26. If you are going to buy a load-type mutual fund, *how can you save money on the sales load*?

27. If you are going to liquidate mutual fund shares, should you use a *mutual fund systematic withdrawal plan*?

28. In your income tax bracket, *would municipal bonds be attractive to you*?

29. *Are tax-sheltered investments (including real estate) attractive to you*? If you have passive activity losses, should you now seek passive activity income to offset them?

30. If you are investing in fixed-income securities, do you have an investment strategy? Short-term? Long-term?

31. Are you taking steps to *protect yourself against bond and preferred stock callability*?

32. If you believe a recession or depression is coming, are you ready for the *contracyclical price movement of high-grade bonds*?

33. Should you consider *professional investment advisory services or other professional management* of your investments?

IV. PLANNING FOR RETIREMENT
(In general, see Chaps. 12 and 13.)

A. What retirement benefits do you now have?

Kind of Plan	Estimate of Benefits (at Retirement)
1. Social security retirement benefits (for yourself and your spouse)	
2. Pension plan (employer-provided)	
3. Savings plan (employer-provided)	
4. Profit-sharing plan (employer-provided)	
5. Nonqualified deferred compensation	
6. Other employee benefits	
7. HR-10 plan	
8. Tax-sheltered annuity (TSA) plan	
9. Individual annuities (fixed-dollar and variable)	
10. Life insurance cash values	
11. IRA plan	
12. Projected general investment fund	

B. How should you plan for your retirement?

1. At *what age* would you like to retire? How old will your spouse be?

2. What *after-tax retirement income do you want:*

   a. While both you and your spouse are alive?

   b. For your spouse if you die first?

3. Do you have enough retirement benefits, along with social security and your general investment fund, to meet your objectives? Too much?

4. If you need *additional retirement income,* how should you provide it?

5. How have you *provided for your surviving spouse* if you should die first?

6. What annuity form should you select for your pension and/or other retirement benefits? Should you and your spouse waive the joint and 50% to the survivor annuity form required by REA?

7. Can you afford to retire early (before age 65) if you desire?

8. How are your qualified retirement plan death benefits payable?

9. To what extent are your employer-provided *pension benefits vested?*

10. How, if at all, are your pension benefits protected against inflation after your retirement?

11. What *vested rights* do you have under any *deferred profit-sharing* or savings plans?

12. Do you have any *loan privileges* under qualified retirement plans? At what interest rate?

13. Are you eligible to adopt an *HR-10 plan?* If you are, should you do so?

14. Are you eligible to participate in a *tax-sheltered annuity (TSA) plan?* If so, should you?

15. Should you consider entering into a *nonqualified deferred compensation plan* with your employer (if offered) to defer income until your retirement?

16. Can you contribute (or contribute more) to qualified savings plans? If so, should you contribute more?

17. What is your *asset allocation* under your qualified retirement plans? Is it consistent with your overall asset allocation strategy?

18. Are you (or can you) make before-tax contributions to qualified retirement plans under a Section 401(k) arrangement?

19. Are you subject to the minimum distribution rules? If so, how much must you take each year?

20. Should you use life insurance settlements options (for cash values) to provide retirement benefits?

21. Should you buy a commercial fixed-dollar annuity or variable annuity?

22. How secure are your retirement benefits? How much is guaranteed? Are you ready for prosperity? Recession? Depression?

V. TAX AND ESTATE PLANNING

A. Income tax planning (In general, see Chap. 11.)

1. What *top income tax bracket* (rate) are you and your spouse now in (federal, state, and local)?

2. Are you taking all the income tax exemptions, deductions, and credits to which you are now entitled (e.g., club dues and fees, costs of a professional library, etc)?

3. Should you file an *amended return* for deductions not taken in the past?

4. What is the *relative advantage* for you and your spouse (considering your top income tax bracket(s)) of *tax-exempt income versus taxable income?*

5. Is *tax-deferred income* attractive to you?

6. Is your present *filing status* (joint return, separate return, etc.) best for you?

7. Check your securities portfolio for possible *tax-loss sale candidates.* Should you use a *tax exchange* to maintain your investment position?

8. Will your alternative minimum tax (AMT) exceed your regular tax, and if so, what planning steps should you consider?

9. How can you postpone the income tax bite?

10. If you are selling stock you have purchased over a period of time, which certificates are best to sell from a tax viewpoint?

11. How can you arrange your life insurance for best income tax savings?

12. If you have a sizable capital gain in securities you own, do you have a "capital gains tax lock-in problem"? If so, how should you deal with it?

13. Which of the following specific tax-saving techniques should you consider (or perhaps are now using)?

   a. Buying *municipal bonds* (Also see "Investment Planning.")

   b. Making *other tax-sheltered investments* (Also see "Investment Planning.")

   c. Adoption of *tax-favored employee benefits* (Also see "Planning for Retirement.")

   d. Making contributions to a tax-deductible IRA if you are eligible, or making nondeductible contributions for the tax-deferred investment growth if not eligible

   e. Giving *appreciated capital gain property* to charity

   f. Using a *charitable remainder trust* or *pooled income fund*

   g. Making gifts of income-producing property (Consider what property and to whom and the effect of the "kiddie tax.") (See Chap. 11.)

   h. Taking a *lump-sum distribution from a "qualified" retirement plan*

   i. Making a tax-deferred rollover from a qualified retirement plan to a rollover IRA

   j. Using U.S. government savings bonds to best tax advantage

14. What tax-planning warnings (caveats) should you consider?

B. Estate planning (In general, see Chaps. 14, 15, 16, and 17.)

1. How large, and what is the nature of, *your estate,* including your *gross estate for federal estate tax purposes,*

your *probate estate,* and the *"net"* estate going to your heirs?

2. How large is, and what is the nature of, *your spouse's estate,* assuming (*a*) your spouse survives you, and (*b*) you survive your spouse?

3. Do *other family members* have sizable estates?

4. What financial obligations will your estate have, including *potential federal estate taxes and state death taxes?*

5. What will be your *estate transfer costs* (*a*) at your death, and (*b*) at your spouse's subsequent death? Can they be reduced by better planning?

6. How *liquid* is your estate? Can it meet its liquidity needs?

7. What *inheritances* (if any) do you, your spouse, or other family members expect in the future?

   a. Can you estimate the amount?

   b. Will it be outright, in trust, or both?

   c. Will any inheritance become part of your or your spouse's gross estate for federal estate tax purposes? (If so, should your estate be "skipped" for federal estate tax purposes?)

   d. Will you or your spouse make any generation-skipping transfers?

8. Are you, your spouse, or your children presently the *beneficiary(ies) of any trusts?*

9. Are you or your spouse currently the donee of any *unexercised powers of appointment?* General powers? Non-general powers?

10. Do you live or have you ever lived in a *community property* state?

11. Who do you want to be the *primary beneficiaries of your estate?* How should they share in it, and in what amounts? Will it be adequate for their needs?

12. Do any of your *dependents have special problems* you should consider in your estate planning?

13. Do you have *dependent parents* (or others) to consider?

14. Are you interested in making any *charitable bequests?*

15. Have you or has your spouse a *closely held business interest* for which you should plan?

16. What *methods of estate transfer*—lifetime and/or at death—are you and your spouse now using? Should you consider others?

17. Have you had an estate planning conference with your lawyer? Banker? Life insurance agent? Accountant? Financial planner? Others? (*Note:* You must have an attorney to give legal advice.)

18. Review your *estate planning objectives.* Is your present plan consistent with them? If not, what changes should be made?

19. Do *you have a will?* If not, why not?

20. *Does your spouse have a will?* If not, why not? Are your wills properly coordinated?

21. Who is *named executor* in your and your spouse's wills?

22. Have you made specific provision for your personal effects?

23. Are *specific bequests in percentages* of your estate, or limited by percentages, rather than in absolute amounts?

24. Are you making *use of the federal estate tax marital deduction* to save estate taxes on your estate? Why or why not? Should you plan on using the full marital deduction in your estate?

25. Is *your estate "overqualified"* for the estate tax marital deduction when the amount of the "exemption equivalent" of the unified credit available to your estate is considered?

26. What method(s) are you now using to *qualify the right amount of property for the marital deduction?* Is a *formula provision* desirable?

27. If you are using *marital* and *non-marital trusts,* what *rights or powers should you give your surviving spouse* (or perhaps others) in one or both of these trusts? Should you consider a Q-TIP marital trust?

28. In general, how much latitude do you want your spouse (or others) to have in dealing with your estate after your death?

29. What provisions (or other considerations), *if any,* do you want to have in the event of *your spouse's remarriage?*

30. When should your *children* (or grandchildren, etc.) *have final control* over their share of your estate?

31. Can you *coordinate* your estate planning with that of *other family members* (parents, grandparents, grown successful children, etc.) who will or do have sizable estates?

32. Are there family members (or others) who may try to unduly influence your spouse or other heirs? How can you deal with this?

33. Do you need any *trusts* in your estate planning? If so, *who should be named trustee* or co-trustees? Should you use *individual or corporate trustees,* or both?

34. Will the trust(s) have enough assets to make naming a corporate trustee economical?

35. Is there a provision in the trust agreement *allowing the beneficiaries to change a corporate trustee?* Should there be one?

36. How have you provided for property that may go to *minor heirs?* (Also see "Life Insurance" above.)

37. Should you leave property to some individuals for their lifetime only (life estate) rather than outright?

38. Have you or your spouse made any *taxable gifts?* Filed a *federal gift tax return?*

39. Should you consider *making some gifts during your lifetime* (inter vivos gifts)? What factors should you consider? Should any *gifts be outright* or *in trust?*

40. If you want to do so, how can you make *lifetime gifts to minors* (children, grandchildren, nieces, nephews, etc.)?

41. What part of your estate goes to your heirs under your will (probate estate) and what part goes outside of your probate estate? How? Should this be changed?

42. Can you *reduce federal estate taxes, state death taxes,* and *estate settlement costs?* Are these important considerations in your case?

43. Should you provide *more liquidity for your estate? How* can this be done?

44. Should you attempt to *"skip the estate"* of one or more *of your heirs* to save estate taxes? Should your spouse attempt to "skip" your estate for the same reason? (Also see No. 7 above.)

45. How should you hold title to your property? In your own name? Jointly? Other? Should any of your present property arrangements be changed?

46. *Should you own the life insurance on your life,* or should someone else or a trust be the owner?

47. *Should you own the life insurance on another's life,* or should someone else or a trust be the owner?

48. *Should you give away any of your existing life insurance?* What factors should you consider in deciding?

49. Should you give away your group life insurance?

50. Should you set up an unfunded irrevocable life insurance trust to own life insurance on your life?

51. How should your life insurance (or other death benefits) be made payable? Should you use *settlement options, an insurance trust, or both?*

52. Is a *revocable living trust* advisable for you and your family? Can it be used to serve as a will substitute in your case?

53. Have you made any of the following arrangements for the management of your property in the event of your physical or mental incapacity?

    a. Existing durable general power of attorney

    b. Springing durable general power of attorney

    c. Power of attorney in connection with a revocable living trust

    d. Funded revocable living trust

54. Have you executed a power of attorney for health care decisions? A living will?

55. Have you made provision for the *common disaster* or short-term-survivorship situation in your estate plan? How would this affect your decision on the use of the marital deduction?

56. If you own a closely held business interest, do you *plan to sell (or liquidate) it, or to retain it, in the event of your death, disability, or retirement?*

57. If you plan to sell your interest, do you have a legally enforceable *buy-sell agreement?* Is it *insured?* Does it deal with both death and disability?

58. If you plan to retain your interest, should you consider a *partial stock redemption (Section 303 redemption)* if your estate would be eligible?

VI. COORDINATION AND REVIEW

A. Do you *regularly review and update* your personal financial planning?

B. Who are your *professional and financial advisors?* Accountant? Attorney? Financial planner? Banker? Broker or investment advisor? Life insurance agent? Property and liability (general) insurance agent or broker? Other?

C. Do you have *adequate and accessible personal financial records?*

D. Do you have a *safe deposit box* or other safekeeping system?

Personal Financial Planning Review Forms

Including the Following Forms:

1. Family Balance Sheet
2. Family Income Statement
3. Insurance Coverages Worksheets
4. Analysis of Investment Portfolio
5. Estimated Retirement Income
6. Tax and Estate Planning Worksheets

How to Use These Forms

These forms can be used in many ways. First, consumers (and their advisors) can use them in conjunction with *Personal Financial Planning* to review their entire personal financial situation in an organized, coordinated manner. By reading the book and then filling out the information that is appropriate for them in these six forms, consumers can identify the areas in which their previous planning has met their financial needs and those of their family, as well as the areas in which there may be gaps, problems, or weaknesses in their present planning.

The information developed in the forms, along with the explanations in the book, also may suggest some possible solutions for these gaps, problems, or weaknesses that individuals and their professional and financial advisors can discuss. Of course, any specific solutions or financial plans should be developed with the aid and advice of professional and financial advisors. The book and these forms are not intended to be a substitute for their services and professional advice.

On the other hand, readers may not wish to complete all the forms at once. Instead, at any particular time they may be interested in reviewing only one or a few areas, such as investments, pension and retirement benefits, or life insurance coverage, for example. In this case, they can review in detail only those forms, or parts of forms, that apply to their particular interests, and then relate the information developed in the form or forms to the specific parts or chapters of the book that explain the area or areas in which they are interested.

The forms also may provide much useful, organized information about personal financial affairs that consumers may need in dealing with their professional and financial advisors. The more these advisors can be told about a person's affairs, the better they can serve that person. Again, of course, these forms are not intended to be a substitute for the more detailed and extensive information that professional advisors may seek in making specific recommendations to their clients in the area of their specialty.

An effort has been made to design these forms to cover as many situations and areas as reasonably possible. Therefore, certain items or areas will not apply to everyone. Also, some items deliberately call for estimates or approximations. In most cases, however, a great deal of the information needed to complete these forms is readily available.

FORM 1
FAMILY BALANCE SHEET (as of present date)

ASSETS

Liquid Assets

Cash and checking account(s)	$ _____
Savings account(s)	_____
Money market funds	_____
Life insurance cash values	_____
U.S. savings bonds	_____
Brokerage accounts	_____
Other	_____
Total liquid assets	$ _____

Marketable Investments

Common stocks	_____
Mutual funds	_____
Corporate bonds	_____
Municipal bonds	_____
Certificates of deposit	_____
Other	_____
Total marketable investments	_____

"Nonmarketable" Investments

Business interests	_____
Investment real estate	_____
Pension accounts	_____
Profit-sharing accounts	_____
Savings plan accounts	_____
IRA and other retirement plan accounts	_____
Tax-sheltered investments	_____
Other	_____
Total "nonmarketable" investments	_____

Personal Real Estate

Residence	_____
Vacation home	_____
Total personal real estate	_____

FORM 1
FAMILY BALANCE SHEET (as of present date) *(continued)*

Other Personal Assets

    Auto(s) ————

    Boat(s) ————

    Furs and jewelry ————

    Collections, hobbies, etc. ————

    Furniture and household accessories ————

    Other personal property ————

      Total other personal assets ————

        Total assets $————

LIABILITIES AND NET WORTH

Current Liabilities

    Charge accounts, credit card charges, and
other bills payable $————

    Installment credit and other short-term loans ————

    Unusual tax liabilities ————

      Total current liabilities $————

Long-Term Liabilities

    Mortgage(s) on personal real estate ————

    Mortgage(s) on investment real estate ————

    Bank loans ————

    Margin loans ————

    Life insurance policy loans ————

    Other ————

    Total long-term liabilities ————

    Total liabilities $————

    Family net worth $————

    Total liabilities and family net worth $————

FORM 2
FAMILY INCOME STATEMENT (for the most recent year)

INCOME

Salary(ies)

    You $_____

    Your spouse   _____

    Others   _____

      Total salaries $_____

Investment Income

    Interest (taxable)   _____

    Interest (nontaxable)   _____

    Dividends   _____

    Real estate   _____

    Realized capital gains   _____

    Other investment income   _____

      Total investment income   _____   _____

Bonuses, Profit-Sharing Payments, etc.   _____

Other Income   _____

      Total income $_____

EXPENSES AND FIXED OBLIGATIONS

Ordinary Living Expenses $_____

Interest Expense

    Consumer loans $_____

    Bank loans   _____

    Mortgage(s)   _____

FORM 2
FAMILY INCOME STATEMENT (for the most recent year)   (*continued*)

    Insurance policy loans   _____

    Other interest   _____

      Total interest expense   _____

Debt Amortization (mortgages, consumer
debt, etc.)   _____

Insurance Premiums

    Life insurance   _____

    Health insurance   _____

    Property and liability insurance   _____

      Total insurance premiums   _____

Charitable Contributions   _____

Tuition and Educational Expenses   _____

Payments for Support of Aged Parents or
Other Dependents   _____

Taxes

    Federal income tax   _____

    State (and city) income tax(es)   _____

    Social security tax(es)   _____

    Local property taxes   _____

    Other taxes   _____

      Total taxes   _____

        Total expenses and fixed obligations   \$_____

Balance Available for Discretionary
Investment   \$_____

FORM 3
INSURANCE COVERAGES WORKSHEETS (How Much Do You Have and Need?)

I. Life Insurance and Other Death Benefits
   A. Individual life insurance policies you own on your own life

Kind of policy (including any life insurance riders)	Net annual premium (gross premium less any policy dividends)	Latest annual increase in cash value	Total cash value	Policy loans outstanding	Net amount of protection (face of policy and additional death benefits less policy loans)
_____	$_____	$_____	$_____	$_____	$_____
_____	_____	_____	_____	_____	_____
_____	_____	_____	_____	_____	_____
_____	_____	_____	_____	_____	_____
_____	_____	_____	_____	_____	_____

   B. Individual life insurance policies that others own on your life

Kind of policy (including any life insurance riders)	Net annual premium (gross premium less any policy dividends)	Latest annual increase in cash value	Total cash value	Policy loans outstanding	Net amount of protection (face of policy and additional death benefits less policy loans)
_____	$_____	$_____	$_____	$_____	$_____
_____	_____	_____	_____	_____	_____

   C. Group life insurance   Face amount

      1. Employer-provided group term life $_____

      2. Other employer-provided group life   _____

      3. Association group life   _____

FORM 3
INSURANCE COVERAGES WORKSHEETS (How Much Do You Have and Need?) (*continued*)

		Lump sum
D.	Death benefits under	
	1. Pension, savings, and profit-sharing plans	$_____
	2. Other employer-provided plans	$_____
	3. HR-10, IRA, and tax-sheltered annuity (TSA) plans	$_____
	4. Personal annuity contracts	$_____
E.	Other death benefits	$_____
F.	Total of other income-producing assets you own that would pass to your heirs (include property you own in your own name, jointly owned property, and community property)	$_____
G.	Total assets available to your family (insurance, employee benefits, and others—sum of A, B, C, D, E, and F)	$_____
H.	Less estimated estate transfer costs (i.e., total estate "shrinkage" because of taxes, expenses, debts, and claims against the estate) (See Chap. 15.)	$_____
I.	Net income-producing assets available to your family	$_____
J.	Estimated annual (or monthly) income available to your family	
	1. Net income-producing assets (I above) × a reasonable, aftertax investment rate of return	$_____
	2. Estimated social security survivorship benefits (See Chap. 4.)	$_____
	3. Other possible sources of income to your family (e.g., nonqualified deferred compensation plan, survivors' income benefit insurance, pension benefits under a joint and last survivor annuity form, income from a likely inheritance, etc.)	$_____
	4. Total estimated income available to your family [Compare this amount with your family's current budget to note any deficiency (or surplus) in the amount they would need.]	$_____
	Estimate from your budget of how much current aftertax income your family would need	$_____

K. The approach used in I and J above is a simplified one that most people can apply for themselves. However, it does not allow for many of the variables that are considered in the more sophisticated *life insurance programming approach* as described in Chap. 4. For example, it does not allow for changing

FORM 3
INSURANCE COVERAGES WORKSHEETS (How Much Do You Have and Need?) (*continued*)

I. Life Insurance and Other Death Benefits (*continued*)

income objectives for your family over time; for family lump-sum objectives, such as education, emergency, and mortgage redemption needs; for the fact that social security survivorship benefits will change for your family as your children and spouse reach certain ages; and that your life insurance, and perhaps other death benefits, can be liquidated in installments or otherwise to increase the current income available to your family.

Therefore, you also should get an estimate of how much life insurance (and other death benefits) you need according to the *life insurance programming approach* (and perhaps also the human life value approach). Both are described in Chap. 4. For this, most people need the services of their life insurance agent or advisor. These amounts can be shown below.

1. Total death benefits needed to meet your stated objectives according to your *life insurance program* $_____

2. Net income-producing assets now available to your family (item I above) $_____

3. Amount, if any, of additional death protection needed to meet your stated objectives $_____

4. For additional reference, if desired, your present human life value $_____

II. Disability Income Insurance and Other Disability Benefits

---

Sources of Monthly Income Available to You and Your Family during Your Total Disability

Source	First month of disability	Next 4 months of disability (i.e., up to 5 months)	After 5 months until your youngest child reaches age 18 or 19	From when your youngest child reaches age 18 or 19 until you reach age 65 (retirement)
A. Social security disability benefits	$—0—	$—0—	$_____	$_____
B. Other government disability benefits	$_____	$_____	$_____	$_____
C. Employer-provided "sick pay"	$_____	$_____	$_____	$_____

FORM 3
INSURANCE COVERAGES WORKSHEETS (How Much Do You Have and Need?) (*continued*)

D. Group disability
   income insurance

   1. Employer-provided
      short-term disability
      insurance $_____ $_____ $_____ $_____

   2. Employer-provided
      long-term disability
      insurance $_____ $_____ $_____ $_____

   3. Association group
      disability insurance $_____ $_____ $_____ $_____

E. Individual disability
   income policies $_____ $_____ $_____ $_____

F. Disability income riders
   added to life insurance
   policies $_____ $_____ $_____ $_____

G. Disability income
   benefits from pension
   and profit-sharing,
   group life insurance,
   nonqualified deferred
   compensation, HR-10,
   and TSA plans $_____ $_____ $_____ $_____

H. Other disability benefits $_____ $_____ $_____ $_____

I. Estimated monthly
   investment income $_____ $_____ $_____ $_____

J. Total estimated
   monthly income during
   disability (sum of A
   through I) $_____ $_____ $_____ $_____

Your Objectives for Monthly Income Available to You and Your Family during Total Disability

Objectives $_____ $_____ $_____ $_____

Amounts, If Any, of Additional Disability Income Benefits Needed to Meet Your Stated Objectives

Amounts $_____ $_____ $_____ $_____

FORM 3
INSURANCE COVERAGES WORKSHEETS (How Much Do You Have and Need?) (*continued*)

III. Medical Expense Insurance and Other Benefits

A. Medical expense insurance and benefits available for you and your family
(include maximum limits and any coinsurance and deductible provisions)

Persons Covered	Type of Need (Objective)				
	"Basic" hospital, surgical, and medical	Health maintenance (HMO)	"Major medical" (or comprehensive)	Medicare (or coverage over age 65)	Other medical coverage
Yourself	_____	_____	_____	_____	_____
Your spouse and children	_____	_____	_____	_____	_____
	_____	_____	_____	_____	_____
	_____	_____	_____	_____	_____
Other dependents	_____	_____	_____	_____	_____

B. Unmet needs for medical expense insurance or duplicate medical expense insurance

_____ _____ _____ _____ _____

IV. Property and Liability Insurance

Need (or exposure to loss)	Present protection (including limits of liability)	Unmet needs

A. Property risks (exposures)

1. Real estate

a. Residence—estimated replacement cost new is
$ _____   _____

FORM 3
INSURANCE COVERAGES WORKSHEETS (How Much Do You Have and Need?) (*continued*)

---

    b. Vacation or other home—
       estimated replacement
       cost new is $_____

    c. Investment real estate

    d. Other real estate (e.g.,
       rented, leased, under
       construction, etc.)

2. Personal property

    a. Regular (or "unscheduled")
       personal property you
       own—estimated current
       value $_____

    b. Special personal property
       (or "scheduled" types of
       personal property)

       (1) Automobiles—estimated
          current values
             $_____
             $_____
             $_____

       (2) Watercraft—estimated
          current value $_____

       (3) Jewelry, furs, etc.—
          estimated current values
          $_____

       (4) Money and coin
          collections—estimated
          current values $_____

       (5) Stamp collections,
          securities, etc.—
          estimated current values
          $_____

       (6) Other high-value
          property (e.g., fine arts,
          antiques, cameras,
          musical instruments,
          etc.—estimated current
          values $_____

       (7) Aircraft

FORM 3
INSURANCE COVERAGES WORKSHEETS (How Much Do You Have and Need?) (*continued*)

IV. Property and Liability Insurance   (*continued*)

Need (or exposure to loss)	Present protection (including limits of liability)	Unmet needs
B. Liability risks (exposures)		
1. Real estate (premises exposures)		
a. Residence	_____	_____
b. Vacation or other home	_____	_____
c. Investment real estate	_____	_____
d. Other premises (e.g., rental, leased, under your care, custody, or control)	_____	_____
2. Automobiles	_____	_____
3. Watercraft	_____	_____
4. Aircraft	_____	_____
5. Snowmobiles or other recreational motor vehicles	_____	_____
6. Business or professional liability	_____	_____
7. Workers' compensation	_____	_____

FORM 4
ANALYSIS OF INVESTMENT PORTFOLIO

I. Present Investment Portfolio (Include Assets Owned Individually or Jointly)

Kinds of assets	Descriptions and amounts of assets	Cost (basis for income tax purposes)	Current market value	Percentage of portfolio (based on current market value)	Net annual income	Current yield	Current yield after taxes	Has asset increased or decreased in value in last year? 5 years?
A. Cash, checking accounts, and brokerage accounts	___		$___					
	___		___					
	___		___					
Subtotal			$___	___%				
B. Money market funds or accounts and savings accounts	___		$___		$___	___%	___%	
	___		___		___	___	___	
	___		___		___	___	___	
Subtotal			$___	___%	$___			
C. Certificates of deposit (CDs)	___		$___		$___	___%	___%	
Subtotal			$___	___%	$___			
D. Life insurance and deferred annuity cash values (See Forms 1 and 3)	___		$___	___%				

FORM 4
ANALYSIS OF INVESTMENT PORTFOLIO *(continued)*

I. Present Investment Portfolio (Include Assets Owned Individually or Jointly)   *(continued)*

Kinds of assets	Descriptions and amounts of assets	Cost (basis for income tax purposes)	Current market value	Percentage of portfolio (based on current market value)	Net annual income	Current yield	Current yield after taxes	Has asset increased or decreased in value in last year? 5 years?
E. Common stocks		$	$		$	%	%	
Total common stocks		$	$	%	$			
F. Mutual funds		$	$		$	%	%	
Total mutual funds		$	$	%	$			
G. Corporate bonds		$	$		$	%	%	
Total corporate bonds		$	$	%	$			

H. Municipal bonds		$___	___	$___	___%	$___	___%
Total municipal bonds		$___	___%	$___		$___	
I. U.S. government securities:		$___	___%	$___	___%	$___	___%
J. U.S. savings bonds		$___	___%	$___	___%	$___	___%
K. Preferred stocks		$___	___%	$___	___%	$___	___%
L. Investment real estate (show mortgages, depreciation, cash flow, etc., if desired)		$___	___%	$___	___%	$___	___%
M. Tax-sheltered investments		$___	___%	$___	___%	$___	___%
N. Profit-sharing, savings, tax-sheltered annuity, HR-10, IRA, and similar accounts		$___					
Subtotal		$___	___%	$___			
O. Business interests owned		$___	___%	$___	___%	$___	___%
P. Other investment type assets		$___	___%	$___	___%	$___	___%
Totals		$___	100%	$___			

FORM 4
ANALYSIS OF INVESTMENT PORTFOLIO *(continued)*

II. Spouse's Present Investment Portfolio (Include Assets Your Spouse Owns Individually or Jointly with Someone Other than Yourself)

Kinds of assets	Descriptions and amounts of assets	Cost (basis for income tax purposes)	Current market value	Percentage of portfolio (based on current market value)	Net annual income	Current yield	Current yield after taxes	Has asset increased or decreased in value in last year? 5 years?

III. Breakdown of Your (and Your Spouse's) Current Annual Investment Income (Use Current or Latest Year as Desired) (Also See Form 2)

Investment source	Ordinary income	Realized capital gains	Tax-free income	Tax deferred income
A. Savings accounts				
B. Certificates of deposit (CDs)				
C. Money market funds or accounts				
D. Common stocks				
E. Mutual funds				
F. Corporate bonds				
G. Municipal bonds				
H. U.S. government securities				
I. U.S. savings bonds				
J. Preferred stocks				
K. Investment real estate				
L. Nonqualified deferred annuities				
M. Other				
_____				
_____				
_____				
Totals	$ _____	$ _____	$ _____	$ _____

FORM 4
ANALYSIS OF INVESTMENT PORTFOLIO *(continued)*

IV. How Attractive Is Tax-Exempt Investment Income (e.g., from Municipal Bonds) to You?

A. Current tax-exempt yield available to you
_____ %

B. Current fully taxable yield (on securities of comparable quality) available to you
_____ %

C. Your highest federal tax rate (and state, etc., if yield in A above also is tax-exempt with respect to these other income taxes)
_____ %

D. Subtract your highest tax rate (shown in C above) from 100%
_____ %

E. Multiply the fully taxable yield (from B above) by the percentage determined in D above, and *compare the resulting aftertax yield with the current tax-exempt yield (from A above).*

FORM 4
ANALYSIS OF INVESTMENT PORTFOLIO (*continued*)

V. Your Investment Objectives

A. Rank the following investment goals in their order of importance to you (1 through 9).

1. Long-term capital growth primarily _____

2. Conservative long-term capital growth with some current income _____

3. Intermediate-term appreciation (up to, say, 12 months) primarily _____

4. Intermediate-term appreciation with some current income _____

5. Maximum current income, accepting the appropriate investment risks ____

6. Safety of capital with as high an aftertax current return as possible (consistent with safety) _____

7. Aggressive, rapid capital growth _____

8. Tax-sheltered investments _____

9. Other _____

B. How much annual income should your investment portfolio provide?
$_____ Yield _____%

C. Does your present investment portfolio meet your stated objectives? _____
If not, why not?_____

D. Can you increase the yield from your portfolio, consistent with your other objectives? _____

If so, how?_____

VI. Asset Allocation of Your Portfolio

A. Outline your *present* and *desired* asset allocation as explained in Chap. 7.

B. Diversification

1. From I and II above of Form 4, what kind of asset (e.g., stocks, bonds, etc.) represents the largest percentage of your present investment portfolio?
Asset _____ Percentage _____

2. Also, what single security is most important?
Security _____ Percentage _____

FORM 4
ANALYSIS OF INVESTMENT PORTFOLIO   (*continued*)

VI. Asset Allocation of Your Portfolio   (*continued*)

   B. Diversification (*continued*)

      3. What other concentrations of assets do you have?

        _____

        _____

        _____

      4. Is your portfolio sufficiently diversified to meet your objectives? If not, why not?

        (See Chap. 7 for the factors you should consider on diversification.)

   C. Liquidity position (emergency fund)

      1. Present liquid assets (see Form 1 for total)
        $ _____

      2. Your liquidity (emergency fund) objective is
        $ _____

VII. Analysis of Your Debts

Obligation (kind and amount)	Maturity date	Interest rate	Periodic payments	Pre-payment privileges	Is interest on debt deductible for federal income tax purposes?
_____	_____	____ %	$ _____	_____	_____
_____	_____	____	_____	_____	_____
_____	_____	____	_____	_____	_____
_____	_____	____	_____	_____	_____
_____	_____	____	_____	_____	_____

   A. Considering your aftertax interest cost, would it be advantageous for you to liquidate any of your present investments and use the proceeds to pay off debt? If so, which ones? _____

   B. Considering available yields, security, and your tax position, should you consider borrowing to acquire any investments (i.e., using leverage)? If so, what obligations should you incur for which investments? _____

FORM 5
ESTIMATED RETIREMENT INCOME

I. Planned Retirement Age: You _____   Your Spouse _____

II. Estimated Monthly Retirement Income Desired

    1. For you (and your spouse) $ _____

    2. For your surviving spouse $ _____

III. Sources of Estimated Monthly Retirement Income Available to You (and Your Spouse)

Source	Age when the income is to begin	Income for you (and your spouse)— amount and duration (if not for life)	Continuing income for your surviving spouse— amount and duration (if not for life)
A. Social security retirement benefits	_____	$ _____	$ _____
B. Other government benefits	_____	_____	_____
C. Pension plan	_____	_____	_____
D. Savings or profit-sharing plan	_____	_____	_____
E. Nonqualified deferred compensation	_____	_____	_____
F. Other employee benefits	_____	_____	_____
G. HR-10 plans	_____	_____	_____
H. Individual retirement annuity or account (IRA)	_____	_____	_____
I. Tax-sheltered annuity (TSA) plan	_____	_____	_____
J. Nonqualified individual annuities (fixed-dollar and variable)	_____	_____	_____
K. Life insurance cash values and the estimated value of any accumulated dividends	_____	_____	_____

FORM 5
ESTIMATED RETIREMENT INCOME   *(continued)*

III. Sources of Estimated Monthly Retirement Income Available to You (and Your
      Spouse)   *(continued)*

Source	Age when the income is to begin	Income for you (and your spouse)— amount and duration (if not for life)	Continuing income for your surviving spouse— amount and duration (if not for life)
L. Estimated investment income from your (and your spouse's) general investment fund, projected at a reasonable rate of return to your planned retirement age	_____	_____	_____
M. Estimated investment income from any expected inheritances	_____	_____	_____
N. Proceeds from any sale or liquidation of a business interest at or during retirement	_____	_____	_____
O. Proceeds from any other planned liquidation of assets during retirement	_____	_____	_____
P. Other sources of retirement income			
_____	_____	_____	_____
_____	_____	_____	_____
_____	_____	_____	_____
_____	_____	_____	_____
Totals		$_____	$_____

IV. Control of Your Estimated Retirement Income

How much of the above sources of retirement income would you retain (control) if
you took an action such as changing jobs (e.g., social security, vested rights in
pension and profit-sharing plans, etc.)?

For you (and your spouse) $_____

For your surviving spouse $_____

FORM 5
ESTIMATED RETIREMENT INCOME (*continued*)

V. What, If Any, Additional Retirement Income (or Guarantees) Do You (or Your Spouse) Need to Meet Your Objectives?

Possible sources	Amounts
	$
	$
	$

FORM 6
TAX AND ESTATE PLANNING WORKSHEETS

I. Income Tax Planning

A. Your top income tax bracket or rate (consider federal, state, and local income taxes) _____ %
(Also see item IV. C of Form 4)

B. Tax planning for capital gains and losses (See Chap. 11 for tax-saving techniques regarding such gains and losses.)

1. *Realized* capital gains and losses for the current year

Capital asset	Capital gains	Capital losses
	$	$
Totals	$	$

FORM 6
TAX AND ESTATE PLANNING WORKSHEETS (*continued*)

I. Income Tax Planning   (*continued*)

  B. Tax planning for capital gains and losses (See Chap. 11 for tax-saving techniques
     regarding such gains and losses.) (*continued*)

     2. *Unrealized* capital gains and losses

Capital asset	Capital gains	Capital losses
_____	$ _____	$ _____
_____	_____	_____
_____	_____	_____
_____	_____	_____
_____	_____	_____
_____	_____	_____
_____	_____	_____
Totals	$ _____	$ _____

  C. Consideration of specific tax-saving techniques, for example:
     (See Chaps. 11, 12, 13, and 17 for discussions of these techniques.)

Technique	Currently used	Not applicable	Would consider	Would not consider
Taking tax losses on securities	_____	_____	_____	_____
Buying municipal bonds	_____	_____	_____	_____
Making other tax-sheltered investments	_____	_____	_____	_____
Giving appreciated capital gain property to charity	_____	_____	_____	_____

FORM 6
TAX AND ESTATE PLANNING WORKSHEETS (*continued*)

Gifts to minors under uniform
gifts (or transfers) to minors acts
or through trusts   _____   _____   _____   _____

Other gifts   _____   _____   _____   _____

HR-10 plans   _____   _____   _____   _____

Individual retirement annuities
or accounts (IRAs)   _____   _____   _____   _____

Tax-sheltered annuity (TSA)
plan   _____   _____   _____   _____

Election of subchapter S
corporation status   _____   _____   _____

Other

_____   _____   _____   _____   _____

_____   _____   _____   _____   _____

_____   _____   _____   _____   _____

II. Estate Planning

    A. Estimating your estate for federal estate tax purposes (See
        Chap. 16 for the calculation of the federal estate tax.)

        Gross estate   \$_____

        Less: deductions from the gross estate   – \$_____

        Adjusted gross estate   \$_____

        Less:

          Marital deduction   \$_____

          Charitable bequests   _____   – \$_____

        Taxable estate   \$_____

        Adjusted taxable lifetime gifts (after 1976), if any   + \$_____

        Tentative tax base   \$_____

        Federal estate tax on the tentative tax base   \$_____

FORM 6

TAX AND ESTATE PLANNING WORKSHEETS   (*continued*)

II. Estate Planning (*continued*)

    A. Estimating your estate for federal estate tax purposes
(See Chap. 16 for the calculation of the federal estate
tax.) (*continued*)

        Less any gift taxes paid on lifetime gifts after 1976   – $_____

        Federal estate tax before application of credits $_____

        Less:

            Unified credit
            State death tax credit
            Other credits   – $_____

        Federal estate tax payable $_____

    B. Your top federal estate tax bracket or rate, if any   %

    C. Estimate of state death taxes payable, if available $_____

    D. Estimate of your estate's liquidity needs (transfer costs):

        1. Federal estate tax $_____

        2. State death tax

        3. Debts   _____

        4. Estimated funeral and estate administration expenses   _____

        5. Other needs   _____

        Total liquidity needs $_____

    E. What part (if any) of your gross estate potentially "qualifies"
for the federal estate tax marital deduction? (See Chap. 16
for an explanation of the marital deduction.)

        1. Property passing outright to your surviving spouse $_____

        2. Property passing to your surviving spouse in trust so as to
qualify for the deduction   _____

        3. Jointly owned property   _____

        4. Life insurance and other death benefits payable to your
spouse so as to qualify for the deduction   _____

        5. Other ways   _____

            _____   _____

            _____   _____

            _____   _____

        Total that potentially qualifies (ignoring, for simplicity,
amounts that may have to be used to pay estate debts,
expenses, and taxes) $_____

    F. Maximum allowable federal estate tax marital deduction
(unlimited amount provided it passes to surviving spouse so
as to qualify) $_____

FORM 6
TAX AND ESTATE PLANNING WORKSHEETS (*continued*)

G. For purposes of the marital deduction, is your estate at present potentially

1. "Overqualified"? (Consider the available unified credit.)

2. "Underqualified"? (Consider whether you have a pre-ERTA formula marital deduction provision in a will or trust.)

H. What part of your estate now must pass through probate?

1. Property you own in your own name (i.e., individually) $_____

2. Life insurance proceeds and other death benefits payable to your estate   _____

3. Your share of property you own as tenants in common   _____

4. Your half of community property   _____

5. Other   _____

   Total probate estate $_____

I. Who will receive your net estate under your present estate arrangements? (Include any special arrangements, such as trusts.)

_____

_____

_____

_____

_____

J. Methods of estate transfer—check the methods you are now using and would consider. (See Chaps. 14, 15, and 16 for discussions of these methods.)

Method	Currently used	Would consider	Not applicable
Outright bequests in your will	_____	_____	_____
Bequests in trust under your will (testamentary trusts)	_____	_____	_____
Jointly owned property	_____	_____	_____
Community property	_____	_____	_____

FORM 6
TAX AND ESTATE PLANNING WORKSHEETS *(continued)*

II. Estate Planning *(continued)*

    J. Methods of estate transfer—check the methods you are now using and would consider. (See Chaps. 14, 15, and 16 for discussions of these methods.) *(continued)*

Method	Currently used	Would consider	Not applicable
Life insurance and other beneficiary designations	_____	_____	_____
Revocable lifetime trusts	_____	_____	_____
Irrevocable lifetime trusts	_____	_____	_____
Outright lifetime gifts	_____	_____	_____
Other			
_____	_____	_____	_____

    K. Arrangement of life insurance in your estate plan

        1. Life insurance (and other death benefits) that you own on your life

Policy or plan	Amount	Beneficiary designations	Settlement arrangements		
			Lump sum	Settlement options	Life insurance trust
_____	$ _____	_____	_____	_____	_____
_____	_____	_____	_____	_____	_____
_____	_____	_____	_____	_____	_____
_____	_____	_____	_____	_____	_____
_____	_____	_____	_____	_____	_____
_____	_____	_____	_____	_____	_____
_____	_____	_____	_____	_____	_____

FORM 6
TAX AND ESTATE PLANNING WORKSHEETS   (*continued*)

---

2. Life insurance that others own on your life

Policy	Amount	Owner	Beneficiary designations	Settlement arrangements
_____	$ _____	_____	_____	_____
_____	_____	_____	_____	_____
_____	_____	_____	_____	_____
_____	_____	_____	_____	_____

3. Life insurance that you own on the life of another

Policy	Amount	Insured	Beneficiary designations	Settlement arrangements
_____	$ _____	_____	_____	_____
_____	_____	_____	_____	_____
_____	_____	_____	_____	_____
_____	_____	_____	_____	_____

L. Lifetime gifts

1. What, if any, significant lifetime gifts have you made? What property, to whom, and how?

_____

_____

_____

2. Have you made gifts that are subject to federal gift taxation?

_____

If so, what is your top federal gift tax rate?_____

_____

Index

About the Authors

G. VICTOR HALLMAN is a member of the Pennsylvania Bar and is also lecturer in financial and estate planning at the Wharton School, University of Pennsylvania. He is the author of many professional books and articles; and consults in the field of financial and estate planning.

JERRY S. ROSENBLOOM is chair and professor, Department of Insurance and Risk Management, at the Wharton School, University of Pennsylvania, and is academic director of the Certified Employee Benefit Specialist Program. He is the author of many books and articles and consults in the field of financial planning.